CITY WALLS
The Urban Enceinte in Global Perspective

The essays presented in this volume describe a phenomenon so widespread in human time and space that its importance is easily overlooked. City walls shaped the history of warfare; the mobilization of manpower and resources needed to build them favored some kinds of polities over others; and their massive strength, appropriately ornamented, created a visual language of authority. Previous collective volumes on the subject have dealt mainly with Europe, but the historians and art historians who collaborate here follow a comparative agenda. The millennial practice of wall building that branched out from the ancient Near East into India, Europe, and North Africa shows continuities and points of contact of which the makers of urban fortifications were scarcely aware; separate traditions in China, sub-Saharan Africa, and North America illustrate universal themes of defensive strategy and the symbolism of power, each time embedded in a distinctive local context.

James D. Tracy is Professor of History at the University of Minnesota. He is author of *Erasmus: The Growth of a Mind*, *Politics of Erasmus*, *A Financial Revolution in the Habsburg Netherlands*, *Holland under Habsburg Rule*, *Erasmus of the Low Countries*, and *Europe's Reformations*. He is also editor of several volumes and author of numerous academic papers, articles, and book reviews.

Studies in
Comparative Early Modern
History

Center for Early Modern History
University of Minnesota

Cambridge University Press

Previously published in series:

CITY WALLS

THE URBAN ENCEINTE IN GLOBAL PERSPECTIVE

Edited by

JAMES D. TRACY
University of Minnesota

CAMBRIDGE
UNIVERSITY PRESS

PUBLISHED BY THE PRESS SYNDICATE OF THE UNIVERSITY OF CAMBRIDGE
The Pitt Building, Trumpington Street, Cambridge, United Kingdom

CAMBRIDGE UNIVERSITY PRESS
The Edinburgh Building, Cambridge CB2 2RU, UK
40 West 20th Street, New York, NY 10011-4211, USA
10 Stamford Road, Oakleigh, VIC 3166, Australia
Ruiz de Alarcón 13, 28014 Madrid, Spain
Dock House, The Water Front Capetown, South Africa

http://www.cambridge.org

© James D. Tracy 2000

First published 2000

Printed in the United States of America

Typeface Palatino 10/12 pt.   *System* DeskTopPro$_{/UX}$ [BV]

A catalog record for this book is available from the British Library.

Library of Congress Cataloging in Publication Data
City walls : the urban enceinte in global perspective / [edited by] James Tracy.
p. cm. – (Studies in comparative early modern history)
Based on a Center for Early Modern History conference held in Oct. 1995.
Includes bibliographical references and index.
ISBN 0-521-65221-9
1. City walls – History – Congresses.   2. Cities and towns – History – Congresses.
I. Tracy, James D.   II. University of Minnesota. Center for Early Modern History.
III. Series
UG405.2.C58 2000
623'.1 – dc21

99-045712

ISBN 0 521 65221 9   hardback

Contents

Figures

Contributors

Catherine B. Asher
Department of Art History, University of Minnesota

Bernard S. Bachrach
Department of History, University of Minnesota

Sheila S. Blair
Art Historian, Richmond, New Hampshire

Jonathan M. Bloom
Art Historian, Richmond, New Hampshire

Graham Connah
Humanities Research Centre, Australian National University

Frederick A. Cooper
Department of Classical and Near Eastern Studies, University of Minnesota

Martin M. Elbl
Department of History, Trent University

Edward L. Farmer
Department of History, University of Minnesota

Richard L. Kagan
Department of History, The Johns Hopkins University

George R. Milner
Department of Anthropology, Pennsylvania State University

Geoffrey Parker
Department of History, Ohio State University

Simon Pepper
School of Architecture & Building Engineering, University of Liverpool

Martha Pollak
Department of Art History, University of Illinois–Chicago

Kathryn L. Reyerson
Department of History, University of Minnesota

Nancy Shatzman Steinhardt
Department of Asian and Middle Eastern Studies, University of Pennsylvania

James D. Tracy
Department of History, University of Minnesota

Wolfgang G. van Emden
Department of French Studies, University of Reading

Michael Wolfe
Department of History, Pennsylvania State University–Altoona

Acknowledgments

THIS volume is based on a Center for Early Modern History conference (October 1995), made possible by a grant from the University of Minnesota's McKnight Special Events Fund. Lucy Simler, assistant director of the Center from 1985 to 1996, gracefully managed the business end of the conference, aided by Kelli Ringhofer. History graduate students who provided reasoned summaries of conference discussions for the use of authors in revising their papers included Mary Beth Ailes, Glen Bowman, Gordon Bynum, Jodi Campbell, Doug Catterall, Dan Doyle, Anna Dronzek, Don Harreld, Lindy Lundgren, Craig Neumeier, and Markus Vink. The authors themselves made an editor's job easy, especially by picking up questions from work by colleagues interested in other parts of the globe, which was part of our purpose. I wish to thank particularly those whose advice and suggestions helped shape the project at various stages: Sheila Blair, Jonathan Bloom, Simon Pepper, Martha Pollak, Paul Solon of Macalester College, Nancy Shatzman Steinhardt, and among my Minnesota colleagues, John Archer, Catherine Asher, Bernard Bachrach, Frederick Cooper, Sheila McNally, Kathryn Reyerson, and Leon Satkowski. Finally, Peter Burkholder compiled the annotated bibliography, and Marguerite Ragnow's finely honed copyediting skills have spared us the embarrassment of errors at many levels. Few projects live up to all of their initial expectations, and we have not in the end been able to include all of the topics we once envisioned. But I believe we have carried out our plan of providing a comparative framework for our topic, which is the walls that men have built around their cities. I hope this juxtaposition of geographically diverse essays on similar issues conveys to readers something of the excitement we have all felt in trying to climb over the walls of the mind that scholars build around their separate regions of the globe.

James D. Tracy,
Director, Center for Early Modern History

Introduction

JAMES D. TRACY

THIS book deals with the association between cities and perimeter walls, an association that is much older than written memory. The earliest settlements that archeological research commonly recognizes as cities are also the earliest cities known to have been walled. Around 8000 B.C. the population of Jericho jumped to approximately 2,000; some five hundred years later the town was girt by a wide ditch and a massive stone wall that is preserved in places to a height of four meters. At Catal Hüyük in Anatolia, a town that flourished between 6500 and 5650 B.C., the blank outer walls of houses presented an unbroken front towards the outside, obviating the need of additional walls.[1] Beginning around 2900 B.C. the cities of ancient Sumer came to be surrounded by massive brick walls, as at Uruk, where the enceinte was approximately 9.5 kilometers in length, and dotted by 900 or more semi-circular towers. The same appears to have been true for the cities of the Indus valley, of a like antiquity or nearly so. At Harappa the mud brick walls were ten to twenty feet high, and forty feet thick at the base.[2] In some later civilizations "wall" and "city" were so tightly linked that one term could stand for the other. In classical Chinese a single character (*cheng*) was used for both city and wall.[3] In early medieval Europe, Gregory of Tours (d. 594) could not understand why the substantial walled community of Dijon was not considered a *civitas*. As the town secretary of Eisenach put it many centuries later (1399), "What has a wall around it, that we call a city." By the same logic, a fifteenth-century map of the proud city of Pisa shows a complete circuit wall that never in fact existed.[4] Whether in China

[1] Horst de la Croix, *Military Considerations in City Planning: Fortifications* (New York, 1972), 12–14.
[2] Song Nai Rhee, "The Sumerian City States," in *The City-State in Five Cultures*, eds. Robert Griffeth and Carol G. Thomas (Santa Barbara, 1981), 7–12; G.N. Pant, *Studies in Indian Weapons and Warfare* (New Delhi, 1970), 212–13.
[3] See Chapter 15.
[4] See Chapter 7; Heinz Stoob, "Die Stadtbefestigung. Vergleichende Überlegungen zur bürgerlichen Siedlungs- und Baugeschichte, besonders der frühen Neuzeit," in *Euro-*

under the Shang dynasty (1511–1100 B.C.) or at Great Zimbabwe in southern Africa or under Egypt's Fatimid caliphs,[5] rulers imposed on their towns the social discipline needed to sustain gigantic building projects that could take decades, even centuries to complete. In some cases, as in parts of medieval Europe or the Hausa city-states of West Africa,[6] townsfolk could impose the same kind of discipline on themselves.

A phenomenon that is global in scope cries out for comparative discussion. This volume is animated by the belief that comparison can enrich the separate histories that make up the history of the globe. Questions that have seemed fruitful in one part of the world may usefully be asked for others, and themes may take on a new importance when it is seen that they recur in many different regions. We leave to others the kind of comparison that seeks to use local or regional histories as foundation stones for a mega-history. It would be dubious in practice to make generalizations on the basis of a comparative scholarship that has been largely confined to European history,[7] and it is arguably dubious in principle to assume that historical processes can be analyzed on quasi-Aristotelian premises, by envisioning a clear-cut distinction between local details or "accidents" and a common "substance" underlying all local manifestations of the process.

Of the nineteen essays presented here, eleven are devoted to Europe or to European settlements overseas, four to the Islamic world, two to China, one to sub-Saharan Africa, and one to North America. Our European focus reflects the fact that most of the work on walled cities is done by Europeanists, but it does not reflect the actual distribution of walled cities in the premodern world, when Europe's fortified towns were probably outnumbered by China's "thousands."[8] We have been selective also in regard to topics, leaving out issues that in themselves are eminently worthy of comparative discussion.[9] The essays

---

päische Städte im Zeitalter des Barock, ed. Kersten Krüger (Vienna and Cologne, 1988), 26, citing Johann Rother: *"Was muren umb sich hat, da heist eyn burgk ader stat"* ("burg" meant the settlement around a castle as well as the castle itself); Wolfgang Braunfels, *Die Mittelalterliche Stadtbaukunst in der Toskana* (Berlin, 1966), 53–4: Pisa, protected by its lagoon, never had more than a partial wall.

[5] See Chapters 15, 1, and 9.

[6] See Chapters 3, 11, and 1.

[7] Cesare de Seta and Jacques Le Goff, eds., *Le citta e le mura* (Rome and Bari, 1989); Ivy A. Corfis and Michael Wolfe, eds., *The Medieval City under Siege* (Rochester, NY, 1995).

[8] See Chapter 15.

[9] For example, the question of the social impact that building a wall has on the urban community so enclosed. The very word "community" may suggest that having a wall fostered among town dwellers a distinctive feeling of urban solidarity: the 1959 *Cassell's New Latin Dictionary* suggests the Latin *communis* apparently derived from *cum*

presented here focus on three issues: What are the circumstances under which towns or their rulers choose to undertake the labor of surrounding cities with enceintes? How are particular programs of wall building – the construction of many urban enceintes in the same area over a relatively short period – linked to particular forms of warfare? And what are the symbolic meanings, cultural and political, that town walls acquire once they are built?

The five essays of Part I, "To Wall or Not to Wall," address the first question. No matter how "natural" it may have seemed for a town to have walls, the sheer labor and expense involved means that wall builders must have had compelling reasons. Most often, it was a matter of defense against anticipated attack. GRAHAM CONNAH's survey of enclosed settlements in premodern tropical Africa finds that the main lines of development, including those leading to the massive mud walls of Benin and the stone towns of the Swahili coast, are indigenous. Full-blown sieges seem to have been rare, with walls and other enclosures intended more for protection against marauders (Chapter 1). GEORGE MILNER's survey of palisaded settlements in eastern North America, from about 1000 A.D. to the seventeenth century, shows a clear distinction between the strongly built enclosures of the Mississippian culture zone, with its powerful chiefdoms, and the more lightly built palisades of northern settlements. The evidence points to scattered local warfare in both regions, albeit of a differing intensity (Chapter 2). These two essays show how a common human experience (warfare) leads to a common response (the enclosure of settlements). Some of these fortifications, like Benin's massive mud walls, were no less demanding in terms of labor and social organiza-

---

= with, and either *moenia* = fortifications or *munus* = office. Discussion about the civic spirit engendered in walled towns is commonplace among Europeanists, and Graham Connah sees evidence of the same phenomenon in the Hausa cities of West Africa, where "the city or town wall, the surrounding ditch or bank . . . gave the contained community a discrete physical identity and strengthened its sense of solidarity" (Chapter 1). On the other hand, internal walls built to separate one population group from another might also be read from culture to culture as evidence of intramural hostility, whether in the Jewish ghettos of medieval Europe, or the thirty-four "twin cities" created by China's Manchu dynasty for cohabitation by ethnically distinct populations; Skinner, *The City in Late Imperial China*, 92. Some urban neighborhoods did not require ethnic differences in order to build barriers against one another: In 1222 Pamplona's dual rulers, the bishop and the king of Navarre, intervened to stop the further construction of internal walls by the city's bitterly divided barrios; James F. Powers, "Life on the Cutting Edge: The Besieged Town on the Luso-Hispanic Frontier in the Twelfth Century," in *The Medieval City under Siege*, 29. In a sense both themes come together in cities like Montpellier (see Chapter 4), where two adjacent walled communities agreed to form a single city and build a "common wall." These are important questions, but they will receive only passing notice here.

tion than the stone or brick walls found in other parts of the world, and no easier to penetrate. Turning to Europe, JAMES TRACY asks which towns got walled and which did not. For medieval Germany there is a scholarly literature rich enough to provide answers for such questions. The towns most likely to build walls were those that had a strong merchant community, or served a territorial ruler's need to secure his borders (Chapter 3). KATHRYN REYERSON develops the perspective of burghers for whom the standing wall was more a present nuisance than a response to dimly remembered past dangers. Montpellier's officials turned a blind eye to the violation of laws aimed at preserving the wall's military function; stricter enforcement began only as war loomed on the horizon again (Chapter 4). Finally, RICHARD KAGAN illumines the phenomenon of wall building by considering its absence in seventeenth-century Spanish America. Here the houses of religious orders and the settlements of converted Indians that clustered round the great cities were described as "spiritual walls," warding off the dangers of idolatry more effectively than any material walls might do (Chapter 5).

Part II, "Walls of War," examines the reciprocal relationship between changes in the character of warfare and what may be called programs of wall building, in which many cities in a given region were fortified over a relatively short period. FREDERICK COOPER shows that massive city walls of ashlar masonry, described by Aristotle as "ornamental as well as useful for war," were an invention not of fifth-century Athens, but of Thebes under Epaminondas (d. 362 B.C.). These fortifications were intended not only to withstand new strategies for siege warfare, but also to secure the forward points of Theban hegemony (Chapter 6). BERNARD BACHRACH points to the enduring legacy of late imperial Rome's program of urban wall building. In the barbarian successor states, as under Roman rule, the capture of fortified cities was the principal objective of warfare. Roman siege techniques were still in use in the Carolingian era, as was the Roman practice of militarizing urban populations by having burghers take responsibility for the defense of their walls (Chapter 7). Turning to Islamdom, JONATHAN BLOOM argues for North Africa that "the notion of the unwalled early Islamic city is a myth." By examining three successive Fatimid capitals, of which Cairo (969) is the best known, he shows that Fatimid architects, sometimes thought to have imported the alien idea of urban wall building, actually drew on North African traditions (Chapter 8). CATHERINE ASHER offers a diachronic survey of the walling of cities built on the site of modern Delhi, from the Indraprashtra of Aryan legend to the Red Fort of Shah Jahan (1639). In most cases, the walls seem intended to hold off marauders rather than to sustain a siege; under the Mughals and their predecessors, Delhi was to be defended at the realm's frontiers (Chapter 9). SIMON PEPPER seeks to dismantle the prejudice that any good work in Ottoman military architecture must have been the work of Christian craftsmen. Fortifications built along the main lines of Islamic-Christian conflict in the second half of the fifteenth century do not anticipate Italy's angled bastions, as has sometimes been argued, but they are designed in other ways both to absorb artillery fire and to provide gun platforms (Chapter 10). Against the view which sees urban fortifications of the costly bastioned trace type as imposed in France by an absolutist monarchy on recalcitrant towns, MICHAEL WOLFE argues that French towns were eager to cooperate with the crown, even during the Religious Wars of the sixteenth century; fortifications in the new style were often built and paid for by the burghers themselves, using customary work-site traditions (Chapter 11). Turning to the projection of European military power overseas in this era, MARTIN ELBL shows the Portu-guese crown resisting as long as possible the expenses of new-style fortifications for its urban outposts in North Africa. Only after several towns had been lost to the Saʿdian dynasty were the three towns that remained under Portuguese rule refortified in the Italian style (Chapter 12). Finally, GEOFFREY PARKER presents a broader view of the significance of the artillery fortress, as part of a military explanation for the rise of the West. In Asia, even old-style fortifications were sufficient to make European outposts virtually impregnable to assault. Only with the advent of Portugal's European rivals, notably the Dutch, did key sites begin to be fortified *alla moderna*. The successful indigenous powers were those that either copied European fortifica-tions, or, like Japanese architects of the Tokugawa era, came up with artillery-resistant designs of their own (Chapter 13).

Part III, "Signifying Walls," examines what standing walls meant to contemporaries in terms of the city's place in the body politic, and in the larger cosmic order. A city wall is almost of necessity a symbol of sovereign power, because no government of more than nominal au-thority will permit the massive mobilization of labor and capital that wall building requires to proceed without its approval. At the same time, the well-ordered city is in many cultures the symbol of a larger cosmic order, and perfectly constructed walls can be the token of this earthly perfection that has meaning beyond itself. NANCY STEIN-HARDT shows that the earliest extant images of Chinese cities, indi-cating perfectly rectangular outer walls and a separately walled gov-ernment city within, bear a striking resemblance to modern

illustrations, and even to conventional Western ideas about Chinese
cities. Through the ages in China, every city must have walls, and
walls that are known to have been irregular are represented as rectilin-
ear, in keeping with an unchanging ideal (Chapter 14). EDWARD
FARMER examines hierarchical relationships among the perfectly
modeled cities in printed gazetteers of the Ming period. Cities of
higher administrative rank are invariably shown as larger than their
subordinates, with larger gates and straighter walls, regardless of
whether these conventions conformed to reality (Chapter 15). SHEILA
BLAIR shows how the massive Roman walls of the city known in the
Islamic era as Diyarbekir were treated as a canvas on which successive
rulers registered their claims to authority in ornate relief inscriptions.
Of particular interest are inscriptions of the Saljuq era (1085–1093), in
which Diyarbekir's ruler used the conventions of language and calig-
raphy to counter the spiritual claims of the rival Fatimid dynasty in
Cairo (Chapter 16). WOLFGANG VAN EMDEN explores images of
the city in French verse of the twelfth and thirteenth centuries. The
distinction between a castle and a fortified city is not always clear, but
both are represented as girt by impregnable walls reaching to the sky,
often crystal white or brilliantly colored; the model for these dream
cities is the New Jerusalem (Chapter 17). SIMON PEPPER considers
the implications of certain customs of siege warfare in Renaissance
Europe: Unsuccessful defenders of fortified places were treated honorably in some cases, hanged in others. The telling point is that sieges
were considered a test of sovereignty, so that he who exceeded the
conventions of "reasonable defense" was deemed to have given offense to the victorious ruler, and was treated accordingly (Chapter 18).
Finally, MARTHA POLLAK examines graphic representations of the
sieges of fortified cities in Europe from the early sixteenth to the late
seventeenth centuries. Over this period, artists adopted mapmaking
techniques for better depiction to scale, and learned to combine a
bird's-eye or ichnographic plan with a curving perspective to display
the wider horizon. Regardless of the techniques involved, the siege
view was both a work of art and a trophy of war, showing forth the
glory of the conquering prince, often portrayed at a central point of
the design (Chapter 19).

Perhaps the most striking common theme to emerge from these
essays is the association between royal power or sovereignty and the
enclosure of towns. In North America it was the towns of the great
Mississippian chiefdoms that had stouter palisades, reflecting a more
organized and sustained pattern of warfare (Chapter 2). The siege and
capture of walled cities was the strategic objective of warfare in the

barbarian successor kingdoms of Europe, as it had been in the late Roman world, and monarchs of the sixteenth and seventeenth centuries used artistic representations of successful urban sieges as a way of publishing their glory to all (Chapters 7 and 19). Even in the Islamic world, often thought to be characterized by open cities, the capitals of great rulers like the Fatimid caliphs were walled as a matter of course (Chapter 8), as was each successive capital built by Delhi's sultans (Chapter 9); rulers also used town walls as a canvas for calligraphic proclamations of their titles and their accomplishments (Chapter 16). In Renaissance Europe, a commander who defended his city more doggedly than the conventions of war prescribed was deemed to have offended the majesty of the town's would-be ruler (Chapter 18). By contrast, the notion that Europe's independent-minded burghers built and maintained their own walls, while not without foundation, has to be deemphasized in light of more recent studies of the relations between townsfolk, their rulers, and their walls (Chapters 3, 4, and 11).

Another important connection among many of the essays is the way programs of wall building are calibrated to perceived dangers represented by the military technology of possible foes. The ashlar masonry of Epaminondas' wall-building campaign represents a response to the torsion catapult (Chapter 6). Late Roman town walls had to be maintained or rebuilt in the early Middle Ages because the contending parties had mastered the techniques of Roman siege warfare (Chapter 7). Ottoman military architects found their own ways of responding to the new threat posed by siege artillery (Chapter 8). And in Europe's overseas expansion, the imperial powers looked at the kind of opposition they might face before deciding whether to build enceintes in the new Italian fashion, to remain content with older-style curtain walls, or not to wall their cities at all (Chapters 12, 13, and 5). Readers will no doubt find other points of contact among the essays, or (perhaps more interesting) omissions that may call for further efforts in the same direction. This collection is meant not as the last word, but as the beginning of a comparative discussion.

Since many (though not all) of the walled cities discussed in this volume may be seen as related to a single grand tradition tracing back to the ancient Near East, it may be useful by way of an introduction to sketch the military-architectural inheritance that finds echoes in the later Christian and Islamic worlds.

Even before the rise of Sumer, the earliest town walls that have left an archeological trace were fitted out with special features that would be copied or reinvented again and again in later civilizations. Jericho's walls – surrounded by a dry moat and overtopped by a tower from which defenders could fire on their assailants – already serve to illustrate the important distinction John Keegan makes between a stronghold and a refuge. Refuges are sanctuaries against periodic raids, strongholds are meant to withstand a sustained siege by a foe capable of supplying his army in the field; hence in Keegan's definition a stronghold must enclose a supply of water, and must provide its garrison the means to wage an active defense. At Babylon, early in the second millennium B.C., active defense was made easier by battlements atop the wall to shield defenders from the missiles of besiegers; by galleries projecting outward that permitted them to cover the base of the wall; and by towers all along the curtain at bowshot intervals that enabled them to rake attackers with flanking fire.[10]

The town walls of the ancient Near East were not only surprisingly "modern" in a military sense, they were often more imposing than anything built subsequently. To my knowledge, no standing wall anywhere in the world can match the sheer opulence of the glazed brick surface of Babylon's Ishtar Gate, with its bright colors and bas reliefs.[11] The city girded by multiple rings of walls, a fantasy suggested to "Utopian" writers of the Renaissance era by Plato's description of Atlantis, apparently existed in reality some centuries before Plato.[12] A Hittite relief from ca. 1280 B.C. shows defenders fighting from battlements on three walls of a besieged city – two curtain walls and an interior citadel. Around 1100 B.C. the Assyrian conqueror Tilgath Pileser boasted of having laid waste "the three great walls" of the city of Hunusa "built with burnt brick." According to Herodotus, Ectabana, once the capital of the Medes, had had as many as seven concentric rings of walls, each overtopping the other; an Assyrian relief of the eighth century B.C., showing the Median city of Kishesim, conforms to this description. Farther to the east, in a document of the second or third century B.C. describing Buddha's birth, the great city of Vaisali is said to have been girt by three walls, each one league distant from the other.[13]

---

[10] John Keegan, *A History of Warfare* (New York, 1993), 140–1; De la Croix, *Military Considerations in City Planning*, 15.

[11] Dating from the sixth century B.C., the front section of the Ishtar Gate is on view in Berlin's Pergamon Museum. For the brightly colored walls of the Heavenly Jerusalem as described by medieval authors, see Chapter 17.

[12] See especially Johann Valentin Andreae, *Christianopolis* (1616; rprt. Stuttgart, 1975).

[13] Sidney Toy, *A History of Fortification from 3000 B.C. to 1700 A.D.* (London, 1955), 9; Victor Davis Hanson, "Genesis of the Infantry, 600–350 B.C.," in *The Cambridge Illustrated History of Warfare. The Triumph of the West*, ed. Geoffrey Parker (Cambridge,

But no structure of brick and mortar was proof against attack, especially as besiegers developed new ways of striking at the walls. Though the battering ram was known in Egypt as early as 1900 B.C., it was the Assyrians, ambitious conquerors, who put the ram on wheels and protected it from defenders' arrows by surmounting it with a turret to accommodate archers. The mobile siege tower was another Assyrian invention. The catapult, first developed by Sicilian Greeks (399 B.C.), was mainly an anti-personnel weapon for use by defenders as well as besiegers. The one-armed onager, better able to fling heavy stones against a wall, came somewhat later in the fourth century A.D.[14] All the known elements of ancient siegecraft came together in the Greek world: Persian invaders brought sappers to undermine the walls, and the earliest recorded use of the battering ram in Greece was in 440 B.C.

Of necessity, Greek wall builders devised countermeasures. For example, the city of Rhodes (ca. 400 B.C.) pioneered a new principle of construction: Instead of having a brick (or stone) outer and inner wall encasing debris between them, the Rhodians built an outer curtain backed by a continuous arcade of deep arches along the inner side; this technique demanded less building material, provided better support for men and machines on the battlements, and also permitted breaches in the curtain to be repaired more quickly. Other Greek cities laid out curtain walls in zigzag segments to facilitate flanking fire from the towers and battlements. Still others (like their Mycenean forebears) built gate-approaches at an angle to the main wall, forcing would-be attackers to expose their right sides (not protected by shields) as they pressed forward. Some time during the fourth century B.C., the casemate or tower chamber fitted with slits for projectiles was developed as a means of protecting defenders' catapults from the effects of rain. In the next century Archimedes (b. 287 B.C.) is thought to have invented the cutting of archer-loopholes into the wall during the siege of his native Syracuse. He also anticipated an element of the bastioned trace system by placing projectile weapons, defended by outworks, in front of the main walls to keep the foe at bay.[15]

1995), 12; Spiro Kostof, *The City Assembled*, (New York, 1988), 29; Pant, *Studies in Indian Weapons and Warfare*, 219.

[14] Keegan, *History of Warfare*, 150; Quentin Hughes, *Military Architecture* (London, 1974), 9–10.

[15] Pierre Ducrey, *Warfare in Ancient Greece*, trans. Janet Lloyd (New York, 1985), 168; Toy, *A History of Fortification*, 14–15, 26; De la Croix, *Military Considerations in City Planning*, 22, 30; Hughes, *Military Architecture*, 10, 17, 21.

The final achievement of Greek wall building came centuries later, in the new eastern capital of the Roman Empire. The land and sea walls of Constantinople, completed during the first half of the fifth century A.D.,[16] have been called "the most formidable development of fortifications systems in the ancient world." The main, battlemented land wall was of solid stone, nearly five meters thick and eleven meters high. Beyond it lay an outer wall fitted along its entire length (5,700 meters) with chambers for catapults, and beyond that a broad ditch supported on both sides by masonry. With suitable repair and improvement over time, the fabled walls of Constantinople withstood seven sieges between 626 and 941, and survived to inspire a later generation of travelers from the West.[17]

The surge of new urban wall building in medieval Europe incorporated some refinements on walls dating from the Roman era, especially after about 1200. The trebuchet, invented between 1180 and 1220, was a siege device that employed torsion and counterweights to achieve several times the throwing power of an ancient onager, but whether it was effective in breaching solid walls is disputed.[18] More likely, changes in the West resulted from what Crusaders saw in the East, especially the mighty double ring of walls that protected Constantinople on the landward side. The principle of concentric fortification was of course more easily applied to castles than to cities. In the Crusader states, the military orders were the first to recognize that a shortage of manpower required unusual attention to fortification. Completed in 1202, Krak des Chevaliers, with a fortified keep and double curtain walls providing three levels from which defenders could fire, stood off twelve attacks by the Saracens before succumbing to a ruse in 1271. Krak and other Crusader fortresses provided the models for England's Edward I (1237–1302), sometimes considered the greatest castle builder of the Middle Ages, whose chef-d'oeuvre was the line of castles built to consolidate his conquest of Wales, as at Harlech and Conway. With sufficient resources, cities too could be protected in the same way, as at Carcassone, where France's Louis IX (1227–1270) surrounded a still-standing Roman enceinte with a formidable outer wall. Even if they could not afford a double wall, towns

---

[16] This project was contemporary with the building of walls at Amida or Diyarbekir: see Chapter 16.

[17] Richard Tomlinson, *From Mycenae to Constantinople. The Evolution of the Ancient City* (London, 1992), 213–22; Jim Bradbury, *The Medieval Siege* (Suffolk, 1992), 7.

[18] See the conflicting views of Philippe Contamine, *La Guerre au Moyen Age* (Paris, 1994), 210, and Michael Toch, "The Medieval German City under Siege," in *The Medieval City under Siege*, 45.

incorporated other ideas from the East, like massive barbicans erected to shield approaches to the gates, or adaptations (machicolation) in the upper part of the curtain wall that permitted the building of projecting platforms from which defenders could fire directly down on an adversary who had reached the wall.[19]

Ancient walls and their medieval refinements constituted as it were a dictionary of possibilities from which builders could draw according to their resources and requirements. The history of battlements – merlons behind which defenders shielded themselves alternating with crenels or open spaces – shows how ancient precedents could leave an imprint on the future even after the cities in question were long since buried by the debris of time. Merlons first appear on representations of Egyptian fortifications from the late third millennium B.C., and are rounded, as if to suggest the shields of soldiers standing atop the wall. Rounded merlons also turn up on bas reliefs showing fortified cities among the Hittites, the Assyrians, and, later, the Phoenicians and their Carthaginian cousins. Triangular or stepped merlons that would seem better suited to a brick wall appear first among the Assyrians, then on reliefs showing fortified cities in post-Mauryan India. The rectangular merlons better known from medieval European fortifications were apparently invented by the Greeks.[20] The venerable antiquity of *merlatura* or crenellation helps to explain why, in sixteenth-century Europe, a ruler could have the battlements stripped from a city's wall as a way of proclaiming that it had forfeited the right of fortification.[21]

Knowing that walls were once built in a certain way does not mean one will necessarily copy the past. For example, the Romans were aware of the Greek practice of building irregular, segmented walls, but chose not to follow it; instead, in walling their cities they often copied the pattern of the rectangular earthen rampart that always surrounded a Roman military camp. When town portals had to be protected in the troubled circumstances of the third century A.D., the Romans did so by building double gatehouses, a solution that was perhaps less daunting to a potential attacker than the an-

---

[19] De la Croix, *Military Considerations in City Planning*, 35; Hughes, *Military Architecture*, 18–45; Heinrich Koller, "Die mittelalterliche Stadtmauer als Grundlage städtischen Selbstbewüsstseins," in *Stadt und Krieg*, eds. Bernhard Kirchgässner and Günther Sholz (Sigmaringen, 1989), 16–17.

[20] Edith Porada, "Battlements in the Military Architecture and in the Symbolism of the Ancient Near East," in *Studies in the History of Architecture Presented to Rudolph Wittkower*, eds. Douglas Fraser, Howard Hibbard, and Milton J. Lewine (London, 1967), 1–12; Pant, *Studies in Indian Weapons and Warfare*, 226.

[21] See Chapter 18.

gled gate-approaches known earlier among the Greeks, but more imposing to the onlooker.[22] The sheer lack of funds was probably a more important reason for not imitating the best of what was known. Military engineers understood perfectly well the advantages of backing a brick wall on the inner side by an arcade of deep arches (as in ancient Rhodes) – in fact a city was hardly defensible without the solid battle platform that such arcades supported. Yet builders could not build more than what the town treasury could afford. For example, in the wall at Leiden, with its 50,000,000 bricks, arcades were added only as funds became available; by the time the Spanish army settled down before the city in 1573, the simple curtain wall was backed by arcades only at a few key points. The fact that Leiden's burghers successfully held off the foe for nearly a year – a victory of great moment in the Dutch Revolt – offers a useful caution against assuming that a town not fortified in up-to-date fashion could easily be taken.[23]

Nonetheless, good fortification did make a difference, and perhaps most clearly so in the age of transition to the fortress architecture *alla moderna*, inaugurated by Italian military engineers of the late fifteenth century. The brilliant success of the "trace italienne" or bastioned trace was preceded and in a way necessitated by the brilliant success of the siege train, as developed by French artillery masters of the fifteenth century. In the last stages of the Hundred Years' War, Charles VII's siege train reduced as many as sixty English-held castles in a single season's campaign (1449); the city of Harfleur took four months to subdue in 1440, seventeen days in 1449.[24] By the 1460s, Italian military enterprisers like Federigo da Montefeltre, Duke of Urbino, were capturing fortified places by the use of mobile field artillery *alla francese*. Italian observers like Francesco Guicciardini, accustomed to a situation in which "the rulers of a state could hardly be disposessed," marveled at how fortresses were cracked open one after the other as

---

[22] De la Croix, *Military Considerations in City Planning*, 30; Hughes, *Military Architecture*, 38; Edward Luttwak, *The Grand Strategy of the Roman Empire from the First Century A.D. to the Third* (Baltimore, 1976), 167.

[23] H.A. van Oerle, *Leiden binnen en buiten de Stadsvesten: de Geschiedenis van de Stedebouwkundige Ontwikkeling binnen het Leidse Rechtsgebied tot het Einde van de Gouden Eeuw*, 2 vols. (Leiden, 1975), 253; and for the successful defense of the city by Dutch rebels in 1573: 844, 278–95. In the absence of a battle platform or *weergang*, loopholes for shooters had to be cut into the wall at ground level.

[24] Simon Pepper and Nicholas Adams, *Firearms and Fortifications. Military Architecture and Siege Warfare in Sixteenth-Century Siena* (Chicago, 1986), 8–11; Hughes, *Military Architecture*, 67.

France's Charles VIII (1484–1498) marched through Italy in 1494, en route to a short-lived conquest of the Kingdom of Naples.[25] It was not just the throw-weight of projectiles that made the cannon of this era so much more effective than the onagers and trebuchets of an earlier time: since the gunpowder missile "travelled in a flat trajectory, it could be directed at the one point where a high wall is vulnerable to collapse, at its foundations."[26]

The new system devised to withstand artillery bombardment had as one of its principal elements a low rampart. In a fully developed bastioned trace, a high curtain wall of medieval vintage was torn down and replaced by a low, stone-or brick-faced rampart that could absorb the shock of incoming cannonballs without giving way. In a less costly variant of the same principle, the old curtain wall remained standing while the suburbs beyond it were cleared to build a new-style rampart or "gun gallery" for the emplacement of cannon.[27] In a pinch, a hastily built earthen rampart could serve to close a breach made by artillery in an old-style curtain wall. This expedient, known in Italy as a *retirata*, was used successfully by Pisa in its defense against the French (1500), by Fra Giocondo, Venice's military architect, in his defense of Padua against the armies of the League of Cambrai (1509), by the duke of Guise in his defense of Metz against Charles V (1552–3), and by the burghers of Leiden against the Spaniards (1573–4).[28]

The second main element of the new system – the bastions properly so-called – was a series of triangular or spear-shaped gun platforms projecting at regular intervals, so constructed that the emplaced cannon could rake the ground at some distance in front of the rampart, while each point along the rampart was enfiladed by covering fire from opposite directions, with the inner loopholes or gunslits protected from besiegers' fire by the bastion's laterally projecting lobes. Fortresses equipped with bastions proved able to stand off or at least delay the advance of immense forces. In 1532 Nicola Jurešić, castellan of Güns in Hungary, held out with his 800 men for twenty-one days

---

[25] Francesco Paolo Fiore, "L'Architettura Militara di Francesco di Giorgio: realizzazioni e trattati," in *Architettura Militare nell'Europa del XVI secolo*, eds. Carlo Cresti, Ameilo Fara, and Daniela Lamberini (Siena, 1988), 38–9; Pepper and Adams, *Firearms and Fortification*, 8–11.

[26] Keegan, *History of Warfare*, 140.

[27] Pepper and Adams, *Firearms and Fortifications*, 20–1.

[28] Christopher Duffy, *Siege Warfare: The Fortress in the Early Modern World, 1494–1660* (London, 1979), 16–17, 52; Geoffrey Parker, "The Gunpowder Revolution, 1300–1500," in *Cambridge Illustrated History of Warfare*, 113.

against the armies of Suleyman the Lawgiver. In Italy, military planners were reluctant to undertake the siege of "artillery fortresses."[29]
By 1530, Michele di Sanmichele, by completely rebuilding the fortifications of his native Verona, had shown how the new principles could
be applied to the defense of a large city.

In practice, however, few cities had the resources to support reconstruction on the massive scale that was required. Taking into account
the outworks as well as the rampart and its ring of bastions, a fully
built bastioned trace could take up as much ground as the area occupied by the city itself. The city as a form of human society was apparently not well adapted to enclosure within such a massive girdle: new
fortress-cities would eventually be built in the *alla moderna* style, but
none ever attained the population level envisioned by its builders.[30] In
fact, the practical need for multiple fortifications in the new style became apparent only as the available supply of heavy guns increased
dramatically in Europe, during the second half of the sixteenth century. Quentin Hughes believes that "nearly all the main towns in Europe were refortified in the second half of the sixteenth or at the beginning of the seventeenth century." But Simon Pepper and Nicholas
Adams take a different view: As late as the end of the sixteenth century, "none of the greatest cities of Europe could boast a complete and
fully bastioned enceinte."[31] Yet if Europe's cities were slow in adopting
the bastioned trace, more costly by far than a curtain wall, military
strategists were even slower in devising means to attack the new fortifications successfully. Not until Vauban, the military architect and
grand strategist for Louis XIV (1660–1715), did planners perfect a system of entrenching that enabled attackers to enclose a city, guard
against reinforcement, and advance step-by-step towards the bastions
that were the key to its defenses. The military balance thus swung
once again in favor of the offense, but at a daunting cost. In Vauban's
opinion anyone expecting to take a properly fortified place needed a
force at least ten times greater than that of the defenders. Hence the
great sieges of the seventeenth century, like the fortifications against
which they were directed, were turned into symbols of the awesome
power of those few princes who controlled the resources of large and
well-governed states.[32]

[29] Luigi Zangheri, "Gli architetti italiani e la difese dei territori dell'impero minacciati
dai turchi," in *Architettura militare nell'Europa*, 245; Duffy, *Siege Warfare*, 25.

[30] Duffy, *Siege Warfare*, 30; Kostof, *The City Assembled*, 31; De la Croix, *Military Considerations in City Planning*, 10, on Palmanova.

[31] Hughes, *Military Architecture*, 112; Pepper and Adams, *Firearms and Fortifications*, 28.

[32] Hughes, *Military Architecture*, 8, 129. On siege maps as a way of glorifying royal
power, see Chapter 19.

One may say in conclusion that the recorded history of town wall building begins with the kings of ancient Sumer and ends with the rulers who disposed over the huge siege armies of seventeenth- and eighteenth-century Europe. The window on that great tradition that this volume affords begins with Epaminondas, the founder of Theban hegemony in Greece, and ends with Louis XIV of France.

PART I

To wall or not to wall

CHAPTER 1

Contained communities in tropical Africa

GRAHAM CONNAH

Illustrations by Jack Simmons, Canterbury, England

INTRODUCTION

THE myth of precolonial Africa as a continent of ephemeral villages persists, not only with many members of the public in Western countries but even occasionally with some non-Africanist scholars. The reality is that the settlements of old Black Africa included everything from tiny hamlets to large cities, which at any point in the continuum could vary from transient, mobile occupation to permanency over long periods. The phenomenon of the city wall, best known from European examples, also occurred in tropical Africa, although to try to understand its African manifestations one must consider them in their broader context. Thus, the crucial issue is not whether a particular settlement constituted a city, a town, or a large village, or indeed whether an enclosure around it could properly be called a "wall." The real issue is whether one is dealing with what this writer proposes to call a "contained community;" that is to say, a group of people who for one reason or another saw fit to separate themselves from other groups by placing themselves in a container, be it of stone, of mud, of earth, of wood, or even of natural vegetation or a body of water. Indeed, an understanding of this practice must not only be sought amongst a wide selection of such settlements, rather than in only a narrowly defined group but, in order to ask questions about the form, function, and meaning of city walls in tropical Africa, one must also consider some of the communities that were not so enclosed.

Some years ago a writer on town defenses in England and Wales complained about the neglect of this subject.[1] It should, therefore,

---

[1] Hilary L. Turner, *Town Defences in England and Wales: An architectural and documentary study AD 900–1500* (London, 1971), 13.

19

come as no surprise that in Africa the enclosure of settlements has even now had very little systematic attention from researchers. In particular there has been no attempt at a synthetic study, although there is a large and scattered body of published material on specific places and areas that is relevant and which has been sampled for this essay. These sources are extremely variable in quality and often difficult to obtain. They also represent a variety of approaches: archaeological, historical, architectural, geographical, and others. A special problem concerns plans and maps, which are so essential for the study of this subject; when included in publications at all, these are often unsatisfactory because of the size and complexity of the area that has to be represented. The more general subject of African urbanization is much better served at the synthetic level, for both the present and the past,[2] and there are numerous more specific studies, of which a selection might be mentioned as of interest here.[3] In such writings African urbanization is often examined in the still broader context of state formation.

As already indicated, the concern of this essay is with tropical Africa, that is, strictly speaking, with that part of the continent that lies between the Tropic of Cancer, which runs through the middle of the Sahara Desert, and the Tropic of Capricorn, which bisects the Kalahari Desert. However, the intention is not to apply the term literally but merely to use it for what is loosely called "Black Africa," and as a means of excluding from consideration Mediterranean North Africa and the Nile below the First Cataract. In recent years there has been

---

[2] For the present, see Anthony M. O'Connor, *The African City* (New York, 1983); for the past: Graham Connah, *African Civilizations. Precolonial Cities and States in Tropical Africa: An Archaeological Perspective* (Cambridge, 1987); Catherine Coquery-Vidrovitch, *Histoire des villes d'Afrique Noire: des origines à la colonisation* (Paris, 1993); and Richard W. Hull, *African Cities and Towns Before the European Conquest* (New York, 1976).

[3] G.H.O. Abungu and H.W. Mutoro, "Coast-interior Settlements and Social Relations in the Kenya Coastal Hinterland," in *The Archaeology of Africa: Food, Metals and Towns*, eds. Thurstan Shaw et al. (London, 1993), 694–704; James Anquandah, "Urbanization and State Formation in Ghana during the Iron Age," in *The Archaeology of Africa*, 642–51; R. Fletcher, "Settlement Area and Communication in African Towns and Cities," in *The Archaeology of Africa*, 732–49; Robert Griffeth, "The Hausa City-States from 1450 to 1804," in *The City-State in Five Cultures*, eds. Robert Griffeth and Carol G. Thomas (Santa Barbara, 1981), 143–80; A. Howard, "Pre-colonial Centres and Regional Systems in Africa," *Pan-African Journal* 8/3 (1975): 247–70; A.L. Mabogunje, *Urbanization in Nigeria* (London, 1968); Susan Keech McIntosh and Roderick J. McIntosh, "Cities without Citadels: Understanding Urban Origins along the Middle Niger," in *The Archaeology of Africa*, 622–41; S. Munro-Hay, "State Development and Urbanism in Northern Ethiopia," in *The Archaeology of Africa*, 609–21; P.J.J. Sinclair et al., "Urban Trajectories on the Zimbabwean Plateau," in *The Archaeology of Africa*, 705–31; and C. Winters, "The Classification of Traditional African Cities," *Journal of Urban History* 10/1 (1983): 3–31.

increasing criticism of the practice of beheading the African continent in this way, and the term "Sub-Saharan Africa" that used to be popular is less frequently used. Nevertheless, the cultural history of North Africa and the lower Nile is so different from that of the rest of the continent that, so far as the present discussion is concerned, it demands separate consideration elsewhere.

FORM

Archaeological evidence indicates that the enclosure of settlements has been a common practice in tropical Africa during the last two millennia, particularly over the last one thousand years (Fig. 1.1). Indeed, one of the earliest examples, that of the Nile city of Qasr Ibrim in the extreme south of Egypt, was first walled in the late eleventh or early tenth century B.C., and remained occupied until the early nineteenth century A.D., with its stone and mudbrick defenses being enlarged, strengthened, or repaired during the Ptolemaic, Roman, Christian, and Islamic periods.[4] Also on the Nile, just inside the northern Sudan, are the remains of the stone-walled city of Faras, dating from the first millennium A.D.,[5] and, much further south, part of the city of Meroë was enclosed with a stone wall by the beginning of the same millennium.[6] These and other examples suggest influences from the Mediterranean world to the north, although archaeological and historical evidence indicates that the practice of settlement enclosure eventually became widespread in parts of Africa far beyond the reach of such influences. Even quite small groups of people would sometimes encompass themselves in this way, such as the largely pastoralist Sotho occupants of the drystone-built Type N settlement units, like Ntsuanatsatsi, studied by Maggs in the Orange Free State and the Transvaal in South Africa.[7] Dated to about the fifteenth century A.D., these structures seem to have been merely family homesteads (Fig. 1.2) and their low enclosing wall must have been principally intended for the pro-

---

[4] W.Y. Adams et al., "Qasr Ibrim 1980 and 1982," *Journal of Egyptian Archaeology* 69 (1983): 45; and Derek A. Welsby, *The Kingdom of Kush: The Napatan and Meroitic Empires* (London, 1996), 46–7.

[5] J. Karkowski, "A few remarks on stone used in Christian constructions at Faras," in *Nubische Studien: Tagungsakten der 5 Internationalen Konferenz der International Society for Nubian Studies Heidelberg 22–25 September 1982*, ed. M. Krause (Mainz am Rhein, 1986), 316.

[6] Welsby, *The Kingdom of Kush*, 45–6, 148–50.

[7] Timothy M.O'C. Maggs, "The Iron Age of the Orange Free State," in *Congrès panafricain de préhistoire, Dakar 1967, Actes de 6ᵉ session*, ed. H.J. Hugot (Chambéry, 1972), 175–81; and Maggs, "Iron Age Patterns and Sotho History on the Southern Highveld: South Africa," *World Archaeology* 7/3 (1976): 318–32.

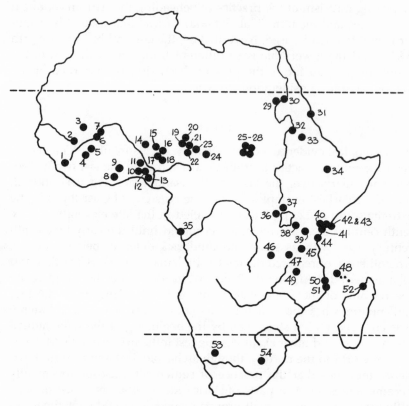

Figure 1.1. Distribution of enclosed settlements mentioned in the text. Tropics of Cancer and Capricorn shown by broken lines. Numbers indicate: 1. Bafodia & Musaia. 2. Mourgoula. 3. Koumbi-Saleh. 4. Tiong-i. 5. Sikasso. 6. Jenne-jeno. 7. Hamdallahi. 8. Kokobin. 9. Kitare. 10. Ife. 11. Old Oyo. 12. Ado-Ekiti. 13. Benin City. 14. Surame. 15. Katsina. 16. Kano. 17. Zaria. 18. Bauchi. 19. Birnin Gazargamo. 20. Garoumélé. 21. Ngala. 22. Amchaka. 23. Goulfeil. 24. Masena. 25–8. Usungra, Namudu, Wima, Mao. 29. Faras. 30. Qasr Ibrim. 31. Suakin. 32. Meroë. 33. Kassala. 34. Harar. 35 Loango. 36. Bigo. 37. Rubaga. 38. Samunge. 39. Kibosho. 40. Gedi. 41. *kaya* settlements. 42–3. Pate and Shanga. 44. Moa. 45. Kalenga. 46. Masala's tembé. 47. Utengule. 48. Itsandra. 49. Kiwaura's tembé. 50. Gomene. 51. Somana. 52. Mahilaka. 53. //Khauxa!nas. 54. Ntsuanatsatsi.

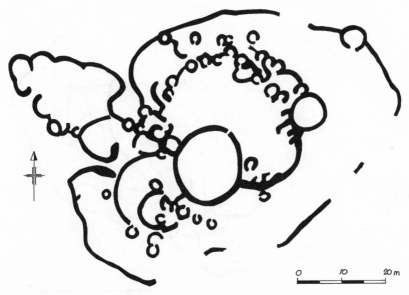

Figure 1.2. Type N settlement unit at Ntsuanatsatsi, South Africa. Scale in meters. After Timothy M. O'C. Maggs, "The Iron Age of the Orange Free State," in *Congrés panafricain de préhistoire, Dakar 1967. Actes de 6ᵉ session.* Chambéry, 1972, Fig. 5.

tection of livestock from wild animals and marauding neighbors. The settlement units occurred in clusters of up to one hundred, comprising small towns of as many as 1,500 people, but the clusters do not seem to have been collectively enclosed. On a larger scale is the stone-walled enclosure of //Khauxa!nas, on a hilltop overlooking a water-hole in southeastern Namibia. This was constructed by Oorlam (Khoi) nomadic pastoralists in the late eighteenth century, apparently in response to the penetration of settlers and merchants from further south.[8] Its perimeter wall is almost 700 meters long, consisting of stones up to two metres in length laid in two parallel rows, with the space in between filled with rubble and earth. Although gunflints found within the enclosure indicate that the inhabitants had firearms, the structure was not a fortification in the narrow sense: most of the wall is little over one meter in height and there are no less than twenty-two entrances. Rather it was a walled herding encampment,

[8] J. Kinahan, "The Archaeology of Social Rank among Eighteenth-Century Nomadic Pastoralists in Southern Namibia," *African Archaeological Review* 13/4 (1996): 225–45.

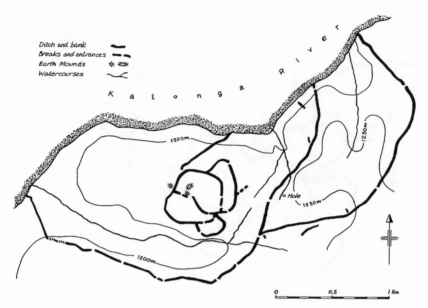

Figure 1.3. Enclosures at Bigo, Uganda. [After Graham Connah, *African Civilizations. Precolonial Cities and States in Tropical Africa: An archaeological perspective* (Cambridge, 1987), Fig. 9.6.]

positioned defensively and meant to impress visitors, both hostile and friendly, although occupied for only a very few years.

At both Ntsuanatsatsi and //Khauxa!nas, our archaeological understanding of the enclosed settlements is aided by historical information, both oral and documentary. In western Uganda, however, are a number of large earthwork enclosures, consisting of banks and ditches, which have also been associated with pastoralism but for which there are only uncertain oral traditions.[9] Most notable of these is Bigo (Fig. 1.3), an extensive and complicated network of enclosures adjacent to the Katonga River, which forms one side of some of them. It has been estimated that the digging of the ditches at Bigo would have required the removal of over 200,000 cubic meters of earth and rock.[10] Dated to the fifteenth and sixteenth centuries A.D., it has been suggested that there was considerable human occupation at the center of this complex, although it seems likely that the outer enclosures were for pen-

[9] E.C. Lanning, "Ancient Earthworks in Western Uganda," *Uganda Journal* 17 (1953): 51–62.
[10] M. Posnansky, "Bigo bya Mugenyi," *Uganda Journal* 33/2 (1969): 144.

ning cattle rather than for defense; it is also possible that the immensity of the earthworks was intended to give prestige to those who lived there. Elsewhere I have called Bigo "the pastoral equivalent of a city,"[11] but it is likely that its occupants were also cultivators, as were those of the nearby (nonenclosed) town of Ntusi,[12] and it has to be admitted that we still do not know enough about any of the western Ugandan earthworks.

Settlements tended to be more permanent in societies where cultivation played a more significant role, as was the case on the clay plains to the south of Lake Chad, in an area that includes parts of southwestern Chad, northern Cameroon, and northeastern Nigeria.[13] Commencing early in the first millennium B.C., continued occupation caused many large settlement mounds to accumulate there; some like Daima in Nigeria were over ten meters in height, and some of these were eventually enclosed with mud walls. One such is the town of Ngala, in Nigeria, where in the 1960s parts of the mudbrick wall could still be seen. In contrast, at the still-occupied mound at Amchaka, also in Nigeria, only slight traces of the ditch survived, although we know from a contemporary written account that the "stockade" surrounding this town (then called Amsaka) was stormed following a siege in 1575.[14] However, some walled towns in this area are not on settlement mounds and Goulfeil in Cameroon is a useful example of these.[15] A map of it made in 1937 shows that most of the community was crammed into the enclosed space by the side of the River Chari. That the walling of towns in the area south of Lake Chad was actually more common than the surviving archaeological evidence would suggest, is apparent from the account of Heinrich Barth's journey through this area in 1852, to which we are particularly indebted for a remarkable plan of the walled town of Masena, now in southwest Chad.[16]

Far to the east of Lake Chad, approximately midway between it and the upper Nile, Musa Mohammed has studied first-millennium A.D. settlement sites in Central Darfur in the Sudan, some of which were

[11] Connah, *African Civilizations*, 225.
[12] A. Reid, "Ntusi and its Hinterland: Further Investigations of the Later Iron Age and Pastoral Ecology in Southern Uganda," *Nyame Akuma* 33 (1990): 27.
[13] Graham Connah, *Three Thousand Years in Africa: Man and His Environment in the Lake Chad Region of Nigeria* (Cambridge, 1981).
[14] A. ibn Fartua, *History of the First Twelve Years of the Reign of Mai Idris Alooma of Bornu (1571–1583)*, trans. H.R. Palmer (Lagos, 1926), 24–8.
[15] M. Griaule and J.-P. Lebeuf, "Fouilles dans la région du Tchad (III)," *Journal de la Société des Africanistes* 21/1 (1951): 1–95.
[16] Heinrich Barth, *Travels and Discoveries in North and Central Africa: Being a Journal of an Expedition Undertaken under the Auspices of H.B.M.'s Government in the Years 1849–1855*, 5 vols. (London, 1857–8), III:foldout facing 388.

also enclosed.[17] Drystone walling was used to enclose small groups of houses, such as those at Usungra, but at Namudu such walling enclosed a space measuring 1 by 0.6 kilometer containing the remains of fifty-five houses, and at both Wima and Mao an embayment in the side of steep hills had its entrance closed by a stone wall behind which larger numbers of houses sheltered. Mao was the bigger settlement, containing about 300 houses and with almost as many again outside the enclosing wall. The occupants of this small town were apparently iron-using cultivators and herders, during a period dated from the tenth to the eleventh century A.D., who seem to have abandoned the place because of environmental deterioration.

Also in the savannah but to the west, in what is now northern Nigeria, lay some of the best known of Africa's enclosed settlements, the many walled cities of the former Hausa states.[18] These seem to have originated early in the millennium just past in an agriculturally rich area that permitted the growth of functional specialization, widening trade networks, and, ultimately, urbanization. Kano, Zaria, Katsina, and other Hausa cities were essentially individual entities, each one controlling the territory around it and comprising a city-state. Constantly in conflict with both powerful neighbors and with one another, these cities shared the distinguishing feature of the mud walls that surrounded them, walls whose primary purpose was clearly defence. In the mid-1820s, explorer Captain Hugh Clapperton, an experienced Royal Naval officer, recorded the length of the Kano city wall as about twenty-four kilometers, and counted fifteen entry gates. The wall rose to heights of over nine meters and had a dry ditch on both the inner and outer sides. The gates were of wood covered with sheet iron, with guardhouses flanking each gate.[19] A plan made by Clapperton shows the "town" of Kano occupying less than half of the walled area, which also included three other "villages," two hills, extensive "gardens," and several water sources.[20] It would appear that Kano was intended to be able to survive a lengthy siege. Much the same impression is given by a plan made by Heinrich Barth in 1851 (Fig. 1.4), and a plan of Katsina that he made in the same year shows it to have been similar.[21] Indeed, for Kano, Barth's text is quite explicit on this point:

[17] Ibrahim Musa Mohammed, *The Archaeology of Central Darfur (Sudan) in the 1st Millennium A.D.*, BAR International Series 285 (Oxford, 1986).

[18] Griffeth, "The Hausa City-States."

[19] Dixon Denham et al., *Narrative of Travels and Discoveries in North and Central Africa, in the Years 1822, 1823, and 1824* (London, 1826): Hugh Clapperton's narrative, 50.

[20] Denham et al., *Narrative of Travels and Discoveries*, Clapperton's narrative, 56.

[21] Barth, *Travels and Discoveries*, II:107, 79, but both reproduced in Anthony H.M. Kirk-

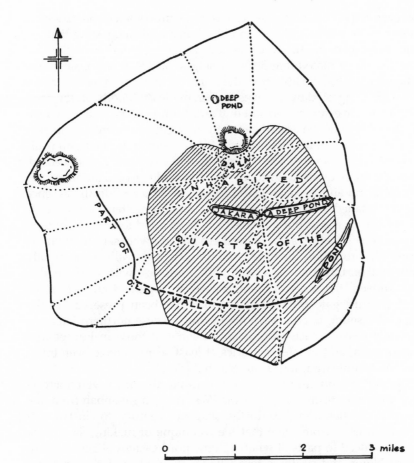

Figure 1.4. Barth's 1851 plan of the walled city of Kano, Nigeria. [After Anthony H. M. Kirk-Greene, *Barth's Travels in Nigeria: Extracts from the Journal of Heinrich Barth's Travels in Nigeria, 1850–1855* (London, 1962), Fig. 3.]

The reason why the fortifications were carried to so much greater extent than the population of the town rendered necessary, was evidently to make the place capable of sustaining a long siege (sufficient ground being enclosed within the walls to produce the necessary supply of corn for the inhabitants), and also to receive the population of the open and unprotected villages in the neighborhood.[22]

Greene, *Barth's Travels in Nigeria: Extracts from the Journal of Heinrich Barth's Travels in Nigeria, 1850–1855* (Oxford, 1962), 94, 108.

[22] Barth, *Travels and Discoveries*, II:119.

However, Barth's map of Kano differed in some details from Clapperton's and also marked part of an older inner wall, suggesting that the Kano walls had gradually expanded as the population of the city grew. (Barth estimated it at 30,000, rising to 60,000 at the busiest time of the year.[23]) That the history of the Kano city walls is indeed complex is strongly suggested by an investigation made by Moody on the basis of both surface examination and oral and documentary sources, which identifies building phases of eleventh to twelfth-, fifteenth-, and seventeenth-century dates.[24] However, Moody's survey of the Kano walls is almost unique so far as northern Nigerian city walls are concerned, although there exists a virtually unobtainable investigation of the walls of Zaria and a sketch-plan of those of Surame.[25] In the absence of other detailed archaeological investigations, only tentative generalizations can be made, but it seems that the city and town walls of both Hausa and some other areas in northern Nigeria were serious attempts to provide protection for their communities. The walls were usually substantial earthen ramparts faced with mudbrick, with solid wooden gates. Indeed, the walls of Surame were of stone and an early nineteenth-century gate from Bauchi, which has been preserved in the Nigeria Museum, Lagos, is wholly of iron.[26] These northern Nigerian city walls were, in fact, reminiscent of some of those in Europe and Western Asia, and in later centuries at least seem to have been influenced by Islamic traditions from North Africa.

Commercial and cultural contacts with North Africa were increasingly important to the people of the West African savannah from late in the first millennium A.D. In the sixteenth century, for instance, it was presumably from there that the technique of making fired brick was introduced to parts of what are now northeastern Nigeria, southeastern Niger, and southwestern Chad.[27] A number of sites in these areas have the remains of important structures of this material and two of them are walled urban sites, of which some record has been made. Best known is Birnin Gazargamo in the Yobe River valley near

[23] Barth, *Travels and Discoveries*, II:124.
[24] H.L.B. Moody, "Ganuwa – The Walls of Kano City," *Nigeria Magazine* 92 (1967): 21; and Moody, *The Walls and Gates of Kano City* (Department of Antiquities, Nigeria, n.d. [1970]), 39–41.
[25] John E.G. Sutton, "The Walls of Zaria and Kufena," *Zaria Archaeology Paper* 11 (1976): 1–18, plus two addenda; and Sutton, "Kebbi Valley Preliminary Survey 1975," *Zaria Archaeology Paper* 5 (1976): 10.
[26] Robert S. Smith, *Warfare & Diplomacy in Pre-colonial West Africa*, 2nd ed. (London, 1989), 101, 118.
[27] J.E. Lavers, "A Note on Birni Gazargamu and 'Burnt Brick' Sites in the Bornu Caliphate," in *Papers Presented to the 4th Conference of West African Archaeologists*, ed. A. Fagg (Jos, 1971), 39–57.

the northern frontier of Nigeria, historically dated to the period ca.
1470–ca. 1810, which is encircled by what appears to be an earthen
dump rampart, although its precise character would only be determined by excavation. This important city was formerly the capital of
the state of Borno.[28] The other site is Garoumélé, in Niger, near the
northwestern corner of Lake Chad.[29] In contrast to Birnin Gazargamo,
it was enclosed by a mudbrick wall of subrectangular plan that appears to have been comparable with the city walls of Hausaland.

Further to the west, on the edge of the Sahara Desert, there were
other examples of walled communities, some of considerable size. The
Islamic influence was strong in these areas; indeed in the case of
Hamdallahi, near Mopti in central Mali, the city was a specifically
religious foundation that lasted for only a few decades in the nineteenth century.[30] The capital of the Fulani Empire of Macina, it has
been claimed to have been "the biggest city of precolonial West Africa."[31] Although only short-lived, Hamdallahi was surrounded by a
mud rampart faced with mudbricks, some of them laid in decorative
courses; the palace in the middle of the city had a stone-built enclosure
wall with at least one angle-tower. However, it would be a mistake to
attribute the origins of city walls in this region to trans-Saharan Islamic influences merely because they were important in later times.
Excavations at Jenne-jeno, in the Inland Niger Delta of Mali, have
shown that the beginnings of urbanization in this part of Africa were
pre-Islamic. A two-kilometer-long city wall of mudbricks and mud
rubble at Jenne-jeno has been claimed to have originated about 800
A.D., although the place was not Islamicized till the thirteenth century,
from which time the site was gradually abandoned and the city
moved to a new location.[32] Another potentially pre-Islamic city wall is

---

[28] A.D.H. Bivar and P.L. Shinnie, "Old Kanuri Capitals," *Journal of African History* 3/1
(1962): 2–3; and Connah, *Three Thousand Years in Africa*, 228–33.

[29] Bivar and Shinnie, "Old Kanuri Capitals," 4–6.

[30] A. Gallay et al., *Hamdallahi, capitale de l'Empire peul du Massina, Mali, Première fouille
archéologique, études historiques et ethnoarchéologiques.* Sonderschriften des Frobenius-
Instituts 9 (Stuttgart, 1990).

[31] A. Mayor, "Hamdallahi, Capital of the Fulani Empire of Macina, Mali: A Multidisci-
plinary Approach," in *Aspects of African Archaeology: Papers from the 10th Congress of
the PanAfrican Association for Prehistory and Related Studies*, eds. Gilbert Pwiti and
Robert C. Soper (Harare, 1996).

[32] Susan Keech McIntosh and Roderick J. McIntosh, *Prehistoric Investigations in the Region
of Jenne, Mali: A Study in the Development of Urbanism in the Sahel. Part i: Archaeological
and Historical Background and the Excavations at Jenne-jeno*, BAR International Series 89
(i) (Oxford, 1980), 63; McIntosh and McIntosh, "The Inland Niger Delta before the
Empire of Mali: Evidence from Jenne-jeno," *Journal of African History* 22 (1981): 17;
and McIntosh and McIntosh, "The Early City in West Africa: Towards an Understanding," *African Archaeological Review* 2 (1984): 91.

that at Koumbi Saleh in Mauritania, thought to have been the capital
of the old state of Ghana in the first millennium A.D., but the wall has
still not been satisfactorily dated. Certainly by the later nineteeth century, walls enclosing towns and cities in some parts of the region just
south of the Sahara were showing clear signs of external influences
and, in an area destabilized by the campaigns of Samori and others,
such walls were numerous.[33] Thus a drawing of Sikasso, in southern
Mali, shows a city enclosed by a high wall with closely set drum
towers that looks almost like something from medieval Europe, an
impression also given by a drawing of Tiong-i in the same area.[34]
Indeed, a series of remarkable French military plans dated to 1881
(Fig. 1.5 of Mourgoula is an example) reinforces this impression of
medieval European walled communities, often huddled around a citadel, in spite of the structures being in mudbrick and located in western Mali and eastern Guinea, where Islamic rather than other influences had determined their form.[35]

Such signs of external influences vanish, however, when one turns
to enclosed West African settlements in the southern savannah, in the
forest, and at the meeting point of the two. In northeastern Sierra
Leone, for instance, there are the remains of numerous fortified towns
dating to the past 400 to 500 years, some protected by a stone wall,
such as Bafodia; others, such as Musaia, by a mud wall and ditch.[36] In
addition, in the forests of the southern Ivory Coast and Ghana are a
number of "entrenchments," consisting of a ditch and one or two
banks surrounding a circular or oval area with an average circumference of two to three kilometers.[37] These appear to belong to the second
millennium and the best known of them is Kokobin, in Ghana. Far
more complex and rather larger is the site of Kitare, in the savannah
woodland of east-central Ghana, which is enclosed by multiple banks
and ditches and has been interpreted as a trading center for gold and

[33] J.F. Ade Ajayi and Michael Crowder, *History of West Africa*, 2 vols. (London, 1974): II:
298–301.
[34] Le Capitaine [Louis Gustave] Binger, *Du Niger au Golfe de Guinée: par le pays de Kong
et le Mossi*, 2 vols. (Paris, 1892), I:95, 171.
[35] C.R. Meillassoux, "Plans d'anciennes fortifications *(tata)* en pays Malinké," *Journal de
la Société des Africanistes* 36/1 (1966): 29–43.
[36] C.R. DeCorse, "An Archaeological Survey of Protohistoric Defensive Sites in Sierra
Leone," *Nyame Akuma* 17 (1980): 49, 51; and DeCorse, "Material Aspects of Limba,
Yalunka and Kuranko Ethnicity: Archaeological Research in Northeastern Sierra Leone," in *Archaeological Approaches to Cultural Identity*, ed. Stephan Shennan (London,
1989), 129, 131.
[37] Oliver Davies, *Archaeology in Ghana* (Edinburgh, 1961), 14–26; Davies, *West Africa
before the Europeans: Archaeology and Prehistory* (London, 1967), 284, 287–90; and James
Anquandah, *Rediscovering Ghana's Past* (Harlow, 1982), 68–9.

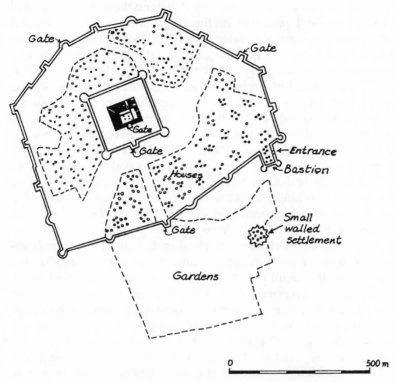

Figure 1.5. French military plan of the fortified settlement of Mourgoula, Mali, in 1881. After C. Meillassoux, "Plans d'anciennes fortifications (*tata*) en pays Malinké," *Journal de la Société des Africanistes* 36/1 (1966): 33.

kola traders during the sixteenth and seventeenth centuries.[38] It is the forest and adjacent regions of Nigeria, however, that have some of the most remarkable enclosed settlements in the more southerly parts of West Africa. For instance, by the nineteenth century the Yoruba of southwestern Nigeria were some of the most urbanized people in Africa, and probably because of the civil wars of that period, most of their towns and cities were surrounded by walls, as at Ado-Ekiti. Although the original character of these enclosures is often uncertain, many seem to have been massive earthen ramparts, perhaps faced with mudbrick or timbering, and some were relatively low, free-standing mudbrick walls, whose disadvantage in such a high rainfall

[38] R.D. Mathewson, "Kitare: An Early Trading Centre in the Volta Basin," in *Congrès panafricain de préhistoire*, 182–5.

area was dealt with in one instance by thatching the top.[39] An external ditch was also usual, planted with thorns or stakes in some cases, and beyond the ditch there was often a belt of forest with thick undergrowth left untouched, so that the gates could only be approached by narrow paths.[40] The antiquity of town and city wall building in Yorubaland is unknown but probably goes back to early in the second millennium. There is evidence that the occupation of Ife, famous for its artwork, commenced late in the first millennium A.D., but its city walls (Fig. 1.6), although they suggest a complex series of phases, have not been adequately dated and at least some of them belong to only the last few centuries.[41] The dating of the walls of Old Oyo, or Oyo Ile as it is also called, is perhaps a little better, because this former capital of the Oyo kingdom is known to have attained the height of its power in the seventeenth and eighteenth centuries and to have been abandoned probably in 1836 or 1837.[42]

By far the most remarkable settlement enclosures of southern Nigeria are those of the extraordinarily complex network of interlocking earthworks in the vicinity of Benin City (Fig. 1.7 shows part only). They have been described as "perhaps the densest concentration of earthworks anywhere in the world."[43] These *iya*, as they are known to the Edo people of the area, consist of complicated combinations of banks and ditches, varying in scale, that cover an area of about 6,500 square kilometers and have been estimated to have a total length of over 16,000 kilometers, implying at least 150,000,000 person-hours of work over a period of several centuries.[44] It would appear that the component enclosures of this network surrounded individual settlements and their agricultural land, although much of the complex had become covered in the dense secondary regrowth that occurs in the West African rain forest following the bush-fallow abandonment of farms, and it was only in the early 1960s that the extent of the earthworks began to be realized. It seems likely that the occupants of each

[39] J.F. Ade Ajayi and R. Smith, *Yoruba Warfare in the Nineteenth Century* (London, 1964), 137.

[40] Ajayi and Smith, *Yoruba Warfare*, 23–8; and Smith, *Warfare & Diplomacy*, 99–119.

[41] Paul Ozanne, "A New Archaeological Survey of Ife," *Odu*, n.s. 1 (1969): 28–45.

[42] Robert C. Soper and P.J. Darling, "The Walls of Oyo Ile," "*West African Journal of Archaeology* 10 (1980): 61–81; B. Agbaje-Williams, "Oyo Ruins in NW Yorubaland, Nigeria," *Journal of Field Archaeology* 17/3 (1990): 367–73.

[43] Soper and Darling, "The Walls of Oyo Ile," 77.

[44] P.J. Darling, *Archaeology and History in Southern Nigeria: The Ancient Linear Earthworks of Benin and Ishan. Part ii: Ceramic and Other Specialist Studies.* BAR International Series 215 (Oxford, 1984), 302–3.

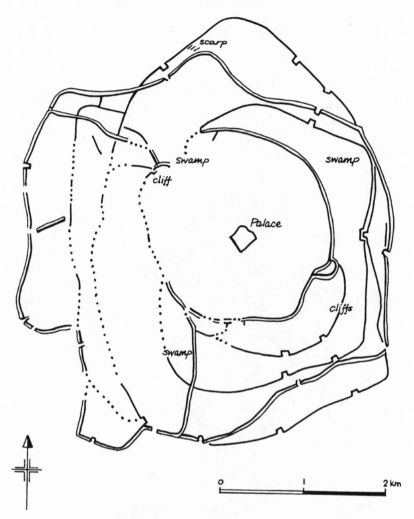

Figure 1.6. The city walls of Ife, Nigeria. After Graham Connah, *African Civilizations. Precolonial Cities and States in Tropical Africa: An Archaeological Perspective* (Cambridge, 1987), Fig. 6.4.

settlement had sought to enclose sufficient forest to provide not only the farmland that was in production at any one time but also the considerable areas that would have to lie fallow in a rotational cycle of some years duration, as well as a share of "wild" forest that could

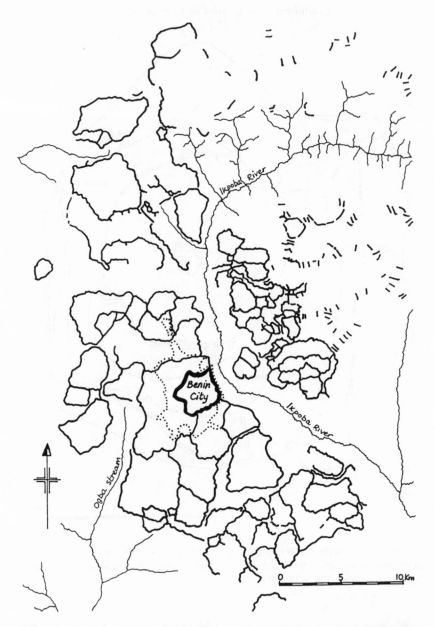

Figure 1.7. Earthwork enclosures in the Benin City area, Nigeria. This map shows only the main part of the complex network. The dotted line indicates the limits of the city in the early 1960s. [After Graham Connah, *African Civilizations. Precolonial Cities and States in Tropical Africa: An Archaeological Perspective* (Cambridge, 1987), Fig. 6.6.]

supply a range of plant and animal resources.[45] Each enclosure may thus be seen as a means of laying claim to the resource base necessary for a settlement's continuance and well being. Therefore it is possible that the concentration of earthworks in the Benin City area is a phenomenon resulting from a particularly successful human adaptation to a rain forest environment, an adaptation in which highly productive, shifting agriculture led to increased population density, of which the extent and scale of the earthworks is surely eloquent evidence.

Towards the southwestern side of this extensive network is Benin City itself, surrounded by part of the complex of earthworks, and with the city enclosed in its own massive bank and ditch with a total height of over 17 meters and a circumference of 11.6 kilometers.[46] Radiocarbon dating, historical documentation, and oral tradition have shown that this was constructed before European contact, quite possibly around the middle of the fifteenth century.[47] It is only this earthwork immediately around the city itself that can properly be called "the Benin City walls." It was presumably this that Dapper was trying to portray in a well known illustration, although the latter is of doubtful accuracy because it fails to show a ditch and shows timber-revetting of the rampart that excavation has not confirmed.[48] Most of the earthworks in the Benin City area have still not been satisfactorily dated, although it would appear that they were constructed at various dates from the thirteenth century onwards, and that they reflect struggles in the formation of the Benin state as well as the emergence of Benin City as an urban center. For instance, the network of enclosures in the vicinity of the city, clustered around the much larger innermost earthwork that encloses the city itself, might suggest that Benin City originated as a concentration of distinct settlements amongst which one became preeminent and was then surrounded by a more substantial defensive work. Alternatively, the enclosures adjacent to this innermost earthwork may merely represent satellite settlements that clustered around the urban center after its emergence; or we might even be looking at a combination of these two processes. This is a matter that will not be resolved until future researchers have accurately dated the various components of the earthwork complex, a task that can

---

[45] Darling, *Archaeology and History in Southern Nigeria. . . . Part i: Fieldwork and Background Information*, 28–30.

[46] Connah, *African Civilizations*, 134.

[47] Graham Connah, *The Archaeology of Benin: Excavations and Other Researches in and Around Benin City, Nigeria* (Oxford, 1975), 88.

[48] Olfert Dapper, *Description de l'Afrique . . . Traduite du Flamand* (Amsterdam, 1686), 308–9; and Connah, *The Archaeology of Benin*, 87–8.

probably only be tackled by archeological means. One thing not in doubt, however, is the defensive character of the massive innermost bank and ditch. Even with superior weaponry and organization, the British attacking forces in 1897 were still held up by one of its gates, which they had to demolish with sixteen pounds of guncotton.[49]

Writers have given so much attention to the enclosed settlements of West Africa that some other parts of the continent have tended to be overlooked. One such area is the coast and islands of East Africa, where the partly stone-built Swahili towns and cities seem usually to have been surrounded by a wall of lime-mortared stonework. Two of the best known examples are Gedi (Fig. 1.8), on the Kenyan coast, and Pate, on the island of the same name in the Lamu Archipelago, also in Kenya.[50] Because the plans of these settlements mark only the stone buildings, one has to imagine most of the blank spaces between them filled with other buildings of mud, wood, and thatch. This would suggest that the strange angular outline of the city walls resulted from the tight enclosure of an irregular mass of extant buildings, indicating indeed that the walls were an afterthought, for why would anyone build a city wall with such an irregular outline otherwise? Allen listed 173 settlement sites with stone ruins from the Somali coast south to the Tanzania–Mozambique frontier.[51] Participating in the Indian Ocean trade, these places originated in the late first millennium A.D. and flourished particularly in the first half of the second millennium. Islam has long been the main religion of this coast, and archaeological, ethnographic, and linguistic evidence suggests strong Arab influence. As a result, it was formerly thought that the Swahili settlements originated from Arab colonization.[52] More recently, their indigenous development has been stressed, particularly as a result of excavations at Shanga, on Pate Island.[53] Thus the city and town walls along the Swahili coast cannot be dismissed merely as resulting from Islamic influence, strong though that influence may have been at times.

To the south of the previously acknowledged Swahili area, recent

[49] Robert Home, *City of Blood Revisited: A New Look at the Benin Expedition of 1897* (London, 1982), 80.

[50] James S. Kirkman, *Men and Monuments on the East African Coast* (London, 1964), and N. Chittick, "Discoveries in the Lamu Archipelago," *Azania* 2 (1967): 37–67.

[51] J. de V. Allen, "Settlement Patterns on the East African Coast, c. AD 800–1900," in *Proceedings of the 8th Panafrican Congress of Prehistory and Quaternary Studies, Nairobi, 5 to 10 September 1977* (Nairobi, 1980).

[52] H.N. Chittick, "The Coast of East Africa," in *The African Iron Age*, ed. P.L. Shinnie (Oxford, 1971).

[53] M.C. Horton, "Early Muslim Trading Settlements on the East African Coast: New Evidence from Shanga," *Antiquaries Journal* 67/2 (1987): 290–323.

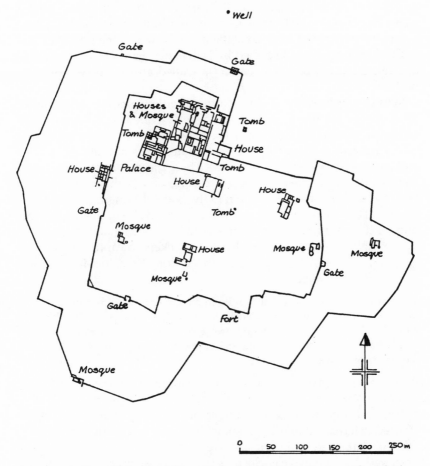

Figure 1.8. Site of the Swahili walled city of Gedi, Kenya. After Graham Connah, *African Civilizations. Precolonial Cities and States in Tropical Africa: An Archaeological Perspective* (Cambridge, 1987), Fig. 7.3.

research along the northern Mozambique coast has revealed two stone-walled settlements that were previously unknown. Although both are small, they make skillful use of the coastal situation: Somana occupying the whole of a small island and Gomene most of a narrow headland. The former seems to have been a Swahili construction with lime-mortared stonework that dates to the period between the twelfth and the fifteenth centuries, but the latter is of drystonework and is thought to be of eighteenth- or nineteenth-century date, built by local rather than Swahili people.[54] To the east of the northern Mozambique coast, the island of Le Grande Comore, out in the Mozambique Channel, had a number of fortified settlements, of which the town of Itsandra has recently been discussed by Dahalani.[55] Farther away, on Madagascar, the town of Mahilaka had a walled area of more than sixty hectares.[56]

In the late nineteenth century, fortified settlements, each surrounded by a mud wall and a ditch, were also described in the area at the southern end of Lake Tanganyika, between Lakes Malawi, Mweru, and Bangweulu, an area that now straddles parts of Malawi, Zambia, and southeastern Democratic Congo. These *chemba*[57] or *tembé*,[58] as they were called, were used by slave traders, and both British-led and Belgian-led forces assaulted them in the hope of bringing that trade to an end. Their defenders seem to have been well supplied with firearms and ammunition, and it appears to have been mainly the possession of light artillery that enabled the attackers to capture them. One of them, "Kiwaura's stronghold" (near Kota Kota in Malawi), was described as follows:

The fortress is a clay wall half a mile in circumference, with a deep dike in front, and the clay wall generously loopholed. . . . The position which the natives held was an exceedingly strong one, and without cannon victory would have been impossible. The place was absolutely impregnable against the efforts of natives.[59]

Another one, "Masala's tembé" (near Moliro in southeastern Democratic Congo), was "composed of thick clay walls twelve feet high, loopholed, and with a ditch."[60] It might be argued that these structures showed external influence, presumably from Arab involvement in the East African slave trade; irrespective of this, however, they also demonstrated that defensive enclosures in tropical Africa could be adapted

---

[54] R.T. Duarte, *Northern Mozambique in the Swahili World: An Archaeological Approach.* Studies in African Archaeology 4 (Stockholm, 1993), 61–8, 70–3.

[55] S.A. Dahalani, "Itsandramdjini: espace et société," in *Urban Origins in Eastern Africa: Proceedings of the 1991 workshop in Zanzibar,* eds. P.J.J. Sinclair and A. Juma (Stockholm, 1992), 180–6.

[56] H.T. Wright, "Trade and Politics on the Eastern Littoral of Africa, AD 800–1300," in *The Archaeology of Africa,* 668.

[57] Harry W. Langworthy, ed., *Expedition in East-Central Africa, 1888–1891. A Report by Carl Wiese,* trans. Donald Ramos (London, 1983), 172.

[58] E.J. Glave, "Glave in Nyassaland. British Raids on the Slave-traders," "Glave's Journey to the Livingstone Tree," and "Glave in the Heart of Africa. Peace and War between Lakes Bangweolo and Tanganyika," *The Century Illustrated Monthly Magazine* 52 n.s. 30 (1896): 589–606, 765–81, 918–33.

[59] Glave, "Glave in Nyassaland," 595–6.

[60] Glave, "Glave in the Heart of Africa," 930.

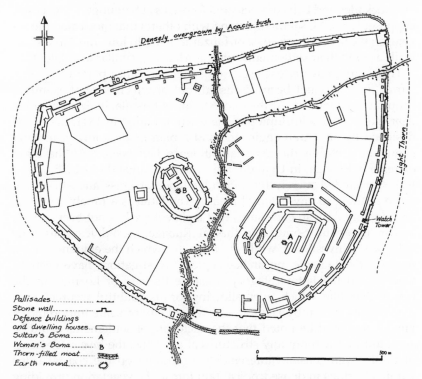

Figure 1.9. The fortified town of Kalenga, Tanzania, in 1894, after being stormed by German forces. After C. Gillman, "An Annotated List of Ancient and Modern Indigenous Stone Structures in Eastern Africa," *Tanganyika Notes and Records* 17 (1944): pl. 3.

to the changing technology of warfare. Indeed, German activities in what is now southwestern Tanzania left plans of the fortified towns of Utengule and Kalenga (Fig. 1.9), which provide strong evidence of this late-nineteenth-century response to colonial expansion.[61] Further north, however, it seems to have been mainly the threat of Masai raids that persuaded the Chagga and Sonjo of northern Tanzania to fortify their settlements during the nineteenth century, the former with drystone walls and ditches, as for instance at Kibosho,[62] and the latter with tim-

---

[61] C. Gillman, "An Annotated List of Ancient and Modern Indigenous Stone Structures in Eastern Africa," *Tanganyika Notes and Records* 17 (1944): 45–6, pls. 2 and 3.

[62] H.A. Fosbrooke, "Chagga Forts and Bolt Holes," *Tanganyika Notes and Records* 37 (1954): 116.

ber stockades and belts of uncleared forest, as at Samunge.[63] It was also
supposedly the Masai threat (along with others) that motivated the Segeju, on the far northern coast of Tanzania, to build lime-mortared stone
walls around their settlements, such as Moa, at a similar late date.[64]

There are, or were, enclosed settlements in other parts of tropical
Africa that have not been discussed, but of which several examples
should be mentioned. At the one extreme is Kassala, in eastern Sudan
near the frontier with Ethiopia; the town, founded in 1841, had walls
designed by an "Arab engineer," and a plan made a few years later
shows how strong the external influence had been.[65] At the other
extreme is Rubaga, in Uganda, the capital of Buganda in 1875, which
was surrounded merely by a circular fence of grass and sticks that
owed nothing to any external ideas.[66] The latter is a timely reminder
of the many African enclosures that archaeology has not been able to
inform us about. Some, like that at Rubaga, would leave us little
evidence to investigate; while at others, for which the evidence might
indeed be obtainable, no archaeological investigations have been attempted. In the latter category must lie the city of Loango, in the
Congo Republic, which, even allowing for his doubtful accuracy with
details, was shown by Dapper as a walled city of some importance.[67]
Finally, it should be noted that the enclosure of settlements could be
accomplished without any structures at all. Thus, the *kaya* settlements
of the Kenyan coastal hinterland were located on the coastal ridge
within clearings in dense tropical rain forest, the vegetation providing
all the protection that was necessary.[68] Another example was the city
of Suakin, in the Sudan, most of which entirely filled a circular island
at the edge of the Red Sea, which provided a natural moat to enclose
the community as effectively as any wall.[69]

FUNCTION

From the above discussion it can be seen that the enclosure of settlements in tropical Africa was a widespread practice over the last mil-

[63] Fosbrooke, "The Defensive Measures of Certain Tribes in North-eastern Tanganyika:
Part IV – Mbugwe Flats and Sonjo Scarps," *Tanganyika Notes and Records* 39 (1955):
5–6.
[64] Fosbrooke, "The 'Masai Walls' of Moa: Walled Towns of the Segeju," *Tanganyika Notes
and Records* (1960): 29–37.
[65] O.G.S. Crawford, *The Fung Kingdom of Sennar: With a Geographical Account of the Middle
Nile Region* (Gloucester, 1951), 96.
[66] Henry M. Stanley, *Through the Dark Continent*, 2 vols. (London, 1878), 1:illus. facing
393.
[67] Dapper, *Description de l'Afrique*, 320–1.
[68] Abungu and Mutoro, "Coast-interior Settlements," 697–8.
[69] Crawford, *The Fung Kingdom of Sennar*, 125.

lennium, and involved communities from small to very large, in environments that ranged from desert to rain forest, using a variety of materials or even natural features. The examples that have been considered are but a tiny sample of enclosed settlements, a sample severely restricted by the limited published information that is available. Nevertheless, these settlements are distributed across tropical Africa (Fig. 1.1) and may be taken as representative of the general practice of settlement enclosure in Black Africa. The question that must now be asked is why did people so often go to so much trouble to enclose their settlement?

The first and inevitable answer must be for protection. However, the scale of protection varied enormously, depending on the real or imagined threat and on the size of the community. To the small number of inhabitants of Maggs's Type N settlement units in South Africa (Fig. 1.2), it was presumably sufficient to be able to protect their livestock from wild animals and their household in general from thieving and murdering neighbors. To the large number of people in the city of Kano (Fig. 1.4), however, it was essential to be able to withstand an attack by a sizable army that would almost certainly include cavalry. Indeed, the walls and other barriers constructed around settlements inevitably reflected the character of warfare in a particular place at a particular time. Thus there were few settlement defenses in tropical Africa that were built to withstand artillery; Burton, for instance, thought that the Harar wall "would crumble at the touch of a six-pounder."[70] The multiple concentric walls of some Yoruba towns and cities (Fig 1.6) suggest that at times defense-in-depth was of more importance than attempting to hold a single, strongly constructed barrier. Foot soldiers and even cavalry did not need much to slow them down or even stop them temporarily, and in the meantime defenders could rally behind their defenses and then burst out in a counterattack. Of relevance here are the comments of Staudinger concerning Hausa warfare:

> But it must be understood that wars here do not amount to wars in our sense of the word. At best they are nothing more than forays and raids, and actual battles hardly ever take place.[71]

He might have said the same thing about formal sieges, or at least about protracted formal sieges, which appear to have been rare in the African past. To understand city walls and other settlement enclosures

---

[70] Richard F. Burton, *First Footsteps in East Africa; or an Exploration of Harar* (London, 1856), 337.

[71] Paul Staudinger, *Im Herzen der Haussaländer* [1889], trans. Johanna Moody as *In the Heart of the Hausa States*, 2 vols. (Athens, OH, 1990), 2:191.

in tropical Africa, one should perhaps rid oneself of Eurocentric ideas of city walls, in which seemingly impregnable urban fortifications, such as those of Carcassonne in France, are closely manned by valiant defenders, who rain death and destruction on the heads of massed, determined attackers, who in turn use every means available to them to break into the city.[72] In fact, such a situation was perhaps more the imaginary ideal than the reality even in Europe; for England and Wales, for instance, Turner has questioned "how far they [city walls] could ever act as a useful and effective barrier against attack."[73] Certainly, in the African situation it would seem that Allen was missing the point when he complained that the town walls of the East African coast "where these exist, are – with a few exceptions – more suitable for excluding dogs and wild pigs than any serious invaders."[74] Many African settlement enclosures were probably more concerned with generalized protection than with formal military defense, and there are many threats (both human and animal) that a community may seek protection from other than organized armies. That the enclosure of settlements in Africa was primarily concerned with protection, at one level or another, is surely confirmed by their distribution: some of the densest groupings are to be found in Hausaland and Yorubaland, both areas of high population with vigorous competition for resources and control of trade. That such protection was at times more psychological than practical is hardly relevant: In our own times the same could be said of the atomic bomb.

Settlement enclosures had functions other than protection, however. They could serve to demarcate land, sometimes on a large scale; as suggested above, this must surely have been one of the functions of the unbelievably extensive network of banks and ditches in the Benin City area. They could also serve as a means of encouraging industry, controlling trade, and exacting taxation, and here the Hausa towns and cities are good examples. Every trader entering such a walled settlement could be asked to pay for permission to do business there, as Paul Staudinger observed to be the case at Zaria in 1885.[75] In addition, some of the enclosing structures clearly had a role as status symbols; they were intended to impress and perhaps intimidate the stranger. Thus Staudinger, visiting Kano in 1885, wrote that the:

... smooth clay walls probably twenty metres high flanked by a protective moat approximately fifteen metres deep, as well as the formidable and sinister

---

[72] C.-L. Salch, *L'atlas des villes et villages fortifiés en France (Moyen Age)* (Strasbourg, 1978), 66.

[73] Turner, *Town Defences in England and Wales*, 76.

[74] Allen, "Settlement Patterns," 363.

[75] Staudinger, *In the Heart of the Hausa States*, 1:177.

gatehouse, called forth an almost uncanny feeling in the traveller who forthwith had to trust himself inside them.[76]

Even Lugard, faced with the task of storming the Kano city walls in 1902, had to admit: "... I have never seen, nor even imagined, anything like it in Africa."[77] Finally, settlement enclosures could be useful for regulating and controlling the people within the enclosed settlements and for keeping out undesirables. In this respect they are an example of how a community's perceived need for security can become a means of curtailing the freedom of the individual. From the point of view of government, a city wall or similar barrier could sometimes be almost as useful for keeping people in, or at least in order, as for keeping people out. Of the five gates in the stone wall around the city of Harar in eastern Ethiopia, for instance, Richard Burton observed: "At all times these gates are carefully guarded; in the evening the keys are taken to the Amir, after which no one can leave the city till dawn."[78]

Light may also be shed on the function of settlement enclosures in tropical Africa by considering some of the communities that were not so enclosed. Most villages and many small towns were open settlements, but some bigger towns and cities also lacked enclosures. For instance, although Harar was walled,[79] numerous towns midway between it and the Gulf of Aden were not.[80] The Asante of Ghana do not seem to have enclosed their settlements either, and even the important pre-eighteenth-century Akan town of Begho was an open settlement. Presumably, if you are powerful enough and do not feel threatened, it may seem pointless to expend labor and resources on walls, banks and ditches, or other barriers. This may, moreover, have been the case with the Ethiopian Aksumite cities of the first millennium A.D., which were also, apparently, unwalled. However, in later times it is known that Ethiopian capitals moved fairly frequently, as their populations of up to 100,000 people exhausted the resources around them, and it is unknown how far this practice goes back in time.[81] Indeed, settlement mobility of varying degrees seems to have occurred widely in Africa and would presumably have inhibited the construction of enclosures, or at least of enclosures substantial enough to be likely to survive in

[76] Staudinger, *In the Heart of the Hausa States*, 1:210.
[77] F.D. Lugard, *Northern Nigeria: Report for 1902.* Colonial Reports: Annual, No. 409 (London, 1903), 28.
[78] Burton, *First Footsteps in East Africa*, 321.
[79] Burton, *First Footsteps in East Africa*, frontispiece and 321–2.
[80] A.T. Curle, "The Ruined Towns of Somaliland," *Antiquity* 11 (1937): 319.
[81] R. Pankhurst, "Ethiopian Medieval and Post-medieval Capitals: Their Development and Principal Features," *Azania* 14 (1979): 1–19.

the archaeological record. Large settlements with dispersed populations were another African phenomenon and again were unlikely to be enclosed, in this case because they were so spread out. Khami, in Zimbabwe, is an example and, indeed, Great Zimbabwe itself would be another, except for the fact that it does have some rather enigmatic incomplete stone walling that may have enclosed it at one stage. Reviewing a sample of open settlements in Africa, one is left with a suspicion that enclosure was more likely to be practised in areas of denser population, where there was greater competition for resources, and where settlement mobility or settlement dispersal was not an option.

MEANING

There are a number of implications of settlement enclosure in tropical Africa, varying with the scale involved. In the case of larger settlements that might be referred to as towns or cities, the expenditure of labor and resources would obviously have been considerable, although relative to population number this would have been so even in smaller settlements. In the bigger settlements, however, the input would have been so great and the organization of effort so complex that direction by some sort of central authority must have existed. In addition, there must have been abundant surplus labor available, if only for part of the year, and at least some functional specialization must have been present in a society to be able to undertake tasks of this sort. In short, it can be argued that major defence systems like those of the Hausa towns and cities are strong evidence for the existence of social complexity and of state development.

Basically, it must have been fear that most commonly drove communities to construct enclosures around themselves, fear of some real or imagined threat. It appears that the greatest concentrations of evidence of enclosed settlements are to be found in areas and at times of tension and conflict between and among population groups. As has been seen, however, there were also other reasons for such enclosure. In addition, the matter was probably complicated in some instances by a socio-psychological desire to be separate and distinct from the outside world, whether it was threatening or not. In the perhaps extreme case of Harar, for instance, Burton observed that it had "not only its own tongue, unintelligible to any save the citizens; even its little population of about 8,000 souls is a distinct race."[82] So it was the

---

[82] Burton, *First Footsteps in East Africa*, 325.

act of enclosure, the creation of a contained community, that was perhaps of most significance for the society involved. The city or town wall, the surrounding ditch and bank, the enclosing stockade – whatever the nature of the barrier, it gave the contained community a discrete physical identity and strengthened its sense of solidarity. Thus both Hausas and Yorubas strongly identified with the particular city or town from which they came: each was unique, shut in by its walls, a world of its own. With enclosed settlements elsewhere in tropical Africa it seems often to have been much the same, wherever there is sufficient evidence to judge. The act of enclosure had the capacity to produce a different sort of community, physically, psychologically, and socially, or to confirm and reinforce pre-existing differences. Life in an open settlement, particularly if it shifted regularly or had a dispersed layout, must surely have been different from that in a contained community.

CHAPTER 2

Palisaded settlements in prehistoric eastern North America

GEORGE R. MILNER

WALLED settlements are one of the few sure signs of intergroup conflicts in prehistoric times. Many of these sites have been excavated in what is now the eastern United States and adjacent parts of Canada, and some of them were mentioned in accounts of early encounters between Europeans and Native Americans. Yet despite the potential contribution of walled sites to studies of the relations maintained among prehistoric peoples, there are few summaries of either the characteristics of defensive works in eastern North America or their geographical and temporal distributions.[1]

Our understanding of hostilities among the kinds of societies – bands, tribes, and chiefdoms – that have dominated most of human existence comes largely from the historical and ethnographic literature.[2] Considerably less is known about the nature of conflicts deep in prehistory, a period of time known only through archaeological research. Conflicts among small societies in relatively recent times in-

James Tracy's invitation to the 1995 City Walls conference at the University of Minnesota served as the impetus for pulling together information on palisaded sites in eastern North America. Some of this information, including unpublished descriptions of palisades, was provided by David Anderson, Brian Butler, Jeff Bursey, John Cable, Victoria Dirst, Eugene Futato, Alan Harn, James Hatch, James Herbstritt, Adam King, Angie Krieger, Jeffrey Mitchem, Cheryl Munson, Christopher Peebles, David Pollack, Thomas Sanders, Margaret Scarry, and Ronald Williamson. This essay was improved by the comments of Claire McHale Milner, Marguerite Ragnow, Sissel Schroeder, and James Tracy.

[1] Robert H. Lafferty, *An Analysis of Prehistoric Southeastern Fortifications* (Carbondale, 1973); Claudine Payne, *Mississippian Capitals: An Archaeological Investigation of Precolumbian Political Structure* (Gainesville, 1994); Gary A. Warrick, *Reconstructing Ontario Iroquoian Village Organization* (Ottawa, 1984).

[2] These commonly used terms pertain to categories that encompass more variation in how societies were organized and functioned than the original definitions by Elman R. Service, *Primitive Social Organization*, 2nd ed. (New York, 1972); see Jon Muller, *Mississippian Political Economy* (New York, 1997), 38–52.

46

clude planned confrontations featuring considerable posturing but little else, the opportunistic killing of situationally vulnerable people, and the massacre of numerous villagers along with the destruction of their property.[3] The form and severity of fighting varied over time. Occasional to frequent encounters involving a few casualties apiece were punctuated by sudden, devastating raids that caused great losses of life. The term warfare is used here to cover all of these different forms of intergroup conflict. It pertains to potentially lethal armed conflicts among separately constituted groups of people living in different communities, the members of which shared common interests furthered and defended through the use of deadly force.[4]

While much is known about the conflicts among band to chiefdom-scale societies of the recent past, several scholars have argued that patterns of warfare described in the historical and ethnographic literature are not necessarily applicable to much earlier times.[5] These sources are said to present a biased view of intergroup relations because they pertain to societies engulfed by warfare spawned directly or indirectly by aggressive states, ranging from early empires to colonizing modern powers. By implication, relations among relatively small societies in the absence of the disruptive influence of expansionistic states were, on the whole, rather peaceful. At the very least, existing archaeological data are apparently viewed as insufficient to determine whether serious intergroup conflicts were ever widespread during prehistoric times.

All scholars would agree that the experiences of prehistoric peoples were different from those of their descendants, who found themselves embroiled in the maelstrom of unprecedented contact-engendered forces that wrought great changes in demographic, economic, and sociopolitical settings. The latter had the misfortune to confront large,

---

[3] Napoleon A. Chagnon, "Life Histories, Blood Revenge, and Warfare in a Tribal Population," *Science* 239 (1988): 985–92; Karl G. Heider, *The Dugum Dani* (New York, 1970), 231; Lawrence H. Keeley, *War Before Civilization* (New York, 1996), 59–69; Andrew P. Vayda, "Warfare in Ecological Perspective," *Annual Review of Ecology and Systematics* 5 (1974): 183–93.

[4] This broad definition follows David Webster, "The Study of Maya Warfare: What it Tells Us about the Maya and What it Tells Us about Maya Archaeology," in *Lowland Maya Civilization in the Eighth Century A.D.*, eds. Jeremy A. Sabloff and John S. Henderson (Washington, DC, 1993), 415–44. For a short discussion of what has been considered warfare among small societies, see Keith F. Otterbein, "The Anthropology of War," in *Feuding and Warfare*, ed. Keith F. Otterbein (Langhorne, 1994), 159–69.

[5] Jeffrey P. Blick, "Genocidal Warfare in Tribal Societies as a Result of European-Induced Culture Conflict," *Man* 23 (1988): 654–70; R. Brian Ferguson, "Tribal Warfare," *Scientific American* 266 (1992): 108–13; R. Brian Ferguson and Neil L. Whitehead, "The Violent Edge of Empire," in *War in the Tribal Zone*, eds. R. Brian Ferguson and Neil L. Whitehead (Santa Fe, 1992), 1–30.

organizationally complex, and technologically sophisticated nations
with the capacity to use overwhelming force to subjugate, disenfran-
chise, displace, and extirpate indigenous peoples. But it does not necessarily follow that precontact peoples always lived in harmony with
one another. Unfortunately, few researchers have attempted to assess
the degree to which the archaeological record conforms to patterns of
warfare described in historical and ethnographic sources.[6] This situation is part of a larger problem: an all too common reluctance by
scholars to acknowledge the existence, let alone the significance, of
evidence for conflicts deep in prehistory.[7]

Eastern North America serves as an excellent example of an intensively studied region where there is no consensus over the frequency,
severity, or effects of prehistoric warfare. The public, in particular,
finds a certain comfort in believing that harmonious relations once
prevailed in those distant times.[8] Scholarly opinion is deeply divided
over the seriousness of warfare in the Eastern Woodlands.[9] It is sometimes assumed that intergroup conflicts were rare, and they had few
if any consequences other than producing occasional casualties. Other
scholars view competition, including outright warfare, as an important component of the evolution of organizationally complex societies.[10] Kroeber's Hobbesian characterization of prehistoric Eastern
Woodlands warfare as "insane, unending, [and] continuously attri-
tional," however, has received little support.[11] Systematic studies of

---

[6] Keeley, *War Before Civilization*; George R. Milner, Eve Anderson, and Virginia G.
   Smith, "Warfare in Late Prehistoric West-Central Illinois," *American Antiquity* 56
   (1991): 581–603.
[7] This issue is covered thoroughly by Keeley, *War Before Civilization*. Scholarly interest
   in prehistoric warfare, however, has increased recently for some culture areas, especially Europe, the Maya region of Mesoamerica, and the southwestern United States.
[8] Kirkpatrick Sale, *The Conquest of Paradise* (New York, 1990), 318.
[9] Sherburne F. Cook, "Interracial Warfare and Population Decline Among the New
   England Indians," *Ethnohistory* 20 (1973): 1–24; Francis Jennings, *The Invasion of America: Indians, Colonialism, and the Cant of Conquest* (Chapel Hill, 1975), 146–70; Alfred L.
   Kroeber, *Cultural and Natural Areas of Native North America* (Berkeley, 1939), 148;
   George R. Milner, "An Osteological Perspective on Prehistoric Warfare," in *Regional
   Approaches to Mortuary Analysis*, ed. Lane A. Beck (New York, 1995), 221–44; Dean R.
   Snow, *The Iroquois* (Oxford, 1994), 31–3, 53–60; Russell Thornton, *American Indian
   Holocaust and Survival* (Norman, 1987), 47–8.
[10] David G. Anderson, "Factional Competition and the Political Evolution of Mississippian Chiefdoms in the Southeastern United States," in *Factional Competition and Political Development in the New World*, eds. Elizabeth M. Brumfiel and John W. Fox (Cambridge, 1994), 61–76; Stephen R. Potter, *Commoners, Tribute, and Chiefs* (Charlottesville,
   1993), 166–8; Helen C. Rountree, *The Powhatan Indians of Virginia* (Norman, 1989), 149–
   50; Snow, *The Iroquois*, 53–60.
[11] Kroeber, *North America*, 148. Kroeber's position is advocated by Cook, "Interracial
   Warfare and Population Decline," 2.

archaeological remains – sites, weapons, and human skeletons – are the only means of resolving debates over the conduct and seriousness of prehistoric warfare, particularly if the challenge to the use of models derived from the historical and ethnographic literature is taken seriously. They also permit the evaluation of whether distant times were as monotonously peaceful or as violent as commonly believed.

This survey of walled settlements in eastern North America was undertaken to identify broad patterns in the construction characteristics of defensive structures, as well as their geographical and temporal distributions. It is an initial step toward identifying patterning in site-related evidence of hostilities during late prehistoric to early historic times. Such an overview is necessary because few scholars, including archaeologists, realize that several hundred palisaded sites have been identified in eastern North America. Descriptions of palisades, many of which were accompanied by embankments and ditches, tend to be deeply buried in reports on single settlements or narrowly defined regions written for specialized audiences.

SETTLEMENT SAMPLE

Excavations at most of the sites included in this overview have revealed signs of wooden palisades that usually surrounded all of the domestic and public buildings that made up these communities. Other sites were included in the sample even though excavations have not confirmed the presence of palisades. These particular settlements were surrounded by embankments and depressions that archaeologists believe were parts of defensive works. They include, among others, large sites in the lower Mississippi Valley where great amounts of occupation debris had accumulated, making the deposits somewhat higher than the surrounding floodplain.[12] Many of these thick middens were encompassed by distinct ditches when they were first described, although plowing has now greatly modified the contours of the sites. The mid-sixteenth-century De Soto expedition visited at least one such settlement where houses were built "on a site somewhat loftier and more eminent than its surroundings, and it has been turned into almost an island by means of a man-made ditch or moat."[13] All of these palisades would have protected people from their enemies; in

---

[12] These settlements are often referred to as St. Francis-type sites; see Phillip Phillips, James A. Ford, and James B. Griffin, *Archaeological Survey in the Lower Mississippi Alluvial Valley, 1940–1947* (Cambridge, 1951), 329–34.

[13] Garcilaso de la Vega, *The Florida of the Inca*, trans. John G. Varner and Jeannette J. Varner (Austin, 1951), 436.

the Eastern Woodlands, there was no need to erect walls to keep dangerous animals at bay.

Data on defensive walls were compiled from both archaeological reports and unpublished notes. Known palisaded settlements were undoubtedly missed because site descriptions often appear only in obscure sources, including limited-distribution reports submitted to government agencies, and the results of many excavations have not been published. Nevertheless, at least some information was found on approximately 370 settlements with defensive works.[14] While they certainly represent most of the palisaded sites that archaeologists have identified, this overview still suffers from having to rely on an availability sample, a common problem with historical and archaeological studies. The most important problem – at least, the most obvious one – is that knowledge of prehistoric eastern North America is uneven, a result of dissimilar histories of archaeological investigations in different places.

The sites are distributed throughout much of eastern North America from the Atlantic Coast to the states bordering the Mississippi River. This area encompasses the Eastern Woodlands, extending into the forest-prairie transition in its western extent. The sites date from the last few centuries of the first millennium A.D. through the seventeenth century. Earlier villages enclosed by clearly defensive structures have not been identified, despite numerous archaeological excavations and the existence of intergroup conflicts as indicated by many skeletons of victims of attacks.[15]

For the purposes of this review, it is useful to compare settlements referred to as Mississippian with generally more northerly sites that belong to the archaeological categories known as Oneota, Fort Ancient, Iroquois, and Monongahela, as well as several mid-Atlantic Late Woodland complexes. The inhabitants of these villages were members of nonhierarchically organized societies, typically considered tribal-scale sociopolitical formations, that were distributed from the upper Midwest eastward through the Great Lakes, middle Ohio Valley, Northeast, and mid-Atlantic regions. Nearby villages, and occasionally several of these spatially separate clusters of sites, were loosely aligned with one another. In contrast, Mississippian peoples, including their immediate predecessors referred to as Emergent Mis-

---

[14] Estimated dates spanning a few centuries, often much narrower intervals of time, were available for most sites; postmold diameters were available for a smaller number of sites.

[15] The osteological evidence for violence has been reviewed by Milner, "Prehistoric Warfare," 221–44.

sissippian, were distributed across much of the Southeast and southern Midwest. For the most part they lived in simple and complex chiefdoms, a distinction denoting the number of levels of control over local communities, that were often larger than the northern societies.[16]

Walls found at archaeological sites can be separated into those that met defensive needs and fences that demarcated spaces underscoring social distinctions. Light weight walls that snaked their way through settlements, setting apart certain sections for highly ranked people or special purposes, were omitted from the sample.[17] They included fences around the bases or summits of earthen mounds that screened socially or ritually significant places associated with important people.[18]

Because this overview focuses on defensive enclosures, earthworks of ritual significance, such as the Middle Woodland circles and squares in Ohio, were omitted. The great size of many of these geometric earthworks would have made their defense impossible. Furthermore, the configurations of both Middle Woodland and somewhat earlier Adena earthworks in the middle Ohio Valley often make no sense in terms of meeting defensive needs.[19] Hilltops in the Midwest and Mid-

---

[16] It is generally agreed that most Mississippian societies were chiefdoms, although some of them approximated tribal sociopolitical systems; see Bruce D. Smith, "The Archaeology of the Southeastern United States: From Dalton to De Soto 10,500–500 B.P.," in *Advances in World Archaeology*, Vol. 5, eds. Fred Wendorf and Angela E. Close (Orlando, 1986), 1–92. There is absolutely no evidence supporting claims that the largest and most organizationally complex Mississippian societies should be labeled states, with all that such a term implies about political centralization, economic differentiation, and population size; see George R. Milner, "The Late Prehistoric Cahokia Cultural System of the Mississippi River Valley: Foundations, Florescence, and Fragmentation," *Journal of World Prehistory* 4 (1990): 1–43; Muller, *Political Economy*.

[17] One such example is a centrally located flimsy fence at the Snodgrass site in the Missouri Bootheel; see James E. Price and James B. Griffin, *The Snodgrass Site of the Powers Phase of Southeast Missouri* (Ann Arbor, 1979), 37.

[18] David G. Anderson, *The Savannah River Chiefdoms* (Tuscaloosa, 1994), 290–4, 302–6; Glenn A. Black, *Angel Site* (Indianapolis, 1967), 228–84; John H. Blitz, *Ancient Chiefdoms of the Tombigbee* (Tuscaloosa, 1993), 80, 84; Joseph Caldwell and Catherine McCann, *Irene Mound Site* (Athens, 1941), 8–29, 33–4; Fay-Cooper Cole, *Kincaid* (Chicago, 1951), 96–7; David L. DeJarnette and Steve B. Wimberly, *The Bessemer Site* (University, AL, 1941), 61; Roy S. Dickens, *Cherokee Prehistory* (Knoxville, 1976), 75, 77; Thomas M.N. Lewis and Madeline Kneberg, *Hiwassee Island* (Knoxville, 1946), 78, pl. 14; Harriet M. Smith, "The Murdock Mound, Cahokia Site," in *Explorations into Cahokia Archaeology*, ed. Melvin L. Fowler (Urbana, 1969), 49–88.

[19] One such example is the Adena site of Mt. Horeb in central Kentucky, where the placement of a ditch and adjacent earthen ridge is reversed from the arrangement needed for defensive purposes; see William S. Webb, *Mt. Horeb Earthworks, Site 1, and the Drake Mound, Site 11, Fayette County, Kentucky* (Lexington, 1941), 148, 167.

south that are partially or completely ringed by generally low ridges of earth or stone are also excluded from the sample.[20] Although often labeled forts – they were once simply assumed to have been places of refuge – their actual purpose is unknown. Late prehistoric ridge and ditch complexes scattered across much of the Great Lakes region from Illinois to New York are likewise excluded, unless they were obviously parts of village defensive perimeters, such as at sites where excavations have revealed the remains of palisades encompassing residential areas.[21]

Eighteenth-century and later fortifications were not included in the sample because they typically incorporated European design features needed to counter new weapons and tactics. They were built in response to demographic settings, political relationships, and economic conditions that were greatly changed from precontact times. Seventeenth-century forts built along European lines were likewise excluded. By the mid-seventeenth century, rectangular enclosures with prominent corner bastions on some or all corners were being erected.[22] Archaeologists have discovered several such sites, and there are references to them in accounts of early encounters between Europeans and Native Americans:

[Early seventeenth-century Jesuits told the Huron] that henceforth they should make their forts square, and arrange their stakes in straight lines; and that, by means of four little towers at the four corners, four Frenchmen might easily with the arquebuses or muskets defend the whole village. They are greatly

---

[20] Most, if not all, of the stone forts, whatever their function, predate the palisaded settlements discussed here; see Jon Muller, *Archaeology of the Lower Ohio River Valley* (Orlando, 1986), 150–3.

[21] Different opinions about the function of these earthworks are covered in Stephanie J. Belovich and David S. Brose, "Late Woodland Fortifications in Northern Ohio: The Greenwood Village Site," *Kirtlandia* 47 (1992): 3–23; Douglas Kullen, "The Comstock Trace: A Huber Phase Earthwork and Habitation Site Near Joliet, Will County, Illinois," *Midcontinental Journal of Archaeology* 19 (1994): 3–38; Lynne P. Sullivan, Sarah W. Neusius, and Phillip D. Neusius, "Earthworks and Mortuary Sites on Lake Erie: Believe It or Not at the Ripley Site," *Midcontinental Journal of Archaeology* 20 (1995): 115–42.

[22] Ralph S. Solecki, "The Archeological Position of Historic Fort Corchaug, L. I., and its Relation to Contemporary Forts," *Bulletin of the Archeological Society of Connecticut* 24 (1950): 3–40; Ralph S. Solecki, "Recent Field Inspections of Two Seventeenth Century Indian Forts on Long Island, Fort Massapeag and Corchaug," *Bulletin of the New York State Archeological Association* 91 (1985): 26–31; Robert L. Stephenson and Alice L.L. Ferguson, *The Accokeek Creek Site, A Middle Atlantic Seaboard Culture Sequence* (Ann Arbor, 1963), 44, 79–81; James A. Tuck, *Onondaga Iroquois Prehistory* (Syracuse, 1971), 188; Lorraine E. Williams, *Ft. Shantok and Ft. Corchaug: A Comparative Study of Seventeenth Century Culture Contact in the Long Island Sound Area* (New York, 1972), 70–7, 84–93.

delighted with this advice, and have already begun to practice it at la Rochelle. . . ."[23]

SETTLEMENT WALLS

In the northern sites, the palisades typically encompassed many domestic buildings that were often, but not always, arranged around small open areas that were the focus of community life.[24] The enclosed areas were no larger than necessary, presumably because of the effort required to erect and repair palisades. Excavations rarely reveal the remains of residential buildings outside village walls.

The walls around the Mississippian sites encompassed residential zones accompanied by large plazas.[25] Many buildings surrounding the

[23] Jean de Brebeuf, "Relation of What Occurred in the Country of the Hurons in the Year 1636," in *The Jesuit Relations and Allied Documents: Hurons 1636*, Vol. 10, ed. Reuben G. Thwaites (Cleveland, 1897), 53.

[24] There are numerous references to such settlements, including the following that pertain to sites where large areas were excavated: Jay F. Custer, Angela Hoseth, Dawn Cheshaek, Mara Guttman, and Karen Iplenski, "Data Recovery Excavations at the Slackwater Site (36LA207), Lancaster County, Pennsylvania," *Pennsylvania Archaeologist* 65 (1995): 19–112; William D. Finlayson, *The 1975 and 1978 Rescue Excavations at the Draper Site: Introduction and Settlement Patterns* (Ottawa, 1985), 60; Richard L. George, "The Gnagey Site and the Monongahela Occupation of the Somerset Plateau," *Pennsylvania Archaeologist* 53 (1983): 1–97; Lee H. Hanson, *The Buffalo Site* (Morgantown, 1975), 10; James T. Herbstritt, "Bonnie Brook: A Multicomponent Aboriginal Locus in West-Central Pennsylvania," *Pennsylvania Archaeologist* 51 (1981): 1–59; Walter A. Kenyon, *The Miller Site* (Toronto, 1968), 12–13; W. Fred Kinsey and Jeffrey R. Graybill, "Murry Site and its Role in Lancaster and Funk Phases of Shenks Ferry Culture," *Pennsylvania Archaeologist* 41 (1971): 7–44; Dean H. Knight, "Settlement Patterns at the Ball Site: A 17th Century Huron Village," *Archaeology of Eastern North America* 15 (1987): 177–88; Howard A. MacCord, "The Brown Johnson Site," *Archeological Society of Virginia Quarterly Bulletin* 25 (1971): 230–72; Trawick H. Ward and R.P. Stephen Davis, *Indian Communities on the North Carolina Piedmont A.D. 1000 to 1700* (Chapel Hill, 1993), 417; Warrick, *Iroquoian Village*, 87; James V. Wright, *The Nodwell Site* (Ottawa, 1974), 5.

[25] Numerous references to these sites include the following: David G. Anderson and Joseph Schuldenrein, "The Rucker's Bottom Site (9EB91) Archeological Record," in *Prehistoric Human Ecology Along the Upper Savannah River: Excavations at the Rucker's Bottom, Abbeville and Bullard Site Groups* (Atlanta, 1985), 251–590; Carl H. Chapman, John W. Cottier, David Denman, David R. Evans, Dennis E. Harvey, Michael D. Reagan, Bradford L. Rope, Michael D. Southard, and Gregory A. Waselkov, "Investigation and Comparison of Two Fortified Mississippi Tradition Archaeological Sites in Southeastern Missouri: A Preliminary Compilation," *The Missouri Archaeologist* 38 (1977): 1–346; Joffre L. Coe, *Town Creek Indian Mound* (Chapel Hill, 1995), 85–99; Melvin Fowler, *The Cahokia Atlas* (Springfield, 1989), 198–205; David J. Hally, "Archaeology and Settlement Plan of the King Site," in *The King Site*, ed. Robert L. Blakely (Athens, 1988), 1–16; Richard R. Polhemus, *The Toqua Site* (Knoxville, 1987), 62; Price and Griffin, *Snodgrass*, 31–41; Lynne P. Sullivan, "The Mouse Creek Phase Household," *Southeastern Archaeology* 6 (1987): 16–29.

plazas were larger than those occupied by ordinary people. Some of the structures fronting the plazas, including residences for highly ranked people and charnel houses containing their ancestors' bones, were built on flat-topped, rectangular mounds. Residential areas frequently were completely encircled by walls, and deep middens formed at a number of large settlements in the lower Mississippi Valley, where walls accompanied by ditches prevented an outward growth of these communities.[26] Houses at some Mississippian sites, however, were located beyond the safety provided by palisades. One such site is Cahokia in southwestern Illinois, where a large, roughly rectangular area encompassing the most important part of this sprawling mound center was enclosed by a strong palisade reinforced with bastions.[27] Despite the length of this wall – it is estimated to have been about 2.8 kilometers long[28] – it did not enclose all residential buildings, wooden public structures, and earthen mounds, many of which were scattered widely across bottomland ridges in the vicinity of the central walled precinct.

Wall characteristics

The posts that made up the palisades stood some distance from one another. Rarely were they placed close enough to form continuous walls of upright posts, and the spaces between posts were often wide enough for people to slip through them. Some form of covering was needed to make the walls effective barriers, although at most sites it is not clear what actually filled these gaps. Branches woven amongst the vertical posts would have strengthened the walls, and presumably some palisades were covered with bark as they were in the early seventeenth century.[29] Occasionally prehistoric palisades were plas-

---

[26] Phillips et al., *Lower Mississippi*, 329–34.

[27] James Anderson, "A Cahokia Palisade Sequence," in *Explorations into Cahokia Archaeology*, ed. Melvin L. Fowler (Urbana, 1969), 89–99; George R. Holley, Neal H. Lopinot, Rinita A. Dalan, and William I. Woods, "South Palisade Investigations," in *The Archaeology of the Cahokia Palisade* (Springfield, 1990), 1–119; William R. Iseminger, Timothy R. Pauketat, Brad Koldehoff, Lucretia S. Kelly, and Leonard Blake, "East Palisade Investigations," in *The Archaeology of the Cahokia Palisade* (Springfield, 1990), 1–197.

[28] Iseminger et al., "East Palisade," 35.

[29] For examples of bark-covered palisades in the Northeast and mid-Atlantic area see Gabriel Sagard, *The Long Journey to the Country of the Hurons*, ed. George M. Wrong, trans. H.H. Langton (Toronto, 1939), 91; John Smith, "Description of Virginia and Proceedings of the Colonie," in *Narratives of Early Virginia 1606–1625*, ed. Lyon G. Tyler (New York, 1946), 73–204.

tered with clay, as indicated by great amounts of daub.[30] These wattle-and-daub walls were encountered by De Soto's expedition, which penetrated deep into the Southeast:

[R]amparts are built in this manner: they sink many thick poles, tall and straight, next to one another; they weave them with some long sticks, and daub them within and without, and they make their loopholes at intervals, and they make their towers and turrets spread out along the curtain and parts of the rampart as suits them; and at a distance, they appear to be one very excellent wall, and such walls are very strong.[31]

In the Northeast, specifically from southern Ontario to western New York and extending south into Pennsylvania, palisade remnants frequently consist of several parallel lines of typically small postmolds that often turn into belts of closely spaced postmolds (Fig. 2.1).[32] These walls are generally thought to have consisted of multiple lines of upright poles. It is obviously difficult from postmolds alone to differentiate sequential lines of posts from a single wall consisting of two or more rows of posts. Yet many walls must have consisted of several rows of posts, judging from the frequent occurrence of multiple lines and belts of postmolds in villages that were occupied for no more than a generation, and often much less. Historical accounts of palisades in this region are consistent with such an interpretation, such as the following early-seventeenth-century description of Huron palisades:

[Many villages are] fortified by strong wooden palisades in three rows, interlaced into one another and reinforced within by large thick pieces of bark to a height of eight or nine feet, and at the bottom there are great trunks of trees placed lengthwise, resting on strong short forks made from tree-trunks. Then above these palisades there are galleries or watch-towers. . . .[33]

Throughout the Eastern Woodlands, the positions of palisades and the areas they encompassed often changed several times at settlements occupied for at least a few decades. New walls were constructed as communities increased or decreased in size. Sections of walls were added to replace posts weakened with rot or to reinforce particularly

[30] One such example is daub, pieces of which were once mistakenly called bricks, scattered along the palisade at Aztalan in southern Wisconsin; see Samuel A. Barrett, *Ancient Aztalan* (Milwaukee, 1933), 42–5.

[31] Rodrigo Rangel, "Account of the Northern Conquest and Discovery of Hernando De Soto," in *The De Soto Chronicles*, Vol. 1, eds. Lawrence A. Clayton, Vernon J. Knight, and Edward C. Moore, trans. John E. Worth (Tuscaloosa, 1993), 288.

[32] Postmolds are dark stains in soil where posts once stood.

[33] Sagard, *Hurons*, 91.

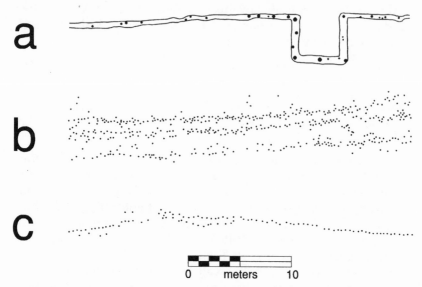

Figure 2.1. Palisade segments from (a) the Mississippian Cahokia site in Illinois where posts were set in a deep trench, (b) the seventeenth-century Huron Le Caron site in Ontario with multiple lines of small posts, and (c) the Late Woodland Shannon site in Virginia with a single line of posts. Redrawn from James Anderson, "A Cahokia Palisade Sequence," in *Explorations into Cahokia Archaeology*, ed. Melvin L. Fowler (Urbana, 1969), 93; Richard B. Johnston and L.J. Jackson, "Settlement Pattern at the Le Caron Site, a 17th Century Huron Village," *Journal of Field Archaeology* 7 (1980): 179; Joseph L. Benthall, *Archeological Investigation of the Shannon Site* (Richmond, 1969), 25.

vulnerable sections of palisades. The close juxtaposition of typically short lines of postmolds paralleling the original walls indicates that such alterations occurred frequently.

The posts forming the main structural supports of the palisades varied greatly in size. Postmold diameters, a crude measure of wall strength, were available for 45 and 163 palisades that surrounded the Mississippian and northern settlements, respectively (Fig. 2.2). When there was evidence of more than one wall at a site – in most instances they were built sequentially – each of the separate palisades was included in the postmold tabulation. Average postmold diameters were used in Fig. 2.2 whenever possible, although range midpoints were substituted when averages were not given in the original publications or could not be computed from data provided in

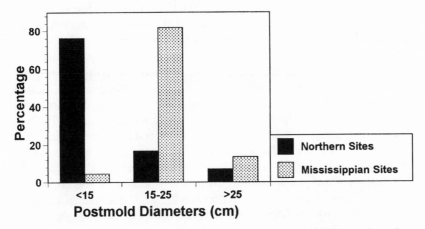

Figure 2.2. Palisade postmold diameters (cm) for Mississippian and northern sites.

them.[34] The overall pattern in postmold diameters is unambiguous: The walls at Mississippian sites were built with larger posts than those used to construct the palisades surrounding the northern sites. Saplings less than 15 cm in diameter were used for most of the northern village palisades, whereas virtually all of the Mississippian walls were erected using more substantial tree trunks.

Bastions reinforced many Mississippian palisades (Fig. 2.1). They were usually square to rectangular, and they jutted out from walls for distances up to twice their width, although bastions composed of tight arcs or circles of posts were also built. A chronicler of the De Soto expedition described one such Mississippi Valley site as "very well palisaded, with towers on the walls, and with a ditch roundabout, and most of it filled with water, which enters through an irrigation ditch that flows from the river."[35] The ditch that headed toward the river must have been an abandoned river channel, although it was not

---

[34] The use of both averages and range midpoints prevents rigorous comparisons of Mississippian and northern site postmold diameters. Available data are suitable only for an exploration of general trends, although a major discrepancy between the postmold diameter distributions would reflect actual differences in the sizes of posts used in the two areas. It is not possible to estimate interobserver variation in the identification of soil stains, but it is unlikely that postmold measurements were affected by systematic biases that invalidate comparisons based on the findings of innumerable excavators at many sites.

[35] Rangel, "De Soto," 301. This settlement corresponds to a St. Francis-type site, following Phillips et al., *Lower Mississippi*, 329–34.

recognized as such by the Spaniards. Bastions were for the most part placed at regular intervals along the walls, although at some sites they were erected in only a few places, as at the sixteenth-century King site in northwestern Georgia.[36] Excavations were sufficiently extensive at fourteen sites to determine the spacing of bastions erected at regular intervals along twenty-two palisades: Aztalan in Wisconsin; Cahokia in Illinois; Snodgrass in Missouri; Angel and Southwind in Indiana; Jonathan Creek and Morris in Kentucky; Sellars and Toqua in Tennessee; Moundville, Lubbub Creek, and Gunter's Landing in Alabama; and Cool Branch and Woodstock Fort in Georgia.[37] Bastion spacing along these walls varied from 21 to 44 meters (mean = 30 m; standard deviation = 7 m), as measured from the middles of the defensive features. These figures are consistent with a 40-pace spacing mentioned in an early-eighteenth-century account of walls in the lower Mississippi Valley.[38]

Bastions were added to palisades at relatively few of the northern sites, and they tended not to be as large or strong as those in the Mississippian area. For example, they consisted of semicircular lines of posts projecting from palisades at Johnston, a Monongahela village in southwestern Pennsylvania.[39] There were exceptions, however, such as the big bastions at Strickler, a seventeenth-century Susquehannock site in southeastern Pennsylvania.[40] This palisaded village was occupied at a time of heightened tensions when guns were readily available. For the most part, bastions were not placed as regularly along the northern village palisades as they were along the Mississippian walls.

[36] Hally, "King," 8.

[37] Anderson, *Cahokia*, 93; Barrett, *Aztalan*, pls. 1–7, 12–15; Black, *Angel*, 121, 132, 158, 215, 220, 222; Blitz, *Tombigbee*, 117; Brian M. Butler, "Sellars: A Small Mound Center in the Hinterlands," *Tennessee Anthropologist* 6 (1981): 37–60; Joseph Caldwell, "Survey and Excavations in the Allatoona Reservoir, Northern Georgia" (Athens, unpublished manuscript); Polhemus, *Toqua*, 84; Price and Griffin, *Snodgrass*, 40; Martha A. Rolingson and Douglas W. Schwartz, *Late Paleo-Indian and Early Archaic Manifestations in Western Kentucky* (Lexington, 1966), 68; Frank T. Schnell, Vernon J. Knight, and Gail S. Schnell, *Cemochechobee: Archaeology of a Mississippian Ceremonial Center on the Chattahoochee River* (Gainesville, 1981), 237; Joseph O. Vogel and Jean Allan, "Mississippian Fortifications at Moundville," *Archaeology* 38 (1985): 62–3; William S. Webb, *The Jonathan Creek Village, Site 4, Marshall County, Kentucky* (Lexington, 1952), 16–17; William S. Webb and Charles G. Wilder, *An Archaeological Survey of Guntersville Basin on the Tennessee River in Northern Alabama* (Lexington, 1951), 41; Thomas R. Wolforth and Cheryl A. Munson, "The Stockade Enclosure," in *Archaeological Investigations at the Southwind Site, a Mississippian Community in Posey County, Indiana,* ed. Cheryl A. Munson (Bloomington, unpublished manuscript).

[38] Antoine Simon Le Page du Pratz, *The History of Louisiana* (London 1774), 375.

[39] Don W. Dragoo, "Excavations at the Johnston Site," *Pennsylvania Archaeologist* 25 (1955): 85–141.

[40] Barry C. Kent, *Susquehanna's Indians* (Harrisburg, 1984), 350.

Instead, they appear to have been built as needed to reinforce sections of palisades that were particularly vulnerable to attack.

Narrow openings have been identified in the lines of postmolds at some sites. These entrances often consisted of long narrow spaces between overlapping walls. Clusters of postmolds have been found near many of them, some of which were probably the remains of defensive towers or platforms, or perhaps baffles that prevented easy passage through the gates. The latter must have been similar to Huron village gates described as being "closed with bars and through which one is forced to pass turning sideways and not striding straight in."[41]

Embankments or ditches accompanied some of the palisades. Most of these features have been obliterated through years of plowing, although a century or more ago many of them were described and mapped. Today the remnants of these now-filled depressions or much-reduced ridges are identifiable as areas of discolored soil in archaeological excavations or on aerial photographs. Many of the embankments and ditches were integral parts of defensive perimeters. Dirt from ditches was piled up to form ridges into which posts were placed, thus increasing the height of the palisades and causing water to flow away from the bases of rot-prone wall supports. Some of the ditches, however, were not important parts of defensive works, although they were related to their construction. These particular ditches are especially well documented at Monongahela Late Woodland sites in southwestern Pennsylvania.[42] The depressions were shallow, often discontinuous, frequently placed inside palisades, and typically filled with village refuse. They were the source of soil heaped up around the bases of nearby wall posts, and these low spots gradually filled with garbage that accumulated over the life of the settlement.

Walls as barriers

Many palisades were no more than screens preventing easy access to communities, especially those in the northern Eastern Woodlands. While some defense was needed from small groups of attackers skulk-

[41] Sagard, *Hurons*, 92.
[42] Deborah K. Catton, *Archaeological Excavations at Bedford Village (36BD90): An Analysis and Synthesis* (University Park, 1994), 91; Dragoo, "Johnston," 91; Richard L. George, "The McJunkin Site, a Preliminary Report," *Pennsylvania Archaeologist* 48 (1978): 33–47; George, "Gnagey," 6–7; Richard L. George, Jay Babish, and Christine E. Davis, "The Household Site: Results of a Partial Excavation of a Late Monongahela Village in Westmoreland County, Pennsylvania," *Pennsylvania Archaeologist* 60 (1990): 40–70.

ing around for targets of opportunity, the walls were not intended to withstand determined assaults by large numbers of warriors intent upon the destruction of entire villages. In the late sixteenth century, such palisades in coastal North Carolina were described as being "compassed abowt with poles starcke faste in the grownd, but they are not verye stronge."[43] All that was necessary was a barrier sufficient to prevent enemies from slipping up on unwary villagers. The possibility of suffering a devastating attack by a strong war party was remote enough that it was not necessary to construct stout walls complete with embankments, deep ditches, and regularly spaced bastions. These people used the smallest posts possible, as indicated by the postmold diameter distribution in Fig. 2.2. Posts any smaller than those actually employed in wall construction would have resulted in palisades that were so weak that they would not have been worth the effort to erect and maintain.

Stronger walls presumably marked places where the possibility of being raided and the likely size of war parties were greater. Walls reinforced with multiple lines of posts were particularly common in the region closely approximating the distribution of historic-period Iroquoian peoples (Fig. 2.1). Bastions and platforms along walls and at gates provided villagers with additional protection from their enemies, although these features might have been manned only when there was some reason to believe that an attack was imminent. In this area, intergroup tensions had a long tradition of flaring into outright warfare. Raids involving many warriors were presumably made possible through alliances that eventually expanded and evolved into the historic Iroquois confederacy.[44]

Regardless of their strength, palisades associated with the northern sites appear to have been thrown up as needed by villagers who worked cooperatively but were free to make expedient choices about the direction and construction of walls in different parts of a single defensive enclosure. No great coordination of effort was needed to gather the numerous small poles they used. Secondary growth, common in long-occupied places such as the area settled by the early-seventeenth-century Huron, was an excellent source of saplings and small trees.[45] Naturally occurring stands of cedars, which tend to have thin straight trunks with few big branches, would have been an excel-

---

[43] Thomas Harriot, *A Briefe and True Report of the New Found Land of Virginia* (1590), 66.
[44] Snow, *The Iroquois*, 53–60.
[45] Conrad Heidenreich, *Huronia* (Toronto, 1971), 153.

lent place to get the many poles needed to construct the palisades and longhouses in Iroquoian villages.[46] In fact, having a convenient source of posts for palisade and house construction was probably an important consideration when choosing a new village location.

The forethought and organization of labor required to build Mississippian palisades – to secure many big posts and to erect walls and reinforcing structures, all according to a reasonably fixed plan – much greater than were those typical of construction efforts at the northern sites. These palisades were often quite substantial constructions, at least by the standards of their time and place (Figs. 2.1 and 2.2). Small posts were not used for a very good reason: Mississippian walls had to be strong to be effective. They often were strengthened by many stout bastions, which would have allowed overlapping fire from arrows, and by substantial embankments and deep ditches. Taken together, these palisade characteristics indicate that Mississippian chiefdoms had the capacity to field more men with some modicum of direction than could be mustered by most of the more northerly located tribal-scale societies. Rival chiefdoms were certainly a force to be reckoned with, and more formidable barriers had to be erected to counter the threat posed by warriors who might do more than simply wait for unwary and outnumbered people. While the possibility of raids by large war parties called forth strong defensive measures, insurmountable logistical problems prevented sustained attacks on settlements.

Sites and societies

Archaeologists have identified many more palisaded settlements in the northern Eastern Woodlands than in the Mississippian area: Almost three-quarters of the fortified sites in the sample were northern villages. It would be wrong, however, to conclude that these numbers indicate that serious intergroup conflicts were much more likely to occur in the north than in the south. Such an interpretation is not consistent with the well-documented Mississippian emphasis on war-related matters. A reputation for prowess and good fortune in war was a means for ambitious men to achieve social recognition and advancement. Artifacts with warfare connotations were closely associated with high-ranking people for whom a minatory demeanor was

---

[46] Richard B. Johnston and L.J. Jackson, "Settlement Pattern at the Le Caron Site, a 17th Century Huron Village," *Journal of Field Archaeology* 7 (1980): 173–99.

essential for their survival.[47] Furthermore, the experiences of sixteenth-century Spaniards indicate that the largest Mississippian groups were able to field, in rather short order, numerous warriors who were organized enough to pose a serious threat to experienced soldiers. The latter generally prevailed through a superiority in arms, but they occasionally found themselves in tight spots when surprised, outnumbered, and attacked in places where their horsemen could not be used effectively.[48]

The discrepancy evident in the simple count of palisaded sites does not take into account differences in settlement longevity and in sociopolitical organization. Large Mississippian settlements were more often ringed by palisades than the many smaller sites distributed around them. The major sites typically were occupied for periods spanning many generations, in contrast to the northern villages that lasted for no more than a generation, and often for much shorter periods of time. More frequent village movement means that correspondingly greater numbers of fortified settlements are likely to be found in the northern Eastern Woodlands.

The numbers of known palisaded settlements also reflect differences in how these sociopolitical systems were organized. The societies scattered across the northern Eastern Woodlands were generally more highly atomized than the chiefdoms to the south. In the northern area, often expedient, sometimes conflicting, and always uncertain relations characterized interactions among the inhabitants of separate communities. These people were left to their own devices when providing for their own defense. It was simply prudent to erect palisades around settlements used for lengthy periods. The demands of building walls could have been met by the inhabitants of these small communities in reasonably short order; all involved had a personal stake in seeing that the work was completed promptly.

It is likely that the objectives of serious Mississippian warfare influenced where and how palisades were constructed. While walls around major sites were erected primarily for defense, they also augmented the aura of strength and sense of legitimacy that successful chiefs sought to maintain. These chiefs would have found it to their advantage to be able to intimidate real and potential enemies, rather than have to rely on tests of strength. Outright conflicts always involved some risk, ranging from actual defeats to pyrrhic victories that eroded

[47] James A. Brown, "The Mississippian Period," in *Ancient Art of the American Woodland Indians* (New York, 1985), 93–143; Wayne W. Van Horne, *The Warclub: Weapon and Symbol in Southeastern Indian Societies* (Athens, 1993).

[48] Vega, *Florida*, 397–403.

the image of prowess in war, a critical component of their positions. There are some hints in the writings of early European explorers that well-planned attacks, as opposed to the opportunistic killing of small numbers of vulnerable people, specifically targeted places where the principal members of chiefly lineages lived. In part, these raids were undertaken to destroy readily visible and highly revered symbols associated with enemy chiefs. De Soto's men had direct experience with such practices when their Indian allies eagerly and thoroughly desecrated their enemies' charnel structures, which contained the bones of important ancestors and other valued items.[49] Such debacles seriously eroded the positions of chiefs for whom success at war was an important justification for the privileged positions they enjoyed. By erecting palisades, chiefs were doing what they could to prevent defeats that might involve a loss of lives, property, and, no less important, the aura of strength and legitimacy that served them well in troubled times.

LATE PREHISTORIC WARFARE

Threatened people in the late prehistoric Eastern Woodlands had several means of protecting themselves: Their strength could be increased through expanded alliance networks; movement could put more distance between hard-pressed people and their enemies; larger settlements could be formed through the aggregation of previously small and dispersed groups; settlements could be moved to more defensible locations; and walls could be thrown up around sites. In some situations, certain responses were undoubtedly preferred over others. Factors likely to have influenced decisions about whether to erect walls around communities included an enemy's ability to field war parties, the village's capacity to counter attacks, and the costs of moving elsewhere. The large number of palisaded sites in late prehistoric times indicates just how frequently mechanisms for mediating disputes between groups failed.

Hard evidence of conflicts – skeletons of victims and fortified villages – indicates that intergroup antagonisms began to flare into outright fighting on a regular basis sometime during the latter part of the first millennium A.D.[50] Data are geographically uneven and distress-

---

[49] Vega, *Florida*, 292–3, 438–9 493.

[50] There were two periods of time when intergroup conflicts occurred fairly frequently in some parts of the Eastern Woodlands, judging from currently available osteological evidence; see Milner, "Prehistoric Warfare." These conflicts first appeared with some regularity among late Middle Archaic to Late Archaic hunter-gatherers, but hostilities

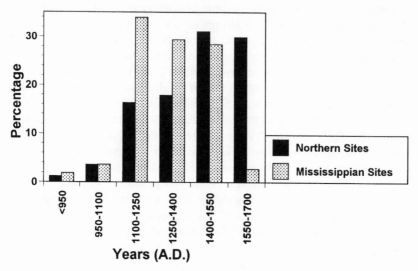

Figure 2.3. The distribution over time of Mississippian and northern walled settlements.

ingly incomplete, but it seems that people were being killed by each other in many places before there was a widespread movement to fortify settlements. Heightened tensions among many groups was perhaps one reason for the rapid spread of the bow and arrow throughout the Eastern Woodlands during the middle of the first millennium A.D.[51] This weapon was ideally suited for stealth-attack tactics, and many late prehistoric skeletons have arrowheads lodged in their bones.[52]

The distributions over time of palisaded settlements shown in Fig. 2.3 are based on the midpoints of occupation spans or archaeological

eventually lessened and by the Middle Woodland period about two millennia ago intergroup fighting rarely took place. Warfare then became more common once again late in the first millennium A.D. among sedentary agricultural peoples, and this period is when palisades were thrown up around many settlements.

[51] John H. Blitz, "Adoption of the Bow in Prehistoric North America," *North American Archaeologist* 9 (1988): 123–45; Mark F. Seeman, "The Bow and Arrow, the Intrusive Mound Complex, and a Late Woodland Jack's Reef Horizon in the Mid-Ohio Valley," in *Cultural Variability in Context*, ed. Mark F. Seeman (Kent, 1992), 41–51; Michael J. Shott, "Innovation and Selection in Prehistory: A Case Study from the American Bottom," in *Stone Tools: Theoretical Insights into Human Prehistory*, ed. George H. Odell (New York, 1996), 279–309.

[52] Milner, "Prehistoric Warfare."

phase affiliations for 109 Mississippian and 251 northern sites.[53] A reliance on only walled settlements is obviously not the best way to identify shifts over time in the likelihood of palisaded communities being present. Unfortunately, there is no way to estimate the proportion of all settlements that had palisades at any particular point in time because it would be difficult, if not impossible, to identify systematically the excavations that were sufficiently large and appropriately positioned to reveal the remnants of palisades if they were once present. Yet despite the shortcomings of existing data, there is no reason to doubt that the distribution over time of the northern palisaded sites differs from that of their Mississippian counterparts.

Mississippian societies

After defensive structures began to be common in the Mississippian area early in the second millennium A.D., they remained a conspicuous part of settlement plans up through the time of initial contact with European freebooters such as De Soto and his men (Fig. 2.3). Apparently, once chiefdoms arose from their organizationally simpler and often less populous antecedents, the need for fortifications became commonplace in what were highly competitive sociopolitical settings. No obvious temporal pattern is evident once palisaded sites began to appear frequently across the southern Eastern Woodlands, although the sample of sites is not as large as one would like and the geographical coverage is uneven. The drop in palisaded sites during the seventeenth century must have been largely a result of the breakdown of once powerful chiefdoms, a consequence of the great loss of life from Old World epidemics and the social disorder that followed in their wake.[54] Marked changes in ways of life and catastrophic depopulation occurred earlier among the Mississippian societies than it did for their more northerly counterparts.[55] Defensive works, however, were still

[53] The most recent estimates of site occupancy or archaeological phase duration were used under the assumption that knowledge about local cultural sequences has improved over time. Thus the estimates used here sometimes differ from dates provided in the original reports, especially when the site descriptions were written several decades or more ago.

[54] For descriptions of culture change in the Deep South during the early historic period see Jeffrey P. Brain, *Tunica Archaeology* (Cambridge, 1988), 264–93; Marvin T. Smith, *Archaeology of Aboriginal Culture Change in the Interior Southeast* (Gainesville, 1987), 54–112.

[55] Compare information presented on different societies in Brain, *Tunica*, 264–86; Jay K. Johnson and Geoffrey R. Lehmann, "Sociopolitical Devolution in Northeast Mississippi and the Timing of the de Soto Entrada," in *Bioarchaeology of Native American*

occasionally needed, and they continued to be constructed until most of the original inhabitants were forced out of the Southeast.[56]

In the Mississippian area, people gravitated toward powerful leaders, abandoning places that were situated between competing chiefdoms.[57] It has been assumed that palisaded settlements were more common on the margins of the chiefdoms, in what could be considered frontier positions, than they were toward the interiors of these societies.[58] Existing information, however, is too spotty to be very informative about the spatial distributions of palisaded settlements within as yet poorly understood sociopolitical units. What is clear is that many of the largest and most important sites that were centrally located within these chiefdoms were protected by palisades, whereas closely associated outlying sites often lacked enclosing walls.

Palisades at major Mississippian centers were probably as important for protection against internal rivals as external enemies. Complex chiefdoms were riven by the divergent interests of competent leaders backed by their own self-sufficient supporters.[59] A chief's grip on his or her subordinates might loosen through an ineffectual handling of internal rivals, an inability to prevent the depredations of external enemies, uncertainty over succession to high office, or hard times from shortfalls in the production of food. These societies were always liable to fragment into their socially and geographically separable components through an irresolute handling of the competing interests of secondary chiefs, who were poised to take advantage of any sign of weakness by the principal chief. The principal chiefs, intent on bolstering their privileged positions, would have done whatever was in their limited power to tilt the military balance in their direction and away

Adaptation in the Spanish Borderlands, eds. Brenda J. Baker and Lisa Kealhofer (Gainesville, 1996), 38–55; Smith, *Interior Southeast*, 54–112; Dean R. Snow, "Microchronology and Demographic Evidence Relating to the Size of Pre-Columbian North American Indian Populations," *Science* 268 (1995): 1601–4; Dean R. Snow, "Mohawk Demography and the Effects of Exogenous Epidemics on American Indian Populations," *Journal of Anthropological Archaeology* 15 (1996): 160–82; Trawick H. Ward and R.P. Stephen Davis, "The Impact of Old World Diseases on the Native Inhabitants of the North Carolina Piedmont," *Archaeology of Eastern North America* 19 (1991): 171–81; Ward and Davis, *North Carolina*, 407–32.

56 Jesse D. Jennings, "Chickasaw and Earlier Indian Cultures of Northeast Mississippi," *Journal of Mississippi History* 3 (1941): 155–226; Thomas M.N. Lewis and Madeline K. Lewis, *The Prehistory of the Chickamauga Basin in Tennessee*, ed. Lynne P. Sullivan (Knoxville, 1995), 562–88.

57 Anderson, *Savannah River*, 326–9; Milner, "Cahokia."

58 Karl T. Steinen, "Ambushes, Raids, and Palisades: Mississippian Warfare in the Interior Southeast," *Southeastern Archaeology* 11 (1992): 132–9.

59 Anderson, "Factional Competition," 61–76; Anderson, *Savannah River*, 102–4.

from upstarts who grasped at any opportunity to further their own objectives. Siphoning off surplus labor to build imposing walls would have given highly ranked chiefs a distinct advantage in internal power struggles by simultaneously reinforcing the impression of their strength while augmenting their defensive position. Such a strategy would have been especially successful if a principal chief managed to limit palisade construction at the sites of potential rivals elsewhere in his, or her, chiefdom.

Northern societies

Fortified settlements in some parts of the northern Eastern Woodlands became common as early as they appeared across much of the Mississippian area (Fig. 2.3). Palisades continued to be thrown up around villages throughout the seventeenth century. The many walled sites in the 1550 to 1700 interval indicate that conflicts frequently occurred at that time, especially considering the rapid seventeenth-century population decline and the correspondingly great reduction in the overall number of settlements.

In contrast to the Mississippian area, the palisaded sites in the northern Eastern Woodlands increased in frequency during the late prehistoric period. This increase was real, unless there were many more sites of all kinds later in time. Such a situation might have arisen if northern populations across a broad area grew rapidly, or if later settlements were smaller or were occupied for shorter periods than the earlier villages. No evidence, however, supports such explanations for changes in the numbers of palisaded villages. Instead, the straightforward inference appears to be the correct one: Proportionally more sites later in time were surrounded by walls. Thus the direction of change is clear, but its magnitude cannot be reliably estimated because of deficiencies in available data.

The geographical distribution of fortified settlements in the northern area – assuming known sites mirror, however imperfectly, past reality – is consistent with a population and resource disparity explanation for the origins of late prehistoric warfare. Villages protected by palisades became common early in the second millennium A.D. in southern Ontario and upstate New York, a region that corresponds closely to the area inhabited by the bellicose historic Iroquoian groups. Palisaded villages referred to as Monongahela Late Woodland were also common at this time across the Allegheny plateau of southwestern Pennsylvania. Both regions were more marginal for agriculture than many other parts of the northern Eastern Woodlands occupied by tribally-organized sedentary agriculturalists.[60] Uncertainty over the yields of critical resources must have aggravated any tensions that existed among neighboring groups. Outright hostilities proving inimical to survival for some groups presumably prompted movement to put more distance between them and their tormentors. Such movements are known to have occurred during the early historic period.[61] Population displacement and a desire for satisfactory alternatives to existing village settings inevitably created new problems elsewhere as dislocated groups infringed on lands claimed or used by peoples farther afield.

By about A.D. 1400, subsistence insecurity was aggravated throughout the Great Lakes region with the onset of the Little Ice Age. The jockeying of ephemeral constellations of villages for advantageous positions took on a new urgency, particularly for the losers in intergroup conflicts. Flight from immediate danger and the priority placed on finding satisfactory land resulted in the movement of some groups that, in turn, displaced more far-flung peoples who were unable to meet the challenge of threatening, and at times desperate, newcomers. Intergroup hostilities soon widened, as indicated by palisades becoming a more common feature of settlements in some parts of the mid-Atlantic states, seemingly earlier in mountainous areas than in the Piedmont and Coastal Plain.[62] The appearance of new archaeological complexes in some places has been interpreted as marking the arrival of culturally distinct groups of people.[63] Yet despite what seem to have

---

[60] For a discussion of risk management see John M. O'Shea, "The Role of Wild Resources in Small-Scale Agricultural Systems: Tales from the Lakes and Plains," in *Bad Year Economics: Cultural Responses to Risk and Uncertainty*, eds. Paul Halstead and John M. O'Shea (Cambridge, 1989), 57–67.

[61] Samuel de Champlain, *The Works of Samuel de Champlain 1615–1618*, Vol. 3, eds. and trans. H.H. Langton and W.F. Ganong (Toronto, 1929), 125.

[62] Wayne E. Clark, "The Origins of the Piscataway and Related Indian Cultures," *Maryland Historical Magazine* 75 (1980): 8–22; Jay F. Custer, "Late Woodland Cultures of the Lower and Middle Susquehanna Valley," in *Late Woodland Cultures of the Middle Atlantic Region*, ed. Jay F. Custer (Newark, 1986), 116–42; Custer et al., "Slackwater," 30; William M. Gardner, "External Cultural Influences in the Western Middle Atlantic: A New-Diffusionist Approach or You Never Know What Went on Under the Rhododendron Bush Until You Look," in *Upland Archeology in the East*, ed. Michael B. Barber (Harrisonburg, 1984), 118–46; Potter, *Chiefs*, 147; R. Michael Stewart, "The Status of Woodland Prehistory in the Middle Atlantic Region," *Archaeology of Eastern North America* 23 (1995): 177–206; Ward and Davis, *North Carolina*, 407–32.

[63] Clark, "Piscataway," 20; Custer, "Susquehanna," 134–8; Custer et al., "Slackwater," 31; Gardner, "Middle Atlantic," 139–40; Howard A. MacCord, "Evidence for a Late Woodland Migration from Piedmont to Tidewater in the Potomac Valley," *Maryland Archeology* 20 (1984): 7–18; Potter, *Chiefs*, 130–2, 136–8, 143–6; Stewart, "Middle Atlantic," 194–5.

been increasingly troubled times, simple screens made up of single lines of small posts usually provided villagers with sufficient protection from their adversaries. Outright fighting rarely reached the feverish pitch seen in southern Ontario and upstate New York, which required the erection of stout barriers consisting of multiple lines of posts.

Farther west, a late prehistoric expansion of upper-midwestern Oneota groups played a part in what had become increasingly bellicose times across a broad area extending far onto the northern Plains.[64] The ramifying effects of bitter fighting may well have pushed expediently aligned village coalitions to new areas while they were being pulled by the lure of resource rich but spottily occupied land. Communities that had the misfortune of finding themselves on the leading edge of this movement sometimes suffered greatly as increasingly desperate people jockeyed for advantageous physical and social positions. In one such village – it was part of a southward expansion of Oneota groups into west-central Illinois – at least one-third of all adults, both males and females, died as a result of warfare.[65]

Archaeologists are only now beginning to delineate the configuration of ever-changing demographic and sociopolitical landscapes across the northern Eastern Woodlands.[66] Knowledge of this broad region is uneven, but it is nonetheless clear that the geographical distribution of small clusters of villages changed throughout the late prehistoric period. People migrated to places where alliances could be made with other groups to augment their strength, or they simply displaced the original occupants, who fled only to spread unrest elsewhere.

CONCLUSION

Much remains to be learned about prehistoric warfare in eastern North America, but hostilities clearly forced people in some places to protect themselves by enclosing their settlements with walls. Despite the strangely persistent image of harmony in prehistory, warfare requiring people to take special measures to protect themselves was common-

---

[64] Guy Gibbon, "Cultures of the Upper Mississippi River Valley and Adjacent Prairies in Iowa and Minnesota," in *Plains Indians, A.D. 500–1500*, ed. Karl H. Schlesier (Norman, 1994), 128–48; Patrick Willey, *Prehistoric Warfare on the Great Plains* (New York, 1990); Patrick Willey and Thomas E. Emerson, "The Osteology and Archaeology of the Crow Creek Massacre," *Plains Anthropologist* 38 (1993): 227–69.

[65] Milner et al., "Warfare in Illinois."

[66] Dean R. Snow, "Migration in Prehistory: The Northern Iroquoian Case," *American Antiquity* 60 (1995): 59–79.

place long before Europeans arrived in force in eastern North America. Furthermore, the temporal and geographical distributions of palisaded sites, as well as the nature of these defensive works, are consistent with variation across the Eastern Woodlands in sociopolitical organization, population size, and subsistence-related uncertainty. Such correspondence, despite the use of coarse-grained geographical, cultural, and temporal categories, should prompt researchers to look more closely at what the abundant archaeological evidence for warfare, including victims of violence and palisaded sites, can tell us about the prehistoric peoples of the Eastern Woodlands.

CHAPTER 3

To wall or not to wall: Evidence from medieval Germany

JAMES D. TRACY

THE labor, the expense, the sheer magnitude of building a city wall can be appreciated from the volumes of built space or estimates of the materials involved. The relatively modest single enceinte at Leiden, a town of some 5,000 people when its wall was built in the fourteenth century, measured approximately 3,700 meters in length and required 50,000,000 bricks. The last and greatest wall of medieval Florence, with a population between 70,000 and 90,000, was some 8,500 meters long and 11.6 meters high, and took forty-six years to complete (1284–1330). Rival Siena, not quite so large or wealthy, began in the 1320s a circuit that involved three miles of new walls and took one hundred and fifty years to complete. Enclosing an imperial capital demanded still greater effort. For the imposing double walls of Caliph al-Mansur's Baghdad, the inner ring was approximately 68 feet high (20.8 meters) and 16,000 cubits (8,280 meters) in circumference; since the wall was ten bricks thick in its lower reaches, a single course required, by the architect's reckoning, 162,000 cubit-long bricks. At Nanking, the walls built by order of the founding ruler of the Ming dynasty were some 39,000 meters long and fifteen to eighteen meters high.[1]

Hence it is hardly surprising that many civilizations found better and cheaper ways of defending their cities. Ancient Egypt had no walled towns, apparently because the pharaohs "relied upon a re-

---

[1] H.A. van Oerle, *Leiden binnen en buiten de Stadsvesten: de Geschiedenis van de Stedebouw-kundige Ontwikkeling binnen het Leidse Rechtsgebied tot het Einde van de Gouden Eeuw*, 2 Vols. (Leiden, 1975), I:251–2; K.A.C. Cresswell, *A Short History of Early Muslim Architecture*, rev. James W. Allen (Aldershot, 1989), 230–1; Wolfgang Braunfels, *Die mittelalterliche Stadtbaukunst in der Toskana* (Berlin, 1966), 64; Simon Pepper and Nicholas Adams, *Firearms and Fortifications. Military Architecture and Siege Warfare in Sixteenth-Century Siena* (Chicago, 1986), 33–4; Chapter 15 of this volume.

gional defense provided by powerful fortresses erected at the only two major access routes into the country, the eastern delta approaches and the Upper Nile valley in Nubia." The Nubian fortresses, dating from the beginning of the second millennium B.C., seem to have been the earliest consciously developed examples of what John Keegan calls a strategic defense system, in which individual strongpoints are "so positioned as to be mutually supporting."[2] The same may be said for Achaemenid Iran. Alexander the Great conducted numerous sieges of walled cities during his Asian campaigns, but none within the confines of Persia: "as befitted a great state, its interior was defended at its periphery." Keegan suggests that wherever a strong central government appears, one almost invariably finds the construction of strategic defenses at the frontiers, like Egypt's fortresses on the Nubian border, or the Great Wall of China, or the Roman *limes*. Based on Catherine Asher's findings, one may add the successive Delhi sultanates to this list.[3] The early Islamic caliphates are sometimes similarly described as providing defense at the frontiers without the need of fortifications on the interior, but this view is in need of revision, as shown by Jonathan Bloom.[4]

The cities of archaic Greece had no walls and no frontier defenses either. Some of the Greek colonies in Sicily and southern Italy began to fortify themselves in the sixth century B.C., but most urban centers in mainland Greece did not. Here the conventions of hoplite warfare dictated giving battle in open country; the object was to defend not just the city but the fields of farmer-hoplites who were themselves citizens of the town.[5] The Romans were familiar with the fortified cities of ancient Etruria as well as those of Greece, yet most of the cities controlled by Rome during the republican and early imperial eras were not walled. The so-called Servian Wall at Rome itself, an exception to the rule, seems to date from the Gallic invasions of the fourth century B.C. A map from the first century A.D. indicates only six walled towns in Roman Spain, eight in Gaul, and seven in Italy. De la Croix believes that the Romans were for several centuries able to rely on their mobile field armies for defense of the empire because, following the final defeat of Carthage in the second century B.C., few

---

[2] Horst de la Croix, *Military Considerations in City Planning: Fortifications* (New York, 1972) 18; John Keegan, *A History of Warfare* (New York, 1993), 142.

[3] See Chapter 8 of this volume. Keegan, *A History of Warfare*, 145, 147.

[4] See Chapter 9 of this volume.

[5] Pierre Ducrey, *Warfare in Ancient Greece*, trans. Janet Lloyd (New York, 1985), 146–7; Victor Hanson, "From Phalanx to Legion," in *The Cambridge History of Warfare. The Triumph of the West*, ed. Geoffrey Parker (Cambridge, 1995), 19.

of the foes that Rome faced were able to organize and sustain the siege of a town.[6]

Thus town walls were usually not built when a central government could easily defend a territory at its frontiers, when potential foes lacked the social organization or the technology to conduct siege warfare, or when the structure of the defenders' society did not support a distinction between protected cities and an unprotected countryside. Conversely, the decision to build a wall – and a fortiori, a ruler's decision to wall a whole series of towns – usually indicates a military problem for which walls seem the only answer, and a political and social configuration in which towns are able and willing to pay for their own fortification. After a brief look at what may be called programs of wall building in earlier eras, this essay will take up the question of "to wall or not to wall" from the standpoint of medieval and early modern Germany, perhaps the one area in this period for which the available scholarship permits a ready determination of which cities were walled and which were not, and some of the reasons why.

In the Early Dynastic era of Sumer (after 2900 B.C.), villagers began congregating in a few large sites that consequently took on an urban character. This redistribution of population is thought to reflect wars between nascent city states that are indirectly evidenced by the massive town walls that now appeared. Towards the end of the third millennium, smaller cities began fortifying themselves as well, in an effort to ward off Assyrian efforts to unify the whole region under a single monarchy.[7] In China it was only under the Shang dynasty (the fifteenth to the eleventh centuries B.C.) that cities began to be walled.[8] In Greece the pattern of hoplite warfare was broken by the Persian invasions of the early fifth century; the introduction of new fighting forces (cavalry and skirmishers) ended the dominance of the farmer-hoplite, even as rivalry between two powers that had

---

[6] Richard Tomlinson, *From Mycenae to Constantinople. The Evolution of the Ancient City* (London, 1992), 150–68; Steven Johnson, *Late Roman Fortifications* (Totowa, NJ, 1983); De la Croix, *Military Considerations in City Planning*, 30–1. But Brian Ward Perkins, *From Classical Antiquity to the Middle Ages. Urban Public Building in Northern and Central Italy AD 300–850* (Oxford, 1984), 12, believes that by the end of the first century A.D. even the smallest Italian towns had walls.

[7] Song Nai Rhee, "The Sumerian City States," in *The City-State in Five Cultures*, eds. Robert Griffeth and Carol G. Thomas (Santa Barbara, 1981), 7–12; Harriet Crawford, *Sumer and the Sumerians* (Cambridge, 1991), 25, 34, 48, 53; Quentin Hughes, *Military Architecture* (London, 1974), 9.

[8] Kwang-Chih Chang, *Shang China* (New Haven, 1980).

fended off Persia, Athens, and Sparta degenerated into full-scale civil war. Mainland towns now fortified themselves, and during the entire period of the Pelopponesian wars there were not more than three or four open-field battles of the old style.[9] In the western provinces of the Roman empire the combination of internal disorders and barbarian invasions around the middle of the third century A.D. marked a turning point; Edward Luttwak believes that the decisive moment came when the Alemannic tribes of southern Germany broke through the imperial frontier in great numbers (259–260 A.D.). With frontier defenses no longer reliable, cities in Rome's western provinces bent every effort to fortify themselves. In the next century or century and a half, some seventy to one hundred towns in Roman Gaul were enclosed by walls, together with forty or more in Spain, and perhaps seventy in Italy. Bryan Ward Perkins notes that the walls now built were in many cases replacements for older walls that had been allowed to fall into decrepitude during two centuries of imperial peace; the new circuits were smaller in circumference and thus more easily defended.[10]

Medieval Europe as a whole – not just the areas that had once been under Roman rule – experienced a second great wave of wall building during the twelfth and thirteenth centuries. Cities with walls of Roman origin built new circuits enclosing more space, while many previously open cities now acquired walls. In England, for example, the number of walled towns roughly doubled, to about 200; in France the great impetus for building or rebuilding walls came somewhat later, in the mid-fourteenth century, as Michael Wolfe points out.[11] Cities in northern and central Italy built a second ring of walls during the twelfth century, and a third, larger still, during the late thirteenth or early fourteenth centuries. On the Rhine, Cologne (the Roman *Colonia Ubiorum*), precocious in this respect, began its second enceinte in 1106 and its third in 1181. The great high-medieval spurt of wall building was not prompted by any new developments in military technology. Rather, wealth accruing from the contemporary commercial revolution meant that towns were now able to afford fortifications of the kind

[9] Hanson, "From Phalanx to Legion," 19–28; for a new perspective, see Chapter 6 of this volume.

[10] Perkins, *From Classical Antiquity to the Middle Ages*, 191 (stressing the rebuilding of older, neglected fortifications); Keegan, *History of Warfare*, 149; Edward N. Luttwak, *The Grand Strategy of the Roman Empire from the First Century A.D. to the Third* (Baltimore, 1976), 168; Johnson, *Late Roman Fortifications*, 10; Bernard S. Bachrach, "On Roman Ramparts 300–1300," in *Cambridge History of Warfare*, 69.

[11] See Chapter 11 of this volume.

that Europe's rural nobles had been putting up for some time, in a wave of castle building that had begun in the eleventh century.[12] But the high curtain walls that were the pride of so many a town became obsolete when battle commanders learned the art of managing siege guns that could batter down an eight-foot-thick wall. Italian military architects developed the bastioned trace in response (ca. 1480–1520), thus providing for other European powers the first models of the "artillery fortresses" discussed here by Professors Wolfe, Elbl, and Parker.

The question of where the political initiative lay in these various programs of wall building does not admit of clear-cut answers. During Sumeria's wall-building era, in the Early Dynastic period, cities were in transition from one form of government to another, from oligarchy to monarchy.[13] In China, the Shang were the earliest dynasty whose unification of the country is a matter of historical record, and the fact that the Shang ideograph for city (*yi*) combined the symbol for a man kneeling in submission with the symbol for an enclosure suggests that the emperor at least had to give his blessing for the fortifying of cities that date from this period.[14] For Greece, urban enceintes dated to the sixth century B.C. have been linked to the contemporary rise of democracy and the awakening of civic consciousness,[15] but Frederick Cooper's dating of the massive walls of ashlar construction from the fourth century seems to point to a military explanation (the strategic thinking of Epaminondas) rather than a political one (the fact that Thebes was an oligarchy).[16] For the later Roman empire in the West, the placement relative to one another of towns that received walls strongly suggests a decision at the center to create a system of strategic defense. Yet scattered indications as to funding point to local initative, or at least local responsibility. Many inscriptions record how town magistrates used public funds to build the walls, while direct imperial patronage of defensive works focused on capital cities or residences; one imperial edict sought to have funds that urban magistrates had

---

[12] Braunfels, *Die mittelalterliche Stadtbaukunst in der Toskana*, 50–73, and *Urban Design in Western Europe*, trans. Kenneth J. Norcott (Chicago, 1988), 24–5; Bachrach, "On Roman Ramparts," 89; Chapter 9 of this volume; Keegan, *History of Warfare*, 149.

[13] Crawford, *Sumer and the Sumerians*.

[14] Keegan, *History of Warfare*, 145; Chang, *Shang Civilization*.

[15] De la Croix, *Military Considerations in City Planning*, 21: "Fortification became a symbol of a free and autonomous body of citizens, and separate strongholds were no longer tolerated in their midst." Ducrey, *Warfare in Ancient Greece*, 150, 167. On the dating of ashlar-built town walls in Greece, see Chapter 6 of this volume.

[16] See Chapter 6 of this volume.

diverted to wall building restored to their original purpose, the provision of games for entertainment of the citizenry.[17]

During the High Middle Ages burghers often accepted formal responsibility for financing a wall, as at Aachen in 1171. Sometimes the cost was apportioned among districts in the town, as at Orvieto in 1327, where each of the town gates was to be paid for by the adjacent quarter. Local funding did not mean, however, that the ruler was a mere spectator. Towns in most areas required permission from the prince to levy new taxes on their burghers, and also to issue the bonds (*rentes*) that were backed by urban taxes; major capital expenditures like wall building required one or the other form of revenue, sometimes both. As princely regimes developed their own panoply of revenues, it also became possible, as in thirteenth-century Castile or fourteenth-century France, to pay for wall building by allowing a town to collect for this end one of the king's taxes.[18] More fundamentally, the right of fortification was one of the prince's prerogatives. Strong rulers were able to enforce a monopoly: In England, royal boroughs were walled, cities under the rule of private lords were not. Even where princely control was less effective, as in the Holy Roman Empire, prudent towns sought a formal grant of *Befestigungsrecht* (the right to fortify) from the emperor, or from the ruler of one of the empire's many princely territories. Northern Italy, where the Lombard League of cities had defeated the emperor and extracted a recognition of their autonomy that was deemed to include the right to fortify (Peace of Constance, 1184), was an exception to the rule.[19]

By granting a town the right to build a wall as well as the right to raise revenues to pay for it, princes in effect transferred control of fortifications to their towns, as Michael Toch has argued for medieval Germany; the towns that were ruled by proud merchant or craft guilds seemed particularly willing to bargain in this way for greater autonomy. Yet the initiative for walling cities in the High Middle Ages did not come only from the towns. The urban fortifications that have most

---

[17] Chapter 7 of this volume; Perkins, *From Classical Antiquity to the Middle Ages*, 10–12, 18, 28.

[18] Braunfels, *Die mittelalterliche Stadtbaukunst in der Toskana*, 72–3; Heinrich Koller, "Die mittelalterliche Stadtmauer als Grundlage städtischen Selbstbewüsstseins," in *Stadt und Krieg*, eds. Bernhard Kirchgässner, Günther Scholz (Sigmaringen, 1989), 11; James F. Powers, "Life on the Cutting Edge: The Besieged Town on the Luso-Hispanic Frontier," in *The Medieval City under Siege*, eds. Ivy A. Corfis and Michael Wolfe (Woodbridge, Suffolk), 29; Albert Rigaudière, *Gouverneur la Ville au Moyen Age*, (Paris, 1993) ch. 10: "Le financement des fortifications urbaines en France du milieu du XIVe siècle à la fin du XVe siècle," 421, 428, 436–7, 447.

[19] Spiro Kostof, *The City Assembled* (New York, 1988), 26; Braunfels, *Die mittelalterliche Stadtbaukunst in der Toskana*, 50; Koller, "Die Mittelalterliche Stadtmauer," 11–12.

impressed later generations, like Carcassone in southwestern France or Montagnan in northeastern Italy, often represent a ruler's decision to strengthen a threatened frontier. From the twelfth century onwards, rulers all over western and central Europe were active in founding new towns, both as nuclei for revenue-producing trade and as strongholds to guard the frontier against a rival prince. In Spain, for example, the success of Christian rulers in planting fortress-towns, and the inability of Muslim rulers to do the same, has been called the "driving force" in the *Reconquista*. From the ruler's standpoint, as Charles Laurent Salch has remarked for thirteenth-century France, a walled town was better than a castle, because the willingness of burghers to pay for the fortification of their own "republic" discharged him of responsibility for building and maintenance costs.[20]

Yet despite the fact that burghers and princes had a common interest in the walling of cities, many of the towns of medieval and early modern Europe were never fortified; for many others there is no reliable documentary or archaeological information one way or the other, suggesting that these towns too were never fortified. Since for the period between roughly 1000 and 1800 the urban history of Germany is better documented than any other part of Europe, it is well to look to Germany to develop a sense of why individual cities were or were not walled. The urban emphasis within German historical scholarship[21] is rooted in the decentralized history of Germany, not unified as a nation until 1871, and was powerfully stimulated by two leading ideas. One was Otto Gierke's argument for the corporate autonomy of the local community.[22] The other was Max Weber's concept of the historical uniqueness of the walled cities of medieval Europe:

An urban "community," in the full meaning of the word, appears as a general phenomenon only in the Occident. Exceptions occasionally were to be found in the Near East (in Syria, Phoenicia, Mesopotamia) but only occasionally and in rudiments. To constitute a full urban community a settlement must display a relative predominance of trade-commercial relations with the settlement as a whole displaying the following features: 1. a fortification; 2. a market; 3. a court of its own and at least partially autonomous law; 4. a related form of

---

[20] Michael Toch, "The Medieval German City under Siege," in *The Medieval City under Siege*, 47; De la Croix, *Military Considerations in City Planning*, 34–7; Powers, "Life on the Cutting Edge," 17; Charles Laurent Salch, *Atlas des Villes et Villages Fortifiées en France (Moyen Âge)* (rprt. Strasbourg, 1978), 13–14. Cf. Jagadish Narayan Sardar, *The Art of War in Medieval India* (New Delhi, 1984), 147: The Bahmanid dynasty of the Deccan, noted for its hill forts, began to neglect them as fortified cities developed.

[21] See Brigitte Schroeder and Heinz Stoob, *Bibliographie der deutschen historischen Stadtforschung* (Cologne, 1986).

[22] See Otto Gierke, *Das deutsche Genossenschaftsrecht*, 4 vols. (Berlin, 1868–1913).

association; and 5. at least partial autonomy and autocephaly, thus an administration by authorities in the election of whom burghers participated. . . . The medieval occidental city presents striking contrasts to its Asiatic counterparts. This was particularly true for urban formations north of the Alps where the Western city developed in its purest form.

In regard to the degree of autonomy that medieval European towns enjoyed, recent scholarship emphasizes the ties that bound even relatively independent towns to their princes a good deal more than Weber did, even if one still finds in the literature echoes of an undiluted Weberian image of self-sufficient towns sheltered behind their walls, ruled by merchant-warriors capable of standing off the prince if need be.[23] In German historical scholarship the lingering influence of Gierke and Weber may be seen in the fact that some of the best recent work on the late medieval and early modern period focuses on the "forms of association" linked with local autonomy, viewed in comparative perspective.[24] Weber's larger claim that the European combination of urban autonomy and urban self-defense is not to be found "as a general phenomenon" in other civilizations is a question that has to be addressed by specialists in Islamic and East Asian history in particular; the jury is still out.[25]

For those interested in urban fortifications, the German tradition has produced some unique monuments of scholarship. One is a large

---

[23] Max Weber, *The City*, trans. and eds. Don Marintale and Gertrude Neuwirth (New York, 1958), 80–1; *The City* is a translation of a lengthy essay Weber first published in 1921; for the most recent German edition, see his *Wirtschaft und Gesellschaft* (Tübingen, 1956), 2:735ff. Cf. Braunfels' argument for the connections between urban self-government and wall building in *Die mittelalterliche Stadtbaukunst in der Toskana*, 64, and *Urban Design in Western Europe*, 25, 32, 52, and also the comment on forms of urban autonomy dating from the eleventh century in Europe by Leonardo Benevolo, *The European City*, trans. by Carl Ipsen (Oxford, 1993), 24: "The appropriation of responsibility – lacking in the Arab and oriental worlds – is the source of the distinctive vital character of European cities, and helped to define European civilization and contribute to its global success." For recent scholarship on the ties between town and prince, see for example, Michael Wolfe, "Walled Towns during the French Wars of Religion, 1560–1630," Chapter 11 of this volume.

[24] For Peter Blickle's concept of "communalism," see *Theorien kommunaler Ordnung in Europa*, eds. Peter Blickle and Elisabeth Müller-Luckner (Munich, 1996), and in English, *Communal Reformation. The Quest for Salvation in 16th-Century Germany*, trans. Thomas Dunlap (Atlantic Highlands, NJ, 1992). For an explicit coming-to-terms with Weber's intellectual heritage, Heinz Schilling, *Konfessionskonflikt und Staatsbildung: Eine Fallstudie über das Verhältnis von religiösem und sozialem Wandel in der Frühneuzeit am Beispiel der Grafschaft Lippe* (Gütersloh, 1981), and "Confessional Europe," in *Handbook of European History 1400–1600*, eds. Thomas A. Brady, Heiko A. Oberman, and James D. Tracy, 2 vols. (Leiden, 1994–5), 2:640–81.

[25] Ira M. Lapidus, *Muslim Cities in the Later Middle Ages* (Cambridge and New York, 1984); Adrian Gerber, "Communalism in Japan," *Journal of Early Modern History* 1/4 (1997): 291–314.

Table 3.1 *Fortified cities in Stoob's* Mitteleuropa

	West of 20th Meridian	East of 20th Meridian	Totals
No information	1,279	396	1,675
Unfortified	1,161	208	1,369
Rampart/palisade	225	45	270
Single wall	1,562	90	1,652
Double wall	234	3	237
Gun platforms	45	6	51
Bastioned trace	349	20	369
Totals	**4,855**	**768**	**5,623**
Total/% fortified*	**2,190/45.1%**	**119/15.5%**	**2,309/41.1%**

*Fortified = single wall, double wall, gun platforms, or bastioned trace; all others counted as unfortified.

multicolored map by Heinz Stoob, director of the Institute for Comparative Urban Research at the University of Münster, on "The Distribution of Cities in *Mitteleuropa*, Development until 1945." *Mitteleuropa* ("Central Europe" does not convey the same meaning) stretches from Calais in the west to the eastern bend of the Vistula, and from southern Scandinavia to the Italian slopes of the Alps, with a southeastern extension as far as Dalmatia. Cities are coded according to symbols that indicate fortification works of various kinds, with each symbol color-coded to indicate the period of construction. Stoob describes the map as a "draft" (*Entwurf*) for what is planned as one of a number of distribution maps in a projected *Deutsches Städteatlas*. Perhaps because there is a definitive version yet to come, he does not provide a numerical summary for the information recorded on this map. Table 3.1 represents my count of walled and unwalled cities according to Stoob.[26] It seems likely that the cities (mostly small) for which no information about walls is available one way or another were not fortified, and in Table 3.1 cities having only a rampart and palisade are also counted as unfortified. Walled cities are counted only once,

[26] Heinz Stoob, "Die Stadtbefestigung. Vergleichende Überlegungen zur bürgerlichen Siedlungs- und Baugeschichte, besonders der frühen Neuzeit," in *Europäische Städte im Zeitalter des Barock*, ed. Kersten Krüger (Vienna and Cologne, 1988), 25–56; the map, approximately 25 in. × 29 in., is folded into the end pocket.

for the most recent kind of fortification. In double-walled cities (as at Carcassone, mentioned above) defenders positioned on the inner curtain wall were able to fire over a lower outer wall. Following Stoob, Table 3.1 also separates cities having a full bastioned trace from those having gun platforms outside the walls (in some cases before 1450) or a partially completed bastioned trace. Since the density of urban settlement thins as one moves into what is now Poland and the eastern parts of the Czech Republic and Hungary, Table 3.1 groups cities on either side of the twentieth meridian, which runs just east of Königsberg and west of Cracow. If the percentage of walled cities falls off sharply in the east, there are also zones in the west and center where far more than forty-five percent of the cities were walled; Stoob notes concentrations of well-fortified towns in the more urbanized regions (Flanders, the Rhineland, Hesse, Saxony), and along contested frontiers (the Dutch Republic, also the borders claimed by the Teutonic Knights and certain territorial princes).

To get a sense of what Germany's urban landscape may have looked like at a given point in time, one may turn to the topographical scholarship of the early modern period. The *Topographica Germanica* series, assembled by Matthaeus Merian (d. 1653) and Martin Zeiller (d. 1661), represents the earliest date at which one can compare hundreds of contemporary engravings of German cities. For all of Germany[27] only a few hundred cities are shown graphically, and of these 264 are represented in sufficient detail to tell that 234 towns are shown as walled. Of the thirty unwalled cities (eleven percent), seventeen have no fortification whatever, nine have an outer ring of houses joined together to form a barrier against intruders (as at Catal Hüyük in ancient Anatolia), three have palisades, and one has a bare earthen rampart. The disparity between Stoob and Merian in terms of the percentage of walled cities is not significant, because most of the towns selected for illustration in Merian were relatively large and important. What is striking is the degree of agreement between Stoob and Merian in terms of the distribution of different types of fortifications, as Table 3.2 shows. In Merian's illustrations one can also see that there were different kinds of single walls. Of the 171 towns in ques-

---

[27] Germany, for purposes of this paragraph, includes Alsace, Austria, Bohemia, Silesia, and Switzerland, on each of which there are volumes in Merian-Zeiller, but not the Italian portion of the Holy Roman Empire or the Low Countries (there is a volume on "Burgundy" but its illustrations are mainly overhead plans rather than the more helpful frontal views found in other volumes). My thanks to Markus Vink for compiling the information presented here, from the reprint of Merian-Zeiller: *Topographica Germanica*, 17 vols. (Kassel, 1959–67).

Table 3.2 *Town fortifications in Merian's Germany and Stoob's*
Mitteleuropa

	Merian's Germany	Stoob's *Mitteleuropa*
Total fortified towns	234	2,190
Single wall	171 (73.1%)	1,562 (71.3%)
Double wall	15 (6.4%)	234 (10.7%)
Bastion or part bastion	45 (19.2%)	394 (18%)

tion, 33 show a bare wall with no sign of battlements, 9 have crenellations, 109 have loopholes for crossbowmen or arquebusiers, and 20 have either the machicolation characteristic of late medieval fortification or a roofed gallery. The fact that some double-ringed cities have a crenellated inner wall and an outer wall with loopholes indicates that the former were of an earlier date. One would think that a bare single wall with no provision for active defense did not afford much protection against attack. On the other hand, unless one is to assume a massive reconstruction of old-style fortifications in the immediate aftermath of the Thirty Years' War (1618–48), what seems most surprising in Merian's illustrations is the number of medieval curtain walls that were still standing and (apparently) maintained in the middle of the seventeenth century.

It is to be hoped that the final version of Stoob's map, especially in combination with other kinds of distribution maps,[28] will provide a solid foundation for the comparative study of urban fortifications. Meanwhile, one can glean a great deal of information about cities walled and unwalled from another monument of German urban scholarship, the series *Deutsches Städtebuch (DSB)*, of which eleven volumes have thus far appeared.[29] Each volume represents the cities of one or more provinces, and each entry covers twenty headings, including the date of the city's charter (if known), the structure of its economy, guild organization, city government, the earliest information on population, and when and how the city was fortified. For purposes

---

[28] For an example of the projects receiving attention at the Institute for Comparative Urban History, see, *Europäische Messen und Marktsysteme in Mittelalter und Neuzeit*, eds. Peter Johanek and Heinz Stoob (Cologne, 1996).

[29] *Deutsches Städtebuch*, eds. Erich Keyser et al. (Stuttgart, 1939–). I am indebted to the late but not forgotten Prof. Bob Scribner of Harvard Divinity School for calling my attention to *DSB*. There is also an *Österreichisches Städtebuch* (Vienna, 1968–), of which nine volumes have appeared.

of this essay, I have used the first four volumes of *DSB*, covering eleven provinces in north and central Germany. *DSB* includes all communities that are described as cities in contemporary sources, down to the time of publication. I have counted only settlements that were recognized as cities before 1800, and on the basis either of a known urban charter, or evidence of the form of government (burgomaster and council) that was considered requisite and proper for a city. Towns surrounded by a rampart and palisade, or a wooden fence or a hedge, or a partial wall are all counted here as unwalled.[30]

In all, 576 of the 1,083 communities identified in this way as cities (fifty-three percent) were walled at one time or another, from Roman times until 1800.[31] Of the remaining 407 communities, 166 are said either never to have had walls or never to have had any fortification at all; 127 had a hedge or a fence, often set atop an earthen rampart; 14 are said not to have needed fortification because of a protected natural site; and 3 began walls which were never finished.[32] Of the 576 walled cities, the *DSB* entries give dates for the building of the (first) wall for only 428, in most cases during the thirteenth or especially the fourteenth century (data from Stoob's map bears out his observation that most walled cities in *Mitteleuropa* were fortified between 1250 and 1450). This chronological concentration fits the political circumstances of medieval Germany, where the period after 1250 has been called the era of the foundation of small cities.[33] It was during this period that the strong monarchy built by Holy Roman emperors of the Hohenstaufen line gave way to an Interregnum (1250–76) and to multiple conflicts among the German princes and cities under the often weak emperors who followed.

The importance of population in determining whether a city would be walled is obvious, if not so easy to demonstrate. The problem is that for cities for which population figures are available before 1800,[34] there is no particular connection between the dating of such estimates

---

[30] I do count cities as walled if surrounded by a wall that includes a side which incorporates some natural barrier against ingress, like a river or a mountain. On Stoob's map, cities that have only a fence or a hedge, usually with a gate to admit visitors or collect tolls, are counted as unfortified.

[31] Of the eleven provinces in vols. 1–4 of *DSB*, only what is called the Rhineland (roughly, the western part of the modern *Bundesstaat* Rheinland-Westfalen) had cities of Roman origin.

[32] This still leaves ninety-six communities, for which no information about fortification is given in the entries.

[33] Evamaria Engel, *Die deutsche Stadt des Mittelalters* (Munich, 1993), 35–7; cf. the comment of F.R.H. Du Boulay, *Germany in the Later Middle Ages* (New York, 1983), 115: "In the thirteenth century the number of German towns increased ten-fold."

[34] Where the information given is a number of dwelling units (houses or hearths) I have assumed a multiplier of five.

Table 3.3 *Dating of city walls*

Date	Cities walled	Percent of total
Before 1100	3	1%
1100–1200	20	5%
1200–1300	126	29%
1300–1400	178	42%
1400–1500	63	15%
1500–1600	26	6%
1600–1700	12	3%
Totals	**428**	**100%**

and the date at which the town's walls were built. Thus Tables 3.4, 3.5, and 3.6 are based on the assumption that cities grew along roughly the same population curve, meaning that information from later centuries would still have some relation to the population when the town was first fortified. Table 3.4 considers the small number of cities for which data are available before 1500. Table 3.5 covers all the cities (including many from Table 3.4) for which population estimates are available between 1500 and 1700. Table 3.6 deals with a smaller number of towns for which there is no information whatever before 1700. What may occasion surprise is the number of tiny communities – many with populations under 1,000 as late as the eighteenth century – that mounted the effort to build a wall. One is reminded of the fact that medieval Germany's sixty-nine imperial cities (those with a right of summons to the Diet) included some that, though they had all the urban trappings, "were not much larger than large villages."[35]

Since the westerly provinces of the Holy Roman Empire (including Hesse and the Rhineland) experienced more rapid urban and economic development during the Middle Ages, it is to be expected that cities in these areas were somewhat more likely to be walled. Conversely, cities were less likely to be surrounded by enceintes in coastal regions of the north (Schleswig-Holstein), where maritime and trading settlements often sprang up in places girt by water or by swampy ground. The low percentage of walled cities in Saxony seems related to that province's role as a mining center, since, as noted below, most mining cities were not walled. (See Table 3.7)

Legal status is another good indicator of whether cities would be

[35] Thomas A. Brady, *Turning Swiss: Cities and Empire, 1450–1550* (Cambridge, 1985), 11.

Table 3.4 *Walled cities by population information from 1200–1500*

Population	Cities	Walled	Percent
Less than 1,000	83	36	43%
1,000–3,000	69	62	90%
3,000–5,000	11	11	100%
5,000–10,000	14	14	100%
Over 10,000	8	8	100%
Totals	**185**	**131**	**71%**

Table 3.5 *Walled cities by population information from 1500– 1700*

Population	Cities	Walled	Percent
Less than 1,000	338	133	39%
1,000–3,000	209	176	84%
3,000–5,000	36	30	83%
5,000–10,000	18	18	100%
Over 10,000	17	17	100%
Totals	**518**	**374**	**72%**

Table 3.6 *Walled cities by population information first available 1700–1800*

Population	Cities	Walled	Percent
Less than 1,000	168	59	35%
1,000–2,000	108	59	55%
Over 2,000	64	43	67%
Totals	**340**	**161**	**47%**

Table 3.7 *Walled cities by province*[1]

Province	Cities	Walled	Percent
East Prussia	76	41	54%
Pomerania	90	42	47%
Brandenburg	120	64	53%
Mecklenburg	48	24	50%
Schleswig-Holstein	30	10	33%
Silesia	131	60	46%
Saxony	138	52	38%
Thuringia	83	54	65%
Anhalt	162	84	52%
Rhineland	73	51	70%
Hesse	132	94	71%
Totals	1,083	576	53%

[1] The order of provinces is given in *DSB*.

Table 3.8 *The walling of chartered cities*

Date of charter	Cities	Walled	Percent
Uncertain	33	15	45%
Before 1200	80	41	51%
1200–1300	361	278	77%
1300–1400	219	122	56%
1400–1500	55	23	42%
1500–1600	46	4	9%
1600–1700	35	3	9%
1700–1800	33	2	6%
Totals	862	488	57%

walled. Of the 1,083 cities considered here, 862 (eighty percent) are known to have received charters of incorporation, usually from a local ruler. While 91 of the 221 nonchartered cities came to be walled (forty-one percent), and 488 of those that were chartered (fifty-seven percent), the percentage rises to seventy-seven percent for cities chartered in the thirteenth century, as Table 3.8 indicates. The thirteenth- and fourteenth-centuries wave of town building moved from west to east,

Table 3.9 *Urban function and city walls*

Type of city	Cities	Walled	Percent
Merchant	70	68	97%
Mining	40	11	27%
Harbor	15	3	20%
Founded by rulers	183	111	61%
Preexisting castle	368	210	57%
Preexisting church	104	56	56%
Village market	124	61	49%
Wild growth	15	6	40%
Totals	921	521	57%

and the entries in *DSB* indicate that many of the new communities were intended by princely founders to serve strategic as well as economic or fiscal objectives. Thus the Teutonic Knights in fourteenth-century East Prussia, like Rhenish counts and bishops in the thirteenth century, planted cities to guard their frontiers, evidently on the principle (as noted above) that wall-building burghers do the job more cheaply than castle garrisons. But as military architecture shifted to the far more expensive bastioned trace, city founders of the sixteenth and seventeenth centuries had to choose very carefully which new settlements were worth fortifying.

Last but not least, a city's social and economic function could also affect its chances of being walled. In Table 3.9, the most dramatic contrast is between towns identifiable as centers of trade (e.g., by membership in the Hanseatic League, or by possession of "staple" rights for exclusive trade in certain commodities), and those that sprang up amid late medieval Germany's copper and silver mining boom. The magistrates of trading cities, many no doubt members of the merchant guild themselves, evidently found it prudent to invest in fortification. Mining settlements were usually open cities, for a number of reasons. Stoob notes that mining towns often experienced rapid growth, sometimes with a haphazard pattern of settlement that would not have been easy to enclose, and that they often declined just as rapidly, draining away the wealth that might have sustained a building program.[36] One may also wonder if potential attackers would

[36] Stoob, "Die Stadtbefestigung. Vergleichende Überlegungen zur bürgerlichen Siedlungs- und Baugeschichte," 30.

not think twice about taking on a population of rough and ready miners. Baltic and North Sea harbor towns were even less likely to be walled, presumably because they had been sited to take advantage of natural protection. In Table 3.9, other cities are grouped under categories of urban origin that are indirectly related to a town's social and economic function. Most cities grew up around a preexisting center (especially a castle or a parish church), others were founded by local rulers, either as towns or as village markets that only later achieved urban status. The few "wild growth" (*aus wilder Würzel*) towns identified in *DSB* were neither based on a preexisting center nor founded by any authority. Here it may be noted that settlements consciously founded as cities by one ruler or another were somewhat more likely to be walled, while "wild growth" towns were usually unwalled.

In sum, apart from its being built on a site not protected from attack by its natural setting, a hypothetical most-likely-to-be-walled city in the northern half of Germany during the medieval and early modern centuries would be: (1) chartered as a city during the thirteenth century, (2) located on a border that its charter-lord wished to guard against his rivals, (3) blessed with a population of 3,000 or more by 1700, and (4) a trading center, with merchants probably having some role in its government. The first two characteristics point up once again the need for correction of Weber's emphasis on the autonomy of medieval towns, but the last two seem to vindicate his stress on the city's trading function and the "form of association" by which it was governed. If town walls were in the prince's mind a cheap substitute for castle building on the frontier, they were also a material expression of a burgher community's will and capacity to organize its own defense.

CHAPTER 4

Medieval walled space: Urban development vs. defense

KATHRYN L. REYERSON

MODERN historians have long recognized the significance of fortifications for medieval inhabitants and their towns. Robert Lopez saw
the essence of the medieval city as "The Crossroads within the Wall,"
the title of his article of 1963.[1] Daniel Smail wrote in his 1994 thesis on
medieval Marseille, "In the middle ages, it was the wall that made the
city."[2] City walls appeared on medieval seals and on the capitals of
Romanesque churches, in medieval Italian frescoes, and in early modern woodcuts, engravings, and etchings of cities. There is no doubt
that urban walls had a symbolic significance as emblems of urban
identity as well as a pragmatic, defensive purpose. My intention in
this essay is to suggest that walled space imposed constraints on
urban inhabitants to which they often reacted with ingenuity, exploit-
ing the fortifications for their own economic ends. Urban authorities,
for their part, had to balance the need to administer the walls for the
purpose of revenue with the maintenance of the defensive capabilities
of the town. This study will examine the often conflicting requirements of urban development and defense in medieval France in the
mid-fourteenth century during the opening phases of the Hundred
Years' War (1337–1453), and then consider, as a case study, the archival
evidence regarding the walls of Montpellier in southern France to
follow the administrative, financial, and military issues of walled
space over the *longue durée*, climaxing in the later fourteenth century.

---

[1] Robert S. Lopez, "The Crossroads within the Wall," in *The Historian and the City*, eds.
Oscar Handlin and John Burchard (Cambridge, MA, 1963), 27–43. For a recent synthetic study of medieval towns, see Jacques Heers, *La ville au moyen âge* (Paris, 1990).
[2] Daniel Lord Smail, "Mapping Networks and Knowledge in Medieval Marseille, 1337–
1362: Variations on a Theme of Mobility" (Ph.D. diss., University of Michigan,
1994), 4.

URBAN FORTIFICATIONS IN MEDIEVAL
FRANCE: THE IMPETUS OF THE HUNDRED
YEARS' WAR

The twelfth through the fourteenth centuries were the great wall-building centuries of the Middle Ages.[3] This period witnessed the incorporation into European walls of fortification strategies derived from the crusades to the Holy Land and exemplified by Richard the Lionhearted's Château Gaillard of the 1190s, the defensive efforts of Alfonse de Poitiers in his *bastides*, built in the western French lands conquered by the Capetians during the Albigensian crusade, and the apogee of medieval fortifications in those castles built by Edward I to solidify his hold on newly acquired Wales in the 1290s and early fourteenth century.[4] Many towns, such as Montpellier, received fortifications during this same period, but some had no walls, or, like Arles, had walls that dated from the Gallo-Roman period.[5] At Arles, as at Nîmes, the Roman amphitheaters served as walled enclaves, cluttered with houses, within the towns.[6] The beginnings of the Hundred Years' War in the mid-fourteenth century witnessed the next concerted activity in fortification. As Michael Wolfe notes in this volume, significant wall building occurred in French cities from the mid-fourteenth century on.[7] When wall restoration began in earnest after 1360 at Arles, the Roman wall on the eastern flank of the town was

---

[3] A 1994 conference, "Les fortifications dans les domaines Plantagenêt de France (XIIème – XIVème siècles)," under the sponsorship of the Centre d'Etudes Supérieures de Civilisation Médiévale at the Université de Poitiers, has served recently to highlight this chronology.

[4] On the *bastides*, see Charles Higounet, "Bastides et frontières," *Le moyen âge* 54 (1948): 113–30, and J.-P. Trabut-Cussac, "Bastides ou forteresses. Les bastides de l'Aquitaine anglaise et les intentions de leurs fondateurs," *Le moyen âge* 60 (1954): 81–137. On English and Welsh castles, see Sidney Toy, *The Castles of Great Britain* (London, 1953); B.H. St. J. O'Neil, *Castles: An Introduction to the Castles of England and Wales* (London, 1973). R. Allen Brown, *English Mediaeval Castles* (Batsford and London, 1954), remains the master of castle history.

On town walls, see the useful studies by Philippe Contamine, "Les fortifications urbaines en France à la fin du Moyen Age: aspects financiers et économiques," *Revue historique* 260 (1978): 23–47, and Albert Rigaudière, "Le financement des fortifications urbaines en France du milieu du XIVe siècle à la fin du XVe siècle," *Revue historique* 273 (1985): 19–95.

[5] Rigaudière, "Le financement des fortifications urbaines," 19, mentioned the case of the Gallo-Roman walls of Arles.

[6] On Arles, see Louis Stouff, *Arles à la fin du moyen-âge*, 2 vols. (Aix-en-Provence, 1986), 1:70. On Nîmes, Robert Michel, "Chevaliers du château des Arènes de Nîmes aux XIIe et XIIIe siècles," *Revue historique* 102 (1909): 45–61.

[7] Michael Wolfe, "Walled Towns during the French Wars of Religion (1560–1630)," Chapter 11 of this volume.

rebuilt.[8] Before the war, urban growth went on apace, but the walls remained relatively unemphasized, providing sometimes an obstacle to urban expansion, sometimes an opportunity for housing or artisanal/industrial use, as is evident in the case of Montpellier below. Beyond the walls, the suburbs of French towns were often among the most economically dynamic sectors, housing the burgeoning population along with their occupations. With the onset of the war and the incredible devastation suffered by towns, in the north of France particularly, a kind of panic set in, which the tension between the needs of urban fortification, on the one hand, and the requirements of urban land for economic expansion and population growth, on the other, crystallized clearly.

The primary field of battle in the Hundred Years' War was the land of France, within which pressures varied from geographic area to geographic area and chronologically, of course.[9] The north and the southwest were the areas most threatened by the English, the north with its proximity to England itself, the southwest in regard to the foothold of the English in Gascony. Before this war, the last military challenge to the north had come with the late-thirteenth-century crisis in Flanders.[10] Thus the 1290s were the last time defensive matters were considered in depth. French fortifications were slowly surveyed beginning in 1335 with somewhat dismal findings. Philip VI, in his campaign of 1339, noted many towns with defensive problems: Noyon, with its ditches and walls in bad shape; Saint-Quentin and Reims with unfinished walls, abandoned in the thirteenth century, leaving the towns open to the countryside in one direction. Towns in the Artois began panicky work on urban fortifications over the years 1337–40. As Jonathan Sumption commented, "The works at Reims between 1337 and 1340, unsatisfactory as they were, cost 10,000 l. t." (*livres*

---

[8] Stouff, *Arles*, 1:72.

[9] Jonathan Sumption, *The Hundred Years' War. Trial by Battle* (Philadelphia, 1990), provides a fascinating study of the early war years. Other useful studies of this war include the classic study by Edouard Perroy, *The Hundred Years' War* (New York, 1965); Jean Favier, *La guerre de cent ans* (Paris, 1980); Christopher Allmand, *The Hundred Years' War. England and France at war c. 1300–c. 1450* (Cambridge, 1988).

It is generally accepted that the Hundred Years' War was a great stimulus to the building of ramparts in the later Middle Ages and in the south of France, in particular. In many places the existing ramparts dated in part from the Gallo-Roman or ninth-century eras and were either replaced or rejuvenated in response to the war. See André Dupont, *Les cités de la Narbonnaise première depuis les invasions germaniques jusqu'à l'apparition du consulat* (Nîmes, 1942), and *Finances et comptabilité urbaines du XIIIe au XVIe siècle*, Acts of the Congress of Blakenberge, 1962 (Brussels, 1964).

[10] See the treatment of this era in Flanders in David Nicholas, *Medieval Flanders* (London, 1992), especially 180–208.

tournois).[11] Towns requested revenues from the king's domain for defense and received them. Taxes on products of consumption and on trade were siphoned off for defensive purposes.[12] Ingenious financing to support the costs of fortifications, including annuities to supplement taxes on real property income, strapped inhabitants for decades. For example, the walls at Saint-Quentin were financed primarily through the sale of annuities, while at Arras, a twenty-five percent tax on real property income covered half of the cost of gate repairs, ditch reconstruction, and the building of outworks, the rest being raised through other financial techniques including annuities. The result was financial crisis for the towns and their citizens.[13]

The problem of financing was exacerbated by the need for ambitious works for which the costs far exceeded the traditional methods of support for wall maintenance.[14] The result was a lengthy period for the completion of some of them – ten years at Villefranche-sur-Rouergue for the consuls to finish fortification work paid for by a tax on merchandise.[15] Finances were a source of continued conflict on the part of towns, and for the royal administration they were outstripped only by conflicts with lords and ecclesiastics, whose exemptions caused considerable difficulties within the context of town defense as well.[16] To defend themselves against the Black Prince's Languedoc expedition, the consuls of Béziers obtained not only royal approval but convinced the count of Armagnac, who was at the time lieutenant of the king in Languedoc, to mandate contributions from all but the mendicant clergy of their town, winning their case against a complaint by the Hospitaliers.[17] Further disputes occurred with surrounding parishes, whose inhabitants sought refuge within the urban fortifications but balked when confronted with paying to maintain them.[18]

---

[11] Sumption, *The Hundred Years' War*, 367. *Tournois* coinage was French royal money. Medieval coinage generally has the denominations of *livres, sous,* and *deniers* (pounds, shillings, and pennies). There were twelve *deniers* to a *sous* and twenty *sous* to a *livre.*

[12] For a general discussion of fortification efforts in this era of crisis, see Jacques Rossiaud, "Crises et consolidations," in *Histoire de la France urbaine,* under the direction of Georges Duby, Vol. 2, *La ville médiévale* (Paris, 1980), 424–38. In regard to taxation, see 432–3.

[13] Sumption, *The Hundred Years' War*, 367. On royal taxation in general, see John Bell Henneman, *Royal Taxation in Fourteenth Century France. The Development of War Financing 1322–1356* (Princeton, 1971), and *Royal Taxation in Fourteenth-Century France. The Captivity and Ransom of John II, 1356–1370* (Philadelphia, 1976).

[14] Pierre-Clément Timbal, *La guerre de cent ans vue à travers les registres du Parlement (1337–1339)* (Paris, 1961), 217.

[15] Timbal, *La guerre de cent ans,* 217 n. 282.

[16] Timbal, *La guerre de cent ans,* 229, the case of Aigueperse.

[17] Timbal, *La guerre de cent ans,* 239–40.

[18] Timbal, *La guerre de cent ans,* 248–9, for a case in Champagne.

The percentage of municipal expenses devoted to defense varied from fourteen to forty-five percent at Saint-Flour in an era of moderate threats to over sixty percent at Tours in difficult times, whereas it reached sixty to eighty percent at Tarascon at the end of the fourteenth century.[19] According to Pierre-Clément Timbal, Charles V was still very anxious about the state of readiness of his fortified sites in 1358 when, in his ordonnance of 14 May, he dispatched his captains to visit all châteaux and to have their lords put them in defensive order, and failing that, to seize them and have them repaired at the expense of their proprietors or level them if there was no way of financing an efficient restoration.[20]

The justification for fortification efforts quickly appeared with the devastating progress of Edward III, John of Hainault, and others in the first decade of the war. Aire and Arques in the Artois were razed; three towns of the Tournaisis, including Saint-Amand, were destroyed. Elsewhere in Normandy there was destruction, while everywhere chaos and fear prevailed.[21] As Sumption remarked, "The scale and system of these destructive expeditions was relatively new to western European warfare."[22] The economic and physical consequences for northern France of these first war years are obvious. Town after town had to see to its ditches and clear a swath through suburbs to prepare for war.[23] The *Registres du Parlement* for the period 1337–69 reveal that towns such as Saint-Omer, Aire, and Lille destroyed their own new and rich suburbs to provide the enemy with as little to work with as possible – a minimum of cover from which to surprise the defenders – but also to free up the ramparts and permit their use in the defense of the town.[24] It was imperative that means of access to towns be cut. In a variation on the scorched earth tactic, bridges and causeways were destroyed by French officials to impede the English progress. Orders went out as early as 1338, but bridges were still being destroyed at Abbeville in 1355 and at Lagny in 1372.[25] Nothing was sacred that stood in the way of refurbishing defenses. Thus, even the main church at Saint-Florentin was destroyed after the battle of Poitiers because it stood in front of the castle, interrupting its defense.[26]

---

[19] Rossiaud, "Crises et consolidations," 427–32.
[20] Timbal, *La guerre de cent ans*, 107.
[21] Sumption, *The Hundred Years' War*, 367–8.
[22] Sumption, *The Hundred Years' War*, 367.
[23] Timbal, *La guerre de cent ans*, 216, for the case of Orléans.
[24] Timbal, *La guerre de cent ans*, 174–258, for the Latin documents of Parlement and Timbal's commentaries.
[25] Sumption, *The Hundred Years' War*, 368, and Timbal, *La guerre de cent ans*, 184 n. 217.
[26] Timbal, *La guerre de cent ans*, 189.

The same fate awaited the fortified collegial church of Saint-Aignan in a suburb of Orléans, which was demolished and the salvaged materials used for city fortifications.[27] Anxieties increased after the defeat at Poitiers and the capture of King John.

Urban inhabitants protested this type of destruction even when indemnification was promised. Moreover, as soon as the danger passed, problems recurred as the bourgeois rebuilt, with royal permission no less, even at as strategically and militarily vital a site as Cherbourg, where houses outside the walls were constructed up against the ramparts.[28] But indemnification for expropriation was not always promised. In 1346, Philip VI allowed the *échevins* of Arras to destroy without restitution.[29] In Languedoc, John, count of Poitiers, the lieutenant of the king in that region, decreed (26 July 1358) that the consuls of southern towns who had made necessary demolitions could not be pursued in the courts, though he did authorize indemnification for damages.[30]

Townspeople offered stubborn resistance to urban defenses when their own special interests were at stake, and, indeed, there was reason for dismay when the haste to destroy in the name of defense leveled some structures unnecessarily.[31] This was the case at Lille when Jean Fiercoq, operating on the orders of the captain Godemar du Fay, burned indiscriminately, destroying houses that were not impeding urban defense. Two important figures – Louis d'Erquery, *maître des requêtes de l'hôtel* and provost of Saint-Pierre-de-Lille, and Godard de Longroy, royal counselor and provost of the church of Furnes – lost their houses. They pursued the matter in court; however an *arrêt* of the royal council determined that action could be brought against the king only if royal orders had been followed to the letter without excess; otherwise, the plaintiffs needed to have his captain punish Fiercoq. The plaintiff Godard succeeded in having the *arrêt* repealed so that the case went further in the Parlement, though P.-C. Timbal could not trace its final dénouement.[32]

If urban inhabitants were resistant to fortification in the later fourteenth century, the attitude of the monarchy, evidenced in its legal inconsistencies and in the authorization of rebuilding in areas sensi-

---

[27] Timbal, *La guerre de cent ans*, 198.
[28] Timbal, *La guerre de cent ans*, 184 and 184 n. 218.
[29] Timbal, *La guerre de cent ans*, 185 n. 221.
[30] Timbal, *La guerre de cent ans*, 239–40. Rigaudière, "Le financement des fortifications urbaines," 30, discussed the issue of expropriation.
[31] Timbal, *La guerre de cent ans*, 187–8.
[32] Timbal, *La guerre de cent ans*, 188 n. 228, lost track of the case and suspected that it was not adjudicated before the Parlement.

tive to defense, recalls the insouciance and naiveté of the ninth century when Bishop Ebbo of Rheims, as Bernard Bachrach points out in this volume, was still tearing down Roman walls for reuse as building materials even as the Vikings threatened.[33] The more astute Charles the Bald fortified bridges on the Seine. Ebbo was an exception, and Bachrach notes that the majority response was one of readiness. During the Hundred Years' War, the French monarchy was again concerned with defense readiness, but the kingdom's capabilities for preparedness were such that royal action was more a matter of reacting to crises than of settled policy.

By the early fifteenth century, artillery had added an additional challenge to wall defense.[34] In all, a definite shortsightedness on the part of both king and townsfolk emerges from the evidence of the Hundred Years' War and a certain contemporary skepticism about the influence of strong fortifications, which seemed to attract attack. As Christopher Allemand stated,

Paradoxically, therefore, instead of providing refuge for those fleeing from the countryside, the very existence of these fortified towns drew the attention of the invader to them. As the narratives of the siege of Rouen, pursued by Henry V between July 1418 and January 1419, underline, the results, both for the civilians who had sought safety there and for the garrison who had led the resistance, could be devastating.[35]

The conflicting requirements of urban expansion and urban defense manifested themselves acutely in time of war and in cases of urban success stories, that is, in towns which enjoyed remarkable expansion, both economic and demographic, in the twelfth through fourteenth centuries. To explore this topic further, I will now turn to a detailed case study that can advance the discussion of medieval walled space.[36]

---

[33] Bernard S. Bachrach, "Imperial Walled Cities in the West: An Examination of the Early Medieval *Nachleben*," Chapter 7 of this volume.

[34] Allemand, *The Hundred Years' War*, 81, cites Christine de Pisan as the source of this information.

[35] Allemand, *The Hundred Years' War*, 79. And, in regard to Poix in the Somme region, the repurchase of its château gave rise to a lengthy dossier in which, among other comments, one finds, "*neque mirandum erat si dictum castrum captum fuerat, cum multa alia castra et fortalicia forcia et bene munita similiter, proth dolor! capta fuissent multis modis sine culpa dominorum ipsorum.*" See Timbal, *La guerre de cent ans*, 108 and 287.

There are a host of other problems attendant on the war and the source of tensions – such as the garrisoning of walled towns and castles – which will not be dealt with in this essay.

[36] The complex topography of medieval Montpellier has enjoyed recent remarkable treatment from scholars of the French Inventaire Général for the Hérault as part of a large multivolume project on the history of urbanism in Montpellier. Ghislaine Fabre and Thierry Lochard, *Montpellier: la ville médiévale*, Etudes du patrimoine (Paris, 1992).

Montpellier provides a laboratory for investigation of the interaction of a burgeoning population (between 35,000 and 40,000 by the year 1300) and growing urban economy with the constraints of city walls and the needs of urban defense.[37] After some initial comments regarding the nature of the medieval fortifications at Montpellier, the pressures of population and industry on the physical space of the walls and their immediate environs and the experience of Montpellier during the early decades of the Hundred Years' War will form the basis of the following analysis.

URBAN FORTIFICATIONS IN MONTPELLIER: THE *COMMUNE CLÔTURE*

The town of Montpellier was composed of two bourgs, Montpellier and Montpelliéret, which were united for the first time under one ruler, Philip of Valois, only in 1349. As early as 1090, information about a complex interlace of holdings linking the two quarters emerged from a dispute between Guilhem V, lay seigneur of Montpellier, and the bishop of Maguelone, Godefroi. Guilhem V held land of the bishop of Maguelone in Montpelliéret, and the bishop had authority over the churches, cemeteries, and their dependencies in the bourg of Montpellier. The gradual de facto fusion of the two bourgs was due, in large measure, to the aggressive initiative of the lay seigneurs. In the twelfth century the perpetual struggle for dominance between the bishop of Maguelone, who controlled Montpelliéret, and the lay seigneurs of Montpellier, the Guilhem family, resulted in occasional changes in the boundaries between the two bourgs.[38] The royal house of Aragon and Majorca, successor to the Guilhem lords, continued to

---

The classic and fundamental study of the topography of Montpellier is Louise Guiraud, "Recherches topographiques sur Montpellier au moyen âge," *Mémoires de la Société archéologique de Montpellier*, 2nd ser., I (1899): 89–355. In addition to her detailed description of the topographical evolution of the town, Guiraud provides several maps of great utility. The volume by Fabre and Lochard outstrips these with excellent illustrations and maps. Still useful are the numerous case studies of Alexandre Germain in the first series of the *Mémoires de la Société archéologique de Montpellier*. There exist additional topographic studies in *Monspeliensia, Mémoires et documents relatifs à Montpellier et à la région montpelliéraine* 1 (1928–9), and in the *Bulletin de la Société languedocienne de géographie*.

[37] The population of medieval Montpellier has been a topic of considerable scholarly discussion. See my article, "The Patterns of Population Attraction and Mobility: The Case of Montpellier, 1293–1348," *Viator* 10 (1979): 257–81, reprinted in Reyerson, *Society, Law, and Trade in Medieval Montpellier* (London, 1995).

[38] For a discussion of the early political struggles, see Bernardin Gaillard, "La condition féodale de Montpelliéret," *Mémoires de la Société archéologique de Montpellier*, 2nd ser., VIII (1922): 344–64.

encroach upon the bishop's possessions.[39] The king of France purchased the bishop's quarter of Montpelliéret in 1293 and the remainder of the town in 1349.[40]

The pattern of fusion of the two quarters is best illustrated by the evolution of the town's fortifications.[41] It may have been that the Guilhem family succeeded in including some parts of Montpelliéret in the first set of fortifications, which date from before 1090 and were enlarged under Guilhem VI (1121–46). This effort seems to have followed the eastern Languedocian pattern of the *circulade*, the circular fortifications that functioned as the initial urban nuclei in numerous towns.[42] The scarcity of documents relating to this fortress leaves much unknown, but Ghislaine Fabre and Thierry Lochard placed the *château-fort* of 1143 in the parish of Saint-Firmin in the quarter of Montpellier.[43]

It was with the construction of the second ramparts, called in the documents the *Commune Clôture* or *Comuna Clausura*, that the coalescence of Montpellier and Montpelliéret became a physical, though not a political or jurisdictional reality (Fig. 4.1).[44] The construction of these ramparts, begun in the twelfth century, continued through the thir-

---

[39] On the political situation at the end of the Guilhem dynasty and the accession of the Aragonese, see A. Germain, *Histoire de la commune de Montpellier*, 3 vols. (Montpellier, 1851). On Montpellier's history within the kingdom of Majorca, see A. Lecoy de la Marche, *Les Relations politiques de la France avec le royaume de Majorque (Iles Baléares, Roussillon, Montpellier, etc.)*, 2 vols. (Paris, 1892).

[40] See Louis J. Thomas, "Montpellier entre la France et l'Aragon pendant la première moitié du XIVe siècle," *Monspeliensia* 1, fasc. i (Montpellier 1928–1929): 1–56.

[41] An early, useful study of the urban fortifications is that of Albert Vigié, "Des enceintes successives de la ville de Montpellier et de ses fortifications," *Bulletin de la Société languedocienne de géographie* 21 (1899): 123–72, 291–323, 459–81.

[42] See Fabre and Lochard, *Montpellier: la ville médiévale*, 40–97. The walling of towns in Languedoc must be put in the context of the general debate about *incastellamento*, which was first articulated by Pierre Toubert, *Les Structures du Latium médiéval: Le Latium méridional et la Sabine du IXe siècle à la fin du XIIe siècle*, 2 vols. (Paris and Rome, 1973). For Languedoc, several studies are pertinent: Fredric Cheyette, "The Castles of the Trencavels, a Preliminary Aerial Survey," in *Order and Innovation in the Middle Ages. Essays in Honor of Joseph R. Strayer*, eds. William C. Jordan, Bruce McNab, and Teofilo F. Ruiz (Princeton, 1976), 255–72; and Cheyette, "The Origins of European Villages and the First European Expansion," *The Journal of Economic History* 37 (1977): 182–206; Ghislaine Fabre and Thierry Lochard, "Topographie de Montpellier aux XIe et XIIe siècles: essai de lecture d'une ville neuve," *Etudes sur l'Hérault*, n.s. 4 (1988): 67–76; Krzysztof Pawlowski, "Villes et villages circulaires du Languedoc: un des premiers modèles de l'urbanisme médiéval?" *Annales du Midi* 99 (1987): 407–27; Monique Bourin-Derruau, *Villages médiévaux en Bas Languedoc: genèse d'une sociabilité*, 2 vols. (Paris, 1987).

[43] Fabre and Lochard, *Montpellier: la ville médiévale*, 87 and 91.

[44] The documents relating to this defense organization are inventoried in Maurice de Dainville and Marcel Gouron, *Fonds de la Commune Clôture et Affaires militaires*, Archives de la ville de Montpellier, Inventaire, Vol. 12 (Montpellier, 1974).

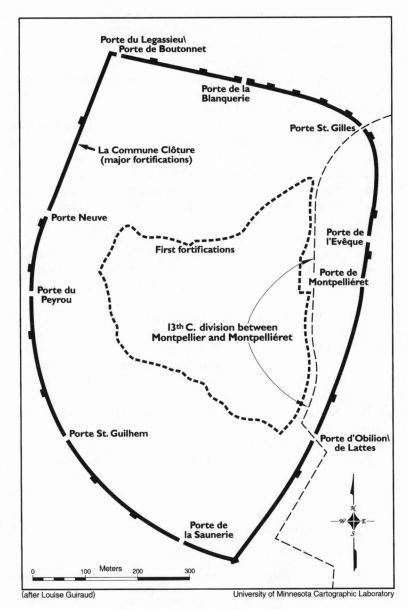

Figure 4.1. Medieval Montpellier.

teenth century. In comparison with the defense organization and fortification of many other southern French towns, the *Commune Clôture*
was a precocious venture, and in its administrative structure, described below, it remained unique.[45]

The early importance of the artisanal and commercial occupations
in Montpellier lies at the origin of the *Commune Clôture*. In an area that
historically had been the victim of invasions by sea, the decision to
fortify for communal necessity is not surprising. By the mid-twelfth
century, Montpellier's commercial function had been established, and
the advantages of a secure urban nucleus must have been evident to
the inhabitants. It was the last ruler of the Guilhem family, Guilhem
VIII, who created in 1196 the defense organization that was to have
responsibility for the ramparts. In a charter of this date, Guilhem VIII
promised eight men, designated as *administratores*, to approve without
exception their decisions concerning the enclosure of the town by
ramparts.[46] The first municipal charter of 1204 provided for the election of the administrators by the city-wide trades and professions
assembled into seven groups or ladders (*échelles, scalae*).[47] Although
this supervisory organization was not described in detail before 1252,
in an entry in the municipal chronicle, André Gouron made a persuasive argument that the 1204 reference indicates the existence of a
rotational system of defense at this time.[48] The defense of the walls
and the gates of the town devolved through a daily rotation upon the
seven ladders, which were composed of a diverse assemblage of
trades and professions based on their individual numerical strength.
While this mechanism provided the personnel to protect Montpellier,
the administrators, soon to be called *obriers* in the documents, were
responsible for the construction and maintenance of the walls.[49]

The ramparts, built of stone from local quarries, were approximately
2,650 meters in circumference. They enclosed an area of about forty-five
hectares.[50] The walls themselves were about two meters wide and seven

---

[45] Fabre and Lochard, *Montpellier: la ville médiévale*, 112–25, traces the emergence of the
Commune Clôture.

[46] The act of foundation is October 1196, EE 1 of the *Commune Clôture fonds* (cited
hereafter with the document numbers EE). Acts relating to the foundation of the
Commune Clôture were assembled in the *Livre des privilèges de la Commune Clôture*, ed.
Achille Montel, *Révue de langues romanes* 2 (1871): 85–108.

[47] The act occurs as Article 94 of the municipal charter of 1204, published in *Layettes du
Trésor des Chartes*, ed. A. Teulet, Vol. 1 (1863), 255–66.

[48] André Gouron, *La Réglementation des métiers en Languedoc au moyen âge* (Paris, 1958),
52–3 and 95–101.

[49] The term *obrier* comes from *obra*, which is the *occitan* version of the Latin word, *opus*,
meaning "work."

[50] Fabre and Lochard, *Montpellier: la ville médiévale*, 122. Scholars tend to use the ballpark
number of 3,000 when speaking of the circumference.

to eight meters high. They had eight gates originally, but three additional gates were added in the thirteenth and fourteenth centuries.[51] In the part of Montpelliéret included in the *Commune Clôture*, on the east and north sides of the fortifications, one finds the Montpelliéret gate, the Porte de l'Evêque, and the gate of St. Gilles. Roads exiting through the latter two gates led to Castelnau in the direction of Nîmes. In Montpellier proper, at the northwest corner of the walls, was the Legassieu gate, also called the gate of Boutonnet, as it was on the road to that settlement, soon to be a suburb of Montpellier. On the western side of town were the gates of the *poterne* of St. Benoît, Porte Neuve, the Peyrou, and St. Guilhem. To the south lay the Saunerie gate on the pilgrimage road leading to Béziers and Spain. Finally, to the southeast lay the commercially important Obilion gate, also termed the gate of Lattes, as it opened towards the sea and Mediterranean trade routes. This gate lay at the southern boundary of the bourgs of Montpellier and Montpelliéret. The quarter of Montpellier was from the beginning a more important concentration of population and industry than Montpelliéret, and it was understandable that the *Commune Clôture* included a larger part of Montpellier than of Montpelliéret (Figs. 4.1 and 4.2).

A pathway called the *Douze Pans*, approximately three meters in width, ran around the interior of the ramparts, while outside there was a large trench, and beyond it, an exterior road termed the *Dougue* or *Douve*. A system of bridges linked the gates with the exterior road. Along the walls were numerous towers and half towers. The geographer Albert Vigié attempted to count the towers and to identify their location. He found as many as twenty-five mentioned in the documents for the *Commune Clôture* fortification and placed twenty-two on his map.[52]

Montpellier experienced the passage from two quarters to one urban nucleus with the creation of the fortifications and the replacement of the seigneurial *circulade*. Although initially a seigneurial initiative,

---

[51] See the forthcoming study of Jean Nougaret, *Montpellier: architecture religieuse, publique et militaire*, Etudes du patrimoine 5 (Paris), MSS 11–12. See also Vigié, "Des enceintes successives," 145–51. Vigié's estimate of the walls' circumference is too low. On the parishes of Montpellier, see L. Guiraud, *La paroisse Saint-Denis de Montpellier* (Montpellier, 1887); and A. Germain, "La paroisse à Montpellier au moyen âge," *Mémoires de la Société archéologique de Montpellier* 5 (1860–9): 1–56.

[52] Vigié, "Des enceintes successives," 153. From the Peyrou gate to the Carmelites' location, he identified four towers; between the Carmelites at the Legassieu gate and the Blanquerie gate, a large tower and a half tower; towers surrounding the Blanquerie gate; five towers between the Blanquerie and Pila-Saint-Gély; four from that point to the Obilion or Lattes gate; three between Lattes and the Saunerie gate; two between the Saunerie and the St.-Guilhem gates; and finally two between the St.-Guilhem and Peyrou gates. See also Nougaret, *Montpellier: architecture religieuse, publique et militaire*, MSS 9–11, who found twenty-four towers and half-towers.

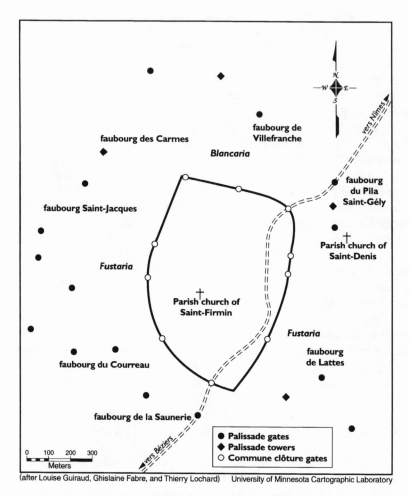

faubourg des Carmes

faubourg de
Villefranche

Blancaria

faubourg Saint-Jacques

Fustaria

faubourg
du Pila
Saint-Gély

Parish church of
Saint-Denis

Parish church of
Saint-Firmin

Fustaria

faubourg
de Lattes

faubourg du Courreau

faubourg de la Saunerie

0   100   200   300
Meters

● Palissade gates
◆ Palissade towers
○ Commune clôture gates

vers Nîmes

vers Béziers

(after Louise Guiraud, Ghislaine Fabre, and Thierry Lochard)   University of Minnesota Cartographic Laboratory

Figure 4.2. Suburban Montpellier.

the walls were embraced by the new consular regime that emerged in 1204 in the political turmoil following the disappearance of the Guilhem family and the entrance of the Aragonese royals. And, although there occurred periodic tensions between the growing suburbs and the central fortified core, the division between town and country, separated by the town's walls, can be overstated. Urban-rural relations remained significant in the economic history of Montpellier.[53]

---

[53] See my article on urban-rural relations, "Urban/Rural Exchange: Reflections on the Economic Relations of Town and Country in the Region of Montpellier before 1350,"

EXPLOITATION AND ADMINISTRATION OF THE WALLS

The *Fonds de la Commune Clôture* of the Archives Municipales contains acts of concession by the *obriers* of towers or half-towers along the walls to private citizens.[54] Beneficiaries included clergy, a leathersmith, a draper, a merchant, a silversmith, several wood merchants, a tawer or dresser of skins, a bourgeois, a knight, a doctor of laws, foreigners, and five men whose occupations are not identified, for a total of seventeen in all. Vigié, in his study of Montpellier's fortifications, stated that these concessions were made on precarious title: the *obriers* reserved the right to take the towers back for the purpose of defense.[55] The list of recipients contains men from middle and upper class trades who would certainly have had considerable stake in the town's defense. It appears in some cases that the wall towers were inhabited by the recipients.[56] And indeed, in Montpellier, the need for housing was great, as it was in many a medieval town that had experienced population growth. Were all of the 40,000 inhabitants of Montpellier to have lived within the 2,650-meter circumference enclosing about forty-five hectares, the density of population would have been over 400 persons per acre.[57] Of course, the suburban growth of Montpellier and its counterparts had been extensive, creating the kinds of problems for defense alluded to earlier. It is also important to consider that not all of urban Montpellier within the walls was inhabited. As is, and was, characteristic of Mediterranean towns, courtyards and unbuilt spaces existed within the walls. Yet even if the density were only 200 persons per acre, the population crush must have been tremendous.[58] Population pressure and local prestige are the logical explanations for tower

---

in *Medieval Urban and Rural Communities in France: Provence and Languedoc, 1000–1500,* eds. Kathryn L. Reyerson and John Drendel (Leiden, 1998), 253–73.

[54] Tower concessions are found in the *Fonds de la Commune Clôture*: 4 October 1265, EE 107; 19 October 1265, EE 109; 25 February 1267, EE 114; 14 October 1267, EE 124; 17 March 1270, EE 126; 30 May 1271, EE 133; 17 April 1271, EE 135; 20 December 1280, EE 145; 25 September 1284, EE 147; 25 February 1291, EE 161; 30 October 1293, EE 166; 29 October 1320, EE 198; 25 September 1343, EE 212; 15 March 1295, EE 251; 6 August 1304, EE 255; 30 October 1251, EE 261; 26 October 1268, EE 275.

[55] Vigié, "Des enceintes successives," 161.

[56] Guiraud, "Recherches topographiques," 99ff. Towers were a common phenomenon in Italian towns, where they represented the strongholds of urban factions. See Jacques Heers, *Le clan familial au moyen âge* (Paris, 1974), and Diane Owen Hughes, "Towards Historical Ethnography: Notarial Records and Family History in the Middle Ages," *Historical Methods Newsletter* 7 (1973): 61–71.

[57] See Fabre, Lochard, and Nougaret, "L'Enceinte médiévale de Montpellier," MSS 2.

[58] The perceived density inside the walls is evident in the 1552 engraving discussed by Ghislaine Fabre in "L'Image et l'idée de Montpellier à la Renaissance d'après une estampe inédite," *Bulletin historique de la ville de Montpellier* 19 (1994): 4–37.

leases. When defense again became a priority, displacement of the individuals living in the towers was inevitable.

The documents speak most commonly of the half tower, defined in 1273 as *"bisturrem seu semiturrem,"* terminology that remains difficult to interpret. Ghislaine Fabre, Thierry Lochard, and Jean Nougaret speculated that what was envisioned was a tower reduced in dimensions by half in relation to other works, with all the characteristics of a tower, but in miniature, a small tower.[59] I would offer another interpretation based on a charter of 1320, in which a silversmith, Johannes Guillelmi, received the grant of a half tower (*bisturrem*) and a space of wall near the gate of St. Gély, of which the other half was said to be his already.[60] Such language would suggest rather a side by side configuration, with the tower broken up vertically into two contiguous units of housing. In this grant the conditions of tenure envisaged that the *obriers* could take back the tower and destroy Guillelmi's house at his expense, if necessity warranted. They also retained rights of entry and exit in and through the tower. The wall and the half tower were to be undamaged, and the trap (probably lowerable wood stairs permitting access to the walls) and the chains that held it were to remain carefully tied above so that men could pass through the gate.[61]

The walls and the road called the *Douze Pans*, around the interior of the fortification, were used intensively by the inhabitants through grants by the *obriers*. These leases with annual fee payment included the *bail à acapt* or *bail à nouvel acapt* as well as certain rentals, *arrentements*. In the years 1200 to 1250 there were three grants, two of these with building permits.[62] In the period 1250 to 1300 there were seventy-four grants, twenty-three of which contained building permits, six with the formula *usum et splecham*, which provided for usufruct, and

---

[59] Fabre, Lochard, and Nougaret, "L'Enceinte médiévale de Montpellier," MSS 3.

[60] See 29 October 1320, EE 198. The document states: *"cuius altera medietas est tui dicti Johannis."*

[61] 29 October 1320, EE 198: *"Retinemus etiam nobis et futuris operariis introhitum et exitum in et per dictam bisturrem causa videndi muram et bisturrem quas non ledatur in aliquo et trappam et cathenas que trapam (sic) tenent que stent bene ligate ut sine perriculo subtus trappam et per portale gentes transire possant."*

Fabre, Lochard, and Nougaret, "L'Enceinte médiévale de Montpellier," MSS 3, noted the archaic character of the Montpellier walls by the fourteenth century, when French royal fortifications were more advanced. In contrast, Montpellier resembled some fourteenth-century Provençal fortifications such as those at Avignon, Ansouis, and Pertuis, with gates flanked by square towers. See also Nougaret, *Montpellier: architecture religieuse, publique et militaire,* MSS 10.

[62] See the *Fonds de la Commune Clôture,* passim. On real estate in general in Montpellier, see my study, "Land, Houses and Real Estate Investment in Montpellier: A Study of the Notarial Property Transactions, 1293–1348," *Studies in Medieval and Renaissance History* 6 (1983): 39–112.

twelve that were recognitions of previous grants. In the years 1300 to 1350 there were thirty-five grants, thirteen of which contained building permits, six with the usufruct formula, while five were recognitions of previous grants. The fact that several of the above acts contained permission to build on or in the town would favor a theory of habitation close to the walls.

The *obriers* were undoubtedly forced to weigh the advantages of additional income gained through new concessions of land or wall use, for which they usually received an entry fee and an annual payment, against the demands of municipal protection. It is undeniable that many of the structures in the *Douze Pans* were located very close to, if not actually touching, the fortifications, and there were some authorizations to encroach upon the walls. Thus, in 1251 a prominent citizen, Raymundus de Conchis, was allowed to cut through the wall for the purposes of his shop near the Montpelliéret tower.[63] In 1262, a Jew was allowed to put a roof over part of the *Douze Pans* road between his house and the town wall.[64] A mercer was permitted a house built up against the Montpelliéret gate.[65] Many were the permissions to build in the *Douze Pans* road, in fact.

On the other hand, one finds a few acts with building permits that specify that the edifice was not to lean on the wall.[66] Abuses of various sorts did occur, however, and their settlement might involve arbitration or compromise. In 1295, a doctor of laws was accused by the *obriers* of having carved holes in the rampart and in the tower of the old Peyrou gate to place timbers for his house. He argued that he had a concession from the time of the Guilhem lords. The arbiter of this dispute, a draper, arranged a compromise that allowed the building of one pillar of the house against the wall and the tower at the doctor's expense. Here, the municipal defense organization did not prevail entirely, in spite of its mandate to police the walls.[67] In 1297, a butcher broke and damaged a stone stair against the ramparts. The *obriers* were able to extract a promise from him that he would repair the damage.[68]

---

[63] 30 October 1251, EE 103.
[64] 22 May 1262, EE 104.
[65] 24 January 1266, EE 111.
[66] Nougaret, *Montpellier: architecture religieuse, publique et militaire*, MSS 4. Conflicting evidence is found in the *Commune Clôture* documents. Thus, in 1295, the *obriers* prevented a Jew from damaging his house, which was located near the walls: 23 October 1297, EE 252. On the other hand, a laborer was granted permission to construct on an area between his house and the wall with the restriction that the construction was not to lean on the wall: 28 April 1267, EE 119.
[67] 15 March 1295, EE 251.
[68] 23 October 1297, EE 252.

In several cases the *obriers* issued fines for the illegal construction of latrines and gutters, and frequently included the prohibition to construct these facilities in their building permits. Since the exterior trench was undoubtedly used for urban waste disposal, the *obriers'* involvement is understandable. Lack of supervision could have weakened the efficacy of the walls. In another case a mason was fined fifty *sous melgoriens* for having built a latrine and a pillar in the *Douze Pans* road.[69] The same year the *obriers* ordered a wood merchant to dismantle the sink he had built up against the fortifications in the *Douze Pans*, on land which he held in tenure from them.[70] The *obriers* of 1284 must have been more assiduous than most, as there were in that year another sink destruction and the destruction of an elevated construction in the tower against the St. Gély gate.[71] This was a point in time when the French king had begun to assert his interests in Montpellier. In 1282, Philip III was able to dictate that his name alone should appear in all notarial acts of Montpellier although he was not in possession of any part of the city.[72] The town inhabitants may have been concerned in the 1280s about the state of the fortifications as a result of the growing penetration of French influence.[73] As of 1293, however, the purchase of Montpelliéret by the French king (Philip IV) was a fait accompli, and the early fourteenth century was again a time of leniency in regard to the use of the walls.[74]

The waste situation and the water supply presented problems for the inhabitants of Montpellier from the second half of the thirteenth century, at least. Two small tributaries of the Lez, the Merdanson, and the Aiguerelle noire flowed near the *Commune Clôture*, but the local water supply was limited, and inhabitants had to rely on the municipal fountains and wells for their domestic needs.[75] In addition, there

---

[69] 22 August 1284, EE 262. *Melgoriens* were local coins of relatively low precious metal content, originally issued by the count of Melgueil.

[70] 14 October 1284, EE 263.

[71] 28 October 1284, EE 264, and 28 October 1284, EE 265.

[72] An era of direct conflict of jurisdiction over Montpellier between the king of Majorca and the king of France opened in 1280. An agreement of 22 July 1282 between the two sides acknowledged the criminal jurisdiction of the king of France in the *sénéschaussée* of Beaucaire-Nîmes, within which Montpellier was an enclave. As a result of this accord, the name of the king of France was to appear alone on all public acts in Montpellier.

[73] On the conflict between France and Majorca, see Lecoy de la Marche, *Les relations politiques de la France avec le royaume de Majorque*.

[74] 24 October 1302, EE 254, where, in contrast, a leather merchant was permitted to rest his house on the wall.

[75] There were a number of fountains and wells in the town and its suburbs. They included the fountains of Pila-Saint-Gély, Burgues, the Saunerie, Latter, Priveirargues, the las Sers bridge, those of the Carmelites and of Saint-Côme, and those called the

were demands on the water supply from the public baths: two establishments at the southeastern corner of the *Commune Clôture* and a second site more centrally located, not far from the eleventh-century fortifications.[76] Municipal legislation provided in 1205 for the deputation of two men to supervise the maintenance of roads, walls of buildings, gutters, and the disposal of garbage.[77] Montpellier was subject to a modified regime of urban servitudes, a legacy of Roman law that remains a part of contemporary French law. Rights of way, possession of rain water, and the passage of light and air were vital considerations in a town where living space was cramped, water in short supply, and the streets extremely narrow. In the vicinity of the walls, the control of latrine placement and water use devolved upon the *obriers*, as revealed in their regulations above.[78] One also finds recorded in their archives occasional permits to build gutters and drainage canals.[79] There exists one case in which the *obriers* ordered the rerouting of water running to the south of the *Commune Clôture* near the road to Béziers.[80] By the same token, from 1267 through the first quarter of the fourteenth century there were attempts by the town consuls to channel water from outside sources into the town.[81]

In the exterior trench, the *Douve*, artisanal/industrial activities were common and posed an additional problem in the case of attack. Such a consideration does not seem to have prevented the *obriers* from making numerous grants to the wood merchants for the stacking of their wood, to cordmakers for their paraphernalia, or to agricultural workers for the cultivation of the land itself. The industrial use of the

---

Carrade fountain, the covered fountain, and the fountain of the Virgin. There were numerous wells, including those of the Esquille, the Palais, the Plan de l'Om, the Chapelle-Neuve, the Barralerie, the Valfère, the Etuves, Espinas, Douarchy, Douzils, and Muguet. Private wells were undoubtedly a source of revenue for the inhabitants also. See Jean Baumel, *Histoire d'une seigneurie du Midi de la France*, Vol. 2, *Montpellier sous la seigneurie de Jacques le Conquérant et des rois de Majorque. Rattachement de Montpelliéret et de Montpellier à la France (1213–1349)* (Montpellier, 1971), 265.

[76] Guiraud, "Recherches topographiques," 179–84.

[77] *Layettes du Trésor des Chartes*, 1:290, article 10. This is also article 10 of the 1205 addition to the municipal charter in *Le Petit Thalamus de Montpellier*, ed. F. Pégat et al. (Montpellier, 1840), 66.

[78] See Nougaret, *Montpellier: architecture religieuse, publique et militaire*, MSS 4.

[79] A drainage canal was authorized in 21 August 1336, EE 258.

[80] 21 March 1232, EE 15.

[81] These attempts were recorded in the *Grand Chartrier* of the Archives municipales de Montpellier. They were inventoried as Louvet nos. 648–53 in *Archives communales de Montpellier antérieures à 1790. Inventaires et documents I: Notice sur les anciens inventaires, inventaire du Grand Chartrier*, ed. J. Berthelé (Montpellier, 1895). On 7 June 1267, the town consuls received from King Jacme of Aragon permission to levy taxes in order to channel water from La Lironde to the king's palace. In later acts it was again a question of channeling-in additional water.

space inside the walls and outside is again explained by the heavy demand placed on land near the center of town.

The wood merchants needed space close to town to avoid transport costs and to warehouse their goods. In 1270, an agricultural laborer and the wood merchants of the Peyrou were authorized to place wood in the ditch on condition that they repair any damage done to the *Douve*.[82] The uses for wood were multiple, requiring different sorts of products: from wine barrels to furniture to building construction. It is possible to get some idea of the size of a private house from a concession by the *obriers*. Included in a 1291 grant of the trench, the wall, and a tower to six wood merchants was the permission to build six houses of about fourteen meters in length and six meters in height with pillars and windows on the trench.[83] These houses would have been only slightly lower than the ramparts themselves. It is generally admitted that the vaulted ground floor of a dwelling in Montpellier was about three and a half meters high.[84] If this consideration is applied to the wood merchants' houses, conveniently located near the ditch where their wood was stored, the probable conclusion emerges that they had two stories, the second floor being about two and a half meters in height.

Cordmakers needed land to stretch and form cords which were employed in multiple contexts, including maritime use. Again, to find adequate expanses of land would have been a challenge in the immediate vicinity of Montpellier. In 1312, cordmaker Bernardus de Popiano received a concession of use of the ditch between the new and old Peyrou gates for ten years to make his cords.[85] The entry fee was twenty *sous tournois* with another twelve *deniers tournois* due yearly at the feast of St. Peter in August, the entire sum to be used for redoing the wall and repairing depredations. It is interesting that there was no provision here for a return of the land to the use of the *obriers* in case it was needed for defense.

Agricultural workers abounded in all medieval towns. The Chronicle of Jacme I the Conqueror numbered them at 6,000 in Montpellier

---

[82] See, for example, 27 December 1270, EE 246.

[83] 25 February 1291, EE 161.

[84] This fact has been substantiated by the *hôtels* of the town whose original vaults have been restored or disengaged from later revision. Shops along the rue de l'Aiguillerie present cases in point. On domestic housing in Montpellier, see Bernard Sournia and Jean-Louis Vayssettes, *Montpellier: la demeure médiévale* (Paris, 1991). The local measures were the *canna*, which equals about 1.987 meters, and the *palmus*, which is one eighth of a *canna*.

[85] 30 October 1312, EE 281.

in 1239.[86] The market for products of truck farming in a large town such as this was enormous. Foodstuffs found ready buyers at the active vegetable market, the *Herberia*, in the center of town. The demand for open, arable land nearby was intense, and the cultivators were candidates for plots on lands near the fortifications. In a 1294 rental, the cultivators of the Legassieu gate were granted part of the ditch from the right side of that gate to the gate leading toward the Ribanson [*sic*] stream for a term of twenty-four years.[87] The payment due yearly at Michaelmas was six *sous melgoriens*. The *obriers* included a clause allowing them to take back the land when common necessity or public use dictated. Here again, as in the case of all of these occupations, the needs of defense were theoretically to deprive inhabitants of vital land use.

In spite of the indiscriminate nature of the *obriers'* concessions, it remained their responsibility to punish misuse of the walls, the trench, and the interior and exterior roads. Stringent control over the number and types of openings in the ramparts was essential in any theory of urban defense. There is evidence that early on (1218) even the Aragonese king had to obtain the authorization of the *obriers* to lean a wall of his castle on the rampart. The bishop also had to get permission to open a door in the wall.[88] The police of the walls was conducted weekly by messengers of the *obriers*, and there was an inspection by the *obriers* in person every three months.[89] Without these inspections, it is stated in an act of 1339, the inhabitants of Montpellier would commit dishonest acts.[90]

THE HUNDRED YEARS' WAR: A NEW DEFENSIVE POSTURE FOR MONTPELLIER

The demographic pressures that converged upon the walls also led to the expansion of the suburbs.[91] Only a portion of the growing town's population actually resided within the *Commune Clôture* fortifications. The development of the town's suburbs and the installation of religious organizations and schools in the outlying areas provided points

---

[86] E. Bonnet, "Les séjours à Montpellier de Jacques le Conquérant roi d'Aragon," *Mémoires de la Société archéologique de Montpellier*, 2nd ser., 9 (Montpellier, 1927): 176–7.
[87] 6 April 1294, EE 279.
[88] Fabre and Lochard, *Montpellier: la ville médiévale*, 177.
[89] Vigié, "Des enceintes successives," 139.
[90] 24 April 1339, EE 58.
[91] On the growth of suburbs, see Fabre and Lochard, *Montpellier: la ville médiévale*, 154–77.

of attraction for the inhabitants of the urban nucleus (Fig. 4.2). As the
town grew, industrial activities were located in the suburbs. There was
a leather treatment area (*Blancaria*) outside the walls. The activities of
wood merchants (*Fustaria*) and cordmakers, as noted above, spilled
out of the urban nucleus into the outer ditch of the *Commune Clôture*.
Another stimulus for townspeople was certainly the desire for greater
space and air. The flow of inhabitants to the suburbs continued until
the 1350s, when the Hundred Years' War reversed the emigration
trend. Hostilities had already begun for Montpellier by then, however.
A first blow to local security came early in the war when the lord of
Montpellier, James II of Majorca, embroiled in a dispute with King
Philip of France, courted Edward III of England and staged a tournament in Montpellier in March 1341, at which one of James II's squires,
with a horse wearing English colors, used the English war cry, "Guy-
enne." This was too much for Philip, whose lieutenants then occupied
the town forcibly.[92]

It is interesting to observe the activity of the *obriers* of the *Commune
Clôture* in the years immediately preceding this crisis. In 1339, in a
reversal of their indulgence of wood merchants' activities near the
walls, the *obriers* prohibited the deposit of wood and stone in the
ditch between the new gate and the church of St. Jacques, on a complaint from one wood merchant accusing a colleague of storing large
timbers and cut stones in the ditch and of damaging the arches of the
bridge and the sides of the ditch.[93] This change of position may have
reflected concern for the condition of the town fortifications in light
of the growing hostility between England and France, and, in particular, of the growing antipathy between the king of Majorca and the
king of France. There was tension between the *obriers* and the lieutenant of the king of Majorca, who, in 1338, had destroyed the coat of
arms of the *obriers* carved in the stone walls between the two Peyrou
gates.[94] For this offense, the *obriers* decided to pursue an action against
the lieutenant in the court of the king of Majorca. That the officers of
the urban defense organization had their arms embossed on the wall
suggests the degree of citizen responsibility for and control over town
defenses.

Beginning in 1336, documents of the *Fonds de la Commune Clôture*
recorded almost yearly *bans* and *criées des murs*. The pronouncements
went out most often in November, in 1336, 1339, 1340, 1342, 1343,

---

[92] Sumption, *The Hundred Years' War*, 378.
[93] 10 July 1339, EE 64.
[94] 16 July 1339, EE 63.

1345, 1347, 1349, 1350, 1351, 1352, 1354, 1356, 1357, 1360, and 1361. These were public proclamations wherein the *obriers* enumerated those prohibited activities that might be prejudicial to the walls and which required proof for holdings in tenure.[95] Water and garbage were not to be thrown into the ditches, blockage of the arrow slits was prohibited, cultivation and tree planting were restricted, as was building construction, stair placement was regimented, high windows were to be closed, and so forth.[96] These pronouncements would be posted in written form at important sites within the town. Certainly, the assiduous nature of the *bans* and *criées* reflects the inception of the war. Then the rhythm of survival of pronouncements was less intense, the next coming in 1373, then 1379, 1382, picking up again in 1391, 1393, 1395, 1396, 1397, 1398, and 1409.[97]

There was reason for concern about fortifications in the region. Mercenary companies began to plague the south of France in the early 1350s. The Black Prince, Edward of Woodstock, raided in the south of France in the fall of 1355, and as Edouard Perroy commented, "The first Anglo-Gascon raid, started from Bordeaux in the autumn of 1355, was able with impunity to ravage Languedoc as far as the gates of Montpellier."[98] Roving mercenary bands, at liberty after the capture of King John at Poitiers, threatened the safety of the suburban residents. In the later fourteenth century, Montpellier witnessed the elaboration of an outer, discontinuous defense system with fortresslike gates at various intervals, called the Palissade (Fig. 4.2). In 1352, the consuls called a general assembly of the inhabitants to hear royal orders regarding the fortifications. The first move was to fortify the suburbs with ditches financed by a tax to acquire the necessary land and a loan of 2,000 florins from the Genoese.[99] Yet in 1356, a plea to the king of France complained of the lack of fortifications and the need for repair.[100] The *Commune Clôture* fortification was probably raised higher.[101] The construction of fortified gates, *portalières*, barring access to the town via its main roads began in 1218 and extended to 1301. The mid-fourteenth-century ditches later connected the reinforced *portalières* with newly constructed stone towers. Fabre and Lochard were not able to plot the full trace of the Palissade in the suburbs; however,

---

[95] Nougaret, *Montpellier: architecture religieuse, publique et militaire*, MSS 4–5.

[96] 10 May 1397, EE 61.

[97] EE 25–44, passim.

[98] Perroy, *The Hundred Years' War*, 129.

[99] Fabre and Lochard, *Montpellier: la ville médiévale*, 194–5, 199.

[100] Fabre and Lochard, *Montpellier: la ville médiévale*, 199.

[101] Nougaret, *Montpellier: architecture religieuse, publique et militaire*, MSS 6.

Figure 4.3. Monspessulanus, Montpellier. Copy on copper of the *princeps* engraving. G. Bruin. 1579. Courtesy of the Bibliothèque Nationale (Cartes et plans). GeDD312 T.I. Pl.9.

they could identify the location of numerous fortified gates.[102] Although there had been considerable intervening destruction, which is difficult to pinpoint, engravings of the mid- and later sixteenth century provide an idea of how the town appeared at its nucleus with the high medieval *Commune Clôture* and the later medieval Palissade, the suburban fortifications. The earliest view is of 1552. Subsequent engravings provide similar views in 1574, 1579, 1598, and 1665 (see Fig. 4.3). In these urban portraits, the inner core of the town is densely built, but the *Commune Clôture* is disengaged, with the exception of a few trees on the exterior, the trench, and the *Douve* or exterior road being clearly visible.[103] While these are undoubtedly idealistic portrayals of the town, the defensive works appear in good shape. But, as Ghislaine Fabre has noted, by the time of the publication of the 1552 engraving in 1564, the suburbs had disappeared, thanks to a siege of

[102] Fabre and Lochard, *Montpellier: la ville médiévale*, 195–9.
[103] Fabre, "L'Image et l'idée de Montpellier," 5, for the 1552 engraving, and 8–9 for other engravings.

1562 in the Wars of Religion. The Protestant commander had caused the destruction of the suburbs to defend the town.[104]

The Palissade provided insufficient protection for the suburbs.[105] Already in 1361 the suburbs were pillaged by *routiers*. Destruction followed, but one must ask whether this was entirely the result of raids or perhaps of deliberate demolition as was general in France in the north, as we have seen, or again at Arles, where by the end of the fourteenth century the countryside began just beyond the walls, all else having been destroyed.[106] At Montpellier the Franciscan convent, which had provided cover for the *routiers*, was damaged, as was the house of the Repenties de Saint-Gilles and the Cluniac house, Saint-Pierre-de-Clunezet. The consuls had already ordered the destruction of the Carmelites' house in 1355 because of its proximity to the *Commune Clôture* and the fact that their church was higher than the walls.[107]

The dangers of war occasioned new efforts on the part of the *obriers* to police the walls, and, in particular, to disengage the structures that had accrued there. In 1363, several documents mentioned the destruction of the suburbs and the need for a new ditch to protect the town. For example, in the notarial register of Pierre Gilles, an act of 20 September 1363 described the decision taken by the French royal governor of the town, the rector of the French quarter, the town bailiff, a judge of the French quarter, the town consuls, and the *obriers* to destroy all the houses contiguous to the walls to avoid the fate suffered by St.-Antonin, St.-Esprit on the Rhône, and Brioude in Auvergne.[108] The act stated that these houses weakened the defensive capabilities of the walls. Patrols on horseback around the walls were not possible given the present placement of these houses. Inhabitants agreed to the measures that followed.[109] An entry in the *Chronicle* of the *Petit Thalamus* for 27 September 1363 indicates that on that day the town councilmen and the *obriers*, followed by a considerable procession, began to disengage the walls, destroying the houses in order to reestablish

[104] Fabre, "L'Image et l'idée de Montpellier," 6.
[105] Fabre and Lochard, *Montpellier: la ville médiévale*, 194ff. Guiraud, "Recherches topographiques," 130–2, lists the Palissade gates.
[106] See Stouff, *Arles*, 100–17, for a description of the experience of Arles in the later fourteenth century.
[107] Fabre and Lochard, *Montpellier: la ville médiévale*, 200, and Louvet no. 1248, *Inventaire du Grand Chartrier*.
[108] BB 4, f. 53r, Archives municipales de Montpellier.
[109] See also Fabre, Lochard, and Nougaret, "L'enceinte médiévale de Montpellier," MSS 3.

the *Douze Pans* or three-meter limit for construction.[110] Some two hundred structures were ordered destroyed.[111]

Documents from other towns in France demonstrate similar initiatives at this time. Not only were the walls disengaged in many towns across France – in the Orléanais, in Provence, in the Périgord – but large swaths were cut in the urban fabric, and there was ruin everywhere.[112] In some cases the chaff of urban housing was removed and the threat of fires as a result, but there was a toll on the fortunes of urban inhabitants whose investments in *rentes* suffered as the value of real estate fell. The suburbs were emptied of population. A downward cycle was initiated and whatever revenues subsisted had to go to the maintenance of the walls.

Undoubtedly because of financial necessity, but with a lack of foresight, the *obriers* of Montpellier continued to make grants of the ditches. In 1367, a wood merchant was granted land between the two Peyrou gates; in 1373, part of the ditch was conceded to a cordmaker; in 1399, a similar concession was made to a cultivator.[113] At times there were limitations of use specified in the *obriers'* concessions. For example, in 1366, one finds the grant of part of a square at the Peyrou gate with the prohibition of construction.[114]

Concessions reflecting military necessity appeared as well. In 1389, the master archer and other archers received land in the ditch, stretching from the gate of Lattes towards the *Douve* at the level of the Babote tower.[115] The tenure entry fee for these archers was two hundred hewn stones to be used for repairs. Here there may have been an instinct of planning at work. The archers may have used the land for practice,

---

[110] *Le Petit Thalamus de Montpellier*, 363:

> Item, a XXVII de setembre, los senhors cossols et obriers de voluntat de totas las III corts temporals et del pobol, comenseron a far derrocar los XII palms dels ostals que si tocon de fra am los murs de Montpellier, et i continueron cascun iorn entre que fo complit, anant per los murs am los curials e portant prumieyras doas bandieyras o estandartz estendudas, la prumieyra dels senhors cossols et apres dels senhors obriers, e menavon am se entorn XL breguans tant de Montpellier quant de Marselha dels cals alcus portavon balestas, els autres portavon glavis am penos de las armas dels senhors cossols, e si estavon soudejatz per la guarda de la palissada, e tot jorn tant cant la dicha obra se ponhet a far, la grand bandieira del cossolat estava estenduda sus la porta del cossolat.

The affair was thus executed with much pomp and circumstance.

[111] Nougaret, *Montpellier: architecture religieuse, publique et militaire*, MSS 9.

[112] Rossiaud, "Crises et consolidations," 434–8. Rossiaud included a pertinent quotation from Falduccio di Lombardo, writing to Francesco di Marco Datini, "'Je suis allé à Salon et à Orgon où il y avait de votre temps de si beaux faubourgs et de si belles hôtelleries, aujourd'hui tout est détruit, ce sont des masures....,'" 434–5.

[113] 5 October 1367, EE 221; 27 August 1373, EE 225; 23 October 1399, EE 227.

[114] 16 February 1366, EE 220.

[115] 31 May 1389, EE 226.

thereby enhancing their skills in defense. They also were required to contribute to defensive repair.

Philippe Contamine has emphasized the financial investment reflected in the new fourteenth-century fortifications throughout France. He also pointed out their significance for medieval urbanism and their aesthetic value.[116] Certainly, with their larger ramparts, they were imposing sights. Yet, there was reflected in the re-utilizations detailed just above a need to make the wall profitable, perhaps for the very maintenance of the structure. Albert Rigaudière has found this phenomenon across France, at Nantes, Troyes, Tours, and at Béziers, where the consuls earmarked the revenues of mills built on the walls for the maintenance of the latter.[117] There is yet another dimension of finance which should be considered in this context. Investment in the walls represented a signficant financial burden for towns and for individual inhabitants, draining from productive use, and from reinvestment in industry or in commerce, profits which might otherwise have occasioned economic growth.[118] Estimating the exact effects of the fiscal impositions to finance fortifications is difficult. However, Jacques Rossiaud argued that they were "de puissants instruments de paupérisation."[119] There was, however, no alternative in late medieval France.

In Montpellier, in spite of many attempts to defend the suburbs with the Palissade, efforts were inadequate. Several factors seem to have been at work. In sociological terms Fabre and Lochard saw the assimilation of the suburban inhabitants with the lower classes of Montpellier, the *populares*. The area within the *Commune Clôture* was privileged, in terms of fortifications, over the suburbs without. The elite, represented by its consuls, spent more on a new consulate building in 1364 than on a loan to fortify the suburbs of a decade earlier.[120] Then too, a lack of will, born in fourteenth-century famine, plague, and war, may have been at the bottom of these half-hearted efforts to fortify.

---

[116] Contamine, "Les fortifications urbaines en France," 43–7.

[117] Rigaudière, "Le financement des fortifications urbaines," 26–7.

[118] See Robert S. Lopez, "Economie et architecture médiévales," *Annales: E.S.C.* 7 (1952): 433–8, for the development of this argument in regard to church construction.

[119] Rossiaud, "Crises et consolidations," 434.

[120] Fabre and Lochard, *Montpellier: la ville médiévale*, 201. On the *populares* of Montpellier, see Jan Rogozinski, *Power, Caste, and Law. Social Conflict in Fourteenth-Century Montpellier* (Cambridge, MA, 1982), and Jean Combes, "Finances municipales et oppositions sociales à Montpellier," *Bulletin de la Fédération Historique du Languedoc méditerranéen et du Roussillon. Vivarais et Languedoc (Congrès, Privas, 1971)* 44 (Montpellier, 1972): 99–120.

Crisis engendered disputes about the fortifications. There is an interesting case of 1357, a crucial moment for conflict between the consuls and suburban inhabitants.[121] The issue was the Lavérune gate, the *portalière* located in the suburb of the Courreau. In their complaint to the town consuls the suburban inhabitants, finding the intermittent fortifications that made up the Palissade inadequate, voiced their desire that the suburbs be fully enclosed with walls. The consuls then criticized the *obriers* for failure to maintain the walls, for their inadequate height, and for the lack of artillery and other equipment and armaments for the ramparts. All three groups agreed to artibration by Pierre Catalan, lieutenant of the governor of Languedoc, acting as a private person. The decision was that the repair of the walls would be financed by the members of the seven ladders of the defense organization, presumably involving inhabitants from both town and suburbs. Five-sevenths of the sums solicited would go for the new walls, two-sevenths to repair the old. Such an arbitrated compromise again reflects the social and financial tensions of this era. Priorities varied when the issue was whether to wall the suburbs or to destroy them, as had been the case in Montpellier and so many other towns. At this moment in time, further fortifications were authorized.

Consuls and *obriers* disagreed again in 1361, when the *obriers* protested that the consuls of the previous year had convinced the people of the need for a tax to finance new construction and repairs, but now the current group of consuls, whose terms ran one year, wanted to prevent this work because of the cost.[122] These new expenditures came for Montpellier and other towns, as Rossiaud has noted, at the very moment when royal and princely demands were at their height.[123] There was not enough by way of revenue to satisfy all.

CONCLUSION

In the end, the threat from marauding mercenary companies (*routiers*) proved less daunting to the population of medieval towns than the onslaught of the plague, which may have claimed three-quarters of the population of Montpellier. The Black Death struck the town hard, initially in 1348 and again in 1361.[124] The most poignant incident in

---

[121] 2 October 1357 and 26 October 1367, EE 71.

[122] 22 November 1361, EE 66.

[123] Rossiaud, "Crises et consolidations," 432ff.

[124] On the experience of Montpellier and the plague, see my article, "Changes in Testamentary Practice at Montpellier on the Eve of the Black Death," *Church History* 47 (1978): 253–69, reprinted in Reyerson, *Society, Law, and Trade in Medieval Montpellier*.

the history of the city walls occurred in 1374, when the inhabitants sought spiritual reinforcement for the physical fortifications.[125] At the order of the town consuls, a great candle running the approximate length of the Palissade walls, 1,900 *cannes* (approximately 3,762 meters), was fabricated and placed in the pilgrimage church of Notre-Dame des Tables, the central spiritual shrine of the town.[126] Reflecting the psychological needs of the inhabitants for divine assistance, it burned day and night for three years. Measurements were retaken and the candle redone again in 1384 and in 1397. To no avail. The walls and the candle failed to protect the town from death and disease at the hands of the mercenary companies and the plague. Frustrations caused the town to revolt in 1379 against royal oppression.[127] Petrarch (+1374) noted a marked change in the character of Montpellier across the forty-year span he had known the town in the mid-fourteenth century. In youth he found it a mighty and proud Majorcan fortress. In old age he was struck by the decay which he, with francophobia, attributed to French conquest.[128] In part he was right. With France came war, as it turned out. The plague only added insult to injury. And against both, the walls proved a poor defense as well as a constraint on urban development.[129]

Montpellier was not to recover its medieval position of prominence as a commercial and financial center in the early modern era. The fortification experience of Montpellier over the thirteenth and fourteenth centuries reveals both the pride and responsibility and the pressures and constraints of walled space for medieval inhabitants. Urban administrators, themselves caught between the need to derive revenue from the walls and the need to maintain them, catered at

---

[125] *Le Petit Thalamus de Montpellier*, 391.

[126] Jacques Fabre de Morlhon, *Le Montpellier des Guilhem et des rois d'Aragon*, 2nd ed. (Montpellier, 1967), 10, gave the same length for the Palissade and the candle. However, Fabre and Lochard, *Montpellier: la ville médiévale*, 194–9, spoke of the difficulties of tracing the extent of the Palissade, giving its length at over 4,000 meters. See footnote 84 earlier on local measures.

[127] Perroy, *The Hundred Years' War*, 173.

[128] *Francisci Petrarchae Florentini Philosophi Oratoris et poetae clarissimi, Opera Omnia*, ed. Henrichus Petri (Basel, 1554), *Rerum senilium*, Liber X: "De mutatione temporum," 960.

[129] Fabre, Lochard, and Nougaret, "L'Enceinte médiévale de Montpellier," MSS 3–4, view the *Commune Clôture* as a constraint on development in the early modern era. After 1627 the citadel construction necessitated the destruction of the eastern part of the wall, but the remaining fortifications persisted until the early nineteenth century. Because of the lack of open space within the old walls, the royal square, dating from the end of the seventeenth century, and the monumental Peyrou park of the eighteenth century were constructed outside the walls.

times to the economic needs of the population, at times to the strict demands of town defense. It took the crisis of the Hundred Years' War to place these conflicting priorities in sharp relief in Montpellier and in other towns of war-torn France.[130]

[130] All that remains above ground of the medieval urban fortifications in Montpellier are two towers: la Tour des Pins and la Tour de la Babotte. In the first languish the incredibly rich municipal archives; the second owed its survival to the construction of an observatory on the site in the eighteenth century. See Ghislaine Fabre, Thierry Lochard, and Jean Nougaret, "L'Enceinte médiévale de Montpellier et ses incidences sur le développement urbain," MSS 8, n. 18. See also Jean Nougaret, *Montpellier: architecture religieuse, publique et militaire.*

In contrast to such southern French towns as Albi and to Languedocian villages such as Saint-Martin-de-Londres and Les Matelles, few buildings still standing in Montpellier are visibly medieval, although close scrutiny reveals medieval elements in many reworked later structures, and archeologists can find traces of the major urban fortifications in the basements of houses and buildings along the boulevards which provide an echo today of the trace of these earlier walls. In the case of Montpellier, the Wars of Religion wreaked havoc with the medieval environment, and the town that remains is essentially of the Ancien Régime with significant hotels of the seventeenth and eighteenth centuries.

CHAPTER 5

A world without walls:
City and town in colonial
Spanish America

RICHARD L. KAGAN

In his influential treatise, *Ten Books on Architecture*, Leon Battista Alberti (1404–72) recognized the importance of city walls. Any city which lacked them he wrote, was "naked."[1] In offering this advice, Alberti was undoubtedly thinking of the important military function that walls, even in the emergent age of artillery, might still play. Yet he was also cognizant that walls served other important, if purely symbolic functions. Throughout fifteenth- and sixteenth-century Europe walls constituted a town's badge of honor, a sign of its grandeur, wealth, and importance. Walls in this sense were architectural manifestations of municipal virtue, an emblem of its *civitas*, or community of citizens banded together, as Aristotle had explained, for mutual benefit and protection. Walls, of course, also served important economic functions; traditionally, they were the places where taxes were imposed on goods entering a town. In addition, walls functioned as a special type of urban prophylactic; city gates were closed whenever plague or other diseases posed a threat. It was also understood that walls served as markers of municipal justice and authority. Although municipal jurisdictions customarily extended well beyond the wall's circuit, encompassing both extramural suburbs and nearby villages, walls constituted a symbolic boundary, delineating the area within which justice, as administered by the municipality, ruled supreme. It was no accident, therefore, that public executions were held and the corpses (and in some cases, simply the heads) of condemned criminals

A preliminary version of this essay was published as "Un mundo sin murallas: la ciudad en la América hispana colonial," in *Imágenes de la diversidad. El mundo urbano en la corona de Castilla (s. xvi–xviii)*, ed. José Ignacio Fortea Pérez (Santander, 1997), 51–86.
[1] Leon Battista Alberti, *Ten Books on Architecture*, ed. Joseph Rykwert (London, 1995), bk. IV, ch. iii, 72. *De Re Aedificatoria*, written ca. 1450, was first published in 1485.

placed on display in areas adjacent to municipal walls and gates. These bodies and body parts conveyed a simple but straightforward message: *intra muros*, justice would be both swift and severe. In other words, for Alberti as well for other Renaissance writers, walls literally defined a town.[2]

In view of Europe's continuing predilection for city walls, the absence of walled cities in sixteenth-century Spanish America is striking. Years ago, George Kubler, in his magisterial study of sixteenth-century Mexican architecture, drew attention to this particular aspect of American urbanization, noting that the towns Spaniards established in the New World were originally conceived as unfortified enclaves that reflected the utopian concerns of the mendicant orders, whose role, both spiritual and secular, in the conquest of New Spain was key.[3] Kubler recognized that in later years, especially after the arrival of northern European corsairs in the New World, American cities gradually hardened their defenses, but his central point was that Spanish American towns, at least at their inception, lacked the walls, fortresses, and bastions that Machiavelli, in his *Art of War*, considered essential components of urban life.[4]

Kubler's observations about the nakedness of America's cities are still widely accepted, although some of today's scholars, while acknowledging the importance of imported European conceptions of the city, would also attribute this particular phenomenon to a continuation of indigenous urban practices. None of the cities that Hernan Cortés encountered in Mexico, for example, were surrounded by walls.[5] On the other hand, there is more than a grain of truth in the argument

---

[2] An early definition of cities as walled enclaves may be found in the *Siete Partidas*, the thirteenth-century legal code compiled by Alfonso X of Castile in which (Partida VII, tit. xxxiii, ley 6) a city was described as "a place surrounded by walls, together with its buildings and suburbs" ("*todo aquel lugar q es cercado de los muros, con los arrabales et los edificios q se tienen con ellos*"). See Julio Valdeón Baruque, "Reflexiones sobre las murallas urbanas de la Castilla medieval," in *Estudios de historia medieval en homenaje a Luis Suarez Fernández* (Valladolid, 1991), 509–22.

[3] George Kubler, *Mexican Architecture in the Sixteenth Century* (New Haven, 1948), 1:11, 81.

[4] Niccoló Machiavelli, *The Art of War*, a revised edition of the Ellis Farneworth translation, ed. Neal Wood (Indianapolis, 1965), 183.

[5] In New Spain, Cortés took note of the hill fortress built by the chief of Tlaxcala as well as the fortified gates at the entrances of Tenochtitlan, but the only stone wall he described was that built by the Tlaxcalans at the frontiers of their territory to defend against Aztec raids. This wall, similar in conception to the Great Wall of China or Hadrian's wall in northern Britain, is described in *Hernan Cortés, Letters from Mexico*, ed. A.R. Pagden (Cambridge, 1971), 57. For more on indigenous fortifications in Mesoamerica, see Ross Haussig, *Aztec Warfare* (Norman, 1988), and his *War and Society in Ancient Mesoamerica* (Berkeley, 1992).

that the absence of walls reflected the utopian concerns of the coloniz-
ers, particularly the Franciscans' efforts to construct communities in
the Americas that were organized around principles of piety and
religion rather than hostility and war.[6] As the Spaniards conceived it,
America was to be a world without walls, a continent whose urban
defenses were to be less material than metaphysical, or what will be
described here, to borrow a phrase from one seventeenth-century
Mexican author, as "spiritual walls." The exact form and shape of
these defenses, themselves part of the intellectual ordering of Spain's
empire in the New World (Fig. 5.1), is the subject this essay – which
may be taken as a gloss upon Kubler's pioneering work – proposes to
address.

MATERIAL WALLS

For all their investment in spiritual walls, Spaniards in the Americas
did not rely upon this kind of protection alone. The threat of Indian
uprisings caused alarm among some early settlers, leading to petitions
for defenses of a more durable sort. In Mexico City, for example, such
a threat persuaded Cortés in 1524 to build a fortified arsenal (*atara-
zanas*) designed to protect the brigantines he had constructed and to
allow Spaniards to escape from the city in the event of attack. Defense
was allegedly also the reason why Cortés and a number of his followers, starting in the 1520s, built *casas fuertes* in and around Mexico
City's main square. Cortés later maintained that these fortified houses
were designed to protect against Indian attack, although there is good
reason to believe that they were actually constructed as a result of
factional infighting among the Spanish settlers.[7] Whatever their precise purpose, Francisco Cervantes de Salazar, writing in 1554, disap-
proved of these *casas fuertes*, evidently regarding these buildings as
incompatible with a community based on the humanistic principles of
communal concord.[8]

The need for defense against a potential native uprising in Mexico
City also gave rise to various other schemes, among them the creation
around the areas inhabited by Spaniards of a kind of no man's land

---

[6] On the utopian strains in Spanish American colonization, the classic statement is by
John Leddy Phelan, *The Millennial Kingdom of the Franciscans in the New World* (Berkeley, 1970).

[7] See Kubler, *Mexican Architecture*, 1:77–8.

[8] Francisco Cervantes de Salazar, *The Dialogues of Francisco Cervantes de Salazar or Life in
the Imperial and Loyal City of Mexico in New Spain*, trans. Minnie Lee Barret Shepard
(Austin, 1955), 39.

Figure 5.1. Map of Spanish America, indicating location of towns mentioned in text.

where attackers could easily be mowed down. There was also a call for the construction of rows of tightly packed fortified houses along two of the causeways leading to the city, which was still an island in the middle of Lake Texcoco. Together these houses would form a defensive barrier (*"casa-muro"*) and also provide a handy escape route.

It should be emphasized, however, that none of these projects – all dating from the 1530s – ever came to fruition, partly owing to official preference for "spiritual walls," partly to the fact that as time passed and the indigenous populations were decimated by disease, natives living in and around Mexico City posed less and less a threat to Spanish settlers.[9]

A similar combination of forces also helps to explain why other early demands for durable defenses were rarely or incompletely realized, or at the very least limited to churches, monasteries, or other stoutly constructed buildings that could be converted into a defensible redoubt whenever necessary. Just such an incident occurred in Guadalajara, for example, when, in 1541, in the teeth of a native revolt, the local Spanish population retreated to the main square where a large house had been hastily fortified.[10] On the other hand, city walls and fortresses remained a rarity as the town descriptions included in the *Relaciones geográficas* of the 1570s and 1580s clearly reveal. Typical in this respect was the description of Tirpitio in Michoacán: "in this town and its district, there is nothing except the mountains that resemble a defensible fortress . . . on no occasion did we ever think about defending ourselves or building a fort or a fortress to defend the Spaniards . . . there is nothing to be afraid of nor reason to build a fort or fortress."[11]

The truth is that most inland communities in the Americas had little incentive to invest in walls and other fortifications of a standard that contemporary European warfare demanded. In fact, with the exception of northern Chile, where native uprisings represented a continuous threat to Spanish settlement well into the seventeenth century, and the "silver frontier" in northern Mexico, where the Spanish established a chain of garrisons (*presidios*) to defend against the warlike Chichimecs, relatively few towns, even port towns in the Caribbean, saw much of a need to erect costly fortifications.[12] This was certainly

---

[9] Details in Kubler, *Mexican Architecture*, 1:77–8. Another failed defensive project was Fray Toribio de Motolinia's plans for walls and a fortress in Puebla. See Fray Antonio de Motolinia, *The Indians of New Spain*, trans. Elizabeth A. Foster (n.p., 1950), 271.

[10] The incident is related in Fray Antonio Tello, *Historia de la Nueva Galicia* (1650), ed. Juan García Icazbalceta, *Colección de documentos para la historia de Mexico* (Mexico, 1866; fasc. ed., Nendeln, 1971), 2:400–4.

[11] *Relaciones geográficas del siglo xvi*, ed. Rene Acuña (Mexico City, 1982), 9:360.

[12] For Chile, see Gabriel Guarda, "Military Influence and the Cities of the Kingdom of Chile," in *Urbanization in the Americas from its Beginnings to the Present*, eds. Richard P. Schaedel, Jorge E. Hardoy, and Nora Scott Kinza (The Hague, 1978), 343–75. The defensive situation on the Mexican frontier is described in Philip D. Powell, *Soldiers, Indians and Silver. The Northern Advance of New Spain, 1550–1600* (Berkeley, 1952). For the Caribbean's haphazard defenses, see Paul E. Hoffman, *The Spanish Crown and the Defense of the Caribbean, 1535–1585* (Baton Rouge, 1980).

true for San Juan (Puerto Rico), where the Jeronymites apparently convinced the town's first settlers that spiritual walls would suffice.[13] In 1529, however, after a surprise Carib raid, local residents demanded a fortress. What came to be known as the *fuerza vieja* was soon built but on a site that one official who came to inspect it deemed totally ineffective: "even if the blind had built it they could not have chosen a more useless spot."[14]

The Caribbean's somewhat haphazard approach towards material defenses changed after European corsairs made their appearance, starting in the 1540s. Spiritual walls may have been sufficient to keep native peoples at bay, but they were practically useless against Protestant pirates arriving in warships. One Spanish admiral – an early advocate of forward maritime defenses – suggested that an expanded armada offered the best protection against these interlopers, but most ports responded to the European threat by constructing new bulwarks, fortresses, and the like.[15] Typical was El Morro, the new artillery fortress begun in San Juan during the 1540s and designed to protect that city's port. El Morro served its purpose well, successfully defending the city against Francis Drake's fleet in 1585.[16] On the other hand, San Juan's failure to protect its land flank with a wall enabled English soldiers commanded by the earl of Cumberland to enter and burn the city in 1598.[17]

Defensive preparations in other Caribbean ports were similarly ill-planned. Cartagena de Indias managed a few gun platforms and some towers after 1574, whereas Santo Domingo, starting around 1556, built a wooden wall meant to forestall land attack. This barricade, however, was so low and so easily breached that it did little to prevent Drake's soldiers from entering and looting the city in 1585.[18]

---

[13] San Juan began as the town of Caparra, founded in 1509 by Juan Ponce de Leon. Caparra had a small *fuerte*, but this was abandoned when the town moved to its present site in 1521. For details, see Adolfo de Hostos, *Historia de San Juan, Ciudad Murada (1521–1898)* (San Juan de Puerto Rico, 1966).

[14] Gonzalo Fernández de Oviedo cited in Hostos, *Historia de San Juan*, 180.

[15] Blasco Núñez Vela also suggested in the event of such attack Spaniards should simply abandon their houses and take refuge in the interior. See Hostos, *Historia de San Juan*, 178.

[16] Drake's defeat is recorded in Thomas Maynarde, *Sir Francis Drake, His Voyage, 1595, together with a Spanish account of Drake's attack on Porto Rico*, ed. W.D. Cooley (London, 1849).

[17] Details in T. Blanco Enrique, *Los tres ataques británicos a la ciudad de San Juan Bautista de Puerto Rico* (San Juan, 1947), and Luis M. Diaz Soler, *Puerto Rico* (San Juan, 1994), 207–10.

[18] The first account of this raid, from the English perspective, was Walter Bigges, *A Summarie and True Discourse of Sir Francis Drakes West Indian Voyage* (London, 1589;

The success of this particular raid – widely-publicized throughout Europe – revealed the weaknesses inherent in the Caribbean's defenses, most of which had been designed to ward off native uprisings rather than cope with Europeans armed with cannons and guns. The Spanish monarchy responded by dispatching to the region two of its finest military engineers, Giovanni Bautista Antonelli and Juan de Texeda, specifically instructing them to design fortifications capable of deterring European-style attack. Antonelli and Texeda both spent years in the region, designing fortresses to meet the particular needs of individual ports.[19] Yet for all of the projects they sent back to Spain for review, the immediate results of this defensive initiative were somewhat mixed, as several surveys done at the start of the seventeenth century clearly indicated. In 1604, for example, it was reported that Panama City, having failed to build a planned fort, had little more to defend itself against corsairs than "the hands, arms and valor of its citizens."[20] The situation elsewhere was not much better. In a secret document presented to King Philip IV in 1632, Nicolas de Cardona praised El Morro and the other fortifications Antonelli designed for Havana ("the best in the Indies"), and he noted that Cartagena de Indias, at the moment of his visit in 1615, "was being surrounded by walls."[21] However, Cardona also discovered that the material defenses of many other ports still left much to be desired. Jamaica City had only a "hill-top lookout," "four pieces of artillery," and "the thickness of the surrounding forest" to protect it, whereas Portobelo (Panama), despite Antonelli's plans for a stone fortress and perimeter wall, marshaled little more than a small fort that was incapable of preventing Dutch ships from blocking access to its port. Cardona was equally pessimistic about Vera Cruz. The small fortress erected there by Cortés had been supplemented, starting in the 1550s, by the supposedly "unassailable" island fortress of San Juan de Ullua. Yet when Cardona

facs. ed., Amsterdam, 1969). See also *Sir Francis Drake's West Indian Voyage, 1585–86*, ed. Mary Frear Keeler (London, 1981).

19 See Diego Angulo Ibañez, *Bautista Antonelli. Las fortificaciones americanas del siglo xvi* (Madrid, 1942), and J.A. Calderon Quijana, "Ingenieros militares en Nueva España durante los siglos xvi y xvii," *Anuaro de Estudios Americanos* 6 (1949): 1–72.

20 Pedro de Valencia, *Relaciones de Indias. 1. Nueva Granada y Virreinato de Perú*, in his *Obras completas*, eds. Francisco Javier and Jesús Fuente Fernández (León, 1993), 5:184–6.

21 See Nicolas de Cardona, *Descripciones geográficas e hidrográficas de muchas tierras y mares del norte y sur, en las Indias, en especial del descubrimiento del reino de California* (Madrid, 1989). The work is also available in English: *Geographic and Hydrographic Descriptions of Many and Southern Lands and Seas in the Indies, Specifically of the Discovery of the Kingdom of California*, ed. and trans. W. Michaels Mathes (Los Angeles, 1974).

inspected the new fortress in 1615, he reported that it offered Vera Cruz "little defense" owing to glaring artillery shortages.[22] Improvements were made, and two additional fortresses were later constructed to protect the city's flanks, but when the Italian traveler Giovanni Francesco Gemelli Careri visited Vera Cruz at the end of the seventeenth century, he reported that its fortifications were still very weak. Careri indicated, for example, that the officials commissioned to wall the city had "blatantly defrauded" the king by constructing only a rather flimsy series of curtain walls. "Horses," he wrote, "can easily jump over them . . . and it is useless to close the gates since the city can be entered from any side." Nevertheless, Careri admitted that "nature makes the port strong, since on both the east and west it is defended by an infinite number of reefs upon which foreigners who do not know them ordinarily wreck."[23]

Despite Careri's remarks, Vera Cruz's reliance on natural as opposed to man-made defenses was rapidly becoming a thing of the past. From about 1540 to 1620, the Spanish Caribbean's main military threat came in the form of the occasional corsair raid, but the strategic climate changed once the Dutch established permanent settlements on the northeast coast of Brazil, starting in the 1620s. English and French colonies soon followed, creating what amounted to a new and permanent threat to Spanish interests in the region. Local officials countered with a new campaign designed to harden urban defenses. San Juan, for example, planned a circuit of walls in the 1640s and managed to enclose the city on at least three sides by 1678.[24] Beginning in 1633, Havana also constructed walls to protect its land flank, whereas Cartagena de Indias erected what was surely among the most impressive arrays of artillery platforms, fortresses, and walls ever constructed in the New World.[25]

---

[22] In 1580 it was reported that the fort of San Juan de Ulloa was soon to become "*una de las más fuertes cosas que hay en el mundo . . . inexpugnable.*" Cf. *Relaciones geográficas del siglo xvi*, 5:331. See also Cardona, *Geographic and Hydrographic Descriptions*, 55.

[23] Giovanni Francesco Gemelli Careri, *Viaje a la Nueva España*, ed. and trans. Francisca Perujo (Mexico, 1976), 154. Confirmation of the weakness of the land defenses of Vera Cruz may be found in Pierre F.X. Charlevoix, *Histoire de l'isle espagnole ou de San Domingue* (Paris, 1730), 2:134.

[24] Eighteenth-century plans of the city suggest that these walls were completed sometime before 1730. See Charlevoix, *Histoire de l'isle espagnole*, 1:223, and Hostos, *Historia de San Juan*, 199.

[25] Havana's walls, described by one visitor as "small and low," were completed at the end of the seventeenth century. See Jean-Pierre Berthe, "La Habana de fines del siglo xvii vista por un italiano," in *Estudios de historia de la Nueva España. De Sevilla a Manila* (Mexico, 1994), 124–49. For Cartagena, see María Carmen Borrego Plá, *Cartagena de Indias en el siglo xvi* (Seville, 1983).

Militarily, however, Spain's Caribbean cities represented something of an exception. In other parts of the Americas cities were slow to invest in material defenses of any sort. Walls, of course, were difficult and expensive to build; they represented considerable investments of labor, resources, and time. Furthermore, in the absence of any serious military threat, municipal authorities may have considered walls as superfluous structures whose construction would necessarily divert indigenous labor from more essential – and productive – tasks, among them, the steady supply of food and the extraction of mineral wealth. These same officials may also have interpreted walls and other fortifications as a potential military threat to their own survival. In the event of an Indian uprising, such structures could potentially be used against the Spaniards themselves.

More needs to be learned about the manner in which individual municipal councils assessed and debated their particular military needs, but whatever decisions were taken, few towns, particularly in the sixteenth century, opted for walls. Acapulco, for example, remained completely "naked" until 1615, when a fleet commanded by the Dutch captain, Joris van Spielbergen, looted the unprotected town. This raid sparked the rapid construction of a fort paid for out of self-imposed taxes on that city's lucrative Pacific trade. Even then, Acapulco remained an open city. Careri reported in 1697 that its defenses were minimal: a small fort and some artillery, but no moat, bastions, or walls of any sort.[26]

The fortifications erected in Spain's other Pacific ports were not much better. Spielbergen's raid led Callao, the port of Lima, to strengthen its fortifications, but the pace of construction at this and other Pacific ports waned until the 1680s, when raids by Henry Morgan, Bartholomew Sharpe, and other English buccaneers threatened the region once again.[27] Plans for the walling of Lima, for example,

[26] See Cardona, *Geographic and Hydrographic Observations*, 75; Engel Sluiter, "The Fortification of Acapulco, 1615–1616," *Hispanic American Historical Review* 29 (1949): 69–80; and Gemelli Careri, *Viaje*, 11. Adrien Boot, a Flemish military engineer, planned the fortress constructed in 1616.

[27] For details, Lawrence A. Clayton, "Local Initiative and Finance in Defense of the Viceroyalty of Peru: The Development of Self-Reliance," *Hispanic American Historical Review* 54 (1974): 284–304, and Guillermo Lohmann Villena, *Defensas militares de Lima y Callao* (Seville, 1974). Despite improvements in Callao's defenses, Fray Buenaventura Salinas y Córdoba, writing in the 1620s, criticized their many inadequacies in his *Memorial de las historia del Nuevo Mundo. Piru. Méritos y excelencias de la ciudad de Lima* (1630; ed. Lima, 1957), 274. It should be noted that Manila was probably the first of Spain's Pacific ports to construct stone walls. It did so, ca. 1600, almost thirty years after its foundation, in an effort to protect itself against Japanese pirates. See Antonio de Morga, *History of the Philippine Islands* (1609), ed. and trans. E.H. Blair and J.A. Robertson (Cleveland, 1907; rprt. ed., New York, 1970), 136, 305.

dated from 1657, but construction did not begin until 1685, apparently because of resistance on the part of local residents, many of whom took pride in their city's "nakedness." Among these holdouts was Fray Juan Meléndez, a local historian who, writing in 1680, openly boasted that "Lima is not enclosed by any walls, moats, nor fortifications," and attributed this both to the city's "grandeur [which] guarantees its security" and the refusal of its citizens to impede the city's expansion and growth.[28] In the end, Lima finally got its walls, thanks to the initiative of the Spanish viceroy, the duke of La Palata, and the labor provided by a small (but underpaid) army of black laborers.[29] It was also in the 1680s that officials in Trujillo, with the help of an Italian engineer, devised an ambitious plan to enclose the central part of that coastal city with bastions and a defensive wall made of adobe. Further south, in Chile, where the rebellious Araucanians still posed a threat, most towns were fortified, although generally with earthen barricades or wooden stockades. Stone walls, however, remained a rarity. Arauco and Cañete built some, and La Serena was walled following an attack by Sharpe in 1680, but Santiago, the region's principal town, abandoned its plan, originally conceived in 1657, to construct a wall.[30] Meanwhile, both Arica and Guayaquil, despite their coastal locations, remained unprotected by walls.[31] This was also true of Buenos Aires, the defense of which, other than a small *fuerte* and a wooden palisade facing the port, consisted primarily of spiritual walls.

[28] Juan Meléndez, *Tesoros verdaderos de las Yndias en la historia de la gran provincia de San Juan Bautista del Peru* (Rome, 1681), 1:157. See also José Sala Catalá, *Ciencia y técnica en la metropolización de América* (Madrid, 1994), 275, where the author cites a 1673 document which reports that "*dice por admiración* [the inhabitants of Lima] *es ciudad abierta, que no tiene muro ni cerca ni centelas de día ni de noche.*"

[29] Work on the wall is reported in *A Chronicle of Colonial Lima. The Diary of Joseph and Francisco Magaburi, 1640–97,* ed. and trans. Robert R. Miller (Norman, 1975), 282, 300. For more on Lima's defenses, see Sala Catalá, *Ciencia y técnica,* 275–86, and Lohman Villena, *Las defensas militares de Lima y El Callao.* Around 1735, the French astronomer Louis Godin observed that these walls offered little defense against a European enemy because they lacked both a moat and "a place suitable for a cannon." As a result, he believed that they had been erected primarily to defend against Indian attack. See Jean-Paul Duviols, "Descripción de la ciudad de Lima . . . ," in *Cultures et sociétés, Andes et Meso-Amérique,* ed. Raquel Thiercelin (Aix-en-Provence, 1991), 268.

[30] For the fortification of Trujillo, La Serena and other Peruvian ports, see Guarda, "Military Influence," 343–75. See also José Luis Romero, *Latinoamérica: las ciudades y las ideas,* (Mexico, 1976), 48–9, who coins the term "*ciudad-fuerte,*" "fortress-city," to describe Valdivia, La Serena, and Chile's other frontier towns. He also applies it to Santa Cruz and Tarija in Bolivia, and Nueva Cádiz and Coro in Venezuela.

[31] Diego Alcedo y Herrera, governor of Guayaquil, complained that construction of a fortress in that city only began in 1707 and resulted in a wooden structure "*poco ajustado a las reglas del arte militar, con materiales muy debiles y temporal duración.*" See his *Compendio histórico de la provincia . . . de Guayaquil* (Madrid, 1741).

Towns located in the interior of the continent deployed similar defenses, although there is evidence that, for a time at least, settlements established in regions that the Spaniards had not fully secured erected barricades to guard against possible native assault. In 1545, for example, Pedro de Valdivia noted that the inhabitants of Asunción managed to finish work on a protective adobe barrier only minutes before the start of such an attack.[32] Similar barriers surrounded newly founded towns in inland regions of New Granada where the Spaniards had also encountered considerable native resistance. Referring, for example, to Espíritú Santo, which was founded by Juan de Pimentel in 1579, a chronicler wrote that the community had "more the aspect of a fort than a town."[33] In more peaceful areas, towns developed without walls or other defenses of a material sort. In 1604, for example, it was reported that Tunja, a mountain town located about 100 miles northeast of Bogotá, not only lacked walls but soldiers as well. "The city's soldiers are the citizens who live and reside there."[34] Nor was the situation in Quito much better. Juan de Velasco, an eighteenth-century chronicler, boasted that Quito "has never even thought about walls, fortresses, artillery pieces, nor companies of soldiers."[35] In the meanwhile, Cuzco had its old Inca walls, but none the Spaniards constructed, and in Potosí, high in the Andes, the municipal council did little more than construct a series of gates that were used primarily for ceremonial purposes.

This world without walls even extended into what is now the southwestern United States. According to a series of eighteenth-century plans (ca. 1768) now in the British Museum, the bastion-shaped presidio of Nuestra Señora del Pilar, "capital de la provincia de los Tejas," was protected by what appears to have been a wooden stockade, but most presidios in the region were not. The plan of the presidio of Nuestra Señora de las Caldas de Caujoquillo (Nueva Vizcaya) had its adobe buildings so tightly arranged around the central plaza that these structures – like a circle of wagons – could probably be used to fend off any attack, but apparently this was the only presidio organ-

---

[32] Cited in Romero, *Latinoamérica*, 48. Note that the first published account of Pedro de Mendoza's expedition to Rio de la Plata in 1536 included a curious drawing of a European settlement labeled Buenos Aires – even though there is no river in sight – protected by a low earthen barrier as well as a palisade. See Ulrich Schmidel, *Wahrhafftige Historian Einer Wunderbaren Schiffart* (1602; Graz, 1962), 9.

[33] José Oviedo y Baños, *The Conquest and Settlement of Venezuela* (1723), trans. Jeanette J. Varner (Berkeley, 1984), 247.

[34] Valencia, *Relaciones de Indias*, 5:271.

[35] Juan de Velasco, *Historia del reino de Quito en la América meridional*, ed. Alfredo Pareja Diezcanseco (1789; Caracas, 1981), 314.

ized in this fashion. The rest were more like Santa Fe, "capital of the
kingdom of New Mexico," a town whose defenses, like those of the
capital of "Old Mexico," were primarily spiritual.[36]

SPIRITUAL WALLS

The Spanish idea of spiritual as opposed to material walls rested in
large part on a literal interpretation of the Book of Isaiah in the Old
Testament. There, referring to Jerusalem, Isaiah wrote that "Thou shalt
call thy walls salvation and thy gates praise" (60.18). Currently, this
verse is customarily understood to mean that the Lord, through Isaiah,
was instructing Jerusalem's inhabitants to give these particular appel-
lations to the city's defenses.[37] In the sixteenth century, however, in
keeping with the literalist school of Biblical exegesis that dominated
the theological faculties of Spain's universities, the verse was taken to
mean that it was religion, not walls, that offered the city its best
protection.[38] In other words, it seems to have been widely understood
that a city with walls but with little faith was as good as lost: "The
defended city," Isaiah wrote, "shall be desolate, and the habitation
forsaken, and left like a wilderness" (27.10).[39] Isaiah was also critical
of the citizens of Jerusalem who, with the approach of Sennacharib's
army, put their faith in fortifications rather than God:

You counted the houses of Jerusalem, and you pulled down houses to
strengthen the wall. . . . But you had no thought for the Maker, no eyes for
Him who shaped everything long ago (22.10).

Interpreted literally, Isaiah's ideas about the inherent superiority of
spiritual as opposed to material walls were integral to the Spanish
conquest of America, especially New Spain, a region where the Franciscans and other mendicants hoped to build a New Jerusalem. There
the region's first viceroy, Antonio de Mendoza (1535–50), defied royal
instructions ordering him to build fortifications in Mexico City as well
as in other towns as a means of guarding against indigenous attack.
Later charged with disobedience, Mendoza vociferously defended the

---

[36] *Maps of the Provinces of New Spain*; British Library, Add. Mss. 17,662.
[37] This is the interpretation offered in *Le Bible de Jerusalem* (Paris, 1974).
[38] See Melquiades Andrés, *La teología española en el siglo xvi*, 2 vols. (Madrid, 1977), 1:
    272; 2: 66, 630–1.
[39] According to the *Jerusalem Bible* (Garden City, NY, 1968), the point of this verse is not
    that cities must be protected by faith but that the Lord's punishment of "Jacob's
    guilt" includes not just exile but also the destruction of fortified cities. I am grateful
    to Prof. Jim Tracy for help in interpreting this biblical passage.

concept that religion and piety represented a city's strongest defense.[40] Mendoza's exact words, apparently uttered or written in 1545 and subsequently reported by Fray Juan de Torquemada in the early seventeenth century, may be apocryphal, but they suggest that Isaiah's ideas about Jerusalem's defenses had a direct influence upon the viceroy's fortification policy:

Towers with soldiers [said Mendoza] were caves of thieves, whereas convents with friars were walls and castles which defended the entire region, because with their [the friars'] example, holy conversation, and prayers the spirit of the Indians was conquered and none of them ever got angry nor rose in revolt; religious houses in the villages were worth far more than soldiers and the convents he had ordered to be built were by far the most secure walls with which his king and Lord could be faithfully served.[41]

Isaiah's ideas about the inherent superiority of spiritual as opposed to material walls may also be found in other sixteenth-century Mexican documents, some of which will be cited below. They also appear in the works of various seventeenth-century writers, among them Fray Baltasar de Medina, a Franciscan responsible for the *Chronicle of the Holy Province of San Diego in Mexico* (Mexico, 1682). Writing specifically with reference to Mexico City's lack of fortifications, Medina expressed an opinion that:

Mexico, although not surrounded by material walls, is nevertheless secure, because, as Isaiah says, its spiritual walls, constructed in the eyes of God, offer ample protection and support, without engines of war or military fortifications, which, like Argus, would be useless sentinels unless God in all his power and these guardian saints [Casiano and Hipólito] did not protect this city and court.[42]

Medina alludes here to the failure of Argus, the all-seeing, to protect Io, then in the shape of a cow, from Hermes. His suggestion, reminis-

---

[40] Charles V had instructed Mendoza to build a fortress in Mexico City as early as 1535. See Juan García Icazbalceta, *Colección de documentos para la historia de Mexico*, 2:76, and José Antonio Calderón Quijano, *Las defensas indianas en la recopilación de 1680* (Sevilla, 1984), 41.

[41] Cited in Fray Juan de Torquemada, *Monarchia indiana* [1615] (Madrid, 1723), 1:605.

Original: "*porque en tiempo en de el Virrei Don Antonio de Mendoca, aviendole mandado el Rei, que hiciese muchos Presidios y Torres, en Pueblos, que conviniesen, para maior seguro de estos Reinos, y no curando de hacerlos, y poniendo en ellos Conventos, y Monasterios de Relgiones, para que administrasen las cosas de la fe, le fue esto puesto en cargo; al qual respondió, que las Torres con Soldados, eran Cuevas de Ladrones, y los Conventos con Frailes, era Muros, y Castillos, con que estaba defendida toda la tierra; porque con su Exemplo, y Santa Conversación, y Amonestaciones, tenian vencido el ánimo de los Indios, y nadie se inquietaba, ni alborotaba, y que mas valían Conventos de Religiosos que Fortaleças de Soldados, en los Pueblos; y que estos Conventos, que avia mandado edificar, eran los Muros mas seguros, con que avia servido fielmente à su Rei, y Señor.*"

[42] Baltasar de Medina, *Crónica de la santa provincia de San Diego de Mexico* (Mexico, 1682), 232.

cent of Isaiah, whom he often cites, is that military fortifications, no matter how strong, would similarly fail to protect Mexico City from a potential enemy. Better, he suggests, to entrust the city's defenses to its two patron saints, Casiano and Hipólito.

The original Franciscan idea of constructing utopia in New Spain had long since faded by the time Medina was writing, but the notion of creating a New Jerusalem protected only by spiritual defenses had not. "Is it necessary," asked Medina rhetorically, "for cities to have walls, bastions, castles, moats, turrets, parapets, and the like?"[43] His answer was unequivocal, at least insofar as Mexico City was concerned. Just as the Spartans, lacking walls, successfully defended themselves against their enemies because of their "loyal spirits," Mexico City was well defended by the virtues of its citizens as well as its faith.[44] Quoting a couplet from an earlier Mexican poet, Medina offered the following observation:

> No ha menester mas muros ni mas torres
> Que la muralla y torre de su amparo;

[The city does not need any walls or towers other than the wall and tower of their intervention.][45]

Although Mexico City was probably not quite as naked as Medina imagined, the city's openness certainly surprised Thomas Gage, an English traveler who was in the city in 1623. His travel diary reads: "all arms are forgotten, and the Spaniards live so secure from enemies that there is neither gate, wall, bulwark, platform, tower, armoury, ammunition or ordnance to secure and defend the city from a domestic or foreign enemy."[46] Yet as Gage himself learned, Mexico City was by no means unique despite its unusual and somewhat defensible lacustrine location. His visit to Oaxaca, for example, elicited the following remark: "this city, as all the rest of America (except sea towns) lieth open without walls, bulwarks, forts, towers, or any castle, ord-

[43] Medina, *Crónica*, 232.
[44] Medina alluded here to Plato's comments about Spartans. See *Laws* (bk. VI, 778–9), trans. R.G. Bury (Cambridge, MA, 1947), 10:481.
[45] Medina, *Crónica*, 232. Medina was quoting from Arias de Villalobos, *Poema de las grandezas de Mexico* (1623).
[46] Thomas Gage, *Travels in the New World*, ed. J. Eric Thompson (Norman, 1985), 65. The only earthwork that Mexico City built for purposes of defense was the dike or *albarradán* constructed during the 1620s to protect the city from flooding. For this and other flood control projects, see Sala Catalá, *Ciencia y técnica*, 99–183, and Luisa Shell Hoberman, "Technological Change in a Traditional Society: The Case of the Desagüe of Mexico City," *Technology and Culture* 21 (1980): 386–407.

nance, or ammunition to defend it."[47] Gage was exaggerating, yet as we have already seen, towns and cities throughout Spanish America, true to their utopian origins, demonstrated a proclivity towards defenses that had little to do with either mortar or brick.

According to the sixteenth-century Spanish geographer, Juan López de Velasco, by 1576 Spaniards had established over 200 towns in the Americas, an achievement second only to that of the Romans whose own empire was grounded upon an extensive urban network.[48] But it is not the aim of this essay to compare Roman and Spanish imperial practices, or to provide a history summarizing the development of Spanish urban foundations in the New World – a topic about which much has already been written. Instead, it will explore some of the intellectual foundations upon which Spanish towns in the Americas rested as these offer a number of clues for understanding – dare I say "deconstructing" – the spiritual walls of the kind to which Medina alluded.

SPIRITUAL WALLS: *POLICÍA*

During the course of the Reconquest, the Christians' centuries-long endeavor to wrest Iberia from Muslim control, towns played a fundamental role. Starting, for example, with the conquest of New Castile in the eleventh century, Castilians generally took possession of lands previously occupied by Muslims by establishing towns and populating them with Christians. Castilians subsequently employed similar practices in the Indies, where the town, starting with Santo Domingo in 1502, served as the principal instrument through which the monarchy organized its newly conquered possessions. During the early stages of the Reconquest, Christians congregated in small urban nuclei in regions they had not yet fully secured. Similarly, in the Americas, towns served as the antidote for what many Spaniards perceived as an alien environment inhabited by hostile peoples. The town, in a sense, constituted a refuge. But the town was also synonymous with order, justice, religion, and organized economic activity in the form of crafts, workshops, markets, and the like. Blended together, these various elements comprised what Spaniards in the Americas commonly referred to as *policía*, a term often translated by historians as polity but one whose meaning was actually far more complex.

---

[47] Gage, *Travels*, 111.
[48] Juan López de Velasco, *Geografía y descripción universal de las indias* (Madrid, 1576), ed. Biblioteca de Autores Españoles (Madrid, 1971).

In the sixteenth century, the Spanish word *policía*, despite its Latin root, *politia*, derived much of its meaning from the Greek, πολιτεία, a complex term which, as used by both Aristotle and Plato, referred to the *polis*, particularly in its public or political aspects. For Spaniards, *policía* signified life in a community whose citizens were organized into a republic. More specifically, again following Aristotle, it implied the subordination of individual desires and interests to those of the community, a subordination guaranteed by ordinances and laws. *Policía* in this sense amounted to the *res publica*, an organized community of citizens governed by law. *Policía* was also good government, especially the order, peace, and prosperity that sound government engendered, and in both cases *policía* was understood to generate its own defense, a concept that Juan de Solórzano Pereira (1575–1655), a legist who spent years in the Indies as a judge on the *audiencia* or high court of Lima, expressed graphically in the form of several emblems included in his *Emblemata Regio Politica* (Madrid, 1653). In one emblem, "Concordia quos unit munit" ("Concord protects those it unites"), Solórzano portrayed a city whose walls were its citizens, gathered, in Spartan like fashion, in self-defense (Fig. 5.2). The accompanying text explains: "What walls does a city need? What powerful crown? Not a stone wall, but a living wall of citizens united by love, and consolidated by concord. With these no city is better protected. . . ." Similarly, Solórzano connected the idea of urban defense with municipal governance in the emblem, "Legum Munia, Urbium Maenia [sic]," ("The protection of laws, fortress of the city"), which depicted a city whose intertwined laws comprised a protective, ever-vigilant palisade (Fig. 5.3). "Law," Solórzano explained, "is like an eye. It provides defense. . . . Laws are the guardians of Cities and States."[49]

Despite these Aristotelian associations, *policía* also had other meanings, more Latin than Greek.[50] Derived principally from Cicero, the word also signified skill, refinement, and manners, all closely tied to another Ciceronian term, *urbanitas*, whose meaning was best understood in opposition to *rusticitas*, or *rusticus*. These words referred to a society or an individual devoid of the virtues associated with urban life, or what one New World missionary referred to as "*policía moral*."[51]

[49] Juan de Solózano Pereira, *Emblemas regio-políticos de Juan de Solórzano Pereira*, ed. Jesús María González de Zárate (Madrid, 1987).

[50] My understanding of the Greek and Latin origins of *policía* derives principally from Emile Benveniste's essay, "Deux modèles linguistiques de la cité," in his *Problèmes de linguistique générale*, (Paris, 1974), 2:272–80.

[51] Gerónimo de Mendieta, *Historia eclesiástica indiana* (1595), ed. Francisco Solano y Pérez-Lila (Madrid, 1973), 2:9.

As Spaniards interpreted it, moreover, *policía* could only be found among town dwellers. Individuals who lived otherwise, as nomads or semi-nomads, were, as Aristotle himself had defined it, barbaric, bestial, subhuman. This kind of itinerant existence was neatly summarized with the contemporary phrase *"vivir alárabe"* ("to live like an Arab"), a concept that Spaniards applied not only to Gypsies and Moors living in Spain and North Africa but also to the indigenous populations of the New World.[52]

Policía thus represented a combination of two concepts: one public, linked to citizenship in an organized polity, the other connected to personal comportment and private life, both inseparable from urban life. The complexity of the term is clearly demonstrated in the definition provided by the Spanish lexicographer Sebastián de Covarrubias in his famous early seventeenth-century dictionary, the *Tesoro de la lengua castellana*:

Policía. A polite, civic term. Police council, that which governs the small things of a city, like adornment and cleanliness. It derives from the Greek term, *res publica*, πολιτεία, meaning polity, the urban, the polite. Also politics, the science and mode of governing a city and a republic.[53]

In addition to Covarrubias' Aristotelian definition, *policía* also contained an important religious component summarized in the term *"policía cristiana."* This concept, derived principally from Augustine's *City of God*, Aquinas's notions about the city as the ideal instrument for evangelization, and the "Christian commonwealth" (*"cosa publica crestiana"*) of the fourteenth-century Catalan theologian, Francesc Eiximenis, linked the city with Christianity.[54] In fact, Christianity and the town were so closely connected in Spanish thinking that Gerónimo de Mendieta and most other sixteenth-century missionaries in the New World believed that it would be impossible to convert natives unless

[52] Two exceptions were the Incas and the Aztecs. Because of cities such as Cuzco and Tenochtitlan, the Spaniards credited them with *policía*, at least in the Aristotelian sense of the term. What they lacked was "policía cristiana."

[53] Sebastián de Covarrubias, *Tesoro de la lengua castellana o española* (1611; fasc. ed., Madrid, 1979), 875. Despite its importance in Spanish political language, *policía* has not yet received the detailed scholarly examination it deserves. See, however, the insightful discussion about its importance for Spanish New World architecture in Valerie Fraser, *The Architecture of Conquest. Building in the Viceroyalty of Peru 1535–1635* (Cambridge, 1990), 23.

[54] In addition to Augustine, see Francesc Eiximenis, *Regiment de la cosa publica* (Valencia, 1499; facs. ed., Valencia, 1991), whose ideas about cities are summarized in Antonio Antelo Iglesias, "La ciudad ideal según Fray F. Eiximenis y Rodrigo Sánchez de Arevalo," *La ciudad hispánica* (Madrid, 1985), 1:19–50. Aquinas's ideas about cities may be found in his treatise, *On Kinship. To the King of Cyprus*, ed. and trans. Gerald B. Phelan (Toronto, 1949), 68–80.

Figure 5.2. Juan de Solórzano Pereira. "Concordia Quos Unit Munit." Emblem. 1653. Solórzano's emblem emphasizes that a united citizenry is a city's strongest defense, or as he explains: "What does a city need? . . . Not a stone wall, but a living wall of citizens united by love, and consolidated by concord. With these no city is better protected."

they were obliged to live in "organized towns" ("*pueblos formados*").[55] Royal officials had similar ideas, among them, Vasco de Quiroga, judge of the *audiencia* (royal court) of Mexico, who in 1531 informed the Council of the Indies that the only antidote for "drunken orgies, idolatries and other evil rites and customs" of the natives was to organize them in towns. The alternative, he warned, would be "chaos and confusion."[56]

Policía, in sum, implied all of the benefits that accrued from urban life: law, order, morality, and religion. In this respect, *policía* was synonymous with civilization itself. *Policía*, moreover, lay at the very core

---

[55] Mendieta, *Historia eclesiástica indiana*, 2:87–8.
[56] Vasco de Quiroga to Council of the Indies, 14 March 1531, published in the *Colección de documentos inéditos relativos al descubrimiento, conquista y organización de América y Oceanea* (Madrid, 1870), 13:423.

Figure 5.3. Juan de Solórzano Pereira. "Legum Munia, Urbium Mænia." Emblem. 1653.

of the empire that Spaniards sought to establish in the New World, an empire which, if examined from a purely jurisdictional perspective, was little more than an "empire of towns," each endowed, in theory at least, with *"buena policía"* and thus with the protection that the concept was thought to provide.

This town-based conception of empire was first manifested when, as early as 1501, Queen Isabella explicitly instructed Fray Nicolás de Ovando, the first royal governor of Hispaniola, to establish towns (*"facer algunas poblaciones"*) on the island so that the Christians living there did not live *"derramados,"* scattered about.[57] Isabella on this occasion did not explain the rationale behind her policy. Issues connected to security and the threat of a native uprising were clearly at stake, but so too was the idea that Christians living outside the municipal *orbis*, that is, devoid of *policía*, would never be successful in their

[57] "Instrucción a . . . Fray Nicolás de Ovando," 16 Sept. 1501, in *Colección de documentos*, 31:17.

efforts to convert the natives to Christianity and a Spanish way of life. Whatever the Queen's precise rationale, from this moment on the Spanish empire in the Americas became an empire of towns, each of which was to embody the basic principles – law, order, justice, religion, an entire way of life – that *policía* implied. By definition, moreover, *policía* generated its own defense, effectively separating – and protecting – a town's inhabitants from the untamed, natural world that began at the perimeter of the municipal *término* or jurisdiction.

The urban policy articulated by Isabella in 1501 had immediate results. The following year Ovando founded Santo Domingo, the first Spanish town in the Americas.[58] Others soon followed, and within a decade or so Spaniards had created more than a dozen towns in various parts of the Caribbean, the most important (and durable) of which were Havana and San Juan.

Isabella's urban policy also appeared in the instructions given to individual captains to *"poblar y pacificar,"* "to settle and pacify" whatever lands they discovered on America's *tierra firme*. *Poblar*, however, entailed far more than the act of settlement, of simply occupying the land, as one scholar has recently (but erroneously) characterized the nature of Spanish New World settlement.[59] *Poblar*'s meaning was much more precise, as it specifically called for the establishment of a *pueblo*, a term derived from the Latin *populus* and one which implied the creation of a municipal corporation, a *civitas* or republic.[60] In 1513, for example, Ferdinand specifically instructed Pedrarías Dávila, who was about to embark on an expedition along the coast of Central America, to ensure that settlement of the region take the form of "ordered" towns.[61] Dávila's expedition came to naught, but six years later, Hernan Cortés officially began the conquest of Mexico when he established the Villa Rica de Veracruz and in so doing transformed his

---

[58] Juridically, La Isabella, Columbus's earlier settlement in Hispaniola, was only a *fundaca*, or trading factory, never a town.

[59] I refer here to Patricia Seed, "Taking Possession and Reading Texts: Establishing the Authority of Overseas Empires," *William and Mary Quarterly* 49 (1992), 196, as well as her *Ceremonies of Possession* (Cambridge, 1995), 69–99, where the *requirimiento*, a declaration of war and the assertion of dominion over people, is presented as if it were a ceremony of possession over land.

[60] According to Covarrubias, *Tesoro*, 874, 886, *"poblar"* derived from the term *"pueblo"* (*populus* in Latin), which he defined as a *"lugar,"* a place in the sense of a hamlet, village, city, or town.

[61] "Instrucción dada por el Rey a Pedrarías Dávila . . . ," 2 August 1513, in *Colección de documentos*, 39:284. The instructions read: "Let the city lots be regular (*ordenada*) from the start, so once they are marked out the town will appear well ordered as to the place which is left for a plaza, the site for the church, and the sequence of the streets; for in places newly established proper order can be given from the start. . . ."

company of soldiers into a municipal council or *cabildo*, whose officers immediately designated Cortés as their *justicia mayor*.[62] In this instance, the formation of a *cabildo* was a brilliant legal stratagem as it allowed Cortés to declare his independence of Diego de Velázquez, the military governor of Cuba who had opposed his expedition.

Most other conquistadors lacked Cortés's savvy, but they also utilized towns as means of organizing their conquests, evidently falling victim to a malady defined by one scholar as "foundation fever."[63] One conquistador who almost certainly succumbed to this particular ailment was Sebastián de Belalcázar. Firm in his belief that newly established cities represented the "center" and "security" of newly acquired provinces, this soldier founded no fewer than twenty new *pueblos* in the course of his conquest of New Granada between 1535 and 1543.[64] Simultaneously, in an unusual expedition sent out directly from Spain, Pedro de Mendoza initiated the conquest of the Rio de la Plata region in 1536 by establishing several "republics," among them Buenos Aires – which had to be re-founded in 1582. Spaniards took possession of other parts of Latin America in similar fashion, founding wherever they went a string of towns, some, *ex nihilo*, as in the case of Potosí, and others, as with Cuzco, Mexico City, and Quito, literally on top of existing indigenous communities.

Integral to this process of urban foundation, and essentially what made a town a town as opposed to a trading factory or military camp (or *presidio*), was the ceremony known as the "act of foundation."[65] Well-established by the 1520s and 1530s, this act was the ritual that miraculously transformed soldiers into citizens and consequently provided military officers with the legal authority – or *regalía* – they needed to exercise jurisdiction over natives within an assigned district or province. Equally important, the act of foundation, by creating a municipal corporation, a polity or republic, created the institution that *policía* needed to take root.

The foundation of Asunción, capital of today's Paraguay, in 1539, is a case in point. The town's creation is generally attributed to Damián Martínez, leader of a Spanish expedition that began in Buenos Aires, proceeded up the Paraná River and then went northwards along the course of the Paragua. If one later Jesuit report is credible, Martínez

---

[62] Cortés, *Letters from Mexico*, xix–xxii, 26–7.
[63] The term is that of Jacques Aprile-Gnoset, *La ciudad colombina* (Bogotá, 1991), 162.
[64] See Lucas Fernández Piedrahita, *Historia general de las conquistas del nuevo reino de Granada* (Madrid, 1688), 211, and Velasco, *Historia del reino de Quito*, 256–98.
[65] The ceremony is summarized in Libro IV of Bernardo Vargas Machuca, *Milicia y descripción de las Indias* (1599; ed. Madrid, 1892), 2:9–47.

founded the town on a site that was "low, sandy, . . . and unhealthy" after the local natives, in an effort to befriend the Spaniards and anxious to make them stay put, offered to give each member of the expedition their daughters as wives. The offer, too good to refuse, persuaded Martínez to found a city, "primarily for family reasons," as the Jesuit graciously put it.[66] Otherwise, Asunción's foundation went by the book. As related by its first historian, Ruy Diaz de Guzmán, Martínez founded Asunción "in the form of a Republic," which is to say that he ordered the creation of a municipal council. The council then elected its officials and decided which among the assembled soldiers were to become citizens or *vecinos* of the newly constituted community. Martínez, as the town's first elected governor, gathered the new *vecinos* at what was to be Asunción's main square, designated the site of its church, laid out the plan of its streets, and parceled out individual plots of land among those assembled.[67] Next, in the shadow of the pillory (*picota*), the newly erected symbol of royal justice and an essential component of *policía*, Martínez began what Guzmán defined as a lengthy harangue in which he exhorted the town's new citizens to "understand the things of our Holy Faith and good *policía*, such as obedience to the King Our Lord, to whom we all owe our loyalty."[68]

The story of Asunción's foundation is important for several reasons. Although the selection of its site was perhaps more serendipitous than most, it exemplifies the process through which the Spanish took possession of much of the American landmass. In addition, and this is crucial to this essay's argument, it suggests that Medina's spiritual walls required not just a town in the physical sense of the term, that is, an *urbs*, but also, and more importantly, a *civitas* or community of

[66] The story of Asunción's foundation is mentioned by Richard M. Morse, "The Urban Development of Colonial Latin America," *Cambridge History of Latin America* (Cambridge, 1984), 2:76. For the original version, which states that the foundation of Asunción was "*mas por via de cuñadasgo, que de conquista*," see "Informe de um jesuita anonimo sobre as cidades do Paraguai e do Guairá espanhóis, indios e mestiços (Dezembro, 1620)," in *Jesuítas e bandeirantes no Guairá (1549–1640)*, ed. Jaime Cortesaõ (Rio de Janeiro, 1951), 163.

[67] This ceremony, which began with the *traza* or design of the new plaza and the location of the church, resembled Roman foundation rituals to the extent that Romulus, founding Rome, began by indicating the site of the *comitium*, meeting place of the *cives* and site of the *mundus*, gateway to the nether world. At this point, however, the Spanish ritual separated itself from the Roman by failing to trace with a plow the outline of the city's future walls, as Romulus did. For the Roman rite, see the life of Romulus in Plutarch, *Lives*, trans. Arthur H. Clough (Chicago, 1952), 19, and Joseph Rykwert, *The Idea of a Town* (Princeton, 1976), 59, 64, 124.

[68] Ruy Diaz de Guzmán, *La Argentina* (1612), ed. Enrique de Gandia (Madrid, 1986), 143.

citizens, organized into a republic, and therefore living in *policía*. Bernabé Cobo, a seventeenth-century Jesuit living in Lima, put it this way: "A town without law, justice, government, and good and just laws does not merit the name of a republic or polity."[69] Meanwhile, other New World authors emphasized the power and strategic value of citizens organized into towns. Francisco Antonio Fuentes y Guzmán, Guatemala's first historian, specifically noted in his *Recordación florida* (1690) that towns guaranteed the "security and constancy of kingdoms that are conquered."[70] José Oviedo y Baños, an early Venezuelan chronicler, was even more emphatic; by creating towns, he wrote, Spaniards not only established order but transformed what had been a "shapeless embryo" into a "formal political entity." This metamorphosis occurred, however, only after the captain in charge "divided up the *repartimientos* [plots of land], designated *ejidos* [common lands], assigned private lands, established archives, issued ordinances, [and] congregated Indians into towns...."[71]

SPIRITUAL WALLS: GRID DESIGN

This last point – the congregation of Indians into towns – will be addressed later in this essay, as it formed yet another block in Medina's spiritual walls. Before that, however, it is necessary to examine, albeit briefly, the particular kinds of cities to which *policía* gave rise. Of crucial importance here is what the Spanish monarchy referred to in the instructions given to Pedrarías Dávila in 1513 as an "ordered" city or town. By this date such a town was generally understood as one laid out according to a grid or checkerboard plan, that is, in symmetrical fashion with a series of straight streets emanating from a central plaza or square endowed with a church, a town hall, a prison, and the pillory – each representing a different yet essential component of *policía* itself.

Much has been written about the relationship between the Spanish grid plan and that of the Roman cities and military encampments, the bastide towns of southern France, and especially Santa Fé, the town

---

[69] Bernabé Cobo, *Fundación de Lima* (1639), part of his *Historia natural de las Indias*, ed. Biblioteca de Autores Españoles (Madrid, 1956), 2:292.

[70] *Recordación florida* (1690; ed. Guatemala, 1932), 1:128.

[71] José Oviedo y Baños, *Historia de la conquista y población de la provincia de Venezuela* (1723; Caracas, 1967), Libro vii, ch. ix, 261. The author referred here to the achievements of Captain Diego de Ossorio who, starting in 1592, began to establish order ["*poner forma*"] in the province of La Guaria.

Ferdinand and Isabella established in the *vega* of Granada prior to that city's conquest in January, 1492.[72] Scholars have also pointed to the connection between the grid design of Spanish cities and medieval conceptions of the ideal city (Augustine, Aquinas, Eiximenis) together with the cities envisioned by Alberti, Filarete, and other Renaissance writers.[73] Another school attributes the orderly design of the Spanish colonial town to the symmetrical layout of indigenous settlements such as a Cuzco or Tenochtitlan. For my purposes, however, the origins of the grid are less important than its function, which, for the Spaniards at least, helped give physical expression to the fundamental principles *policía* entailed.

An "ordered" town in the sixteenth century was necessarily a grid town, or one like Santo Domingo, the first to be laid out in this fashion, which at least attempted to adhere to the regularity and symmetry of such a design.[74] Grid plans were not always possible, especially in hilly or mountainous areas, yet a town laid out *por cordel*, through careful measurement, was clearly the ideal throughout the Americas. In fact, urban chroniclers of later eras were forever making excuses if their particular community possessed what was commonly referred to as *"desigualidades,"* or irregularities. With reference to Asunción, for example, Diaz de Guzmán felt obliged to explain that the city, although otherwise a fully constituted Republic, was not built with "equal squares and plots" but with "wide and narrow streets, that criss-cross each other, as in some villages in Castile."[75] Juan de Velasco, historian of Quito, also apologized for the *"desigualidades"* of his city, whereas Lima's historians, pointing proudly to the checkerboard design of their city's center, confessed that its peripheral areas were considerably less orderly but that this mattered little because

---

[72] The literature on this topic is abundant. Recent titles include Richard M. Morse, "Some characteristics of the Latin American Urban History," *American Historical Review* 67 (1962): 317–38; J.M. Houston, "The Foundation of Colonial Towns in Hispanic America," in *Urbanization and its Problems*, eds. R.P. Beckinsale and J.M. Houston (Oxford, 1968), 352–90; Ramón Gutiérrez, *Arquitectura y urbanismo en Iberoamérica* (Madrid, 1983); and *Historia urbana de Iberoamérica* (Madrid, 1987), Vol. l.

[73] Among other studies, see Gabriel Guarda, "Santo Tomás de Aquino y las fuentes del urbanismo indiano," *Boletín de la Academia Chilena de la Historia* 72 (1965): 5–29, and Richard M. Morse, "A Framework for Latin American Urban History," in *Urbanization in Latin America: Approaches and Issues*, ed. Jorge E. Hardoy (Garden City, NY, 1975), 57–108.

[74] On the early history of this and other grid towns in the Caribbean, see Erwin W. Palm, *Los monumentos arquitectonicos de La Española*, 2 vols. (Trujillo, República Dominicana, 1955). For the "ordered" town, see Allen R. Brewer-Carías, *La ciudad ordenada* (Madrid, 1997), which reprints many of the royal instructions pertinent to the foundation of towns in the Americas.

[75] Diaz de Guzmán, *La Argentina*, 143.

these sections of the city were inhabited primarily by natives and blacks.[76]

Implicit in these *apologiae* was the notion that *policía* and the grid plan were one. The order and symmetry of the grid seemingly offered settlers a measure of security in what was otherwise a natural environment only marginally subject to Spanish authority and control, and Philip II's regulations on town building in the Americas, although promulgated in 1573, or well after hundreds of towns had already been founded, underscored this principle by requiring all future towns to be laid out on a grid. Of particular interest is the ordinance ordering settlers not to permit any Indians to even approach their town (*"población"*) until "it is built, defended [*"puesta en defensa"*], and organized, so that when the Indians see the towns, it sparks their admiration, allows them to understand that the Spaniards living there are not transients but staying for good, and creates such respect that, rather than dare to attack the Spaniards, they will seek out their friendship."[77]

The language of this particular directive might have been a bit clearer, but it suggests that the Spaniards knew there was more to intimidating people than military prowess alone. Architecture could be equally intimidating, a concept clearly understood by the Spanish military governor in Florida, who, in 1580, reported that whitewashing houses made them appear "fortified to the Indians."[78] With respect, however, to the design of cities, the Spanish also attributed defensive capabilities to the grid plan, apparently interpreting the harmony and order implicit in such a design as a town's first line of defense against a possible attack by natives living in surrounding areas.

Illustrating this particular point are several of the *pinturas* or maps included in the *Relaciones geográficas*, the geographical reports for the Indies ordered by the monarchy starting in the 1570s. Only several dozen of these *pinturas* survive, among them the map of Texúpa (or Santiago Tejúpan, Oaxaca), in which the contrast between the town – rendered in European fashion as a perfect grid – and the surrounding

---

[76] For Quito, see Velasco, *Historia del reino de Quito*, 308. For Lima, Cobo, "Fundación de Lima," 306, where he admits to a certain "disorder" in the city's *arrabales*, which are composed primarily of "*ranchos viles de indios y gente de servicio.*"

[77] Antonio de León Pinelo, *Recopilación de las Indias*, ed. Ismael Sánchez Bella (Mexico, 1992), 3:2023. My translation of this ordinance is somewhat different from that in Dora P. Crouch, Daniel J. Garr, and Axel I. Mundigo, *Spanish City Planning in North America* (Cambridge, MA, 1982), 18.

[78] Cited in Verne E. Chatelain, *The Defenses of Spanish Florida, 1565 to 1763* (Washington, DC, 1941), 129.

hills, done in the more florid and colorful style of indigenous artists – is particularly sharp. In this instance, the town, represented as a grid, constituted an emblem of the *policía* the Spaniards introduced into a region that was still largely beyond their jurisdiction and control[79] (Fig. 5.4).

SPIRITUAL WALLS: RELIGIOUS HOUSES AND *REDUCCIONES*

If *policía*, epitomized by a town constituted as a republic, planned according to a grid (and, just possibly, whitewashed as well), contained the essential components of a town's spiritual defenses, religion was even greater importance. Friars such as Medina naturally placed their trust in religion, and we have seen how he regarded Saints Casiano and Hipólito as Mexico City's first line of defense. Yet many other urban dwellers in the Americas also depended upon spiritual walls, relying on them to protect them from what they perceived as their principal enemy: the diabolical beliefs of the natives.

Essential to the defeat of this particular foe was the *convento*, or religious house, the sole institution with the power – the spiritual power, that is – to crush native religion and to spearhead the spread of Christianity. The mendicants, of course, were the principal exponents of this position, but as the quotation of Viceroy Mendoza cited earlier in this essay suggests, secular officials were also quite prepared to entrust their defense to convents rather than bastions of the traditional sort. "Religious convents," wrote the newly created *audiencia* of New Spain, "are . . . the citadels, the walls, and the castles of this kingdom."[80] This attitude may also explain why, starting in the 1530s, both the Franciscans and the Dominicans strategically situated their religious houses adjacent to the main roads leading to Mexico City. These *casas de camino* evidently served many of the same functions as blockhouses and presidios that Spaniards, starting in the 1560s, erected – but soon abandoned – to protect the Mexico City-Zacatecas road from the rebellious Chichimecs.

Another key feature of the Spaniards' spiritual walls was the policy

---

[79] For more on this map, see Joyce Waddell Bailey, "Map of Texúpa (Oaxaca, 1579): A Study of Form and Meaning," *Art Bulletin* 54 (1972): 452–79. Somewhat similar are the *pinturas* of Chicoloapa (Mexico, 1579), the present Chicoloapan de Juarez (Mexico, 1579), and Teutenango (Mexico, 1582), the present Tenango de Arista. For more on these and other maps from the *Relaciones Geográficas*, see Barbara J. Mundy, *The Mapping of New Spain* (Chicago, 1996).

[80] Cited in Kubler, *Mexican Architecture*, 1:81.

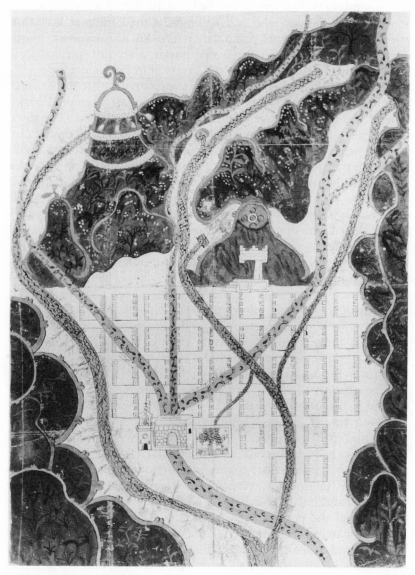

Figure 5.4. Map of Texúpa (Oaxaca). 1579. Real Academia de la Historia, Madrid. The town in this map, as in many other maps of New Spain, is represented as a grid in keeping with Spanish notions of the "ordered" city.

of surrounding their towns with a buffer zone dotted with settlements populated by natives who had embraced Christianity, at least outwardly. These settlements, commonly referred to as *reducciones*, constituted a town's outward defensive perimeter, a kind of spiritual Dew Line guarding against idolatries still rampant in the countryside.

In this context it is perhaps worth remembering that the town in Spanish America was far more than an instrument of empire, a convenient means of exercising jurisdiction over new land. The town served also as an instrument of indoctrination, the mechanism through which America's natives were to be converted and acculturated to the Spanish way of life. Starting in Hispaniola, missionaries recognized that native religious beliefs would be impossible to eradicate if the native population lived scattered in small, inaccessible hamlets. Christianization required urbanization. Such was the policy Queen Isabella announced to Ovando, the island's governor, in 1501 and subsequently promulgated in the Laws of Burgos (1512–13), which specifically ordered that all chiefs and Indians "shall be brought from their present dwelling places to the villages and communities of Spaniards who reside ... on the said island [of Hispaniola]."[81]

So began a policy of obligatory resettlement that the Habsburg monarchy, with encouragement from the missionaries, gradually implemented throughout its American empire. In 1521, Charles V ordered his officers in Castilla del Oro (Panama) to make certain that the natives lived "in towns and just like Spanish Christians in order that they may be saved."[82] In 1530, the monarch extended the policy to New Spain so that the natives of that region could "begin to understand our way of life, both in matters of governance as in *policía* and public life." Mexican church officials thought along similar lines: "if Indians are truly to become Christians and civilized [*políticos*] like rational men, it is necessary to congregate and organize them in towns and prohibit them from living scattered about and dispersed in the mountains and hills." There, it was said, "they lived more like beasts than rational and political men."[83]

The monarchy pursued a similar policy of urban resettlement in Peru. A royal order of 9 October 1549 instructed local magistrates to cooperate with church officials in order "to reduce, little by little, the Indians into towns" with the hope of teaching them "*policía humana*"

---

[81] *The Laws of Burgos of 1512–13*, ed. and trans. Lesley Bird Simpson (San Francisco, 1960), law II, 16.
[82] Cited in Pedro Borges, *Métodos misionales en la cristianización de América, siglo xvi* (Madrid, 1960), 213. *Cédula* dated Burgos, 6 September 1521.
[83] Borges, *Métodos*, 217–18.

and making them Christians. A few such Indian communities, often referred to as *"repúblicas,"* were established on the outskirts of both Quito and Popayán, and by 1570 Spanish officials in those cities reported that the Indians living there "have begun to become civilized [*ser políticos*]." Yet they hastened to remark that most of the region's Indians continued to live *"alárabe,"*[84] a situation which prompted Viceroy Francisco de Toledo to begin a "general reduction" of the natives starting in 1571. Toledo was influenced by Juan de Matienzo's *Gobierno del Peru* (1567), a set of instructions written expressly for his benefit and one in which Matienzo, a strong proponent of "reductions," advocated that "they [the Indians] can neither be instructed in the faith nor can they become men if they are not gathered into towns"[85] (Fig. 5.5). Toledo announced his own intentions in a letter of 1572: "the reduction of the Indians to villages and parishes makes them easier to manage, to be governed, and given religious instruction."[86] He subsequently forced thousands of Indians to regroup in towns situated on the outskirts of others already inhabited by Spaniards. In the region of Huarochirí, as Karen Spalding has shown, Toledo's "reduction" concentrated Indians who formerly lived in 121 hamlets into eleven new towns, each with a population of approximately 200–250 households. Matienzo had earlier provided the viceroy with a sketch of how these communities might be constructed, and it seems that most were laid out accordingly. The plan itself called for a village laid out as a grid and centered around a plaza containing a church, a municipal council, and a prison. Natives brought to the *reducciones* were also required to abandon their traditional dwellings – which tended to be round – for squared houses of Spanish design.[87]

For a time, Spanish officials in charge of these new settlements reported success. Over the long run, however, *reducciones* rarely managed to retain population on a permanent basis. Natives assigned to these communities tended to drift away, often in the hope of returning to their old hamlets and former way of life. "They are friends of their

---

[84] *Relaciones histórico-geográficos de la audiencia de Quito*, ed. Pilar Ponce Leiva (Madrid, 1991), 1:30, 72, 87.

[85] Juan de Matienzo, *Gobierno de Peru*, ed. Guillermo Lohmann Villena (Paris/Lima, 1967), 48.

[86] Cited in Karen Spalding, *Huarochirí. An Andean Society under the Inca and Spanish Rule* (Stanford, 1984), 214.

[87] Note that in New Granada, several *reducciones*, though described by one official as having *"calles formadas al uso de los españoles,"* tended to be elongated rather than square. Houses were aligned in perfect order along a central street at the end of which, overlooking the entire community, was the parish church. See Aprile-Gniset, *La ciudad columbina*, 242–3.

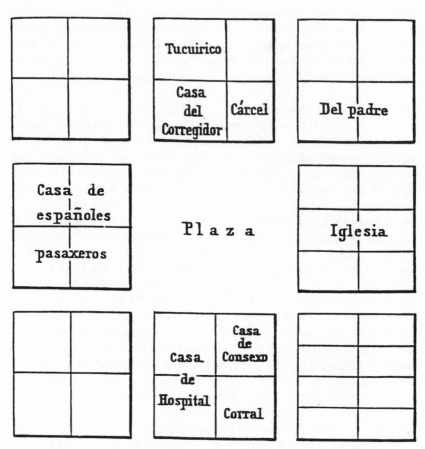

Figure 5.5. Juan de Matienzo. Plan of a Reducción. 1567. In order to help instill notions of *policía* among the indigenous population of Peru, Matienzo envisioned them living in "ordered" villages planned in accordance with this design.

lands," one disgruntled Spanish official was forced to admit.[88] Despite such slippage, Toledo firmly established the principle of the general "reduction" of the indigenous population into "ordered" towns, a policy subsequently adopted by the Jesuits in their mission settlements along the Paraná River as well as by Spanish officials in other parts of

[88] *Relaciones históricas de Quito,* 1:37.

the Americas.[89] In most cases, however, *reducciones* met only with very limited success.[90]

Notwithstanding these failures, Isabella's original policy of promoting *policía* among the natives by means of forced urbanization represented an important component in the spiritual wall Spaniards used to protect their own communities. The Franciscan missionary town at Acámbaro (Michoacán) in New Spain developed with a perimeter of outlying Indian villages meant to provide the pueblo not only with a ready source of labor, but also with a modicum of protection against native raids. Much the same can be said of the town of Huexutla (today's Huejutla de Reyes, Hidalgo) (Fig. 5.6). Lacking walls, this community deployed a spiritual bulwark in the form of a ring of nine villages, each populated by Christianized natives living in *policía*. Further north, in the area around Zacatecas, where the Chichimecs remained a serious threat until the 1580s, *reducciones* served a similar defensive purpose, supplemented by a string of *presidios* and other towns populated mainly by soldiers. It is worth noting, however, that peace with the Chichimecs was not fully achieved until the marquis de Villamanrique, starting in 1585, initiated a policy of peaceful coexistence that led to the removal of soldiers ("lazy, licentious people" in his words) and their replacement by officials who, in addition to teaching the natives to plough and to cultivate, were instructed to treat them kindly, and provide them with food and clothes. Five years into this program, Villamanrique could confidently report that commerce and population in the region were growing whereas the Chichimecs were "adapting to culture and the 'political' life."[91]

[89] For the design of the Jesuit *reducciones*, see Hernán Busaniche, *La arquitectura en las misiones jesuíticas guaraníes* (Santa Fe, Argentina, 1955). Also of interest are the views of the *reducción* of San Javier in the mid-eighteenth century by the Austrian Jesuit Florian Baucke (or Paucke). See Florian Paucke, *Hacia allá y para acá*, trans. Edmundo Wernicke, 4 vols. (Tucuman-Buenos Aires, 1942), and Florian Baucke, *Iconografía colonial rioplatense 1749–1767*, ed. Guillermo Furlong (Buenos Aires, 1935).

[90] An early critic of the policy of *reducciones* was Fray Agustín Dávila Padilla, a sixteenth-century Mexican-born Dominican who warned that these new settlements made the natives more susceptible to plague and other diseases. See his *Historia de la fundación y discurso de la provincia de Santiago de Mexico de la orden de predicadores* (Madrid, 1596), 125.

[91] "Advertimientos generales que el marqués de Villamanrique dió a Luis de Velasco, 14 Feb. 1590," in *Los virreyes españoles en América durante el gobierno de la casa de Austria*, ed. Lewis Hanke, *Biblioteca de autores españoles* (Madrid, 1976), 259–76. In the 1530s, Juan de Zummáraga, the first archbishop of México, had recommended policies similar to those later instituted by Villamanrique, but the Council of the Indies had rejected them, recommending instead a "war of fire and blood." See Alonso de Zorita, *Life and Labor in Ancient Mexico*, trans. Benjamen Keene (New Brunswick, 1963), 50.

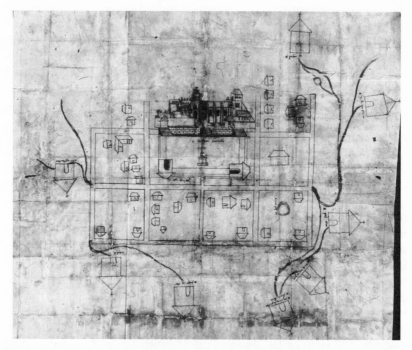

Figure 5.6. Map of Heuxutla (México). 1580. Archivo General de las Indias, Seville. Inhabited by Christianized natives, the *reducciones* surrounding this Mexican town constitute a kind of "spiritual" wall that offers protection from the idolatries that Spaniards associated with Indians living outside the municipal orbit.

SPIRITUAL WALLS: MADONNAS AND SAINTS

Faith in the fundamental tenets of Roman Catholicism formed the last but probably the most important component of America's spiritual walls. As Medina suggested, Mexico City's defense consisted primarily of the protection afforded by its two *patrones*, Casiano and Hipólito. Other towns invoked other saints, creating a complex religious patchwork modeled on the type of "local religion" that William A. Christian, Jr. has described for sixteenth-century Castile.[92] This meant that individual towns appropriated particular manifestations of Jesus and identified with particular saints, integrating them into the fabric of the community through the use of votive paintings, processions, and

---

[92] William A. Christian, Jr., *Local Religion in Sixteenth-Century Castile* (Princeton, 1981).

prayers, both individual and collective. In turn, these *patrones* and *patronas* rewarded the faithful by serving as their *defensores*, offering them divine guidance together with protection against disaster, both natural and man-made.

Worship of the Virgin proceeded along similar lines with the appearance of a series of local madonnas starting with that of Our Lady of Guadalupe, in 1531, on the hill of Tepeyac, above Mexico City.[93] Over time a handful of these virgins, notably Guadalupe, who was declared patroness of the "Mexican nation" in 1734, and Our Lady of Copacabana, who attracted wide appeal throughout the Andes, gained a broad regional following, but for the most part worship of these madonnas remained localized. Many, as in the case of Our Lady of the Candelaria at Cayma, Our Lady of Cocharcas (Fig. 5.7), Our Lady of Quinche, or Our Lady of Gúapulo – all in the Andes – were associated with particular communities and the object of local pilgrimages. *Cuzqueños* therefore invoked Our Lady of Mercy to save their city from further destruction during the great earthquake of 1649, just as *quiteños* relied upon the nearby Our Lady of Gúapulo to rescue them from duress, while residents of Arequipa, seeking protection from the volcanic eruptions of El Misti, paraded the figure of Our Lady of Cayma through their city's streets.

As in medieval Europe, moreover, where the regular procession of holy images through the streets of a town was designed to strengthen a community's particular relationship with the divine, in the towns and cities of Spanish America public worship centering upon the Christian cult was specifically intended, albeit with varying degrees of success, as a substitute for indigenous religious practices and beliefs. In this respect the open-air churches of sixteenth-century Mexico, designed to bring thousands of worshipers together in chapels strategically situated on former temple sites, constituted important components in a city's spiritual armor.[94] Public rogations involving thousands of converted natives of the kind Mendieta described in sixteenth-century Mexico and Tlaxcala played a similar defensive and possibly purgative role.[95] So did the great procession organized by church authorities on the festival of Corpus Christi in Cuzco. Al-

---

[93] For the history of this Virgin, see Stafford Poole, *Our Lady of Guadalupe. The Origins and Sources of a Mexican National Symbol, 1531–1797* (Tuscon, 1995).

[94] See the perceptive comments on the role of these open chapels in James Lockhart, *The Nahuas after the Conquest* (Stanford, 1992), 419–20. The best comprehensive architectural accounts of these chapels is John McAndrew, *The Open-Air Churches of Sixteenth Century Mexico* (Cambridge, MA, 1964).

[95] Mendieta, *Historia eclesiástica indiana*, 2:53–4.

Figure 5.7. Anonymous. *Our Lady of Cocharcas*. Early 18th century. Brooklyn Museum. Local incarnations of the Virgin Mary, like this in central Peru, formed an important part of the spiritual defenses of many New World towns.

though it is undoubtedly true that natives initially encrusted this celebration with beliefs and rituals drawn from the pre-Hispanic harvest festival of Intip Raimi which it was intended to replace, by the seventeenth century this and similar religious processions were becoming more Christian, and were interpreted, even on the part of native worshipers, in terms of the power and protection that Christianity bestowed.[96] Not surprisingly, this era also marks the appearance of the first New World saints, especially Santa Rosa de Santa María (canonized 1671), whose cult was initially tied to Lima, the city in which she was born.[97]

It is difficult, if not impossible, to measure the efficacy of this type of spiritual defense, let alone the extent to which spiritual walls substituted for those of a more durable sort. Nevertheless, it appears that towns relied heavily on spiritual walls so long as they considered the idolatrous beliefs of the natives a major threat. Echoing Isaiah, urban chroniclers regularly boasted about the piety of the local citizenry, and in 1690 Agustín de Vetancourt, calculating the amount of money Mexico City spent on votive candles, fixed that it was by far the most pious city in Christendom.[98] Such exaggerated remarks were obviously intended to flatter a local readership, but it is undoubtedly true – although I lack the statistics to prove it – that Mexico City in the seventeenth century invested a greater proportion of its resources in spiritual walls than material ones. Other Spanish American cities did likewise, evidently confident that the piety of their citizens would offer them the protection necessary to keep idolatry at bay.

What this brief survey of Spanish New World fortification in the sixteenth and early seventeenth centuries suggests is that the occasional corsair raid did not justify the time and expense the construction of stone walls and imposing fortresses required. With the exception of Chile, the threat of Indian uprisings was sufficiently remote that it could easily be dealt with by the kind of spiritual walls Viceroy Mendoza originally envisioned and this essay has attempted to describe. In the Andes, the Tupac Amaru uprising of the 1780s helped to change this utopian way of thinking, and along with it the intellectual

---

[96] An interesting interpretation of this festival may be found in Sabine MacCormack, *Religion in the Andes: Vision and Imagination in Early Colonial Peru* (Princeton, 1991), 420–1.

[97] Santa Rosa was Isabel Flores de Lima (1584–1617), a *beata* who in 1607 joined the Third Order of the Dominicans. For her cult and its spread, see Brading, *First America*, 337–9.

[98] Agustín de Vetancourt, *Grandeza mexicana* (1697; ed. Madrid, 1960), 193.

ordering of Spanish America experienced a fundamental change. Previously, however, Alonso de Ovalle, a Jesuit active in seventeenth-
century Chile, was essentially correct when, in a comment about New
World towns, he observed that Spaniards were like Solomon, "who
began building the temple and house of God even before he built his
own palace." In this context it is telling – but not surprising – that
Ovalle's description of the region made no mention of city walls.[99]

[99] Alonso de Ovalle, *Histórica relación del reyno de Chile* (Roma, 1646; rprt ed., Santiago
de Compostela, 1969), 175. The translation is from *An Historical Account of the Kingdom
of Chile* (1649), in John Pinkerton, *A General Collection of Voyages and Travels* (London,
1813), 14:171. Although Ovalle did not mention any walls, he did admit that Pedro
de Valdivia, shortly after founding the city of Santiago de Chile in 1541, "constructed
a fort in the city for the protection and defense of its citizens." It is curious that this
fort, supposing that it still existed in the seventeenth century, did not figure in the
"Plan and Prospective" of Santiago that Ovalle published in his book. On the other
hand, Ovalle carefully pinpointed the location of each of the city's churches and
monasteries, referring to these temples as "the principal part of a Christian republic."

PART II

Walls of War

CHAPTER 6

The fortifications of Epaminondas and the rise of the monumental Greek city

FREDERICK A. COOPER

IN a short essay written a decade ago, I proposed a fundamental revision to the history of Greek fortifications by stating: "the Theban general Epaminondas created the first enceinte of massive and cut-stone blocks, the genre which soon became epidemic throughout the Greek world."[1] Until the time of my essay, this extraordinary program of fortification built under Theban military purview in Central Greece and the Peloponnesos had been mentioned in passing by several

In memoriam Charles Edwards. A small troupe, Charles Edwards, Jane Carter, Georgia Cooper, and myself, investigated West Boiotian coastal forts in the summer of 1985. These awesome sites and beaches are all but inaccessible, but the long treks went quickly and more profitably, as always, because of the companionship and insights of Charles.

List of Abbreviations

AJA	*American Journal of Archaeology*
AthMitt	*Mitteilungen des Deutschen Archäologischen Instituts, Athenischen Abteilung*
BSA	*The Annual of the British School at Athens*
CAH	*Cambridge Ancient History*, eds. D.M. Lewis, J. Boardman, S. Hornblower, and M. Ostwald, 2nd. ed., Vol. 6 (Oxford, 1994)
FGrHist	F. Jacoby, *Die Fragmente der griechischen Historiker* (Berlin and Leiden, 1923–58)
IG	*Inscriptiones Graecae*
RE	Pauly-Wissowa, *Real-Encyclopädie der classischen Altertumswissenschaft*
SEG	*Supplementum Epigraphicum Graecum*
Syll.[3]	W. Dittenberger, *Sylloge inscriptionum graecarum*, 3rd ed. (Leipzig, 1915–24)
Tod	M.N. Tod, *A Selection of Greek Historical Inscriptions*, Vol. 2, *From 403–323 B.C.* (Oxford, 1948)

[1] That is to say, blocks laid in isodomic (regular coursed) ashlar or isodomic trapezoidal stone construction from wall socle to parapet or battlement. R. Ginouvrè and R. Martin, *Dictionaire méthodique de l'architecture grecque et romaine*, I (Rome, 1985), s.v. "*appareil rectangulaire isodomic*," 97–9. Frederick A. Cooper, "Epaminondas and Greek Fortifications," *AJA* 90 (1986): 195.

scholars, but had never been the subject of study.[2] Rather, scholarship on the topic relied on a number of suppositions. Some were basic to the course of scholarship on Greek fortifications, while others were linchpins to one or another history of classical Greece. For instance, a major handbook, *Greek Aims in Fortifications*, by A.W. Lawrence, describes the underlying method of interpretation on this subject.[3]

One widely held assumption has been that, over the centuries from the Geometric (eighth century B.C.E.) through the Hellenistic periods (first century B.C.E.), political entities had coherent, stratigraphic policies that led to the planning and construction of fortification walls.[4] I never found this to be the case: Most Greek cities did not begin with fortifications. Rather, rural defenses developed haphazardly as need arose over generations, and these show no similarity of practice.[5] In other words, Greek fortifications were built without an overall plan with the important historical exception of the Boiotian contribution.[6] This exception deserves to be specified: a set of fortifications built between ca. 370 B.C.E. and 338 B.C.E. in Boiotia and Arkadia, and particularly at the new foundation city of Messene (Figs. 6.1 to 6.3). Boiotians built these enceintes under the generalship of Epaminondas and they were an essential ingredient behind his military policies and a crucial component of the Theban hegemony. As early as 394/5 B.C.E., Boiotian craftsmen were in the employ of Athens and their last masterpiece dates to shortly before 338 B.C.E. This essay clarifies my position and amplifies the point that Boiotians had become supreme when it came to the craft of fortification construction through most of the fourth century B.C.E.[7]

Josiah Ober offered a rebuttal to my original essay.[8] In contesting

---

[2] Jean-Pierre Adam, *L'Architecture militaire grecque* (Paris, 1982), 15 n. 7: "*Sur ce vaste programme il n'existe pas encore d'étude spécifique exclusivement consacrée à l'architecture militaire engendrée par les conquêtes thébaines.*"

[3] A.W. Lawrence, *Greek Aims in Fortifications* (Oxford, 1979).

[4] For instance, Josiah Ober, *Fortress Attica: Defense of the Athenian Land Frontier, 404–322 B.C.*, Mnemosyne Supplement 84 (Leiden, 1985), ch. 2: "Methods of Waging War."

[5] A. Wasowica, "Le système de défense des cités grecques sur les côtes septentrionales de la Mer Noire," in *La fortification dans l'histoire du monde grec*, eds. P. Leriche and H. Tréziny (Paris, 1986), 93, and A. Snodgrass, "The Historical Significance of Fortification in Arachic Greece," in *La fortification*, 128.

[6] Frederick Winter, "A Summary of Recent Work on Greek Fortifications in Greece and Asia Minor," in *La fortification*, 26–8.

[7] H.M. Hack, "The Rise of Thebes: A Study of Theban Politics and Diplomacy, 386–371 B.C." (Ph. D. diss., Yale University, 1975), 167: "The sources . . . show the same confusion in regard to the terms 'Thebes' and 'Boeotia' after 379 as they did before 386 (Diod., 15.32.2; 51.4; 55.3; 71.2; 16.7.2; Xenophon *Hellenika* 5.4.62). It is clear, however, that whichever name the sources use, the policy enunciated at any time was Theban."

[8] J. Ober, "Early Artillery Towers: Messenia, Boiotia, Attica, Megrid," *AJA* 91 (1987): 601–3.

my position, Ober used a line of argument braced by the very approach to Greek military history and the topography of Attica that I had called into question. An impressive border fort, popularly known as Gyphtokastro, lies on or close to the ancient border between Boiotia and Attica (Figs. 6.4, 6.5, 6.15). A name for the Attic deme site, and thus of this fort, has always been troublesome, usually divided in scholarly opinion between Eleutherai or Panakton.[9] By any name, Gyphtokastro is held by Ober to be Athenian built. I agree with Ober and those other scholars who accept Gyphtokastro as Eleutherai, but the identification is incidental to my contention that the fortress at the mouth of the Kaza Pass on the principal route from central Boiotia and Thebes to Athens was a Theban garrison.[10]

Early observations led me to believe that fifth-century Athenian forts consisted of rubble and mud construction and this conclusion made sense when I first realized that the imposing enceinte at the Attic-Boiotian border, Gyphtokastro, is neither fifth century B.C.E. in date nor Athenian.[11] Because Ober was unable to elicit from the historical record evidence that Gyphtokastro was Boiotian for any length of time, let alone for the period in question (the second quarter of the fourth century B.C.E.), he disallows it as a Boiotian construction and makes it Athenian.

In a separate essay, Ober published pottery scatters from a selection of Attic border forts and used this evidence to further support a Gyphtokastro of Athenian origin.[12] Ober also adopts a hypothetical strategy, "it is always preferable to build the fortress on one's own side of the pass. . . ." This not being the case for Gyphtokastro, he ruled against a Theban stronghold and returned to the long-standing assumption.[13]

An equally impressive fortification at Aigosthena (modern-day Porto Germeno) commands the head of a long inlet off the Bay of

---

⁹ Recent adherents of Gyphtokastro = Panakton: Lawrence, *Greek Aims*, 174; Adam, *L'Architecture militaire*, 217; Yvan Garlan, *Recherches de poliorcétique grecque; Bibilothèque des écoles francaises d'Athènes et de Rome* 223 (Paris, 1974), 8 n. 5. For identification of Gyphtokastro as Eleutherai, see M.H. Munn, *The Defense of Attica. The Dema Wall and the Boiotian War of 378–375 B.C.* (Berkeley, 1993), 9 n. 15.

¹⁰ Today a highway traverses this corridor; see C. Edmondson, "KOITH AKTAIONOS," *Journal of Hellenic Studies* 89 (1969): 153–5, fig. 1. Munn, *The Defense of Attica*, 16–21, reviews scholarship on the military defense of passes: no discernible rule is followed.

¹¹ Followed by John Camp, "Notes on the Towers and Borders of Classical Boiotia," *AJA* 95 (1991): 199; Munn *The Defense of Attica*, 8 n. 12.

¹² J. Ober, "Pottery and Miscellaneous Artifacts from Fortified Sites in Northern and Northwestern Attica," *Hesperia* 56 (1987): 215–20.

¹³ I concur with Munn's observation: "there is no hint that forts along the border prevented or even delayed the arrival of the invaders outside the walls of Athens." Munn, *The Defense of Attica*, 21.

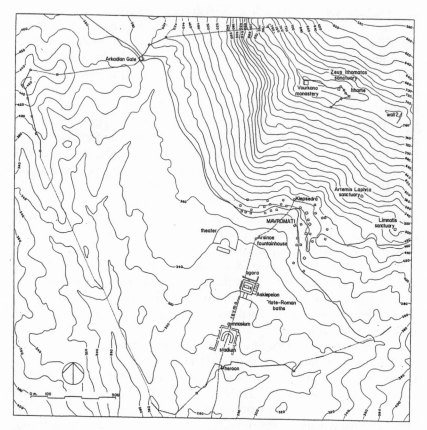

Figure 6.1. Messene, plan of site and walls. Drawing by Pieter Broucke.

Corinth (Fig. 6.6). By geographical position it is situated somewhere near the border between Megarian and Boiotian territories and approximately fifteen kilometers west of Gyphtokastro, putting it approximately the same distance from the border of Attica.[14] A difficult and narrow coastal route connected Aigosthena with Boiotian Kreusis (Fig. 6.12) and Siphai (Figs. 6.10 and 6.11) to the northwest. Since it was the single access from the south, Kleombrotos took this route in

---

[14] E. Vanderpool, "Roads and Forts in Northwestern Attica," *California Studies in Classical Antiquity* 11 (Berkeley, 1978): 227–45; map in S. Van de Maele, "Le réseau mégarien de défense territoriale contre l'Attique à l'époque classique (Vᵉ et IVᵉ s. av. J.-C.)," in *Fortificationes antiquae*, eds. S. Van de Maele and J.M. Fossey, *Monographes en archéologie et histoire classiques de l'Université McGill* 12 (Amsterdam, 1993), 96, fig. 5.2.

Figure 6.2. Messene, view of Arkadian Gate and Tower L. Drawing by Miry Park.

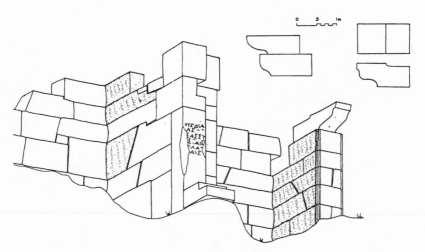

Figure 6.3. Gyphtokastro, Portal B. Drawing by Joanne Mannell.

Figure 6.4. Gyphtokastro, view of N wall from N. Photo: F. Cooper.

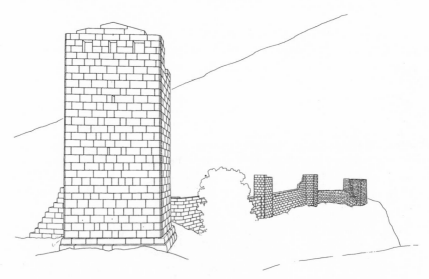

Figure 6.5. Aigosthena, E wall from SE. Drawing by Pieter Broucke.

Figure 6.6. Boudoron, walls. Photo: F. Cooper.

371 B.C.E. on his way to the Spartan disaster at Leuktra.[15] The site also controls the entire coastal plain (Mallia Psatha) and the natural border formed by the promontory of Mount Mytikas at the south and west.[16]

At the time of the Battle of Leuktra, Aigosthena was a *hora* of Megara and a Megarian decree of 306 B.C.E. honored an officer under the command of Demetrius Poliorcetes placed at Aigosthena.[17] Hence, in 306 B.C.E., too, Aigosthena was clearly a *hora* of Megara, and the fort was already in place. Yet, there are no historical reasons against Aigosthena being part of the Boiotian hegemony of the fourth century

[15] Xen., *Hell.* 5.4.17–18; 6.4.25–6. Hack, *The Rise of Thebes*, 154 n. 31; W.K. Pritchett, "The Battle of Leuktra," in *Studies in Ancient Greek Topography I*; University of California Publications, Classical Studies 1 (Berkeley and Los Angeles, 1980), 57, fig. 4; J. Buckler, *The Theban Hegemony* (Cambridge, MA, 1980), 48–66; V.D. Hanson, "Epameinondas, the Battle of Leuktra (371 B.C.) and the 'Revolution' in Greek Battle Tactics," *ClasAnt* 7 (1988): 190–207; C.D. Hamilton, *Agesilaus and the Failure of Spartan Hegemony* (Ithaca, 1991), 202–3, 205 n. 87.

[16] L. Robert, "Hellenica," *Revue de Philologie*, series 3, 13 (1939): 116–17, pls. 7–9; Ober, *Fortress Attica*, 169 n. 85; and Ober, "Two Ancient Watchtowers Above Aigosthena in the Northern Megarid," *AJA* 87 (1983): 387. Van de Maele, "Le réseau mégarien de défense," 95–100, and n. 93. A regional survey by J. Bintliff and A. Snodgrass, "The Development of Settlement in South-West Boeotia," in *La Béotie antique*, Colloques internationaux du Centre National de la Recherche Scientifique (Paris, 1985), 49–70.

[17] Xen. *Hell.* 6.4.26; *Syll.*³ 331.

B.C.E. As Louis Robert points out, Aigosthena was only rarely under the jurisdiction of Megara; at times it was independent.[18] During the Hellenistic period, ca. 243–146 B.C.E., Aigosthena was a member of the Boiotian League.[19] Who built the fort at Aigosthena is another matter of dispute. Most scholars hold Aigosthena to be Athenian, while others claim it as a border fort of Megara, or even a Macedonian creation built at the end of the fourth century B.C.E. under Demetrius Poliorcetes.[20] In other words, when I voiced my contention that Gyphtokastro and Aigosthena are Theban forts, this stirred an already vexed problem in Athenian topography.[21]

My position in 1985 was tenable, but a persuasive presentation meant undoing years of accepted scholarship on the topography of Attica and Athenian military policies.[22] Then in 1991, John Camp

---

[18] Xen. *Hell.* 5.4.18; 6.4.26.

[19] Robert, "Hellenica," 118–22 n. 39. P. Roesch, *Thespies et la confédération béotienne* (Paris, 1965), 50, 68–71; Van de Maele, "Le réseau mégarien de défense," 99 n. 16, ascribes the decree to Demetrius II.

[20] Ober, "Early Artillery Towers," 603; Ober, *Fortress Attica,* 169 n. 85: "The circuit was built with Athenian help in ca. 343 B.C." Ober narrows the date from an earlier estimation of 350–275 B.C.; *Fortress Attica,* 169, 391 n. 83. L. Karlsson, *Fortification towers and masonry techniques in the Hegemony of Syracuse, 405–211 B.C.,* Acta Instituti Romani Regni Sueciae, series 4, 49 (Stockholm, 1992), 78, questions Ober's attribution: "I find it unlikely that the Athenians were responsible for the erection of Tower A at Aigosthena." A Theban construction is the far more likely, given their attested and admired wall construction until 338 B.C. (see below). For Megara, see N.G.L. Hammond, "The Main Road from Boeotia to the Peloponnese through the Northern Megarid," *Annual of the British School at Athens* 49 (1954): 110; R.P. Legon, *Megara* (Ithaca, 1981), 32–3; Van de Maele, "Le réseau mégarien de défense," 99–100. For a Macedonian attribution, see Lawrence, *Greek Aims,* 389 n. 79. Demetrius was a "sieger of cities," a master of siege craft. While there is no direct evidence that he built permanent fortifications, some scholars have attributed walls to him, e.g., Halos: R. Reinders, "Investigations at Halos and Zereleia, Preliminary Report, 1982," *Bulletin antieke beschaving* 58 (1983), 91–100.

[21] M.H. Munn, review of *Fortress Attica: Defense of the Athenian Land Frontier, 404–322 B.C.,* by J. Ober (Leiden, 1985), in *AJA* 90 (1986): 365, reviews the sources and concludes: "The Attica system is not as comprehensive as Ober claims."

[22] The following bibliography contains some of the repartee: J. Ober, review of *Greek Aims in Fortification* by A.W. Lawrence (Oxford, 1979) in *Classical Philology* 78 (1983): 56–61; M.H. Munn, review of *Fortress Attica,* 363–5; P. Harding, review article of *Fortress Attica,* in "Athenian Defensive Strategy in the Fourth Century," *Phoenix* 42 (1988): 61–71; J. Ober on Cooper's "Epaminondas and Greek Fortifications," 195; Ober, "Early Artillery Towers," 601–3; and "The Defense of the Athenian Land Frontier: A Reply," *Phoenix* 43 (1989): 294–301; M.H. Munn, "New Light on Panakton and the Attic-Boiotian Frontier," in *Boiotika, Vorträge vom 5, internationalen Böotien-Koloquium zu Ehren von Professor Dr. Siegfried Laauffer. Institut für Alte Geschichte, Ludwig-Maximilians-Universität München 13.-17. Juni 1986;* Münchener Arbeiten zur Alten Geschichte, Vol. 2, eds. H. Beister and J. Buckler (Munich, 1989), 231–44; Munn, "Studies on the Attica-Boiotian Frontier: The Stanford Skourta Plain Project, 1985," in *Monographs in Classical Archaeology and History 7;* Boeotia Antiqua 1 (Amsterdam, 1989), 73–127; and Munn, "On the Frontiers of Attica and Boiotia: The Results of the Stanford Skourta Plain Project," in *Essays in the Topography, History, and Culture of*

reopened these questions in a focused study of Attic and Boiotian border forts and towers. He wrote:

The identification of the forts at Oinoe and Gyphtokastro now seems clear, though Gyphtokastro needs further attention in view of the recent suggestion that the well-preserved fort might be of Boiotian construction, perhaps dated to the time of Epaminondas.[23] This goes against the views of almost all earlier commentators and has recently been challenged;[24] yet evidence from Gyphtokastro itself, as well as considerations of Oinoe and the Mazi tower, suggests that the idea has considerable merit.[25]

Camp also addressed the question of Gyphtokastro's political affiliation: "The ancient literary sources concerning Gyphtokastro indicate that at times it was Attican and at times Boiotian." Furthermore, he pointed to the high percentage of classical Boiotian *kantheroi* with one example inscribed in a Boiotian dialect. Camp correctly concluded that the archaeology of Gyphtokastro was Boiotian during the last classical period.[26]

Camp's essay, together with a series of studies on Boiotian forts and towers in the years since 1986, bolstered my position and very much streamlined the extensive argumentation for my proposition that the first massive fortification walls of ashlar masonry (squared stone) were developed and exploited under Epaminondas. In the most recent overview of the development of fortifications in the Greek world, Lars Karlsson introduces new evidence in support of Epaminondas's role. More precisely, the first true *emplekton* walls (ribbing between inner and outer curtains) in Greece occur in fortifications of three cities associated with Epaminondas: Megalopolis, Mantinea, and Messene (Figs. 6.1 to 6.3, 6.13, 6.14).[27]

A BRIEF HISTORY OF GREEK FORTIFICATIONS, ESPECIALLY IN ATTICA

The Greek settlement enclosed by a wall begins in the Neolithic period or late fourth millennium B.C.E. (e.g., Dimini).[28] Thereafter, the walled

---

Boiotia, *Teiresias* Supplement 3 (Montreal, 1990), 33–40; P. Harding, "Athenian Defensive Strategy Again," *Phoenix* 44 (1990): 377–80; and Ober, "Review of M. Munn, *The Defense of Attica*," in *AJA* 98 (1994), 374–5.

23 Cooper, "Epaminondas and Greek Fortifications," 195.

24 Ober, "Early Artillery Towers," 601–3.

25 Camp, "Notes on the Towers and Borders," 199.

26 Camp, "Notes on the Towers and Borders," 199.

27 Vitruvius 2.8.7: "... at intervals they lay single stones which run through the entire thickness of the wall." R. Tomlinson, "Emplekton Masonry," *Journal of Hellenic Studies* 81 (1961): 133–40. Karlsson, *Fortification Towers and Masonry Techniques*, 73.

28 G.H. Hourmousizidis, *To neolithiko Dimini* (Volos, 1979).

village or city continues as a common occurrence until modern times with Greek independence from Ottoman rule beginning in the 1820s. For the most part, when these enclosing walls occur, they are interpreted as fortifications or enceintes serving to protect the inhabitants from attack. Although examples of prehistoric and historic Greek enceintes are both numerous and varied, not all city walls are fortifications.

An interest in Greek fortifications began with the early European travelers through Greece (ca. 1800–ca. 1830s), such as Dodwell and Leake.[29] *The Expédition Scientifique de Moreé archéologique et topographique* published the first measured drawings of a selection of walls, as did William Gell.[30] In the past fifty years, the study of fortifications of the classical and Hellenistic periods (fifth through first centuries B.C.E.) has become a separate field of scholarship (distinct from prehistoric, Roman, and medieval)[31] and has received considerable attention in the form of monographs, articles, and published conference papers.[32] Publications devoted to this subject range from the authoritative overviews of Robert Scranton, Frederick Winter, Yvan Garlan, A. W. Lawrence, and Jean-Pierre Adam to several excellent regional studies focused on Attica.[33] Recent conferences and publications on the topography of Boiotia by John Fossey and others, and the topography of the Megarid by Arthur Muller and S. Van de Maele, help put into balance a view previously skewed towards Attica alone.[34]

---

[29] E. Dodwell, *A Classical and Topographical Tour through Greece during the Years 1801, 1805, 1806*, 2 vols. (London, 1819); W.M. Leake, *Travels in Northern Greece*, 3 vols. (London, 1835).

[30] A. Blouet, *The Expédition Scientifique de Moreé archéologique et topographique* (Paris, 1831–8). *Probestücke van stadtemauern des alten Griechenlands* (Berlin, 1831); cf. W. Gell, *The Itinerary of Greece: Containing One Hundred Routes in Attica, Boeotia, Phocis, Locris, and Thessaly* (London, 1819).

[31] S. Iakovidis, *Late Helladic Citadels on Mainland Greece* (Los Angeles, 1983).

[32] P. Leriche and H. Tréziny, eds., *La fortification*, with important review by A. McNicoll, "Colloque International sur les fortifications grecques," *RA* (1983): 347–52.

[33] Robert Scranton, *Greek Walls* (Cambridge, MA, 1941); F. Winter, *Greek Fortifications* (Toronto, 1971); Garlan, *Recherches de poliorcétique grecque*, and *Guerre et économie en Grece ancienne* (Paris, 1989); Lawrence, *Greek Aims*; Adam, *L'Architecture militaire*; W. Wrede, *Attische Mauern* (Athens, 1933); H. Mussche, "La fortresse maritime de Thorikos," *BCH* 85 (1961): 176–205, and "L'Architecture civile et militaire," in *Monumenta Graeca et Roma* (Leiden, 1963); J. McCredie, *Fortified Military Camps of Attica, Hesperia*, Supplement 11 (Princeton, 1966); M. Langdon, "Some Attic Walls," in *Studies in Attic Epigraphy, History and Topography Presented to Eugene Vanderpool; Hesperia*, Supplement 20 (Princeton, 1982); J. Pouilloux, *La fortresse de Rhamnonte*, in *Bibliothèque des Écoles Françaises d'Athènes et de Rome* 179 (Paris, 1954); Ober, *Fortress Attica*; H. Lauter, H. Lohmann, and H. Lauter-Bufe, *Attische Festungen: Beiträge zum Festungswesen und zur Siedlungsstruktur vom 5. bis zum 3. Jh. v. Chr.*, in *Attische Forschungen III*, Marburger Winkelmann-Programm (Marburg, 1989); Munn, *The Defense of Attica*.

[34] A. Muller, "Megarika," *BCH* 106 (1982): 379–407; Van de Maele, "Le réseau mégarien

Freestanding towers dot the landscapes of Attica, Boiotia, the Megarid and other regions of Greece, sometimes in proximity to barrier walls of one sort or another. Some scholars have interpreted the function of these military-looking constructions as agrarian, others claim it was martial.[35] Adherents of the latter view go further and describe these regional fortifications and freestanding towers as coherent and strategic fire-signal systems of communication.[36] Opinion differs more on the date of the implementation of a fire-signal system than on whether or not such a system ever existed.[37]

Archaeological investigations of specific sites provide an objective basis for a reassessment of the development and chronology of regional fortification designs and styles.[38] Maier's compilation of Greek inscriptions concerning the construction and repair of walls presents valuable evidence for an understanding of costs, techniques, and chronology.[39] Marsden looks at technological development of the catapult from the time of its invention in 399 B.C.E. and into the Roman period.[40] Overall size, plan, and configuration of embrasures of fortification towers built in the fourth century B.C.E. through the Hellenistic period can be seen as responses to advances made in the engineering power of the catapult (nontorsion to torsion, arrows to bolts to stone

de défense," bibliography, 107, and Camp, "Notes on the Towers and Borders," 193 n. 4.

[35] For a recent and brief review of the discussion, see H. Lohmann, "Agriculture and Country Life in Classical Attica," in *Agriculture and Country Life in Classical Attica,* ed. B. Wells, *Acta Instituti Atheniensis Regni Sueciae,* ser. 4, 42 (Stockholm, 1992), 29–60, esp. 39–42, and notes for bibliography.

[36] See particular essays in *Fortificationes antiquae.*

[37] Ober, "Early Artillery Towers," 568–604, and "The Defense of the Athenian Land Frontier," 294–301; Munn, *Defense of Attica,* 94–5. J. Fossey, "The Development of Some Defensive Networks in Eastern Central Greece During the Classical Period," in *Fortificationes antiquae,* 114–15, insists that the Rhakes Tower could not date to the late 370s because it lacks sightlines to other towers and forts.

[38] H. Kienast, *Die Stadtmauer von Samos,* in *Samos XV* (Berlin, 1978); R. Martin, "Les enceintes de Gortys d'Arcadie, *BCH* 71–2 (1947–8): 81–147; A. Von Gerkan, *Milet II 3: Die Stadtmauern* (Berlin, 1935); R. Carpenter, A. Parsons, and A. Bon, *Corinth II 2: The Defenses of Acrocorinth and the Lower Town* (Cambridge, MA, 1936); S.C. Bakhuizen, "Salganeus and the Fortifications on its Mountains," in *Studies of the Dutch Archaeological and Historical Society* (Groningen, 1970); A. Akarca, *Neandreia Kuzey ege' de Arkaik ve kasik caglara ait bir sehir* (modern Turkish) (Istanbul, 1977); W. Jobst, "Hellenistische Aussenfortifikationen um Ephesos," in *Studien zur Religion und Kultur Kleinasiens; Festschrift für F. Dörner* (Leiden, 1978); K. Krischen, *Milet III 2: Die Befestigungen von Herakleia am Latmos* (Berlin and Leipzig, 1922).

[39] F. Maier, *Griechische Mauerbauinschriften,* 2 vols. (Heidelberg, 1959–61).

[40] The engineers of Dionysos II of Syracuse invented the mechanism and deployed it first against Motya in 397 B.C.E. (Diod. 14.47–53). In 369 B.C.E. and again in 368 B.C.E., Dionysos II sent relief forces of 2,000 mercenaries and 50 cavalry to the Peloponnesos in aid of the Spartan cause (Xen. *Hell.* 7.1.20, 28; Diod. 15.70.1). D.M. Lewis, "Sicily, 413–368 B.C.," *CAH,* 120–3; J. Roy, "Thebes in the 360s B.C.," *CAH,* 192.

throwers).[41] The catapult provides a chronological fix beyond that of masonry style or even that of a synchronism between surviving sources and the physical survival of a fort.

Camp and Ober have compiled useful typologies of tower shapes, dimensions, fabrics, and apertures of extant Attican and Boiotian towers.[42] Going further afield, Anthony McNicoll considers posterns and the heights and thicknesses of curtain walls in Hellenistic Asia as a chronological indicator. The elegant and lofty "great circuit" at Herakleia is a prime example of the second-generation fortification. McNicoll finds that fortifications group not only into regional characteristics but also into distinct periods.[43] Recently, Lars Karlsson has added significantly to the field by his researches on the development of the *emplekton* technique in fortification design (Figs. 6.9d and 6.9e show tie-blocks, e.g., *emplekta*, at Sounion, set as headers through the faces of the outer curtains).[44]

Epaminondas has not been recognized as a major innovator in military architecture and engineering because of three misconceptions widely held by scholars writing on the subject: (1) that the character of masonry for city walls advanced alongside the development of temples and other civic architecture; (2) that styles of masonry indicate dates; (3) that Attic fortifications of the late fifth century already had taken monumental form in cut-ashlar stone blocks, bonded without mortar, thus following the impulse of contemporary architecture on the Athenian Akropolis.

WALLS OF ATTICA

While the Athenians developed ashlar masonry for their public buildings and monuments through the fifth century B.C.E., there is no reason to believe that they typically extended this form of construction to their forts in Attica. For example, the anti-Spartan walls built under Themistokles in 479/8 B.C.E. consisted of a broad, humble construction

---

[41] W. Marsden, *Greek and Roman Artillery: Historical Development*, 2 vols. (Oxford, 1969). Summary in Ober, *Fortress Attica*, 41–4, and A. McNicoll, "Developments in Techniques of Siegecraft and Fortifications in the Greek World ca. 400–100 B.C.," in *La fortification*, 305–13.

[42] Camp, "Notes on the Towers and Borders," 193–202; Ober, "Early Artillery Towers," 569–604, and Ober, "Towards a Typology of Greek Artillery Towers: The First and Second Generations (ca. 375–275 B.C.)," in *Fortificationes antiquae*, 147–69.

[43] A. McNicoll, "Some Developments in Hellenistic Siege Warfare with Special Reference to Asia Minor," in *Proceedings of the X International Congress on Classical Archaeology* I (Ankara, 1978), 405–19; McNicoll, "Developments in Techniques of Siegecraft," 308–9.

[44] Karlsson, *Fortification Towers and Masonry Techniques*, 21.

composed of rubble and earth on a stone socle. An apt description comes from Thucydides: "the foundations are made of different sorts of stone, sometimes not shaped so as to fit, but laid down just as each was brought up at the time; there are many stelai taken from tombs and fragments of sculpture mixed in with the rest."[45] A few stretches of the Themistoklian wall have been excavated and they are indeed built from rubble and reused sculpture.[46]

Fifty years later, rubble walls with earth fill continued as a norm for Athenian fortification construction. A naval outpost at Boudoron provides the necessary evidence.[47] Boudoron, the site of an event during the Peloponnesian War, occupies a ridge on Salamis overlooking Megara. Thucydides' description of the episode in 427 B.C.E. allows for no other location.[48] Today, the stretches of walls and towers of packed stone and rubble are eroded to low running mounds (Fig. 6.6). These walls have been rejected as fifth-century Attic simply because of their non-ashlar construction, but I argue that their form is typical of Athenian fifth-century fortifications.[49]

The site of Sounion furnishes another example of Athenian fortification construction that continues to the end of the fifth century. Thucydides states that the cape was fortified in 413–12 B.C.E. (Figs. 6.7 and 6.8).[50] The extant stretches of mixed construction can be clearly differentiated: some have a hurriedly built appearance, other sections have coursed ashlar, while still other stretches are in trapezoidal masonry.[51] Obviously different building periods are involved (Figs. 6.7 and 6.8). Nonetheless, the published studies assign the ashlar stonework to the date mentioned by Thucydides.[52] I contend that the heaped rubble walls that lie behind this ashlar construction, like those of the late fifth

---

[45] Thucydides 1.89.3; 1.93.2; trans. R. Warner, *Thucydides, The Peloponnesian War* (London, 1954).

[46] For major excavation reports, see I. Threpsiades, *Praktika* (1953): 61–71, and Threpsiades, *Deltion* 16 *Chronika* (1960): 22–7; G. Gruben, "Die Ausgrabungen im Kerameikos," *Archäologischer Anzeiger* (1964): 390–419, and a summary with bibliography in I. Travlos, *Pictorial Dictionary of Athens* (Tubingen and New York, 1971), 158, 162; also in S. Hornblower, *A Commentary on Thucydides* I (Oxford, 1991), 137–8. The fabric and finds from the Themistoklian wall deserve further study.

[47] W.E. McLeod, "The Walls of Boudoron," *Hesperia* 29 (1960): 316–23; McCredie, *Fortified Military Camps of Attica*, 32–3; Hornblower, *A Commentary on Thucydides*, 371.

[48] Thuc. 2.93–4.

[49] Lawrence, *Greek Aims*, 174.

[50] Thuc. 8.4.

[51] Review of bibliography in Karlsson, *Fortification Towers and Masonry Techniques*, nn. 73 and 96; 278–81, 406–15; Mussche, "L'Architecture civile et militaire," 35.

[52] Scranton, *Greek Walls*, 173, 180; Mussche, "L'Architecture civile et militaire," 35; H. Lauter, "Some Remarks on Fortified Settlements in the Attic Countryside," in *Fortificationes antiquae*, 78; Lauter, Lohmann, and Lauter-Bufe, *Attische Festungen*, 123–6.

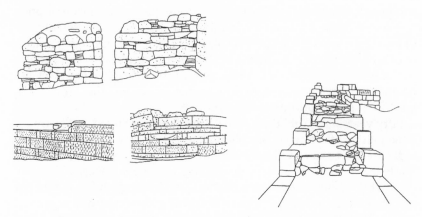

Figure 6.7. Sounion, masonry styles. Drawing by Miry Park.

Figure 6.8. Sounion, earlier rubble wall encased in later isodomic construction. Photo: F. Cooper

century at Boudoron, were laid out in 412 B.C.E., and subsequently encased in ashlar at some later date (Fig. 6.8).[53] The walls at Thorikos show many traits found at Sounion, which also lead to a mistaken dating of Thorikos to the fifth century B.C.E.[54]

The multi-enceinte in multi-style masonry and tower design at Rhamnous defies a chronological fix for any given stretch, let alone one that securely predates the years prior to Epaminondas' ascendancy.[55] Parts of the acropolis wall, especially those to the south, "suggest" an older date according to Lauter, but the presence of ladder- or stackwork indicates a fourth-century or later date for the entire fabric (Fig. 6.9a–e).[56]

Mark Munn argues that Athenian action for the physical defense of Attica intensified during the Boiotian War of 378–5 B.C.E. or a generation after Ober's date of 404 B.C.E. According to Munn, the enigmatic Dema Wall represents an impressive strategic system of barrier walls and signal towers. Built in fieldstone and rubble, the low-lying (about two meters high) Dema Wall blocks a pass in the southern foothills of Mount Parnes, north of Athens and east of Eleusis. Beyond Munn, the study of the Dema Wall has attracted more than its share of scholarly attention but a secure date and explanation of function remains elusive.[57] In any event, the generic, rubble-built Dema Wall pales sadly when compared to the new-age Theban fortifications. My own preference is to associate the Dema Wall with a comparable construction at Koroni in central Attica and other barrier walls thrown up during the Chremonidian War, 267–1 B.C.E.[58]

A crucial problem lies in the accepted methodology for establishing a chronology for Greek fortifications of the fourth century B.C.E. Estimations of dates for published encientes rely heavily on a correlation

---

[53] Karlsson, *Fortification Towers and Masonry Techniques*, 97: "the filling is probably from the old wall even though the face was rebuilt."

[54] Mussche, "La fortresse," 176–205; and "Note sur les fortifications de Sounion," *BCH* 88 (1964): 423–32; and "L'Architecture civile and militaire," 43; Lauter, Lohmann, Lauter-Bufe, *Attische Festungen*, 11–33, and Lauter, "Some Remarks on Fortified Settlements in the Attic Countryside," 78–9.

[55] Detailed treatment with dimensioned drawings by Pouilloux, *La fortresse de Rhamnonte*, 43–66, who proposes a date in the third quarter of the fourth century B.C.E. Munn, *The Defense of Attica*, 19–20, distinguishes between the enceintes of garrisons, fortified demes, and barrier walls. Garrisons, such as Boudoron, are attested in ancient sources by the fifth century B.C.E. Accompanying barrier walls are a later development.

[56] Lauter, "Some Remarks on Fortified Settlements in the Attic Countryside," 80–1.

[57] Ober, "Review of M. Munn," 374–5.

[58] McCredie, *Fortified Military Camps of Attica*.

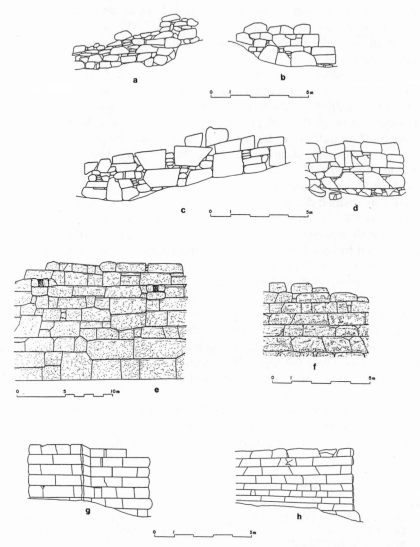

Figure 6.9. Rhamnous, masonry styles. Drawing by Diane Fortenberry and Miry Park.

between a stylistic classification of masonry and its chronological approximation to record battles, sieges, or hostilities. Scranton first systemized and refined this approach.[59] His chapter headings illustrate the way he went about the task of dating walls: (1) "The Stylistic Development of Masonry Jointing and Tooling," (2) "Lesbian Masonry," (3) Polygonal Masonry," (4) "Trapezoidal Masonry," and (5) "Ashlar Masonry." The chapter divisions cover four phases in the stylistic development of Greek walls over a period of six generations, beginning with the early sixth and ending in the later fourth century; thence, "330–300 . . . under the influence of Macedonian armies, old fortifications were repaired and rebuilt, and some new walls were constructed, characterized principally by the use of tooled isodomic ashlar with beveled joints."[60] According to Scranton's view, the stylistic evolution of Greek fortification runs lock-step with the development of the whole of Greek architecture, mainly temple construction. Later scholars, with very few exceptions, have not deviated from Scranton's thesis.[61]

The occasional stretch of polygonal masonry appears to be a norm in most solid-stone fortifications of post-fifth-century date, yet scholars routinely assert that polygonal masonry is a good sign of archaic or early classical construction, as Lauter does for Rhamnous (Fig. 6.9a).[62] In actuality, polygonal pointwork became a prevalent style in the fourth century, probably under Theban influence, and lasted into the Hellenistic period.[63] It appears in the retaining walls of fourth-century graves in the Kerameikos and, as Adam clearly demonstrated, it is a pervasive style within the ashlar and coursed, trapezoidal fortification walls dated to the fourth and later centuries.[64] My own observations lead me to believe that it is a particular feature of Boiotian fortifications prior to 338 B.C.E.[65] For instance, the walls of Boiotian

---

[59] Scranton, *Greek Walls.*
[60] McNicoll, "Colloque International," 347–52, clarifies the distinct changes in design of fortifications between ca. 300 B.C.E. and 200 B.C.E.
[61] Jean-Pierre Adam is among the first to recognize that archaisms such as polygonal masonry are not an indicator of early date: Adam, *L'Architecture militaire*, 23 n. 16; and "Approche et défense, des portes dans le monde hellénisé," in *La fortification*, 5–43. Y. Garlan, "Les fortifications grecques: bilan et perspectives de recherches," in *La fortification*, 16–17, notes that sixteen different types of masonry are common to fortification design and construction, making any sorting a subjective consideration.
[62] Cf. J. Fossey and J. Morin, *Khostia 1983* (Amsterdam, 1986).
[63] J. Fossey, *The Ancient Topography of Eastern Phocis* (Amsterdam, 1986), 121–31, esp. 125 and fig. 26.
[64] Adam, *L'architecture militaire*, 23–6.
[65] J. Fossey and H. Giroux, "Two Fortified Sites in Southern Boiotia," *Tiresias* 9A (1979):

Orchomenos probably date to the years following 335 B.C.E. (based on the advanced technique of *emplekton*), and those at Chaironeia may date somewhat earlier, to ca. 353 B.C.E.[66] These alterations in masonry type are not a matter of eclecticism in style but a result of good engineering. I have observed that polygonal masonry generally occurs above areas liable to settlement, such as footers crossing earth-filled gulleys, hollows, and the like. In these cases, polygonal jointing allows stones to rotate when shifted in a vertical plane, as in heaving or settlement, whereas stones laid in isodomic courses resist such twisting and thus the rock mass is subject to greater stress and shear and the likelihood of cracking.

Excavation of fortification walls and towers has produced uneven results. Those fortifications located away from continuously occupied habitation sites provide the most satisfactory archaeological evidence for date which, inevitably, turns out to be later than those previously deduced from masonry style alone.[67] A chronological fix on this order is available with the walls at Messene, which represent one of the remarkably few instances where the ancient sources are unambiguous in describing the historical circumstances. Under the direction of Epaminondas, the Thebans built the walls for the foundation city of the Messenians during the winter and spring of 370–69 B.C.E.[68] Scholars dispute an absolute chronology for the nine years between the Battles of Leuktra, 371 B.C.E., and Mantinea, 362 B.C.E. Precise dates vary by one or two years and do not affect the fact that many publications of the Greek fortifications reviewed in the preceding sec-

---

1–18; Camp, "Notes on the Towers and Borders," 194–5. R.M. Kallet-Marz in "The Evangelistria Watchtower and the Defense of the Zagaora Pass," *Boiotika, Vorträge vom 5. internationalen Böotien-Kolloquium*, 301–11, compresses the date of the Siphai network into the period of the Third and Fourth Sacred Wars, 354–40 B.C.E.

[66] Karlsson, *Fortification towers and masonry techniques*, 78. J. Fossey and G. Gauvin, "Les fortifications de l'acropole de Chéronée," *Actes du 3e congrès internationale sur la Béotie antique, Montreal 1985* (Amsterdam, 1985), 41–75, rprt. in J.M. Fossey, *Papers in Boiotian Topography and History* (Amsterdam, 1990), 100–24. Fossey on the other hand, dates those at Chaironeia, albeit with hesitation, to the Archaic period (115–16).

[67] R. Martin, "Les enceintes de Gortys d'Arcadie," *BCH* 71–2 (1947–8): 81–147. Mc-Credie, *Fortified Military Camps of Attica*, correctly lowered the date to the Hellenistic period of many Attic fortifications based on the evidence of excavation at Koroni, which Lauter, "Some Remarks on Fortified Settlements in the Attic Countryside," 77–8, wants to restore to the fifth century B.C.E.

[68] Plutarch *Ages.* 34.1–2; Plut. *Pelop.* 24.5; Nepos 15.8.5; Diod. 15.66.1–67.1; Isokrates *Lykourgos Against Leokrates* 5.28, 5.49, 6.25; Aelian *v.h.* 2.42; Pausanias 4.19.3, 20.4, 26.5–27.7; Dio Chrysostomos 15.28. C. Roebuck, *A History of Messenia from 369 B.C. to 146 B.C.* (Chicago, 1941), 31–4. Overview of discussions of walls at Messene: J. Ober, "Toward a Typology of Greek Artillery Towers," 148, and Karlsson, *Fortification Towers and Masonry Techniques*, 74.

tion recognize Epaminondas's fundamental role in the development of coursed, cut-stone walls.[69]

EPAMINONDAS

We know little of Epaminondas's life. Plutarch's biography of the Theban leader unfortunately is lost and only those episodes that overlap the lives of Pelopidas and Agesilaos supply any biographical detail.[70] Xenophon barely mentions Epaminondas in his heavily biased *Hellenika* and when he does, it is late in the narrative (366 B.C.E.) and with faint praise.[71] Moreover, Xenophon never mentions the founding of Messene.[72] Diodorus provides the most information but this is untrustworthy unless backed by independent confirmation.[73] In short, our knowledge of Epaminondas must be pieced together from inferences in fragmentary sources or later compilations such as that by Cornelius Nepos. New to the formula of Boiotian fourth-century history is a look at the physical presence of a lasting accomplishment – monumental Greek fortification.

Ephoros, the historian and contemporary of Epaminondas, was a great admirer of the Theban.[74] Plutarch, who used Ephoros as his primary source, favorably compared Epaminondas with the sage lawgivers and leaders of the Greek past: Solon, Themistokles, and Peri-

[69] The argument centers on a high (earlier) date of 369 B.C.E. and a low (later) date of 368 B.C.E. for the second invasion of the Peloponnesos by Epaminondas and, for the third invasion, a high date of 367 B.C.E. and a low date of 366 B.C.E. J. Wiseman, "Epaminondas and the Theban Invasions," *Klio* 51 (1969): 177–99, opens with a salvo in favor of a low chronology (see his chronological table, 197–9), but G.L. Cawkwell, "Epaminondas and Thebes," *Classical Quarterly* 22 (1972): 277, and Buckler, *The Theban Hegemony*, 87–9 and 233–4, strenuously argue for the higher dates. I adopt the higher chronology even though this detail of absolute chronology does not affect the arguments put forward here.

[70] Diod. 15.39.88; Strabo 9.40.1; Justin 6.8. Cawkwell, "Epaminondas and Thebes," 254–78; Buckler, *The Theban Hegemony*, 270–2; H. Volkmann, s.v. "Epameinondas," *Kleine Pauly* 2 (1979): cols. 280–2.

[71] Xen. *Hell.* 7.1.41–3; 7.5.8; 7.5.18–20.

[72] C.J. Tuplin, "The Failings of Empire: A Reading of Xenophon *Helenica* 2.3.11–7.5.27," *Historia Einzelschrift* 76 (1993): 163–80. Buckler, *The Theban Hegemony*, 263–8, counters the many attempts to excuse Xenophon's bias against Epaminondas.

[73] On the low reliability of Diodorus, see Hamilton, *Agesilaus*, 6; Buckler, *The Theban Hegemony*, 268–70, and 6; R. Drews, "Diodorus and His Sources," *American Journal of Philology* 83 (1962): 382–92; C.J. Tuplin, "Two Proper Names in the Text of Diodorus Book 15," *Classical Quarterly*, n.s., 29 (1979): 347–57; Lewis, "Sicily, 413–368 B.C.," 120–3; Buckler, *The Theban Hegemony*, Appendix 2:B, 268–70.

[74] F. Jacoby, *FGrHist* 70 Komm., 31; C.J. Tuplin, "'Pausanias' and Plutarch's Epaminondas," *Classical Quarterly* 78 (1984), 346–58.

kles, among others.[75] The noble characterization of Epaminondas persisted through antiquity. He was also described as steeped in Pythagorean philosophy, and as accomplished in music and dance.[76] A statue in the old agora at Thebes commemorated Epaminondas as a renowned flutist.[77] Cicero reflects: "Epaminondas, to my mind the leading man in Greek history was, we are told, an accomplished singer to the accompaniment of the harp."[78] Generals and liberators, such as Timoleon, Scipio Africanus, and Hadrian, marveled at his innovative military science.[79] Indeed, while the young Philip II was incarcerated in the house of Epaminondas's protégé, Pammenes, Philip may have received his first lessons in military science; and it is said that Alexander the Great adopted many of his strategies from those of Epaminondas.[80]

Athens, one of Epaminondas's former enemies, memorialized his heroic death at Mantinea in 362 B.C.E. in a public mural.[81] The famed artist, Euphranor, painted the event.[82] A copy, perhaps commissioned by Hadrian, was set up at Mantinea.[83] Statues of Epaminondas stood in two sanctuaries at Messene; another stood at Delphi as part of a commemoration of the founding of Messene by the Argives.[84] In the first century C.E., the Messenians flattered Tiberius by an inscription at Olympia declaring the emperor, "the new Epaminondas."[85]

THEBAN HEGEMONY OF THE SEA

Ephoros claimed that Boiotia was geographically well suited to be a sea power: its shores were lined with many natural harbors having access to sea lanes leading towards the west and east.[86] In the fifth

[75] Plut. *de garrul.* 22.514. J. Buckler, "Plutarch on the Trials of Pelopidas and Epameinondas (369 B.C.)," *Classical Philology* 73 (1978): 36–42; and *The Theban Hegemony*, Appendix 2:2, 270–2.
[76] Plut. *Mor.* 583C, 585E; Diod. 10.11.2, 15.39.2; Paus. 9.13.1; Nepos 15.2.1. Athen. 4.184E; Nepos *Praef.* 1.
[77] Paus. 9.12.5.
[78] Cicero *Tusc.* 1.2; trans. J.E. King, *Cicero. Tuscan Disputations* (London, 1966).
[79] Plut. *Tim.* 36; *Philip* 3; *Sc. Afr.*; Paus. 8.11.8; 8.8.12.
[80] Plut. *Pelop.* 26.4; Diod. 15.67.3–4, 16.2.22–3; Ael. *v.h.* 13.7; Justin 7.5.1. H. Svoboda, s.v. "Epameinondas," *RE* 5 (1905): col. 2702. A recent summary is in E. McQueen, "Why Philip Won," in *The Greek World*, ed. A. Powell (London, 1995), 323–46. Cf. J.R. Ellis, "Macedon and North-West Greece," *CAH* (Cambridge, 1994), 730, on the over-speculation on these Theban influences on Philip II.
[81] Ael. *v.h.* 7.14; Strabo 9.2.5; Nepos 15.9.2.
[82] Paus. 1.3.3–4; Plut. *de glor. Athen* 2. O. Palagia, *Euphranor* (Leiden, 1980), 50–4.
[83] Paus. 8.9.8.
[84] Paus. 4.31.10, 4.32.1., 10.10.5.
[85] W. Dittenberger and K. Purgold, *Olympia* V: *Die Inscriften* (Berlin, 1896), no. 477.
[86] *FGrHist* 70 F 119.

century, the Boiotians had a strong naval presence, never equal to that of Athens, but widely underestimated in modern scholarship.[87] Events of 371 B.C.E. and afterwards, however, prompted changes in Theban strategy. In that year the Boiotians docked ten or twelve triremes at fortified Kreusis.[88] The Spartan commander, Kleombrotos, captured the walls and the ships on his march to Leuktra.[89] There is no way of knowing whether the Boiotian fleet was more extensive than this, but it is clear that over the next several years Epaminondas developed a naval policy aimed at neutralizing Athenian control of the seas.[90] In 367–6 B.C.E., the Theban assembly sent Pelopidas and Hismenias to the court of the Persian king Artaxerxes in a diplomatic maneuver meant to upstage Thebes's rivals, Athens and Sparta. Pelopidas's fame preceded him to Susa and, once there, he promoted before the king several clauses for a new treaty: (1) the independence of Messene, and (2) the deactivation of the Athenian fleet.[91]

These provisions turned out to be unenforceable, but shortly thereafter, probably in 366 B.C.E., Epaminondas persuaded the Theban assembly to form a naval empire, "a hegemony of the sea," and to build 100 triremes and the dockyards necessary to accommodate the fleet.[92] By 364–3, Epaminondas took his ships on an expedition to Byzantium and Herakleia.[93] Some scholars doubt that the allocation of 100 triremes was ever fulfilled but, as Buckler points out, "Enough Boiotian ships actually took to the sea to frighten off an Athenian commander with a large fleet, so it is reasonable to conclude that the building program was substantial."[94] In any event, physical remains of a dockyard facility at Siphai show that this provision was also implemented.

THE NEW CITIES OF EPAMINONDAS

After Epaminondas's death, the Thebans glorified their hero with an elegiac epitaph:

[87] Thuc. 8.3.5, 8.106.; Roesch, *Thespies*, 100–12, summarizes Boiotian naval strength in the late fifth, fourth centuries. For the position of *navarch* during this period, see 124, 125.

[88] Diod. 15.53; Xen. *Hell*. 6.4.3.

[89] Xen. *Hell*. 6.4.3–4.

[90] Demosthenes 49.14–15. Cawkwell, "Epaminondas and Thebes," 273.

[91] Nepos 16.4.3. Xen. *Hell*. 7.1.35–7; Plut. 14.30.2–4; Aeschines 2.105. J. Cargill, *The Second Athenian League, Empire or Free Alliance?* (Berkeley, 1981), 164–6.

[92] Diod. 15.78.4, 15.79.1; Buckler, *The Theban Hegemony*, 161–75.

[93] Aes. 2.105; Justin 16.4.3–4; Isok. 5.53.

[94] E.g., Cawkwell, "Epaminondas and Thebes," 270–3; F. Carrata Thomes, *Egemonia boetica e potenze maritima nella politica di Epaminonda* (Turin, 1952), 28–9. Buckler, *The Theban Hegemony*, 308 n. 19.

> By my counsels was Sparta shorn of her glory,
>   And holy Messene received at last her children.
> By the arms of Thebes was Megalopolis encircled
>   with walls,
> And all Greece won independence and freedom.[95]

The last line is a flourish, but the founding of Messene by Epaminondas is a fact beyond dispute.[96] The general sent Pammenes to Megalopolis to supervise construction of the walls in either 370 B.C.E. or 368 B.C.E. Plutarch, Diodorus, Nepos, Aelian, and Pausanias each provide an account.[97] Diodorus places the founding of Megalopolis in 368 B.C.E., but there is some evidence that the event occurred two years earlier.[98] After 350 years of subjugation by the Spartans, during the winter of 370–69 B.C.E. Epaminondas freed the Messenian people, who had served as *helots* and *perioikoi* to their Spartan overlords.[99] Epaminondas not only personally supervised the construction of fortification walls at Messene, but also recalled Messenian exiles from Libya, Naupactos, Messana, and Sicily.[100]

The ascendancy of Thebes corresponds to the life of Epaminondas. Unlike the first and second Athenian and Spartan empires, the Theban hegemony never extracted tribute, nor did it install *Kleruchies* or governors in member cities.[101] For revenue Thebes depended upon fickle handouts from the Persian king and his satraps.[102] Despite Athenian propaganda to the contrary and with the exceptions of Plataia, Thespiai, and Orchomenos in 378–1 B.C.E., the Thebans did not level or interfere with the walls of Boiotian confederate cities.[103] Instead, the main objective of Theban foreign policy after 378 B.C.E. was to eliminate vulnerability to attack and to halt the installation of foreign (Spar-

---

[95] Paus. 9.15.6, trans. W.H.S. Jones, *Pausanias Description of Greece* 4 (London, 1965).

[96] See the section, Epaminondas, this chapter.

[97] Plutarch *Pelop.* 24.5, *Regnum et imperatorum apotphthegmata* 23; Diod. 15.72.4, 15.94.1–3.; Nepos 15.8.4–5; Ael. *v.h.* 8.42; and Paus. 6.12.8, 8.27.1–7, 9.14.4–5, 9.15.2–6. Also Marmor Parium (Tod 205, *FGrHist* 239, A73), and Stephanus Byzantius, s.v. "Megale polis."

[98] Diod. 15.72.4; Wiseman, "Epaminondas and the Theban Invasions," 198 n. 1 for 370 B.C.; S. Hornblower, "When Was Megalopolis Founded," *BSA* 85 (1990): 71–7.

[99] Diod. 16.55.1; Isok. 5.28. J. Chambers, "On Messenian and Laconian Helots in the Fifth Century B.C.," *Historian* 40 (1978): 271–85.

[100] Diod. 15.66.1; Paus. 4.26.5–8; 4.27.5–9. Hamilton, *Agesilaus*, 235–40.

[101] R. Meiggs, *The Athenian Empire* (Oxford, 1972); P.J. Rhodes, *The Athenian Empire*; Greece and Rome New Surveys in the Classics 17 (Oxford, 1985); P.A. Cartledge, *Aesilaos and the Crisis of Sparta* (London, 1987), 86–98.

[102] For instance, Tod, 160; M.M. Austin, "Society and Economy," in *CAH*, 551–2; S. Hornblower, "Persia," in *CAH*, 94.

[103] Iso. 14.9, 19, 35; Buckler, *The Theban Hegemony*, 20–2.

tan and Athenian) garrisons.[104] What is implicit in these sources, yet little recognized in modern scholarship,[105] is that Epaminondas originated the Greek idea of a monumental walled city, the very type admired by Aristotle:

Not only should cities have walls but care should be taken to make them ornamental, as well as useful for warlike purposes, and adapted to resist modern inventions . . . more especially now that catapults and siege engines have been brought to such perfection.[106]

THEBAN EPILOGUE UNDER PAMMENES, 362–35 B.C.E.

Ancient testimonia on the affairs of Thebes and Boiotia are particularly sparse for those years prior to the battle of Chaironeia in 338 B.C.E. According to Ephoros, the death of Epaminondas wrought the collapse of the Theban hegemony;[107] in this opinion, modern scholars concur with but minor hesitation.[108] Ephoros provides a reason: "(the Thebans) belittled the value of learning and of intercourse with mankind and cared for military values alone," a view shared by Aristotle and Arrian.[109]

Modern scholars seek other reasons for the rapid failure of the Theban hegemony, usually finding an explanation based on politics.[110] Pausanias, however, records one notable undertaking that has escaped the attention of scholars on Greek fortifications. In the months leading up to the battle, the Thebans fortified the Phocian city of Ambrossos with a set of walls that Pausanias compares to the best of fortifications. In other words, Boiotian expertise in wall construction persisted after the death of Epaminondas. What has been obscured is the Theban role in events leading up to the battle at Chaironeia. Indeed, Theban hegemony over Boiotia remained intact through the Social War, 357–5 B.C.E., the Third Sacred War, 355–45 B.C.E., and the Fourth Sacred War, 340–38 B.C.E.; and Thebes continued to be active in Peloponnesian

---

104. Hack, *The Rise of Thebes*, 168.
105. Buckler, *The Theban Hegemony*, 67, is an exception: "To protect the area from sea-borne invasion, the Boiotians began [ca. 370 B.C.E.] to fortify their cities with fine ashlar masonry and to build watch towers and signal towers at strategic points."
106. Aris. *Politics*, 1330b–1331a; trans. B. Jowett, *The Politics* (London, 1932).
107. *FGrHist* 70 F 119; Nepos 15.10.4.
108. Buckler, *The Theban Hegemony*, 220–1.
109. Aris. *Rhet*. 2.23.11; Arrian 1.94.
110. Buckler, *The Theban Hegemony*, 226–7; Cawkwell, "Epaminondas and Thebes," 274–5.

affairs.[111] During the post-Epaminondas period of Theban history, the Attic orators make clear that the city remained a worry, if not a major military threat, to Athens and Sparta.[112]

Epaminondas groomed Pammenes to be his successor; and, while Pammenes never achieved the exalted reputation of his mentor, he nonetheless was highly regarded by posterity. Plutarch praises Pammenes and equates him with the likes of Aristides and Agesilaos.[113]

As a young man, Pammenes was entrusted with the construction of the walls at Megalopolis in 368–7 B.C.E.,[114] and sometime during this period he held the teenage hostage Philip of Macedon under house arrest.[115] The two maintained mutual respect for each other, perhaps a friendship, lasting from their early years together at Thebes.[116] Suffice it to say, Pammenes remained a significant force in Greek politics until his death in 354–3 B.C.E.[117] At least five of his victories are recorded.[118] In 361–60 B.C.E., Pammenes returned with 3,000 troops and 300 cavalry to Megalopolis to quell an insurrection.[119] There was a significant Theban presence at the end of the Social War in 355 B.C.E., and in 354–3 B.C.E. Pammenes brilliantly led two military successes with a contingent of 5,000 Boiotian troops to Phrygia.[120]

These maneuvers and experiences make it reasonable to assume that Pammenes continued fortification construction and that he oversaw the building of an undetermined number of Boiotian walls in the post-Epaminondian period. During these years, tower and rampart designs kept pace with advances in siege warfare, and I identify Aigosthene as a Boiotian arsenal of this later period.

In 352–1 B.C.E. the Thebans returned to Arkadia with a contingent of 4,000 foot soldiers and 400 cavalry under the command of Cephesion, the probable successor to Pammenes.[121] The Sacred Band,

[111] Diod. 15.94, 16.39–30; Strabo 9.2.5.
[112] Isok. 12.159, 15.248. Cargill, *The Second Athenian League,* 51: "after 362/1, the chief enemy of Athens was Thebes."
[113] Plut. *Mor* 805 E–F.
[114] An inscription, *IG.* V, ii, 440–1, dated to second half of the second century B.C.E., records the repair of the Megalopolis walls. A German expedition under the direction of H. Lauter has resumed excavations at Megalopolis.
[115] Plut. *Pel.* 26. See page 174 of this chapter.
[116] Diod. 16.34; Demosthenes, *Against Aristokrates,* 183.
[117] Diod. 16.34.1–2.
[118] Polybius 5.16.1–5.
[119] Diod.15.94.1–3.
[120] Cargill, *The Second Athenian League,* 178–9; Ellis, "Macedon and North-West Greece," 741–2. Diod. 16.34.1–2; Dem. 23.183. P. Cloché, *Thèbes de Béotie. Des origines à la conquête romaine;* Bibliothèque de la faculté de philosopie et lettres de Namur 13 (Namur, 1952), 173–4.
[121] Diod. 16.39.

organized in 379 B.C.E., went undefeated in battle until the Battle of Chaironeia in 338 B.C.E., when 300 were killed fighting the phalanx commanded by Alexander.[122]

The standing assumption has been that Thebes was extinguished as a potent force in Greek politics after 362 B.C.E. Rather, it was not until 335 B.C.E., when Alexander, with the complicity of Boiotian cities, namely Plateia and Thespiae, took revenge and razed Thebes to the ground and sent surviving citizens into exile.[123]

The glory that was Thebes certainly diminished with the death of Epaminondas in 362 B.C.E., but the real final calamity occurred with the Macedonian destruction of the city in 335 B.C.E., an event that became a literary topos as a disaster of disasters, ranked with the defeat of the Athenian fleet in 404 B.C.E., the decimation of Sparta at Leuktra in 371 B.C.E., and the leveling of Corinth in 146 B.C.E.[124] This is the moment that closes the book on the history of Theban skill in the design and construction of fortifications. The events make it clear, however, that the patches of surviving wall, towers, and portals can just as easily date to the refoundation of the city under Kassander in 316 B.C.E.[125] A century of excavation has exposed portions of an inner and outer circuit, the first around the base of the Dadmeia, the second extending into the surrounding plain. A portion of the Elektra Gate and a trace of wall nearby show a wall socle built of isodomic masonry intended for a mudbrick superstructure. This and the circular entrance court have similarities with the fortification of Peiraeus, Mantinea, and Megalopolis.[126]

WALLS OF THE THEBAN HEGEMONY: SIPHAI, KREUSIS, KORSIAI

Proof of a Theban origin for the massive cut-stone fortified circuit begins with the walls at Siphai (Figs. 6.11 and 6.12), Kreusis (Fig. 6.12), and Korsiai, not even mentioned by Winter, Lawrence, Marsden, Adam, or Karlsson in their works on Greek fortifications. Before 386

---

122 Paus. 940.5; Plut. *Pelop.* 18.7; Strabo 9.2.37; Justin 9.3–9.4.6.
123 Diod. 17.15.1; Plut. *Alexander* 11.5–12; Arrian *Anab.* 1.9.9; Justin 11.3.8. A.B. Bosworth, *A Historical Commentary on Arrian's History of Alexander I* (Oxford, 1980), 84, 89–95.
124 Arrian *Anab.* 9.1.8; Poly. 18.1.3. For an estimate of depopulation, see S. Symeonoglou, *The Topography of Thebes from the Bronze Age to Modern Times* (Princeton, 1985), 206, fig. 6.1.
125 Diod. 19.53–4; Paus. 9.7.1. Cloché, *Thèbes de Béotie*, 202–7.
126 Winter, *Greek Fortifications*, 225, fig. 238, and Symeonoglou, *The Topography of Thebes*, 117–22, with bibliography of excavations. Symeonoglou, following the scholarly trend as outlined above, decided on an initial construction date before 446 B.C.E.

B.C.E., Siphai, Kreusis, and Korsiai were administered by Thespiae; from 371–62 B.C.E. they were part of the Theban hegemony, and became independent after 338 B.C.E.[127]

Siphai, modern-day Aliki, commands a protected bay along the north shore of the Corinthian Gulf, deep in Boiotian territory (Figs. 6.10 and 6.11). There, a circuit of stout masonry encloses a small but high *akropolis* with steep slopes on all sides. A counterwall or *hypoteichisma* runs down a spine from the heights to the shore, originally going into the water. Wide, parallel cuttings in the beach rock spread along the shore, probably serving as slips for ships. The use of a counterwall is a typical feature of a Theban fortified port. Today, one sees at this spot the dockyards legislated by Epaminondas's decree in 367–36 B.C.E. A portal passes through the counterwall at the foot of the *akropolis* above an entrance corbeled by a pair of hefty but profiled consoles (Figs. 6.11a–6.11c). These voluted consoles reappear in other Theban forts as well (cf. Fig. 6.3). Brushwork and pick-work are the preferred manner of dressing the masonry. Outside-corner returns bear drafted margins and the coursing and jointing mixes ashlar with trapezoidal polygonal jointwork, a style that occurs generally in Boiotian forts of this time (Fig. 6.10).

Ernst-Ludwig Schwandner, who published a work on the beautiful and beautifully preserved walls at Siphai, argues for a date within the Theban hegemony.[128] Karlsson develops a point not elucidated by Schwandner, that the curtain walls of Siphai display the *emplekton* technique as a dating indicator and as a hallmark of Epaminondas-period design (cf. Fig. 6.7).

Another powerful but smaller and less well-preserved fortification exists at Kreusis (Fig. 6.12).[129] Kreusis lies approximately halfway between Siphai, around the promontory to the north, and Aigosthena, on the next bay to the south (Fig. 6.15). Its fortification plan mixes styles of masonry including the *emplekton* technique, catapult towers, and window designs. In fact, nearly all the elements found at Siphai are found also at Kreusis.

A third coastal fort lies at Korsiai (modern-day Kostia). Little is left of the main circuit at the east precipice, but a well-preserved gate and

---

[127] Xen. *Hell.* 4.5. Roesch, *Thespies*, 50–2, 54–8. Buckler, *The Theban Hegemony*, 22.

[128] Ernst-Ludwig Schwandner, "Die Böotische Hafenstadt Siphai," *Archäologischer Anzeiger* 92 (1977): 513–51.

[129] J. Fossey and G. Gauvin, "*Livadhostro*: un releve topographique des fortifications de l'ancienne Kreusis," in *La Béotie antique*, CNRS (Paris, 1985), 77–85, reprinted in Fossey, *Papers in Boiotian Topography and History*, 157–8; Roesch, *Thespies*, 218, fig. 4.

tower at the southeast indicate the use of coursed-ashlar masonry, typical of this set of Gulf forts. Phocians destroyed the site in 347–6 B.C.E., an event supported by archaeological evidence.[130] Excavations also indicate that Korsiai was probably in place in the years following the battle at Leukra or by the early 360s B.C.E.[131]

These three sites are part of a fortified coastal system that lies entirely within Boiotian territory, and the physical attributes link these forts with the Boiotian walls at Messene.[132] On historical grounds these military installations must be constructions of the Theban hegemony, a chronology supported by the excavation evidence from Korsiai, as noted above.[133] All construction features of the Boiotian coastal forts at Siphai, Kreusis, and Korsiai apply as well to the fort at Aigosthena, on or near the Megarid border. The similarities include the presence of the polygonal masonry that misled Scranton to posit an early-fourth-century date for Aigosthena (Fig. 6.5).[134] Recent discussions, nonetheless, conclude with a date in the second half of the fourth century B.C.E.[135] The fort at Aigosthena (Fig. 6.5) has hybrid, but rather more developed, construction features resembling a combination of those at Messene (Figs. 6.1 and 6.2) and Gyphtokastro (Figs. 6.3 and

---

[130] Diod. 16.58.1. J. Fossey and G. Gauvin, "*Mali en Boétie du Sud*: un site des 'Dark Ages'," reprinted in Fossey, *Papers in Boiotian Topography and History*, 93.

[131] J. Fossey, ed., "Khóstia 1980 A: Preliminary Report on the First Season of Canadian Excavations at Khóstia, Boiotia, Central Greece," *McGill University Monographs in Classical Archaeology and History* 1 (1981): 51–61.

[132] I reserve opinion on the inland fort on Mount Mavrovouni, discussed by John Fossey and R.A. Tomlinson, *Annual British School at Athens* 65 (1970): 243–63, reprinted in Fossey, *Papers in Boiotian Topography and History*, 130–56. A plan of the rectangular enceinte can be made out of the collapsed heaps of stone. A nearby, freestanding tower rises to a height of 6.5 m, which Camp, "Notes on the Towers and Borders," 197, considers to be a Boiotian compartment tower.

[133] Fossey, "The Development of Some Defensive Networks," 116–17; Ober, "Early Artillery Towers," 577 n. 25; Camp, "Notes on the Towers and Borders," 202; and Cooper, "Epaminondas and Greek Fortifications," 195, and bibliography in Kallet-Marx in "The Evangelistria Watchtower," 301–11. J. Fossey and G. Gauvin in "Les fortifications de l'acropole de Chéronée," 41–75, and Fossey, "The Development of Some Defensive Networks," 112, advance the attractive but insupportable suggestion that a set of small walled forts on the perimeter of the Copaic Basin were emplacements for defense against the pre-Leuktra maneuvers of Kleombrotos.

[134] Scranton, *Greek Walls*, 81; Karlsson, *Fortification towers and masonry techniques*, 86, rightly argues that Hellenistic walls of the third century B.C.E. return to classical polygonal style.

[135] J. Ober, "Two Ancient Watchtowers," 391, gives 350–275 B.C.E. and narrows it to ca. 343 B.C.E. in Ober, "Early Artillery Towers," 586. Karlsson, *Fortification Towers and Masonry Techniques*, 78: ca. 338 B.C.E.; Marsden, *Greek and Roman Artillery*, 163; Winter, *Greek Fortifications*, 142 n. 56: end of the fourth, early third B.C.E.; and F.G. Maier, "Das Stadtmauer von Thisbe," *AthMitt* 73 (1958): 24.

Figure 6.10. Siphai, view of tower. Photo: F. Cooper.

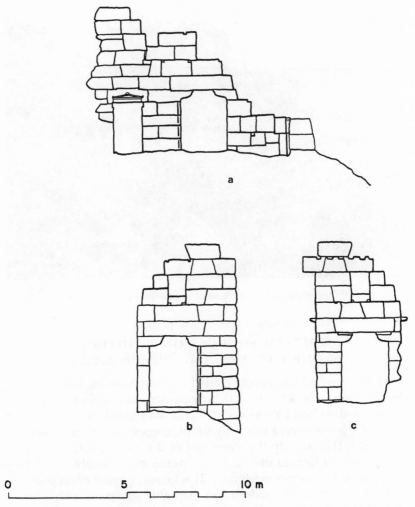

Figure 6.11. Siphai, view of consoles at portal. Drawing by Joanne Mannell.

6.4). I therefore include it as a Theban fortification, built after the death of Epaminondas, perhaps under his protégé, Pammenes, or even as late as the outbreak of war with Philip II in 338 B.C.E.[136]

---

[136] In a further refinement of his typology based on wall thickness and chamber size, Ober divides towers and walls into two generations: I. 370–50 B.C.E. (defense against nontorsion catapults), and II. 325–285 B.C.E. (torsion catapults perhaps engineered under Philip II); Ober, "Toward a Typology of Greek Artillery Towers," 149, 161.

Figure 6.12. Kreusis, view of tower. Photo: F. Cooper.

WRITTEN SOURCES ON BOIOTIAN
STONEWORKERS, CA. 395–38 B.C.E.

The imposing and beautifully crafted walls at Messene form a circuit about 9.5 km in length (Fig. 6.1). Any modern assessment of the man-hours taken to build these walls would lead to an excessively high estimate. For instance, a relatively simple consolidation and rebuilding of tower L (Fig. 6.2, up the slope east of the Arkadian Gate) in 1994 took a crew of four to five workmen nearly nine months – and they were assisted by heavy machinery. This expenditure of effort puts into contrast the report of Diodorus on the lightning speed with which a long wall at Syracuse was constructed in 402 B.C.E. under Dionysos II.[137] An unspecified number of quarrymen supplied the material for 60,000 men, divided into crews of 200 each, to construct a 9-km-long wall at the northern edge of the Syracusan plateau in twenty days.

Accordingly, Aigosthena falls into the last phase of the first generation or is transitional to the second phase, a moment I think suitable, but not under Athenian oversight, as believed by Ober.

[137] Diod. 14.18. F.E. Winter, "The Chronology of the Euryalos Fortress at Syracuse," *AJA* 67 (1963): 363–87; Adam, *L'Architecture militaire*, 248–51; Garlan, *Recherches de poliorcétique grecque*, 186–8.

While the figures of Diodorus may seem exaggerated, they are consistent with the four- to six-month period of Theban encampment at Messene during the spring of 370–69 B.C.E.[138] Experienced masons, not just sheer manpower, made possible this architectural accomplishment.

In 417–16 B.C.E., it was Athens that supplied technical assistants and stone workers for construction of fortifications at Argos, perhaps a set of long walls running to the sea.[139] These walls have disappeared; they may have been of the sort described above as typical fifth- and fourth-century Attic, as at Boudoron (Fig. 6.6). Preserved wall stretches on the Aspis and Larissa at Argos date from the first half of the third century B.C.E. A short stretch of Lesbian-style polygonal masonry on the Larissa at Argos probably is earlier in date, but cannot be associated with the crews of Athenian stone workers.[140] By the beginning of the fourth century, Athens apparently had lost her masons in the catastrophic events of 404 B.C.E. and had to look to Boiotia for assistance in stone wall construction.

The walls at Peiraeus offer a secure point of departure for an assessment of the technological advances in fortifications. Earlier stretches of walls date from the time of Themistokles,[141] but these were demolished in 404 B.C.E. at the end of the Peloponnesian War.[142]

Clear evidence shows that a generation prior to Epaminondas's achievement at Messene in 370–69 B.C.E., Boiotian contractors and crews were already skilled in the construction of fortification walls. In 395–4 B.C.E., Konon launched a program for the rebuilding and modernization of the walls of Athens, including the refortification of Peiraeus.[143] Some of the expense accounts for its construction survive.[144] Two are embedded in the wall itself,[145] the rest are preserved in reused marble roof tiles found over greater Athens, including the Akropolis and Agora.[146]

The Peiraeus accounts of 394–3 B.C.E. reveal an important moment in the tradition of Boiotian masons: "The contractor for the transport

---

[138] Ober so thinks, but gives no evidence for his position. *Fortress Attica*, 59.
[139] Thuc. 5.82.6.
[140] Scranton, *Greek Walls*, 34, 160.
[141] Themistokles 1.93.4, and those at Athens cited above. R. Garland, *The Piraeus* (London, 1987), 163–5; bibliography, 222.
[142] Xen. *Hell.* 2.2.23.
[143] Xen. *Hell.* 4.8.9–10; Diod. 14.85; Nepos 9.4.5.
[144] *IG* II² 1656–64. Maier, *Griechische Mauerbauinschriften*, I:17–21, nos. 1–9; Garland, *The Piraeus*, 40, 185 (bibliography).
[145] *IG* II² 1656, 395–6 B.C.E. and 1657, 394–3 B.C.E.
[146] M. Walbank, "Greek Inscriptions from the Athenian Agora: Building Records," *Hesperia* 64 (1995): 315–23.

and laying of stones was Demosthenes the Boiotian."[147] This epigraphic evidence is confirmed by Xenophon and Nepos, who write that the Peiraeus walls were re-erected with the help of Boiotian volunteers.[148] The Oxyrhynchus Historian gives a slightly different account: "500 Boiotian craftsmen and masons."[149] The inscribed contract, II² 1657, gives greater weight to the latter version, which notes that skilled professionals were under contract.[150]

Long stretches of the Peiraeus wall socle survive. A double-curtain stone socle forms the base for a superstructure of mudbrick. The socle is of isodomic trapezoidal masonry with blocks about 0.50 m in height and rising two to four courses (six courses at towers). The interval between the curtains was filled with earth and aggregate.[151] This is to say, the Peiraeus fortifications did not rise in solid stone; not until a generation later does Epaminondas's design at Messene achieve that distinction. Yet this stone socle and mudbrick (*plinthon*) superstructure design persisted until 371 B.C.E., used for the new walls at Mantinea (Figs. 6.13 and 6.14) and, a year later, for the circuit built at Megalopolis.[152]

Pausanias was awed by the impressive walls at Ambrossos during his visit to the town.[153] The walls at Ambrossos were built as a part of a Boiotian-Athenian venture into Phocis, just before the Battle of Chaironeia in 338 B.C.E.[154]

This brings me to another important clarification: Boiotian specialization in stone-wall construction continued for a generation after the death of Epaminondas in 362 B.C.E., a date modern scholars perhaps

---

[147] *IG* II² 1657. Tod, 107. Translation of *IG* II² 1657 by J. Wickersham and G. Verbrugghe, *Greek Historical Documents: the Fourth Century B.C.* (Toronto, 1973), no. 10.

[148] Xen. *Hell.* 4.8.10.; 9.4.5. R. J. Buck, *Boiotia and the Boiotian League, 432–371 B.C.* (Edmonton, 1994), 48.

[149] P. Oxy. 842A, col. 1, lines 5–13 and *apud* Diod. 14.85.3.

[150] I.A.F. Bruce, *A Historical Commentary on the Hellenica of Oxyrhynchus* (Cambridge, 1967).

[151] Wrede, *Attische Mauern*, 29, pls. 69–70; Scranton, *Greek Walls*, 117–19; Mussche, "L'Architecture civile et militaire," 35; Karlsson, *Fortification Towers and Masonry Techniques*, 97–8.

[152] *IG* II² 1658, line 5: 1659, line 6; 1661, line 4. Karlsson, *Fortification Towers and Masonry Techniques*, 73, claims "the first true *emplekton* walls (Vitruvius 2.8.7; see note 27) in Greece occur in the walls of the cities associated with Epaminondas: Megalopolis, Mantinea and Messene."

[153] Pausanias 4.31.5; 10.36.5. Kleombrotos withdrew to Ambrossos in Phocis after his march into Boiotia in 371 B.C.E. and was thwarted by the Thebans at Chaironeia (Diod. 15.527). From Ambrossos the Spartans entered Boiotia over Mount Helicon on their way to Kreusis and Leuktra (Paus. 9.13.1).

[154] Demo. 18.215–16.

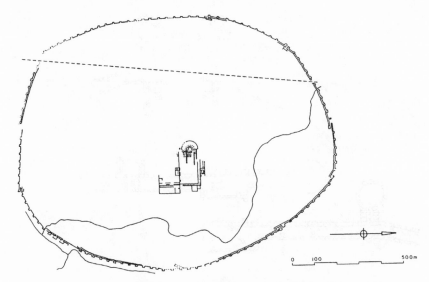

Figure 6.13. Mantinea, plan. Drawing by Helen Foster.

too easily fix as the end of Theban hegemony.[155] Pausanias enthusias-
tically describes these walls at Ambrossos: "On going to war with
Philip and his Macedonians the Thebans drew around Ambrossos a
double wall. It is made of a local stone, black in colour and very hard
indeed."[156] Unfortunately, the walls at Ambrossos, modern-day Disto-
mon, have been entirely robbed. Vestiges are reported by Dodwell and
John Fraser.[157] Today, all that remains are one or two courses of short
stretches of extant ashlar and polygonal walls in the village and ashlar
blocks built into medieval and later constructions.[158] In other words,
although monumental Boiotian walls after ca. 395 B.C.E. were a reality,
we must rely on Pausanias's words that here at Ambrossos in 338
B.C.E. was a masterpiece second only to Messene.

Round Messene is a wall, the whole circuit of which is built of stone, the
towers and battlements upon it. I have not seen the walls at Babylon or the

---

[155] Buckler, *The Theban Hegemony*, 220–7; Cawkwell, "Epaminondas and Thebes," 254–
78; Roy, "Thebes in the 360s B.C.," 206.
[156] Paus. 10.36.5.
[157] Dodwell, *A Classical and Topographical Tour*, 250. J. Fraser, *Pausanias's Descriptions of
Greece* V (London, 1913), 449.
[158] A. Nikopoulou, *Deltion* (1968): 2708; J. Fossey, *The Ancient Topography of Eastern Phocis*
(Amsterdam, 1986), 30–1, 128; brief description in Lawrence, *Greek Aims*, 447 n. 11.

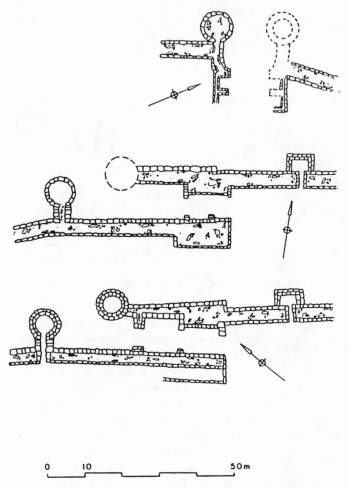

0   10   50m

Figure 6.14. Mantinea, detail of portals and walls. Drawing by Helen Foster.

walls of Memnon at Susa in Persia, nor have I heard the account of any eyewitness; but the walls at *Ambrossos in Phocis,* at Byzantium and at Rhodes, all
of them the most strongly fortified places, are not so strong as the Messenian
wall.[159]

This means that the Boiotians were supreme in fortification construction for nearly sixty years, 395 to 338 B.C.E.

---

[159] Translation Jones, italics mine.

PELOPIDAS AT SUSA AND ASSYRIAN FORTIFICATIONS

A strong similarity in overall appearance exists between the enceintes of the Assyrian empire, 999–666 B.C.E. (northern Iraq), and those under discussion.[160] These Mesopotamian forerunners had no direct influence on Greek fortification design through the fifth century, but in the fourth century, Theban, Spartan, and Athenian emissaries traveled to the Persian court and Greek-led mercenary armies marched through these lands.[161] Xenophon was overwhelmed by the size of Nimrud and greatly impressed by Ninevah.[162]

As noted above, Pelopidas was not only a Theban general but also an emissary who travelled to the court of the Persian king Artaxerxes at Susa in 367/366 B.C.E. The trip probably took about six months and the most convenient route went through central Anatolia (Phrygia) to the upper valley of the Tigris and Euphrates Rivers and hence towards the southeast to Susa. It is likely that Pelopidas saw the imposing vestiges of the Assyrian empire, such as those of the palace of Assurbanipal at Ninevah. Even though Pelopidas's delegation went abroad about two years after the construction of the walls at Messene, there may be a connection. Perhaps the idea for the visually impressive and intimidating Messenian fortifications came to Greece via this route.

CONCLUSION

An Athenian perspective pervades recent scholarship on Greek fortifications, which has obscured the Theban contribution. Boiotian masons established the practice of solid stone-socle fortification construction by the early fourth century B.C.E. and became itinerant specialists in stone socles for fortification walls and towers. Epaminondas's rise to power, his stunning victory at Leuktra, and the arrival of the catapult from Syracuse led to a major advance in the architecture of war:

[160] W.A.P. Childs, *The City-Reliefs of Lycia* (Princeton, 1978), 49–54, discusses iconographic history of the earlier Assyrian city sieges; more germane is A. Gunter, "Representations of Urartian and Western Iranian Fortress Architecture in the Assyrian Reliefs," *Iran* 20 (1982): 103–12.

[161] Lawrence, *Greek Aims*, 13–30, devotes an introductory section to "Fortifications in Western Asia," specifically Assyrian reliefs, ca. 885–681 B.C.E. A.M. Snodgrass, in "Historical Significance," 127, comments: "that wall-builders of the ninth and eighth centuries had actually studied the great fortifications of [Assyria] seems to me on reflection unlikely."

[162] *Xen., Anab.* 3.4.7; 3.4.10–11.

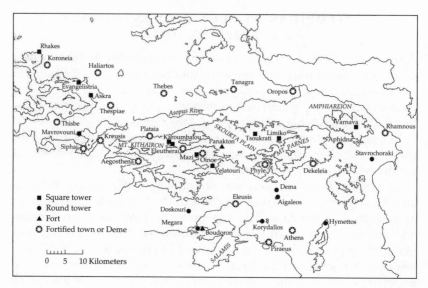

Figure 6.15. Attica and Boiotia, plan of sites. Drawing by Michael Nelson, after Camp.

full-scale stone walls and towers.[163] The death of Epaminondas did not curtail Theban wall building which, in fact, continued to ca. 338 B.C.E. These three generations are documented by ancient sources and the physical evidence of surviving examples (Fig. 6.15).

In the first generation, 395–70 B.C.E., came the stone-socle walls at Peiraeus, Mantinea, Megalopolis, and perhaps, Thebes. In Epaminondas's generation, 370–62 B.C.E., there are the enceintes at Messene, the Boiotian coastal ports on the Corinthian Gulf (Siphai, Kreusis, and Korsiai), and Gyphtokastro. In the last generation, which embraced the later career of Pammenes and then Cephesian, 361–38 B.C.E., there are the constructions at Aigosthena and Ambrossos. According to this prescription, fifth century and earlier dates for all-stone fortifications must be revised downwards, a process already taking place with the recent studies by Adam and Karlsson.

With the conquests of Alexander, wall building spread quickly throughout the Greek world and continued apace henceforth.[164] In this essay, I cannot canvass the entire architectural history of Greek fortifications, but at the beginning of the period, the Syracusan convention

---

[163] Garlan, "Les fortifications grecques," 19.
[164] Lawrence, *Greek Aims*, 460–83, lists over 500 sites.

of the non-torsion catapult and siege tower opened new possibilities for warfare. The shift in military science came with adaptation to these weapons under Epaminondas, whose strategy was to pursue the defeated and to cause destruction of property along the way.[165]

In the first stages and perhaps later as well, Epaminondas employed a new version of temporary fortifications-within-enemy-territory or *epiteichismos*.[166] The early form of the *epiteichismos* was a stationary garrison built of rubble and earth.[167] Plato had in mind walls such as these when he expressed deep reservations about their utility:

> As to the walls . . . I agree with Sparta in thinking that they should be allowed to sleep in the earth . . . besides, how ridiculous . . . that we should surround ourselves with a wall, which in the first place, is by no means conducive to the health of cities, and is also apt to produce a certain softness in the minds of the inhabitants, inviting men to run thither instead of repelling their enemies.[168]

Plato wrote this at the very time Epaminondas was in the process of advancing Greek military tactics by the creation of the quick and flexible *epiteichismos* for his Peloponnesian campaigns, "wherever Thebans encamped they at once threw down in front of their lines the greatest possible quantity of trees which they cut down, and in this way guarded themselves."[169] The counterpoint to the new-era *epiteichismos* and to Plato was the massive, stone-built walls for Epaminondas's foundation of Messene, the first monumental Greek city and the very kind much admired by Aristotle.

---

[165] Ober, *Fortress Attica*, 4.
[166] *Epiteichesmos*, Thucydides 1.122.1; 1.142.2.
[167] H.D. Westlake, "The Program of Epiteichismos," *Classical Quarterly* 33 (1983): 12ff, and *Studies in Thucydides and Greek History* (Bristol, 1989), ch. 3. Additional examples in Lawrence, *Greek Aims*, 175; Ober, *Fortress Attica*, 60.
[168] Laws 6.778B–E.
[169] Xen. *Hell*. 6.5.30.

CHAPTER 7

Imperial walled cities in the West: An examination of their early medieval Nachleben

BERNARD S. BACHRACH

Writing during the early seventh century, Isidore of Seville made the observation "... urbs ipsa moenia sunt," that is, "The *urbs* is made by its defensive walls."[1] Isidore's understanding of the topographical features that were essential to the existence of an *urbs* is far indeed from that of the Roman republic and early empire. The vast majority of Roman *urbes* during the first two and a half centuries of the empire either were not walled or their walls had been left to decay during the *pax Romana*.[2] For the Romans, as Robert Lopez observed, "the test of cityhood ... was the existence of a public square for political meetings and discussion, of a public bathhouse for the comfort of the body, and a theatre or arena for the pleasures of the mind."[3]

The process by which the *forum*, *thermae*, and *amphitheatrum* gave way to the *moenia* as the basic topographical element that gave definition to the *urbs* is also the process by which the ancient world ended and the medieval world began. The well-known complex of civil wars and foreign invasions which has come to be known, even in textbooks,

---

[1] Isidore, *Etymologiae*. xv, ii. 1; *Isidorii Etymologiae*, ed. W.M. Lindsey (Oxford, 1911). Donald A. Bullough, "Social and Economic Structure and Topography in the Early Medieval City," *Settimane di Studio del Centro Italiano di studi sull'alto Medioevo* I (1973), 350, is correct in observing that Isidore emphasized the community of people living in the city as well as the walls.

[2] See Paul-Albert Février, "Permanence et héritages de l'antiquité dans la topographie des villes de l'occident durant le haut moyen âge," *Settimane di Studio del Centro Italiano di studi sull'alto Medioevo* I (1973), 41–138. Jean Hubert, "Evolution de la topographie de l'aspect des villes de gaule du Ve au Xe siècle," *Settimane di Studio del Centro Italiano di studi sull'alto Medioevo* VI (1959), 529–58, is still of value.

[3] Robert Lopez, "Of Towns and Trade," in *Life and Thought in the Early Middle Ages*, ed. R.S. Hoyt (Minneapolis, 1967), 31.

as "the crash of the third century" led the imperial government to alter in a radical manner the physiognomy of the *urbes* throughout the greater part of the empire, but most especially in the western provinces. In Gaul, for example, some eighty percent of the one hundred and fifteen *urbes* that are listed in the *Notitia Galliarum* were drastically reduced in size and became the beneficiaries of massive walls that averaged ten meters in height and four meters in thickness at the base. These fortifications were generally strengthened with equally massive towers, which on average were placed at twenty-five-meter intervals along the walls, and elaborate fortifications to protect the gates. This entire complex was usually further reinforced with an internal citadel, i.e., the *arx* or *praetorium*. Finally, in order to enhance the defenses, it was not uncommon to have ditches dug around the walls, which were then filled with water by having nearby streams or rivers diverted.[4]

Intensive examination of these defenses or their remains during the past century and a half by both antiquarians and trained scholars has made clear that these walls and towers were built, at least in part, from the stones that previously had served as the buildings and the monuments of the forum, the baths, and the amphitheater.[5] Thus, in a material sense the new imperial *urbes* were built not on the ruins of the Roman empire but with the remains of its ancient cities. Those characteristics that had defined the *urbs* of the Roman world reappeared during the later empire in a new and fundamentally different form and thereby gave shape to the early medieval city.[6]

For more than six centuries, and in some places for some seven

---

[4] Regarding the monumental physical infrastructure see, for example, the general survey by Stephen Johnson, *Late Roman Fortifications* (Totowa, NJ, 1983). For special focus on Britain, Gaul, and the Rhineland, see H. von Petrikovits, "Fortifications in the North-Western Roman Empire from the third to the fifth centuries A.D.," *Journal of Roman Studies* 61 (1971): 178–218. Special attention is given to Gaul by R.M. Butler, "Late Roman Town Walls in Gaul," *Archaeological Journal* 116 (1959): 25–50; Albert Grenier, *Manuel d'archéologie gallo-romaine* (Paris, 1934), 6:1; Carl-Richard Brühl, *Palatium und Civitas: Studien zur Profantopographie spätantiker Civitates vom 3. bis zum 13 Jahrhundert*, I *Gallien* (Cologne and Vienna, 1975), II, *Belgica I, beide Germanien und Raetia II* (Cologne and Vienna, 1990); and Adrien Blanchet, *Les enceintes romaines de la Gaule* (Paris, 1907).

[5] See particularly Grenier, *Manuel d'archéologie gallo-romaine*, 6:1.

[6] It should not be assumed, however, that the attributes of the ancient city disappeared in the Western half of the empire completely and suddenly everywhere at the same time. Rather, within the reduced confines of the late Roman city there were considerable continuities. See, for example, Bullough, "Social and Economic Structure and Topography," 353; Février, "Permanence et héritages de l'antiquité," 41–138; and Brian Ward Perkins, *From classical antiquity to the Middle Ages: Urban Public Building in Northern and Central Italy, AD 300–850* (Oxford, 1984).

hundred years or more, these walls not only survived but continued, more often than not and in more places than in fewer, to be maintained at great expense in defensible condition.[7] Indeed, local pride in the defenses of these cities is evidenced by surviving *encomia* written during the eighth century and not only in Italy, which might be expected.[8] Somewhat of a surprise is Alcuin's poem on York, in which Charlemagne's adviser wrote:

> York, with its high walls and lofty
> towers, was first built by Roman
> hands . . . secure for its masters,
> and an ornament to empire, was a
> dread bastion against enemy attacks,
> a haven for ocean-going ships. . . .[9]

Writing about the *Nachleben* of these massive defenses from a somewhat different perspective, Donald Bullough observed: "Once built they were for centuries a constant factor in the topographical evolution of the towns. Hardly less important than natural features such as sea-coasts, rivers, marshes and prominent hills. . . ."[10]

The fundamental reason for this huge building program was the need perceived by the emperor and his advisors, i.e., those in decision-making positions, to provide for the security of the cities of the empire in the event of an attack. Indeed, without imperial action no building or rebuilding of city walls could legally take place. As the *Codex Justinianus* put it, based upon Ulpian:

It is unlawful to rebuild the walls of municipalities without the authorization of the emperor or the governor, nor is it legal to build anything onto or on top of them [without such authorization].[11]

---

[7] Regarding the medieval use of these walls see, for example, Carl-Richard Brühl, *Palatium und Civitas*, vols. 1 and 2; and Bernard S. Bachrach, "Early Medieval Fortifications in the 'West' of France: a technical vocabulary," *Technology and Culture* 16 (1975), 531–69.

[8] See, for example, regarding Milan and Verona, *Versus de Verona, Versum de Mediolano Civitate*, ed. G.B. Pighi (Bologna, 1980).

[9] Alcuin, *Versus de patribus regibus et sanctis euboricensis ecclesiae*, lines 19–27, in *Alcuin, The Bishops, Kings, and Saints of York*, ed. and trans. Peter Godman (Oxford, 1982).

[10] Bullough, "Social and Economic Structure and Topography," 352.

[11] *The Digest of Justinian*, Latin text ed. Theodore Mommsen with Paul Kruger and English trans. Alan Watson, 4 vols. (Philadelphia, 1985), bk. I, ch. viii, para 9. See the discussion by Février, "Permanence et héritages de l'antiquité," 74. Cf. Petrikovits, "Fortifications in the North-Western Roman Empire," 203, who takes the fact that there was no great uniformity in building styles as evidence that there were no "central directives from the Emperor or his ministers." This line of reasoning is based upon an unnecessary set of assumptions, that is, if the emperor were to order that a

Would-be clandestine efforts to build massive fortifications by local authorities, contrary to governmental policy, could hardly remain secret for very long given the magnitude of the efforts at issue.

The *urbes* of the Roman empire historically had been the primary centers of governmental administration, population density, manufacture, trade, and culture. The ravages of the third century had made clear to the imperial authorities that those cities which were not adequately defended by walls were exceptionally vulnerable to enemy attack.[12] Therefore, it was concluded that extraordinary efforts had to be undertaken if the needs of local urban defense were to be met.

In this context, it is important to emphasize that not all the *urbes* that survived the crash of the third century were provided with the kinds of fortifications that have been described above. In the south of Gaul, for example, Eauze, Aire, Lectoure, Tarbes, Oloron, Lodève, Frèjus, and Javols either were not given walls or their old walls were not repaired.[13] Such undefended cities either disappeared completely during the period under discussion here – generally before the end of the sixth century – or disappeared only to reappear again more as villages than as urban centers during occasional interludes of relative peace.[14] In many of the unwalled *urbes* the Church, which seems to have been committed in general to the establishment of bishoprics in the erstwhile Roman cities, either abandoned the unfortified ones completely as episcopal sees or the bishops followed the uncertain fate of the unprotected settlements and disappeared for long periods of time.[15]

The building of the walls was intended, in large part, to thwart the efforts of the so-called "barbarians" from beyond the frontiers to loot and ravage the cities of the empire. It was widely believed by military

particular city have a wall built, he also is assumed to have sent a set of plans, and if he did, it is further assumed that plans for all of the fortifications would be sufficiently uniform for modern scholars to detect this uniformity.

[12] Blanchet, *Les enceintes romaines de la Gaule;* and Grenier, *Manuel d'archéologie,* 6:1, provide a good introduction regarding the ravages suffered by unwalled cities during the crash of the third century. As our knowledge is increasing from the archaeological evidence, it is becoming more clear that this building effort did not begin only as the crash of the third century came to an end; attempts were made to build and repair walls during the time of troubles as well. See, for example, Petrikovits, "Fortifications in the North-Western Roman Empire," 178–218; and Johnson, *Late Roman Fortifications,* 1–30.

[13] Johnson, *Late Roman Fortifications,* 83.

[14] Auguste Longnon, *Géographie de la Gaule au VIe siècle* (Paris, 1878), under the names cited above.

[15] Élie Griffe, *La gaule chretienne a l'époque romaine,* 3 vols. (Paris, 1947–65).

experts that these various *gentes*, who were viewed as threats to the peace of the empire, had developed neither the technological sophistication nor the logistic infrastructure adequately to lay siege to strongly built and well-defended fortifications. For example, Ammianus Marcellinus portrays a relevant incident involving the Visigoths:

> Then Fritigern [the Visigothic leader], seeing that his men, who were ignorant of the manner in which to conduct a siege, were suffering serious casualties . . . reminded them to be at peace with the walls and persuaded them to attack and loot the rich and well stocked countryside. . . .[16]

Indeed, for the barbarians, as imperial military commentators saw the matter, learning how to deal with fortifications was the *sine qua non* for being civilized in military terms. Flavius Merobaudes (d. before 467), a Roman of at least nominal Frankish origin who was raised in Spain, owned land in northern Gaul, and likely was a descendant of the famous general of the same name who flourished during the fourth century, earned fame and fortune both as a general and as a writer.[17] Not unexpectedly, he was also an acute observer of the military scene and noted that the Visigoths, during the two generations following their flight from *Gothia*, their trans-Danubian homeland, had learned a great deal regarding the proper conduct of war. Merobaudes observed that the Visigoths' military establishment was very different from that of the "Teutons" whom Caesar had fought. These Teutons, according to Merobaudes, had only a "crude command of warfare ("ad bella rudem") and were inexperienced in its developed art." By

---

[16] *Codex Theodosianus*. bk. XXXI, ch. 6, para. 4 (hereafter *CTh*). *Theodosiani Libri cum constitutionibus Sirmondianis et Leges Novellae*, eds. T. Mommsen and P. Meyer, 2 vols. (Berlin, 1905). Cf. *The Theodosian Code and Novels and the Sirmondian Constitutions*, trans. with commentary by Clyde Pharr et al. (Princeton, 1952).

[17] Regarding various details of Merobaudes's life and career, see Ferdinand Lot, "Un diplome de Clovis confirmatif d'une donation de patrice romain," *Revue belge de philologie et d'histoire* 17 (1938): 906–11; Karl. F. Stroheker, "Spanische Senatoren der spatrömischen und westgotischen Zeit," *Madrider Mitteilungen* 4 (1963), followed by Fredrich Prinz, *Frühes Mönchtum im Frankenreich: Kultur un Gesellschaft in Gallien, den Rheinlanden und Bayern am Beispiel der monastichen Entwicklung (4. bis 8 Jahrhundert)* (Munich-Vienna, 1965), 70–1; and Frank M. Clover, *Flavius Merobaudes: A Translation and Historical Commentary* in *Transactions of the American Philosophical Society* n.s. 61/1 (Philadelphia, 1971), 7–10. Merobaudes's good classical education is well documented through the surviving poems and panegyrics which he authored. His military service is highlighted by campaigns in the Alps during the early 430s, in connection with which he was given the rank of *comes rei militari* or that of *dux*, as evidenced by his appointment as a count of the Consistory, and appointment in 443 to the rank of *magister utriusque militiae*, which he exercised in Spain as successor to his father-in-law, Austurius. Merobaudes's honors included the award of the name *Flavius* for distinguished military service, admission to the senate of Rome, the title of *patricius*, and a bronze statue erected in Rome by imperial order.

contrast, the Goths, Merobaudes implies, came to be both sophisticated and experienced in the mature art of warfare (*"adulto marte
probatum"*) after their settlement within the empire.[18]

As Merobaudes saw the situation, the Goths were no longer "a race
from a barbarian land" but "enemies equal [to the Romans] in war."
Among those mature skills in the art of war which the Goths had
acquired and which particularly convinced Merobaudes that this *sem-
inium barbaricae terrae* had learned a great deal, was the ability to
defend fortifications (*castra*) of the type which dotted the landscape of
the Roman empire, and citadels (*arces*). The *arx* was the specially
constructed stronghold within each great fortified city (*urbs*) that
served as the civil, military, and ecclesiastical capital of the *civitas*. It
might even be argued from Merobaudes's account that the Visigoths
had learned something of the art of constructing fortifications, as
well.[19] This is a point of considerable interest when one evaluates the
history of the defenses of southern Gaul and Spain, where there were
an abundance of important walled fortress cities under Visigothic
control.[20]

More particularly, the imperial planners conceived of defending the
empire with a strategic system that we now call "defense-in-depth."
This required the radical transformation of the *urbes* of the later Roman empire into "hardened" centers of military strength which had
four interrelated military functions: (1) supply depots; (2) control
points on key land and water routes; (3) coordination of rear area
security and intelligence; and (4) self-contained strongholds with mobile field forces.[21] So, it is perhaps fitting that Isidore of Seville, that

---

[18] *Panegyricus*, II, lines 144–5 in *Flavius Merobaudes reliquiae*, ed. F. Volmer, *Monumenta
Germaniae Historica, Auctores Antiquissimi* (Berlin, 1905), 14:1–20. See the discussion by
Bernard S. Bachrach, "The Education of the 'officer corps' in the Fifth and Sixth
Centuries," in *La noblesse romaine et les chefs barbares du IIIe au VIIIe siècle*, eds. Fran-
çoise Vallet and Michel Kazanski (Paris, 1995), 7–13.

[19] *Panegyricus*, II, lines 149–51.

[20] E.A. Thompson, *The Goths in Spain* (Oxford, 1969), remains basic regarding the political history. The military role of the *urbes* in Spain during the early Middle Ages is not
effectively covered. However, José Maria Lacarra, "Panorama de la historia urbana
en la peninsula iberica desde el siglo V al X," *Settimane di Studio del Centro Italiano di
studi sull'alto Medioevo* VI (1959), 319–57; and Claudio Sanchez-Albornoz, "El gobierno
de las ciudades en España del siglo V al X," *Settimane di Studio del Centro Italiano di
studi sull'alto Medioevo* VI (1959), 359–91, provide useful background material.

[21] Edward N. Luttwak, *The Grand Strategy of the Roman Empire* (Baltimore, 1976), 126–
90, and esp. 132–4, where Luttwak outlines five major elements. However, it would
seem reasonable to suggest that Luttwak's point five, that is, "conservation of the
strength of *mobile* forces," can reasonably be subsumed under point four. Luttwak's
major contribution to our understanding of late Roman military strategy has predict-
ably attracted the attention of small-minded quibblers. However, their arguments are
effectively dismissed in a magisterial study by Everett L. Wheeler, "Methodological

compiler of so-called ancient knowledge for the Middle Ages, should, as noted above, tell his readers that the *urbs* is made by its walls.

This century-long effort to convert vast numbers of undefended or ill-defended cities into massively walled fortifications was carried out only at an immense cost in both human and material resources. For example, an *urbs* such as Bordeaux, with a perimeter of approximately 2,330 meters, required well in excess of 200,000 tons of stone, much of it neatly cut into building blocks of various sizes, for the construction of its foundation, walls, towers, and gate emplacements.[22] Forests of trees were consumed simply to burn the tons of limestone that were needed in order to create lime so that mortar might be mixed to hold the stones together.[23] The man-hours of labor expended to carry out the myriad tasks required for such building projects runs into the millions.[24]

The physical changes wrought by Roman policy on the cities of the empire were sustained and supported by changes in military organization which, in the present context, focused on the extensive militarization of the civilian population.[25] Thus, for example, the legislation establishing urban militia forces, and especially the urban militia of Rome, was already very well attested in 440 when Emperor Valentinian III clarified the existing situation in the following manner:

We decree . . . that all are to know . . . that no Roman citizen or member of a guild is to be compelled to do [expeditionary] military service. Indeed, he is required to do armed service only on the walls and at the gates [for the defense of the city] whenever the necessity arises. The regulations made by the Illustrious Prefect of the City are to be obeyed by all.[26]

Limits and the Mirage of Roman Strategy," *Journal of Military History* 57 (1993): 7–41, 215–40.

[22] Concerning Bordeaux see Robert Étienne with the collaboration of P. Barrère, *Bordeaux Antique* (Bordeaux, 1962), 204–10.

[23] For a discussion of the cost of building fortifications see Bernard S. Bachrach, "The Cost of Castle-Building: The Case of the Tower at Langeais, 992–994," in *The Medieval Castle: Romance and Reality*, eds. Kathryn Reyerson and Faye Powe (Dubuque, IA, 1984), 46–62, where particular attention is given to the costs of burning lime among other tasks.

[24] With regard to the calculation of man-hours of labor see the efforts by Hans Hubert Hofmann, "*Fossa Carolina* Versuch Einer Zussammenschau," in *Karl der Grosse: Lebenswerk und Nachleben*, I, eds. W. Braunfels and Helmut Beumann (Düsseldorf, 1965), I: 437–53, with the literature cited there; and Bachrach, "The Cost of Castle Building," 46–62.

[25] See, in general, Bernard S. Bachrach, "Grand Strategy in the Germanic Kingdoms: Recruitment of the Rank and File," in *L'armée romaine et les barbares du IIIe au VIIe siècle*, eds. Françoise Vallet and Michel Kazanski (Paris, 1993), 55–63, with the literature cited there.

[26] *Nov. Val*. V.2

This process, however, went on not only in the cities. For example, in 406 Emperor Honorius ordered:

We exhort that . . . slaves shall offer themselves for war. . . . Of course we especially encourage the slaves belonging to men who are in the imperial armed forces, and also the slaves of federates . . . , because it is clear that these slaves already are making war alongside their owners.[27]

The Roman government clearly recognized and, indeed, encouraged the widespread militarization of the civilian population, both slave and free, before the middle of the fifth century. Thus in 440, upon receiving intelligence regarding a forthcoming Vandal invasion by sea, the emperor Valentinian took steps for his regular soldiers and his federate allies to guard the cities and shore, and for a mobile force to be put in the field. He then ordered:

. . . because the opportunities presented by navigation in the summer make it uncertain at which shore the enemy ships would land, we admonish each and all to defend their property with their own men against the enemy if the circumstances require it. They are to use those weapons which they have available on the condition that public order is preserved. Thus, they are to guard our province and their own fortunes. . . . Whatever a victor takes away from an enemy shall belong to him without any doubt.[28]

The great Antiochene rhetorician, Libanius, was not happy with these policies, which in part, at least, based military defense upon fortified cities and relied on irregulars for local defense. Consequently, he harangued Emperor Theodosius I so that he might institute "reforms":

[Recent] disasters make clear that we have been deserted by fortune. . . . The natives, who live outside of the walled cities, have been taken off as prisoners. Those who are on the inside eat up everything that they have and then . . . die of starvation. . . . Up until now the Goths were accustomed to cringe when they heard about the skill of the Romans in the art of war. But now they are victorious. . . . Now that those who have spent their lives as soldiers are no longer available, we base our defense on farmers.[29]

The die was cast and the situation that Libanius lamented was not materially altered either by Theodosius or his successors.

At various times from the sixth century into the eleventh century the danger of attack was a continuing threat for the inhabitants of

[27] *CTh.* VII.13.16
[28] *Nov. Val.* 9.1.
[29] *Oratio*, no. 24, 15–16. Libanius, *Opera*, ed. R. Förster (1903–27), vol. 2 of 12; and cf. Libanius *Orationes*, ed. and trans. A. Norman, 2 vols. (Cambridge, MA, 1969).

much of Western Europe. For example, Franks, Alamans, Burgundians, Vandals, Alans, Goths, Saxons, Huns, Lombards, Avars, Magyars, Muslims, and Vikings, to mention only the most prominent groups, raided, pillaged, besieged, and fought throughout various parts of the western half of the erstwhile Roman empire for more than half of a millennium. Indeed, it is rather difficult to find a decade during which some part of the West and more particularly one or another western *urbs*, which had been fortified during the later Roman empire, was not under attack. The endemic nature of this danger, as Georges Duby has shown in a discussion of the southeast of France, elevated the importance of the *urbs*. He correctly emphasized the usefulness of the massive fortifications as places of refuge and observed that their already existing character as military strongholds was greatly strengthened by the uncertainty of the time.[30]

At the end of the fourth century, when the mortar was not yet dry, metaphorically speaking, the great Gallo-Roman rhetorician, Ausonius, discussed and, in fact, praised the walled cities as though they had always been.[31] If an inference may be permitted, it seems to me that Ausonius believed that these walled cities would always be. It should be expected then, that Cassiodorus, the Italo-Roman scholar and head of Theodoric the Great's government, also knew that the walls were fundamental to the *urbs* and observed somewhat pedantically, "they are an adornment in time of peace and a precaution in a time of war." At the time, Cassiodorus was defending the military budget for 518.[32]

Gregory of Tours, Cassiodorus's younger contemporary, believed that massive fortifications were the *sine qua non* for a city. Indeed, he simply could not find an explanation when in a particular circumstance this generalization was not borne out. Thus, he observed regarding Dijon, which was considered a *castrum* rather than an *urbs* or a *civitas*:

It is a fortified place (*castrum*) with very strong walls ("firmissimis muris"), built in the middle of a plain. . . . Four gates ("portae") face the four corners of the earth ("quattuor plagis mundi sunt positae") and thirty-three towers ("torres") guard the [circuit] walls. These towers are built of squared stones to a height of twenty feet and above these are courses of small stones. The total

---

[30] Georges Duby, "Les villes du sud-est de la Gaule du VIIIe au XI siècle," *Settimane di Studio del Centro Italiano di studi sull'alto Medioevo* VI (1959), 231–58.

[31] Ausonius, *Ordo Nobilius Urbium*, ed. K. Schenkl, *Monumenta Germaniae Historica, Auctores Antiquissimi* (Berlin, 1883), V.2.

[32] Cassiodorus, *Variae*, I, xxviii (*Casidorii Variae*, ed. Theodore Mommsen, *Monumenta Germaniae Historica, Auctores Antiquissimi*, XII [Berlin, 1894]).

height of the walls comes to thirty feet and they have a thickness of fifteen feet. Why this place is not called a *civitas* I do not know.[33]

The dissolution of imperial government in the West did not bring with it the disintegration of the late Roman city as the focus of military life. The grand strategies or military policies that were developed by men such as Theodoric the Great, the Ostrogothic king and imperial governor of Italy, and Clovis, the *rex Francorum* and *consul*, generally showed no inclination to dismantle the vast physical infrastructure of fortified cities, fortresses, ports, and roads that had been created by the empire.[34] In addition, these rulers and their advisers, who were responsible for military decision making in the Romano-German kingdoms of early medieval Europe, found that the corpus of ancient military science, available in books such as Vegetius's *De re militari*, which was known in the West from the edition made at Constantinople in 450, reinforced these tendencies toward continuity.[35]

During the Middle Ages, Vegetius's handbook was the most frequently copied secular text of late antiquity.[36] Further reenforcement of late antique military ideas came as a result of the substantial direct contact of Westerners with the Byzantines and later with the Muslim military, both heirs of Rome's martial legacy.[37] In a reciprocal manner, access to information concerning the past provided additional stimuli for military commanders in the West to take advantage of the physical legacy bequeathed to them by the empire.[38]

It should be emphasized, moreover, that "foreign" invasion was not

---

[33] Gregory of Tours, *Historiarum libri X.*, bk. III, ch. 19; *Gregorii episcopi turnonsis Historiarum libri X*, eds. Bruno Krusch and Wilhelm Levison, *Monumenta Germaniae Historica, Scriptores rerum Merovingicarum*, I.1 (Hanover, 1951).

[34] Johnson, *Late Roman Fortifications*, provides a useful introduction to this very important topic along with considerable bibliography. For a more specialized approach see Brühl, *Palatium und Civitas*, Vols. 1 and 2.

[35] See, for example, Bernard S. Bachrach, "The Practical Use of Vegetius' *De Re Militari* During the Early Middle Ages," *The Historian* 47 (1985): 239–55, with the literature cited there.

[36] The most comprehensive study remains Charles R. Shrader, "A Handlist of Extant Manuscripts Containing the *De Re Militari* of Flavius Vegetius Renatus," *Scriptorium* 33 (1978): 280–395, but it is not exhaustive.

[37] Bernard S. Bachrach, *The Anatomy of a Little War: A Diplomatic and Military History of the Gundovald Affair (568–586)* (Boulder, 1994), for consistent Western involvement with the Byzantines. For a later period see two articles by Krijnie Ciggaar, "England and Byzantium on the Eve of the Norman Conquest," and "Byzantine Marginalia to the Norman Conquest," in *Anglo-Norman Studies* V (1982): 78–96, and IX (1986): 43–63, respectively.

[38] See, for example, two articles by Bernard S. Bachrach, "On the Origins of William the Conqueror's Horse Transports," *Technology and Culture* 26 (1985): 505–31, and "Some Observations on the Military Administration of the Norman Conquest," *Anglo-Norman Studies* VIII, ed. R. Allen Brown (Woodbridge, Suffolk, 1986), 1–25.

the only military threat that increased the value and importance of these great mountains of stone with which the Romans had so fundamentally marked the strategic landscape of Western Europe. An examination of political activity within Rome's successor states throughout the West, i.e., Gaul, Italy, Spain, and even Britain, makes clear that the *urbs* was the key to domination of the area around it, i.e., the *civitas* or *pagus*.[39]

Throughout the early Middle Ages and, indeed, during the entire medieval period, warfare was dominated by sieges. By comparison, important battles in the field were very rare. For example, a ruler such as William the Conqueror, who was thoroughly engaged in military operations throughout his entire career, fought only two major battles in the field. From the perspective of the manpower engaged in warfare, sieges, in general, saw the deployment of a great many more warm bodies than battle in the field.[40]

The focus of war very often was based upon an effort to gain control of one or more *civitates*. The *civitas* (Gk. *polis*), which consisted of the *urbs* or city with its surrounding area, was the fundamental unit of political, military, economic, and religious organization during the Roman empire, and as mentioned above, it continued to play that role in the West during the Middle Ages. For centuries thereafter, under such names as *pagus*, *Gau*, *comté*, and "county," the *civitas* dominated local governmental and administrative organization in Western society. From a political perspective the *civitates* were the basic building blocks of the state. Several *civitates* frequently were united to constitute a duchy, while several more were gathered up to create a kingdom.[41]

The prizes of diplomacy and by extension of war were viable *civitates* with their highly developed economic resources of a rural nature, as well as their fortified *urbes* and lesser fortified places such as *castra* and *castella*, which provided protection for their inhabitants who did much of the manufacturing in each region. The *urbs* also served as the administrative capital, religious center, and focus for commercial activity within each *civitas*. Campaign strategy, and to a lesser extent battle tactics, recognized the primary importance of keeping the de-

---

[39] Dick Harrison, *The Early State and the Towns: Forms of Integration in Lombard Italy*, AD 568–774 (Lund, 1993), 67–73, 141–3; 197–202.

[40] Jim Bradbury, *The Medieval Siege* (Woodbridge, 1992); and Bachrach, "Medieval Siege Warfare: A Reconnaissance," *The Journal of Military History* 58 (1993): 119–33.

[41] Bernard S. Bachrach, "The Middle Ages," *Cambridge History of Warfare*, ed. Geoffrey Parker (Cambridge, 1995).

struction of both people and resources to a minimum and of avoiding unnecessary damage when possible. Massacred farmers and artisans, burned buildings, devastated vineyards, broken canals, and destroyed bridges merely undermined the value of victory as taxes would fall in arrears and productivity would slump.

The growing sophistication of the Germanic newcomers in regard to adapting to the conditions that they found within the empire can be traced as a kind of evolutionary process. As we have seen, Fritigern was intent upon plundering the countryside because his men were unable to carry out a productive siege of a fortress city. His successors learned the art of siegecraft, but the lesson still to be learned was how to integrate a successful siege into a grand strategy, that is, how to maximize the benefits of conquest. In this context, the *desideratum*, in strategic terms, was unambiguously voiced by Aridius, a Gallo-Roman magnate in the Burgundian kingdom, when he is reported to have observed to Clovis while the latter was laying siege to the massively fortified *urbs* of Avignon:

O king, if the glory of your highness (*gloria celsitudinis*) deigns to hear from me a few words of humble advice, though, indeed, you have little need of counsel (*consilium*), I will offer them in complete faith; and it shall be useful to you, in general, and to the districts (*civitates*) through which you intend to pass. Why, he said, "do you keep this army (*exercitus*) in the field when your enemy (*inimicus*) sits in this exceptionally strong place (*loco firmissimo*)? You depopulate the fields, you consume the meadows, you hack down the vines, you fell the olive trees, and all the fruits of this region you completely destroy. Yet you do not prevail against your enemy. Rather send a *legatio* to him and impose on him a yearly tribute (*tributum . . . annis singulis*) that he will pay to you so that this region may be saved. You will be lord (*domineris*) with the tribute (*tributa*) being paid *in perpetuum*."[42]

In effect, Aridius's advice encapsulates rather clearly the differences between the putative actuality of "barbarian" warfare and the teachings of ancient military science, while at the same time affirming the centrality of the *urbs*. The purpose of war for the "barbarian" is presumed to have been primarily the taking of booty in order to provide for his sustenance, as well as irrationally and arbitrarily spreading terror to and wreaking destruction on the human and material resources that were within reach. By comparison, the goals of late imperial strategy and early medieval strategy required the preservation of both human and material resources whenever possible, in order to

---

[42] Gregory, *Hist.*, bk. II, ch. 32.

obtain tribute or taxes from one's adversaries on a regular basis.[43] Corollary with the fundamental effort to develop secure and continuing sources of income was the imposition of an institutional structure through which the tribute payers recognized the *dominium* of those to whom they were thus subjected.

Consistent with this view, which was basic to the traditions of Western civilization, Alexander the Great kept his soldiers from ravaging Asia and is reported to have told them "they ought not destroy what they were fighting to possess."[44] Closer in time to the events at hand and more relevant to the Salian Franks, in particular, is a policy attributed by Eunapius to the emperor Julian. The latter is reported to have "ordered the Romans to harm none of the *Salii* nor to ravage or plunder their territory. He told them [the Romans] that they should understand that all the land they had won without fighting and toil was theirs: thus while they must regard as enemy territory that which belonged to those at war with them, they must treat as their own that which belonged to those who had submitted to them."[45]

Clovis, himself, made clear that he had accepted the new way of doing things, as advised by Aridius, when he invaded Aquitaine in 507 and issued an order (*edictum*) that his troops should take only water and grass from the lands they traversed. When some soldiers violated this order, Clovis is reported to have had the malefactors executed.[46] This tradition of not despoiling the countryside (or if of necessity some damage was done, giving compensation) can also be seen to have been followed by Pepin and his son Charlemagne.[47]

The centrality of siege warfare focused upon the *urbs* during the

---

[43] Some scholars believe that during the early Middle Ages the "barbarians" practiced "primitive" warfare. For a critique of this view, see Bernard S. Bachrach, "Anthropology and Early Medieval History: Some Problems," *Cithara* 34 (1994): 3–10.

[44] J.F.C. Fuller, *The Generalship of Alexander the Great* (London, 1958), 285.

[45] Eunapius, *fr.* 18, *The Fragmentary Classicising Historians of the Later Roman Empire: Eunapius, Olympiodorus, Priscus and Malchus*, ed. and trans. R.C. Blockley, 2 vols. (Liverpool, 1981).

[46] Gregory, *Hist.*, bk. II, ch. 37. Gregory sets Clovis's views on the preservation of resources within the framework of proper religious observance and respect for God as is echoed in a speech Gregory attributes to King Guntram (bk. VIII, ch. 30): "How . . . are we to win victory in our day when we no longer keep the observances of our fathers?" Cf. the discussion by Martin Heinzelmann, "Histoire, Rois et Prophètes. Le rôle de éléments autobiographiques dans les *Histoires* de Grégoire de Tours: un guide épiscopal à l'usage du roi chrétien," in *De Tertullien aux Mozarabes: antiquité tardive et christianisme ancien (IIIe-VIe siècles). Mélanges offerts à Jacques Fontaine* I (Paris, 1992), 547.

[47] See *Capitularia Regnum Francorum*, ed. Alfredus Boretius, *Monumenta Germaniae Historica, Leges* II.1 (Hanover, 1883), no. 18, ch. 6, where Charlemagne confirms Pepin's general order that troops are permitted to take only water, grass, and wood from the countryside.

early Middle Ages is massively documented.[48] In Italy, from the Byzantine reconquest to the fall of the Lombard kingdom, wars were fought for the control of the *urbes*, and sieges abounded.[49] In Spain, the fall of the great fortress cities of Seville, Cordova, and Toledo to the Muslims and their Jewish allies in 711 effectively marked the end of the Visigothic kingdom.[50] Clovis's conquest of what is now the greater part of France during the later fifth and early sixth centuries was based upon his ability to lay effective siege to fortress cities such as Verdun, Paris, Avignon, Albi, Rodez, Clermont, Arles, Bordeaux, Toulouse, and Angoulême.[51] When Clovis's sons, grandsons, and great-grandsons fought their exhausting civil wars, the *urbes* remained the focus of their military activity.[52] The situation did not change under the Carolingian mayors of the palace as, for example, when Charles Martel besieged Avignon twice and Narbonne once, all in 737, or when his son Pepin, as king, attacked Narbonne in 752, 757–9, Pavia in 755 and 756, Clermont-Ferrand in 761, and Bourges in 762.[53] Under Charlemagne, Carolingian armies besieged Saragossa, Lérida, Barcelona, and Pavia.[54]

Under Charlemagne there was a brief hiatus in what may be characterized as the endemic civil wars of the *regnum Francorum*.[55] But the internal upheavals that marked the reign of Louis the Pious and continued during the reigns of his sons, Lothair, Louis the German, and Charles the Bald, exposed many of the *urbes* in the *regnum Francorum* to the dangers of civil war. The danger was substantially exacerbated by Viking, Muslim, Magyar, and Breton attacks.[56]

Ebbo, that foolish archbishop of Rheims, who during this era used

---

[48] Bradbury, *The Medieval Siege*; and the review article by Bachrach, "Medieval Siege Warfare: A Reconnaissance."

[49] Harrison, *The Early State and the Towns*, 197–202.

[50] Bernard S. Bachrach, *Early Medieval Jewish Policy: 476–877* (Minneapolis, 1977), 25.

[51] Bachrach, *Merovingian Military Organization, 481–751* (Minneapolis, 1972), 1–17.

[52] Bachrach, *Merovingian Military Organization*, 18–73; and for additional detail, Bachrach, *The Anatomy of a Little War*, esp. 119–48.

[53] See two articles by Bernard S. Bachrach, "Charles Martel, Mounted Shock Combat, the Stirrup and Feudalism," *Studies in Medieval and Renaissance History* 7 (1970): 49–75; and "Military Organization in Aquitaine Under the Early Carolingians," *Speculum* 49 (1974): 1–33. Both are reprinted in *Armies and Politics in the Early Medieval West* (London, 1993), with the same pagination.

[54] Bernard S. Bachrach, "Charlemagne's Cavalry: Myth and Reality," *Military Affairs* 47 (1983): 181–7 (reprinted in Bachrach, *Armies and Politics in the Early Medieval West*, 1–20); and Bachrach, "Military Organization in Aquitaine," 1–33.

[55] Bachrach, "Military Organization in Aquitaine."

[56] Regarding *Francia occidentalis*, see Janet Nelson, *Charles the Bald* (London, 1992), and for *Francia orientalis*, see Timothy Reuter, *Germany in the Early Middle Ages, c. 800–1056* (London, 1991).

some of the stones from the Roman wall to rebuild his church, deserves notice.[57] He apparently trusted in the defense of God and his
saints and is worthy of note only because he was so far out of step
with the vast majority of both lay and ecclesiastical magnates who,
through the six centuries under consideration here, saw to the ongoing
repair and defense of the massive Roman fortifications that defended
their cities and provided them with a vital margin of security. It hardly
needs to be added that follies of this kind were rectified in the sober-
ing circumstance of a growing Viking menace and the increasing perils
of civil war.[58]

In the post-Carolingian era the *urbes*, in particular, and siege warfare, in general, continued to dominate military activity throughout
the West. Although William the Conqueror's best known military
exploit is undoubtedly his victory at the battle of Hastings on 12
October 1066, his subsequent capture of Dover, Winchester, and London was crucial to the conquest of England.[59] Fulk Nerra, count of the
Angevins and William of Normandy's elder contemporary, laid under
siege directly or had his allies invest Nantes, Tours, Melun, and Poitiers. In fact, the great Roman walls of Poitiers were besieged several
times during the latter part of the tenth century.[60] The success of the
First Crusade rested upon the capture of Antioch and Jerusalem after
lengthy sieges.[61] Many pages could be taken up merely with lists of
the sieges carried out against erstwhile Roman fortifications during
the early Middle Ages.[62]

In light of the importance of the walled *urbes* for defensive purposes
and the role of the fortified city as a refuge for the people of the surrounding area, it will hardly be surprising to learn that the inhabitants
of these strongholds as well as those who lived in the shadow of the
walls were mobilized for local defense during the early Middle Ages as
they had been during the later Roman empire. It was common for separate ethnic groups, artisan groups, and merchant groups, among others, to occupy rather exclusive "neighborhoods" within the city.[63] Thus,

[57] Cf. the discussion by Ferdinand Vercauteren, *Etude sur les civitates de la Belgique seconde*
(Brussels, 1934), 63–4; and Février, "Permanence et héritages de l'antiquité," 74.

[58] Brühl, *Palatium und Civitas*, I:53–72.

[59] David Douglas, *William the Conqueror* (Berkeley and Los Angeles, 1967), 181–210, esp.
205: "The key to William's success . . . is to be found in his appreciation of the strategic importance of London."

[60] See Bernard S. Bachrach, *Fulk Nerra, The Neo-Roman Consul, 987–1040: A Politcal
Biography of the Angevin Count* (Berkeley, Los Angeles, and London, 1993).

[61] John France, *Victory in the East: A Military History of the First Crusade* (Cambridge,
1994).

[62] Bradbury, *The Medieval Siege*, and Bachrach, "Medieval Siege Warfare."

[63] Bullough, "Social and Economic Structure," 306–72, with the literature cited there.

it was the norm for the city authorities to assign to the inhabitants of each district within the *urbs* the duty of defending that section of the wall that specifically protected their community. The importance of this duty meant that even Jews, who often were exempted from normal military service, were required to defend the walls.[64]

In addition to the local militia, which was organized for the defense of the city, each *urbs* generally had a garrison of professional soldiers settled either within the walls or in camps (*castra*) in the immediate environs. We catch a glimpse of both the militia organization and the garrison at Arles, an important fortified city in the Visigothic kingdom, which was laid under siege by the armies of Clovis in 507–8. Thus the contemporary author of the *Life of Bishop Caesarius of Arles* first calls attention to contingents of Gothic troops, who were temporarily billeted in the residence of the bishop, and then goes on to discuss the "Jewish troops stationed along that part of the city wall that the Jews were responsible for guarding."[65]

A third group that played an important role in the defense of the fortified cities of the early medieval West was formed by the armed followers of the urban lay magnates. First among these great men usually were the counts. These officials not only governed the *civitates* from their citadels (the erstwhile *praetoria* and *arces* of the late Roman era, located in the *urbs* or capital of each region), but also led the armies raised within their jurisdiction in both defensive and offensive operations.[66] Below the count were other important men who are referred to in the sources by various terms: e.g., *maiores civitates, seniores, primates urbis,* and *primores civitatis*.[67] Some of these important men might even be merchants rather than landed aristocrats.[68]

Generally, however, all but the most important laymen were greatly overshadowed in terms of wealth, power, and armed forces by the bishop of the city.[69] Indeed, it was generally agreed that two-fifths or

---

[64] See the discussion by Bachrach, *Early Medieval Jewish Policy*, 33–4, 44–5; and Guido Kisch, *Forschungen zur Rechts- und Sozialgeschichte der Juden in Deutschland während des Mittelalters* (Sigmaringen, 1978), 16–31, for the later period.

[65] See, for example, *Vita Caesarii episcopi Arelatensis libri duo*, ed. Bruno Krusch, *Monumenta Germaniae Historica, Scriptores rerum Merovingicarum* III (Hannover, 1896), bk. I, chs. 30, 31, respectively.

[66] Regarding the centrality of the count, see F.L. Ganshof, *Frankish Institutions under Charlemagne*, trans. B. and M. Lyon (Providence, 1968), 26–34, for a basic guide. Note: the Anglo-Saxon "earl" is a translation of Latin *comes* and the Anglo-Saxon "sheriff" is a translation of the Latin *vicecomes*.

[67] Bullough, "Social and Economic Structure," 362–7.

[68] Bullough, "Social and Economic Structure," 388.

[69] See Martin Heinzelmann, *Bischofsherrschaft in Gallien. Zur Kontinuität römischer Führungsschichten vom 4. bis zum 7 Jahr. soziale, prosopographische und bildungsgeschichtliche*

forty percent of episcopal income as well as that of other religious institutions was to be used for the defense of the *res publica*. In the later ninth century, Hincmar of Rheims, a well-known defender of church freedom and reform, not only recognized that traditional military obligations were regularly assumed by bishops and other ecclesiastical leaders, including abbesses, but vigorously supported the legitimacy of these obligations.[70] Therefore, it is hardly surprising that bishops, in addition to serving as the spiritual pastors of their flocks during times of stress, maintained arsenals for their troops and played a major military role in the defense of their cities when enemies laid siege.[71]

The *urbes* not only served as bases for the local defense but also as centers of military organization. Numerous inscriptions as well as the *Notitia Dignitatum*, which preserves within it the only surviving order of battle for the later Roman empire, indicate that during the later fourth century and into the first quarter of the fifth century the imperial government based substantial numbers of troops in and around the newly fortified *urbes*.[72] This practice was followed throughout Western Europe during the early Middle Ages. Local levies, which numerically dominated the military organization of the empire's Romano-German successor states in the West, were called up for service by the count or his subordinate, whether assigned only to the defense of the *civitas* or obligated to perform expeditionary duties, and were comparable to the great and select *fyrds*, respectively, in Anglo-Saxon England.[73]

Aspecte (Munich, 1976); and more recently, Heinzelmann, "Bischof und Herrschaft vom spätantiken Gallien bis zu den karolingischen Hausmeiern. Die institutionellen Grundlagen," *Herrschaft und Kirche. Beiträge zur Entstehung und Wirkungsweise episkopaler und monastischer Organisationsformen*, ed. Fredrich Prinz (Stuttgart, 1988), 23–82.

[70] Hincmar of Rheims, *De Ecclesiis et Capellis*, ed. W. Gundlach, *Zeitschrift für Kirchengeschichte* 10 (1889): 135, who may be considered a ferocious defender of ecclesiastical independence and the church's property rights in ninth century *Francia*, was willing to sustain this *divisio* of church wealth, which clearly was customary by his time. See the discussion by Janet Nelson, "The Church's Military Service in the Ninth Century: A Contemporary View?" *Studies in Church History* 20 (1983), 15–30, and reprinted in Janet Nelson, *Politics and Ritual in Early Medieval Europe* (London, 1986), 117–32. For the arithmetic see p.124.

[71] *Cap. reg. Franc.* no. 74, ch. 10, 167, regarding arsenals and Hincmar, *De Ecclesiis et Capellis*, ed. Gundlach, 135, regarding the *casati*. In general, see Friedrich Prinz, *Klerus und Krieg im Früheren Mittelalter* (Stuttgart, 1971), and the review by Bachrach, *Catholic Historical Review* 60 (1974): 478–9.

[72] Dietrich Hoffmann, *Das spätrömische Bewegungsheer und die* Notitia Dignitatum, *Epigraphische Studies* 7/1–2 (Düsseldorf, 1969–70).

[73] See, for example, Bachrach, *Merovingian Military Organization*, and C. Warren Hollister, *Anglo-Saxon Military Institutions on the Eve of the Norman Conquest* (Oxford, 1962), 25–102.

In the later ninth and early tenth centuries, Alfred the Great and Edgar the Elder experimented with some new ways to provide well-trained garrisons for the fortifications of their kingdom. Thirty-three strongholds were surveyed, thirty in Wessex and three in Mercia, and each of 27,000 men were assigned the income from one hide of land (the amount of land required to support a single family), so they might serve on a regular basis as garrison troops. The formula that was used was based upon calculations derived from the effectiveness of early medieval military technology, particularly the traditional Western short or self bow. This analysis resulted in the formula that required that one man be assigned to defend 4.125 feet of wall. For example, the old Roman city of Winchester, the most important of these fortifications, was assigned 2,400 hides in order to provide enough men to defend a perimeter wall of 9,954 feet. A two percent error can be detected as having been made by the Anglo-Saxon surveyors and their staffs. An analysis of the "fire power" that could be generated by the garrison deployed on the wall of the city's perimeter makes clear that any attacking force which enjoyed less than a four to one advantage in effectives could not under normal conditions expect to storm the fortifications successfully.[74] Thus, for example, if only the 2,400 garrison troops who were assigned to defend Winchester were available, and this is a highly unlikely occurrence, then a force of at least 9,600 effectives would be required to storm the walls.

These data were calculated and organized by the highly sophisticated agents of the late ninth- and early tenth-century Anglo-Saxon bureaucracy, the forerunners of the men who were responsible for the making of Domesday Book at the end of the eleventh century and the descendants of the men who carried out the assessments for the "Burghal Hidage" in the eighth century.[75] The estimates made by the royal agents for the Burghal Hidage not only were implemented but worked very well as the Vikings were unable to take these fortresses, which provided what today we would call a system of defense-in-depth for the kingdom of Wessex.[76] In addition, these estimates provide a sound basis for calculating the minimum in terms of fighting men required

---

[74] Bernard S. Bachrach and Rutherford Aris, "Military Technology and Garrison Organization: Some Observations on Anglo-Saxon Military Thinking in Light of the Burghal Hidage," *Technology and Culture* 31 (1990): 1–17.

[75] James Campbell, "Some Agents and Agencies of the Late Anglo-Saxon State," in *Domesday Studies: Papers read at the Novocentenary Conference of the Royal Historical Society and the Institute of British Geographers: Winchester, 1989*, ed. J.C. Holt (Woodbridge, Suffolk, 1987), 201–18; and the review article by Bachrach on the "Novocentenary of Domesday Book," *Albion* 20 (1988): 450–5.

[76] Bachrach and Aris, "Military Technology and Garrison Organization."

for the effective defense of all types of fortifications, not only old Roman *urbes* and not only during the later tenth and early eleventh centuries. Indeed, these ratios, that is, one man needed for the defense of each 4.125 feet of wall and at least a four to one superiority required effectively to storm a fortification so defended, are valid throughout the early Middle Ages because there were no significant technological developments of either an offensive or defensive nature from the later Roman empire to the First Crusade.[77]

The decision to maintain the walls of the *urbes* in defensible condition and to defend them, as we have seen above, required the massive militarization of the civilian population beginning in the later Roman empire and continuing for centuries into the Middle Ages. In addition, from the offensive perspective, the new Romano-German governments of the early Middle Ages had to be prepared to capture by siege these great fortifications. In order to do this, the logistic and technical infrastructures that had been developed in the ancient world, and which were manifested in the West during the later Roman empire, had to be preserved and maintained.

To illustrate the impact that these erstwhile Roman fortifications had upon warfare, thus providing some insight regarding the sophistication of early medieval sieges, in the remaining pages I will examine the efforts undertaken in 762 by the Carolingian king, Pepin I, to capture the fortified city of Bourges, which belonged to Waiofar, the duke of the Aquitanians.

Since Merovingian times, Bourges had been a major military base and key to the control of northeastern Aquitaine.[78] The Roman walls, which had been built during the fourth century, enclosed approximately 26 hectares within a roughly oval-shaped form. These defensive walls were 2,600 meters in circumference. There were forty-six semi-circular projecting hollow towers distributed at roughly fifty-meter intervals along the walls and four gates have been identified, each with two "U"-shaped towers to provide additional protection. The walls averaged between approximately three and a half to four meters in thickness and were of the same type of exceptionally strong ashlar construction commonly used throughout the late Roman world for building urban defenses.[79]

---

[77] Bachrach and Aris, "Military Technology and Garrison Organization."

[78] See Bachrach, *The Anatomy of a Little War*, 80, 81, 102, 106, regarding the strategic position of Bourges in the Merovingian era. A more general picture is to be found in Dietrich Claude, *Topographie und Verfassung der Städte Bourges und Poitiers bis in das 11. Jahrhundert*, Historische Studien 380 (Lübeck and Hamburg, 1960), 40–7, 64–75, 104–10.

[79] Claude, *Topographie und Verfassung der Städte Bourges und Poitiers*, 40–7, remains the basic work. There is some controversy regarding the length of the walls. See the

The capture of Bourges by force would thus require not only a substantial force of men but an exceptionally sophisticated siege train, and Pepin took elaborate precautions for the investment of the city.[80] First, the Carolingians established fortified encampments (*castra*) in strategic positions around Bourges.[81] These *castra* served two purposes at once. First and foremost such camps provided immediate protection for the army. Thus it is clear that Pepin was following procedures for operations of this type that had been standard in the West for centuries.[82] Second, it is very likely that these *castra* were sited in a position to interdict entry and exit from the city, at least in a preliminary manner, and thus constituted the initiation of the siege.

The main fortified encampment built by the Carolingians was almost certainly erected about three hundred meters southeast of the *urbs* at Bourges, opposite the gate now called the Port de Lyon, along the old Roman road to Nevers.[83] The likely locations for the placement

discussion by Carl-Richard Brühl, *Palatium und Civitas*, I:163–4, with the additional literature cited there.

[80] Fredegar Continuator, ch. 42; *The Fourth Book of the Chronicle of Fredegar with its continuations*, ed. and trans. J.M. Wallace-Hadrill (London, 1960), provides information regarding the composition of the forces at Bourges. See the discussion by Bachrach, "Military Organization in Aquitaine," 11–12; Claude, *Topographie und Verfassung der Städte Bourges und Poitiers*, 66 n. 634, observes that the account by Fredegar's Continuator is particularly detailed.

[81] Fredegar Continuator, ch. 43; and Claude, *Topographie und Verfassung der Städte Bourges und Poitiers*, 66.

[82] See, for example, Vegetius, *De re Militari*, bk. I, ch. 24, and bk. III, ch. 8; *Epitoma rei militaris*, ed. Carl Lang (Leipzig, 1885).

These procedures were well documented in the military handbooks. See, for example, Maurice, *Strategikon*, bk. X, *Das Strategikon de Maurikios*, ed. G. Dennis (Vienna, 1981); Anon., *Strategy*, ch. 29, and Anon. *Book on Tactics*, ch. 1: both can be found in *Three Byzantine Military Treatises: Text, Translation, and Notes*, ed. G. Dennis (Washington, DC, 1985). See also *Maurice's Strategikon: Handbook of Byzantine Military Strategy*, trans. G. Dennis (Philadelphia, 1984).

The handbooks and histories, which along with practical experience provided by operations in the field, served as the basis for the education of military commanders in the West from the ancient world through the Middle Ages and beyond. Regarding the education of the officer corps in the late antique world and the early Middle Ages, see Bachrach, "The Education of the 'Officer Corps'," 7–13.

[83] The traditional view that this *fortification* was built by the Romans is accepted by Claude, *Topographie und Verfassung der Städte Bourges und Poitiers*, 47, who provides references to earlier literature. By contrast, Brühl, *Palatium und Civitas*, I:165, though recognizing that Fredegar's Continuator, ch. 43, provides the only references to external fortifications, argues by analogy with *castra* constructed at Arras and Tours for a date sometime between the ninth and eleventh centuries. Until an exhaustive archaeological examination of the site is undertaken there will be no certainty regarding the date of construction and perhaps none even after excavations have been completed.

Of course, Nevers had been the main base for Pepin's operations in eastern Aquitaine during the previous two years and was the fortified city under Carolingian control closest to Bourges. The remains of a rectangular *castrum* 200 by 160 meters, which encloses the seventh-century church of Saint Austregisel, can still be discerned on this site dominating the road to Nevers. Indeed, the only literary mention of of the Carolingians' other *castra* in the environs of Bourges were opposite the remaining three gates: Port Saint-Andre in the north wall, which opened onto the road leading to Orléans, Port d'Auron in the west, which led to Tours, and Port Gordaine in the east wall, which led to Saint-Satur (*Cortunum Castrum*). Although no compelling archaeological evidence has yet been uncovered to sustain this hypothesis, Pepin's intention to besiege the *urbs* required blocking each of the main gates so as to interdict access to the city by any considerable relief force or supply train.[84]

Once the Carolingian army was in its defended emplacements, a thoroughgoing foraging operation was undertaken throughout the surrounding area. Again this followed standard operating procedure for the initiation of a siege.[85] The region was very well foraged in order to augment stores and to prevent a potential enemy relief column from obtaining logistic support from the land. However, it became obvious after these efforts had been carried out that a protracted siege would be necessary and that additional steps would be required both to perfect the interdiction of relief to the city and to protect the besieging army. Consequently, a second and far more costly and time consuming initiative was undertaken. The *castra* discussed above were linked by lines of vallation that established a circuit of siege walls completely around Bourges.[86]

---

fortifications being constructed beyond the walls of the *urbs* of Bourges are the *castra* discussed by Fredegar's Continuator.

[84] Claude, *Topographie und Verfassung der Städte Bourges und Poitiers*, 43.

[85] For further discussion of early medieval siege techniques, see Bachrach, *Anatomy of a Little War*, 119–48. Fredegar's Continuator, ch. 43, with some obvious hyperbole, depicts the region as being devastated as a result of these foraging efforts. See also Claude, *Topographie und Verfassung der Städte Bourges und Poitiers*, 66. Unfortunately, a distinction is very rarely made by medieval writers, and Fredegar's Continuator is no exception, between regular foraging operations, which were intended to augment an invading army's supplies, and an intentional effort to destroy the productivity of a region for a lengthy period of time. The latter, for example, necessitated the cutting down or burning of grape vines and olive trees. In light of the available technology, such destruction could not be accomplished easily either in a fit of absence of mind or as the normal byproduct of a regular foraging mission. Rather, extensive devastation of capital resources had to be the result of a predetermined policy to which the perpetrator would have to dedicate considerable planning, effort, and time. Since it was Pepin's clear intention not only to conquer the Berry but also to integrate it directly into that part of the *regnum Francorum* which he ruled, it is highly unlikely that he departed from traditional wisdom by destroying the capital infrastructure of the region. Concerning the difficulty in destroying agricultural resources see Victor D. Hanson, *Warfare and Agriculture in Classical Greece* (Pisa, 1983). The technology available to the armies of the early medieval West for the purpose of destroying capital infrastructure was no better than that available to the armies of classical Greece.

[86] Fredegar Continuator, ch. 43; and Claude, *Topographie und Verfassung der Städte Bourges und Poitiers*, 66.

It is very likely, in addition, that lines of contravallation were also put in place in order to protect the besieging forces from attack by an enemy relief force. The possibility that Waiofar could put an army into the field similar to the one that had operated effectively the previous year in Burgundy could not be ignored by the Carolingians. Indeed, the refusal of Chunibert, the count of Bourges, to surrender his city on favorable terms prior to the initiation of hositilities and in the face of a very formidable Carolingian army may perhaps be considered prima facie evidence that he believed not only that the duke of Aquitaine had the capacity to send an army capable of relieving the siege but that Waiofar very likely would do just that.[87]

The task of preparing the siege of Bourges, as briefly described above, provides important insights into the Carolingians' military infrastructure. The anonymous "Continuator" of Fredegar, a very well informed court source, makes clear that Pepin's army fully encircled Bourges with a wall. This wall, undoubtedly of earth but probably constructed with wooden supports and topped by a rampart, had, according to the Continuator, two main purposes: (1) to stop all traffic in and out of Bourges, and (2) to serve as a protected firing platform for the catapults and other siege engines that were to be used by Pepin's men to batter the walls of the city and kill enemy personnel.[88]

For these purposes to be accomplished the Carolingian vallation had to have a circumference of a minimum of 3,200 meters and could have been perhaps as long as 4,400 meters. The former figure puts the siege wall roughly 100 meters from the outer defenses of the city of Bourges itself. The latter scenario puts the vallation 300 meters from the city and permits it to be linked directly to the *castrum* on the road to Nevers, which has been discussed above. If, as is likely, Pepin's forces also constructed contravallation, at least twenty meters between the two walls was required so that artillery might be maneuvered into place, wagons provided with easy access and turning room, and perhaps even space provided for the protection of horses.[89]

---

[87] Fredegar Continuator, ch. 43. It was Pepin's intention to lure Waiofar's field army far to the west of Bourges by a *ruse de guerre*, which threatened that a major attack would be launched either against the *castrum* of Thouars or perhaps against the great fortress-city of Poitiers, which dominated the duke's defenses in the northwest of Aquitaine. This ruse, if successful, would provide time for the Carolingian army to establish the siege at Bourges without an enemy force in the field nearby.

[88] Fredegar Continuator, chs. 43, 46.

[89] Vallation of the type traditionally used in the West from ancient times did not require the sophisticated level of engineering knowledge and surveying skills that Charlemagne so obviously commanded only three decades later when he undertook the building of a Rhine-Main-Danube canal. Concerning this project see Hofmann, "*Fossa Carolina*," 437–53.
Nevertheless, the construction of four major siege *castra* as well as at least a siege

As with the armies of the later Roman empire and their Byzantine contemporaries, the equipment for building fortifications while on campaign was a standard part of the *impedimenta*, along with a great many other items, carried on what may surely be called Carolingian war carts. A partial list of those implements that were useful for building *castra* and siege walls conveniently is to be found in one of the few surviving Carolingian military *capitula*. It reads:

> In your carts (*carris*) there are to be various kinds of equipment, i.e., hatchets (*cuniada*), saws for stone cutting (*dolaturia*), augers (*tarratros*), carpenter's axes (*assias*), spades for ditch digging (*fosorios*), iron shovels (*palas ferreas*) and all the rest of the tools (*utensilia*) which are necessary for an army on campaign.[90]

With equipment of the type that traditionally was part of a Carolingian baggage train, as well as with sufficient manpower and engineers, the building of the siege works mentioned by Fredegar's Continuator could easily be carried out.[91]

Roman military handbooks, such as Vegetius's *De re militari*, provided detailed information regarding fortified encampments of a type that were to be constructed "when enemy forces present a more serious danger." Such encampments may have ditches anywhere from nine to seventeen feet in breadth. In more elaborate fortified camps "battlements and turrets" were placed on the embankment.[92] A ditch

---

wall of more than 3,000 meters in length, if not a contravallation of a somewhat greater circumference, required considerable manpower and large numbers of basic tools. In addition, the building of fortified camps for the establishment of a siege as well as other purposes was standard operating procedure for the Byzantines with whom the Carolingians had substantial direct contact. Concerning Byzantine standard operational procedure in this context see Maurice, *Strategikon*, bk. X; Anon. *Strategy*, ch. 29; and Anon., *Book on Tactics*, ch. 1.

[90] *Cap. Reg. Franc.*, I, no. 75. Cf. Vegetius, *De re Militari*, bk. I, ch. 24, bk. III, ch. 8.

[91] Vegetius, *De re Militari*, bk. I, ch. 24. The various types of earthen walls with ramparts and ditches, which were commonly used during the later Roman empire, are briefly discussed, for example, by Vegetius; for example, defenses which are to be used "when there is no pressing danger," that is, the kind of fortified encampment that might be built "for one night or for brief occupation in the course of a march." For this very temporary type of ditch and wall fortification two methods are described, either: "sods are cut from the earth and from these a type of wall is built, three feet high above the ground." Then on the top of this "rampart . . . stakes or wooden posts are set up . . ." (bk. III, ch. 8) or "when the earth is too loose for it to be possible to cut the turf like a brick, the ditch is dug in 'temporary style,' five feet wide, three feet deep, and with the rampart rising on the innerside . . ." (bk. III, ch. 8); and the simple ditch without a wall which Vegetius suggests be "nine feet wide and seven feet deep" (bk. I, ch. 24).

[92] Vegetius, *De re Militari*, bk. III, ch. 8. Apparently, it was most common:

> to fortify the perimeter of the camp with an appropriate ditch, i.e., one that is twelve feet wide and nine feet below ground level. Above the ditch, embankments are built [of wood] and . . . filled with the earth that has been dug out from the ditch; these walls rise to a height

and wall complex – even one that was far below later Roman and contemporary Byzantine standards (and we have no reason to believe that Pepin was given to skimping) – required a substantial amount of highly organized labor and a substantial number of the best iron tools available. What we may perhaps consider a minimum effort, i.e., a 3,000 meter wall with a ditch three meters in breadth and perhaps two meters deep, would require that 18,000 cubic meters of earth be excavated. This task alone is estimated under optimal conditions to have required 27,000 man-hours of labor, that is, 2,700 man-days of digging.[93]

This estimate does not include the labor needed for cutting and preparing the wood with which to build the revetments within which the earthen walls were held, nor does it include cutting and shaping the wood for building the palisade or rampart that crowned the earthen wall. If, as is very likely, a comparable contravallation was also built, the very minimum labor figures suggested above would have to be more than doubled and still no account will have been taken of the labor, equipment, and resources used to build the *castra*, or the shelters for the men, for the horses, and for the safe storage of supplies.[94] In short, rather than a mere 2,700 man-days of work, the Carolingian siege complex at Bourges, built by Pepin's forces during

of four feet. Thus the ditch is thirteen feet deep [from the bottom to the top of the wall] and twelve feet wide. On top of the wall stakes of very strong wood are fixed. . . .

These data provided by Vegetius and confirmed by other handbooks as well as by contemporary Byzantine usage are intended to provide merely a glimpse of the order of magnitude of the task which lay before Pepin as he planned and executed Carolingian siege emplacements at Bourges. Thus, for example, we are not informed whether Pepin ordered nine foot ditches or twelve foot ditches to be dug or whether the earthen embankments his men constructed were three feet or four feet above ground. We do know, however, that there were ditches and earthen walls and that the latter were topped by ramparts. In addition, we also know that the earthen walls were sufficiently solid in their construction not only to support the weight of the artillery that Pepin had placed on them, but also that these embankments withstood the recoil of the catapults when these were used. Finally, Pepin's wall was, at the least, that is, excluding the *castra* and contravallation, more than 3,000 meters in circumference.

93 Bernard S. Bachrach, "Logistics in Pre-Crusade Europe," in *Feeding Mars: Logistics in Western Warfare from the Middle Ages to the Present*, ed. John A. Lynn (Boulder, 1993), 65–72. Cf. Hofmann, "*Fossa Carolina*," 437–53, whose calculations are based on experiments done with nineteenth-century hand tools. Although the modern tools, of course, are far superior to later eighth-century equipment, Hofmann tries to figure out ways to compensate for this. However, Hofmann calculates greater food costs because he uses basic modern military diets as his models and not lowest case nutritional values in terms of wheat equivalent calories. Probably, the actual costs to Charlemagne were somewhere between the minima that I have calculated and the less brutal figures used by Hofmann.

94 Bachrach, "Some Observations on the Military Administration of the Norman Conquest;" Bachrach, "The Cost of Castle-Building," 46–62 (four plates).

the campaigning season of 762, may have required well in excess of 20,000 man-days of labor.

The manpower problems inherent in conducting a highly sophisticated siege of a major fortified city almost any time between the fourth and eleventh centuries in the West were very similar, due in large part to the rather static nature of the available military technology.[95] This technology, as seen above, dictated the minimum number of troops required to defend the walls of a fortification and also had a substantial impact on the size of any army that was mobilized by a commander who sought to capture a city such as Bourges by military force. According to these early medieval calculations, the 2,600-meter wall of Bourges required a normal complement in the neighborhood of 2,500 urban militia men for its defense. However, as Fredegar's Continuator makes clear, Bourges was at this time defended not only by its local militia but by garrison troops who had been stationed there by Waiofar, as well as by Gascons who most likely were mercenaries.[96] The exceptionally elaborate precautions taken by the Carolingian army that have been discussed here make clear that the enemy forces defending Bourges were regarded as a formidable lot, with a predictable capacity to sally against a besieging force should the latter fail to operate in a tactically sound manner.

In light of Pepin's actions, which would seem to have been well planned and thus based upon extensive intelligence data, it would perhaps not seem an exaggeration to put the order of magnitude of the forces defending the *urbs* at Bourges at about 5,000 effectives. This force would be comprised of some 2,500 local levies drawn from among the residents of the *urbs* and its environs, whose normal task as part-time soldiers was to defend the walls of their city, and another 2,500 fighting men including both the regular troops whom Waiofar dispatched to defend Bourges and a noteworthy force of Gascon mercenaries.[97] Not included in this very loose estimate are the ubiquitous personal armed followers, both free and unfree, who served in the entourages of the important magnates of the city and the countryside.[98]

---

[95] Bachrach, "Medieval Siege Warfare," 119–33.

[96] Fredegar Continuator, ch. 43.

[97] Fredegar Continuator, ch. 43, regarding special troops and Gascon mercenaries with the discussion by Bachrach, "Military Organization in Aquitaine," 5–8.

[98] For the background on Carolingian military demography, see Karl Ferdinand Werner, "Heeresorganization und Kriegsführung im deutschen Königreich des 10. und 11. Jahrhunderts," *Settimane di Studio del Centro Italiano di studi sull'alto Medioevo* 15 (Spoleto, 1986), 791–843; for some further methodological observations, see Bachrach, *The Anatomy of a Little War*, 161–7.

By contrast, Pepin's army at Bourges had to be considerably larger than the forces that defended the city. The besieging army of Carolingians had to be of sufficient size not only to build the extensive siege works described by Fredegar's Continuator, but to defend those who undertook the construction work necessary to make the *castra*, and then the siege wall or walls, defensible. Once a minimum 3,000 meter siege wall had been completed, some 3,000 fighting men were required simply to defend it from enemy attack. However, no early medieval besieging army, as noted above, could expect to capture a substantial and well-defended enemy fortification, such as the *urbs* at Bourges, with an army that was not at least four times greater in size than the forces assigned to the defense.[99]

Indeed, Pepin had demonstrated his ability during the previous year to launch very effective attacks and take sophisticated fortifications by storm.[100] This, in itself, suggests his ability to raise rather large forces from throughout the *regnum Francorum*. To place Pepin's army at Bourges much below 20,000 men would likely be a serious underestimate.[101] A force of this order of magnitude compares favorably with the now well-accepted estimates for the size of Carolingian armies in the reign of Charlemagne, Pepin's son, made by K.F. Werner and accepted by Philippe Contamine.[102]

Despite the foraging done in the region of Bourges, there was no way that Pepin's forces could live off the land for a significant length of time. In addition, there is little likelihood that Pepin's baggage train could have carried the foodstuffs necessary to feed both the personnel and the animals required for a protracted siege. For example, a twenty days' supply of victuals for an army of some 20,000 men required approximately 400 cart loads of wheat pulled by 800 horses or oxen.[103] In short, Pepin's army had to be regularly supplied through the late spring and summer from his forward base at Nevers by wagon trains

---

[99] Bachrach and Aris, "Military Technology and Garrison Organization," 1–17.

[100] Fredegar Continuator, ch. 42.

[101] Einhard, *Annales regni Francorum, an. 762, Annales regni Francorum, inde ab a. 741 usque ad a. 829: qui dicuntur Annales laurissenses maiores et Einhardi*, ed. G.H. Pertzii with Fridericus Kurze (Hannover, 1895), contrary to the usual topos of trying to portray the victories of one's own side as being won by small forces, calls attention to the large size of Pepin's army, but gives no explicit figure.

[102] Werner, "Heeresorganization und Kriegsführung," 819–21; and Philippe Contamine, *La guerre au moyen âge*, 4th ed. (Paris, 1994), 102–3.

[103] Concerning rations and their transportation, see, Donald Engels, *Alexander the Great and the Logistics of the Macedonian Army* (Berkeley, 1978), 14–16, 120–1, who deals with the problems of foraging from a logistic perspective; and Bachrach, "Animals and Warfare in Early Medieval Europe," *Settimane di Studio del Centro Italiano di studi sull'alto Medioevo* 31 (1985), 716–29.

carrying a minimum of 10,000 kilograms of wheat to feed the men alone.[104]

Some indication of the success of Pepin's logistic operations in support of his siege of Bourges and the capacity of his siege train, can, of course, be gleaned from the fact that he ultimately captured that great fortress city. More important, however, is the reaction of Pepin's adversary, Duke Waiofar of Aquitaine, to the overwhelming nature of the Carolingians' ability to wage siege warfare. As Pepin's court chronicler put it:

When Waiofar, the ruler of Aquitaine, saw how the king had stormed the stronghold at Clermont and had taken Bourges, the most strongly fortified city in Aquitaine, with siege machines and that he had been able to do nothing to stop this, he [Waiofar] had the walls of all of the Aquitanian cities under his control, Poitiers, Limoges, Saintes, Périgueux, Angoulême and many other cities, as well as smaller strongholds, rendered indefensible.

Needless to say, Pepin had them all repaired and sent men to serve as garrisons in the strongholds throughout Aquitaine.[105]

To conclude, the centrality of the newly fortified *urbes* to the political, military, economic, social, and religious life of the later Roman empire has been well studied. By contrast, misunderstandings regarding what is meant by the concept "the fall of the Roman empire" combined with unsubstantiated assumptions regarding the backwardness of the so-called "barbarians" continue to obscure the significance of these *urbes* during the early Middle Ages. It has been the purpose of this essay to illuminate the fact that the fortress cities built during the later Roman empire fundamentally conditioned military life in the Romano-German successor states of the early Middle Ages and beyond as they had during the epoch of their original construction. The walled cities of late antiquity in the West provide an important way to study the basic continuities that connect the Roman world and the Middle Ages.

---

[104] See the recent discussion of logistics by Charles Bowlus, *Franks, Moravians, and Magyars: The Struggle for the Middle Danube, 788–907* (Philadelphia, 1994), 25–30.
[105] Fredegar Continuator, ch. 46.

CHAPTER 8

Walled cities in Islamic North Africa and Egypt with particular reference to the Fatimids (909–1171)

JONATHAN M. BLOOM

IT is generally believed that walled cities, with a few notable exceptions, became important features of the Islamic lands in the late tenth
and particularly the eleventh centuries, the period to which many sets
of impressive walls in several regions date. Before that time the security provided by the central government – first the Umayyad caliphate
of Damascus (r. 661–750) and then the Abbasid caliphate of Baghdad
(r. 749–1258) – meant that cities in the Islamic heartlands had no need
to defend themselves with walls, although frontier posts were regularly fortified against foreign incursions, notably in Syria against the
Byzantines. At the end of the first millennium, however, the waning
power of the central government permitted local powers to emerge,
and they surrounded their capitals with defensive walls against enemy attack. These domestic and foreign enemies ranged from roving
bands of Persian, Turkish, and Kurdish condottieri looking for a nice
place to settle to armies of European Crusaders organized to wrest the
Holy Land and whatever else they could find from Muslim hands.[1]
The most notable exception to this model is the Round City of Baghdad, founded by the Abbasid caliph al-Mansur (r. 754–75) as the new
administrative center of his empire. An even more prominent exception to this rule is the series of three walled capital cities founded by
the Fatimid dynasty (r. 909–1171) of North Africa and Egypt. Unlike
most contemporary dynasties, which established a single capital and

---

[1] The classic formulation is to be found in K.A.C. Creswell, "Fortification in Islam Before
A.D. 1250," *Proceedings of the British Academy* 38 (1952): 89–125. For a recent view, see
Yasser Tabbaa, "Military Architecture and Fortification, IV. Islamic Lands, 1. Before c.
AD 900," in *The Dictionary of Art*, ed. Jane Turner (London, 1996), s.v.

219

Figure 8.1. Map of the Mediterranean region showing sites mentioned in the text.

then stayed put, the Fatimids established three successive capitals within a brief half century. The Fatimids, who claimed descent from the Prophet Muhammad's daughter Fatima through Isma'il, the seventh Shi'ite imam, gained a foothold in what is now Tunisia in the early tenth century. They were attempting to wrest power from the Abbasids of Baghdad and others whom they considered usurpers of the power that should rightfully be theirs. By the middle of the century this Isma'ili Shi'ite dynasty nominally controlled most of North Africa, and in 969 the Fatimid general Jawhar conquered Egypt for his master, the Fatimid caliph al-Mu'izz (r. 953–75). A few years later, al-Mu'izz abandoned North Africa for Egypt, and for the next two centuries the Fatimids ruled a realm of steadily decreasing size from Cairo, their splendid capital there.

Mahdia, a walled city constructed from 916 to 921 on a peninsula on the Mediterranean coast halfway between Sousse and Sfax, served as Fatimid capital until 947–8 (Figs. 8.1 and 8.2). The dynasty then moved to Mansuriyya, a walled city built in the suburbs of Kairouan, the traditional capital of the region. Just two decades later, in 969, Jawhar began construction of the walls of what would become Cairo, the Fatimid capital in Egypt. It is generally thought that this succession of walled enclaves had a new purpose, to separate the Shi'ite Fatimid rulers from their hostile Sunni subjects and provide a stage for elaborate rituals.[2] A careful examination of the Fatimid walled capitals in the context of the urban history of Islamic North Africa and Egypt reveals, however, that the walled Fatimid cities were not anomalies but the product of a tradition of walling cities since the very beginnings of Islam.

There can be many different reasons for spending vast sums on

---

[2] See, for example, Paula Sanders, *Ritual, Politics, and the City in Fatimid Cairo* (Albany, NY, 1994).

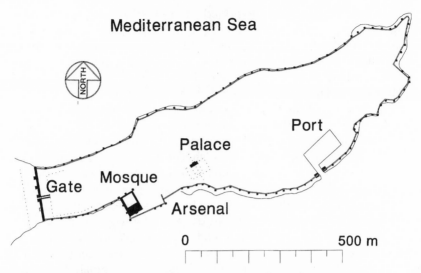

Figure 8.2. Plan of Mahdia in the early tenth century.

constructing city walls. In Islamic history the most obvious justification has been the location of a city on a frontier, usually defined as the
line between the Islamic and non-Islamic lands (*dār al-Islām and dar al-
ḥarb*). The multiplying social divisions in the first four centuries of
Islam, however, created a range of internal frontiers, as the egalitarian
ideal of early Islam was replaced by the hierarchical realities of the
middle period. The powerful and rich sought refuge from the weak
and poor, the claimants to local power sought refuge from the central
power, and the adherents of one sect sought security from those of
another. As in many other times and places, the building of physical
barriers, such as walls, was a practical response to the growing divisions within society.

THE FATIMIDS

Shi'ites believe that the leadership of the Muslim community was
transferred from the Prophet Muhammad through his daughter Fatima and son-in-law 'Ali, the fourth caliph, to their descendants. Following the death of Muhammad's great-great-great grandson, the
Shi'ite *imam* (leader) Ja'far al-Sadiq, in 765, the Shi'ites were divided
over the succession, because Ja'far's son Isma'il, whom he had already
designated as his heir, had predeceased him. Some of Isma'il's follow-

ers denied his death and expected his return as a Messiah (*mahdī*, "right/just guide"), while others transferred their allegiance to Isma'il's son Muhammad or Ja'far's eldest son 'Abdallah. The following century of the Isma'ili movement is shrouded in mystery until 899, when a certain 'Ubayd Allah assumed leadership of the Isma'ili movement in Syria. He claimed to be the messianic figure who would reveal the inner truths of the true religion of Islam. Some Isma'ilis, however, rejected his claim to the imamate and followed another figure, a certain Hamdan Qarmat; his followers became known as Qarmatians.

Missionaries secretly spread the Isma'ili doctrine in several regions of the Islamic lands. One such missionary, known as Abu 'Abdallah, proselytized the Kutama Berbers of Ifriqiya, the province roughly corresponding to modern Tunisia, which was ruled for the Abbasid caliphs by the oppressive Aghlabid dynasty of governors (r. 800–909). When 'Ubayd Allah, the Isma'ili leader, was forced to leave Syria, he made his way secretly across Egypt to North Africa where 'Abu 'Abdallah had incited the Kutama to rebel against the Aghlabids. 'Ubayd Allah attempted to rendezvous with Abu 'Abdallah at Ikjan, a Kutama citadel in northern Algeria, but he was forced to skirt not only the territories of the Aghlabids in Tunisia but also those of the Zanata Berbers in central Algeria (who were ruled by the Kharijite Rustamids of Tahart), as well as those of the Sunni Umayyads and Idrisids in northern Morocco. Only the small Midrarid realm centered at Sijilmasa in the Tafilalt oasis of southern Morocco offered a potential haven, so 'Ubayd Allah rented a fine house and resided there unnoticed for nearly five years, while Abu 'Abdallah and the Kutama Berbers put an end to the hated Aghlabid dynasty and proclaimed his regency for the long-awaited Isma'ili imam. In 909, Abu 'Abdallah attempted to bring his master from Sijilmasa to the former Aghlabid capital, but just at that moment the Midrarid ruler learned of 'Ubayd Allah's true identity; he was imprisoned until Abu 'Abdallah's show of force compelled the ruler to release his prisoner. The army then returned with 'Ubayd Allah across North Africa to Kairouan, where the advent of the new world order under the Fatimid caliph was proclaimed on 26 January 910.[3]

'Ubayd Allah, who as caliph took the regnal name al-Mahdi, "the

---

[3] The principal accounts of this period are Farhat Dachraoui, *Le Califat fatimide au Maghrib: 296–362/909–973; histoire politique et institutions* [Thèse principale pour le doctorat d'etat présentée à la Sorbonne] (Tunis, 1981), and Heinz Halm, *Das Reich des Mahdi: Der Aufsteig der Fatimiden, 875–973* (Munich, 1991), trans. Michael Bonner as *The Empire of the Mahdi: The Rise of the Fatimids* (Leiden, 1996).

right guide," initially occupied the Aghlabid palace at Raqqada outside of Kairouan, the capital of the region since the late seventh century. After al-Mahdi treacherously had Abu 'Abdallah murdered, hostilities broke out in Kairouan between supporters of the new regime and fierce local opponents of Shi'ism, for Abu 'Abdallah had been able to broker a truce between the remnants of the Aghlabid army and the Kutama Berbers. In addition, apart from the Kutama, who had much to gain from Fatimid rule, many Berbers, especially those from the Sanhaja confederation, saw the Fatimid caliph as just another in a long series of foreign powers seeking to dominate the region.

Al-Mahdi sent out the Fatimid army and navy – which he had inherited from the Aghlabids – to ensure the submission of the provinces and begin the conquest of the rest of the Muslim world to the Fatimid cause.[4] The Zanata tribes of North Africa were uneasily kept under control. Sicily, which had been an Aghlabid province, unsuccessfully attempted to throw off the Fatimid yoke by sending a naval expedition against the city of Sfax while the Fatimid navy was helping in the ultimately unsuccessful conquest of Egypt in 914–15. Another attempt on Egypt made in 919–21 was repulsed by an Abbasid fleet sent from Tarsus. Al-Mahdi probably also intended to extend his power to the west and take Spain from the branch of the Umayyad dynasty that ruled there (756–1031), for their ancestors had likewise usurped power from al-Mahdi's forebears.[5]

Imagining that Egypt and Spain, not to mention Syria and Iraq, would fall as quickly as had North Africa, al-Mahdi must have believed that his sojourn in Ifriqiya was only temporary, and he initially made do with the Aghlabid administrative and residential facilities in and near Kairouan. His decision to begin searching for the site for a new capital must be understood as representing a change of plan. While he still expected the Fatimid realm to expand to include all of North Africa from Spain to Egypt and beyond, it was not going to be as easy as he had first thought. Although it is said that he began his search for a site in 912, construction of the new city did not begin until 916, the year following the abortive Egyptian campaign. The decision to protect the new capital city with walls should be understood in the context not of developing Fatimid ceremonial but of urbanism in the region during the Islamic period.

---

[4] For the Aghlabid navy, see Mohamed Talbi, *L'Émirat aghlabide 184–296/800–909, Histoire politique* (Paris, 1966), 384ff.
[5] On the foreign policy of al-Mahdi, see Dachraoui, *Le Califat*, 138–60.

WALLED CITIES IN EARLY ISLAM

Like Basra and Kufa, the first Muslim garrison cities in Iraq, Kairouan had been founded as an unwalled camp (*al-qayrawān*) to control the relatively narrow strip of fertile land that stretches across the north of Africa between the Sahara Desert and the Mediterranean Sea. Kairouan's unprotected status, however, left it open to attack from the residents of the region, known to outsiders since antiquity as Berbers. By the eighth century and the definitive defeat of Berber resistance to Islam, a "frontier" in the sense of a concrete border between Muslim and non-Muslim territories would have been difficult to draw, although the cities from which caliphal authority was expressed remained constantly under threat of Berber attack. The Berbers adopted Islam relatively quickly, but they tended – in contrast to the Arab settlers – to join Kharijite or Shi'ite sects, which challenged the authority of the central caliphal government and its local representatives. The remoteness of North Africa from metropolitan centers of power made it an attractive refuge for those seeking to challenge the status quo, such as Kharijite or Shi'ite leaders, and they often found a ready ear among the Berbers.

According to Strabo and Herodotus, in antiquity the Berbers fought with swords and short, heavy iron javelins and carried round leather shields, and they continued to do so well into the Islamic period.[6] These strategies were used during the early Islamic conquests of Iraq and Egypt, when garrison towns (*miṣr/amṣar*) were built next to the open desert. Since it was expected that the early Islamic state would always remain on the offensive, these garrisons had neither walls nor ditches to serve for defense.[7] Scarcely had Kairouan been founded, however, when it had to be evacuated for fear of a Berber attack.

Walled cities had, however, been common in classical times, for cities were normally protected by impressive sets of walls and gates. In the classical world, walls and gates provided not only security and an appearance of strength, but a fitting dignity as well. Indeed, they were the proper expected dress of classical towns, which can be defined schematically as walled enclosures pierced by one or more trunk roads leading directly to the main square.[8] Walled cities were particu-

---

[6] David Nicolle, "An Introduction to Arms and Warfare in Classical Islam," in *Islamic Arms and Armour*, ed. Robert Elgood (London, 1979), 16.

[7] Saleh Ahmad El-Ali, "The Foundation of Baghdad," in *The Islamic City*, eds. A.H. Hourani and S.M. Stern (Oxford, 1970), 90.

[8] William L. MacDonald, *The Architecture of the Roman Empire II. An Urban Appraisal* (New Haven and London, 1986), 18.

larly important in such frontier regions as North Africa, where the Berbers viewed the settlers as just another in a continuous succession of foreign conquerors who had come, settled, and eventually gone without deeply penetrating the life of the region.[9] Many classical cities in the North African interior were built with walls (e.g., Timgad) or came to have walls (e.g., Volubilis in Morocco or Sbeitla in Tunisia) when imperial power weakened and the cities contracted in the Byzantine period.

Despite the common belief that early cities in the Islamic heartlands were unwalled, the notion of unwalled early Islamic cities is a myth. Although neither Mecca nor Medina had walls in the time of the Prophet, Medina was given a wall for the first time as early as 683, when the Meccan anti-caliph Ibn al-Zubayr revolted against Umayyad authority.[10] Fustat, the unwalled garrison city in Egypt founded in 641, was given a defensive ditch about two kilometers long in 684 during the same revolt.[11]

The virtually continuous series of raids and counter-raids between the Muslims and Byzantines meant that most Syrian cities were considered to lie on a frontier, and their walls were restored under Islamic rule in the late seventh and early eighth centuries. For example, the port of Ascalon, which had been destroyed by the Byzantines, was rebuilt and fortified by ʿAbd al-Malik (r. 685–705), along with Caesarea, Tyre, and Acre in 688.[12] The fortifications of Latakia were restored in 718–19 after another Byzantine attack.[13] In 702–3, ʿAbdallah, son of the ruling caliph, rebuilt the walls of Massisa (Mopsuestia), a frontier post, to check any Byzantine advance on Antioch. Nearby, to the east of Pyramus River, Marwan ibn Muhammad built wooden houses around which he erected a wall with a wooden gate and dug a moat.[14] The walls of the cities of Homs and Baalbek were destroyed by Marwan II in 744–5 during his struggle for the caliphate.[15] In 747–8, al-

---

[9] Abdallah Laroui, *The History of the Maghrib, an Interpretive Essay*, trans. Ralph Mannheim (Princeton, 1977).

[10] K.A.C. Creswell, *The Muslim Architecture of Egypt*, 2 vols. (Oxford, 1952–9; rprt. New York, 1979) [hereafter *MAE*], 2:374, and al-Masūʿdī, *Kitāb al-tanbīh waʾl-ishrāf*, ed. M.J. de Goeje, Bibliotheca Geographorum Arabicorum, vol. 8 (Leiden, 1894; rprt. 1967), 305.

[11] Wladyslaw B. Kubiak, *Al-Fustat: Its Foundation and Early Urban Development* (Cairo, 1987), 86–7.

[12] Abūʾl-ʿAbbś Aḥmad ibn Jābir al-Balādhuri, *The Origins of the Islamic State* [*Kitāb futūḥ al-Buldān*], trans. P.K. Hitti (New York, 1916; rprt. 1968), 219–20.

[13] Balādhuri, *Origins*, 1:204.

[14] Balādhuri, *Origins*, 1:256.

[15] K.A.C. Creswell, *Early Muslim Architecture*, 2 vols. (Oxford, 1932–40; 2nd ed. of Vol. 1 in 2 parts, Oxford, 1969; rprt. New York, 1979) [hereafter *EMA*], 2:378, and *The Encyclopaedia of Islam*, 2nd ed. (Leiden, 1954–) [hereafter *EI/2*], s.v. "Marwān II."

Walid b. Hisham reconstructed the citadel of Marʿāsh on the Byzantine border.[16] Walled cities were not, however, limited only to the Syrian frontiers. In 715–17, a walled city named al-Maḥfūẓa ("the well-guarded") was built in Sind as a refuge for Muslims,[17] and in 751–2, Abu Muslim ordered the construction of walls for the ancient city of Samarqand in Central Asia.[18]

In North Africa, Kairouan itself was first fortified in August 761 by the governor Muḥammad ibn al-Ashʿath under directions from the Abbasid caliph al-Mansur. This first wall, which the eleventh-century geographer al-Bakri estimated to be ten cubits (5 meters) thick and 13,600 cubits (7.5 km) long, was begun in February 762 and finished in September-October of the following year. Kairouan's wall, however, did not save the town, for it was besieged in 771 by a coalition of Berbers of both Sufri and Ibadi Kharijite affiliation, who reduced the inhabitants to eating their domestic animals. The town was stormed after its gates had been set on fire and a breach made in the wall.[19] In the following century Kairouan's walls were repeatedly razed and replaced. For example, in 810 Ibrahim I, the Aghlabid governor of the region from 800 to 812, had the ramparts taken down and its gates removed in order to punish the city for having dealt with army rebels. By 824 the gates must have been restored, for in that year the inhabitants opened them to the rebel Mansur al-Tunbudhi, in return for which the Aghlabid Zidadat Allah I (201–23/817–38) razed the brick and clay walls of the town until he had made them "level with the ground."[20] Such assertions, however, should not necessarily be taken literally, for it would have been foolish to dismantle such massive constructions, especially when they would soon be needed again.[21]

The construction of Kairouan's walls seems to have been part of a larger program of fortification throughout the Muslim lands in the late eighth century, and even outside the Abbasid realm walls seem to have become of greater importance at that time. Most of these projects

---

[16] *EI/2*, s.v. "Marʿash." The defenses were rebuilt in June 952 by the Hamdanids.

[17] Baladhuri, *Origins*, 2:229.

[18] Abū Jaʿfar Muḥammad ibn Jarīr al-Ṭabarī, *Tārīkh al-rusul wa'l-mulūk*, ed. Muḥammad Abū Faḍl Ibrāhīm, 10 vols. (Cairo, 1387/1967), 7:464.

[19] In response, Yazīd b. Ḥātim al-Muhallabī (155–71/772–88) was dispatched from the east to put an end to the Kharijite threat. *EI/2*, s.v. "Ḳayrawān," 4:827.

[20] Yaʿqūbī, *Les Pays*, trans. Gaston Wiet (Cairo, 1937), 209; Ibn ʿIdhari al-Marrākushī, *Kitāb al-bayān al-mughrib (Histoire de l'Afrique du Nord et de l'Espagne Musulmane)*, eds. G.S. Colin and É. Lévi-Provençal, 4 vols. (Leiden, 1948; rprt. Beirut, 1967), 1:109, and *EI/2*, s.v. "Ḳayrawān," 4:827.

[21] See, for example, Max van Berchem, Josef Strygowski, and Gertrude Bell, *Amida* (Heidelberg, 1910).

can be associated with the Abbasid caliph al-Mansur. For example, ʿUmar ibn Hafs, the governor of the city of Tobna in eastern Algeria during his reign, built the ramparts of that city in 771, undoubtedly to protect it from attack by Kharijite Berbers. According to al-Bakri, the city was surrounded by a brick wall with several monumental stone portals with iron gates. The town was dominated by a Roman fortress, built in the time of Septimius Severus when Tubuna had been a *municipium*.[22] Along the Syrian frontier, the walls of Massisa, which had been shattered by an earthquake, were restored by al-Mansur at the hands of Jibriʾil ibn Yahya al-Khurasani in 757–9. At the same time (757–8) the walls of Malatya were rebuilt and refortified by Salih ibn ʿAli on order of al-Mansur, after having been leveled in 750, when the Byzantine emperor Constantine Copronymus captured the city. ʿAbd al-Wahhab ibn Ibrahim al-Imam, who had been in Khurasan, was appointed governor of Mesopotamia and its frontier fortresses. He went to Malatya gathering workmen from various places and started construction. The renowned scholar Al-Hasan ibn Qahtaba, himself, would sometimes carry a stone and hand it over to the mason, and would also provide the workers with meals at his own expense. Al-Hasan used to announce to the workmen that he who, in building a wall, got first to the crown of a cornice would receive so much, which made them put forth a special effort so that the town was rebuilt in six months.[23]

Few if any of these massive construction projects survive. One exception is the city of Raqqa in northern Syria, which was fortified by the construction of a new city alongside the old known as al-Rafiqa, "the companion." This D-shaped construction (covering somewhat more than 1 km²) was protected by a massive wall (nearly 5 km long), with 132 projecting round towers, an advance wall, and a moat. Three axial entrances with massive or metal-plated doors provided access to the interior. One of the doors was said to be spoils from the Byzantine

---

[22] These included *Bāb Khaqān* ("the emperor's portal"), a handsome stone structure, and *Bāb al-Fatḥ* ("portal of victory"), situated on the west side of the city. Both were closed with iron gates. A street lined with houses connected these two gates. The *Bāb Tahūda* ("the portal of the Tahuda"), which opened to the south, was an imposing structure of iron. *Al-Bāb al-Jadīd* ("the new portal") was of iron. *Bāb Kutāma* ("the portal of the Kutama") was situated to the north of the city. Outside the Bab al-Fath was a vast open space, about two thirds the size of the city, surrounded by a wall. See Abu ʿUbayd al-Bakrī (Abou-Obeïd El-Bekri), *Description de l'Afrique Septentrionale*, trans. Mac Guckin de Slane (Paris, 1911–13; rprt. 1965), 108; text. 50, and *The Encyclopaedia of Islam*, 1st ed. (Leiden, 1913–36; rprt. 1987) [hereafter *EI/1*], s.v. "Tobna."

[23] Baladhuri, *Origins*, 1:292.

city of Amorion in Anatolia.[24] While many of these cities could be considered to lie on some sort of frontier, fear of external enemies does not explain the widespread construction of walls in cities far from the line of fire. In Spain, the Umayyad amir ʿAbd al-Rahman I surrounded his capital city of Córdoba with a thick and strong wall in 767–8, and the work continued for the greater part of his reign.[25] In Iraq, such previously unwalled cities as Kufa and Basra were surrounded with ditches and walls in 772, the cost of these works being assessed to the people of each town.[26]

The walls of Raqqa were undoubtedly modeled after al-Mansur's most famous project, the Round City at Baghdad, although they seem to have served a different purpose. In 762, the caliph had ordered construction of a circular and walled administrative center at Baghdad. Known officially as Madinat al-Salam ("City of Peace"), this center was designed to replace a series of unfortified administrative centers along the lower Euphrates near Kufa-Hira, Qasr ibn Hubayra, and al-Anbar.[27] The Round City at Baghdad was located on the west bank of the Tigris, a wide river that could not be forded, in the midst of an intricate network of canals that provided a barrier against an attacking army. The city's fortifications comprised a moat sixty feet wide and two protective walls, the inner of which was a massive affair, perhaps forty meters high, with numerous and elaborate defensive arrangements concentrated around four gates set at the northeast, northwest, southwest, and southeast.[28] The elaborate gateways included bent entrances surmounted by royal reception halls. The five iron gates from the city walls of Wasit in lower Iraq were transported to Baghdad; four were set into the gateways of the Round City and the fifth placed at the entrance to al-Mansur's palace.[29] The walls of Baghdad enclosed two annular zones surrounding a central court in which stood the caliph's palace and the congregational mosque. Commercial and industrial establishments were excluded from the interior, government functionaries were housed in residential quarters in the outer ring, accessible only from a road running just within the walls. The inner ring, housing government offices, was even more secure. It was accessible only from the central court, itself accessible only by

---

[24] In 838 they had been transported by the caliph al-Muʿtasim to Samarra; at the end of the ninth century they were moved to Raqqa/Rafiqa, and a half century later they were incorporated in the Bab al-Qinnasrīn (Qinnasrin Gate) at Aleppo.

[25] *EMA* 2:380.

[26] Tabari, *Tārīkh* 8:46.

[27] Jacob Lassner, *The Shaping of ʿAbbāsid Rule* (Princeton, 1980), ch. 4.

[28] Lassner, *Shaping*, 184–5.

[29] Lassner, *Shaping*, 180–1.

heavily guarded market streets leading from the four gates. The main commercial areas, however, lay outside the Round City in al-Karkh, directly to the south and easily accessible by several canals.

The walls of Baghdad were not meant to protect the city from foreign invaders; rather, they were elaborate defenses to separate the ruler and his court from the populace outside. The violence that had brought the Abbasids to power could just as easily be used to oust them, and this strongly walled city center was meant to provide the caliph and his administration with elaborate security. There is no question that the threat was real: just as the caliph was supervising the construction of Baghdad in 762–3, he faced a serious Shi'ite revolt in which the residents of Kufa joined. Although the revolt temporarily delayed construction of the new, more secure capital, al-Mansur was able to transfer his household and the government to the new city in the following year, and the outer fortifications were completed within three years.[30] Nevertheless, the design had serious flaws: While the impressive fortifications may have provided the caliph with necessary security, they did not allow for the normal functions within the residential and working areas of the city.[31] First it was found necessary to allow public access to the government offices, so access was cut directly to them from the streets. Then the location of the congregational mosque in the most secure part of the complex meant that the populace inundated the heart of the complex every Friday. The caliph was trapped in an architectural cul-de-sac, for it would have been just as difficult for him to escape to safety as it was to reach him. To solve these problems, the caliph had a new mosque built in the market suburb, transferred the markets from the Round City, and returned security forces to the flanking rooms. Shortly thereafter, however, he abandoned the Round City altogether and moved to a new residence immediately to the northwest of the Round City in al-Khuld. Construction was also begun on another, even larger palace on the opposite bank at al-Rusafa; although it was surrounded by a protective wall and moat, the caliph's primary protection derived from the large numbers of troops quartered nearby.[32]

As at Baghdad and Raqqa, where walled suburbs, some of them containing palaces, came to dominate the older parts of the city, walled suburbs became an important feature of Kairouan in the ninth century, as the Aghlabid governors aped the luxury and pomp of their

[30] Lassner, *Shaping*, 160–1.
[31] Lassner, *Shaping*, 195.
[32] Lassner, *Shaping*, 204–5.

masters' courts. In 801, Ibrahim I began to construct a walled palace suburb to which he gave the name of al-ʿAbbāsiyya, in homage to the Abbasids, his suzerains. It was, it is believed, the *fossatum* where, following Einhard, the envoys of Charlemagne were received whilst reclaiming the body of Saint Cyprian. During the revolt of ʿImran ibn Makhlad, Ibrahim gave al-Abbasiyya a ditch. As a residential administrative center it was modeled on the idea of al-Mansur's Round City at Baghdad, and similarly underwent a spatial and functional evolution. Al-Abbasiyya was not only a princely residence, it became a veritable city surrounded by a wall with gates. Of the town's five gates, the most important was Bab al-Rahma (mercy) in the east. Others included Bab al-Hadid (iron), Bab Ghalbun (attributed to al-Aghlab b. ʿAbdallah b. al-Aghlab, relative and minister of Ziyadat Allah I), Bab al-Rih (wind), and Bab Saʿada (happiness) in the west. Within the walls were baths, bazaars, caravanserais, etc.[33] In 876, the Aghlabid ruler Ibrahim II began construction of Raqqada, located five kilometers beyond Abbasiyya to the south of Kairouan, to replace Abbasiyya. Raqqada's walls, which at ten kilometers long (according to Bakri) contained an area almost as large as Kairouan itself, enclosed mostly gardens, although there were also a congregational mosque, baths, and souks necessary for urban life.[34]

Kairouan and its walled suburbs served as the capital of the Aghlabid province of Ifriqiya, but the strong agricultural base of the region supported an unusually large number of cities, most of them coastal foundations with classical antecedents. Although the location of these cities may have made them less liable to Berber attack, their situation on the frontier between the African mainland – controlled by Muslims – and the Mediterranean Sea – still dominated by the Byzantine navy – made them vulnerable to attack. In consequence, a type of fortified military-religious institution known as a ribat (*ribāṭ*) developed in medieval Islamic times along several frontiers, particularly the coast of Ifriqiya. These ribats served to reinforce the coastal defenses against raids launched from the Christian shores of the north and to serve as bases for the conquest of Sicily, begun in 817.[35]

The oldest ribat is commonly said to be that of Monastir, built by the governor Harthama ibn Aʿyan in 796–7, at a particularly fine anchorage on the Mediterranean coast of Tunisia. Increasing raids by Byzantine fleets as well as by those of the newly established maritime

---

[33] *EI/2* s.v. " ʿAbbāsiyya," and Georges Marçais, *Architecture musulmane d'occident* (Paris, 1954), 26–7. It was also known as *qaṣr al-qadīm*, "the old fort."

[34] Marçais, *Architecture*, 27–8.

[35] *EI/2*, s.v. "Ribāṭ."

powers of Naples, Amalfi, and Gaeta had prompted the caliph Harun al-Rashid (r. 786–809) to instruct local governors to fortify the Mediterranean coast, and these fortifications were linked in a chain of signal towers said to stretch from Alexandria to Tanjiers.[36] The sea ramparts of Tripoli (Libya), for example, were erected by Harthama ibn A'yan under the direction of Zakariya ibn Qadim.[37] In Tunisia, the ribat of Sousse (Susa), the ancient Hadrumetum, is commonly dated by its guard tower, known to have been erected by the Aghlabid governor Ziyadat Allah in 821. The ribat itself may actually predate that of Monastir, as it was founded during the governorship of Yazid b. Hatim (772–88). In this period, Tunis too had a wall of brick and clay, except on the side facing the sea, where the ramparts were of stones apparently brought from the nearby ruins of Carthage. As at Kairouan, however, the walls of this city were demolished by Ziyadat Allah during the revolt of Mansur Tunbadhi.[38]

In 844–45, the Aghlabid governor Muhammad I (r. 841–56) built a fortress (*qaṣba*) at the high point overlooking the harbor of Sousse, and in 859 the entire city, including the arsenal and the interior port, was surrounded by a continuous rampart enclosing thirty-two hectares. The walls have vaulted recesses on their inner side to economically support the rampart walk, a technique known from pre-Islamic Byzantine fortifications in the region.[39] The fortifications of Sousse belong to a general program of improvement of the defense of Mediterranean ports undertaken in 853 by order of the caliph al-Mutawakkil (r. 847–61), following a successful Byzantine attempt to capture the arsenal of the Egyptian port of Damietta.[40] On al-Mutawakkil's order the city of Barqa in Libya, for example, was given ramparts with iron gates and a surrounding ditch.[41] Sfax, located on the coast between central and southern Tunisia, acquired its first (and last) fortifications between 860 and 863, on the order of the future qadi, the jurisconsult 'Ali ibn Sālim,

[36] *EI/2* s.v. "Monastir," and Talbi, *L'Emirat*, 394–5.
[37] Al-Bakri, *Description*, 25.
[38] Ya'qūbī, *Les Pays*, 211.
[39] As at Tebessa. See *EMA* 2:271–3.
[40] *EMA* 2:271, and Alexandre Lézine, *Sousse: Les Monuments musulmans* (Tunis, 1968), 11. Damietta suffered repeated naval raids, first from the Byzantines and then from Crusaders. After an attack in June 853, al-Mutawakkil ordered the construction of a fortress at Damietta as part of a general plan to fortify the Mediterranean coast. The city, as the key to Egypt, played a particularly important part in the conflicts between the Franks and the Muslims at the end of the Fatimid period and in Ayyubid times. The Mamluks decided to end its military importance by demolishing the walls and town (except the mosque) and blocking the river mouth to seagoing ships. *EI/2* s.v. "Dimyāṭ."
[41] Ya'qūbī, *Les Pays*, 202.

a disciple of the Imam Sahnun. The quadrilateral space (600 × 400 m) enclosed by these ramparts remained unchanged until the eighteenth century, and according to the geographer Ya'qubi, ships were able to sail right up to the ramparts.[42]

MAHDIA AND MANSURIYYA

The foundation of a fortified coastal city such as the first Fatimid capital seems, therefore, to fit squarely in the local context. Although the early life of the Fatimid leader 'Ubayd Allah in Syria remains a matter of much speculation, it is clear that he had no interest in building cities or the opportunity to build one in Syria. He lived there in relative obscurity to avoid attracting the notice of the Abbasid rulers, and fancy houses, let alone cities, were out of the question. After his escape from Syria, the Fatimid leader's peregrinations through Egypt and most of North Africa to temporary refuge at Sijilmasa in Morocco undoubtedly familiarized him with contemporary cities throughout the region, which, as we have seen, were virtually all walled, with the notable exception of Fustat, the capital city of Egypt. Even after Abu 'Abdallah, his propagandist, had brought the Aghlabids to an end and revealed the new era of the Mahdi, or expected one, in 910, 'Ubayd Allah remained content to reside and administer his realm from the Aghlabid palaces at Raqqada outside Kairouan for an entire decade until the new capital was completed in 921.

The site selected for Mahdia (from *al-Mahdiyya*, "the Mahdi's [city]") is a rocky spur located on the Mediterranean coast between Sousse and Sfax. Virtually an island, it projects about 1,400 meters into the Mediterranean and is linked to the mainland only by a narrow isthmus. Unlike other Ifriqiyan coastal cities, the site does not seem to have been occupied in pre-Islamic times, perhaps because there was no ready supply of drinking water. Under the Fatimids, cisterns were excavated in the rock and a stone wall approximately 8.3 meters thick was erected along the coast. It was reinforced with approximately 110 towers spaced every twenty meters, a massive project which would have taken several years to accomplish. Two large towers in the seawall controlled access to a rectangular port excavated within the enceinte, much like the ancient ports of Carthage and Utica, and a shipyard or arsenal (*dār al-ṣina'a*) seems to have been located between the mosque and a site identified as that of the palace. Access from the

---

[42] *EI/2* s.v. "Safākus."

mainland was controlled by a strong wall 175 meters long across the isthmus. An advance wall some forty meters away offered further protection. According to a reconstruction based on later sources, the main wall had polygonal towers at either end where it met the sea-wall, projecting towers, and an elaborate gate with iron fittings in the center. The gate, now known as al-Saqīfa al-kaḥla ("the dark vesti-bule") because of its long vault on the interior, controlled entry to the city. An extensive suburb called Zawila grew up on the mainland outside the city walls.[43] Zawila itself was surrounded by a ditch by the second Fatimid caliph, al-Qaʾim (r. 934–46), during the revolt of Abu Yazid, the Kharijite opponent to Fatimid rule.

Abu Yazid, an Ibadi Kharijite of Zanata Berber descent, began his revolt against the Fatimids in 943, towards the end of al-Qaʾim's reign. Abu Yazid quickly conquered several North African cities and was even supported at first by the Sunnis of Kairouan, who despite doctri-nal differences saw an ally in their enemy's enemy. The most danger-ous moment of the rebellion was in 946, when Abu Yazid besieged Mahdia itself, just as the Fatimid caliph al-Qaʾim died. Keeping al-Qaʾim's death secret, his son al-Mansur (r. 946–53) forced Abu Yazid to withdraw to Kairouan, whose population eventually excluded him from the city. Al-Mansur eventually defeated Abu Yazid in 948 near the site of the future Qalʿat Bani Hammad in Algeria.[44]

According to the geographer, merchant, and Fatimid missionary Ibn Hawqal, who visited North Africa between 947 and 951, just after the defeat of Abu Yazid, Mahdia had a wall of stone and two unusual gates (perhaps to be understood as referring to a double gate), as well as many palaces, fine residences and houses, baths, and caravanserais. Far from suggesting that this was, like Baghdad, an administrative center restricted only to the Fatimid courtiers and administrators, Ibn Hawqal suggests that the city was like other cities, with all the stan-dard and necessary urban functions.[45] A native of Nasibin in Upper Mesopotamia, Ibn Hawqal quite naturally compared the gates to those of Raqqa in the same region. The slightly later geographer al-Muqaddasi (985) picturesquely compared the city to an island ap-proached by a single road like a shoelace.[46]

---

[43] Alexandre Lézine, *Mahdiya: recherches d'archéologie islamique* (Paris, 1965).

[44] *EI/2*, s.v. "Abū Yazīd al-Nukkārī."

[45] Abū'l-Qāsim ibn Hawqāl, *Kitāb ṣūrat al-arḍ*, ed. J.H. Kramers, Bibliotheca Geographo-rum Arabicorum II (Leiden, 1873, 1938; rprt. 1967), 73.

[46] Shams al-Dīn Abū ʿAbdallah Muḥammad ibn Ahmad ibn Abī Bakr al-Bannāʾ āl-Muqaddasī, *Aḥsan al-taqāsīm fī maʿrifat al-aqālīm* [*Descriptio Imperii Moslemici*], ed. M.J. de Goeje, Bibliotheca Geographorum Arabicorum III (Leiden, 1877, 1906; rprt.), 226.

The creation of a walled city on the Tunisian coast as the first Fatimid capital is therefore a logical product of historical circumstances and local traditions. While much has been made of the Fatimids' desire to distance themselves from the hostile Sunni atmosphere of Kairouan in the choice and defensive design of the new capital, the important roles of the Fatimid navy and maritime commerce in early Fatimid times should not be underrated. To see the foundation of Mahdia as merely a defensive response to the hostility of Kairouan's *ulema* (religious establishment) underestimates al-Mahdi's global aspirations for his new regime. These are clearly voiced in a poem composed to celebrate the inauguration of the new city, which specifically expresses the impermanence of this "camp in a hospitable land" before the expected conquest of the remaining lands of Islam.[47]

Following the defeat of Abu Yazid (who died of his wounds in the summer of 947), al-Qaʾim's son, Ismaʿil, publicly announced the death of his father and assumed the caliphate with the regnal name al-Mansur, "the victor." Later in that year the new caliph ordered a new capital, al-Mansuriyya – "the victorious" – constructed a short distance southwest of Kairouan at a site known as Sabra. Ibn Hawqal identified the site as the location of the camp from which al-Mansur had defeated Abu Yazid, but this does not seem to be a sufficient reason to found a new capital.[48] Mansuriyya was the Fatimid capital from May 949, when the government was transferred there, to 972, when al-Muʿizz departed for Egypt, and the Fatimids' Zirid successors continued to use it as their capital for another eighty-five years.[49]

The city, which is known almost exclusively from medieval geographers' accounts, was round in plan with an enclosing wall twelve cubits thick. The basic structure has been confirmed by aerial photography. There were four or five gates with iron fittings, and like those of al-ʿAbbasiyya, the former Aghlabid capital nearby, they had special names, such as Bab Wadi al-Qassarin ("Gate of the Qassarīn stream"), Bab al-Futuh ("Gate of Conquests"), or Bab Kutama and Bab Zuwayla (both the names of Berber tribes who had supported the Fatimids). In contrast to Mahdia, the city had a copious supply of water and numerous and extensive garden palaces, private houses, a congregational mosque, baths, and fine markets.[50] The contemporary geographer al-Muqaddasi compared it to the Round City of Baghdad, for the palace

---

[47] The full translation of the poem is given in Jonathan M. Bloom, "The Origins of Fatimid Art," *Muqarnas* 3 (1985): 24.
[48] Ibn Hawqal, *Kitāb*, 72; Dachraoui, *Califat*, 217.
[49] *EI/2*, s.v. "Ṣabra or al-Manṣūriyya."
[50] *EI/2*, s.v. "Ṣabra or al-Manṣūriyya."

and mosque were located in its center, separated from the surrounding walls by an *intervallum*. This comparison is all the more telling because Baghdad had been built by the other Mansur, the Abbasid caliph, and this comparison was not lost to other medieval historians, such as the Egyptian al-Maqrizi (1364–442), who said that both Mansurs successfully surmounted the disruption of the state, the threat of war, and the loss of the caliphate.[51]

The North African historian Ibn Hamadu (d. 1231) described the palaces of Mansuriyya as lofty and splendid structures with marvelous plantings and tamed waters. The buildings bore grandiose names which echoed those of the great Islamic palaces of the past. Verses by the Fatimid court poet 'Ali ibn Muhammad al-Iyadi lyrically extol the beauties of the palaces in terms very different from the frankly martial tone associated with the first capital at Mahdia, and suggest that Mansuriyya was a very different type of city. Mansuriyya was, like Baghdad and the Aghlabid satellites of Kairouan, a physical manifestation of the ruler's power over a populace from whom he was largely separated by massive walls. Whereas Mahdia's walls were essential to its role as a fortress and stronghold, those of Mansuriyya reflect the new sense of pomp and majesty with which the Fatimid caliph surrounded himself following the triumphant defeat of Abu Yazid.[52] Abu Yazid's siege of Mahdia had shown the deficiencies of that site: As at Baghdad, it was just as difficult to escape to safety as it was to take the city. Had security been his only concern, however, it is unlikely that the Fatimid caliph would have chosen to return the seat of his government to the frankly hostile atmosphere of Kairouan. Rather, his primary concern must have been, like many other medieval Muslim potentates, to construct a theme park within high walls for his private pleasure.

Al-Mansur died in March 953 and was succeeded by his son, Ma'add, who assumed the regnal name al-Mu'izz li-Din Allah (r. 953–75). The new and ambitious caliph needed to pacify North Africa, particularly Algeria and northern Morocco, where the Umayyads of Spain had actively been challenging the Fatimids through Berber intermediaries, so as to be able to extend his hegemony. For most of his reign, al-Mu'izz continued to live at Mansuriyya, adding palaces and razing the remains of Raqqada so that only its gardens remained.[53] His greatest achievement, however, was his realization of his ances-

---

[51] Taqī al-Dīn al-Maqrīzī, *Itti'āẓ al-ḥunafā' bi-akhbār al-a'immat al-fāṭimiyyīn al-khulafā'*, ed. Jamāl al-Dīn al-Shayyāl, 3 vols. (Cairo, 1967–73), 1:91.

[52] Bloom, "Origins," 30.

[53] Bloom, "Origins," 31.

tors' dream by displacing the Abbasid usurpers from Egypt, southern Syria, the Hijaz, and the Yemen. Al-Muʿizz was also anxious to get to Egypt before the Qarmatians of Bahrain did, for they too wanted to take advantage of the power vacuum in Egypt at that moment. The expedition, led by Jawhar in the spring of 969, was meticulously organized with an immense army and strong supporting fleet; it reached Alexandria in late June and Fustat in early July. Immediately following the Egyptians' surrender, Jawhar began tracing the outlines of the third Fatimid walled city to the northeast of Fustat.[54]

CAIRO

The history of Cairo (Fig. 8.3), from the Arabic *al-Qāhira* ("The Victorious"), is complicated by the renown that this third Fatimid capital later acquired when, following the Mongol invasions of the late thirteenth century, it came to replace Baghdad as the great center of Arab-Islamic civilization. Historians then looked back on the founding of Cairo in the tenth century to find the seeds of its later greatness, and when no seeds were visible, they were often planted in retrospect. Revealing the early history of Cairo therefore requires careful separation of contemporary reports from retrospective interpretation. The fourth city established in Islamic times at the head of the Nile Delta, Cairo was the first of them to be walled, and its city walls and gates remain one of its most distinctive features. Indeed, several sections of these walls and gates, dating to the reconstruction of the city's defenses in the second half of the eleventh century, are deemed masterpieces of medieval Islamic military architecture.

This walled city is commonly thought to belong to a specific type of Islamic city, the princely town founded to mark the birth of a dynasty and to affirm its authority.[55] Specifically, Cairo was "a royal refuge within whose secure enclosure an alien [and Shiʿite] caliph and his entourage could pursue their lives" and rule over a largely Sunni population.[56] Indeed, a recent study considers the walled city of Cairo a "ritual city," which served as a stage for the elaboration of Fatimid ceremonial.[57] Although the Fatimid walled city may eventually have come to serve as a ceremonial stage in the later part of the dynasty's 200 years of rule in Egypt, when fancy-dress parades to mosques

[54] *EI/2*, s.v. "Muʿizz li-Dīn Allāh."
[55] Janet L. Abu-Lughod, *Cairo: 1001 Years of the City Victorious* (Princeton, 1971), 14, quoting Xavier de Planhol, *The World of Islam* (Ithaca, 1959), 4.
[56] Abu-Lughod, *Cairo*, 19.
[57] Sanders, *Ritual, Politics and the City.*

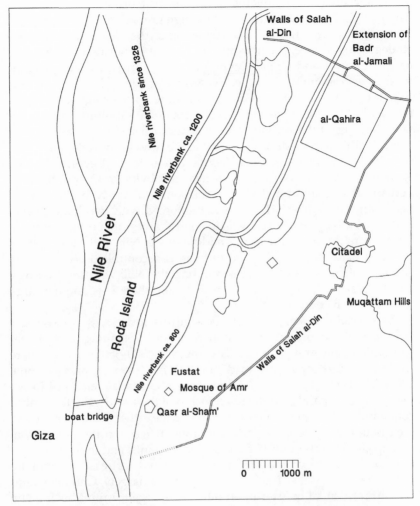

Figure 8.3. Schematic plan of Cairo and the surrounding districts.

replaced military-dress parades to war, the city was certainly not created as one, and the enormous effort of building a city wall was a practical response to very real threats.

Cairo is located on the east bank of the Nile at the juncture of the Nile valley and its delta. To the east and west of the river are vast expanses of inhospitable desert. Just before the Nile valley widens into the delta, the steep scarp of the Muqattam hills on the east constricts the valley floor into a relatively narrow belt of alluvial land. This narrow strip is closed on the south by high ground, but is largely open to the delta on the north. This narrowing of the valley had immense strategic importance, for not only did it control north–south passage between Lower and Upper Egypt, but it also provided the northern-most easy crossing of the Nile. Even travelers, from Syria to Alexandria, for example, preferred the longer route with a single crossing at the head of the delta over the shorter route with multiple and uncertain crossings of the several Nile branches further downriver.

Fustat, the first Muslim settlement at the head of the delta, had been founded in 641 by ʿAmr b. al-ʿAs, the conqueror of Egypt, outside a Roman fortress known to the Muslims as Babylon or Qasr al-Shamʿ.[58] Perhaps as a result of a change in the course of the Nile, the fortress had been rebuilt under Trajan and reinforced with two huge towers and a moat. Its primary role was to control access to a bridge of boats leading first to an island in the middle of the Nile and ultimately to the west bank of the Nile. The fortress also controlled access to the Amnis Trajani, Trajan's canal connecting the Nile with the Red Sea. On the plateau to the southeast of Babylon, there was another large fortress which controlled the valley.[59]

ʿAmr's camp town, set up to besiege the fortress, was loose and flexible with no preconceived notion of town planning, except that tribal and ethnic groups, probably comprising 300–350 men each, were sparsely settled separately in districts (*khiṭṭa*) over an area of some 600-800 hectares (5–6 × 1–2 kilometers); the spatial relationship between districts paralleled the relationship of their settlers to the central command.[60] Once the conquest was complete, other settlers arrived to seek riches, and there was a tremendous increase in the population, perhaps to several hundred thousand inhabitants, and in the density – but not the area – of the settlement.[61] The old fortress was initially garrisoned by Arabs, but it soon became a largely Christian (and Jewish) residential quarter in an otherwise largely Arab Muslim city; although it retained its walls, the quick pacification of the countryside meant that there was no need for walls elsewhere. Each district had a

---

[58] This fortress, of which parts still remain, was a rectangular structure located on the east bank of the Nile. The wall was built of baked brick and was about 2.7 meters thick and 12 meters high. Rounded rectangular towers projected from the wall on the north, east, and south, but not on the west where the river would have provided necessary protection. For Fustat, see Wladyslaw B. Kubiak, *Al-Fustat: Its Foundation and Early Urban Development* (Cairo, 1987).

[59] Kubiak, *Al-Fustat*, 53–7.

[60] Kubiak, *Al-Fustat*, 65–71.

[61] Kubiak, *Al-Fustat*, 83.

mahras, perhaps to be understood as a guardhouse for those tribesmen on active duty, somewhat like the frontier ribats, but the settlement was principally the home base for military expeditions elsewhere, such as North Africa.[62]

Temporary defensive fortifications were, however, introduced within a few decades, as the political and military situation changed. A fortress, probably a *castrum* constructed of dressed stone taken either from the Pyramids or the ruins of Memphis, was built in Giza (on the west bank of the Nile) on the order of the caliph ʿUmar in 642–3. It not only sheltered the Arab settlers there in case of attack but also protected the western end of the bridge of boats.[63] In 684, a protective ditch was dug on the orders of ʿAbd al-Rahman ibn ʿUtaba ibn Jahdam, governor for the anti-caliph Ibn al-Zubayr, anticipating an attack by the Umayyad claimant Marwan ibn al-Hakam, who was encamped at ʿAin Shams to the northeast.[64] Perhaps in recollection of ʿAmr's conquest of Egypt, the northern ditch was complemented by a second ditch to the southeast, on the side of the city apparently impregnable because of the Muqattam cliffs. A corvée of 30,000 men completed the work within a month. As it was the season of the Nile flood, the deeper parts of the ditch filled with water. Gates were constructed, presumably to allow people to cross it when it was dry.[65]

In the two centuries following the victory of the Abbasid army over the Umayyads in 750, the unusual geography of the region continued to provide adequate security, for neither the second nor the third cities were protected by walls. Very little is known about al-ʾAskar ("the army"), founded for the Abbasid troops in 750. The third, al-Qitaʾiʿ ("the allotments"), focused on a mosque, government house, maidan, and private palace, was built in 870 by Ahmad ibn Tulun (r. 868–84), the semi-independent governor of Egypt for the Abbasids. He, like his nominal Abbasid suzerains in Iraq, seems to have relied on the sheer number of troops quartered around him for security. This comparison was apparent in medieval times, for the tenth-century geographer Ibn Hawqal compared the then ruined district of al-Qitaʾiʿ to Raqqada, the Aghlabid palace-city outside Kairouan.

Although Jawhar arrived in Egypt with an army whose size would have made Egyptian resistance suicidal, he approached security in quite a different fashion, for he built a walled enclosure in which he and his troops were housed. The site was the closest sizable (1,100 ×

---

[62] Kubiak, *Al-Fustat*, 123.
[63] Kubiak, *Al-Fustat*, 122, and Creswell, *EMA* 2:373.
[64] Kubiak, *Al-Fustat*, 86–7.
[65] Kubiak, *Al-Fustat*, 86–7.

1,150 meters) piece of dry and flat ground to the northeast of Fustat. The enclosure was oriented approximately twenty degrees to the northeast to take advantage of the extra defense the canal might provide. This desire for protection was underscored in the following year when a moat (*khandaq*) was dug to further protect the northern flank of the enclosure in anticipation of an invasion by the Qarmatians.

The primary importance of the wall is apparent in the lost account of Ibn Zulaq (d. 996), one of the few contemporary sources to the founding of Cairo, which is partially preserved in later texts. Ibn Zulaq states that immediately after crossing through Fustat in July 969, Fatimid troops camped in the spot that al-Muʿizz, who was still resident in Tunisia, had marked out (*rasama*) for Jawhar. Al-Muʿizz must therefore have provided Jawhar with a map of the environs of Fustat, which would probably have been prepared for the caliph either by a Fatimid geographer or by a missionary-spy already resident in Egypt.[66] The site, presumably meaning the circuit of the walls, was drawn out (*ikhtaṭṭa*) and the army spent the next weeks establishing houses there in which they resided.[67] In retrospect, later writers elaborated and embellished the simple facts of this story. For example, it was said that astrologers were called in to determine the exact moment when work on the city walls should begin. A system of cords and bells was set up so that all the workmen could begin digging at the most propitious moment; unfortunately a crow alighted on the cords, tinkling the bells at the wrong moment and casting a malign influence on the city. The historian Masʿudi (943) had, however, told the same story several decades earlier about the founding of Alexandria, so this story is just that.[68]

The enclosure wall was of sun-dried brick (*labin*), broad enough for two horsemen to ride abreast.[69] When the historian al-Maqrizi saw the last remaining section of this wall in 1400, he was astounded at the

---

[66] It is tempting to imagine that the noted geographer Ibn Hawqal (fl. 943–73), who was certainly a Fatimid sympathizer, if not a missionary, could have provided such a map. For Ibn Hawqal, see A[ndré] Miquel, "Ibn Ḥawḳal" *EI/2*, 3:787–8; for Ibn Hawqal's maps, see Gerald R. Tibbetts, "The Balkhī School of Geographers," in *Cartography in the Traditional Islamic and South Asian Societies*, Vol. 2, bk. 1, *The History of Cartography*, eds. J.B. Harley and David Woodward (Chicago: University of Chicago Press, 1992), 108–36, especially fig. 5.14, showing a schematic view of the Nile delta based on later rescensions of Ibn Hawqal's text.

[67] Jonathan Max Bloom, "Meaning in Early Fatimid Architecture: Islamic Art in North Africa and Egypt in the Fourth Century A.H. (Tenth Century A.D.)" (Ph.D. diss. Harvard University, 1980), ch. 3.

[68] Creswell, *MAE* 1:23ff.

[69] Taqī al-Dīn al-Maqrīzī, *al-Mawāʿiẓ waʾl-iʿtibār bi-dhikr al-khiṭaṭ waʾl-āthār*, 2 vols. (Cairo, 1853; rprt. Beirut, n.d.), 1:377, lines 31–5.

size of the bricks: each measured a cubit (roughly 50 cm) square and two-thirds of a cubit thick. The site would have provided a virtually unlimited supply of earth and water from which to make mud bricks. According to later accounts, the first Fatimid enceinte had eight gates, two on each wall, but not all of the gates were planned from the outset. The Bab al-Futuh (Gate of Conquests) and Bab al-Nasr (Gate of Victory) stood on the north, the Bab al-Barqiyya (Gate of the Barqa regiment) and Bab al-Qarratin (Gate of the clover merchants) on the east, Bab Zuwayla (Gate of Zuwayla) and Bab al-Faraj (Gate of Joy) on the south, and Bab Saʿada (Gate of Felicity) and Bab al-Qantara (Gate of the Bridge [over the canal]) on the west. It is likely that the gates were constructed of stone, not mud brick, for later observers noted the presence of Kufic inscriptions (although not the texts themselves) on two of them (Bab al-Futuh and Bab al-Qantara). It would have been difficult for inscriptions to have been worked (or to have survived) in mud brick.[70] No trace of these walls or gates remains.

Ibn Zulaq called the new settlement a fortress (*qaṣr*), for its main feature was a defensive wall. In Ramadan, the following month, and long before construction of the wall could possibly have been finished, Jawhar ordered a festival prayer ground (*muṣallā*) laid out outside one of the gates on the north side of the city in preparation for celebrating the end of the Ramadan fast. Only in the spring of the following year was construction of a congregational mosque begun in the center of the enclosure. This mosque, now known as al-Azhar, was inaugurated two years later on 22 June 972. Oddly enough, the supposed center-piece of the complex, the sovereign's palace, was apparently something of an afterthought, for it was not begun until January–February

---

[70] Creswell, *MAE*, 1:23–33, with particular reference to al-Maqrīzī, *Khiṭaṭ* 1:362, lines 2–4; 376, lines 7–8; and 1:381, lines 27–9. According to Creswell, the nineteenth-century urban historian ʿAli Mubarak Pasha saw a Kufic inscription on the Bab al-Qantara before it was demolished in 1878. It is conceivable, but not likely, that the gates could have been built of *baked* brick, for inscriptions can be worked into baked brick, as on the roughly contemporary mosque of Bab Mardum (1000–1) in Toledo, for which see G.R.D. King, "The Mosque Bāb Mardūm in Toledo and the Influences Acting upon It," *Art and Archaeology Research Papers* 2 (1972): 29–40. The only Egyptian examples of inscriptions worked in brick known to me, however, are on some eleventh-century minarets in Upper Egypt, which are related not to the architecture of Lower Egypt (i.e., Cairo) but to that of the Hijaz. See Jonathan M. Bloom, "Five Fatimid Minarets in Upper Egypt," *Journal of the Society of Architectural Historians* 43 (1984): 162–7. Therefore I conclude that these inscriptions were engraved on stone. Considering the date of the gates to which these "public texts" were affixed, they predate by several decades the Mosque of al-Hakim, which is, according to Irene Bierman, the first example of "visually prominent writing" displayed on the exterior of a Fatimid monument. Bierman's [unpublished] views are quoted in Sanders, *Ritual, Politics, and the City*, 55.

Jonathan M. Bloom

973 in preparation for the arrival of the Fatimid caliph al-Muʿizz in Egypt five months later, in June of that year. At this time the name of the city was apparently changed from al-Mansuriyya to al-Qahira.[71]

The planning of the Fatimid camp outside Fustat must have been the work not of general Jawhar, but of the caliph, who remained in Ifriqiya until the work was largely complete. Considering the care given the Egyptian campaign in general, al-Muʿizz would have planned the Fatimid camp long in advance of Jawhar's arrival in Egypt. Indeed, we know that al-Muʿizz had indicated the spot where Jawhar should build. Some accounts state that al-Muʿizz was displeased when he first saw that Jawhar had built the Egyptian city on the plain rather than along the river or on the hills dominating Fustat, but this seems to be a later and anecdotal interpolation by local historians to the story.[72] The choice of site was fine: It was located to the northeast of the earlier settlements on what had been largely agricultural lands lying along the east bank of the canal. Although the course of the Nile has, over the centuries moved substantially to the west, in the tenth century this site controlled the only land route from Syria and the east to Fustat. While Fatimid sights were set on quickly expanding into Syria, the threat from the Qarmatians was real enough. Indeed, al-Maqrizi wrote that Cairo was erected as a fortress (ḥisn) to protect Fustat from capture by the Qarmatians.[73]

The chronology and sequence of construction suggests that practical considerations were always foremost in al-Muʿizz's mind: The walled camp was founded not as a new Fatimid capital in the center of the realm but as a frontier fortress at its dynamic edge; it would serve not only to protect the Fatimid realm from enemy invasion from the east, but also as a base from which further Fatimid advances to the east could be made. Al-Muʿizz had no greater attachment to Egypt than

---

[71] Al-Maqrīzī, *Ittiʿāz*, 1:133. The caliph al-Muʿizz arrived with his family members, "gold and silver, jewels, jewelry, carpets, vases, clothing, weapons, baskets, sacks, saddles and bridles," according to the contemporary historian Ibn Zulaq. See *Ittiʿāz*, 1:135 and *Khiṭaṭ*, 1:385. At that time the palace comprised a structure called the New Iwan (the [old] Iwan palace was in Tunisia), a courtyard, a two-story gateway, and a dynastic mausoleum. Fatimid family members were assigned standing buildings elsewhere in the city or built their own structures. See Bloom, "Meaning," 82–3.

[72] Bloom, "Meaning," 64, with reference to al-Maqrīzī, *Ittiʿāz*, 1:112–13.

[73] Al-Maqrīzī, *Khiṭaṭ*, 1:361, lines 30–1. Another reason for choosing the site may have been the relatively healthier climate there; according to Ibn Ridwan, physician to the Fatimid caliph al-Hakim (r. 996–1021), Fustat, which lay directly on the bank of the Nile, was distinctly unhealthy, with narrow streets, high houses, fumes from the chimneys of bathhouses, dead animals rotting in the streets, and latrines draining directly into the river. Indeed, fish swimming upriver from the Mediterranean were said to die from the polluted water when they reached the vicinity of the city. See Neil D. MacKenzie, *Ayyubid Cairo: A Topographical Study* (Cairo, 1992), 5–6, 11.

had his ancestors to Ifriqiya: Their sights were set on conquering the central Islamic lands and the holy cities of Arabia. Therefore, scarcely had Jawhar established Fatimid power in Egypt than he set forth for Syria to battle the last of the enemy troops who had escaped from Egypt and deliver Syria from the Qarmatian threat. Unfortunately, in this last task the Fatimid army was severely beaten and the dreams of easy penetration to the heart of the Abbasid empire dashed. Jawhar then retreated to his new stronghold in Egypt, for he preferred to give battle to the Qarmatians from a position of strength. Al-Mu'izz's decision to join Jawhar on the banks of the Nile must be attributed to the seriousness of the Qarmatian threat to the unity of the Isma'ili cause and prestige of the Fatimid caliphate in the east. He therefore transferred the seat of the imamate to Egypt and left Ifriqiya forever in 973.[74] During the last years of his life in Cairo, al-Mu'izz continued to be occupied with Syria, particularly the Qarmatian threat but also that of the Byzantines. He died in December 975 without having taken the Syrian capital permanently or opening up the Fatimid route to the east.

The geographer Ibn Hawqal, who visited Egypt for the second time after 976–7, confirms this reading of events:

The Maghribis recently built a city (*madīna*) which they call al-Qāhira. Jawhar, the Maghribi general, built it when he entered Egypt for his army, his supplies and his entourage. Already it includes residential quarters and markets, as well as places for livestock, baths and inns, palaces and utilities. It is surrounded with a high wall enclosing three times the built-up area. Thus, there are open spaces which can be used for the grazing of livestock in the event of danger. In it are the Egyptian administrative offices and a congregational mosque which is handsome and elegant and generously supplied with caretakers and muezzins.[75]

According to Ibn Hawqal, therefore, the Fatimid foundation was a new city with a variety of functions and much open space enclosed by what we know to have been a powerful set of walls.

Construction in and around the Fatimid city flourished under al-Mu'izz's successor, al-'Aziz bi'llah (r. 975–96), when magnificent mosques, palaces, pavilions, baths, houses, and markets were erected.[76] A second and much larger congregational mosque, now

---

[74] *EI/2* s.v. "Mu'izz," 488.

[75] Ibn Hawqāl, *Kitāb*, 146–7.

[76] The building activities of al-'Aziz are enumerated in his obituary, for which see al-Maqrīzī, *Itti'āz*, 1: 294–5. There are scattered textual references to private houses and baths within the city walls (e.g., *Itti'āz*, 1:149), a market (*Khitat*, 1:100), and two synagogues (*Khitat*, 2:409, 471).

known as the mosque of al-Hakim, was erected directly outside the Bab al-Futuh, one of the northern gates of the city, and the first Fatimid congregational mosque, known as al-Azhar, became a center of Fatimid teaching.[77] The distinctive arrangement of two palaces facing each other across the city's main north–south street (known consequently as *bayn al-qaṣrayn*, "between the two palaces") can be dated to al-'Aziz's reign, but the city had not yet assume a restricted character.[78] For example, it is recorded that under al-'Aziz's successor, the erratic caliph al-Hakim (r. 996–1021), riders were prohibited from entering the city, sitting at one of the palace gates, or walking between the two palaces. Such prohibitions, like all sumptuary laws, serve as an invaluable index of contemporary behavior, and indeed these prohibitions were quickly repealed because merchants (presumably in the Fatimid city itself) objected to the effect on their trade.[79]

During the long caliphate of al-Mustansir (r. 1035–94), a civil war erupted between the Berber troops, who had come from North Africa with the Fatimids, and the Black and Turkish mamluks (slave troops), whom the Fatimids had purchased in Egypt to serve in their army. The ensuing civil war involved all of the country by the 1060s, and its effects were exacerbated by widespread and horrific famine caused by the repeated failure of the Nile to flood. The famine and ensuing epidemic resulted in the abandonment, looting, and eventual destruction of many buildings throughout the city. A cosmetic wall was built to hide the ruins from the caliph's gaze when he passed from Cairo to Fustat, and a second wall of similar function was built near the mosque of Ibn Tulun.[80] In 1073, the caliph sent in desperation for Badr al-Jamali, an Armenian military slave (*mamluk*) who was serving as the governor of the city of 'Akka in Syria. He arrived in January–February 1073 and quickly established his dominion over the delta and as far up the Nile as Aswan, restoring law and order and establishing a far-sighted tax policy. Meanwhile in Syria, Damascus had fallen into the hands of the Saljuq Turks by the summer of 1075, and in 1076–7 the Saljuq chieftain Atsiz attacked Cairo itself, followed by further attempts in 1078–9, 1085–6, and 1089–90. It was in this context that Badr al-Jamali decided in 1087–8 to rebuild the walls and gates of Cairo.

---

[77] The location of the mosque immediately outside the city gate suggests that, as in medieval Italy, the area beyond a gate assumed some particular spatial importance. The continuing importance of this type of space can be seen in the similar location outside Bab Zuwayla, chosen some two centuries later by al-Salih Tala'i' for his mosque. For this latter mosque, see Creswell, *MAE*, 1:275–88.

[78] Al-Maqrīzī, *Khiṭaṭ*, 1:457.

[79] Al-Maqrīzī, *Ittiʿāz*, 2:57; *Khiṭaṭ*, 2:58.

[80] Al-Maqrīzī, *Khiṭaṭ*, 1:305.

The relative position of the gates remained essentially unchanged, and the walls were moved somewhat further out, but the amount of new territory enclosed was not significant, probably because so much of the city remained devastated from twenty years earlier. On the west, the wall was moved a bit closer to the canal, enough to enclose a north–south street known then (and now) as Shariʿ Bayn al-Surayn ("street between the two walls"). The new northern wall encompassed the Harat al-Rihaniyya and the Mosque of al-Hakim, the eastern wall enclosed the Harat al-Bataliyya, and the southern wall was extended to the present Bab Zuwayla.[81] Three of the gates – Bab al-Futuh and Bab al-Nasr on the north and Bab Zuwayla on the south – along with the parts of the adjacent wall, constitute one of the greatest master-pieces of military architecture to survive in the Islamic lands.[82] It was said that the gates were built by three brothers who were engineers or architects (*muhandis*) from al-Ruha (Urfa or Edessa in northern Meso-potamia),[83] and there are many similarities to military architecture of northern Syria and Mesopotamia.[84]

The walls of Cairo were restored once again after the defeat of the Fatimid dynasty by Saladin, founder of the Ayyubid dynasty of Syria and Egypt. In 1168, during the last days of the Fatimids, Saladin ordered Fustat burned to prevent the Crusaders from using it as a base from which to attack the walled city of Cairo. He also began to restore Badr al-Jamali's walls, but upon assuming the sultanate in 1171, he dropped this scheme for a much more ambitious one, in which Badr's walls were incorporated in Saladin's project of a single massive wall constructed to enclose the cities of al-Qahira and Fustat and connect them with a citadel built on a spur of the Muqattam hills overlooking Cairo from the east. This wall enclosed the four earlier capitals and set the basic plan for the development of Cairo for the next six centuries.[85] In this new scheme, the seat of power was moved from the interior of the walled enclosure to a citadel set along its edge, as at the Syrian citadels of Damascus and Aleppo.

CONCLUSION

Although the Fatimid dynasty erected three walled cities within fifty years, one should not speak of a Fatimid tradition of walling cities. Rather, in North Africa by the tenth century virtually all cities and

[81] MacKenzie, *Ayyubid Cairo*, 13.
[82] Creswell, *MAE*, 1:160–217.
[83] Al-Maqrīzī, *Khiṭaṭ*, 1: 381, lines 5–9.
[84] Creswell, *MAE*, 1:207ff.
[85] MacKenzie, *Ayyubid Cairo*, 27.

royal foundations were walled, and the Fatimid foundations were built very much within the local idiom. The first capital, Mahdia, was a Mediterranean port and naval center fortified against the Byzantine naval threat. The second capital, Mansuriyya, in contrast, was built in the style of Baghdad as a royal and administrative complex on the outskirts of a functioning commercial center. Although comparatively little is known about it, Mansuriyya seems to have undergone some substantial changes over the century of its existence, as commercial functions were transferred there from Kairouan after the departure of the Fatimids to Egypt. Cairo, ultimately the most successful of the Fatimid foundations, for it has grown to become the largest city in Africa and the Middle East, was begun as a temporary walled garrison for the Fatimid troops on the outskirts of Fustat, the capital of Egypt. Changed political circumstances, however, meant that the original enclosure was soon provided with a residence for the commander-in-chief and spiritual leader of the Fatimid community. Had the Fatimids' original intention been to build a royal and administrative suburb near Fustat, it is unlikely that it would have been walled, for the natural defenses of the site had made walls unnecessary in the past.

The history of Cairo itself presents several different concepts of walling, as the function of the wall changed along with the nature of what it enclosed. Unlike many other cities elsewhere in the early Islamic lands, the pre-Fatimid city had been unwalled, although it had grown up around the kernel of a walled Byzantine fortress. The city first got walls when its human geography changed, and the region – for centuries in the heartland of Islam – suddenly found itself on a frontier between the Fatimids and their Syrian enemies. The second phase of walling, when the original mud-brick walls were rebuilt in stone under the direction of Badr al-Jamali in the late eleventh century, was designed specifically to protect the core of the Fatimid settlement from another Syrian enemy, the Saljuk Turks. Parallels for this type of walled city are found in northern Mesopotamia, particularly Diyar-bekir.[86] The final phase, in which the ethnically-differentiated troops and ruler were quartered in a citadel set astride ramparts that enclosed the entire urban agglomeration, is paralleled by developments in Ayyubid and Mamluk cities in Syria and seems to represent as much a means of controlling the populace as it does a means of protecting it.

[86] See, for example, Sheila Blair's contribution to this volume (Chapter 16).

CHAPTER 9

Delhi walled: Changing boundaries

CATHERINE B. ASHER

INTRODUCTION

DELHI is traditionally said to consist of seven cities, most of them
once walled; Lutyens's new capital for the British, inaugurated in
1931, might be described as the eighth city (Fig. 9.1). While in fact
Delhi has consisted of many more cities, most of them walled, the
number seven first proposed by European authors was probably a
reference to the proverbial seven cities of Rome.[1] Thus India's past
was linked with what would have been perceived as a foundation of
European civilization. This number also probably appealed to Indian
Muslims, since it associates the city with the seven levels that comprise
the Islamic concept of heaven.[2] Further linking Delhi's cities with the
concept of heaven are these words painted on the palace walls of the
seventh of these cities: "If there is a paradise on earth, this is it, this is
it, this is it."[3]

Delhi today is a vast modern city, about 1,500 square kilometers,
built on the foundations of a series of older cities. What is ironical is
that few traces of any city walls survive, including those of the so-

[1] The first reference to the seven cities of Delhi appears to be Alexander Cunningham,
ed., *Archaeological Survey of India Reports*, 23 vols. (Calcutta: Office of the Superinten-
dent of Government Printing, 1871–87), 1:133 (hereafter *ASI*). He cites William Finch,
who traveled to Delhi in 1608, as saying there were seven castles or Delhis. However,
William Finch in Samuel Purchas, *Hakluytus Posthumus or Purchas His Pilgrimes*, 20
vols. (Glasgow, 1905–7), 4:48, actually mentions nine castles. Most writers after Cunningham credit Delhi with seven cities. Good examples include H.C. Fanshawe, *Delhi
Past and Present* (London, 1902), and Gordon Hearn, *The Seven Cities of Delhi*, 2nd ed.
(Calcutta, 1928).
[2] For example, see Sheila S. Blair and Jonathan M. Bloom, eds., *Images of Paradise in
Islamic Art* (Hannover, 1991), 81.
[3] *List of Muhammadan and Hindu Monuments: Delhi Province*, 4 vols. (Calcutta: 1916–22),
1:19 (hereafter known as *List*). My translation varies slightly from that given in the
List. This inscription appears on the Diwan-i Khass, that is, the Private Audience Hall
in what is today called Delhi's Red Fort.

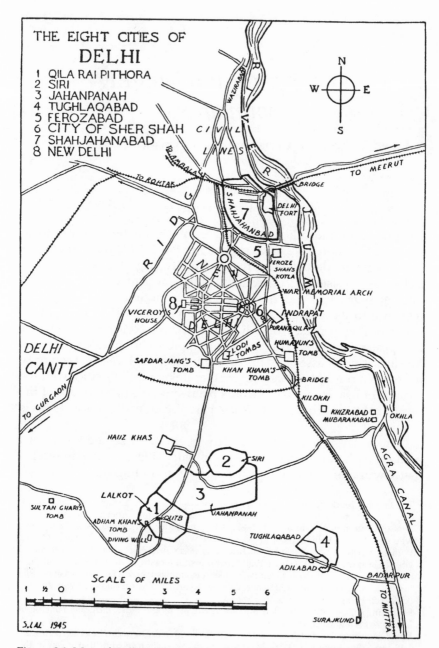

Figure 9.1 Map of Delhi's "Eight Cities." From H. Waddington, "Adilabad: A Part of the 'Fourth' Delhi," *Ancient India* I (1946): 61. Courtesy of the Archaeological Survey of India.

called seventh city, Shahjahanabad, which in common parlance today is still called the "walled city." The boundaries of Shahjahanabad's no-longer-existent walls are understood perfectly. For example, when curfew was imposed in 1987 in the "walled city" due to communal riots, there was no question in Delhi dwellers' minds what this area comprised.[4] Boundaries formed by walls, even those no longer extant, thus remain potent markers.

Delhi is situated on a rich alluvial plain almost in the center of north India. The Aravalli range demarcates much of Delhi's northern, southern, and western limits; the Jumna river running north–south flanks the city on its east. Further to its west is the great Thar desert of Rajasthan. Delhi's central location, essentially equidistant from important frontiers on the northwest and the rich Doab of the Jumna-Ganges valley, along with its naturally protected setting, explains why it has been continuously inhabited since at least the sixth century B.C.E.

Delhi's rich history can be traced by its shifting walls. These walls were at times defensive but more often symbolic because warfare, with one exception, was waged on the plains well outside of Delhi's gates. Nevertheless, the walls served as important markers. My purpose in this study – the first to propose a connected account of Delhi's walls – is to see them not so much as physical entities but as indicators of political, military, and social significance.

INDRAPRASHTA TO QILA RAI PITHORA

Delhi's oldest city is known from the great epic, the *Mahabharata*, as Indraprashta, literally the city of the God Indra. The epic relates that this city was situated on the banks of the Jumna on a high hillock. The literary description of the site's topographical features matches those of the fort today known as the Purana Qila. The fort as it presently appears is a sixteenth-century product, but its builders would have known the lore that associated it with the ancient site of Indraprashta.[5]

---

[4] I was just commencing for the first time to do extensive field work in the old walled city when these riots broke out in 1987. Everyone I met, even those living a considerable distance away in New Delhi, was able to explain to me precisely what areas were under curfew. The various local newspapers, I recall, also assumed that these boundaries were commonly understood.

[5] M. Athar Ali, "Capital of the Sultans: Delhi During the Thirteenth and Fourteenth Centuries," in *Delhi Through the Ages*, ed. R.E. Frykenberg (Delhi, 1986), 36, says the lore of Indraprashta (Indrapat) was known in the thirteenth and fourteenth centuries. Also see Y.D. Sharma, *Delhi and Its Neighbourhood*, 2nd ed. (New Delhi: Archaeological Survey of India, 1974), 9, for an inscription dated 1328, which includes the name Indraprashta for this site.

This is where the comparison ends, for the *Mahabharata* describes a splendid and magnificent fortified royal city:

The Pandavas . . . selected a beautiful place and made it second heaven. They selected an auspicious region, performed certain propitiatory ceremonies and measured out a piece of land for their city. Then surrounded it by the trench, wide as [the] sea and walls reaching high up to [the] heavens. . . . It was protected with gateways looking like clouds and as high as the Mandara mountain. There were walls furnished with darts and other missiles. The turrets along the walls were filled with armed men. . . .There were . . . numerous other machines on the battlements. Decked with innumerable mansions, the city became like unto Amaravati and came to be called Indraprashta.[6]

Excavations, however, have revealed nothing of this grandeur.[7] They have yielded only uneven findings of painted gray pottery characteristic of the eleventh century B.C.E.; no signs of a built environment, much less of fortifications, have been revealed.[8]

Many archaeologists, especially those who advocate Hindu supremacy in India, as well as some more even-handed scholars writing since the initial excavations in the 1950s, have tried to rationalize this discrepancy in context.[9] Yet for the purposes of understanding Delhi as a walled city, this is irrelevant. Whether Indraprashta existed as described in the *Mahabharata* matters not; but as we shall see, the site of Indraprashta and the lore associated with it were well known to the citizens and rulers of Delhi, especially from the fourteenth century on.[10] It is this knowledge that plays a role in the city's subsequent development.

More elusive than Indraprashta is Delhi as a city during the long period from the early centuries B.C.E. to the twelfth century. We do know, however, that the city we today call Delhi remained an urban center all the way through the twelfth century, as indicated by continuous archaeological strata. The items discovered are those used by

---

[6] G.N. Pant, *Studies in Indian Weapons and Warfare* (New Delhi, 1970), 218.
[7] Trial excavations were carried out in 1955 by the Archaeological Survey of India in the Purana Qila (Indraprashta). A four season excavation followed in the late '60s and early '70s whose findings were briefly published in *Indian Archaeology: A Review* (1954–5): 13–14; (1969–70), 4–6; (1970–1): 7–8; (1972–3): 8–9. Also see A.K. Narain, "On the Proto-History of Delhi and Its Environs," in *Delhi Through the Ages*, ed. R.E. Frykenberg (Delhi, 1986), 9–15.
[8] The gray ware suggests occupation as early as the eleventh century B.C.E., although other findings show continuous habitation only from the sixth century B.C.E. See Narain, "On the Proto-History," 14.
[9] For an overview, see Narain, "On the Proto-History," 3–17.
[10] Athar Ali, "Capital of the Sultans," 36.

sophisticates, not rural dwellers.[11] The city lay on a major commercial route during much of this time. For example, a royal edict issued by the great third-century B.C.E. ruler Aśoka, found in south Delhi, indicates the importance of this location since all his edicts were placed at strategic sites along India's major trade routes.[12]

Little from Delhi's past between the third century B.C.E. and tenth century C.E. survives above the ground, probably because most structures were of mud or brick construction. This is a situation characteristic of much of north India from Delhi all the way east to the Bay of Bengal. Thus it is not possible to speak of city walls during this period.

By the tenth century the Rajput Tomars settled in the south of Delhi, making it their capital. Two remarkable hydraulic works suggest that they first settled in an area today known as Suraj Kund.[13] For reasons unknown, in about 1060 the Tomars shifted their capital ten kilometers west, establishing a walled citadel known as Lal Kot.[14] Extant remains and excavations reveal that the original citadel was oblong, about four kilometers in circumference, and composed of thick rubble-built walls surrounded by a ditch.[15] These walls were covered with brick to give them an elegant appearance. The citadel is pierced with three surviving gates, although more probably existed before the citadel or fort was further enlarged by another Rajput group about a century later.

The choice of this location seems odd. True, it is on a raised, rocky ridge, which may have been favorable in terms of defense, but it is a considerable distance, more than eighteen kilometers, from the nearest river, the Jumna. The only water source would have been deep, stepped wells known as *baolis*. Several of these survive in the area, although they may post date the Tomar period. In addition, near Lal Kot was a large tank or reservoir called the Anang Tal for catching and storing water.[16] Although the fort's location so far from the river

---

[11] See *Indian Archaeology: A Review* (1969–70): Figs. X–XVII. These items include pottery, coins, baked bricks, terracotta figurines, agate rings and discs, sealings and beads among others.

[12] Sharma, *Delhi and its Neighbourhood*, 105–6. This area of Delhi today is known as Srinivaspuri.

[13] Today this area is actually in Haryana about three kilometers south of Tughluqabad. The two works are Suraj Kund itself, a semicircular, deep stepped well that was probably associated with a Surya temple, and a reservoir and sluice system known as Anangpal. No other traces of habitation remain. See Sharma, *Delhi and Its Neighbourhood*, 100–1, for concise descriptions.

[14] Sharma, *Delhi and Its Neighbourhood*, 50–1, and *ASI*, 4:6 and figs. I and II for plans and sections.

[15] Sharma, *Delhi and Its Neighbourhood*, 50–1.

[16] *ASI*, 1:152. This means the Tank of Anangpal Tomar, that is, the name of the ruler who provided the reservoir.

may seem strange, it is a pattern that will reoccur. Possibly in this case it can be explained by the Tomars' Rajasthani origins. In their desert homeland there is virtually no source of continuously flowing water; thus reliance on tanks and deep wells was the tradition.

We know virtually nothing about how the fort was used nor even by whom, except for the Tomar rulers. But the only surviving structures within the fort – parts of temples – may provide clues. Inside the walls of Lal Kot is the site of Delhi's earliest mosque (1192–3), which may have been built on the remains of a temple enclave.[17] While possibly not all of these temples date to the Tomar period, an architectural member of one incorporated into the mosque bears a Tomar-period date.[18] Possibly of greater significance was the existence of at least a shrine, if not a full scale temple, dedicated to the tutelary goddess of Delhi, Yogamaya.[19] A number of inscriptions indicate that this area, as well as larger parts of Delhi, was known as Yoginipura, that is, the city of the Yogini; inscriptions also attest to the name Dhilli, a precursor of Delhi.[20] Thus the site of Lal Kot, a considerable distance from the Jumna river, may have been considered auspicious since the shrine of Yogamaya, the protective goddess of Delhi, resided there. Exactly who had access to these temples and the Yogamaya shrine is not clear, but to exclude devotees, among them common people, from the city's tutelary goddess would have been most unusual. Thus it is likely that the fort was intended against siege, not to keep out ordinary persons.

By the 1160s, the Chauhans, another Rajput group, had wrested Delhi from the Tomar rulers; Prithviraja Chauhan (also known as Rai Pithora) enlarged the older Lal Kot with massive rubble walls and ramparts, although his capital was Ajmer, in Rajasthan. The enlarged Lal Kot was called Qila Rai Pithora (fort of Rai Pithora);[21] it is approximately twice the size of Lal Kot. The walls, like the earlier fortification, were surrounded by a wide ditch, but these walls were more massive and higher than the earlier ones. The walls of the two forts together total more than six and a half kilometers. Qila Rai Pithora

---

[17] This was proposed by Cunningham in *ASI*, 1:152. A fuller exploration of this area including excavation needs to be done for verification.

[18] *ASI*, 1:153. Sharma, *Delhi and Its Neighbourhood*, 56, cites oral tradition claiming that the fourth-century iron pillar, now part of the mosque, was placed there by Anang Pal Tomar.

[19] The present temple was rebuilt in the nineteenth century, but the site is considered age-old. See Sayyid Ahmad Khan, *Asar as-Sanadid*, 2nd ed. (reprint 1854; Delhi, 1965), 344–6.

[20] Sharma, *Delhi and Its Neighborhood*, 15–16.

[21] *ASI*, 4:160, and Sharma, *Delhi and Its Neighbourhood*, 51–2.

must have served as a city proper with Lal Kot remaining the citadel. We know from a fourteenth-century history that thirteen gates (three of which still survive)[22] pierced the walls of Qila Rai Pithora, suggesting considerable movement within and without its walls. We have, however, no more information on how the city and its citadel were used than we did with the earlier Tomar enclave.

DELHI DURING THE EARLY SULTANATE

Only thirty years later Prithviraja's Chauhan dynasty came to an end as it was defeated by Afghans. The new ruling house brought with it a highly refined Persian Islamic culture, infusing Delhi with an innovative richness just as the Kushanas, Śakas, and others had added to South Asia's cultural diversity in the past. This Afghan house, the Ghurids, seized Delhi in 1192 when their leading general, Qutb al-Din Aibek, defeated Prithviraja Chauhan. He occupied Qila Rai Pithora, which he renamed Dilhi, reviving a much older name.[23] It became the capital of Ghurid India. The fort's perimeter or walls remained unchanged under Aibek and his immediate successors. This is probably because its layout as modified under the Chauhans, a fortified city with a citadel, corresponded closely enough to the Iranian *shahristan* (walled city and citadel) that changes to the city's perimeters were not required.[24]

Considerable changes, however, were made to the religious structures in the city's interior in an attempt to give the formerly Hindu city a new Islamic Persian character. Among Aibek's first acts was the construction of a Jami mosque, today known as the Quwwat al-Islam, in the citadel of the former Chauhan and Tomar rulers. A Jami mosque, that is, a mosque for community prayer, was necessary, for it was here that the *khutba*, which includes the ruler's name, was read in the Friday prayer, thus legitimizing his power.[25] Hence the mosque had to be constructed quickly. Usually when Islam was introduced to an area, mosques were constructed with readily available materials. So it comes as no surprise that the mosque, according to Persian

[22] These are the Hauz Rani, Barka, and Badaun Gates. See Sharma, *Delhi and Its Neighbourhood*, 51.

[23] From now on Dilhi will be synonymous with Qila Rai Pithora; Delhi will refer to the areas which today are part or all of modern Delhi.

[24] For example, the city of Ghazna under the Ghaznavid ruler Sebuktakin was a *shahristan* with walls, four gates enclosing a citadel (*arg* or *qal'a*) in the center of the town. See C.E. Bosworth, "Ghazna," *Encyclopaedia of Islam*, ed. H.A.R. Gibb et al., 2nd ed. (Leiden, 1960-[95]), 1048.

[25] This is a practice that continues today in parts of the Islamic world.

inscriptions dated between 1192 and 1196, was made from the components of twenty-seven temples – probably those from the citadel.[26]
The mosque in this phase was modeled loosely on near-contemporary
Iranian mosques. But because *spolia* dominated and the building was
not constructed according to arcuated principles common to Islamic
architecture, Aibek, the patron, was dissatisfied with its appearance.[27]
In 1198 he had an enormous stone screen pierced with five corbeled
arches placed in front of the original prayer chamber. This was an
attempt to emulate the great arched entrances into the mosques of
Iran.[28]

Concurrent with the construction of the mosque's screen, construction of an enormous minaret, today known as the Qutb Minar, was
commenced to the mosque's south.[29] Completed under Iltutmish
(1211–36), the Qutb Minar was (and still is) the tallest minaret in the
world.[30] Its tapering form and height echo the minaret at Jam (Afghan-
istan), erected in 1132 by an Afghan rival, although the Qutb Minar is
even taller.[31] On one level, the Delhi minaret may be interpreted as an
expression of this new political power's supremacy in India. The historical inscriptions on the minaret indicate that first the Afghan
Ghurid overlords and then their successors, Aibek and Iltutmish, considered themselves part of the greater Persian and Islamic world. The
rest of the inscriptions, however, are of a very different nature. They
are all Quranic verses indicating the doom that will befall non-
believers on the Day of Judgment and the paradise promised to the
faithful.[32]

The transformation of Qila Rai Pithora from a Hindu Rajput capital
to Dilhi, that is, an Islamic Ghurid and later independent Islamic
capital is made symbolically clear by the transformation of the temples

---

[26] For an exhaustive survey of the entire mosque complex, see J.A. Page, *An Historical Memoir of the Qutb: Delhi*, Memoirs of the Archaeological Survey of India, no. 22 (reprint ed. 1926; New Delhi, 1970). For a more recent analysis, see Tokifusa Tsukinowa, "The Influence of Seljuq Architecture on the Earliest Mosques of the Delhi Sultanate Period in India," *Acta Asiatica* 43 (1982): 37–49. Also see Catherine B. Asher, *The Architecture of Mughal India* (Cambridge, 1992), 3–5.

[27] The mosque is not built according to principles of arching; rather it is trabeated (that is, constructed on the post and lintel technique).

[28] Tsukinowa, "The Influence of Seljuq Architecture," 60.

[29] Page, *An Historical Memoir*, fig. 1, provides an excellent plan.

[30] Page, *An Historical Memoir*, 19–20, indicates that the top two stories were provided and repaired by the Tughluqs and Lodis.

[31] A. Maricq and G. Wiet, *Le Minerat de Djam: La Decouverte de la Capitale des Sultans Ghorides (XII-XII Siecles)* (Paris, 1959), 21.

[32] Page, *An Historical Memoir*, 30–4.

into a mosque and the towering presence of the minaret and its inscriptions. Knowledge of the temples' destruction would doubtless
have been widespread. The minaret was visible from far beyond the
city's walls, but who would have seen the inscriptions that clearly
related to non-Muslims?[33] Who, in essence, was allowed inside the city
walls? Who lived there on a permanent basis?

These are not easy questions to answer. Art historians have tended
to write about the monuments as if no walls ever surrounded them,
and hence the message of the minaret, for example, would have been
clear to all.[34] Some historians, basing their work on Persian texts that
simply ignore the presence of Hindus, assume only foreign-born Muslims lived within these walls.[35] India, however, was very unusual
among Muslim-ruled countries since it did not witness wide-scale
conversion to Islam. Among those who did convert, in all probability,
were *chandalas*, that is, noncaste Indians.[36] The minaret's message
promising paradise was likely directed at them, at least in part, and
was successful not so much because the *chandalas* sought paradise
after Judgment Day, but rather because they sought social mobility.
They gained, only modest stature, however, for they were treated little
better than their unconverted counterparts.

Other sectors of Hindu society played a major role in India's so-
called Islamic cities. These were represented by the bankers, creditors,
transport merchants, and market merchants who controlled the economic life of the city as well as the sultanate. Without them the
administrative machinery run by the foreign-born Muslim elite would
have come to a sudden standstill.[37] The messages of the minaret also
were directed at this highly influential group.

How the city was organized is not known, although most writers
have assumed that it was divided into quarters according to occupation, much like contemporary Middle Eastern cities and later Indian

[33] No Hindu could read the Arabic script and few probably could read Nagari either;
however, since oral transmission of knowledge was the norm, the script would
present no unusual problems.

[34] For example, see Anthony Welch, "Qur'an and Tomb: The Religious Epigraphs of
Two Early Sultanate Tombs in Delhi," in *Indian Epigraphy: Its Bearing on the History of
Art*, eds. Frederick M. Asher and G.S. Gai (New Delhi., 1985), 257–67.

[35] For example, K.A. Nizami, *Some Aspects of Religion and Politics in India During the
Thirteenth Century*, 2nd ed. (Delhi, 1974), 85–6, treats cities as solely Muslim sponsored
and populated.

[36] M. Habib's introduction to Nizami, *Some Aspects of Religion and Politics*, xx, and K.S.
Lal, *Early Muslims in India* (New Delhi, 1984), 118.

[37] Mohammad Habib and Afsar Umar Salim Khan, *The Political Theory of the Delhi
Sultanate* (Allahabad, 1961), v.

ones.[38] What is clear, however, is that access to water continued to be a problem. In response, Iltutmish provided a large tank, the Hauz-i Shamsi, about 1230, which impressed Ibn Battuta, a Moroccan traveler in the fourteenth century.[39] This tank, located immediately south of the city walls, suggests that while the city walls protected against marauders, the city would not have been able to withstand a long siege. We can only guess why the tank would have been placed outside the city walls. Likely it served agricultural needs, for Delhi is largely irrigated desert.

Delhi was not to be defended at her own walls, but on the frontier, especially on the northwestern frontier, the only break in north India's otherwise naturally secure boundaries.[40] For example, when the Mongol Abd Allah invaded India in 1291–2, the Delhi Sultan Jalal al-Din Firuz Shah Khalji marched with his troops to the northwest frontier to meet the Mongol.[41]

DELHI IN THE FOURTEENTH CENTURY

The Khaljis: 1286–1320

Delhi was synonymous with Aibek's *shahristan* of Dilhi, until the late thirteenth century, when the last pre-Khalji ruler Sultan Muizz al-Din Kaiqubad (1286–90) commenced his city of Kilokhri on the banks of the Jumna. No trace of it remains, but archaeologists have located it south of the area that now is the site of Humayun's tomb.[42] The fourteenth-century writer Barani suggests it was essentially the ruler's palace, not a city.[43] He describes it as an enclave for the elite and the sultan, who, in his words, "gave himself up entirely to dissipation and enjoyment."[44] Barani further indicates that the inhabitants of "old

---

[38] See, for example, Lal, *Early Muslims in India*, 117–18; Nizami, *Some Aspects of Religion and Politics*, 85.

[39] Ibn Battuta, *The Travels of Ibn Battuta, A.D. 1325–1354*, trans. H.A.R. Gibb, 3 vols., The Hakluyt Society (Cambridge, 1956–71), 3:624.

[40] A.B.M. Habibullah, *The Foundation of Muslim Rule In India* (Allahabad, 1976), 169–86, discusses the measures taken to defend Delhi on this front in the early Sultanate period. Apart from this northwestern frontier, India either fronts on the sea or is protected by tall mountains, most notably the Himalayas.

[41] S.K. Lal, *History of the Khaljis* (New Delhi, 1980), 30.

[42] *ASI*, 4: 75–6.

[43] Zia ud-Din Barani, "Tarikh-i Firuz Shahi," in *History of India as Told by Its Own Historians*, eds. H.M. Elliot and John Dowson, 8 vols. (London, 1867–77): 3:126.

[44] Barani, "Tarikh-i Firuz Shahi," 3:126.

Delhi" disliked Kilokhri, thereby suggesting that the old city retained its central importance.[45]

The first sultan of the Khalji dynasty, Jalal al-Din Firuz Shah (1290–6), resided in Kilokhri as well, completing the palace, its river-front garden, and evidently building a fortified wall around the site.[46] Barani's very brief text reveals two important facts about Kilokhri. One regards the fort's defenses: "the erection of its defenses was allotted to the nobles, who divided the work of building among them."[47] This probably refers to *alang*, a practice in which nobles each took responsibility for a portion of a fort's construction. Such a project is successful only when there is careful and detailed adherence to a master plan.[48]

The second point Barani relates is that the nobles and subjects were not eager to move to Kilokhri.[49] He indicates that they did shift, albeit reluctantly, and "in three or four years houses sprung up on every side, and the markets became well supplied."[50] Again no elaboration is provided. One likely reason for the reluctance to move was the considerable distance of Kilokhri from the main urban center of Dilhi, some nine kilometers away. A second reason might have had to do with the location. Kilokhri is one of only two of the many Sultanate cities of Delhi located on the river. Initially this seems strange, especially considering the shortage of water in Delhi's cities; for example, later in the fourteenth century the creation of artificial lakes and *bunds* (dams) becomes a major enterprise. Hence it seems likely that the problem is the river itself. Even in modern times when there are a number of canals and dams that control the spate of the river, the Jumna has a history of very heavy flooding.[51] The danger

---

[45] Barani, "Tarikh-i Firuz Shahi," 3:126.

[46] Barani, "Tarikh-i Firuz Shahi," 3:136.

[47] Barani, "Tarikh-i Firuz Shahi," 3:136. Spellings have been Americanized.

[48] Mehrdad Shokoohy and Natalie H. Shokoohy, *Hisar-i Firuza: Sultanate and Early Mughal Architecture in the District of Hisar, India* (London, 1988), 9, for this technique when used under Firuz Shah Tughluq. Unfortunately, I was not able to learn more about the specific responsibilities of each noble under the *alang* system. I do assume, however, that Mirza Nathan, *Baharistan-i-Ghaybi*, trans. M.I. Borah, 2 vols. (Gauhati, 1936): 2:765, is describing an aspect of the *alang* system when describing the construction of a seventeenth-century Mughal fort in Bengal. "Ten thousand men consisting of builders, labourers, and diggers were engaged. Every twenty yards was assigned to one of the officers and the work was expedited."

[49] Barani, "Tarikh-i Firuz Shahi," 3:136.

[50] Barani, "Tarikh-i Firuz Shahi," 3:136.

[51] Prabha Chopra, ed., *Delhi Gazetteer* (Delhi, 1976), 10. Reginald Heber, *Narrative of a Journey Through the Upper Provinces of India from Calcutta to Bombay, 1824–25*, 3 vols. (reprint ed. 1827; Delhi, 1985), 2:286, confirms heavy flooding for 1824.

of flooding and the subsequent resulting marshes would have been breeding grounds for mosquitoes and malaria. Thus health and comfort may have had a role in the nobles' reluctance to settle in Kilokhri.

Even though Muizz al-Dins' Kilokhri and Aibek's Dilhi were walled, the importance of a fortified frontier as a guarantee of Delhi's security is underscored by an encounter between Ala al-Din Khalji and the Mongol invader, Taraghai. He entered India in 1303 when the city of Delhi was essentially unprotected by troops.[52] Ala al-Din Khalji was engaged with his troops in western India, while much of the rest of his army was in eastern India. Taraghai was able to reach the edges of Delhi just about the time Ala al-Din returned with his exhausted army. Nevertheless, the Khalji army was able to hold off the Mongols by strong defensive action. Although the Mongols had successfully blocked all roads and river fords, thus preventing access to supplies of food and water, they suddenly returned to Central Asia after just a few months. For strategic reasons they could not be away for long periods of time.[53]

That Delhi was spared is short of a miracle as even contemporary texts relate.[54] Galvanized to action by this near disaster Ala al-Din immediately built a new, strongly fortified citadel on the plain of Siri north of the original city, repaired the walls of the old city, and perhaps most significantly:

. . . issued orders that forts on the line of march of the Mughals [Mongols], which had gone to ruin, should be erected wherever they were required, and distinguished and able governors appointed to all these strongholds in the direction whence the inroads of the Mughals [Mongols] occurred. He further commanded that they should make up numerous warlike engines, enlist expert marksmen, establish magazines for arms of all kinds and accumulate stores of grain and fodder after the manner of granaries within the ramparts; that numerous picked and chosen troops should be enrolled at Samanah, and Deopalpur, and kept ready for service, and that the districts in the direction of the Mughal [Mongol] inroads should be confided to experienced nobles, and firm and energetic chiefs.[55]

---

[52] For this event see Zia ud-Din Barani, *The Reign of Alauddin Khilji. Translated from Zia ud-Din Barani's* Tarikh-i Firuz Shahi, trans. A.R. Fuller and A. Khallaque (Calcutta, 1967), 97–9. For secondary accounts see Lal, *The History of the Khaljis*, 140–3, and Jackson, "Delhi: The Problem of a Vast Military Encampment," in *Delhi Through the Ages*, ed. R.E. Frykenberg (Delhi, 1986), 18–20, who includes dates for other Mongol invasions.

[53] See Lal, *History of the Khaljis*, 143.

[54] Barani, *The Reign of Alauddin Khilji*, 99.

[55] Barani, *The Reign of Alauddin Khilji*, 99–100.

For Ala al-Din, Taraghai's invasion underscored the importance of fortifying the frontier, since Delhi, despite its walls, would have been unable to withstand a concerted onslaught. This clearly was recognized as well by Ala al-Din's successors, the Tughluqs.

Ala al-Din's new city, Siri, was built on the plain of Siri, located to the northeast of the old city and southwest of Kilokhri, where earlier he had defeated the Mongol Taraghai.[56] Its foundation on the site of victory probably was intended to glorify his successful expulsion of Mongol forces. Extant portions of Siri's strong rubble-built wall indicate that it was oval shaped. These walls, surmounted with loopholes for arrows and battlements, were pierced by seven gates. Traces of a mosque survive within the walls, but nothing else to suggest that Ala al-Din took seriously his orders to supply his fortifications with provisions. In fact the site's choice remains problematic, for the nearest source of water was a tank or reservoir that the sultan had provided for his own private use at Hauz Khass. This tank, praised by Ibn Battuta, was still more than three kilometers west from Siri.[57]

Ala al-Din, in his efforts to protect his subjects, repaired the walls of old Delhi, the area first known as Qila Rai Pithora and subsequently as Dilhi. This protection was genuinely needed, for the Mongols continued to be a very real threat.[58] In the past they had reached Delhi's walls, and in spite of a newly fortified frontier, there remained fear that this could happen once again. Ala al-Din also began an ambitious enlargement of the first mosque built by Aibek that was intended to increase its size by four times.[59] Adjacent to this mosque is the shell of a second minaret which, when completed, would have dwarfed the Qutb Minar. Of the mosque's additions, only the south gate, known as the Alai Darwaza and dated 1311, was ever completed (Fig. 9.2). Introducing a new aesthetic of red and white stone, this gate would serve as an important visual source for Delhi's sixteenth-century cities. Ala al-Din built this gate after he improved Delhi's fortifications and as part of a campaign to restore the citizens' morale after their near defeat by Taraghai, the Mongol. The mosque, its sheer size a statement of the sultan's and Delhi's strength, essentially underscored the message sent by the restoration of the city's walls and the construction of a new palace.

[56] *ASI*, 1:207–12.
[57] Ibn Battuta, *The Travels*, 3:625. There also must have been *baolis*, wells and shallow catchment basins for water, but they are no longer extant.
[58] See Jackson, "Delhi," 18.
[59] For Ala al-Din's additions, see Page, *An Historical Memoir*, 14–18, and Asher, *Architecture of Mughal India*, 6–7.

Figure 9.2 Alai Darwaza, Jami (Quwwat al-Islam) Mosque Complex.

The Delhi of Ghiyas al-Din and Muhammad Shah Tughluq (1325–51)

The construction of fortified and walled enclaves continued, in fact escalated, under the Tughluqs, the fourteenth-century successors of the Khaljis. From the founding of the Tughluq house in 1320 to the accession of the third Tughluq ruler in 1351, at least three, new, fortified walled enclosures were added to Delhi (Fig. 9.3). First, Ghiyas al-Din (1320–5) constructed the massive fortress known as Tughluqabad, which included a citadel, palace area, and huge residential area about eight kilometers east of the original city of Dilhi.[60] His successor, Muhammad Shah (1325–51), added a fortress known as Adilabad, essentially a military headquarters and storage area, to the southwest of Tughluqabad. The two fortified areas were originally linked by a *bund* (dam) intended to contain rainwater. The walls of the fortress, the dam, and the outcropping of the rocks ideally formed a catchment for a large artificial body of water.

Then in 1327, Muhammad Shah added to Delhi yet another city

---

[60] For Tughluqabad and Adilabad, see H. Waddington, "Adilabad: A Part of the 'Fourth' Delhi," *Ancient India* 1 (1946): 60–76, and Anthony Welch and Howard Crane, "The Tughluqs: Master Builders of the Delhi Sultanate," *Muqarnas* 1 (1983): 127–8.

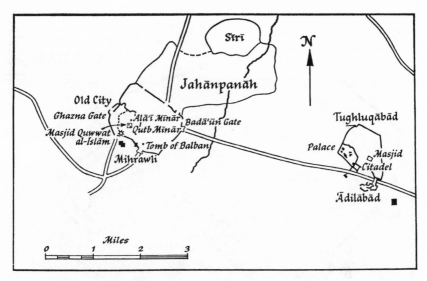

Figure 9.3 Map of Qila Rai Pithora, Siri, Tughluqabad, and Jahanpanah. From Ibn Battuta, *The Travels of Ibn Battuta*, A.D. 1325–1354, trans. H.A.R. Gibb, 3 vols. (Cambridge, 1956–71), 3:620.

called Jahanpanah (world refuge).[61] This city, provided with massive walls, was sandwiched between Siri and Dilhi, thus uniting three of Delhi's important cities.[62] Muhammad Shah wished to expand the walls to link Tughluqabad with Siri, Jahanpanah, and Dilhi, but they were never completed due to the vast expense.[63] Outside the walls were suburbs, including one called Indrapat – the ancient Indraprashta – which still remain to be studied.[64]

Ibn Battuta, the Moroccan *qadi* (judge) who stayed in Delhi for seven months during Muhammad Shah's reign, gives testimony to Delhi's magnificence:

... we arrived at the royal residence of Dilhi [Delhi], the metropolis of the land of al-Hind, a vast and magnificent city, uniting beauty with strength. It is surrounded by a wall whose equal is not known in any country in the world, and is the largest city in India, nay rather the largest of all the cities of Islam in the East.[65]

---

[61] See Welch and Crane, "The Tughluqs," 128–9.
[62] Ibn Battuta, *The Travels*, 3:619–21.
[63] Ibn Battuta, *The Travels*, 3:621.
[64] See Jackson, "Delhi," 19. Indrapat is the same as Indraprashta.
[65] Ibn Battuta, *The Travels*, 3:618.

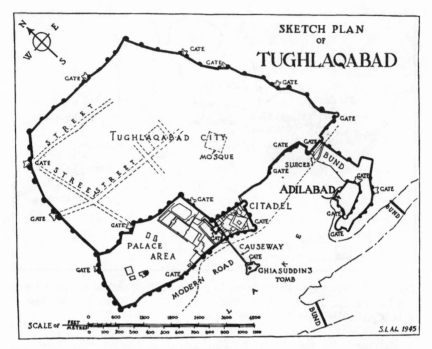

Figure 9.4 Sketch plan of Tughlaqabad. From H. Waddington, "Adilabad: A Part of the 'Fourth' Delhi," *Ancient India* I (1946): 63. Courtesy of the Archaeological Survey of India.

Thus, by 1334, Delhi was clearly an impressive and large city composed of a series of walled units linked, ideally at least, by one extensive wall.

Tughluqabad

The invasion of the Mongol Taraghai right up to the walls of Dilhi underscored, among other things, the importance of strong fortifications around the city. Ala al-Din himself added the fortified walls of Siri and repaired the walls of Dilhi, but Ghiyas al-Din Tughluq only a few years later produced one of the most massive fortified cities on the Indian plain, Tughlaqabad (Fig. 9.4). It is even possible that Tughluqabad could have withstood an attack at its very walls and was planned with this in mind. What is particularly remarkable about this achievement is that he did this within a five year reign.[66] The fortified

---

[66] Ibn Battuta, *The Travels*, 3:655.

area corresponds roughly to an Iranian *shahristan*: a citadel on the city's south with a large palace area and an enormous city covering over 300 acres.[67] The role of the third component of the traditional *shahristan*, the suburbs, is less clear.

Tughluqabad's walls, 6.5 kilometers in perimeter, remain intact, although the interior structures are largely in ruins. In spite of the site's size and significance, no archeological or detailed studies of Tughlaqabad have been produced.[68] The extensive ruins situated on streets are assumed to be largely dwellings, although businesses, too, must have existed. Aerial photos reveal that the city streets were designed as a grid with streets running from a gate on one side to a gate on the opposite side. The order and regularity of the streets' layout is highly unusual for an Indian city, perhaps a testimony to its military nature. The foundations of a large mosque survive, but little else is easily identifiable except wells.[69] There are *baolis* (step wells) in all parts of the city, and storage bins measuring 7.6 meters in diameter are located inside each gate.[70] This indicates that concerns for adequate water and food were taken seriously and would have served the city well in time of siege, a marked contrast with Delhi's earlier walled cities.

The exterior walls, ten to fifteen meters high, are marked by bastions and pierced by gates, including one escape door leading from the citadel area. This door would have been obscured when the original earth glacis was still in place.[71] The massive size of the exterior stones was obviously meant to impress any enemy. For example, in 1838 C.J. French praised the walls of Tughlaqabad:

The spectator is struck with the dimensions of the blocks of black stone . . . with which these forts [Tughlaqabad and Adilabad] were built. . . . Their colossal size would certainly impress the ignorant with an idea of their being of Cyclopean construction . . . The forts of Tughlaqabad . . . must have been almost impregnable.[72]

This is a compliment indeed, for usually Europeans were highly critical of Indian forts and their ability to withstand a siege.

In addition to curtain walls and a glacis, the city also was protected, at least in theory, by an artificial lake. A stretch in the fort's south wall

[67] Waddington, "Adilabad," 63–4.
[68] See Waddington, "Adilabad," 60–4, and Sidney Toy, *The Strongholds of India* (London, 1957), 116–19, for brief reports. Unfortunately there are no other studies.
[69] Waddington "Adilabad," 64.
[70] Waddington, "Adilabad," 64. Madhi Husain, *Tughluq Dynasty* (New Delhi, 1976), 613, claims these are wells. However, since no further excavations were done after Waddington this seems an unsubstantiated claim.
[71] Waddington, "Adilabad," 64.
[72] C.J. French, *Journal of a Tour in Upper India Performed During the Years 1838–39* (Simla, 1872), 14.

is fitted with sluices that appear to allow water to fall from a huge catchment basin from the fort's interior to the terrain below, thus forming a shallow lake.[73] The water was contained by dams, an engineering project generally believed to have been successful.[74]

Delhi, however, is situated on the edge of the great Thar desert; rain essentially only falls at the monsoon. Much of the year this so-called lake was probably at best an irrigated field; at the worst it was a mosquito-breeding marsh or completely dry. In fact, the provision of water was always a primary concern for the Tughluq rulers. For example, at his walled city of Jahanpanah, the next Tughluq ruler, Muhammad Shah, tapped a stream that ran through the city and fed the water through seven massive sluices into a tank outside the city walls.[75] Thus by the mid-fourteenth century, three of Delhi's cities – Dilhi, Jahanpanah, and Tughlaqabad – each had tanks of water outside the walls that were intended to provide for the citizens' needs. Ibn Battuta, however, makes no reference to those at Tughluqabad or Jahanpanah, suggesting that these projects were less successful than intended.

The location of these tanks was strategic if not for military purposes – indeed, their extra-mural location would have had serious consequences in time of siege – at least to serve agriculture in the plains below the city and to distance mosquito-breeding water from the city's population. After all, the city was so rarely threatened by siege that primary consideration had to be given to the population's needs for food and health.

Situated within the Tughlaqabad lake and attached to the fort's south wall via a long arched bridge is the tomb of Ghiyas al-Din (or Ghiasuddin) Tughluq, known from an interior inscription and contem-

---

[73] Sultanate period waterworks are most fully described and discussed in volume three of T. Yamamoto, M. Ara, and T. Tsukinowa, *Delhi: Architectural Remains of the Sultanate Period*, 3 vols. (Tokyo, 1967–70). For these sluices, see 3:46–54 and Figs. 19 and 20. These three volumes are rare, and in Japanese, making them relatively inaccessible for most Western scholars, but a summary of their findings is in Ara and Tsukinowa, "Outline of Surveys and Studies of the Architectural Remains of the Delhi Sultanate Period," *Acta Asiatica* 43 (1982): 92–109; see 98 for the waterworks. Also Waddington, "Adilabad," Fig. XI, provides an aerial view of Tughlaqabad where the catchment basin is visible. Also see Anthony Welch, "Hydraulic Architecture in Medieval India: The Tughluqs," *Environmental Design* 2 (1985): 75, and Welch and Crane, "The Tughluqs," 127–8.

[74] See, for example, Welch, "Hydraulic Architecture," 75–6.

[75] This is known as Sat Pul. See Yamamoto, Ara, and Tsukinowa, *Delhi: Architectural Remains*, 3:56–7 and Figs. 23–34. Welch, "Hydraulic Architecture," 76, 78. Hamida Khatoon Naqvi, *Agricultural, Industrial and Urban Dynamism Under the Sultans of Delhi, 1206–1555* (New Delhi, 1986), 34, indicates the Jumna was tapped by the city via an underground method.

porary texts as Dar al-Aman (the Abode of Peace) (Fig. 9.4).[76] The tomb is surrounded by fortified pentagonal walls. Provided with a good well and storage areas for grain, it has been likened to a small fort.[77] While I find it difficult to understand how this considerably smaller fort could withstand a siege if the larger one failed, this view remains essentially unchallenged.[78] If the lake were dry or essentially a marsh, the small fort would be vulnerable.

All the same, Ghiyas al-Din's Tughluqabad was well fortified with stronger walls than other forts except for the adjacent Adilabad. While the walls of Siri and Jahanpanah have largely vanished, those of Tughluqabad remain intact.[79]

French, in his observations on Tughluqabad, notes that these walls must have taken years to build and required considerable expense.[80] In fact, near contemporary chronicles indicate that Tughluqabad was constructed during Ghiyas al-Din's five-year reign.[81] In spite of the availability of cheap labor and the presence of nearby quarries, this achievement seems remarkable. The fort surely was built on the principle of *alang*, which probably had been used at Kilokhri and certainly later in the fourteenth century at Hisar.[82] Who paid for the walls and interior structures is not revealed by texts, but probably funds came from the imperial treasury. Until nearly the beginning of the Tughluq period, the policy of the Delhi sultans to attack and loot independent Hindu states was a lucrative one, for it filled the royal coffers without incurring long-term administrative responsibilities.[83] During Ghiyas al-Din's short five-year reign, the coffers would have been adequately full to construct Tughluqabad's walls; it was only beginning in the reign of his son, Muhammad Shah, that serious contraction of the state's resources occurred.[84]

The walls, the palace area, the citadel, and the city's Jami mosque were probably state financed. But likely some individual components of the city, such as *baolis*, wells, houses, and *madrasas* (schools for

---

[76] Muhammad Ashraf Husain, *A Record of All the Quranic and Non-Historical Epigraphs on the Protected Monuments in the Delhi Province*, Memoirs of the Archaeological Survey of India, No. 47 (Calcutta, 1936), 72.

[77] Waddington, "Adilabad," 64, and Toy, *The Strongholds*, 119.

[78] Only Asher, *Architecture of Mughal India*, 8, has questioned this view.

[79] Waddington, "Adilabad," 64–7, has studied the six-stage construction of Adilabad's massive stone walls and the methods used at Tughluqabad seem essentially comparable.

[80] French, *Journal of a Tour*, 14.

[81] Ibn Battuta, *The Travels*, 3:619, 655.

[82] See Shokoohy, *Hisar-i Firuza*, 9 and n. 47.

[83] Jackson, "Delhi," 22.

[84] Jackson, "Delhi," 23–4.

religious instruction), were paid for by private individuals.[85] This follows the normal pattern of patronage in sultanate India. Certainly this
appears to be the case in Muhammad Shah's Jahanpanah, where the
large Jami mosque was erected by the sultan, but the city's smaller
mosques were constructed by important officials.[86]

To build Tughluqabad in less than five years surely meant a highly
organized building campaign executed by large numbers of laborers –
the sort that only a ruler could muster. In fact legend claims that the
well-known sufi, Nizam al-Din Auliya, was unable to find labor for
the construction of his own *khanqah* (hospice) at this time, since every
available man or woman was working on Tughluqabad.[87] He is said
to have cursed the sultan, thus causing his death. The point here is
that Ghiyas al-Din's complete control of all labor was mandatory for
the completion of Tughluqabad, even if the story is apocryphal.

Tughluqabad may indeed be an exception among the various cities
of Delhi whose walls played generally more of a protective than defensive role. This massive walled city, complete with an elaborate
water system (whether it worked or not is another matter), a glacis,
and curtain walls was probably built to be adequately strong to withstand attacks at its very walls. This may indeed explain the praise
French has for Tughluqabad versus the disregard held by most Europeans for the walls of the later Mughal Shahjahanabad (Delhi).[88]

Jahanpanah

Ghiyas al-Din died in a freak accident in 1325.[89] He was succeeded by
Muhammad Shah, who within two years of his accession began to
build yet another Tughluq walled city in Delhi, Jahanpanah.[90]

Why build all these walled enclosures within such a short period of

---

[85] Ara and Tsukinowa, "Outline of Surveys," 98.

[86] This Jami mosque is called the Begumpuri mosque today. See Welch and Crane, "The
Tughluqs," 130–40, for all the Tughluq mosques. Ibn Battuta, *The Travels*, 3:665.

[87] For the story of the relationship of Nizam al-Din and Ghiyas al-Din, see Husain,
Quranic and Non-Historical Epigraphs, 81–3, 628–31. Also see Waddington, "Adilabad,"
62.

[88] There has been no study of Tughluqabad from a militarily defensive point of view.
I'm grateful to Jim Tracy for suggesting that the favorable comments of Europeans
about this city's walls as well as the elaborate water arrangements tend to suggest
that the walls were genuinely protective. See footnote 163 for comments about Shahjahanabad's walls.

[89] For the events surrounding his death, see Husain, *Quranic and Non-Historical Epigraphs*, 77–87.

[90] Jackson, "Delhi," 25.

time? This question is especially pertinent since it is generally believed that Muhammad Shah, at the very time he was constructing Jahanpanah and its great connecting wall, forced the entire population of Delhi to move 650 kilometers south to his second capital, Daulatabad.[91]

Jackson recently has argued that the move to Daulatabad as well as Muhammad Shah's construction of Jahanpanah, Adilabad, and the unifying wall are misunderstood.[92] At the outset of his reign, Muhammad Shah embarked on an ambitious project of subduing Khurasan in order to limit Mongol power. To do so demanded an enormous army, larger than any gathered to date, even under the sultans of Delhi who were renowned for their ability to muster troops. Muhammad Shah needed both his newly established walled areas as well as the older parts of Delhi to house his troops.[93] Thus to make room Muhammad Shah ordered the Muslim elite of Dilhi, with their massive households, to move south. However, within a year the entire Khurasan project was abandoned.[94] After a few years most of the Muslim elite who had moved to Daulatabad returned to Delhi, finding that a city was in place. It consisted of walled enclaves within walled enclaves that provided for the subjects' every need, except possibly adequate water.

Who were these people? Certainly we have the Muslim elite and service class living within these walls. It is they who would benefit from the reputed sixty or seventy *madrasas*, mosques, and *khanqahs* that made Delhi a seat of Islamic learning (*qubbat al-Islam*).[95] But by the reign of Muhammad Shah we have Hindus in high administrative positions.[96] From this it would follow that Hindus of all classes lived in these cities. Some were in the army, while others serviced Delhi's tremendous mercantile and industrial activities, acting as merchants, laborers, and, of course, bankers and moneylenders.[97]

Finally, while it appears that movement between the various walled areas of the city was fairly free, some areas did seem to have specific functions. Tughluqabad, or at least the palace/citadel area of that city,

---

[91] Husain, *Quranic and Non-Historical Epigraphs*, 145–6. Ibn Battuta, *The Travels*, 3:707–8.

[92] Jackson, "Delhi," 18–27.

[93] Jackson, "Delhi," 20–1, 24.

[94] See Jackson, "Delhi," 25–6, for details.

[95] See Naqvi, *Agricultural, Industrial and Urban Dynamism*, 176, and Jackson, "Delhi," 19.

[96] For example, see Barani's negative views on Hindus in society in Habib and Khan, *The Political Theory*, 46–50. He is essentially reacting to Hindus taking over administrative positions formerly allotted to Muslims.

[97] See Naqvi, *Agricultural, Industrial and Urban Dynamism*, 146–76; Jackson, Delhi," 25.

was used as a treasury under Muhammad Shah.[98] Given the unique strength of these walls this seems logical. Jahanpanah, according to Ibn Battuta, was the residence of Muhammad Shah;[99] that is, it served as a citadel. Here was his Sar Dara Palace, which contained multiple chambers, including his immense public audience hall known as the Hazar Setun or Thousand Pillared Hall. Today, what little remains of the palace is known as the Bijay Mandal in a locality called Begumpur.[100] The type of ceremonial described by Ibn Battuta, consisting of a progression from semi-public to increasingly private chambers until one reaches audience with the sultan, is characteristic of much of Islamic palace architecture.[101]

Firuzabad

To this already well developed and large city of Delhi the third Tughluq ruler, Firuz Shah, added yet another city (Fig. 9.1). It has an unprecedented number of extant structures, including a newly-constructed walled citadel named Firuzabad, hunting pavilions, water works and canal systems, and *madrasas*. At the same time, he encouraged the nobility to provide mosques, which they did generously, among other buildings. Around the populated areas were orchards and gardens – a contemporary text claims the sultan alone provided 1,200 orchards and gardens.[102] The new garden city, stretching sixteen kilometers north of Muhammad Shah's Delhi, essentially extended from the oldest part of Delhi, Indraprashta, to the northern ridge. To travel the considerable distances between Delhi's farthest ends, all now fully populated, official arrangements for transport were made:

During the forty years of the reign of the excellent Sultan Firoz, people used to go for pleasure from Delhi to Firozabad to Delhi, in such numbers, that every *kos* [3.2 kilometers] of the five *kos* between the two towns swarmed with people, as with ants or locusts. To accommodate this great traffic, there were public carriers who kept carriages, mules, and horses which were ready for hire at a settled rate . . . so the traveler could make the trip as seemed to him

[98] Jackson, "Delhi," 25.
[99] Ibn Batutta, *The Travels*, 3:658–68, provides a description of the palace and the ceremonial practiced in it.
[100] For a secondary account with illustrations, see Welch and Crane, "The Tughluqs," 148–9.
[101] Ibn Battuta, *The Travels*, 3:658–60.
[102] Shams-i Siraj Afif, "Tarikh-i Firoz Shahi," in *The History of India as Told by Its Own Historians*, eds. H.M. Elliot and John Dowson, 8 vols. (London, 1867–77), 3:345.

best and arrived at the stated time. Palankinbearers were also ready to convey passengers. . . .[103]

Delhi, anticipating the present, consisted of two cities: the old – a series of interconnected walled cities – linked to the new.

The citadel, Firuzabad, was the only walled portion of the new city.[104] It was located, unlike any sultanate city in Delhi since Kilokhri, on the banks of the Jumna. From this point, every walled city of Delhi would be situated on the alluvial soil of the Jumna in an area north of the Aravalli rocky soil.[105] Each of these cities was on elevated land, providing some protection against mosquitoes. Perhaps in these northern areas flooding was less violent.

Why the larger city of Firuzabad was unwalled is not clear. Threats from Central Asia still remained a very real problem. For example, on Firuz Shah's accession day as he proceeded to Delhi, Mongols eager for booty attacked the emperor's entourage with considerable success.[106] Likely the older walled city, still clearly inhabited, was considered a suitable refuge in time of attack.

Firuz Shah marked the two ends of his city not with walls, but with public references to India's ancient past.[107] To the north end, he transported an enormous stone monolith dating to the third century B.C.E. The complexity of this operation was so great that it was recorded in several contemporary texts; one even included illustrations, which is extremely rare for this period.[108] A second such column was erected as a minaret at his mosque in the Firuzabad citadel. While Firuz Shah did not know the actual dates or historical events associated with the pillars, he was aware that they were of considerable antiquity – so old that the script written on them, which today we know is Brahmi, could be deciphered by no living person.[109] The southernmost limit of

---

[103] Afif, "Tarikh-i Firoz Shahi," 3:303.

[104] Accounts of Timur's invasion make clear the walled portions of Delhi included Jahanpanah, Siri, and Dilhi, but not Firuzabad. See Amir Timur, "Malfuzat-i Timuri," in *The History of India*, 3:441.

[105] Athar Ali, "Capitol of the Sultans," 41–2.

[106] Barani, "Tarikh-i Firuz Shahi," 266–7.

[107] For two recent articles on Firuz Shah's appropriation of India's past, see Anthony Welch, "Architectural Patronage and the Past: The Tughluq Sultans of India," *Muqarnas* 10 (1993): 311–22, and William Jeffery McKibben, "The Monumental Pillars of Firuz Shah Tughluq," *Ars Orientalis* 24 (1994): 105–18.

[108] The text and illustrations are included in J.A. Page, *A Memoir of the Kotla Firoz Shah, Delhi with a Translation of Sirat-i Firozshahi*, Memoirs of the Archaeological Survey of India, No. 52., trans. M. Hamid Kuraishi (Delhi, 1937), 33–42, figs. VIa–VId, 19–20 of the Persian text portion.

[109] Page, *An Historical Memoir*, 34, and Afif, "Tarikh-i Firoz Shahi," 3:350–3.

Firuz Shah's city was Indraprashta,[110] a site imbued with antiquity whose implications Firuz Shah would have known well.

It is also important to understand that Firuzabad was only one of Firuz Shah Tughluq's new cities, and not the first one at that. He first built a new walled city and citadel at Hisar, 150 kilometers northwest of Delhi on the main road to Multan.[111] The citadel, much of which still survives, was of tremendous strength according to a contemporary observer.[112] Surrounded by a ditch and glacis, the fort appears to have been made to withstand enemy attack. In addition, Hisar was further protected by the founding of Fatehabad, forty-five kilometers to the northwest. The city walls of Fatehabad encompassed a small walled citadel.[113] Situated near the Saraswati River, the town was clearly intended to afford further protection to Hisar and areas south such as Delhi. In addition, a series of older defenses north of Delhi at Panipat, Sonepat, and Sirhind, among others, strengthened Delhi's security.[114]

About the same time as Hisar was constructed, Firuz Shah excavated two canals, still in use today, which transported water from the Jumna and Sutlej Rivers.[115] Hisar and its surrounding area were transformed from an arid area into a highly arable one. The increase in crops brought considerable wealth to the Tughluqs, thus allowing even more construction.[116] Firuz Shah also constructed a third canal that brought water directly from a northern branch of the Jumna to Delhi.[117] In addition, a number of waterworks were provided by Sultan Firuz Shah, both inside the perimeters of his city as well as in the suburbs, transforming Delhi into a garden city.[118] Thus for the first time since Delhi's foundation, water was not a problem. The citadel on the river's bank set a pattern for future Delhi cities. Now thanks to canals and tanks, orchards and fields could flourish in Delhi's dry terrain – in both city and suburb alike.

The reign of Firuz Shah is painted by contemporary chroniclers as one of prosperity and peace;[119] in fact, he abandoned an expansionist

---

[110] Afif, "Tarikh-i Firoz Shahi," 3:302.
[111] Afif, "Tarikh-i Firoz Shahi," 3:298–300. For the city and its walls, see Shokoohy, *Hisar-i Firuza*, 14.
[112] Afif, "Tarikh-i Firoz Shahi," 3:299.
[113] Afif, "Tarikh-i Firoz Shahi," 3:299; Naqvi, *Agricultural, Industrial and Urban Dynamism*, 100; Shokoohy, *Hisar-i Firuza*, 116–18.
[114] Naqvi, *Agricultural, Industrial and Urban Dynamism*, 118, 124, 125.
[115] Afif, "Tarikh-i Firoz Shahi," 3:300.
[116] Afif, "Tarikh-i Firoz Shahi," 3:301.
[117] Afif, "Tarikh-i Firoz Shahi," 3:354, but he remains imprecise on the canal's source.
[118] Afif, "Tarikh-i Firoz Shahi," 3:354–5, and Welch, "Hydraulic Architecture," 76–7.
[119] See Afif, "Tarikh-i Firoz Shahi," 3:344–7.

policy in favor of retreat. This was a policy which, by the end of the fourteenth century, was to have disastrous effects. Firuz Shah was seen as a champion of Islam, although in fact he had policies that essentially treated Muslims and non-Muslims equally.[120] He was regarded as a great builder; his most important contribution was his canals, which continue to water north India even today. Nevertheless, despite the beneficial aspects of his building program, the policy itself was essentially a cover for his politically weak regime and rapidly shrinking domain.[121]

Although Firuz Shah's reign was in many respects the calm before the storm, his vision of Delhi was to make a profound mark on Mughal visions of Delhi. Three things in particular stand out. One was to place the citadel on the Jumna. A second was to evoke Delhi's past as a basis for Delhi's present. And a third was to provide sufficient water for the population's needs and for creating green gardens and orchards around heavily populated areas.

Firuz Shah died in 1388. By the end of the fourteenth century, Tughluq rule and Delhi's defenses were so weakened that Timur (known in English literature as Tamerlane), a Barlas Turk from Central Asia, was able to take the city in 1398.[122] Timur rode around the city so impressed by the edifices in Siri, Jahanpanah, and Dilhi that he ordered all the artisans and engineers to be taken to Samarqand to build a Jami mosque for him there.[123] He then had his name read in the *khutba*, thus establishing himself as Delhi's legitimate ruler.[124] After Timur's sack of Delhi, the city lost virtually all of its status until the mid-sixteenth century. Except for a vast number of tombs that dot the area between Jahanpanah and Firuzabad, we know little about Delhi as a city during the fifteenth and early sixteenth centuries.

DELHI: 1526–1639

It was not until the Mughal period (1526–1858) that Delhi once again became a flourishing center and twice the capital of Hindustan. After the defeat of Sultan Ibrahim Lodi in 1526, the first Mughal, Babur,

---

[120] K.A. Nizami, *Supplement of Elliot and Dowson's History of India*, vol. 3, *The Khaljis and Tughluqs* (Delhi, 1981), 3:16.
[121] Catherine B. Asher and Thomas R. Metcalf, eds., *Perceptions of South Asia's Visual Past* (New Delhi, 1994), 8.
[122] For Delhi during this period, see Gavin Hambly, "The Twilight of Tughluqid Delhi: Conflicting Strategies in a Disintegrating Imperium," in *Delhi Through the Ages*, 45–62.
[123] Timur, "Malfuzat-i Timur," 3:448.
[124] Timur, "Malfuzat-i Timur," 3:444.

proclaimed himself ruler of Hindustan. Although today we call the dynasty that Babur founded the Mughals, in fact they were Timurids, related to Timur, the great Iranian ruler who had sacked Delhi in December 1398.[125] Now some 125 years later, Babur essentially traced his famous ancestor's steps in making his own claim to Delhi, the traditional capital of north India. He visited first the tomb of Nizam al-Din Auliya, the very saint associated with causing the death of Ghiyas al-Din.[126] After partaking of Nizam al-Din's *baraka* (spiritual essence), Babur proceeded to the old walled cities of Tughluqabad, Siri, and Jahanpanah, and to the saints' tombs in those cities.[127] Only a few days later the *khutba* was read in his name, as he reenacted Timur's steps toward legitimacy. Thus in this legitimizing act Babur combined sanctity with Delhi's past and present as well as with his Timurid legacy.[128]

In spite of the significance of visiting the ancient walled cities of Delhi as a statement of legitimacy and appropriation, Babur established his capital at Agra. It had been the capital of the defeated Lodis, and its fort was simply reused by the Mughals. In 1533, Humayun, Babur's son and successor, made Delhi the Mughal capital. Likely he wanted a newly constructed capital, and at the same time to move the Mughal line of defense further north.

The site chosen was Indraprashta, Delhi's epic city situated on a hillock overlooking the Jumna (Fig. 9.1).[129] Just a kilometer to the south is the tomb of Nizam al-Din Auliya, perhaps an inspiration for the city's name, Din Panah, Refuge of the Faith (today the fort is called the Purana Qila or Old Fort). The setting, combining India's ancient past with Islamic sanctity, must have been consciously chosen, but the topography as well may have played a role. Timurid citadels, for example that of Herat, a city Humayun knew and admired, were elevated above the *shahristan* proper;[130] the setting of Indraprashta was a plains' version of a Timurid ideal.

---

[125] The Mughals were related both to the Timurids and Mongols. Mughal is simply an Indian corruption of Mongol; both the Mughals and Mongols are Chaghtai Turks. See John F. Richards, *The Mughal Empire* (Cambridge, 1993), 9.

[126] Zahiru'd-din Muhammad Babur, *Babur Nama*, trans. Annette S. Beveridge (reprint ed. 1922; New Delhi, 1970), 475 [hereafter *Babur Nama*].

[127] *Babur Nama*, 475–6; see also Ebba Koch, "The Delhi of the Mughals Prior to Shahjahanabad as Reflected in the Patterns of Imperial Visits," in *Art and Culture: Felicitation Volume in Honour of Professor S. Nurul Hasan*, eds. Ahsan Jan Qaisar and Som Prakash Verma (Jaipur, 1993), 4.

[128] Koch, "The Delhi of the Mughals," 4, argues Babur had with him a copy of the *Zafar Nama*, the book of Timur's great victories.

[129] Muhammad Khwand Amir, *Qanun-i Humayun*, trans. Baini Prasad (Calcutta, 1940), 61.

[130] Howard Crane, "Military Architecture and Fortification, Islamic Lands, IV, 3 (iv):

The walled citadel was commenced after "taking omens and religious advice;"[131] but how much of it was completed before the Afghan upstart Sher Shah Sur usurped the throne in 1538 is unclear. Khwand Amir, a noble in Humayun's court, reports that by 1534 the "walls, bastions, ramparts and gates" of Humayun's Din Panah were nearly completed, adding his hope that the "great and lofty buildings of the city soon would be completed."[132] It is difficult to tell from Khwand Amir's effusive prose exactly how much of the city was really ready by 1534; and it is virtually impossible to judge how much was completed before Sher Shah's accession to the Delhi throne in 1540, for Humayun constantly was engaged in defending the Mughal domain and struggling to maintain his crown.

Sher Shah almost doubtless completed Humayun's Din Panah, renaming it Shergarh (Fort of Sher Shah) and constructed its interior Qala-i Kuhna mosque. This would be in keeping with his general pattern of patronage across north India. During his short seven-year reign, he staged a massive building campaign intended to underscore his image as an ideal sultan concerned with the public and the maintenance of Islam.[133] By building public works such as city walls – as well as roads, serais, wells, and forts – Sher Shah bolstered his image as a ruler concerned with public welfare and the execution of justice. In order to do this, Sher Shah often capitalized on pre-existing structures or routes that he repaired or completed.[134] For example, his road system was based on ancient trade routes that he paved and lined with trees. So, too, his Delhi citadel appears to rest on the foundations begun by Humayun. There is a definite break about halfway up the walls suggesting a change of hand;[135] probably here Sher Shah resumed construction of the former Mughal citadel with stones taken from Old Delhi, meaning probably Jahanpanah.[136] The splendid so-called Humayun Darwaza of the citadel is almost surely Sher Shah's, as suggested by contemporary grafitti written on the interior walls.[137]

Eastern Islamic Lands, after c. 1250," in *Dictionary of Art*, ed. Jane Turner (London, 1966), 588.

[131] Khwand Amir, *Qanun-i Humayuh*, 61.

[132] Khwand Amir, *Qanun-i Humayuh*, 59–62.

[133] Catherine B. Asher, "Legacy and Legitimacy: Sher Shah's Patronage of Imperial Mausolea," in *Shari'at and Ambiguity in South Asian Islam*, ed. Katherine P. Ewing (Berkeley, 1988), 79–82.

[134] Catherine E.B. Asher, "The Patronage of Sher Shah Sur: A Study of Form and Meaning in 16th-Century Indo-Islamic Architecture" (Ph.D. diss. University of Minnesota, 1984), 41–2.

[135] *List*, 2:87.

[136] See Abbas Khan Sarwani, *Tarikh-i Sher Shahi*, ed. and trans. S.M. Imam al-Din (Dacca, 1974), 173.

[137] *List*, 2:97. Humayun here means auspicious and is not a reference to the Mughal emperor, Humayun. This inked inscription is dated A.H. 950/1543–4 C.E.

The citadel walls and gates appear imposing; in fact, they are comparable to those at Tughluqabad and Adilabad. But those cities had been erected before the advent of gunpowder and cannon. Din Panah/ Shergarh, however, was built just as knowledge of explosive gunpowder and modern weaponry reached India; Babur was the first to use such weapons, which played a major role in his success against the much larger army of Ibrahim Lodi.[138] All the same, the Mughals, like their Timurid predecessors, continued to build highly conservative military architecture.[139] There is, for example, little use of the curtain wall or attempts at adaptation of the kind seen in Europe with the beginning of the bastioned trace. This is a pattern that continues with the second great Mughal city of Delhi, Shahjahanabad.

Sher Shah commenced the walls of Shergarh about 1540. Two extant gates (the Sher Shah Darwaza on the Mathura Road near the Purana Qila and the Kabuli Gate on Mathura Road near Firuz Shah Kotla) are part of the city that stretched as far north as the Firuzabad citadel and south past the tomb of Nizam al-Din Auliya.[140] We know nothing of how the city functioned under Sher Shah and his Sur successors. In fact, Sher Shah essentially never lived in Delhi since he was continuously on campaign to conquer and consolidate additional territory.[141]

Sher Shah did, however, provide the splendid Qala-i Kuhna mosque in the citadel's interior; its decorative program suggests that Sher Shah drew upon Delhi's past as part of an attempt to revive its status as a major city.[142] Today the approach to the mosque is from the fort's Bara Darwaza, the main gate; the viewer does not grasp how it was intended to be seen in pre-modern times, that is, from the river, a major mode of transport. From this vantage, the magnificent single-aisled mosque would stand out on the horizon. The contemporary viewer would immediately understand that the mosque, built in the manner of Afghan congregational mosques and quite distinct from contemporary Mughal ones, was a political statement as well as a religious one.[143] On closer inspection the contemporary viewer would see its

[138] Jagish Narayan Sarkar, *The Art of War in Medieval India* (New Delhi, 1984), 134–5; *Babur Nama*, 463, 469–73.

[139] Christopher Tadgell, "Military Architecture and Fortifications, VI, I: West Central Asia," in *Dictionary of Art*, 591.

[140] For the walls, see *List*, 2:87; see 68–9 for the Kabuli Gate and 53–4 for the Sher Shah Darwaza.

[141] See *List*, 2:300, for Salimgarh, the fortified enclave that Sher Shah's son and successor built to the city's north.

[142] For a discussion of this mosque, see Catherine B. Asher, "The Qal'a-i Kuhna Mosque: A Visual Symbol of Royal Aspirations," in *Chhavi* II, ed. Anand Krishna (Varanasi, 1982), 22–17.

[143] Asher, *Architecture of Mughal India*, 12–13.

carved calligraphic bands and contrasting colored stones on the richly textured exterior and interior. Those who were attuned would be aware that these recall the appearance of Ala al-Din Khalji's Alai Darwaza, this early-fourteenth-century ruler's extension at the first Delhi mosque.

Why did Sher Shah build in his own citadel such a carefully crafted mosque that evokes Delhi's past? Sher Shah, a low-ranking upstart holding few of the perquisites required for kingship, revived many of Ala al-Din's administrative practices in his own government; moreover, he associated these features with the revival of the Delhi Sultanate's prestige. Even Abu al-Fazl, the Mughal Akbar's official chronicler, guardedly applauded these revived administrative practices in spite of Mughal contempt for this Afghan upstart.[144]

In 1555, the Mughals returned to power. Humayun occupied Sher Shah's city and citadel (once again renamed Din Panah) making minor improvements before his death a year later. Din Panah briefly served as the capital of his successor, Akbar, before he moved to Agra. Although Delhi did not resume its role as a royal residence until 1639, it still continued to be called Dar al-Mulk Dilhi (Seat of the Empire), underscoring its continued significance.[145] While ruling from Delhi, Akbar continued to reside in Din Panah, commenced under Humayun and essentially completed under Sher Shah. In very close proximity to the citadel and within the city's walls, leading members of Akbar's court built mosques, schools, and tombs.[146]

Even after Akbar moved the imperial headquarters to Agra, Delhi remained a vital urban center. For example, Akbar, in 1572, after his move to Agra, gave orders for the restoration of the mosque at Nizam al-Din Auliya's *dargah* (shrine), indicating the Mughals' continued close ties with this sufi order. Nizam-al Din was the saint associated with the fourteenth-century Ghiyas al-Din's demise. Babur had paid the saint homage as did the later Mughals.

Not only was Nizam-al Din's *dargah* within Delhi's walls, thus giving the city a sense of legitimacy, but also the largest and most important structure erected in Akbar's Delhi, the tomb of the deceased emperor Humayun, finished in 1571, was within those walls.[147] Situ-

---

[144] Abu al-Fazl, *Akbar Nama*, trans. H. Beveridge, 3 vols. (reprint ed. 1907–39; Delhi, 1972–3), 2:399.

[145] Koch, "The Delhi of the Mughals," 3.

[146] Asher, *Architecture of Mughal India*, 41–7. Examples include the Khair al-Manazil, Atagah Khan's tomb, patronage at the tomb of Nizam al-Din Auliya, and Humayun's tomb, among other structures.

[147] Al-Badayuni, *Muntakhab al-Tawarikh*, trans. G.S.A. Ranking, W.H. Lowe, and W. Haig, 3 vols. (reprint ed., 1884–1925; Patna, 1973), 2:135.

ated just south of the Din Panah citadel (Purana Qila) and close to the esteemed *dargah* of Nizam al-Din, the mausoleum dominates its surroundings. Its Timurid appearance, strikingly different from any other structure in Delhi, suggests that it was intended as a dynastic tomb, that is, a tomb not only for Humayun but for future Mughal rulers as well.[148] The tomb then can be seen as a continuation of a theme that ties Delhi's religious and historical past to a Timurid present and future. The fact that Akbar visited his father's tomb and that of Nizam al-Din Auliya nine times after his move from Delhi underscores the importance of these two landmarks in the city.[149]

SHAHJAHANABAD

Under the fifth Mughal emperor, Shah Jahan, Delhi again became the Mughal capital and remained so until 1858. Much has been written on the Shah Jahan's walled city, Shahjahanabad, and its citadel, today known as the Red Fort (Fig. 9.1).[150] Here I will focus largely on the walls and their role in defining what this newly built and planned city meant for the emperor, as well as for the later Mughals and even the British.

Shahjahanabad, literally the Abode of Shah Jahan, was an entire walled city and fortified palace built as the new Mughal capital. Located north of Din Panah and Firuzabad, Shah Jahan's citadel was built on a bluff overlooking the Jumna river. The city surrounded it on three sides. The site was chosen with considerable care once the emperor decided to abandon Agra, whose streets he complained were too crowded and not adequate for ceremonial processions. Fully conscious of Delhi's past in historic and religious terms, Shah Jahan perceived the site as a symbolic center of the earth, an *axis mundi*.[151] Shahjahanabad's foundations were laid in 1639 at an auspiciously chosen moment. The plans for the roughly semicircular city and rectangular fortified palace mainly were designed by Ustad Hamid and Ustad Ahmad; as with his other architectural projects, Shah Jahan was actively involved. He approved the designs and later visited the site,

---

[148] Asher, *Architecture of Mughal India*, 46.
[149] Koch, "The Delhi of the Mughals," 8.
[150] For example, see Stephen P. Blake, *Shahjahanabad: The Sovereign City in Mughal India, 1639–1739* (Cambridge, 1991), for social and economic aspects of the city. Narayani Gupta, *Delhi Between Two Empires, 1893–1931: Society, Government and Urban Growth* (Delhi, 1981), is excellent for Shahjahanabad in the nineteenth and twentieth centuries. Art historical coverage is in Asher, *Architecture of Mughal India*.
[151] Blake, *Shahjahanabad*, 29–30.

ordering changes in the plans.[152] The result was a walled city balanced by mansions, markets, broad tree-lined streets, canals, and many gardens. The traditions commenced by Firuz Shah Tughluq continued; in fact, one of his canals, restored by Shah Jahan, was the basis for Shahjahanabad's greenery.[153]

The chroniclers of Shah Jahan's reign have written about his architectural and building projects in tremendous detail. It is not uncommon for detailed measurements of each project, for example, the Shahjahanabad palace and citadel, to be included in contemporary histories.[154] These chronicles, however, are remarkably silent about the walls of Shahjahanabad. We know that they were first mud-built, but after suffering damage in the heavy rains of 1653, they were rebuilt in red stone and completed by 1657.[155] This information, extremely scanty in relation to other projects in Shahjahanabad and elsewhere, has led one modern scholar to say the walls simply were not very important.[156] How accurate is this analysis?

Why would Shah Jahan build mud walls around the city? It is well established that mud walls were actually better at protecting against attacks by cannon than were stone walls, since the mud would simply absorb the ball;[157] perhaps that is one reason for this seemingly unusual choice. All the same, no imperial Mughal city had mud walls. Agra had stone walls;[158] Lahore's walls were brick. But the walls of some major Timurid cities (*shahristan*), including Herat, were of mud construction.[159] Both Babur and Humayun had spent considerable time in Herat and were deeply impressed by the city's beauty.[160] Shah Jahan, of all the Mughal rulers, was the most proud of his Timurid

---

[152] See Asher, *Architecture of Mughal India*, 191–2, for the above information.

[153] Blake, *Shahjahanabad*, 64–5.

[154] For example, Muhammad Salih Kanbo, *Amal-i Salih*, 3 vols. (Lahore, 1967), 3:21–36, provided detailed information about the palace's construction and measurements.

[155] Kanbo, *Amal-i Salih*, 3:184, and Inayat Khan, *The Shah Jahan Nama of Inayat Khan*, trans. A.R. Fuller; eds. W.E. Begley and Z.A. Desai (Delhi, 1990), 537.

[156] Samuel V. Noe, "Old Lahore and Old Delhi: Variations on a Mughal Theme," *Ekistics* 295 (1987): 314.

[157] *Observations on the Attack of Mud Forts* (Calcutta, 1813), 106; Martha D. Pollak, *Turin, 1564–1680: Urban Design, Military Culture and the Creation of an Absolutist Capital* (Chicago, 1991), 217.

[158] I can find no Mughal account or contemporary European account that mentions any city walls of Agra, but *ASI* 4:115–16 traces the extent of these walls which were no more than five feet in thickness. The material is not given, but since they were still standing and Agra is a quarry rich area, they must have been stone.

[159] See Crane, "Military Architecture and Fortification," 588–9, and Terry Allen, *A Catalogue of the Toponymns and Monuments of Timurid Herat* (Cambridge, MA, 1981), 26–30.

[160] *Babur Nama*, 304–6; Sukumar Ray, *Humayun in Persia* (Calcutta, 1948), 9–14.

heritage and even borrowed portions of Timur's title as his own. Perhaps the Timurid link, already seen in the site's topography, explains why the walls of this splendid new city were mud.

Nevertheless, mud is not a visually impressive material, and after a year Shah Jahan ordered the mud walls replaced by stone ones. Enclosing an area of about 1,500 acres, the walls were about six kilometers long, about eight meters high and four meters thick.[161] The walls were pierced by seven main gates and a number of smaller ones, thus providing easy entrance and egress. Some of the gates survive; only portions of the wall are extant.

How strong were these walls – those of the city and the citadel? Could they, in fact, protect the city and its subjects in case of attack? Mughal texts claim the unprecedented strength of these walls, but such hyperbole is common and not to be taken literally.[162] The Frenchman François Bernier visited Delhi in 1663 and wrote of Shahjahanabad's walls:

The fortifications, however, are very incomplete, as there are neither ditches nor any other kind of additional defence, if we except flanking towers of antique shape, at intervals of about one hundred paces, and a bank of earth forming a platform behind these walls. . . . Although these works encompass not only the city but the citadel, yet their extent is less than is generally supposed. . . . The walls of the fortress [Red Fort] likewise excel those of the town in height, strength and thickness, being capable of admitting small field pieces, which are pointed toward the city. Except on the side of the river, the citadel is defended by a deep ditch faced with hewn stone, filled with water and stocked with fish. Considerable as these works may appear, their real strength is by no means great, and in my opinion a battery of moderate force would soon level them with the ground.[163]

Sixteen sixty-three, the year of Bernier's observations, corresponds to the period when Aurangzeb, the sixth Mughal ruler, was strengthening the fortifications of the Delhi and Agra citadels.[164] So why is this European, usually generous in his comments, so critical of Delhi's walls and fortifications?

In part the answer is cultural. While weapons and artillery were constantly undergoing improvement in Europe, a highly conservative attitude was taken toward weapons in Iran, Central Asia, and Mughal

---

[161] Blake, *Shahjahanabad*, 31.
[162] Kanbo, *Amal-i Salih*, 3:184.
[163] François Bernier, *Travels in the Moghul Empire, 1656–1668*, trans. A. Constable, 2nd ed. rev. (London, 1916), 242–3.
[164] Asher, *Architecture of Mughal India*, 261–2.

India.[165] Once heavy arms and the giant, unwieldy siege cannon were adopted, there was no interest in updating these weapons. In fact, those in power feared that abandoned weapons could be used to overthrow their authority.[166] Thus as cumbersome, slow, and difficult as it might be to move enormous cannon, they remained the pride of the Mughal army. Hill forts were taken by mining and sapping, but not really by decisive use of heavy artillery.[167] Cities might be walled, but they were not fortress cities. Among other things, new-style European fortresses were extraordinarily expensive to build, and were not well suited to the Indian defense approaches, which demanded multiple fortifications across a frontier into the heartland. To construct these new-style fortified cities simply would have bankrupted the Mughals and other South Asian states.[168] Moreover, none of the decisive battles of empire or succession in Mughal India were fought at the walls of Delhi. For example, the battles of Samugarh (1658), Karnal (1739), and Panipat (1761) all were fought on the plains outside of Delhi. All these battles were cavalry competitions. To the victors of these cavalry battles, Delhi was much more of a prize than a further obstacle. It was then relatively easy to find someone who would open the city gates once the armies had fought on the plains.[169]

If that were the case, why wall Delhi at all? The Mughals were not aware that European military equipment was more advanced and could take their city within hours. Moreover, the Mughals, like the ruling houses before them, had no intention of defending the city at its very walls, but rather on the open plains and at the borders. Thus walls were needed to keep out marauders, not full-scale armies. But in the long run, the tradition of a walled Delhi, if not a city served by these walls, was so strong that to break with it was probably unthinkable.

The walls were damaged in 1720 by an earthquake. They were repaired, however, between 1804 and 1811 once the British gained control of the city.[170] Bishop Heber, visiting Delhi in 1838, was im-

---

[165] William H. McNeill, *The Pursuit of Power: Technology, Armed Force and Society Since A.D. 1000* (Chicago,1982), 98.

[166] McNeill, *Pursuit of Power*, 98.

[167] I am most grateful to Stewart Gordon for these observations.

[168] This information was kindly conveyed to me by John A. Lynn in private correspondence of May 26, 1996. For information on the rise of these new-style fortresses in the larger cultural setting of Europe, see his "The Trace Italienne and the Growth of Armies: the French Case," *Journal of Military History* (July 1991): 297–330.

[169] Correspondence with Stewart Gordon dated June 1, 1995. This is not to say that cities were never attacked at their walls; Delhi, for example, in the early fourteenth century was attacked at its walls, but this was the exception and not the norm.

[170] Toy, *The Strongholds*, 130–2.

pressed with the "embattled wall which the British Government have put into repair and now are engaged in strengthening with bastions, a moat and a regular glacis."[171] The great irony of this is that during the Uprising of 1857 the walls had been so strengthened that it was four months before the British were able to liberate the captured city.[172]

British reaction to what they called the Mutiny was aggressively anti-Indian. Walls of all sorts were torn down to prevent Indians from once again rising against them. These included the east wall of the Agra Jami mosque, entire portions of forts such as the one in Jaunpur, and many buildings within the city of Shahjahanabad between the fort and the city's Jami mosque.[173] Left, however, after much debate were Delhi's walls, for it was argued that with the British now controlling the Red Fort, the city's walls afforded protection.[174] Eventually, however, in the name of progress – the introduction of the railroad and for reasons of health, among others – vast portions of Shahjahanabad's walls and gates came down.[175] By the twentieth century little was left of the city walls.

DELHI IN THE TWENTIETH CENTURY

In 1911, George V stunned India's subjects by announcing that once again Delhi, which he referred to as the "ancient capital," was to be India's capital.[176] The combined genius of Herbert Baker and Edwin Lutyens was engaged to plan yet another Delhi. This one was consciously situated across from Indraprashta and approximately midway between Shahjahanabad and Jahanpanah (Fig. 9.1). It was to be the new British capital of India, to rise like a phoenix amidst the ruins of Delhi's past.[177] Plans for the city were commenced soon after King George's announcement in 1911; but due to World War I it was not finished or officially inaugurated until 1931, when British authority was clearly declining in India. Lutyens's city, intended as a statement of modernity and progress, was not walled.

---

[171] Heber, *Narrative of a Journey*, 2:285; for a similar view, see Edward Archer, *Tours in Upper India, and in Parts of the Himalaya Mountains*, 2 vols. (London, 1833), 1:105.

[172] Narayani Gupta, "Military Security and Urban Development: A Case Study of Delhi, 1857–1912," *Modern Asian Studies* 5/1 (1971): 62.

[173] For example, see Gupta, "Military Security and Urban Development," 62–5; *ASI*, 4: 170; 11:120–1.

[174] Gupta, "Military Security and Urban Development," 67.

[175] Gupta, "Military Security and Urban Development," 70–7.

[176] G.H.R. Tillotson, *The Tradition of Indian Architecture* (New Haven, 1989), 103. Calcutta until then had served as the capital of British India.

[177] Robert Grant Irving, *Indian Summer: Lutyens, Baker and Imperial Delhi* (New Haven, 1981), 53.

Yet nearly a century after the walls of Shahjahanabad were largely torn down and as Delhi expands to the east, west, and especially the south, every Delhite still knows what is meant by the "walled city," that is, the area formerly comprising Shahjahanabad. Delhi is, in the minds of many, a series of walls, not so much defensive walls, but simply protective ones. Today the city is vast, covering 1,500 square kilometers. The old Delhis are largely covered with modern developments, or colonies as they are called. Some, such as Kalkaji in south Delhi, a residential area for the up-and-coming middle class, even have walls around them with gates that are closed and locked at night. Delhi as a refuge – a notion we have seen in a number of her former cities – is evoked as the middle class seeks protection from the anonymity and vast size of an increasingly impersonal city.

CHAPTER 10

Ottoman military architecture in the early gunpowder era: A reassessment

SIMON PEPPER

OTTOMAN military architecture has had a bad press. The military construction that marked the phenomenal expansion of the Ottoman empire during the fourteenth, fifteenth, and sixteenth centuries has generally received little attention, and that almost entirely critical. The sole exception seems to be in the field of military communications, where the Ottomans continued the Seljuk tradition of elegant civil engineering as they laid down the infrastructure which allowed them to move enormous bodies of fighting men from one frontier to the other across their vast empire, leaving roads and bridges that are admired today. Fortifications themselves are generally either ignored or scorned.

Mallet set the tone for subsequent critical coverage when he wrote just after the last siege of Vienna: "*Le Turcs qui sont fort ignorans dans les belles Lettres, ne sont pas plus éclairez dans tous les Arts, & moins dans celui des Ingenieurs que dans les autres, aussi ne le voit-on fortifier aucune Place dans les Regles de l'Art,*" before going on to assert that most Ottoman frontier posts had been fortified by Christian princes, lost because of the foolishness of the inhabitants, or the weakness of their garrisons, and then neglected and ruined in the belief that Christian disunity would prevent a serious challenge. When obliged to fortify a

An early version of this essay was presented to a faculty seminar of the Departments of History and Art History at Vassar College in April 1996. I am most grateful to Professor Nicholas Adams and his colleagues at Vassar for their hospitality, and for the opportunity to receive valuable feedback. I am also very grateful to Professor Christopher Allmand of the University of Liverpool and to Professor Geoffrey Parker of Ohio State and Yale University for helpful comments and suggestions.

place, the sum total of their science consisted of enclosing it in the tightest possible circuit, in raising a terrace *"au maniere de rempart"* all around, and putting forward towers in some places the better to flank the walls. As for bastions, the "infidels" constructed none unless some [Western] renegade had set them out, sometimes contrary to the rules. Such was Turkish ignorance, declared Mallet, that, provided the work was high enough, it was accepted, even though it might not be properly flanked.[1] Like other military writers, he was impressed by Turkish discipline, bravery, camp hygiene, and by aspects of their artillery founding. But the mathematics instructor to the pages of His Majesty's *Petite Ecurie* and former engineer and sergeant-major of artillery in Portugal – writing in the flush of victory following the events of 1683 – was moved to indignation by the sorry state of former Christian strongholds in Ottoman hands.

The charge of incompetence stuck. In his important book on the Venetian fortresses in Greece, Kevin Andrews so often identifies Turkish work from its poor construction and design (in sharp contrast to the presumed high quality of Venetian or other Frankish military building) that disparagement practically becomes a methodology for attribution: good work Christian; shoddy work Turkish.[2] Christopher Duffy quotes with evident approval Major-General von Valentini, who was writing in the 1820s:

> With regard to the art of fortification among the Turks, little can be said in its praise. They have no idea of a regular system either of bastions or of lines, or outworks or covered ways, nor of conforming the height of the works to the nature of the ground in front. When we find anything of this kind in a Turkish fortress, we may be assured that it has been in the hands of some European power, by which it has been improved or originally constructed.[3]

General Valentini wrote when Turkey was firmly stigmatized as the "sick man of Europe," and before Osman Pasha's epic resistance at Plevna (1877) forced Western powers to re-evaluate Ottoman defensive capabilities and their imaginative use of field fortifications.[4] Fernand Braudel's views, however, carry real weight and this great

---

[1] Alain Manesson Mallet, *Les Travaux de Mars ou l'Art de la Guerre*, 3 vols. (Paris, 1684), III:bk. vi, ch. 1, 318.

[2] Kevin Andrews, *Castles of the Morea* (Princeton, NJ, 1953).

[3] General von Valentini, *Military Reflections on Turkey* (London, 1828), 53, quoted by Christopher Duffy, *Siege Warfare: The Fortress in the Early Modern World, 1494–1660* (London, 1979), 216.

[4] For the Turkish defense against the Russian siege operations at Plevna, in modern Bulgaria, from 20 July to 10 December, 1877, see William Von Herbert, *The Defence of Plevna, 1877, written by one who took part in it* (Ankara, 1990). The book was first published in 1895.

scholar dedicates a substantial section of *The Mediterranean* to a comparison between the Western and the Eastern approaches to frontier defences, which addresses a much earlier period but reaches fundamentally similar conclusions.

To meet the Turkish threat, Mediterranean Christendom erected a chain of fortresses, now to be one of the characteristic marks of its approach to war. As well as fighting, it was constantly extending its defensive and protective lines, encasing itself within a shell of armour. It was a policy both instinctive and unilateral: *the Turks built neither very many nor very effective fortifications.*[5]

The Ottomans certainly built fortifications differently from the Christian West, and this paper will explore some of those differences in the early stages of the Renaissance military architectural revolution. Yet the Ottoman Turks were generally so successful in their military operations during the centuries of expansion that it seems unwise to dismiss such differences as evidence of ignorance or technical incompetence. In other military fields – notably their tactical employment of artillery and other firearms, and their rapid development of naval tactics and warship design – the Ottomans borrowed designs but quickly set standards envied by apparently more advanced western cultures. The Ottomans were also particularly receptive to talent or expertise from abroad. The fifteenth- and sixteenth-century revolution in fortification design, which introduced the pointed-bastion-and-rampart system, is therefore a particularly good area in which to debate technology transfer, or its apparent failure. From its origins in Italy, the new military architecture spread very quickly throughout Europe and Europe's overseas empires and is seen by many contemporary historians as a key element in the world wide success of the technically advanced colonial powers. During the formative period of the new bastioned fortifications, moreover, the Turks had opportunities to witness some of the more advanced western prototypes as they took shape in Rhodes, Bodrum, and other outposts of the Knights of St. John – probably the most advanced fortress builders in the region – as well as in the Aegean naval stations of the Venetian Republic and the Genoese colonies.

It behooves us, therefore, to look more closely not merely at the different types of fortifications actually built by the Ottomans in their heyday, but at the strategic and tactical roles that these fortresses played. Function thus becomes a key to the understanding of form. These are the questions which this essay sets out to address.

---

[5] Fernand Braudel, *The Mediterranean and the Mediterranean World in the Age of Philip II*, trans. Siân Reynolds (London, 1972), II:844–5. My emphasis.

Fourteen fifty-three was a decisive date on more than one level, for it signaled not only the end of the Eastern Roman Empire, but marked what was certainly the most celebrated (if not necessarily the most significant) achievement of a new gunpowder artillery technology over one of the most impressive fortifications of the ancient world. It also brought into sharp focus new tactical roles for coastal guns and the permanent installations that accommodated them. What the fall of Constantinople did not mark, of course, was the opening up of southeast Europe to the Ottomans. This had already been achieved long before 1453. It may well be helpful, therefore, briefly to place the end of the Byzantine empire into a wider strategic context.

The original Ottoman heartland was the northwest corner of Anatolia, around Bursa. By the mid-fourteenth century the Ottoman state was, in Inalcik's words, still "no more than one of many frontier principalities, but events after 1352 so firmly established its superiority over the others that, within thirty years, they had become Ottoman vassals."[6] In 1352, Süleyman, son of Orhan and grandson of Osman, the founder of the dynasty, crossed the Dardanelles in the mercenary service of one of the warring Byzantine factions, and took possession of Tzympe on the Gallipoli peninsula. Despite efforts to dislodge him, Süleyman persisted in the occupation of Tzympe until, on the night of 1–2 March 1354, an earthquake destroyed the walls of Gallipoli, allowing the Turks to seize and hold the principal fortress on the peninsula.

The occupation of Gallipoli gave the Ottomans a vital foothold in Europe. By the end of the fourteenth century, Constantinople itself was a Byzantine island in an Ottoman sea that extended northwards to the Danube and westward almost to the shores of the Adriatic.[7] The Palaeologi were Ottoman vassals and, when summoned by Sultan Bayezid I (Yilderim, the Thunderbolt) to reaffirm their feudal ties in 1394, they absented themselves, fearing treachery, and brought down upon Constantinople the first serious Turkish siege of 1394–1402. The crusade of Nicopolis (1396) was to have relieved Constantinople from this siege. Bayezid's total victory on the battlefield of Nicopolis not only decimated the flower of European chivalry, but confirmed Ottoman control of the southern Balkans. It would probably have led to the loss of Constantinople too, had not the situation been saved for the Byzantines by the invasion from the east of Timur (Tamerlane), who defeated and captured Bayezid at Ankara on 28 July 1402, and

---

[6] Halil Inalcik, *The Ottoman Empire: The Classical Age 1300–1600* (London, 1973), 9.

[7] For the expansion of the Ottoman sphere of influence and its precise chronology, see Donald Edgar Pitcher, *An Historical Geography of the Ottoman Empire from the Earliest Times to the End of the Sixteenth Century* (Leiden, 1972).

exhibited the "Thunderbolt" in an iron cage. Bayezid died soon afterwards, probably by his own hand.[8]

Bayezid's defeat at Ankara halted Ottoman expansion while his successors struggled for the succession. Briefly, moreover, the European-based Ottomans and the Byzantines shared a community of interest in a defensive pact, the Treaty of Gallipoli (1403), which ensured that Timur's ravaging of Asia Minor remained east of the Bosphorus and the Dardanelles. At this time the Venetians considered plans to seize Gallipoli as an advanced base from which to defend their interests in the region.[9] As Sultan Mehmed I (1413–21) emerged victorious from the post-1402 Ottoman succession struggles and began once again to make inroads into the Balkans, the western powers went onto the offensive. In 1416 Pietro Loredan, Venetian Captain of the Gulf, attacked the Ottoman fleet in the Dardanelles, sinking or capturing all of the Turkish vessels and destroying the Ottoman fort at Lapseki, on the Asian shore opposite Gallipoli.[10] The build-up of Ottoman naval forces and the development of their fleet tactics date from this period, and over the next seventy-five years were to change the balance of naval power in the Mediterranean. In the meantime, the Ottomans remained from time to time dependent on the Genoese (the other significant western naval power in the region) for protected passage between Europe and Asia.

When Mehmed I died in a hunting accident in 1421, he had pacified Anatolia and in the north had secured the Danubian fortresses of Isaccea, Giurgiu, Novo Selo, and Turnu Severin. In Albania he had

[8] Donald M. Nicol, *The Last Centuries of Byzantium 1261–1453* (Cambridge, 1993), 315. Doukas (sometimes, Ducas), *Decline and Fall of Byzantium to the Ottoman Turks*, trans. H.J. Magoulias (Detroit, 1975), ch. 16, 12, says Bayezid was at first honorably treated and chained only after an unsuccessful rescue attempt and (ch. 17, 7) that he was rumored to have taken poison at Qara Hisar on 9 March 1403 because of plans to send him alive to Persia, "first to exhibit him as a spectacle and to parade him about, and then after he had suffered much torment, to take his life."

[9] The plan to occupy Gallipoli was discussed by the Venetian Senate on 22 September 1402, dropped the next day, but revived in October 1402 when Tomas Mocenigo was commissioned to study its feasibility. De Clavijo's description of Gallipoli in October 1403, "a castle strongly fortified with a large garrison . . . [and a] . . . fleet of ships and galleys, forty in number," suggested to one author that the Venetian plan was perhaps over-ambitious. Colin Imber, *The Ottoman Empire 1300–1481* (Istanbul, 1990), 57.

[10] Imber, *Ottoman Empire*, 88. Doukas, *Decline and Fall*, ch. 19, 2, records that the "enormous tower" at Lampsakos, on the promontory opposite Gallipoli (which must be the same as Lapseki), was built for Süleyman shortly after the defeat of Bayezid by a Genoese noble, Salagruzo de Negro (or Negri). Doukas, ch. 21, 8–9, also indicates that the Venetian attack damaged, but did not actually destroy the tower, which was pulled down by the Turks after the Venetians' departure. Does the employment of a Genoese indicate a perceived lack of expertise in military architecture amongst the Turks?

taken the fortress of Gjirokaster and established the first Ottoman foothold on the Adriatic at Valona/Vlore (1417). Murad II (1421–37) consolidated the Ottoman position on the Danube with the seizure of the fortress of Golubats in 1427, and in 1435–8 gained control of Smederovo, a newly-built fortress on the Danube between Golubats and Belgrade, the "key to Hungary."[11] The Bosnian fortresses of Borach, Zvornik, and Srebrnica all fell to Murad in 1438. On the Aegean front, 1430 saw the Ottoman capture of Thessaloniki, which had been under siege since the summer of 1422.[12] Some of these places subsequently changed hands in the ebb and flow of frontier warfare, or were exchanged by treaty. At the time of their capture, however, all of them represented important milestones in the Turkish advance. The almost unbroken run of Ottoman military success was only interrupted by their failure to take Belgrade in 1440, when the Hungarians relieved the fortress-city after a six-month siege. As the Turks withdrew they established a fortress at Avala (now part of the suburbs of Belgrade) to maintain a blockade from the south.[13]

Janos Hunyadi's successful defense of Belgrade in 1440, and his defeat of what turned out to be relatively minor Turkish incursions into Transylvania in 1441 and 1442, encouraged the European powers to mount a series of major counteroffensives.[14] In October 1443 an army of Hungarians, Vlachs, and Poles crossed the Danube and fought its way towards Edirne through a scorched landscape devastated by the retreating Turks. The advance was stopped in the pass of Zlatiza in a notably bloody encounter, and the invaders retreated through the snows to Belgrade with further heavy losses.[15] While the exhausted

[11] Imber, *Ottoman Empire*, 116: "It was probably in order to acquire the use of this fort as a defence against Hungarian attack and a crossing-point for raids into Hungary, that Murad established his suzereinty over George Brankovich, Despot of Serbia, in 1435." In 1438 Smederovo was captured after a three-month siege.

[12] Thessaloniki had been ceded to Venice in 1423 by the Byzantine Despot, who felt unable to sustain the city's defence, and Venice's inability to hold the most important city in northern Greece was widely seen as yet another landmark in the decline of Western power in the Eastern Mediterranean.

[13] D. Djurdjev, "Belgrade" in *Encyclopedia of Islam*, new edition (London, 1986), I:1163–5, which also discusses the fortifications carried out by the Turks after their capture of Belgrade in 1521.

[14] The most exhaustive general source for the Crusades in the Balkans and the Eastern Mediterranean is Kenneth M. Setton, *The Papacy and the Levant (1204–1571)*, Transactions of the American Philosophical Society, 4 vols. (Philadelphia, 1976–84), which offers much more than the title promises. The same author's *Venice, Austria and the Turks in the Seventeenth Century*, Transactions of the American Philosophical Society (Philadelphia, 1991), continues the military and diplomatic story to the Peace of Passarowitz.

[15] See Doukas, *Decline and Fall*, ch. 32, 1, for the Hungarian invasion which ended at the Battle of Zlatiza (otherwise, Izladi or Zlatica). The Ottomans had been shaken badly

Hungarians were negotiating and signing a peace treaty at Edirne, the Venetian, papal, and Burgundian allies launched a naval campaign by blockading the Dardanelles and the Bosphorus. The emir of Karaman had been encouraged to revolt, drawing Murad and the main army into Asia Minor, where the Christian alliance hoped to keep him. The Hungarians promptly repudiated the very recent Treaty of Edirne and marched along the Danube toward the Black Sea coast. With much of the Ottoman army still cut off in Anatolia, the situation was critical and the Ottoman European capital, Edirne, hitherto unfortified and treated as an open city, was rapidly surrounded by a new ditch. The Genoese of Galata (and perhaps some Venetians, too) provided vital assistance for Murad by shipping his army across the Bosphorus while shore batteries kept the blockading Burgundian and Byzantine galleys away from the crossing point.[16] Reinforced by Murad's army, the Ottomans met the Crusaders in a decisive battle at Varna (10 November 1444), which saw the Hungarians defeated, King Vladislav killed, and all but the youths under the age of twenty amongst the prisoners massacred. Hunyadi himself escaped and in the following year cooperated with the allied galley squadron in the campaign that became known as the Crusade on the Danube. Its results were limited to the capture of a number of Ottoman fortresses on the great river. The events of the 1440s convinced the Ottomans that so long as Constantinople remained in Christian hands there would be further Western attempts to liberate the Byzantine capital. When Murad died on 3 February 1451, the youthful Mehmed II determined to move against Constantinople.

During the siege of 1394–1402, Bayezid had built the fortress known as Anadolu Hisar (the Castle of Anatolia) on the Asian shore of the Bosphorus where two small rivers – the "sweet waters of Asia" – entered the seaway at its narrowest point (Fig. 10.1a). The fortress was little more than a keep, joined to the curtain wall of a fishing village.[17] Its main function was almost certainly to protect the mooring and

by this invasion and, under the terms of the Treaty of Edirne, returned Smederovo, Novo Brdo, and Golubac to the Despot of Serbia, who reciprocated by honoring the terms of the treaty and – unlike the other Christian princes, who were absolved from their oaths by the pope – failed to join the crusaders at Varna. See also Setton, *The Papacy and the Levant*, II:76–84.

[16] Setton, *The Papacy and the Levant*, II:89 and nn. 28 and 29.

[17] The best general account is still Albert Gabriel, *Châteaux turcs du Bosphore* (Paris, 1934), which corrects a number of errors and misunderstandings in works published just before by Sidney Toy, "Castles on the Bosp[h]orus," *Archaeologia* (1930), and Hans Högg, *Türkenburgen an Bosporus und Hellespont* (Dresden, 1932).

embarkation points for boats used to ferry Turks across the Bosphorus to the European shore. There was no question in Bayezid's time of Anadolu Hisar being used to block the Bosphorus passage since the Ottomans did not yet have gunpowder artillery.[18] But the protection of a ferry port was vital, as the recent events of 1444 had shown. The Burgundian galley squadron of ten Venetian-built vessels commanded by De Waverin had succeeded in preventing Murad's Anatolian army from crossing into Europe to meet the Crusade of Varna until the Genoese of Galata had provided a fleet of thirty vessels to ferry the Ottomans. The crossing had been supported by some 7,000 to 8,000 Turks on the European shore, with a number of additional cannon and culverins that had also been supplied by the Genoese. Murad's force on the Asian shore included camels bearing gunmetal, which the Turks cast overnight into cannon. The crossing of Murad's army was covered from both banks by cannon fire, which sank one Byzantine ship and prevented the more numerous Burgundians from intervening.[19]

In the spring of 1452 Mehmed II began the construction of another fortress on the steep slopes facing Anadolu Hisar from the European shore.[20] Rumeli Hisar (the Castle of Europe) was very much larger

---

[18] David Ayalon, *Gunpowder and Firearms in the Mamluk Kingdom: A Challenge to a Mediaeval Society* (London, 1955), argues that the Ottomans had acquired artillery and other firearms relatively late, probably in the early years of the fifteenth century, but subsequently had developed their use with spectacular speed. Paul Wittek, in a separate appendix, 142: "I am inclined to believe that before 1400 the Ottomans had no knowledge of firearms." Wittek shows that the Ottomans used artillery in sieges during the 1420s, although at the siege of Constantinople of 1422 the guns were very big, but not very effective. By 1453, of course, their effectiveness was much improved. Wittek has more difficulty in identifying the first use of firearms in the field. At Varna in 1444, the Christians had artillery but the Ottomans apparently none. By the second battle of Kossovo (1448) there is evidence that the Ottomans brought guns into the field (142). By 1465 muskets must have been well known to the Ottomans and were no longer regarded as a novelty (143). Further light on this aspect of Ottoman military development is shed by Djurdjica Petrovic, "Firearms in the Balkans on the Eve of and after the Ottoman Conquests of the Fourteenth and Fifteenth Centuries," in *War, Technology and Society in the Middle East*, eds. V.J. Parry and M.E. Yapp (London, 1975), 164–94, who generally supports Wittek in identifying the third decade of the fifteenth century for the first Ottoman use of large siege cannon at Constantinople (1422) and Novo Brdo (1427), but believes that research will probably put back by one or two decades the introduction of the arquebus. See also Halil Inalcik, "The Socio-political Effects of the Diffusion of Firearms in the Middle East," in *War, Technology and Society*, 195–217.
[19] Imber, *Ottoman Empire*, 312–13.
[20] Doukas, *Decline and Fall*, ch. 34, 7, tells us that by March 1452 the furnaces of Kataphygia were in daily use making slaked lime, that timber was brought from Nikomedia and Pontoheraklea, and the stones came from the East (later indicating the Asian shore of the Bosphorus).

Figure 10.1a. Ottoman fortifications at Constantinople (redrawn after Gabriel). Top: Anadolu Hisar, the Castle of Anatolia, built ca. 1400 and extended by the addition of a water-level battery in 1452–3. Bottom: Rumeli Hisar, the Castle of Europe, built in 1452 to close the Bosphorus waterway. Rumeli Hisar is drawn at approximately one-third the scale of Anadolu Hisar (above), i.e., it is three times bigger. Its walls also carry battlements, but these cannot be shown at this scale.

than Anadalu Hisar, with two great towers high above the waters of the Bosphorus on the ridge line of the first range of heights, thus preventing the castle from being overlooked on the landward side (Fig. 10.1a). These round towers were connected by curtain walls and a series of smaller towers to a third great round tower near the beach.[21] An inscription on the southwestern tower confirms that Zaganos, one of the sultan's leading military advisers, finished it in July–August 1452, and the castle was probably completed in September.[22] A garri-

---

[21] Doukas, *Decline and Fall*, ch. 34, 8: "These three towers, serving as citadels for purposes of defense . . ." perhaps indicates that they were built first in order to secure the site against any action from the city.

[22] Nicoló Barbaro, *Diary of the Siege of Constantinople 1453*, trans. J.R. Jones (New York, 1969), 9, gives the month of August 1452 for completion, and March for the commencement of construction. George Sphranzes, *The Fall of the Byzantine Empire: A Chronicle by George Sphranzes 1401–1477*, trans. Marios Philippides (Amherst, MA,

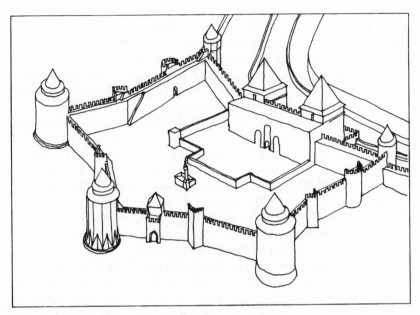

Figure 10.1b. Ottoman fortifications at Constantinople (redrawn after Gabriel). Yedikule, the Castle of the Seven Towers, 1457–8, bird's-eye view from inside the Theodosian Walls. For the plan, see Fig. 10.2a (*top*).

son of "four hundred youths" was left in the fortress under Firuz Aga, "one of his (Mehmed's) most trusted slaves."[23] Mehmed had quarters prepared for himself in one of the towers and apparently used it at times during 1453. Afterwards they became the most feared of Ottoman Turkey's dungeons. Even in the derelict state of the photographs taken by Gabriel in the 1930s, Rumeli Hisar was an impressive monument. When its lead-sheathed conical roofs were in place over the round towers, it must have been one of the most picturesque of late medieval castles.

In military terms, however, the most significant part of the new fortress was a relatively low and unimpressive length of wall enclos-

1980), ch. 35, 69, gives 26 March for the start and 31 August for completion. Franz Babinger, *Mehmed the Conqueror and His Time*, trans. Ralph Manheim, ed. William C. Hickman, Bollingen Series 96 (Princeton, 1978), 76, dates the start of construction to 15 April and stresses the personal contribution of the young sultan to the design of the fortress. Babinger again: "As architect a certain Muslihuddin, surely a renegade, is mentioned, but also a christian monk converted to Islam." No reference is given for this intriguing remark.

[23] Doukas, *Decline and Fall*, ch. 34, 12.

ing a strip of land outside the main defences and just above the waterline. Part of this lower wall has clearly been lost, and the early photographs show buildings on the foreshore, which are themselves no longer standing and whose builders may well have been responsible for the destruction. It is also not entirely clear whether the low wall formed part of the original scheme or was added shortly after 1452–3. What remains, however, contains three, very large, semicircular arched openings, with a radius of about one meter, and seven smaller openings to the north (i.e., toward the Black Sea) ending in a gateway. The complex is often described as a barbican, and the protection of the gate was obviously one of its functions. A similar outer screen wall with identical openings was added to Anadolu Hisar at the same time, and here the angling of the openings makes it quite clear that these were gun embrasures for very large cannon located so as to allow them to fire across the Bosphorus channel.[24] This, of course, was the main purpose of both sets of outworks.

No doubt other cannon were mounted on the battlements of the towers, turrets, and curtains as reported by the Greek chroniclers Doukas and Kritovoulos of Imbros.[25] But the floor space in these higher works was restricted and any guns placed there could not have been very big. The lower batteries, which were located outside the main works and protected only by low, thin walls, could mount very long and heavy guns directly on the ground. Firing from only a few feet above the waterline, as Kritovoulos reports, "they hurled immense round stones that went along the surface of the seas as though

---

[24] In 1955, Babinger published an annotated sketch of the Bosphorus fortresses, which he found in the Biblioteca Trivulziana in Milan (Codex Membr. 641), and which had previously been misidentified as a view of Constantinople because of a misreading of one of the annotations. He dates it to 1452–3 or very closely thereafter, and attributes it to a Venetian spy because of the military nature of the notes. The view is taken from the Asian side, with Anadolu Hisar in the foreground and Rumeli Hisar (shown very much larger as the focus of interest) occupying all of the upper half of the sheet. The sketch confirms most of the details of the surviving work (except for some differences in the roofs over the north and seaside towers, which are shown with dome-like coverings). But the barbicans on both sides of the channel are missing, although the drawing clearly shows very large cannon on flatbed mountings facing the seaway. This raises the possibility that the screen walls of the barbicans were added later, either after the events of 1453, or just after the sketch had been made. See Franz Babinger, "Ein Venedischer Lageplan der Feste Rumeli Hisari," *La Bibliofilia* 57 (Florence, 1955): 188–95.

[25] Doukas, *Decline and Fall*, ch. 34, 12, says that in the tower of Halil Pasha (i.e., the tower by the water) were placed "bronze tubes capable of discharging balls weighing over six hundred pounds," (199) but I take leave to doubt that the towers held guns of this size. For Kritovoulos see Imber, *Ottoman Empire*, 147.

they were swimming." This strongly suggests that they could skim stone balls along the surface of the Bosphorus like Lord Nelson's ricochet fire or Barnes Wallace's "bouncing bombs," used in the Dam Busters' raid in World War II. It bespeaks a sound grasp of the principles of coastal battery gunfire on the part of the Ottoman planners and prompts the question: Was this kind of technique employed elsewhere at the Dardanelles or on the Danube? At the Bosphorus, the gun batteries went into action for the first time in November 1452, when a Venetian ship bringing food from the Black Sea was sunk by gunfire.

The main events of the final siege of Constantinople are sufficiently well known not to demand detailed repetition. Closely invested since early in 1452, the city faced Turkish siege lines that were brought up to the Theodosian Walls early in April 1453. The Ottomans' heaviest artillery piece, so the story goes, was cast in Edirne in January by a Hungarian in the sultan's service named Urban.[26] It was dragged to Constantinople in February to reach a point five miles from the city by March. The biggest guns bombarded the walls for almost two months before the final successful assault on 29 May 1453, causing much damage to defensive towers as well as making the breach which was finally stormed.[27] The inherent effectiveness of the very big and probably old-fashioned Ottoman siege guns has recently been questioned by DeVries, and it is likely that this aspect of the Turkish performance has been exaggerated by contemporary reporters, as well as by later historians, seeking to soften the loss of Constantinople by attributing the disaster to a new technology supplied by renegade Christians.[28] The Byzantines used cannon of their own in defense, of course, and accounts mention the damage done to the Theodosian

[26] Doukas, *Decline and Fall*, ch. 35, 1 and 3, for the construction and testing of the cannon at Adrianople by the Western artificer who had, apparently, previously offered his skills to the emperor, but had been unpaid and was forced by hardship to work for the "barbarian."

[27] Doukas, *Decline and Fall*, ch. 38, 11 (216), for details of the bombardment technique employed, again on the advice of a Christian, the ambassador from the king of Hungary.

[28] Kelly DeVries, "Gunpowder Weapons at the Siege of Constantinople, 1453," in *War and Society in the Eastern Mediterranean, 7th–15th Centuries*, ed. Yaacov Lev (Leiden, New York, Köln, 1997), 342–62. M. Balard, "Constantinople vue par les témoins du siège de 1453," in *Constantinople and Its Hinterland*, eds. Cyril Mango and Gilbert Dagron (Aldershot and Brookfield, VT, 1995), 169–77, is also a valuable corrective to some of the exaggerations and contradictions amongst contemporary accounts; for the best collection of which, see A. Pertusi, *La Caduta di Costantinopoli* (Verona, 1976).

towers by the shock of the discharge and recoil, albeit from the relatively small weapons that could be accommodated at high level.[29] But the Turks did not rely entirely on cannon fire to bring down the walls. Accounts of the siege mention numerous underground mines which were successfully countermined by the defenders, and mining was certainly a tactic that the Turks used to good effect in other sieges, notably the two great sieges of Rhodes in 1480 and 1522.[30] At Constantinople the enormous numerical superiority of the Turks over the defenders was without doubt the decisive factor in the victory, for it allowed the attackers to wear down the defense by fighting along the entire length of the Theodosian land front, as well as the much weaker walls facing onto the Golden Horn. The latter were exposed to attack once the besiegers had hauled their galleys from the Bosphorus over the slipway prepared behind the Galata hill to open up this section to a massed waterborne assault, which was little different from the tactics that proved successful for the Venetians and their Frankish crusader allies in 1204.

Following the capture of Constantinople, Mehmed immediately repaired the damaged walls and, interestingly, made no fundamental changes to the Theodosian system.[31] This comprised two complete circuits of walls, the lower wall and its towers being overlooked from the rear by a second higher wall and towers spaced to dominate the

---

[29] Doukas, *Decline and Fall*, ch. 38, 3, mentions defensive fire from the walls with crossbows, ordinary bows and arrows, and guns firing lead balls,

> which were propelled by powder, five and ten at a time, and as small as Pontic walnuts. These had tremendous perforating power and, if one ball happened to penetrate an armor-clad soldier, it would transpierce both shield and body, passing through and striking the next person standing in the way. Passing through the second individual, it would strike a third until the force of the powder was dissipated. Thus, with one shot it was possible to kill two or three soldiers. The Turks learned of these weapons and not only employed them but had even better ones.

[30] Barbaró, *Diary*, entries for 16–17 May (50–1), 22 May (55), 23 May (56), 24 May (57), 25 May (58) record the discovery of separate mines. See also Makarious Melissenos (otherwise Melissourgos, or Pseudo-Sphranzes) in Sphranzes, *The Fall of the Byzantine Empire*, trans. Philippides (Amherst, MA, 1980), 104 and nn. 23 and 47, for the roles played by a foreigner (either German or Scottish) named John serving with the Byzantines, and the Serbian miners employed by the Ottomans. Quentin Hughes and Athanassios Migos, "Rhodes: The Turkish Sieges," *Fort* 21 (1993): 3–17, concentrate on the underground operations in the sieges of 1480 and 1522.

[31] Doukas, *Decline and Fall*, ch. 42, 3, lime slakers were required to work throughout the month of August 1453 on the main land front. The land walls of Galata had been ordered overthrown only five days after the fall, but the walls along the harbor on this side of the Golden Horn were allowed to stand (ch. 42, 2). It is not clear whether the orders to demolish Galata's main wall were carried out; certainly the Genoese tower survives and sixteenth-century Turkish illustrations indicate other towers and curtains.

interval in the outer circuit.[32] They are sometimes described as "triple walls" by including the inside face of the dry ditch, which was carried up to form a parapet on the wide ledge that ran outside the outer, lower curtain.[33] It was probably on this ledge "next to the gates" that guns were placed by the Ottomans when their new capital was threatened. If so, the solution was not very different from that adopted only a few years later by the Aragonese in their refortification of the Angevin Castelnuovo in Naples[34] and by the Venetians in their late-fifteenth-century improvements to the fortress of Modon.[35]

In the winter of 1457–8, the Golden Gate – the official entry point for Byzantine emperors arriving by land at the Sea of Marmara end of the Theodosian Walls – was transformed into the centerpiece of a new fortress complex.[36] The Castle of the Yedikule (Seven Towers) was one of the very few early Ottoman fortifications to be laid out on formal geometrical lines (Fig. 10.1b). With only slight deviations caused by irregularities in the original Byzantine walls, the castle forms a pentagon, with each of the four new curtains facing into the city cranked inwards to form an interior angle which was fortified by a small triangular tower. The three great towers facing into the city, like those at Rumeli Hisar, were roofed on the two upper levels, where guns could be accommodated on a platform three-and-a-half meters wide. The timber interior floors of the great towers (now missing) would probably not have borne artillery, and in any event the embrasures through the

[32] The best general source is still A. Van Milligen, *Byzantine Constantinople: The Walls of the City and Adjoining Historical Sites* (London, 1899).

[33] A number of early descriptions have suggested that the ditch was flooded, and it was clearly subdivided into discreet sections by "dams," often combined with water conduits going into the city from the aqueducts. None of the siege accounts support the view that the ditch was anything other than a dry one, which was deepened in 1452–3. Van Millingen, *Byzantine Constantinople*, 56–8.

[34] Simon Pepper, "Castle and Cannon in the Naples Campaign of 1494–95," in *The French Descent into Renaissance Italy, 1494–95: Antecedents and Effects*, ed. David Abulafia (London, 1995), 263–93, and the detailed references to other recent works as well as Riccardo Filangieri's numerous papers on the Castelnuovo.

[35] Simon Pepper, "Fortress and Fleet: The Defence of Venice's Mainland Greek Colonies in the Late Fifteenth Century," in *War, Culture and Society in Renaissance Venice: Essays in Honour of John Hale*, eds. David S. Chambers, Cecil H. Clough, and Michael E. Mallett (London, 1993), 29–55.

[36] Doukas, *Decline and Fall*, ch. 45, 11: "That winter [1458] the tyrant began to construct a fortress at the far end of the city at the Golden Gate. This was the fortress that old Emperor John wished to build but Bayazid, the tyrant's grandfather, prevented him from doing" (257). Doukas's translator, Magoulias, argues (320–1n. 315) that work had taken place at the Golden Gate in the reign of John V, despite threats to Manuel Palaeologos (1391–425) who was a hostage at the Ottoman court at the time. If so, Mehmed's scheme would be a restoration. However, Gabriel and others all accept that Yedikule was substantially a new fortress.

immensely thick walls were too narrow for a useful field of fire. However, the curtain wall provided an uninterrupted level platform about five metres wide which, unlike that of Rumeli Hisar, could well have mounted cannon. The triangular and semicircular subsidiary towers also provided suitably wide and open platforms for guns and, again unlike those of Rumeli Hisar, were built out from the main curtain gallery so that the passage around the walls was not interrupted.

The towers that formed part of the Golden Gate and the adjacent section of the Theodosian Wall took their form from a much earlier time and, in the cases of the two flanking octagonal towers, were rebuilt in 1754–5 according to an inscription cited by Gabriel.[37] The massive towers of the Golden Gate were modified to form a keep with some residential accommodation, but the aga commanding the fortress occupied a house in an area of formal, walled garden just "inside" the Golden Gate. The garden also accommodated the guards' quarters. On the central axis of the fortress was placed a mosque. The overall pentagonal geometry (Fig. 10.2a), which has been analyzed by Gabriel, finds echoes only in the most formal of Western European medieval schemes (e.g., the Hohenstaufen Castel del Monte in Apulia) and in a much later generation of Italian-inspired bastioned works. Some of Yedikule's detailed military architecture is highly formalized, too; in particular the faceted masonry on the central great tower, with its elaborate fluted base mouldings (very similar to those on the base of the Castelnuovo in Naples). The precise geometrical detail and the overall sense of order at Yedikule are exactly what one expects of Ottoman public architecture. It may be that this citadel, which was started nearly ten years before the Ottoman sultans began the construction of the Topkapi Palace and made it their favored state residence, incorporated such features of "polite" architecture as a result of its special status as a royal fortress that initially housed the treasury and many of the more distinguished state prisoners.

It has recently been proposed by Necipoğlu that "this star-shaped fortress [was] designed according to new Italian theoretical concepts of ideal planning."[38] She cites Restle and Raby in support of this contention.[39] Mehmed II's interest in Western history and his appoint-

[37] Albert Gabriel, *Chateaux turcs du Bosphore* (Paris, 1934), 97–8.
[38] Gŭlru Necipoğlu, *Architecture, Ceremonial and Power: The Topkapi Palace in the Fifteenth and Sixteenth Centuries* (Cambridge, MA, 1991), 10.
[39] Marcell Restle, "Bauplanung und Baugesinnung unter Mehmed II Fatih," *Pantheon* 39/4 (1981): 361–7; and Julian Raby, "A Sultan of Paradox: Mehmed the Conqueror as a Patron of the Arts," *Oxford Art Journal* 1 (1982): 3–8.

ment to the Ottoman court of Western scholars, artists, and artisans is well known. It has even been suggested that Filarete himself may have joined the Ottoman court in about 1465.[40] However, the geometry of Yedikule's walls and towers predates by some years the earliest tentative Italian drawings of star-shaped castles and fortified cities in the manuscript treatises of Filarete and Francesco di Giorgio Martini (Fig. 10.2b).[41] Even if Filarete did travel to Constantinople in 1465, he would have arrived long after the completion of Yedikule. The first Italian radially planned fortress cities appeared on the ground well into the sixteenth century and were always far outnumbered by paper projects.

All of this, however, is not to deny the significance of Yedikule's formal geometry and its other architectural features. The first Ottoman palace complex in Constantinople had been built in great haste between 1453 and 1458 on the vacant site of the Theodosian Forum Tauri, covering an area that included much of the present Grand Bazaar and main Istanbul University campus. It took the form of a vast park, containing as many as twenty-five dispersed timber palace pavilions and other buildings, surrounded by an unfortified wall with a length (according to different accounts) of one to two miles. Shortly after its completion, Mehmed embarked on the construction of what was then known as the New Imperial Palace (now the Topkapi), on Seraglio Point. Although the Topkapi was walled and is sometimes described as a fortress, Necipoğlu argues that (like its immediate predecessor the Old Imperial Palace) it was never intended to serve as a serious military fortification. Its walls were much too narrow to mount or resist artillery. Its gates and towers, however, were full of meaning for those able to read the symbolism. The design of its outer Imperial Gate made reference in its central and side openings to the Roman triumphal arch, and in its lead-roofed, turreted, and gilded-domed internal superstructure to ceremonial palace gatehouses in Abbasid Baghdad and Byzantine Constantinople. The Middle Gate, with its vestigial merlatura and its flanking octagonal pepper-pot towers has long been seen as a distinctive (and to the eyes of many, northern)

---

[40] Necipoğlu, *Architecture, Ceremonial and Power,* 15, citing Restle, "Bauplanung und Baugesinnung." Babinger, *Mehmed the Conqueror,* 504–7, is skeptical and, 465, dismissive of Filarete's possible involvement.

[41] Horst De La Croix's "Military Architecture and the Radial City Plan in Sixteenth Century Italy," *Art Bulletin* 42 (1960): 263–90, and "The Literature of Fortification in Renaissance Italy," *Technology & Culture* 6 (1963): 30–50, provide a general context for this debate.

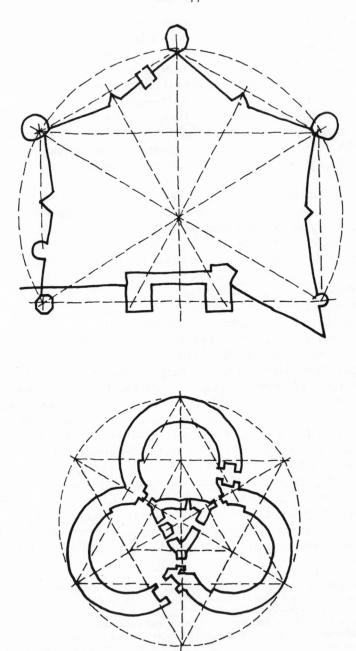

Figure 10.2a. Fortification plans. Top: Yedikule, Constantinople (after Gabriel); Bottom: Kilid Bar, near Gallipoli (after Restle).

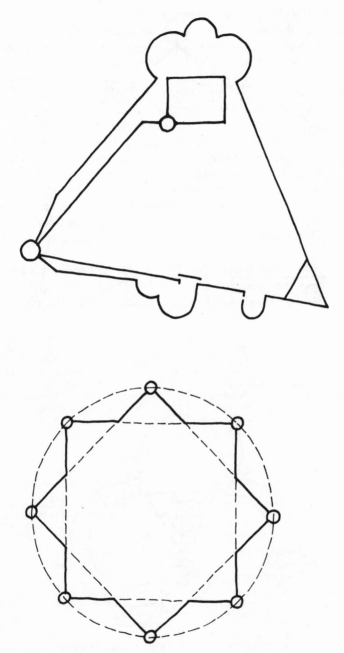

Figure 10.2b. Fortification Plans. Top: Filarete's Sforzinda; Bottom: the Castle of the Morea, straits of Patras (after seventeenth-century Venetian survey in Andrews).

style of architecture.[42] The octagonal flanking towers picked up local references to the seaside Gate of Santa Barbara (the Cannon Gate), which led from the waterfront of Seraglio Point into the Byzantine palace gardens, and which itself reflected the Golden Gate and its octagonal flanking towers.[43] Yedikule, on the other hand, was defensible by the standards of the 1450s and already included the Golden Gate, traditionally the most important of Constantinople's imperial entrances. It was not necessary here to make oblique references, only to conserve it with its distinctive octagonal flanking towers. By incorporating both gate and towers (which were again specially conserved in the eighteenth century), and by employing the conical roofs which featured on a number of the sultan's key residences and their gateways, the geometrical fortress of Yedikule made a useful defensive contribution to the land front of Ottoman Constantinople and assumed a special architectural significance in the conquered city.[44]

Ever since its occupation in the 1350s, Gallipoli had been a key position for the Ottomans, as well as for their opponents. It was briefly held in 1366 by Amadeus VI of Savoy, who handed the place to the

---

[42] Necipoğlu, *Architecture, Ceremonial and Power*, 31–52. The outer Imperial Gate was burnt down and is today seen without its superstructure, but the Middle Gate, flanked by thin octagonal towers with pepper-pot roofs is still extant. "The Nuremberg woodcut shows this gate . . . with its two towers, so we know they were there by the late fifteenth century. It is often erroneously assumed that they were added in the sixteenth century by Süleyman I, who had been inspired by the castles he saw during his campaigns in the Balkans. This notion has no textual evidence to support it" (50–1). The author marshals solid chronicle evidence for the construction of "two towers in the European mode (*iki frengī burğāz*) flanking both sides of the gate" in 1478.

[43] Van Millingen, *Byzantine Constantinople*, 249–50: The gate was

> known as the Gate of St. Barbara . . . after a church of that dedication in the vicinity; the presence of a sanctuary consecrated to the patroness of firearms at this point being explained by the fact that the Mangana, or great military arsenal of the city, stood a little to the south of the gate. As became its important position, it was a handsome portal, flanked, like the Golden Gate, by two large towers of white marble, and beside it, if not in it, Nicephoras Phocas placed the beautiful gates which he carried away from Tarsus as trophies of his Cilician campaigns. On two occasions it served as a triumphal entrance into the city. . . .

The gate disappeared when the coastal railway line was built.

[44] Van Millingen, *Byzantine Constantinople*, 67–70, stresses the preeminence of the Golden Gate as both an entrance and a fortress.

> It was, however, on the return of an emperor to the city after a victorious campaign that the Porta Aurea fulfilled its highest purpose, and presented a brilliant spectacle of life and splendour. However, victorious generals below Imperial rank were not allowed to enter the city in triumph through this gate. [Belisarius and others had their triumphs in the Hippodrome and the Great Street.] But besides serving as a state entrance into the city, the Porta Aurea was one of the strongest positions in the fortifications. The four towers at its gateways, the deep moat in front, and the transverse walls across the peribolos on either hand, guarding approach from that direction, constituted a veritable citadel.

One account says it was provisioned for three years.

Byzantines, who returned it to the Ottomans ten years later as the price of their support in one of Byzantium's many civil wars. Except for these few years, Gallipoli remained in Ottoman hands. The fortifications and harbor installations were almost entirely Ottoman, albeit on older foundations. The defensive works at Gallipoli, which developed into the Ottomans' chief naval base and arsenal, merit serious attention, but this is not the only part of the picture to remain incomplete.[45]

Gallipoli, however, could not block the straits. This was accomplished in the years 1459–62 by the construction of two new Ottoman fortresses at the narrows where Europe and Asia are only 1,200 meters apart. The fortress of Kilid Bar (Key to the Sea) stood on the European shore, and Cianak Kale (sometimes Sultaniye Kale) on the Asian side in the modern town of Cianakkale. The two fortresses are strikingly different in form (Figs. 10.3a and 10.3b), indicating a lively spirit of experimentation in the 1450s (which is by no means unlikely), completely separate designers and builders (which is less likely), or peculiarities in topography that persuaded the designers to adopt quite different solutions.

Cianak Kale is rectangular in plan, with round corner towers and multifaceted semicircular intermediate towers on its outer enceinte. In the center, a substantial rectangular keep with a broad platform on its roof is equipped with a thick, curved parapet, indicating that this platform, like the mural towers, was designed to mount artillery. Fresne-Canaye, in 1573, was not permitted to enter the castle but from outside observed many guns mounted on the central *terrazza*.[46] Culverins were still mounted on the central platform in 1702 when Dapper described the fort. The general proportions of the fortress are much lower and squatter than Yedikule or Rumeli Hisar, which is to be expected in a purposefully built artillery fortress accommodating heavy weapons in the fortress itself, rather than in the outworks seen only a few years earlier on the Bosphorus. Unfortunately, the side facing the seaway was substantially modified in the nineteenth and twentieth centuries to house modern coastal artillery, some of which saw service in 1915. Dapper says that the towers on the sea side were

[45] Ermanno Armao, *In giro per il mar egeo con Vincenzo Coronelli* (Firenze, 1951), 73, provides a list of visual sources. Another important aid to researchers in this area is Stephane Yerasimos, *Les Voyageurs dans l'empire Ottoman (XIV^c–XVIe siècles): Bibliographie, itinéraires et inventaire des lieux habités* (Ankara, 1991).

[46] Philippe Du Fresne Canaye, *Le Voyage Du Levant de Philippe Du Fresne-Canaye (1573)*, publié et annoté par M.H. Hauser (Paris, 1897): *"Egli é cinto di profondi fossi nelli quali corre il mare. In mezzo di esso si vede una terrazza con molte artilarie ma non vi lasciano entrar nessuno sapendo molto bene che queste sono le chiavi di Const^{li} et che tutta la sicurta dell'imperio Turchesco si riposa sopra queste due fortezze."*

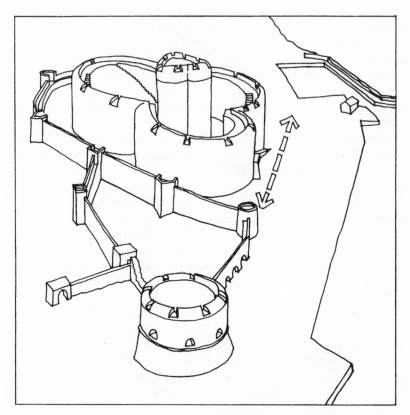

Figure 10.3a. Ottoman fortifications at the Dardanelles. Kilid Bar, near Gallipoli. The original clover-leaf complex is shown above, with a round sixteenth-century tower in the foreground. The broken line between the arrows indicates the probable position of the original water-level gun battery.

square and that most of the guns on this side were mounted at water level.[47] Tournefort, who visited the region in 1700–2, recorded a long series of semicircular openings facing the sea, very similar in their appearance to the embrasures in the Bosphorus forts.[48] Although lacking the picturesque silhouette of the Ottoman fortresses built earlier in the same decade at Constantinople, Cianak Kale is very clearly a product of the new gunpowder age.

Kilid Bar has a central trefoil plan keep (six floors high from the evidence of embrasures), surrounded by a larger trefoil curtain, which

---

[47] Olfert Dapper, *Description exacte des îles de l'Archipel* (Amsterdam, 1703), 488.
[48] I.P. de Tournefort, *Relation d'un voyage du Levant*, 3 vols. (Lyons, 1717), II:260 and 263.

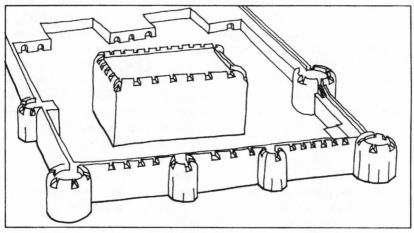

Figure 10.3b. Ottoman fortifications. Top: Cianak Kale, Asia Minor shore, seen from the landward side. The works in the background face the seaway and have been considerably changed by nineteenth- and twentieth-century improvements. The interior of the castle now contains many buildings added since the original mid-fifteenth-century construction. Bottom: The White Tower of Thessaloniki, shown with the *chemise* that was destroyed in the early twentieth century. For disputed dating see text.

itself towers over lower outer works (Figs. 10.2a and 10.3a). The keep and its trefoil curtain are skillfully rotated so that a series of separate courtyards are formed at ground level and the gun positions on parapets have a large number of overlapping fields of fire. Formally, the geometry of the plan is sophisticated, tempting Restle to speculate on Western influence here as well as at Yedikule.[49] Both the inner keep and its trefoil curtain are equipped with the same curved parapets as

[49] Marcell Restle, "Bauplanung und Baugesinnung," 361–7.

at Cianak Kale, but a much smaller proportion of the gun embrasures bear onto the sea. On the Aegean side of the castle, however, an extensive triangular outwork still stands, with the same large, semicircular arched openings at ground level that we have seen before on the Bosphorus gun batteries. A lengthy section of this wall is now missing directly in front of the keep and its trefoil curtain, where a modern quay has been built. The views published by seventeenth- and eighteenth-century travellers (as well as the anonymous fifteenth-century drawing published by De Seta which illustrates both castles[50]) all show that the fifteenth-century gun battery wall extended right across the front of the castle to where a gate now gives access to the waterfront quay. With so much of the battery missing, the extent of the armament can only be estimated from illustrations and the reports of the travelers who were stopped at the forts for security checks on their way to and from Constantinople. Philippe Du Fresne-Canaye, writing in 1573, reported twenty-five guns on the waterfront battery.[51] Le Brun, writing in 1700, suggested that Kilid Bar was better armed than Cianak Kale, where he had estimated about thirty guns.[52] This kind of increase is to be expected, given the time that had elapsed between the two visits. However, the artillery was seen by later reporters as antique, often mounted directly on the ground on stone or timber blocks, and without the wheeled carriages that would have allowed them to be run in for reloading. Many of the dimensions by then seemed monstrous and it does seem that the state-of-the-art, mid-fifteenth-century coastal batteries had been scarcely modernized since their installation. The precise chronology of the works surrounding the central complex is difficult to determine without closer inspection on site. The round tower at the southern end of the extant low-level battery is clearly a later addition, probably dating from the early sixteenth century.

The common feature in both of these very different designs is the use of a central keep (rectangular in one case, trefoil-shaped in the other), surrounded by curtains. From the location of the largest arched

[50] Cesare De Seta, "Le mura simbolo della città," in *La città e le mura*, eds. Cesare De Seta and Jacques Le Goff (Roma-Bari, 1989), 11–57. Figure 30 is taken from the Museo Correr codex: *Turcherie*. Although undated, the evident early date of this generally rather accurate view makes it certain that the rows of water-level emplacements were early, and probably original, components of the schemes.

[51] Fresne-Canaye, *Le Voyage du Levant*, 285: "... et si stende lungo il lito dove sone da 25 artilarie che guardano il passo di quella banda."

[52] Corneille Le Brun, *Voyage au Levant* (Delft, 1700), 156: "L'autre Château qui est du côte d'Asie en Natolie est bâti dans une plaine. . . . Autant que je le pus (sic) remarquer, il n'etoit pas si bien fourni de canon que l'autre. Nous en estimames le nombre à environ trente pièces, dont la pluspart pouvoient porter jusqu'à l'autre rive. . . ."

openings it seems certain that the heaviest artillery was located in both cases only a small distance above water level. The obvious comparison is with the *bourtzi*, or sea forts, that still survive off Modon and other Greek sites. At Modon, a Venetian tower had been equipped by the Ottomans after 1500 with a broad apron to accommodate heavy guns.[53] Descriptions of late-Mamluk coastal fortifications cited by David Ayalon refer to towers surrounded by walls, and it may be that this had become a standard Islamic fortification type in the second half of the fifteenth century.[54] If there was a Mediterranean prototype, it is possibly to be found in works carried out by the Ottomans at Thessaloniki.

The White Tower at Thessaloniki stands isolated on the waterfront and, together with the Chain Tower on the heights near the citadel, was for many years attributed to the Venetians, who were ceded the city in 1423 by the Byzantine despot. By then Thessaloniki was already under Turkish siege, and Venice was hard-pressed to defend the city until its capture by the Ottomans in 1430. Recent scholarship, however, attributes both towers to the Ottomans. The White Tower is dated to the mid-fifteenth century, probably between 1450 and 1470, possibly a few years earlier or later.[55] A photograph taken in the early

---

[53] Pepper, "Fortress and Fleet," 35; Nicolaos Lianos, "Il castello di Mare di Methoni," in *Dieci tesi di restauro (1982–1985)*, eds. Giovanni Carbonara and Franca Pietrafitta (Rome, 1987), 61–74; and Samuel Tamari, "The Venetian-Ottoman fort-castel da Mare in Modon," *Atti dell'Accademia Nazionale dei Lincei, rend. morali*, series viii, 33 (1978): 7–12 and 527–52.

[54] David Ayalon, *Gunpowder and Firearms in the Mamluk Kingdom: A Challenge to a Mediaeval Society* (London, 1956), 112 n. 4: "The most conspicuous measure taken by Qatbay in connection with artillery was the building of his famous tower (*burj*) in Alexandria in 884/1479. The tower, which was intended to protect the town from the incursions of the Frankish corsairs and was strongly fortified, was *surrounded* by a large number of guns." Also 113 n. 18: "The two expeditionary forces sent by the Mamluks against the Portuguese had an additional assignment: each was accompanied by a large group of masons, carpenters, and other workers. The first expedition built towers (*abraj*) surrounded by walls in the harbour of Jidda." Towers were also built at Nakhl, at ʿAjrud, and at Aznam, while at Yanbuʿ a tower and a wall was built, which was the formula adopted for the works at Rosetta. Ayalon distinguishes between fortress (*qalʿa*) and towers (*abraj* or *burj*), which avoids the problem of largely interchangeable terms in Turkish.

[55] J.P. Braun, N. Faucherre, and J.M. Spieser, "Deux tours Turques de Thessalonique," *MAKEΔONIKΩN* (1983): 1–23, and Braun et al., "La Tour Blanche et la Tour du Trigonion de Thessalonique," *Byzantinische Forschungen* 11 (Amsterdam, 1987): 269–70. The much lower, round Tour du Trigonion (or Chain Tower) is located in the upper town where the Ottomans broke through the Venetian defenses in 1430. This certainly dates from the sixteenth century, possibly from the last quarter of the century, when the Ottomans strengthened their coastal works following their defeat at Lepanto.

years of this century, and reproduced in Braun, Faucherre, and Spieser's paper, shows the White Tower surrounded by a low apron of works (known as the *chemise*) which would have housed the heavy guns sweeping the port and its landing areas. Their dating for the tower, it has to be said, is contested by Kiel, who dates it to 1535–6 on the basis of an inscription.[56] The French group, however, believe the inscription refers only to the *chemise*, which they accept as sixteenth century in origin, and which they believe to have been a replacement for earlier outworks. If Braun, Faucherre, and Spieser are correct in their analysis, the White Tower at Thessaloniki, and any first generation outworks, are amongst the earliest surviving Ottoman gunpowder fortifications in the Mediterranean theatre. Kiel's dating would bracket the White Tower with a similar high tower built at Valona/ Vlore in the 1530s, when the Ottomans reinforced their advanced Albanian naval base prior to the campaign against the Venetian colony of Corfu.[57] The continuing uncertainty about the dating of such a prominent surviving work illustrates very clearly the difficulties surrounding the evaluation of Ottoman Renaissance military architecture.

The White Tower is similar in scale to the larger, rounded towers of Yedikule and Rumeli Hisar (Fig. 10.3b). The main cylindrical drum has a diameter of twenty-three metres and rises twenty-seven meters above ground level, surmounted by a turret with a diameter of twelve metres and a height of six meters. A spiral ramp cum stair in the thickness of the wall serves a number of embrasures; others are

---

[56] Machiel Kiel, "A Note on the Exact Date of Construction of the White Tower of Thessaloniki," *Balkan Studies* 14 (1973): 352–7. It was Jean-Michel Spieser (of the French team) who actually discovered a photograph taken in 1912 of an Ottoman inscription which was deciphered by Kiel to give a construction date of 1535–6. Kiel also believes that the architect may have been Sinan, who is credited by Babinger with authorship of a similar tower in Valona/Vlore in 1537 (see footnote 57). Kiel, in a postscript to his 1973 paper, republished in the Variorum collection as *Studies on the Ottoman Architecture of the Balkans: A Legacy in Stone* (Aldershot, 1990), ch. 6, refers to a more recent dendrochronological analysis of timbers in the White Tower by Cecil Lee Striker and Peter Kuniholm, but not by then published. Their analysis confirms that the trees were cut down in 1535. This might seem conclusive, but it is possible for a substantial rebuilding to introduce later timber. The dangers of reading too much into plaques fixed on buildings are well known.

[57] The citadel at Valona/Vlore was demolished with the other sixteenth-century fortifications in 1906, but Albanian archaeologists have attempted to reconstruct the fortress with the aid of early descriptions and Venetian maps. An unusually regular octagonal enceinte, with six-sided polygonal towers at the corners, and a wet moat connected to the harbor, surrounded an irregularly developed town. A large, round tower (similar in scale to the White Tower at Thessaloniki, and the three main towers at Rumeli Hisar) formed a citadel inside the walls. A construction date of 1531 is given by Apollon Bace, "Kalaja e Vlores," *Monumentet* 5–6 (1973): 43–57.

reached from the central room on each of the six upper floors. The turret provides a platform with a ten-meter diameter, and the open gallery on the upper level on the main tower is about five meters wide. Early illustrations show a conical roof covering both platforms, as at Yedikule and Rumeli Hisar. Although no trace remains of the *chemise*, a surviving photograph shows that this low battlemented apron enclosed an area at least three times the diameter of the main tower. It was fortified by octagonal turrets at the corners (somewhat larger than the sentry posts known as *echaugettes* in the seventeenth century). What appear to be *caponiers* can be seen at ground level. These were pillboxes, from which low-level flanking fire could be delivered along the base of the apron. It is impossible to say whether the *chemise* demolished in 1917 formed part of an original scheme, whatever its date, or was added later as a replacement for primitive low-level gun batteries, like those at Rumeli Hisar and Anadalu Hisar. The *chemise* would, as Braun et al. point out, protect the White Tower from the sea, which comes very close, and it is certainly possible (as they seem to suggest) that this was its prime function. It would also provide much the best low-level gun positions for heavy artillery sweeping the waterfront and the harbor from just above the waterline. Ottoman practice elsewhere in the Bosphorus and the Dardanelles would tend to support this last hypothesis.

The island of Lesbos fell to the Ottomans in 1461 after a fiercely contested siege of the Gattilusi stronghold of Mitylene. The Ottomans embarked quickly on a refortification scheme, which added a new enceinte to the upper bailey, with a wide gun platform running parallel to the main walls, and four semicircular bastions projecting forward to provide flanking fire. The biggest corner bastion has a plan and section that can be found in French fifteenth-century fortification, namely, an outer masonry retaining wall with two levels of gun emplacements for small guns, surrounding a broad central earth platform, built to the same level as the upper, outer gun gallery, but capable of mounting much larger guns firing over the outer masonry fortifications.[58] An air gap between the central platform and the outer masonry walls allows the lower gun positions to be lit and ventilated. The masonry is of relatively low quality and this may convey a primitive impression. But this line of Turkish bastions and the long wide

[58] The author has inspected very similar works at Clisson and Murol, in France, both dating from the second half of the fifteenth century.

platform it retains under the early medieval fortress is equal to anything constructed in Italy, France, or Spain in the same period.[59] Moreover, it worked. The new outer enceinte resisted Christian attacks by Orsano Giustiniano in 1464, by Pesaro in 1499, and by a Franco-Rhodian fleet in 1501. The large island also contains numerous remains of forts and watchtowers constructed by the Byzantines and the Genoese, many of which have been refortified by the Turks.[60] The most important of these outer fortresses is Methymna (Molivos), which contains another semicircular Turkish artillery bastion. The bastions at Methymna and Mitylene are amongst the first Western-style Ottoman fortifications to be built in this part of the Mediterranean.

Generally, the Turks did not adopt Western models for their artillery fortifications, but in some places they anticipated them. During Bayezid II's campaign against the Venetians in Greece, the Ottoman fleet captured Lepanto (Naupactos) in the Gulf of Corinth and wintered there in 1499–1500 before the victorious naval and land campaign of 1500, which captured Modon and Coron – "the eyes of Venice" – at the southern end of the Messenian peninsula.[61] To protect his fleet against the Venetians patrolling off Patras, Bayezid defended the "Dardanelles of Lepanto" by means of two fortresses. On the northern shore, the Castle of Rumelia took the form of an irregular triangle, and although much deteriorated, it can still be identified as a simple coastal battery, with slender outer walls once pierced in their lower levels for big gun embrasures similar to the lower works at Kilid Bar, Rumeli Hisar, and Anadalu Hisar. The Castle of the Morea on the Peleponnesian side of the narrows is also basically triangular in plan but more complex, bearing a marked resemblance in parts to the trefoil keep at Kilid Bar (Fig. 10.2b). When Kevin Andrews did his fieldwork during the Greek Civil War, the Castle of the Morea was in use as a prison and not open for visitors (Fig. 10.4). But if the additions made by the Venetians in their late-seventeenth-century reoccupation of the Morea, and by the French in their early-nineteenth-century

[59] A plan and photographs are to be found in F.W. Hasluk, "The Monuments of the Gattilusi," *Annual of the British School in Athens* 15 (1908–9): 248–69.

[60] E. Armao, *In giro per il mar egeo*, ch. 8, 108–16, for full list. L.A. Maggiorotti, *Architetti e architetture militari* (Rome, 1933), 410, gives a description of the citadel at Mityline. Mitylene and Molivos are the only two fortresses on Lesbos which I have been able to visit, albeit very briefly. This Greek island, and its Turkish neighbor, Tenedos/Bozcaada, would repay further attention.

[61] For the 1499–1500 campaign, Pepper, "Fortress and Fleet," 48–9, and Frederic Lane, "Naval Actions and Fleet Organisation, 1499–1502," in *Renaissance Venice*, ed. J.R. Hale (London, 1973).

interventions are both discounted, the castle, now much lower and squatter in its proportions than Kilid Bar, presents an extraordinarily advanced response to the needs of the moment.[62] The triangular trace provides almost complete all-round flanking fire, while the cluster of towers forming the land-gate and sea-gate complexes provide developed examples of smoothed-off, shot-deflecting curved surfaces that are only rivaled in my experience by the turn of the century Spanish castle at Salses (now in southern France), or in King Henry VIII's English south coast defenses dating from the 1540s.[63] Although Ottoman military architecture had by 1500 made no commitment to the angle bastion, which was already being explored by advanced Italian architects, some of the Ottoman buildings that survive from this period are well-developed examples of a new military architecture designed both to resist the impact of cannon balls and to accommodate the new weapons.

Italian military architects set the pace in the evolution of bastioned systems and it is against their achievements that fifteenth- and sixteenth-century fortress designs tend to be measured. By the formal "rules" of Western military engineering, Mallet was rightly critical of Ottoman military architecture that made little use of pointed bastions, and may well have transgressed many of his maxims. Certainly most early modern Ottoman fortifications on the Hungarian front employed rounded bastions. I have attempted to resist the tendency simply to condemn such differences. What emerges from this survey of the early Ottoman Mediterranean fortresses is a distinctively non-Italian approach to early gunpowder fortification by the Turks who, nevertheless, experimented widely in the designs that emerged from their mid-fifteenth-century building program. This conclusion prompts numerous further questions, not all of which can yet be answered. Were foreign "experts," as Babinger assumes, involved in Ottoman fortress design as they evidently had been in the formative stages of heavy artillery fabrication?[64] Can anything as public and as international as

---

[62] Andrews, *Castles of the Morea*, ch. 12, 130–4.
[63] For Salses, Philippe Truttmann, *La Forteresse de Salses* (Paris, 1980); for the Henrician castles, Andrew Saunders, *Fortress Britain: Artillery Fortification in the British Isles and Ireland* (Liphook, 1989), 34–52.
[64] Although Franz Babinger, *Mehmed the Conqueror*, 465, was dismissive of the possible involvement in Ottoman projects of Filarete and other foreign architects, elsewhere he assumes Italian influence in both fortification and bridge building:

> Thus far, we have no knowledge whatever of the names and works of the architects and builders of fortifications, chiefly Italian, it may be presumed, whom Mehmed employed.

Figure 10.4. Castle of the Morea, straits of Patras, 1499–1500. Trefoil cluster of artillery towers at the seaward end of the castle. For plan, see Fig. 10.2 (*top*) Photograph by the author.

fortification be entirely self-referential? If not from Italy, then from where were the strongest external influences on Ottoman designers likely to have come?

One possibility that cannot be safely ignored is that external influences came from the Middle East.[65] This area is relatively unexplored and may still hold surprises for us. However, a much more likely source of ideas about weapon and fortification technology was the north. The initial Ottoman incursions into Europe took them quickly to the Danube, which they reached as early as 1365.[66] The Danube and its tributaries remained a major theatre of war for more than three centuries, and brought the Ottomans continuously into contact with the central European, medieval fortification tradition, with its emphasis on tall towers (and later multitiered gun towers) rather than the low, squat, pointed bastions that were eventually to be perfected in Italy.[67] It has been suggested that the conical-roofed towers which featured so prominently at Thessaloniki, Rumeli Hisar, and Yedikule were influenced by a more local example, the medieval Genoese fortifications of Pera, one tower of which has survived in modern Istanbul with its distinctive conical pepper-pot roof.[68] But the so-called Genoese Tower at Pera is not typical of Italian medieval fortifications, even in Genoa.[69] The early Ottoman use of tall towers (with or without roofs)

Equally unknown are the bridge builders, whose works often suggest Italian influence although they are usually attributed to Greeks or Bulgarians. Their resemblance to Italian bridges of the same period leaves no doubt that Italian architects were employed. . . . (507)

[65] There is evidence of direct eastern as well as Byzantine influence in Seljuk military architecture, which is well illustrated by the medieval fortress complex at Alanya ("Turkey's Gibraltar"), where a miniature Theodosian wall constitutes the main land front, terminating at one end in the Kizil Kule (the Red Tower). The Red Tower is a polygonal structure with box machicolations, built by a Syrian (possibly the architect of the Citadel in Aleppo), who is known to have executed similar work in Sinop in 1215. Seton Lloyd and D. Storm Rice, *Alanya* (London, 1958), 11–15.

[66] Fernc Szakaly, "The Hungarian-Croatian Border Defense System and its Collapse," in *From Hunyadi to Rakoczi: War and Society in Late Medieval and Early Modern Hungary*, eds. Janos M. Bak and Bela K. Kiraly (New York, 1982), 141–58.

[67] In the sixteenth century, of course, Italian-style fortifications were imported into Hungary's border zones, often by emigre Italian architects themselves. But in the fifteenth century this process had not begun, despite the presence of a distinguished Florentine soldier, Pipo Scolari, commanding the Danube sector of Hungary.

[68] J. Sourdel-Thomine, "Burdj: Military Architecture in the Islamic Middle East" in *Encyclopedia of Islam*, I:1318.

[69] S. Eyice, *Galata ve Kulesi: Galata and its Tower* (Istanbul, 1969). The Genoese tower was perhaps the first of Constantinople's towers to boast a conical roof. Although the evidence of early pictures has to be treated with caution, it is clear that conical roofs appear with increasing frequency in sixteenth-century images of Constantinople. One of the very earliest and best known picture-maps of the city, that of Bondelmontius (or Buondelmonti) in 1422, shows only the Genoese tower with this kind of roof. Buondelmonti's *Liber Insularum Archipelagi* (MSS in the Biblioteca Marciana, Venice)

at Thessaloniki, Rumeli Hisar, Yedikule, and Kilid Bar was much more likely to have been influenced by military experiences gained in the Danubian and Transylvanian theatres of operations.

Here much of the physical evidence is often confused, if not altogether missing. Many Hungarian castles (particularly in Slovakia, Upper Hungary, and Transylvania) were systematically demolished by the Austrians in the early eighteenth century in the program of repression following the defeat of Rakoczi's rebellion, and much useful information on the process of transition from medieval to early modern fortification has been lost. By Rakoczi's time, the Ottoman front line had retreated once again to the Lower Danube, where a new generation of frontier defences was constructed on post-Vauban principles, often built over earlier Bulgarian, Wallachian, Serbian, and Ottoman works, and thus eliminating even more potentially interesting transitional work from the fifteenth and sixteenth centuries. Others, like Smederovo, were severely damaged in World War II. But some generalizations can still be advanced. Although Danubian and Transylvanian Europe contains many of the classic, late medieval towering castles of stone and brick which may well have provided models for the fifteenth-century Ottoman builders, this tradition evidently existed side by side with an even older tradition of timber-reinforced earthwork construction that could well have survived from Roman times. Even after the mid-fifteenth-century adoption of cannon, incendiary fire continued to be used with great frequency by the Ottomans and their opponents in Balkan sieges. This supports the view that many, if not most, of the fifteenth- and sixteenth-century fortifications on both sides of the Croatian-Hungarian-Transylvanian defended frontier were constructed on the so-called *palanka* method of timber and earthwork. Of these works little trace now remains because of the ravages of weather. But late-sixteenth- and early-seventeenth-century illustrations of Hungarian towns and sieges show quite clearly that *palanka* construction was widely used even for substantial urban fortification, by both Christians and Ottomans, as well as for the smaller forts and towers of the frontier *limes* that Braudel saw as characteristic of Western defense policy in the sixteenth century.

What of Braudel's assertion that the Turks built few fortifications? That the Ottomans focused many if not most of their offensive Balkan campaigns on the acquisition and consolidation of fortifications is beyond doubt. Kritovoulos discusses more than once the Ottomans'

is discussed in Giuseppe Gerola, "Le vedute di Constantinopli di Cristoforo Buondelmonti," *Studi Bizantini e Neoellenici* 3 (1931): 247–79.

concern to occupy fortresses wherever these gave strategic advantages, in particular where river crossings or passes were involved.[70] Real efforts were made to secure Nikopolis, Golubats, and Smederovo on the Danube. The struggles for Jajce and Sabac in Bosnia, and above all for Belgrade, were epics of endurance on both sides and speak volumes for the vital importance of fortified positions in the inland Balkan campaigns. When necessary, the Ottomans built new fortresses of their own. We have seen that Avala, south of Belgrade, was constructed in 1440 to maintain pressure on the "key to Hungary" after Murad's siege had been raised. Sabac, on the River Sava in Bosnia, is described as a Turkish foundation, although the fortress changed hands so frequently that initial ownership is difficult to identify. Elbasan in Albania was apparently built de novo south of Scanderbeg's stronghold of Kruje in 1466–7, in the words of Kritovoulos:

to maintain control of the region which [Mehmed II] had devastated. The garrison in the new fortress could prevent refugees in the mountains from descending to the winter pastures and cultivated lands of the plain, as well as protecting the [Turkish] settlers in the new town around the citadel.[71]

Mehmed II, to keep the Hungarians out of any Western plans to relieve Constantinople, agreed to a special additional clause in his treaty of 1451 with Hunyadi, forbidding the sultan from building fortifications along the Danube.[72] For Hunyadi, it seems, the threat of

---

[70] Kritovoulos of Imbros, *History of Mehmed the Conqueror by Kritovoulos*, trans. Charles T. Riggs (Princeton, 1954), 99, 135, and 157.

[71] Quoted in Imber, *Ottoman Empire*, 195. The strategic intent is clear from the report of Sphranzes, *The Fall of the Byzantine Empire*, ch. 43, 87–8: ". . . the sultan, the lord of the impious, marched against Albania, put its lord, Scanderbeg, to flight, seized and destroyed the territory, and built a fortress near its capital, called Kroya, in order to wage war against him." James Pettifer, *Blue Guide: Albania* (London, 1994), 224–5, describes it as a "massive four-sided castle with a deep moat and three gates" and gives the etymology of the name as *Ilibasan* or "strong place" in Turkish. There were twenty-six towers, nine metres high, regularly spaced at intervals of forty meters. It was dismantled by Reshid Pasha in 1832, although the south wall is relatively undamaged, showing the scale and strength of Mehmed II's fortifications. Despite the apparent solidity of these authorities, Albanian archaeologists now believe that Mehmed constructed his "new" fortress on the foundations of a castrum built between A.D. 380 and the mid-fifth century. Gjerak Karaiskaj, "Kalaja e Elbasanit," *Monumentet* 1 (1971): 61–77, and "Të Dhëna Të Reja Për Datimin e Kalasë Së Ebasanit," *Monumentet* 3 (1972): 147–57. There is continued uncertainty about the identity of the Jenidjekela (or new citadel) listed in the Ottoman census of the sandjak of Albania in 1431–2, and located by Inalcik at Bradashesh, just west of Elbasan, but evidently slighted by Scanderbeg's Albanian rebels sometime after 1432. Was this a different fortress from the castrum rebuilt by Mehmed II to the east of Elbasan, or does it represent an early-fifteenth-century restoration and demolition of the same ancient works? Kasem Biçoku, "Kështjella e re (Jenixhekalaja) dhe Elbasan," *Monumentet* 3 (1972): 159–61.

[72] Babinger, *Mehmed the Conqueror*, 99.

new Ottoman fortifications on the Danube was real enough. For obvious reasons, however, the great majority of Ottoman works in Europe are likely to have been repaired or modernized, captured Christian fortresses.

Despite what at times must have seemed their unstoppable forward progress, the Turks needed fortresses. The defense of harbors, and the control of strategic waterways were both obvious priorities, particularly in the fifteenth century when Western naval supremacy constituted one of the chief threats to Ottoman domination of the eastern Mediterranean. It is no surprise to find so many of the important early Ottoman fortresses close to the sea. Secure crossings on the main river barriers could also serve as bases where weapons and munitions could be stockpiled for offensive or defensive campaigns.[73] Fortresses were needed to protect the infrastructure of Balkan roads and bridges and the riverside arsenals housing the Ottoman Danube galley fleet, amounting to some 100 vessels, which allowed the army to move quickly to the front in time for a campaigning season that usually focused on one or more sieges. For in Croatia and Hungary, the Ottoman invaders were confronted by a series of fortified defense lines that could always be penetrated by raiders, but which formed a real barrier to the passage of an invading army and its logistical tail.[74] It was the fortified frontier that prompted Braudel to contrast the defensive mentality of sixteenth-century Western Europeans with that of the Ottomans, who at that time were implicitly more inclined to the offensive than to sit behind strong walls. The Christian approach, suggests Braudel, was "a policy both instinctive and unilateral."[75] Only on the Persian front, he concedes, did the Turks defend their frontier conquests with newly built fortifications because here the Ottomans enjoyed advantages over the Persians in the firearms their economy could support.[76] Braudel here confuses the Western obsession with new fortress construction on an enormous scale along threatened frontiers, with the less visible but equally strong Ottoman concern to hold strategically placed fortified positions and, if necessary, build them for themselves. Ottoman policy, moreover, was highly

---

[73] Geoffrey Parker, *Europe in Crisis 1598–1648* (London, 1979), 79–80, gives a brief but illuminating sketch of the logistical factors involved in moving men, draft animals, food on the hoof, and other supplies in the Danube campaigns.

[74] G.E. Rothenburg, *The Austrian Military Border in Croatia 1527–1747* (Urbana, IL, 1960), is the standard source on the structure and administration of the border defenses and the garrison population, but contains very little information on the fortifications themselves.

[75] Braudel, *The Mediterranean*, II:844–5.

[76] Braudel, *The Mediterranean*, II:846.

selective about which of their captured castles to keep and which to demolish. Once the northern frontier had been stablized, however, the Ottoman settlers, who were surprisingly thin on the ground in many parts of the occupied Balkans, were not immune from the need to shelter behind walls. Near to the Hungarian frontier, in particular, the Ottoman timar-holders living outside established settlements were obliged to fortify themselves against Christian raiders, often led by the dispossessed nobility or their agents, who sought from exile to extract taxes from their former serfs.[77] The *palanka* defenses erected throughout Ottoman-occupied Hungary perhaps represent a late turning point in Turkish thinking, from the offensive spirit which took the crescent standards twice to the gates of Vienna, to a more defensive posture, which foreshadowed the long retreat of Ottoman Turkey from Balkan Europe.

---

[77] Gustav Bayerle, "One Hundred Fifty Years of Frontier Life in Hungary," in *From Hunyadi to Rakoczi*, 227–42.

> The lightning raids and ambushes of the new hussar troops posed a serious threat to the Ottoman landlords who planned to live on their Timar properties. Trade also suffered. The saphis had to withdraw from their villages into fortified enclaves, and the merchants needed military escorts to transport their wares to the market place of Buda eyalet. Eventually the Turks had to erect a defensive line of frontier defences similar in design to the Habsburg line of defence (232).

CHAPTER 11

Walled towns during the French wars of religion (1560–1630)

MICHAEL WOLFE

With the revival of urban life after the eleventh century, inhabitants of provincial towns known as the *bonnes villes* gradually assumed the attributes of lordship long associated with kingship, the feudal nobility, and the church. Among these was the right of self-defense. The remains of French urban fortifications, be they the splendidly reconstructed walls of old Carcassonne or the deserted, lushly overgrown confines of the seventeenth-century citadel built by the crown to "protect" Amiens, still convey an impressive sense of potency, representing at base a defiance of the outside world. Such defensive complexes also represented the single greatest investment of resources that a town ever made. The return on this investment has to be measured not just in terms of the protection a town gained, but also in terms of the conflicts engendered and sacrifices required to raise the walls and extend the works ever further into the *faubourgs* (suburbs) and beyond. Early modern municipal fortifications thus intimately shaped – and were in turn shaped by – the urban communities they were constructed to protect. As this essay will show, the exigencies of war, from the late medieval conflicts with the English through the Wars of Religion (1562–1629), helped to define the outer contours as well as the inner makeup of French *bonnes villes*, thereby affecting their identity and relationship with the outside world. In addition to this long-term continuity, French towns demonstrated a remarkable resiliency when responding to the military threats raised by the spasms of violence that descended upon France after the mid-sixteenth century. Lastly, the numerous sieges of the Wars of Religion gave rise to an enormous amount of occasional literature that reflected the clashing values and visions at play in French public opinion about what constituted a well-ordered, godly community.

Easy generalizations about the *bonnes villes* mask the essential par-
ticularism of the 240 urban agglomerations that go by this name.
Ranging anywhere in size from 5,000 to 50,000 inhabitants, the *bonnes
villes* exhibited a remarkable diversity that developed out of the complex interactions between terrain, local social and political makeup,
economic growth, and cultural traditions.[1] Along with a charter detailing supposedly age-old privileges, each town had an expressive,
individualized profile created by a town's public buildings ringed by
a curtain of walls, turrets, and, by the sixteenth century, bastions.
Joachim Duviert's *Recueil de vues de diverses villes de France* (Meaux,
1610) offers numerous examples of the distinctive cityscapes found
throughout early Bourbon France, as do earlier collections, such as
François de Belleforest's *Cosmographie universelle* (Paris, 1575) and Gabriel Tavenier's *Théâtre françois* (Paris, 1594).[2] Scenographic depictions
of the urban landscape conveyed many different messages. A traveler
returning to his hometown, for example, found a comforting, inviting
familiarity in its walls, gates, church spires, and civic buildings as he
approached from afar; a foreign visitor might likewise remark on the
sense of grandeur and prosperity communicated by a town's outer
face. By contrast, a would-be conqueror might, it was hoped, think
twice before tackling the formidable task of attacking a fortified town,
while a peasant or itinerant merchant on his way to market might
begrudgingly search his purse to pay the toll levied at the town gates;
for in addition to its obvious military functions, a town's walls also
delineated its legal and fiscal jurisdictions. Besides shaping relations
with the outside world, municipal fortifications also powerfully struc-
tured the urban ensemble contained within them, determining street
layouts, drainage systems, the location of public places, neighborhoods and districts, and a family's place in the local hierarchy. Any
analysis of the *bonnes villes'* encircling shell of walls and outworks
must constantly keep in mind this dialectic between the external and
internal aspects of municipal fortifications; indeed, if stones could
speak, those contained in a town's walls would probably tell us the
most about the community within them.[3]

[1] Bernard Chevalier, *Les bonnes villes de France du XIVe au XVIe siècles* (Paris, 1982); G.
Maudvech, "La 'bonne ville': origine et sens de l'expression," *Annales économies, socié-
tés et civilisations* 27 (1972): 1441–8; and Yves Durand, "Les républiques urbaines en
France à la fin du XVIe siècle," *Annales de la société d'histoire et d'archéologie de
l'arrondissement de Saint-Malo* (1990): 205–44.
[2] See Mireille Pastoureau, *Les Atlas français XVIe–XVIIe. Repertoire bibliographique et étude*
(Paris, 1984).
[3] For an introduction to this topic, see Spiro Kostof, *The City Shaped: Urban Patterns and*

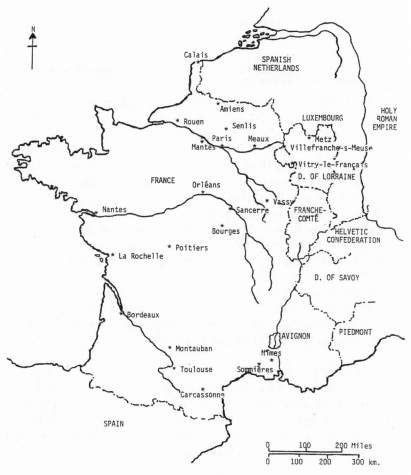

Figure 11.1. Map of fortified towns.

Municipal fortification programs (see Fig. 11.1) represented an ongoing concern for *bonnes villes* as they struggled to adapt to the advent of gunpowder weaponry, new tactics, and the escalating size of armies, all of which combined after 1400 to create what historians now call the Military Revolution. Recent debates have considerably revised, though not overturned, the original thesis presented by Michael Rob-

Meaning through History (Boston, 1991), and Kostof, *The City Assembled: The Elements of Urban Form through History* (Boston, 1992).

erts forty years ago and recently updated, with modifications, by Geoffrey Parker in his eponymous work published in 1988.[4] Whether the emphasis is on technology, logistics, or administrative innovations, virtually all historians agree that these novel forms of warfare marked a decisive new stage in the development of European states. The magisterial works of Philippe Contamine and André Corvisier clearly posit a connection in France between the growth of monarchical authority from the late Middle Ages to the reign of Louis XIV and the crown's burgeoning capacity to wage war. The history of French military institutions during the intervening period, from Charles VIII's invasion of Italy in 1494 on through the Thirty Years' War, remains relatively murky, however.[5] A look at the evolving military role of the *bonnes villes* helps to fill this lacuna and offers important insight into the impact of the Military Revolution on both the French state and society. We do well to avoid the artificial distinction drawn between *"état"* and *"ville"* by historians like Pierre Chaunu and Bernard Chevalier, who mistakenly equate the emerging governing apparatus with the monarchy, when in fact it represented a wide array of complex, ongoing relationships between the crown and urban notability, never mind the nobility and church. This relationship, based as much on cooperation as coercion by all parties, shaped the history of fortified towns from the late Middle Ages down to the early seventeenth century.[6]

This history begins with the long-term insecurities caused by the Hundred Years' War and then revisited during the Wars of Religion. If control of territory hinged on control of its towns (a fact that remained unchanged until the late eighteenth century), then a town's ability to resist a siege ultimately determined who controlled that territory. The military independence associated with the walled city

---

[4] Michael Roberts, "The Military Revolution, 1560–1660," in Roberts, *Essays in Swedish History* (Minneapolis, 1967), 195–225, and Geoffrey Parker, *The Military Revolution: Military Innovation and the Rise of the West, 1500–1800* (Cambridge, 1988). The literature on this debate is vast. See, for example, Clifford J. Rogers, "The Military Revolutions of the Hundred Years War," *The Journal of Military History* 57 (1993): 241–78, and David Parrott, "The Military Revolution in Early Modern Europe," *History Today* 42 (1992): 23–46.

[5] Philippe Contamine, *Guerre, état et société à la fin du Moyen Age. Etudes sur les armées des rois de France, 1337–1494* (Paris and The Hague, 1972), and André Corvisier, *L'armée française de la fin du XVIIe siècle au ministère de Choiseul, Le soldat,* 2 vols. (Paris, 1964). Excellent monographs exist for the intervening period as does a recent, though by no means definitive synthesis in *Histoire militaire de la France,* ed. Philippe Contamine (Paris, 1992), vol. 1.

[6] Pierre Chaunu and Robert Gascon, *L'État et la Ville,* Vol. I of *Histoire économique et sociale de la France,* eds. Fernand Braudel and Ernest Labrousse (Paris, 1970), and Chevalier, *Les bonnes villes.*

was in France largely a product of the long dynastic struggle between the French and English between 1337 and 1453. Urban fortifications in France had developed sporadically until then because there was no pressing need before the Hundred Years' War for towns to invest heavily in their own defense.[7] Philip Augustus' decision in the late twelfth century to enclose Paris within a ring of walls was exceptional, yet even here urban growth in the capital soon burst out of its new confines.[8] Many towns in France simply did not have walls; those that did often had walls dating back to Gallo-Roman times which, if they still stood, did little more than define the city's original core. Even the handful of towns that had walls of fairly recent construction often let them fall into disrepair given the sizable ongoing costs required for their upkeep.[9] Several reasons explain why the *bonnes villes* displayed such a patent disregard for their own safety. These included the lack of immediate threats before the 1330s; the ill-defined nature of municipal government and jurisdiction, particularly in relation to the competing claims of crown, church, and local seigneurs; underdeveloped revenue sources to provide the necessary capital for fortifications; uncertainty as to where to draw the line between the city, with its sprawling *faubourgs*, and the outside world; and, last, an unwillingess on the part of the citizenry to shoulder the enormous financial and physical burdens entailed by self-defense.

When circumstances finally compelled townspeople to begin building walls, they did so in earnest after the mid-fourteenth century. The age of cathedrals then gave way to an age of urban fortifications that permanently changed the country's political landscape. In the process, the *bonnes villes* put in place mechanisms of military protection that lasted in evolving form down to the reign of Louis XIII. The actual construction of urban fortifications is the least known aspect of siege warfare during the Hundred Years' War, as it is for the later Wars of Religion.[10] To begin, any town that wished to construct a wall had to receive permission from the crown, if only because the right to fortify

---

[7] J. Scheider, "Problèmes d'histoire urbaine dans la France médiévale," *Bulletin philologique et historique* 3 (1977): 23–54, and Michael Wolfe, "Siege Warfare and the *Bonnes Villes* of France during the Hundred Years War," in *The Medieval City Under Siege*, eds. Ivy A. Corfis and Michael Wolfe (Suffolk, 1995), 49–66.

[8] Roger Rottmann, *Murs et mémoires: la construction de Paris* (Paris, 1988), and A. Bonnardot, *Dissertations archéologiques sur les anciens enceintes de Paris, suivies de recherches sur les portes fortifiées qui dependaient de ces enceintes* (Paris, 1852).

[9] F.L. Ganshof, *Étude sur le développement des villes entre Loire et Rhine au Moyen Age* (Paris, 1943), 39–45.

[10] See the essays in *La construction au Moyen Age* (Paris, 1973), and the extended essay by Marcel Aubert, "La construction au moyen âge," *Bulletin monumental* 118 (1960): 241–59, 119 (1961): 7–42, 81–120, 181–209, 297–323.

had long been recognized by feudal law as a royal prerogative. Town councils, it seems, usually appointed a comptroller to oversee the project, subcontracting different tasks to specialized groups like masons, carpenters, ropemakers, and haulers. A remarkable (and exceptional) series of municipal account books on the *ouvrages* of Amiens chronicles the annual expenses incurred by self-defense from the fourteenth through the seventeenth centuries, thus demonstrating some of the underlying continuities in municipal fortifications.[11] By the midfifteenth century, virtually every *bonne ville* possessed the distinctive curtain wall, often machicolated and replete with towers and fortified gates, fronted by either a ditch or moat. If funds permitted, *faubourgs* were often encompassed by the works, along with adjoining pastures, cultivated fields, and vineyards. Demographic contraction after the Black Death further reduced any constricting pressures that late medieval municipal fortifications might have had on urban communities. The popular modern image of the medieval city as an unplanned, overcrowded jumble more appropriately fits cities during the sixteenth and early seventeenth centuries, as the swelling defense-in-depth associated with the bastioned trace stifled any tendency toward urban growth by militarizing substantial acreage on the periphery. Indeed, the shift from the vertical emphasis of late medieval fortifications to the horizontal orientation of early modern defenses, a process fueled by ongoing refinements in gunpowder weaponry, represented one of the most significant structuring factors in the development of premodern French cities.[12]

A town's walls and related defensive emplacements, including outlying forts and eventually in the sixteenth century a bastioned trace, required for their construction the mobilization and organization of enormous resources in a society wracked by the horrors of war, the Black Death, and all their attendant economic traumas.[13] Given their vulnerability, towns needed little prompting from either the English or French crowns to initiate these projects, as royal wishes usually coincided with local needs. The key development here lay in the new cooperative arrangements made to defray the considerable costs of

[11] The records are organized in the series CC, "Impôts et Comptabilité," at the Bibliothèque Municipale of Amiens.

[12] The literature on this topic is quite extensive. See in particular, Christopher Duffy, *Siege Warfare: The Fortress in the Early Modern World, 1494–1660* (London, 1979), and the introductory essay by Martha Pollak in her *Military Architecture, Cartography and the Representation of the Early Modern City: A Checklist of Treatises on Fortification in The Newberry Library* (Chicago, 1991), xi–xxxvi.

[13] Philip Benedict, ed., *Cities and Social Change in Early Modern Europe* (London, 1989), introduction, and Jan de Vries, "Studying Cities in Their Context," *Urban History Review* 18 (1990): 193–9.

wall construction and upkeep. Despite the haphazard nature of wall construction, it seems clear that after the 1340s the French monarchy, along with local feudatories and church officials, ceded to the towns the right to levy taxes and surcharges as well as sell bonds (*rentes*) to finance fortifications. At first limited to set periods of time, these tax concessions eventually became perpetual, thus allowing the towns to gain more power over the labor and property of residents in and around the community.[14] Even if it had wished, the crown could do little to monitor how local authorities actually used the monies so raised as long as the walls went up. And go up they did, judging from the frenzied building activity evident throughout urban France during the late Middle Ages.[15]

These ad hoc arrangements between crown and towns evolved into an informal, highly individualized system of relationships akin in many ways to the kinds of affective ties binding the king and the nobility. Although in principle delegated by royalty, the increasing powers of town governments to undertake such large-scale projects hinged on the willingness of residents to make these tremendous ongoing investments of capital and labor. In this manner, a town's walls stood first and foremost as evidence of local public-spiritedness that gave real life to the puffed up rhetoric about civic liberty found in municipal charters. Such communal cooperation was by no means confined to the towns; indeed, throughout this period on through the Wars of Religion, the need for self-defense extended to the countryside and resulted in the construction of fortified peasant villages and rural churches, as well as the small planned towns known as *bastides*.[16] This massive investment in protection, while not a guarantee against a successful siege, raised considerably the stakes of such an undertaking by the enemy, be he a local seigneur, a marauding mercenary commander, or the king. No change in behavior fostered by these perennial insecurities proved more long lasting than a readiness to accept new forms of taxation levied by local authorities for the community's fortifications. Granted, there were occasionally violent instances of

[14] E.A.R. Brown, "*Cessante causa* and the Taxes of the Last Capetians: The Political Applications of a Philosophical Maxim," *Studia Gratiana* 15 (1972): 565–87; Brown, "Customary Aids and Royal Fiscal Policy under Philip IV of Valois," *Traditio* 30 (1974): 191–258; and J.B. Henneman, "Financing the Hundred Years War: Royal Taxation in France in 1340," *Speculum* 42 (1967): 275–98.

[15] Philippe Contamine, "Les fortifications urbaines en France à la fin du Moyen Age: aspects financiers et économiques," *Revue historique* 260 (1978): 23–47.

[16] C. Higounet, "Bastides et frontières," *Le moyen âge* 49 (1948): 113–30; Alain Giradot, "Les forteresses paysannes dans le duché de Bar aux XIVᵉ et XVᵉ siècles," *Annales de l'Est* 38 (1986): 3–55; and Sheila Bonde, *Fortress-Churches of Languedoc: Architecture, Religion and Conflict in the High Middle Ages* (Cambridge, 1994).

fiscal resistance against agents of the crown and municipal government, from the rural Jacqueries and urban uprisings of the 1350s and 1360s down to the riotous struggles against the *gabelle* (salt tax) and other excise taxes during the sixteenth and seventeenth centuries.[17] And there was no doubt plenty of less dramatic, though no less costly, tax dodging on the part of individuals. Such deviance should not blind us to the more significant evidence of compliance embodied in the walls and towers that ringed nearly all French towns from the mid-fifteenth century to the early seventeenth century. The principle of royal taxation was very much in its infancy during this period, especially in the towns; if anything, in fact, this principle only became solidly established there once the crown conceded to municipal authorities intermediate control over direct and indirect levies for the express purpose of building fortifications and related military support services in the areas of supply and procurement.[18]

As Albert Rigaudiére has recently noted, the growth of municipal government after 1400 dovetailed with the emerging monarchical state, with which it shared a wide array of interests as well as skilled personnel. In this way, the walls of the *bonnes villes* did not represent a challenge to royal authority, but testifed to a longstanding partnership with the crown that lasted through the Burgundian Wars (1463–77) and the Italian Wars (1494–1559).[19] While this relationship certainly broke down during the ensuing Wars of Religion, especially for the towns that embraced Calvinism, cooperation from the *bonnes villes* was as necessary to Louis XIV's martial ambitions as it had been for Charles VII's expulsion of the English. In prudent partnership with the crown and aristocratic provincial governors, the *bonnes villes* provided the infrastructure upon which French military power rested from the fourteenth to the eighteenth centuries, complementing rather

---

[17] For an introduction to early modern fiscality and the state, see Martin Wolfe, *The Fiscal System of Renaissance France* (New Haven, 1972), and Philip T. Hoffman, "Early Modern France, 1450–1700," in *Fiscal Crises, Liberty, and Representative Government, 1450–1789*, eds. Hoffman and Kathryn Norberg (Stanford, 1994), 226–371. On urban revolts, see A. Leguai, "Émeutes et troubles d'origine fiscale pendant le règne de Louis XI," *Le moyen âge* 73/3–4 (1967): 447–87; V.I. Raytses, "Le programme d'insurrection d'Agen en 1514," *Annales du Midi* 93 (1981): 255–77; and L.S. Van Doren, "War Taxation, Institutional Change, and Social Conflict in Provincial France – The Royal *Taille* in Dauphiné, 1491–1559," *Proceedings of the American Philosophical Society* 121 (1977): 7–96.

[18] J. Glénisson and Charles Higounet, "Remarques sur les comptes et sur l'administration financière des villes françaises entre Loire et Pyrenées (XIVᵉ–XVIᵉ siècles)," in *Finances et comptabilité urbaine du XIIe au XVIe siècle* (Brussels, 1964), 38–69.

[19] Albert Rigaudière, *Gouverner la ville au Moyen Age* (Paris, 1993).

than countering the monarchy's moves under Charles VII and his successors to build a standing army and strengthen the crown's fiscal hold on the peasantry. In meeting the challenge of siege warfare, town governments throughout France, as Paul Solon has shown, secured greater control over the local population and economy, marshaling the resources necessary to build walls, develop armaments industries, form urban militias, and requisition food supplies from the countryside for the king's army. In exchange, the crown acknowledged the towns' new measure of autonomy. A town's walls thus hardly symbolized independence from the crown, but rather freedom from the prevailing insecurities that lurked beyond them. This helps to explain the seeming contradiction found in town charters, especially evident during the fractious struggles of the religious wars, that municipal liberty rested on dutiful submission to the king.[20]

Despite this underlying continuity from the late Middle Ages onward, several new developments during the first half of the sixteenth century significantly affected the position of French fortified towns. Renewed economic and demographic growth after 1500 meant that many towns simply outgrew their existing fortifications, which occasionally were dismantled in piecemeal fashion or allowed to fall into disrepair. The long domestic peace that France enjoyed after the Burgundian Wars also encouraged this negligence, as municipal authorities understandably invested less heavily in self-defense, except along exposed areas of the Franco-Imperial frontier. Thus, the most sustained period of urban expansion in France since the Black Death was not, in general, accompanied by any concerted program to upgrade municipal fortifications, except for those towns so identified and then financed by the crown.[21] The administration of royal buildings (*bâtiments royaux*) from Louis XII to Henri II included a growing number of urban projects, though never anywhere on the scale or in the quantity of those initiated by the *bonnes villes* during the Hundred Years' War or later in the Wars of Religion. Even so, this intermediate period introduced important innovations in the areas of organization and design. In the first half of the sixteenth century, large-scale fortification projects financed by the crown became increasingly bureaucratic; the

---

[20] Paul Solon, "War and the *Bonnes Villes*: The Case of Narbonne, ca. 1450–1550," *Proceedings of the Annual Meeting of the Western Society for French History* 17 (1990): 65–73.

[21] Gaston Zeller, *L'organisation défensive des frontières du nord et de l'est au XVIe siècle* (Paris, 1928), and Kelly DeVries, "The Impact of Gunpowder Weaponry on Siege Warfare in the Hundred Years War," in *The Medieval City Under Siege*, 227–44.

previous wide latitude, enjoyed by master masons in particular, was hemmed in by first business administrators (*intendants des bâtiments royaux*) and then, in 1536, the central oversight office of the Superintendant, significantly first held by Philibert de la Bourdaisière, chief finance minister to François I.[22] The next crucial change came with the heightened prestige of specially trained architect-engineers for specific projects, beginning with the appointments of Fra Giocondo in 1505 and Pacello da Mercogliono, a Neapolitan garden designer, in 1507. By the mid-1530s, another Italian, Sebastiano Serlio, served as the king's chief architectural consultant for all royal building projects. With the influx of Italian architect-engineers came the introduction of Italian-style fortifications, notably the applied geometry of the celebrated *trace italienne*, during the 1540s. The construction of Vitry-le-François and Villefranche-sur-Meuse, both designed by the Bolognese engineer Girolamo Marini, for example, certainly foreshadow the *villes-fortresses* later designed by Vauban.[23] Although Italians continued to dominate the field for the rest of the century, French design specialists, beginning with Philibert de l'Orme in the 1540s, began to appear with increasing frequency. Thus, new trends toward the professionalization of both construction and design, as well as a mathematically grounded defense-in-depth intended to negate the deleterious effects of gunpowder weaponry, emerged during the first half of the sixteenth century, but were not emulated by the *bonnes villes* until the outbreak of the Wars of Religion, in large part because of the expenses they entailed.[24]

Sieges, of sorts, framed the long internecine struggles of the Wars of Religion, beginning with the 1562 massacre at Vassy of Huguenots who had barricaded themselves in an old barn against rampaging Catholics, and ending with the dramatic fall of La Rochelle in October 1628 to Louis XIII and Cardinal Richelieu. Scores of sieges punctuated the intervening years – a fact that has contributed to the longstanding, but mistaken view by historians that the monarchy strove to subjugate the towns during this period in its drive to become "absolute." According to Bernard Chevalier, the Wars of Religion represented the last days of the *bonnes villes'* independence from the crown, which

[22] Myra Nan Rosenfeld, "The Royal Building Administration in France from Charles V to Louis XIV," in *The Architect in History: Chapters in the History of the Profession*, ed. Spiro Kostof (New York, 1977), 161–79.

[23] Pierre Lavedan, *Histoire de l'urbanisme. Renaissance et temps modernes* (Paris, 1959), 76–118.

[24] Didier Dubant, "Fortifications urbaines en France au XIVe et XVIe siècles. État de la question," *Sites* 45 (1991): 4–17, and Catherine Wilkinson, "The New Professionalism in the Renaissance," in *The Architect in History*, 124–60.

after 1630 forcibly began to have city walls razed, except along frontier areas in the emerging *pré carré*.[25] Such blanket generalizations based on individual instances of conflict between specific towns and the king, of which there are admittedly many, nevertheless pale beside the fact that the vast majority of the some 240 *bonnes villes* never overtly resisted the king's men except during the intense, but short-lived struggle between Henri IV and the Catholic Holy League (1589–93). Calvinist strongholds from La Rochelle across the Midi to Nîmes in Bas-Languedoc certainly flouted royal authority on more than one occasion; nevertheless, the crown's efforts to subdue these Calvinist towns in the 1570s and 1620s relied upon the active, often quite enthusiastic, support of Catholic towns in these same regions. The royal sieges of La Rochelle in 1573 and 1628 could not have occurred but for the strategic support provided by rival port cities like Bordeaux and Nantes; likewise, the monarchy's attempts to take Montauban in 1562 and 1621 received substantial assistance from Toulouse. The same pattern can be discerned in the case of Catholic cities like Paris, besieged during the summer of 1590 by Henri IV, who received the willing and vital support of smaller towns in the *bassin parisien*, such as Mantes, Meaux, and Senlis, against the capital, then in the hands of the Holy League. Arguments by historians such as Janine Garrisson that Calvinist sympathies in southern France represented some sort of broader protonationalist identity overlook these complicated regional cleavages.[26] Robert Descimon's suggestion that both Calvinist and Catholic towns clung to an older, civic republican tradition increasingly threatened by the growth of royal government neglects the longstanding, synergistic relationship between municipal and royal authority since the Hundred Years' War.[27] The abiding continuity in the urban notability across the *bonnes villes* of France from the late fifteenth through the seventeenth centuries, open as it was to the occasional inclusion of new families from commerce or even the rural nobility, reflected a broad-based strategy aimed at controlling customary official positions in town government as well as receiving through court patronage or purchase the newer fiscal and judicial offices created by the crown. My point is this: during the Wars of Religion, urban elites and the monarchy sought to perfect, not break, the traditional partnership that had for centuries tied them together.

Far from another decisive step in the creation of the centralized

---

[25] Chevalier, *Les bonnes villes*, 319–36.
[26] Janine Garrisson-Estèbe, *Protestants du Midi, 1559–1598* (Toulouse, 1980).
[27] Robert Descimon, "La Ligue à Paris (1585–1594): Une révision," *Annales économie, société, civilisation* 37 (1982): 72–111.

monarchical state, siege warfare involving the *bonnes villes* during the Wars of Religion reflected the continuing regional and military importance of urban centers across the realm. Indeed, the confessional frontiers that so profoundly shaped French politics over the next century basically reflected the urban alignments for or against Calvinism of the 1560s. Perhaps the best sign of the *bonnes villes'* vitality was the rapidity with which they responded militarily to the threatening insecurities spawned by confessional conflict after 1560. Although subject to the same factional infighting then tearing the rest of the country apart, many towns managed within a very short time to overhaul and upgrade their defenses, often incorporating in a pragmatic fashion many of the new principles of Italian fortification design by employing professional architect-engineers as well as new, more bureacratic forms of project oversight. This was as true of towns that embraced Calvinism as those that remained staunchly Catholic. In 1569, La Rochelle, for example, hired the Friulian engineer Scipio Vergano to design bastions on the landward, eastern perimeter of the city; four years later, ironically, the crown paid him to direct siege operations against the Calvinist stronghold.[28] Significantly, these innovations still unfolded largely within the framework of municipal self-protection inherited from the Hundred Years' War.

The frenzy of urban military construction after 1560 has left its mark on many French provincial towns down to this day. The wide boulevards and large plazas ringing the older downtown districts of Amiens, Bourges, Nîmes, or Montauban – to name just a few – though usually built in the nineteenth century, reflect almost as a palimpsest the broad plain of earthen outworks thrown up beyond the late medieval curtain walls during the sixteenth and seventeenth centuries. Archival records, where they survive, document the enormous labors and costs incurred by the *bonnes villes*, many of which nearly went bankrupt as a result of fortification expenditures. An account book for two bastions built in 1585–6 in Montauban, along with a 1627 contract with a syndicate of local masons to build a new wall along the Tarn, offer a rich vantage point from which to gauge the new urbanism spawned by civil unrest.

With a population of around 10,000 and an economy based on artisanal manufactures and transshipment, Montauban was a leading center of Calvinist militancy in southern France, besieged as early as 1562 by the dreaded Blaise de Monluc and then again in 1621 by Louis

---

[28] Louis-Etienne Arcère, *Histoire de la ville de La Rochelle et du pays d'Aulnis*, 2 vols. (La Rochelle, 1756), I:378.

XIII. During this sixty-year interval, Montauban, like many other *bonnes villes*, committed huge resources and energy to safeguarding its security. One way town consuls did so after 1568, when Calvinists finally consolidated control over Montauban, was to invest heavily in new Italian-style bastion defenses to reinforce the dilapidated medieval curtain walls, which were all too vulnerable to gunpowder artillery. This was accompanied by other measures, such as fortifying outlying smaller towns and châteaux in the vicinity, expanding the militia, stockpiling arms and creating their own armaments industry. Like so many other *bonnes villes* at the time, Montauban's sporadic campaigns to upgrade and extend urban fortifications – in 1577, 1585–6, 1614, and 1620–1 – profoundly reconfigured existing urban space and its relationship with the immediate hinterland and faubourgs; in moving their defensive works beyond the older medieval core, cities such as Montauban entered a new stage of urban development (Fig. 11.2).[29]

Essential to the construction of municipal fortifications was, of course, money. A surviving account book from 1585–6 kept by Pierre de France, a consul, his son-in-law Jehan Fournier, and their secretary Guillaume Voyr, details receipts and expenditures for two new bastions hurriedly built at the Portes de Campagnes and de Moustier on the northeastern side of Montauban. Other parts of the city received attention, too, though records of these works unfortunately do not survive.[30] Town consuls, as well as Henri de Navarre, who as Protector of the Reformed churches authorized the project, fully expected a rapid renewal of hostilities with the newly revived Catholic Holy League. The section on *"Comptes Receus"* is quite unusual, in that it shows the city's reliance during an emergency on a special levy to raise the money necessary for these defenses. As such, it departed from the conventional methods of raising money for fortifications that had existed since the Hundred Years' War.[31] It should be noted, how-

---

[29] See Hélène Guicharnaud, *Montauban au XVIIe (1560–1685). Urbanisme et architecture* (Paris, 1991). A contemporary political history of the city can be found in H. Le Bret, *Histoire de Montauban*, 2 vols. (Montauban, 1668).

[30] On Montauban's fortifications, see Maurice Langevin, "La visite de Charles IX à Montauban," *Bulletin archéologique, historique, et artistique de la société antiquaire de Tarn-et-Garonne* 101 (1976): 9–21; Émile Forestié, "Les fossés et les portes de la ville de Montauban," *Bulletin archéologique . . . Tarn-et-Garonne* 10 (1882): 263–76; Le Commandant Delavel, "Les anciennes fortifications de Montauban et le siège de 1621," *Bulletin archéologique . . . Tarn-et-Garonne* 31 (1904): 73–90, 193–209, 357–82; and Hélène Guicharnaud, "Les fortifications de Montauban," *Bulletin archéologique . . . Tarn-et-Garonne* 103 (1978): 7–23.

[31] "Comptes receus et compte, Montauban." 3 EE 1, liasse 25, Archives Départementales (hereafter AD) Tarn-et-Garonne.

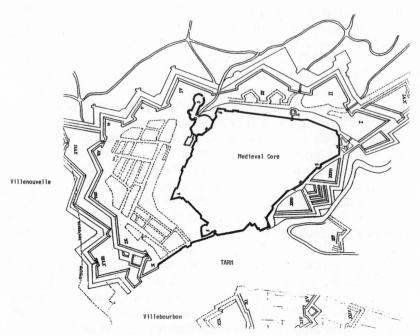

Figure 11.2. Montauban's fortifications in 1621. I: Bastion at Porte de Campagne. II: Bastion at Porte de Moustier. *Source:* Le Commandant Delavel, "Les
anciennes fortifications de Montauban et le siège de 1621," *Bulletin archéologique . . . Tarn-et-Garonne* 31 (1904): 80.

ever, that many towns that never overtly opposed the crown, such as
Amiens and Bordeaux as well as a host of lesser *bourgs*, still financed
their extended fortifications within this older framework. These longstanding methods usually entailed lengthy negotiations with local
feudatories and the crown, which – for a price – would authorize a
diversion of local excise taxes, a special levy, or sale of *rentes* to defray
the huge expense of municipal fortifications. Sometimes, the crown
might even send start-up funds directly, with the balance of payments
to be covered later by the town. As seen above, these conventional
methods had begun as temporary expedients during the Hundred
Years' War which, like so many other aspects of the emerging governing apparatus knitting the royal court with wider French society, soon
coalesced into a permanent, albeit clumsy system of municipal fortification financing, lasting in many cases until the end of the Ancien
Régime. But not for Montauban after the 1560s: In joining the Re-

formed movement, towns like Montauban upset these established procedures of revenue collection and reallocation; royal tax officials in the *généralité* refused to authorize fund transfers, while Catholic Toulouse – Montauban's great urban rival to the south – did what it could to divert trade along the Garonne and Tarn from stopping at Montauban.[32] As a result, the town consuls fell back upon such expedients as seizing church lands and revenues (something other Calvinist towns, such as La Rochelle and Nîmes, did as well), then the property of people, invariably Catholics, who had fled the city, and finally special direct levies on the townspeople.

The list of contributors for these two bastions reflects how much municipal self-defense during the Wars of Religion represented a community-wide effort, just as it had in the Hundred Years' War. From 24 December 1585 to 9 May 1586, Pierre de France and his son-in-law collected some 600 *livres* to defray their cost; whether the city eventually had to repay these forced loans, and under what terms, remains unclear. They tabulated the contributions monthly and identified by name, title and/or occupation every individual donor. Residential addresses were not provided, though with fortification construction proceeding in other parts of the city, especially across the river in the *faubourg* Villebourbon and to the northwest in the *faubourg* Villenouvelle, it seems likely that the donors paid for the works nearest their neighborhood. Over the six-month period in question, some 247 separate contributions were listed, with a high of seventy-seven in February and a low of thirty-eight in January; rates were calculated on the basis of the daily pay scale for one male laborer, which was 4 *sols*. The amounts assessed ranged from 36 *livres* paid by a Monsieur de Saliot on 4 February to much smaller, but more numerous contributions of 1 to 3 *livres*. Many multiple entries for the same person are also found; Saliot, for example, forked over another 28 *livres* on 5 March. Factoring out multiple entries reduces the total number of individuals contributing to the works by about a third. Even so, a total of 160 individual donors must represent a fairly high percentage of the households in the neighborhood near the Portes de Campagnes and de Moustier. Like the fortification account books for fifteenth-century Amiens, the wide degree of social involvement in funding the bastions is confirmed by the modest nature of the many contributions in the 1 to 3 *livres* range, as well as the humble occupational status of a large number of the donors, many of whom were hatters, cobblers,

---

[32] On militant Catholicism in Toulouse, see Robert Schneider, *Public Life in Toulouse, 1463–1789: From Municipal Republic to Cosmopolitan City* (Ithaca, 1989).

and tailors. Along with such artisanal groups are references to a municipal *conseiller*, several merchants, and a retired consul. Women also figure occasionally as donors; most are married or widows, and thus acted as heads of household.[33]

Another interesting feature of the accounts receivable record is the fact that some contributors paid on behalf of others. An entry on 24 December of *"Jehan Palauze pour Marye de Petit, 1 livre,"* is typical in its intriguing brevity. In some cases, the affiliation is stated or obvious, as when, for example sons and wives paid in lieu of the household head. Thus, on 24 February, Monseiur Escorbain, *conseiller*, paid 3 *livres "par mains de son filz,"* while three days later Philip Molyier chipped in 12 *sols "par mains de sa fame."* In other more ambiguous instances, I suspect (but cannot yet prove) that private debts were being settled in the collection of fortification donations. Modes of payment could vary, with most made in coin but a number paid in kind, usually by donating household and personal items given a monetary value by the collector. Raimond Confimat, for example, gave clothes worth 1*l* 9*s* 5*d*, then a few weeks later a *"habitz"* valued at 4 *sols*. Whether this was personal attire or clothes inherited from some recently deceased relative or neighbor (a common enough practice) is impossible to tell. Other kinds of donated household items so scrupulously recorded include an enamel cook pot given by Madame de Bongnon, the wife of a notary; other women gave or pawned valuable cookware and table items, such as painted serving platters, washbasins, and linens. Artisans in the metal trades occasionally donated scrap iron, while a wholesale meat merchant sold four veal calves to raise his 1 *livre* contribution. Some contributors apparently dealt in false or clipped coins when making their contributions – a fact duly noted in a special section at the end of the account book for miscellaneous items. The gravity of the situation facing Montauban in the mid-1580s can thus be seen in the willingness of residents to donate even modest personal possessions to meet the urgent needs of municipal defense. Fortification account books for Montauban and other towns, Calvinist and Catholic alike, reflect the vital, widely shared sense of community in the towns during the Wars of Religion that belies any notion that the *bonnes villes* were in decline during this period.[34]

The organization of such a large worksite represented a remarkable feat of logistics and planning. Evidence of this can be seen in the

---

[33] 3 EE 1, liasse 25, AD Tarn-et-Garonne.

[34] André Corvisier, "Le pouvoir militaire et les villes," in *Pouvoirs, villes et sociétés en Europe de 1650 à 1750, Actes du Colloque de Strasbourg* (Paris, 1982), 11–20.

second half of Pierre de France's account book, which details the multifarious expenditures entailed by constructing these two earthen bastions in 1585–6. Unlike in the late Middle Ages, when master masons generally headed such projects, Pierre de France and his son-in-law acted both as auditors and as general contractors for the project. As the account book shows, they arranged to purchase indirectly through a variety of middlemen large amounts of timber, limestone, and sand (to make mortar), and bricks to be used at the site. Barges had to be rented, dockhands hired, and land transport arranged to move this materiel – sometimes from as far away as thirty miles – to the worksite.[35] In addition, de France hired two agents to oversee the mustering and payment of workgangs of men and women assembled for the project. Not surprisingly, they were paid widely divergent rates (Fig. 11.3). Tabulating this information in graphic form allows us to reconstruct the rhythm of work at the site (Fig. 11.4). Activity proceeded in definite spurts and could take place any day of the week, save Sunday. Weather, too, does not seem to have been much of a factor, since it is never mentioned in the account book as a reason for not working. The initial burst of activity by male workgangs from late December to mid-January cleared away residential structures and excavated the fronting ditch for the two bastions. The one month lull then enabled the site engineer (if there was one) and skilled craftsmen, like masons, to survey and lay out the proposed construction; it also allowed de France and his team to assemble the necessary capital to pay for the works. Male, then female, workgangs attacked the site over the next month (mid-February to mid-March), with the men clearing and excavating, and the women, using primarily baskets, hauling and piling earth and debris to form the bastions. After mid-March came nearly six weeks of terracing and facing the outworks – a job requiring smaller numbers of laborers; another account book (de France closed his in mid-May) indicates that this finishing work continued well into the summer. A handful of daily muster sheets survives, which show a strong continuity among the people making up the labor force; occasional family affiliations, even among the women, are also suggested by the surnames when mentioned together. Although individually paid a pittance, these day laborers received in toto a sizable portion of the adjoining neighborhood's movable

---

[35] "Recepte faicte par Guillaume Darassus Commis par Messieurs les consulz de la Presente Ville de Montauban et leurs conseillers des deniers tant des tailles Que les autres deniers emploies à la fortification de la presente ville ceste année 1586," 9 CC 3, AD Tarn-et-Garonne.

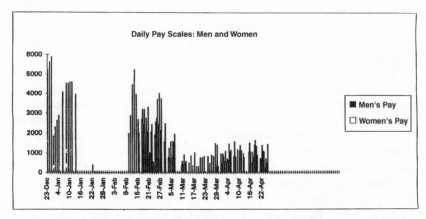

Figure 11.3. Montauban 1585–6. Bastion construction at Portes de Campagne and de Moustier. Men's pay: 4 sols/day. Women's pay: from 1 sol 6 deniers to 2 sols 6 deniers/day. February 21 to 24, the work gangs worked half-days only, thus explaining the dip noticeable in that section.

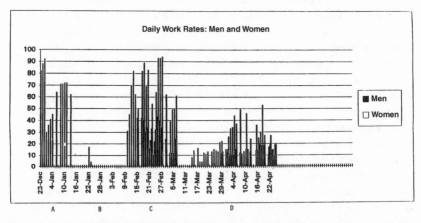

Figure 11.4. Montauban 1585–6. Bastion construction at the Portes de Campagne and de Moustier. A. Demolition of residental properties and initial excavation of fronting ditch. B. Site engineer and master masons survey and layout proposed construction. C. Further excavation and piling of earthen bastions. D. Terracing and facing of bastion and related works in vicinity.

wealth, thus reflecting a significant redistribution of resources from the standpoint of the city's political economy.

New-style bastion defenses, while sophisticated in design, were anything but in construction, which was essentially a matter of large-scale earth moving, then terracing and facing the work with either brick or stone. This practice, so often associated with the fortification projects in the Low Countries, was actually very common in French towns from the 1560s onward. Earthen fortifications were markedly cheaper to construct and well suited to absorbing the impact of artillery; they were also surprisingly durable when reinforced with grassy plantings and fascines, which were wattle constructions in timber and reed. Professional experts in the new geometric military designs coming out of Italy devoted attention to the utility, as opposed to the aesthetic quality, of earthen fortifications in the second half of the sixteenth century, beginning with Giacomo Lanteri's *Due dialoghi del modo di desegnare le piante delle fortezze* (1557) and *Due libri del modo di fare le fortificazione* (1559).[36] No engineer or designer is associated with the bastions raised in Montauban in the 1580s; such an absence is often encountered in the fortification records of other *bonnes villes* during this period, though Italian and French military engineers do occasionally crop up. Such a lack of prominence on the part of professional designers, who certainly craved as much publicity as possible when it came to royal projects in which they participated, suggests that French towns undertook new-style defenses, both in their design and construction phases, still largely within the existing framework of municipal building-trade associations and conventions.[37] In the realm of urban military architecture, at least, a rough parity therefore existed between old and new until well into the seventeenth century.

Evidence of this abiding continuity in the construction of urban defenses can be found when *bonnes villes* contracted the services of skilled masons, carpenters, haulers, and others to carry through the project. The rising importance of trained engineers to design the geometric "defense-in-depth" characteristic of the *trace italienne* did not displace the essentially medieval character of the worksite.[38] This con-

---

[36] Quentin Hughes, *Military Architecture* (New York, 1974), 105–11.

[37] On the emergence of military engineering in late-sixteenth-century France, see David Buisseret, "Ingénieurs du roi Henri IV," *Bulletin de la section de géographie, Comité des travaux historiques et scientifiques* 87 (1964): 12–81.

[38] Yves Bruant, "Les traités d'architecture militaire français à la fin du XVIe et au début du XVIIe siècle," in *Les traités d'architecture de la Renaissance* (Paris, 1988), 477–84. The continuity with medieval fortification construction methods can be discerned in Alain Erlande-Brandenbourg, "Organisation du conseil d'architecture militaire et du corps

trast between the innovative nature of urban planning and the traditional modes by which it could be realized comes through quite well in the contracts. Whereas professional engineers, some Italian, others French, might occasionally dominate the initial design and layout phases of the work in question, town councils, which paid for the project, in every instance entrusted its actual building to master masons. The conventions of awarding building contracts can be seen in a series of documents from late 1627 regarding the construction of a new wall along the Tarn.[39] On 8 November of that year, the two town syndics, Messieurs Benediction and de Constans, in consultation with an unidentified site engineer, submitted the contract terms and site specifications for the town consuls to review and approve. The contract described in very precise language the proposed dimensions of the wall, stipulating its height and width, the depth of the fronting ditch, the extent of the talus, etc. It also specified the construction materials to be used and the procedures for apportioning cost through subcontracting. Whoever won the contract was responsible for providing all tools and day laborers – a difference with the project overseen by Pierre de France back in 1586. The town council retained the right to procure all tile and brick facing as well as mortar destined for the ramparts; whether this was to relieve the master mason of this duty or try to control costs is not clear. An advance of 150 *livres* would be awarded to the winning bidder, with the balance of the project costs to be paid upon completion. The party awarded the contract was forbidden to quit the project on pain of paying all outstanding costs and damages incurred by the city to complete the project.

This contract does not differ all that substantially from several I have found from fifteenth-century Amiens, and reflects the persistence of medieval public-works traditions going back to the age of the cathedrals. The contract was presumably circulated among interested masons, who could then inspect the proposed site and reckon their own costs for the bid, which was scheduled ten days later on 18 November. At 3 P.M. on that day at the Hôtel de Ville, the syndics publicly read the contract to nineteen master masons who represented different syndicates of masons. Five bids were then submitted; why the other fourteen in attendance did not bid is unclear. Perhaps there had been collusion; perhaps the others hoped to offer their services as subcontractors to the winning party. The bids ranged wildly, from a high of

des spécialistes sous Philippe Auguste," in *Artistes, artisans et production artistique au Moyen Age*, ed. Xavier Barral i Altet, 2 vols. (Paris, 1987), II:221–4.

[39] "Bail pour batir la muraille le long du Tarn," November 8–18, 1627, 3 EE 1 liasse 42, AD Tarn-et-Garonne.

3 *livres* per *"centain carré"* (a regional unit of measurement roughly comparable to square footage) by the mason Jean Borier to a low of 20 *sols* per *"centain carré"* put in by Jean Fagon, who was naturally awarded the contract. Information on this particular project ceases here; it is impossible to tell how far along construction of the wall proceeded before Cardinal Richelieu, a year later, after the crown's stunning victory over La Rochelle, ordered Montauban and all other Calvinist cities to begin dismantling their walls.[40] Ironically, a contract for fortification demolition in Montauban, dated 28 November 1633, was awarded by the crown to the mason Jean Bourgeois, who six years earlier had attended the public bid for the contract to build the wall along the Tarn.[41]

Numerous other account books and building contracts on early modern urban fortifications exist in departmental and municipal archives across France; additionally, comprehensive surveys of residential structures in the *faubourgs*, demolished in order to extend a city's "defense-in-depth," as well as judicial records on civil suits brought by property owners to contest such demolitions or challenge compensation rates, also cast light on the morphology of the early modern city.[42] In reshaping the contours and existing spatial relationships of a city in such fundamental ways, fortification construction and demolition, which began in earnest during the seventeenth century, tangibly expressed the redefinition of the *bonne ville*, in forms sometimes still discernible today. These evolving urban forms, so much a product of a city's political and military circumstances, economic infrastructure, and social relations, in turn provided a new, enlarged terrain upon which French cities gradually shed their medieval character in the sometimes brutal, sometimes quite subtle transition to modernity.

Printed siege accounts provide another way to gauge the changing character and significance of early modern urban fortifications. Hundreds of these ephemeral publications appeared between 1562 and 1628, detailing in a wide variety of formats the trials and tribulations of townspeople during the Wars of Religion. Through the mid-1590s, a rough balance existed between pamphlets sympathetic to Huguenot and Catholic Leaguer towns, often produced by printers within the

---

[40] Letters concerning the demolition of Montauban's fortifications after 1628 can be found in 3 EE 1 liasse 47, AD Tarn-et-Garonne.

[41] 3 EE1 liasse 42, AD Tarn-et Garonne.

[42] Over 200 residences in the *faubourg* of Villenouvelle in Montauban, for example, were razed in the early 1620s to extend defensive outworks. A complete inventory of the demolitions is contained in 3 EE 1 liasse 40, AD Tarn-et-Garonne.

walls of the very towns under siege, and those that promoted a royalist perspective of events. These publications invariably construed the principles at stake in the familiar rhetoric of lawful resistance, the just war, dutiful obedience to God and king, and the heinous nature of sedition, all of which resounded in pamphlets dealing with confessional factions or rebellious noblemen.[43] In nearly every case, it was the king's army that besieged the town, though such instances of conflict between a town and the crown must not be generalized upon too loosely, since the vast majority of *bonnes villes* never took up arms against the king. More effective censorship policies under Henri IV and Louis XIII eventually gave the crown a virtual monopoly on printed siege accounts by the early seventeenth century. The 1628 siege of La Rochelle, which brought the religious wars to a close, saw only a handful of pamphlets favoring the besieged, while nearly two hundred titles boosting the crown's cause poured off the presses.[44] The monarchy's growing domination of this form of occasional literature thus mirrored the steady eclipse of the independence long enjoyed by walled towns in France.

Literary depictions of siege warfare go back to the very origins of Western culture. Early modern French exponents of the genre could, and often did, readily draw on the treasure trove of rhetorical conventions that writers had long used to portray a city under assault. As a literary form, siege accounts participated in an epic tradition first developed in the West in Homer's *Iliad*.[45] Another source upon which writers drew was the romance literature of the High Middle Ages, such as stories about the Cid or the *Roman de la rose*.[46] Given the renewed importance of Scripture in sixteenth-century France, siege accounts could also find inspiration in Old Testament exemplars, like the siege of Jericho. Siege accounts from the Hundred Years' War, such

---

[43] In general, see Myriam Yardeni, *La conscience nationale en France pendant les guerres de religion* (Louvain, 1971), and Jeffrey K. Sawyer, *Printed Poison: Pamphlet Propaganda, Faction Politics, and the Public Sphere in Early Seventeenth-Century France* (Berkeley, 1990).

[44] Hélène Duccini, "Pamphlets et censure en France au XVIIe siècle," *Lendemains* 13 (1979): 93–102; Alfred Soman, "Press, Pulpit, and Censorship in France before Richelieu," *Proceedings of the American Philosophical Society* 120 (1976): 439–63. On the siege of La Rochelle, see David Parker, *La Rochelle and the French Monarchy: Order and Conflict in Seventeenth-Century France* (London, 1980).

[45] R.W. Southern, *The Making of the Middle Ages* (New Haven, 1953), 219–57.

[46] Richard Cooper, " 'Nostre histoire renouvellée': The Reception of Romances of Chivalry in Renaissance France," in *Chivalry in the Renaissance*, ed. Sydney Anglo (Woodbridge, 1990). Also Michael Harney, "Siege Warfare in Medieval Hispanic Epic and Romance," in *The Medieval City Under Siege*, 177–90, and Heather Arden, "The Slings and Arrows of Outrageous Love in the *Roman de la rose*," in *The Medieval City Under Siege*, 191–206.

as the struggles over Calais (1356) and Orléans (1429), and the six-teenth-century Hapsburg-Valois struggles in Italy, tended to form part of regnal histories or local chronicles rather than stand as discrete episodes. The works of Christine de Pisan, Jean Froissart, and Martin Du Bellay, to cite three fairly well-known writers of this earlier period, typify this manner of depicting siege warfare.[47] Another place where siege narratives could be found prior to the Wars of Religion was in noble memoirs, such as those of Boucicaut and Jean de Bueil's *Le Jouvencel*. This genre helped adjust conventional notions of chivalric *prouesse*, held so dear by the aristocracy, to meet the new, more technical requirements of a protracted siege.[48]

A new style of portraying siege warfare emerged in France in 1553 with the publication of Bernard de Salignac's lengthy account of the siege of Metz (1552). Although elements of these earlier literary traditions clearly influenced Salignac's work, it broke new ground with its explicit bid to encourage French public opinion to support Henri II's brazen act of aggression against the Holy Roman Empire. This is made abundantly clear in his dedicatory epistle to the king. Salignac's book was in the most literal sense of the term a *livre d'occasion*, and as such established a model for siege accounts printed later during the Wars of Religion. In terms of men and materiel, the siege of Metz was the largest operation of its kind in French history prior to the reign of Louis XIV. As an officer in the duc de Guise's occupation force, Salignac enjoyed privileged access to field reports and correspondence with the crown; likewise, French intelligence provided him fairly detailed information of Charles V's huge army of 80,000 men. Pitched primarily to a noble audience, Salignac's book combined vignettes of individual valor with strategic analysis of Metz's importance to the crown. He also discussed logistical aspects of the siege and provided a detailed analysis of Guise's rapid upgrade of the city's fortifications. All of this was supplemented by a pictorial depiction of the city's walls and principal buildings as well as the surrounding territory, replete with numbers and letters marking the main sites mentioned in the text. Tiny figures representing infantry and cavalry formations, as well as artillery emplacements, also helped

---

[47] Michael Wolfe, "Siege Warfare and the *Bonnes Villes* of France during the Hundred Years War," in *The Medieval City Under Siege*, 49–66.

[48] M.G.A. Vale, *War and Chivalry: Warfare and Aristocratic Culture in England, France, and Burgundy at the End of the Middle Ages* (Athens, 1981). Germany and the Low Countries also drew on these various traditions. See W. Rheinhard, "Humanismus und Militarismus. Antike-Rezeption und Kriegshandwerk in der Orangischen Heeresreform," in *Krieg und Frieden im Horizont der Renaissance-humanismus* (Wernheim, 1986).

to set the stage for the reader, who could easily follow the sequence of events. This became a common manner of depicting urban warfare over the next century. One notable difference with siege accounts from the later Wars of Religion, however, was the relative absence of the townspeople of Metz from Salignac's description. They only entered into Salignac's account insofar as they supported or obstructed Guise's efforts to hold the city for the king. This would change once the *bonnes villes* took matters into their own hands ten years later.[49] Then the good bourgeois and more generally the "people" assumed a more central role in warfare and its subsequent depiction in print.

The general format established by Salignac was loosely adapted to relate the story of individual sieges over the next eighty years. The dedications to either the king or some grand personage, such as a high ranking aristocrat, with which so many siege pamphlets begin, laid out the moral lessons conveyed in the narrative that followed. In Salignac's case, the siege of Metz stood as a dramatic example of the aristocracy's valor and loyalty to the crown. This pitch to men of the sword recurred time and again in many later siege accounts that took the royalist perspective; many of them, in fact, tabulated in a sort of honor roll all of the noble officers killed or wounded in action. By contrast, Jean de Léry's *Histoire du siège de Sancerre*, published in 1576, shifts away from a celebration of noble values to an ethnographic analysis of the tragic dissolution of community bonds, culminating in cannibalism, that sustained violence forces upon people who try to fight the good fight.[50]

Despite their dwindling variety, these different readings of urban warfare sprang from a like treatment of individual sieges as theatrical events. Mounting a siege, at least in literary form, was in many respects akin to staging a play. Like a play, a siege held a significance beyond the immediate action at hand, and thus served as a convenient vehicle for commentaries about political ideology, conflicting social values, or the inexorable unfolding of God's will through battle. As in theatre, siege accounts devoted close attention to describing the setting where the *dramatis personae* acted out their assigned parts. Detailed descriptions of municipal fortifications, long since demolished, furnish historians with a valuable source for reconstructing the changing urban fabric of early modern cities. Likewise, important information on

---

[49] Bernard de Salignac, *Le siège de Metz* (Paris, 1553), and the full-length study by Gaston Zeller, *Le siège de Metz* (Metz, 1929).

[50] Jean de Léry, *Histoire du siège de Sancerre* (n.p., 1574). A modern edition by Gerald Nakam was published in 1978. Other accounts include Jean La Gessée, *Nouveau discours sur le siège de Sancerre* (Paris, 1573).

the disposition of besieging forces, which in some cases even outnumbered the inhabitants of the besieged town, helped contemporary readers – and helps us – envision what it was like to attack a town. Like a play, a siege unfolded in discrete acts, beginning with the assembly of the players, their harried preparations for the parts they would play, and then their dramatic entry on to the stage. Assaults and counterassaults, as well as the occasional face-to-face parlay, punctuated the drama of the siege as it ineluctibly moved toward its denouement of either capitulation or successful resistance. Thereupon the players exit the stage, leaving the author – much like a Greek chorus – to summarize the principal lessons that readers should take away with them.

Theatrical depictions of siege warfare were not artificial devices imported by the authors of siege accounts. In fact, siege warfare was (and had always been) a highly ritualized form of combat regulated by longstanding conventions and laws of war.[51] Pictorial representations of siege warfare from the crown's viewpoint, for example, sometimes portray the king's leadership in explicitly directorial terms, as at the 1597 siege of Amiens (Fig. 11.5). There, with but a sweep of his hand, Henri IV as dramaturge motions the serried ranks of his soldiers to their appointed places as the action begins. The elaborate movements of advance and retreat, when artistically depicted, bear a striking resemblance to graphic portrayals of courtly cavalcades and the tournament. Allegorical images of siege warfare also drew on traditions of the stage, as seen, for example, in a print of a triumphal arch celebrating the sea wall built at La Rochelle in 1628 (Fig. 11.6). This aspect comes through clearly, too, in stylized renderings of the surrender of La Rochelle (Fig. 11.7). These and other similar depictions of siege warfare followed many of the well-established traditions of ceremonial procession and entry that had developed during the Renaissance.[52]

Siege warfare, like stagecraft, required machinery to move the action forward. From the Trojan Horse and Gabriel's Trumpet to the advent of gunpowder weaponry, descriptions of siege warfare had long evinced an abiding interest in military technology and treachery

---

[51] Maurice Keen, *The Laws of War in the Late Middle Ages* (London, 1965), and *The Laws of War: Constraints on Warfare in the Western World*, eds. Michael Howard, George J. Andreopoulos, and Mark R. Shulman (New Haven, 1994), 40–58.

[52] Lawrence M. Bryant, *The King and the City in the Parisian Royal Entry Ceremony: Politics, Ritual, and Art in the Renaissance* (Geneva, 1986); Marie-France Gueusquin, "Le guerrier et l'artisan. Rites et représentations dans la cité en France du Nord," *Éthnologie française* 14 (1985): 45–62; and D. Worfthal, "Jacques Callot's Misères de la Guerre," *Art Bulletin* 59 (1977): 222–33.

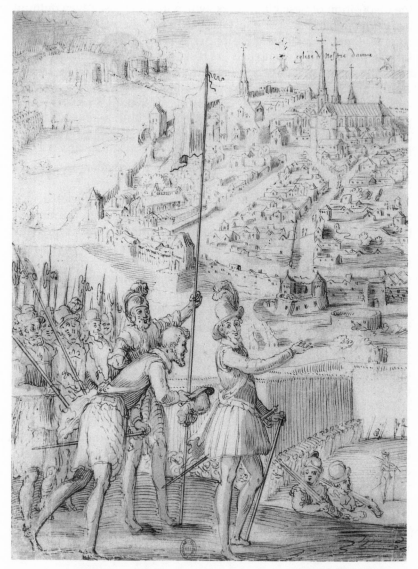

Figure 11.5 Siege of Amiens. 3 April 1597. Collection Hennin G 151474. Courtesy of the Bibliothèque nationale de France.

Figure 11.6. Arc de triomphe sur la magnificence du Roy. Collection Hennin G152861. Courtesy of the Bibliothèque nationale de France.

Figure 11.7. La justice et la clemence sont agenouillées. Collection Hennin G152878. Courtesy of the Bibliothèque nationale de France.

– two aspects of warfare more closely related than is sometimes realized. Printed siege accounts from the Wars of Religion provide an excellent source for tracing the progressive evolution of bastion defenses and corresponding modifications in assault tactics.[53] Here again important continuities with classical antiquity and the Middle Ages existed. Siege manuals by Romans such as Vegetius and Frontinus, once they were translated in the sixteenth century, provided a ready technical vocabulary to describe complicated siege operations and engines.[54] Another source of innovation appeared in the 1550s with French translations of Italian military-science treatises (which of course many in France could read in the original anyway), which were shortly thereafter followed by similar works by French authors, culminating in the work of Jean Errard in the 1590s. "Do-it-yourself" lesson books in practical mathematics and geometry supplemented these works in military design. Practical treatises on arithmetic and geometry, inspired in part by sixteenth-century French translations of Vitruvius's works on architecture and Euclid's *Elements*, broadened

[53] Bert S. Hall, "The Changing Face of Siege Warfare: Technology and Tactics," in *The Medieval City Under Siege*, 257–76; David Buisseret, "Sully, Henri IV et les machines de guerre," *Bulletin de la société des amis du château de Pau* 22 (1990): 3–7; Guillaume de la Perrière, *Le théâtre des bons engins: la morosophie* (Brookfield, VT, 1993).

[54] Vegetius, *Epitome of Military Science* (*Epitoma rei militaris*), trans. and foreword N.P. Milner (Liverpool, 1993); Frontinus, *Juli Frontini Strategemata*, ed. Robert I. Ireland (Leipzig, 1990); Charles C. Peterson, "The *Strategikon*: A Forgotten Military Classic," *Military Review* 72 (1992): 66–79. In general, see Kelly DeVries, *Medieval Military Technology* (New York, 1992). R.H.C. Davis, *The Medieval Warhorse: Origins, Development, and Redevelopment* (New York, 1989), discusses the evolution of animals used for combat and transport – another important continuity with the past.

public appreciation – and perhaps even understanding – of warfare as not simply an art but also a science. These works, as evidenced in the writings of Bernard de Palissy, provided sufficient information for local artisans involved in the construction industry to adapt the new bastion designs into the fabric of existing municipal defense. As we have seen, manuscript materials on actual projects in the *bonnes villes* during the Wars of Religion show that this process of adoption and adaptation usually proceeded independently of the crown. The common assumption that the new technologies and "scientific" expertise associated with the Military Revolution only benefited the state at the expense of groups in society like townspeople may bear reconsideration.

Because siege warfare constituted the most direct experience that people had of combat during the French Wars of Religion, it furnished civilians a unique, if frightening, opportunity to participate in early modern war. Printed siege accounts thus provide us with an early instance of how "the people" at war could be depicted before the Revolution of 1789. The lower orders, usually relegated by historians to the role of helpless victim, could compete and occasionally prevail against the nobility and professional soldiery during a siege. They could even be given voice, as in the patois declamation by a refugee peasant related in Martin Liberge's *Le siege de Poictiers* (1570):

Vrement o nous in falet d'y qualé Menistres, pré nous fere anse mangy et tuy lé uns lé autre. Gnen avan ouy goulée de pù qu'ils sont en icou pois, qu'ò ne no' et cousti mes de chaquin in écu.

[Truly, these ministers have only encouraged us to eat and kill one another so that just before we've gulped each other down, they'll be able to offer to sort out our weighty differences at the modest cost of one *écu* per person.][55]

The leveling effect of siege warfare also came through in descriptions of combat. Léry, for example, catalogued those Sancerrois as well as refugees who died while defending the town. They came from all walks of life, and included a vintner, a tailor, an innkeeper, a butcher, a lawyer, a dyer, a notary, a haberdasher, and a parchment preparer.[56]

---

[55] Martin Liberge, *Le siege de Poictier et ample discours de ce qui s'y faict et passé és mois de Juillet, Aoust et Septembre 1569; avec les noms et nombre des Seigniors, Chevaliers, Capitaines, Gentilshommes et compaignes tant estrangeres que Françoises, qui estoient dedans la ville durant le siege, et de ceulx qui y ont esté blecez ou tuez: Ensemble les Epitaphes Latins et François de quelques-uns des occis* (Poitiers, 1570), 18–19; Jean-Marie Constant, "Le langage politique paysan en 1576: les cahiers de doléances des bailliages de Chartres et de Troyes," in *Représentations et vouloir politique: autour des États-Généraux de 1614*, eds. Roger Chartier and Denis Richet (Paris, 1982).

[56] Léry, *Histoire du siège de Sancerre*, 232.

Ordered thus by Léry, this list of occupations showed how social differences all but dissolved in the common struggle against a town's foes. The honor roll of the wounded similarly defied any hierarchical order reflective of urban society; servants were mingled among sergeants, women among men. The involvement of women in constructing and defending municipal fortifications also recurs in many siege narratives. Gender lines often blurred in descriptions of these "manly" women. At the siege of Sommières in 1578, for example, a group of women of "the lowest condition," dressed as men wearing hats with paper plumes, bravely defended a section of wall assigned to them by the militia captain, beating back a Catholic assault as well as any battle-hardened soldiers. Mentioned, too, was a band of fearless children who stood fast upon the ramparts.[57] At the 1573 siege of La Rochelle, women of the city apparently inflicted heavy casualties on an assault party made up primarily of noblemen. At another point in the action, women from the ranks of the urban notability grabbed picks and shovels to repair a damaged wall.[58] Later in 1621, in fact, La Rochelle organized a battalion of women to act as auxiliaries to the urban militia.[59] Siege warfare could also shrink the boundaries of urban community, however, especially when food supplies ran low, thus compelling town fathers to expel the people they labeled "useless mouths" (*bouches inutiles*). Rarely did the besieging army allow such people to pass through their lines unhindered, since to do so enabled the defenders to hold out longer. The fate of such *bouches inutiles* was consequently a piteous one, trapped between enemy trenches and the city walls they had often helped to build. Nowhere were the brutal contradictions of urban warfare more apparent.

Printed siege accounts from the French Wars of Religion offer us a rich source from which to reconstruct the reality as well as changing

[57] Estienne Giri, *Histoire des choses memorable advenues en la ville de Sommieres en Languedoc à ces derniers troubles. Où sont compris les deux sièges l'un contraire à l'autre qu'elle a souffert, les massacres et inhumanitez qui y ont esté executées, pendant l'un et l'autre siege, l'ordre et place des Gouverneurs qui ont commandé en icelle. Les exemples de la vengeance de Dieu sur les habitans avec le Siege et avitaillement de la Ville de Montpellier* (Lyons, 1578), 36.

[58] Anonymous, *Discours et recueil du siege de la Rochelle en l'année 1573 contenant les assaux donnez à ceux de la ville, ensemble les sorties par eux faictes, avec le nombre des Chefs plus remarquables qui y sont morts de l'ordre qui fut donné pour les blessez le tout fidellement recueilly et mis par ordre de moys à moys et jours par jours* (Lyons, 1573), 6.

[59] Anonymous, *L'exercise militaire fait à présent par les femmes de La Rochelle, avec les ordonnances à ce sujet; ensemble les fortifications qu'elles ont faites, et tout ce qui s'est passé en ladite ville jusqu'à présent* (Paris, 1621). In general, see B.C. Hacker, "Women and Military Institutions in Early Modern Europe," *Signs: Journal of Women in Culture and Society* 6 (1980–1): 27–45; and Megan McLaughlin, "The Woman Warrior: Gender, Warfare and Society in Medieval Europe," *Women's Studies* 17 (1990): 193–209.

perception of urban warfare during the early modern era. Although beholden to longstanding traditions of depicting the city under assault, these ephemeral publications provided authors new ways to confront – in their narratives – the changing nature and context of war and its corresponding impact on the community and its values. The dramatic potential of siege warfare offered them an opportunity to address a diverse audience of readers who together formed that nebulous entity we call public opinion. Yet as cities lost their walls after 1630, so too did this startlingly innovative form of *littérature engagée* lapse into the deceptively intriguing, but more narrowly conceived combative genre epitomized by the *mazarinades* of the Fronde.[60] Thereafter the "city" virtually disappears from print culture as an independent entity and voice in Ancien Régime France; its social, economic, and cultural importance was not correspondingly diminished, however. As urban politics became increasingly subsumed under the complex, negotiated accommodations of the *système louisquatorzien*, so antiquarian interest in the city rose. Intendants' reports from the 1690s commented upon the dilapidated condition of municipal defenses in towns throughout the interior of the country, evincing at times an almost archaeological curiosity in the ruins.[61] Until the Revolution, the vast majority of publications on French cities focuses on the hoary past, not the present. Even the brief recrudescence of municipal liberty during the Revolution did little more than bring down the wrath of the Jacobins and then Napoléon. These were but murmurous reminders of the earlier age of the *bonnes villes*, faint voices soon drowned out once and for all not so much by the "state," but by Haussmann's Paris in the nineteenth century.[62]

This brief excursis into the fortifications of early modern French towns suggests just some of the ways in which the wall's immediate military importance shaped the entire fabric of the urban community. A town's unique identity, as expressed in its physical form from the delineation of urban public space to its relations with the outside world, grew out

---

[60] Marie Noël Grand-Mesnil, *Mazarin, la Fronde et la presse* (Paris, 1967); Hubert Carrier, *La Presse de la Fronde (1648–1653): les mazarinades. La Conquête de l'opinion* (Geneva, 1989); and Christian Jouhaud, *Mazarinades: la Fronde des mots* (Paris, 1985).

[61] André Corvisier, *Les français et l'armée sous Louis XIV d'après les Mémoires des Intendants* (Paris, 1975), 105–30, and Claire Dolan, "L'identité urbaine et les histoires locales publiées du XVIe au XVIIIe siècle en France," *Canadian Journal of History* 27 (1992): 277–98.

[62] Ted Margadant, *Urban Rivalries in the French Revolution* (Princeton, 1987). In general, see Charles Tilly and Wim P. Blockmans, *Cities and the Rise of States in Europe, A.D. 1000–1800* (Boulder, 1994).

of the imposing structures within which townspeople encased their communities from 1350 to 1630. Progressive adaptation of the urban form to ongoing improvements in gunpowder artillery, seen in the spreading use of the bastioned trace after 1560, unfolded within the existing framework of how *bonnes villes* had, since the mid-fourteenth century, planned, financed, constructed, and then defended their ramparts against outside threats. Archival and printed sources clearly show that French towns met the military challenge of the religious wars after 1560 both energetically and creatively, modifying the existing traditions of municipal fortification where necessary. Despite the trend toward a more exclusive urban oligarchy that dominated municipal governments from the fifteenth century onward, the perennial need for self-defense, especially after 1560, offered many opportunities for towns to articulate an equally significant sense of the city as an inclusive community of interests, subject to factions to be sure, but also capable of sustained bursts of public unity transcending class and confession. The image of humble fishermen working side by side with great merchants in repairing and then defending the walls of La Rochelle in 1628 offers a compelling, though by no means unique, case in point. Likewise, spectacular examples of conflict between individual towns and the monarchy stand out as exceptional; throughout this long period, fortified cities and the crown for the most part accommodated each other's interests and needs, though this relationship underwent considerable strain during the Wars of Religion. The *bonnes villes* much preferred strong kings to weak ones, believing that their cherished liberties could only be secure if the monarchy was stable. Municipal fortifications, therefore, never represented a defiance of state authority, but rather a localized expression of it. When the walls began to be torn down or, as more often occurred, were allowed to fall into desuetude after 1630, urban notables fairly quickly recognized the pecuniary and proprietary advantages afforded by converting the vast acreage consumed by "defense-in-depth" into more lucrative uses. As a result, the long-standing image of the fortified *bonne ville* gradually gave way to a new discourse on *la commerce* and the city after 1650, which has continued by and large down to the present.

CHAPTER 12

Portuguese urban fortifications in Morocco: Borrowing, adaptation, and innovation along a military frontier

MARTIN M. ELBL

THE transition from medieval defensive works to the bastioned gunpowder fortifications of the early modern era, spanning roughly the years 1450–1530, represented a crucial transformation in military architecture. Unlike the high towers and vertical curtain walls of the previous era, the new fortifications not only offered a much stouter resistance to siege artillery, but also provided a solid platform for the defenders' guns, thus changing the balance of offensive and defensive forces. Gone was the previous component of vertical defense against scaling or sapping in the form of a curtain of missiles dropped on the enemy from overhanging machicolations or timber hoarding. Systematically devised flanking fire took over as the sole means of protecting the curtain walls, and unlike the old tower, the angle bastion no longer had to assure most of its own short-range defense: Its faces were now effectively enfiladed from gunports in the flanks of adjacent bastions. The aggressively projecting bastion also carried defense forward by opening up as wide a field of fire as possible for the defenders' heavy pieces, to break up or halt the attackers' advance at a safer distance. As a final step, the battle was taken far out toward the enemy by throwing forward a phalanx of geometrically designed and mutually supporting outworks.

The rise of the new design in its Italian heartland and the spread of its earliest mature forms across Europe was a gradual and uneven process. In town walls the use of bastions was hesitant, lagging behind its use in fortresses. Modernizing entire urban enceintes represented a

349

leap of faith and a massive capital investment justified only if the town in question possessed considerable strategic or political value. Adopting the bastioned trace was more easily rationalized in self-contained forts. Not only did their smaller size, compared to an urban enceinte, make the proposition relatively cheaper, but their importance as pivots of defence against external and internal enemies continued to be universally acknowledged. Whether medieval castles or bastioned fortresses bristling with artillery pieces, strongholds remained indispensable elements of the defence grid required to hold a territory.[1]

The introduction of the bastion in Europe was followed very quickly by its adoption along the outer frontiers of European military expansion. Here, however, builders of fortifications faced obstacles seldom encountered back home. Laboring far from support bases, often under constant threat of counterattack, they were beset by problems that ranged from daunting logistics to dearth of skilled labor, inadequate supplies, unsuitable material, and the vagaries of imperial policy. The combination of institutional, material, geopolitical, and accidental constraints that prevailed at any given time and place was a factor that influenced very heavily the rate at which the most advanced designs were adopted. The challenges involved in maintaining and modernizing defenses along an overseas military frontier come into particularly sharp focus if we consider the case of a frontier at a very short distance from the homeland, but exposed to onslaughts by an opponent who begins, at a certain point, to move quickly and decisively up the learning curve in the use of modern weaponry. One such frontier, garrisoned by the Portuguese, stretched along the Atlantic coast of Morocco, from the Straits of Gibraltar south to the edge of the Sahara (Fig. 12.1), and it deserves a closer look for three basic reasons.

First, except for the earliest conquest, that of Ceuta in 1415, the Portuguese occupation of Moroccan coastal sites spans the years 1458–1550, conveniently coinciding with the main sweep of change in European fortification design. The expansion gathered momentum with the taking of Alcácer Ceguer (Qaṣr al-Ṣaghīr) in 1458, which was followed in 1471 by the occupation of Arzilla (Azīla) and Tangier (Ṭanjā). Safi (Asfī) came under Portuguese influence sometime in the

---

[1] See, e.g., Simon Pepper, *Firearms and Fortifications: Military Architecture and Siege Warfare in Sixteenth-Century Siena* (Chicago, 1986); *Architettura militare nell'Europa del XVI secolo: Atti del convegno di studi, Firenze, 25–28 Novembre 1986*, ed. Carlo Cresti (Siena, 1988); Amelio Fara, *Il sistema e la città: Architettura fortificata dell'Europa moderna dai trattati alle realizazzioni, 1464–1794* (Genoa, 1989); Martin Hubert Brice, *Stronghold: A History of Military Architecture* (New York, 1985).

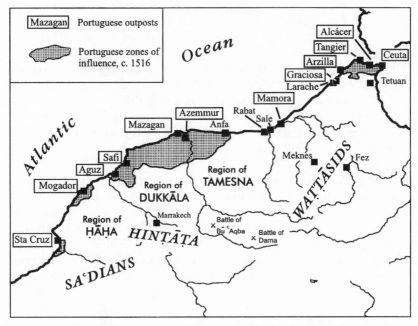

Figure 12.1. Morocco in the early sixteenth century.

late 1470s and its *qāʾids* became vassals of the Portuguese crown. Weakened by internal partisan struggles, it finally fell under direct Portuguese control in 1507–8, after a wave of anti-Portuguese riots.[2] In Azemmur (Wazmūr), a trading post (*feitoria* or factory) was founded in 1486, after the town, threatened by Castilian naval raids, had agreed to accept Portuguese suzerainty and pay a yearly tribute.[3] The town let its ties with Portugal lapse in 1502, renewed them in 1504, withstood an unsuccessful attempt at conquest in 1508, and

---

[2] For the recognition of vassalage in 1488, 1496, and 1500, see J.M. da Silva Marques, ed., *Descobrimentos Portugueses. Documentos para a sua história, 1057–1500*, 4 vols. (Lisbon, 1944–71), III:346–7 (doc. 230), 473 (doc. 310). Concerning the Portuguese takeover, see Arquivo Nacional da Torre do Tombo [henceforth ANTT], Corpo Cronológico [henceforth CC] I–6–69, Diogo de Azambuja to the King, 12 December 1507; Leo Africanus, *Description de l'Afrique*, ed. A. Epaulard, 2 vols. (Paris, 1956), 118–20; J. Goulven, *Safi. Au vieux temps des Portugais* (Lisbon, 1938), 33–5.

[3] García de Resende, *Crónica de Dom João II e Miscelânea*, ed. J. Veríssimo Serrão (Coimbra, 1798; reprinted Lisbon, 1973), Cap. 60; A. Braamcamp Freire, ed., "Cartas de quitação de el-Rei D. Manuel," *Archivo Histórico Português*, IV: 446, doc. 484 (quittance to Martim Reynel, ANTT, *Chancelaria de D. Manuel* [henceforth CDM], Livro 17, fo. 105v).

finally capitulated in 1513.[4] Apart from seizing these six Moroccan towns, the Portuguese built from the ground up six forts intended to double as trading posts. Four of these had only a short lifespan: Graciosa (1489),[5] São João da Mamora (1515),[6] Mogador (Castelo Real; 1506–10),[7] and Aguz (1520/1–25).[8] The two remaining, Santa Cruz do Cabo de Gué (Agadir; founded in 1505–6),[9] and Mazagan (founded in 1514–17),[10] eventually evolved into enduring urban settlements. The Portuguese permanently lost or evacuated most of their Moroccan holdings between 1541 and 1550, keeping only Ceuta, Tangier, and Mazagan. Only Arzilla was briefly reoccupied in the later sixteenth century (1578–89).[11]

Second, Portuguese Morocco offers a good opportunity to observe the transition to gunpowder-age fortifications in the specific environment of a military frontier strung out along a hostile shore and consisting exclusively of seaports and fortresses, whose main lines of communication and supply were maritime ones. The strategic hinterland of these installations, the source of men and military materiel, lay overseas. Their natural local hinterland had shrunk to a thin strip

---

[4] Leo Africanus, *Description*, 125–7; Vergilio Correia, *Lugares d'além: Azemôr, Mazagão, Çafim* (Lisbon, 1923), 34; Vitorino de Magalhães Godinho, *Os descobrimentos e a economia mundial*, 4 vols. (Lisbon, 1987), III:257.

[5] Tomás García Figueras, "Expedición de los portugueses al río de Larache y fundación de la fortaleza 'La Graciosa' en el Lucus (1489)," in *Miscelánea de estudios varios sobre Marruecos* (Tetuan, 1953), 7–33; Weston F. Cook, Jr., *The Hundred Years' War for Morocco. Gunpowder and the Military Revolution in the Early Modern Muslim World* (Boulder, 1994), 117–18.

[6] See construction particulars in ANTT, CC I–18–39, Mestre Duarte to the King, 19 June 1515; Pierre de Cénival, "L'expédition de La Mamora (juin-août 1515)," in *Les sources inédites de l'histoire du Maroc, Ière série – Dynastie Sa'adienne, Archives et bibliothèques du Portugal*, eds. Pierre de Cénival, D. Lopes, and R. Ricard (Paris, 1934–), I:695–702 [further as *Sources, Port.*]; Cook, *Hundred Years' War*, 148–9.

[7] Goulven, *Safi*, 30; David Lopes, *A expansão em Marrocos* (Lisbon, 1989), 29; Cook, *Hundred Years' War*, 144–5.

[8] Damião de Góis, *Crónica do felicissimo Rei D. Manuel*, eds. J.M. Teixeira de Carvalho and D. Lopes, 4 vols. (Coimbra, 1949–55), Parte III, Caps. 12, 14, 32, 35, 47, 49; Parte IV, Caps. 44, 59, 85; *Sources, Port.*, I:171–3, 223, 246, 252, 280; Lopes, *A expansão*, 29.

[9] Joaquim Figanier, *História de Santa Cruz do Cabo de Gué (Agadir), 1505–1541* (Lisbon, 1945), 30–1; Lopes, *A expansão*.

[10] ANTT, CC I–15–14, 30–1 March 1514; Correia, *Lugares*, 57. Portuguese crown factors periodically traded at Mazagan throughout the early years of the century (e.g., A. Baião, ed., *Documentos do Corpo Cronológico relativos a Marrocos, 1488–1514* [Coimbra, 1925], 11–2 [ANTT, CC I–3–123, 6 December 1502]).

[11] Safi was evacuated in October 1541; Azemmur, also abandoned in October 1541, was briefly reoccupied and finally abandoned in 1549; Santa Cruz was lost to the Muslims on 12 March 1541. *Sources, Port.*, III:ix–x. The evacuation of Arzilla proceeded in stages: the first was completed by the end of August 1549, the final one on 24 August 1550. Alcácer was abandoned in June 1550. R. Ricard, *Etudes sur l'histoire des Portugais au Maroc* (Coimbra, 1955), 374–5.

of territory patrolled by long-range scouting parties. Beyond this lay a gray zone, access to which depended on shifting alliances with the region's tribes or with local Muslim power-holders, and on the assertiveness of rulers and groups aspiring to control the interior and reclaim the occupied coastal areas. Underneath a façade of belief in the permanency of Portuguese presence in Morocco, the thinking of those who maintained and improved the fortifications was necessarily dominated by short-term tactical concerns. The solutions they devised were further constrained by bureaucratic rigidity, compounded in the sixteenth century by competition for resources between the various parts of the far-flung Portuguese empire. Moreover, the necessity to defend occupied urban centers from the very first moment against counterattack made it difficult to dispense with or extensively redesign the existing Muslim defenses. The result was a peculiar juxtaposition of Islamic, Portuguese, and ultimately Italianate military architecture, ranging from somewhat archaic medieval works, through transitional-style fortifications showing various traces of gunpowder-age concepts, to mature angle bastion fortifications in the Italian fashion.

Third, despite the changes wrought by decay and rebuilding, enough survives of the various original structures to make coastal Morocco a valuable repository of Portuguese transitional-period military architecture. A complete urban time capsule even exists at Alcácer which, unlike the other sites of Portuguese Morocco, remained a ghost town after its evacuation in June 1550. In the case of the site worst affected by the passage of time and men, Tangier, relatively detailed sketches and engravings of the old Muslim and Portuguese fortifications were made before their demolition by the British in 1683–4.[12] Some sections of the defenses, moreover, proved too stout to be brought down completely, and may still be studied at Tangier today. This architectural evidence remains to be fully exploited and confronted with both published and as yet unused archival sources.

The existing literature on the Portuguese outposts in Morocco offers neither detailed descriptions of the defenses, nor coherent comparative analyses of their development.[13] The archaeology of the fortifica-

---

[12] E.M.G. Routh, *Tangier. England's Lost Atlantic Outpost, 1661–1684* (London, 1912), 262–5.

[13] Correia, *Lugares*; Figanier, *Santa Cruz*; Goulven, *Safi*; Adolfo L. Guevara, *Arcila durante la ocupación portuguesa* (Tangiers, 1940); David Lopes, *História de Arzila durante o dominio Português* (Coimbra, 1924–5); J. Goulven, *La place de Mazagan sous la domination portugaise (1502–1769)* (Paris, 1917); António Dias Farinha, *História de Mazagão durante o período Filipino* (Lisbon, 1970); Robert Rézette, *Les enclaves espagnoles au Maroc* (Paris, 1976).

tions has been sorely neglected. Systematic excavations have been carried out only at Alcácer, and the publication of the results unfortunately stopped short of closely correlating archaeological and archival data.[14] Despite recent advances,[15] we are still far from a balanced understanding of the Portuguese military frontier in Morocco and of its role in the broader history of the Portuguese overseas empire. The purpose of this study is not to undertake the daunting task of filling the gaps, but to present a bird's-eye view of the evidence and outline a general chronological framework capturing the main trends.

The development of the Portuguese fortifications in Morocco may be usefully divided into four phases. The first one – Phase A – is an operational stage (in military terms) without fixed chronological frame. Representing the early period of occupation, it necessarily varies in starting point and duration from one town or fort to another. In the more southerly localities, it partly overlaps with the subsequent period (Phase B). Nonetheless, this initial phase embodies a distinctive bundle of choices and constraints that deserve to be singled out. It provides a baseline in terms of immediate, pragmatic solutions, and of the relative speed with which the Portuguese were able to begin overcoming the most dangerous weaknesses of the inherited Muslim infrastructure, or of the terrain chosen for new construction. No matter how awkward, the temporary expedients adopted during the early months and years of Portuguese presence created a self-justifying framework in terms of how defensive elements were arrayed across the terrain, and how much land was actively defended.

In urban centers, the first phase was marked by urgent necessity to secure the conquered area, organize defense, and repair existing Muslim fortifications. More extensive changes were attempted only once initial hostilities had subsided: thus at Alcácer and Azemmur, new construction was in progress within a year of the Portuguese conquest, and at Safi within two years.[16] Substantial refurbishing and strengthening of the defenses followed later still. In Arzilla and Tangier, it

---

[14] Charles L. Redman, *Qsar es-Seghir. An Archaeological View of Medieval Life* (New York, 1986). This failure of archaeology and history to work hand in hand when it comes to medieval, and especially late medieval Islamic sites, is a perennial source of frustration. See R. Stephen Humphreys, *Islamic History. A Framework for Inquiry* (Princeton, 1991), 59–63.

[15] Above all Cook, *Hundred Years' War*, a valuable study of the Moroccan assimilation of gunpowder technology and a perceptive analysis of the military aspects of Portuguese involvement in North Africa. Cook, however, offers very little regarding fortifications.

[16] For Alcácer, see Rui de Pina, *Crónica do Rei D. Duarte*, ed. António Borges Coelho (Lisbon, 1966), Cap. 34; for Azemmur, ANTT, CC I–14–30, Nuno Gato to the King, 18 December 1513; for Safi, Correia, *Lugares*, 80–3.

seems to have gathered momentum only under D. João II (1481–95) and in the very first years of the reign of D. Manuel I (1495–1521), more than fifteen years after the towns had been seized by the Portuguese. In the case of the six brand new forts, Phase A represented either (a) the building of an initial stone castle, generally of a simple and archaic design, as in the case of the first fort of Mazagan (Mazagan I),[17] or (b) the building of a wooden fort from prefabricated sections brought on board expeditionary vessels, followed later on by a transition to a more solid stone structure.[18] Time, resources, size of the expeditionary force, and degree of expected local resistance dictated the choice of one or the other alternative.

Phase B covered roughly the decade 1508–18 and witnessed the first great wave of concerted surveying, repairs, and new construction at all the Portuguese sites. This coincided with a determined military expansion, a surge of economic activity in the colonies, and a bout of civilian building. As the renewed Portuguese expansion ran into stubborn Moroccan resistance, it quickly became clear that existing fortifications, whether previously held or newly seized, would have to be brought more closely in line with the new standards required by gunpowder warfare. The most serious threat to the Portuguese outposts was the increasingly numerous and efficacious artillery of the Waṭṭāsid sultan of Fez, Muḥammad al-Burtuqālī (1504–26). The Hintāta rulers of Marrakech and the Saʿdian Sharīfs in the extreme south lagged behind the Waṭṭāsids in the acquisition of firearms and remained seriously handicapped in tactical terms, but as early as 1510 the Portuguese crown was greatly concerned about the smuggling of powder and metals into southern Morocco by French, Castilian, and Genoese interlopers.[19] Throughout Portuguese Morocco, skilled *mestres das obras*, stonemason-architects, now grafted new elements in the style typical of the reign of D. Manuel onto both existing Muslim city walls and the first set of fifteenth-century Portuguese additions erected in the northern localities.

The third stage, Phase C, spanned the 1520s and 1530s and repre-

---

[17] See page 376, this chapter.
[18] One of these prefabricated wooden fortifications was the first fort of Santa Cruz do Cabo de Gué, erected in 1505–6 by João Lopes de Sequeira. Figanier, *Santa Cruz*, 29; *Sources, Port.*, III:xi–xii.
[19] For the general context, see Cook, *Hundred Years' War*, 138–56. On the smuggling of weapons, *Hundred Years' War*, 170–1; Andrew Hess, *The Forgotten Frontier. A History of the Sixteenth-Century Ibero-African Frontier* (Chicago, 1978), 53; *Sources, Port.*, I:256–8. The heightened economic activity and resurgent civilian construction, which cannot be extensively discussed or documented here, because of the sheer abundance of archival sources, has also been remarked upon by Redman, *Qsar*, 176.

sented a decisive, fatal period of hesitation and inaction that in the end sealed the fate of Portuguese Morocco. The slugging match of the preceding decade had eroded the commitment of the Portuguese crown and estates to an aggressive policy in North Africa, despite the fact that the rapid assimilation of gunpowder battle tactics by the Sa'dians from the early 1520s onward, in emulation of the Waṭṭāsids, worried policymakers. Castile and Portugal alike were haunted by the possibility of an alliance between Morocco and the Ottoman Turks, especially after the fall of Algiers to the corsairs of Khayr-ed-Dīn Barbarossa in 1529.[20] In 1526–9, the Portuguese crown even began to retain the services of Italian or Italian-trained architects with a view to improving some of the Moroccan fortifications. Yet things never progressed beyond the planning stage. The problem was to decide where to concentrate the modernizing effort, given that Portugal's role in Morocco was an object of disagreement at court, and that D. João III (1521–57) increasingly favored retrenchment. As political waffling stalled construction projects, the Manueline military infrastructure was allowed to fall into disrepair.

It was at this point, from ca. 1530 onward, that the Sa'dians resumed attacks against the Portuguese in the south, all the while still battling the Waṭṭāsids in the north. The previous ten years had brought significant changes in the Sa'dian manner of waging war, and in 1534 their forces laid siege to Safi using a sizable artillery train, a modern system of trenches, dug-in gun emplacements, and earthwork redoubts.[21] By 1536, government firearms workshops in Sa'dian territory were catching up with those owned by the Waṭṭāsids, and gun shops flourished in Marrakech. Scarce materials, parts, and expertise were supplied by merchants and artisans from Spain, France, and even Portugal by expatriate Iberian *morisco* and *marrano* craftsmen, and by Christian slaves and prisoners. When Santa Cruz do Cabo de Gué fell to the Sa'dians in 1541, the victory was largely due to their artillery, and João III of Portugal was forced to acknowledge reluctantly that in terms of armaments Sa'dian forces no longer lagged behind what the Portuguese could field against them.[22]

The loss of Santa Cruz and a mutiny at Azemmur, reduced to

---

[20] Despite incessant rumors of an Ottoman-Waṭṭāsid alliance, a tentative agreement did not materialize until 1532. Cook, *Hundred Years' War*, 180; Svat Soucek, "The Rise of the Barbarossas in North Africa," *Archivum Ottomanicum* 3 (1971): 238–50.

[21] Francisco de Andrade, *Crónica de D. João III*, trans. R. Ricard, "Les Portugais et l'Afrique du Nord sous le règne de Jean III (1521–1557), d'après la Chronique de Francisco de Andrade," *Hespéris* 24 (1937), 259–345; and *Sources, Port.*, II:608–29.

[22] Cook, *Hundred Years' War*, 193, 197; *Sources, Port.*, III:356–62, João III to Cristovão de Sousa, April 1541.

desperate straits although it had successfully repelled a Saʿdian attack that same year (1541), ushered in Phase D.[23] Only this phase, somewhat ironically, brought to Portuguese Morocco the innovative and by now essentially mature Italian angle bastion design. The innovations were applied, however, only to the three outposts the Portuguese crown decided to keep. The entire military frontier was crumbling. The fall of Santa Cruz sealed the fate of Safi and Azemmur, evacuated shortly thereafter. The fratricidal war between the two Saʿdian brothers, Aḥmad al-ʾAʿraj and Muḥammad al-Shaykh, in 1541–4, gave the Portuguese some respite, but with Muḥammad emerging as the winner the worst-case scenario feared in Lisbon, a Morocco united under one ruler, came one step closer to reality. The decisive defeat of the Waṭṭāsid sultan Abū ʾl-ʿAbbās by the forces of Muḥammad al-Shaykh at the Battle of Darna in 1545 and the Saʿdian conquest of Fez in the winter of 1548–9 prompted an accelerated evacuation of Arzilla and Alcácer.[24] The advanced fortification features made indispensable by the pervasive dissemination of gunpowder technology throughout Morocco, a process that had taken barely fifty years, were implanted mainly at Mazagan and Ceuta, and to a lesser extent at Tangier.

Let us now return in some detail to the beginnings of Portuguese presence in Morocco, to the first phase most heavily marked by the reuse of Muslim fortifications. In the form in which the Portuguese found them, the Muslim urban defenses mostly dated back to the twelfth through fourteenth centuries.[25] They consisted of vertical curtain walls with square or round defensive towers placed at regular intervals. The towers were either open-backed or comprised an upper and lower domed chamber. The elaborate town gates were mostly of the double bent-axis type, with flanking rectangular towers that were frequently solid to the parapet level. One of the inner chambers of the bent-axis gateway usually remained open to the sky and was surrounded by a parapet that allowed missiles to be hurled down at attackers.[26] The larger cities generally possessed a complex array of

[23] Cook, *Hundred Years' War*, 194–9; Luís de Sousa, *Anães do Rei D. João III*, trans. R. Ricard, *Les Portugais et l'Afrique du Nord de 1521 à 1557* (Rabat, 1940), 152–60; and Ricard, "L'évacuation des places portugaises du Maroc sous Jean III," in *Etudes*, 357–81.

[24] Cook, *Hundred Years' War*, 199–211; Hess, *Forgotten Frontier*, 53–5; Lopes, *A expansão*, 74–5.

[25] J. Vallvé Bermejo, "Descripción de Ceuta musulmana en el siglo XV," *al-Andalus* 27 (1962): 396–442; A.M. Turki, "La physionomie monumentale de Ceuta: un hommage nostalgique à la ville par un de ses fils, Muḥammad b. al-Qāsim al-Anṣārī (traduction annotée de son Ikhtiṣār al-akhbār)," *Hespéris-Tamuda* 20–1 (1982–3): 113–63; Redman, *Qsar*, 49–57.

[26] Redman, *Qsar*, 49–57.

defenses, incorporating a fortress (*qaṣba*) placed either so as to dominate the highest point of the city (Tangier, Ceuta, Safi), or to defend
the port (Arzilla). The residential palace (*qaṣr*) might, however, also
function as a link in the chain of defenses (e.g., the Alcázar of Ceuta).[27]

As a rule, the Portuguese parsimoniously reused whatever was in
good shape or could be salvaged. Only excessively fragile tapia (pisé)
walls found in the more southerly localities, for instance throughout
the *qaṣba* of Safi, were replaced as soon as possible with dressed stone
and rubble.[28] No attempt was made to rebuild from the ground up
compact Muslim fortifications of solid brick, heavily mortared stone
and rubble, or coursed rubble masonry with leveling brick- or stonework. The only major problem was the quality of local mortar. Muslim
builders often heavily plastered or stuccoed their masonry, not only
for decorative purposes, but also, according to Portuguese military
engineers, to seal mortar in the joints. The Portuguese usually found
it necessary to repoint and repair heavily decayed segments of walls.[29]

Several factors account for the extensive reuse of Muslim structures.
First, in the immediate aftermath of the Portuguese conquest there
was hardly any time, or resources, for more than hasty small-scale
changes designed to confuse the enemy and make the perimeter defensible with a reduced number of men, such as walling-in sally ports
and secondary gateways, or opening new sally-ports in unexpected
places.[30] Second, even had money been available, repeated enemy
raids and constant fear of siege did not leave much latitude for extensive rebuilding, and there often was considerable uncertainty about
how long political commitment to holding the places would last.
Third, the main wall trace had to continue answering the defensive
needs of established urban agglomerations. A drastic reshaping was
seldom an option. Most of the Muslim population having fled, all

---

[27] Ceuta, with its unusual topography, had both a *qaṣba*, located on top of the Almina
hill that dominates the tip of the elongated peninsula, and a *qaṣr* at the root of the
peninsula, where it could both control access from the mainland and protect the port.
Work on the *qaṣba* started in the late tenth century, and continued under the Almoravids. Vallvé Bermejo, "Ceuta musulmana," 432.

[28] Tapia walls were made of mud, packed and rammed between forms in successive
layers. Paradoxically, when it came to resisting the fire of light field artillery, tapia
was somewhat more effective than stone and rubble. The projectiles simply embedded themselves in the walls, instead of shattering them. Cook, *Hundred Years' War*,
204. Decayed tapia, however, offered little real protection.

[29] Baião, *Corpo*, 75–8 (ANTT, CC I–15–14, Francisco and Diogo de Arruda and Vasco da
Pina to the King, 30–1 March 1514).

[30] At Alcácer, the small gate of Bāb al-Fās was walled in sometime early during the
Portuguese occupation, and a sally port was knocked through the city wall in the lee
of the gate. This was in turn sealed later on. See Redman, *Qsar*, 57–8.

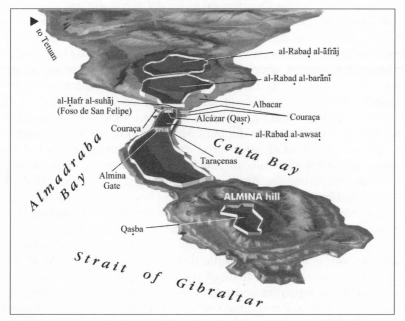

Figure 12.2. Perspective model of Muslim and Portuguese Ceuta, fifteenth–sixteenth centuries.

choices were in principle open, without any messy problems involving compensation to property owners. The crown, however, viewed the empty towns as valuable assets, hoping that they would quickly fill up with Portuguese merchants, settlers, and exiled convicts (*degredados*) so as to ensure the economic and military viability of each colony. The prospect of abandoning any section of the main built-up area usually gave rise to acrimonious debates.[31]

The Portuguese were nonetheless in no position to waste resources on the defense of outlying suburbs that represented the furthest extension of urban settlement before the plague epidemics of the fourteenth century and the internal troubles that afflicted fifteenth-century Morocco. A particularly dramatic retrenchment occurred at Ceuta. In the immediate aftermath of the 1415 conquest, the Portuguese decided not to occupy the mainland suburbs of al-Rabaḍ al-āfrāj (also known as al-Manṣūra, or as Ceuta la Vieja) and al-Rabaḍ al-barrānī (Fig. 12.2). The latter, located at the very root of the Ceuta peninsula, closer to the

---

[31] As at Azemmur, for instance; see footnote 36 below.

city core (the Middle Quarter, or al-Rabaḍ al-awsaṭ), became a no-man's-land completely cleared of its gardens and villas in order to deny cover to the enemy.[32] The city thus retreated seaward to the broad ditch of the Muslim Ḥafr al-Suhāj (the later Foso de San Felipe), filled with sea water, which had served to separate the peninsula from the mainland already in the eleventh century.[33] The decision was made easier by the fact that although the five gate towers of the Rabaḍ al-barrānī were still standing, the walls had been pulled down long ago, in 1328–9, when the Marīnid sultan Abū Saʿīd ordered the building of the palace suburb of al-Āfrāj.[34] The Portuguese however, did not de-molish the decaying walls of al-Āfrāj and their prominent fortified gateway complexes: the Arzilla Gate, and the great Fez Gate (Bāb al-Fās), added by the Marīnid sultan Abū 'l-Ḥasan. The suburb periodi-cally served Muslim forces and tribal raiders as a convenient base from which to harass the Portuguese garrison.[35]

At Azemmur, the small size of the first garrison, the small number of those who volunteered to settle there initially, and the dilapidated state of the *madīna* walls, made of tapia, left only one alternative – to concentrate on repairing and improving the *qaṣba*, which became the nucleus of the new Portuguese settlement. There were too few houses inside the old *qaṣba* to hold the garrison, prompting a decision to enclose part of the *madīna* within the new improved walls, but the Portuguese commanders nonetheless sought to limit the size of the settlement in order to make the perimeter more defensible. The ruin-ous state of many houses, neglected by their previous owners as they

---

[32] Gomes Eanes de Zurara, *Chronica do Conde Dom Pedro de Menezes* (Lisbon, 1792), Part I, Cap. 16, 260; Carlos Posac Mon, *La última decada lusitana de Ceuta* (Ceuta, 1967), 24.

[33] Abū ʿUbayd ʿAbd Allāh b. ʿAbd al-Azīz al-Bakrī (d. 1094), *Description de l'Afrique septentrionale*, ed. and trans. MacGuckin de Slane (Algiers, 1911–13), 103–4.

[34] E. Lévi-Provençal, "Un nouveau texte d'histoire mérinide," *Hespéris* 5 (1925): 63; Walī al-Dīn ʿAbd al-Raḥmān Abū Zayd Ibn Khaldūn (1332–1406), *Histoire des Berbères et des dynasties musulmanes de l'Afrique septentrionale*, trans. P. Casanova, 4 vols. (Paris, 1925–56), IV:201; Vallvé Bermejo, "Ceuta musulmana," 429. The gate towers are reasonably well shown in the vista included in Georg Braun and Frans Hogenberg, *Civitates orbis terrarum* (Cologne, 1572).

[35] The two key gates of the Rabaḍ al-āfrāj were known to the Portuguese in the fifteenth century as the Torre de Fez and the Porta de Alvaro Mendes. Fernão Lopes, *Chronica de el-Rei D. João I*, Vol. III (Lisbon, 1900), Cap. 85, 60–1. The Marīnid palace complex in the Rabaḍ was originally given in apanage to the count of Barcelos, natural son of João I of Portugal, on 20 September 1415, but was left abandoned and by 1458–63 lay almost completely in ruins. See Ricard, *Etudes*, 18–19. The dilapidated suburb wall still existed in the times of Jerónimo Mascarenhas (1630s and 1640s); see D. Jerónimo Mascarenhas, *História de la ciudad de Ceuta*, ed. A. de Dornelas (Lisbon and Coimbra, 1918), Cap. 3, 12. For a reference to the eighteenth-century *Plano no. 4735, hoja 18* of the S.G.M. in Madrid, which still shows the position of the old walls, see Vallvé Bermejo, "Ceuta musulmana," 431 n. 99.

gradually lost faith that the town would remain in Muslim hands, favored such retrenchment.[36] Ceuta and Azemmur were exceptions, however. At Alcácer, the Portuguese took over the entire, relatively small, circular fortified enclosure (150 meters in diameter). At Tangier, the suburbs had been abandoned long before the Portuguese conquest of 1471. A zone of gardens and villas west of the Upper Castle (*qaṣba*), toward Cape Spartel, had stood uninhabited since the mid-fourteenth century at the latest, and the settlement of Ṭanjā al-Bālī (Old Tangier), on the eastern side of the Bay of Tangier, was empty by 1436–7.[37] At Arzilla, the Portuguese settled both the walled town (*madīna*) and the *qaṣba*.[38] Safi, enclosed within a belt of walls stiffened by seventy-five towers, was likewise taken over in its entirety, from the sea front to the *qaṣba* on the high ground above the city.[39]

The first Portuguese additions to existing defensive works undertaken during the initial phase of occupation reflected mainly changes in the strategic position of the conquered towns. First, it was necessary to strengthen the landward defenses. At Ceuta, this was achieved merely by pulling the frontline back to the Ḥafr al-Suhāj, defended by an old curtain wall with nine towers and by the Muslim Qaṣr (Alcázar).[40] At Tangier, the monumental Muslim western gateway that became the St. Catherine Gate (Fig. 12.3) was strengthened by adding an enclosed outer ward and a barbican,[41] and at Alcácer the entire landward enceinte was reinforced by walling in the small Fez Gate, and adding three bastions to provide artillery platforms (Fig. 12.4).[42] The *qaṣba* of Tangier, which had easily withstood the Portuguese in 1436–7, probably needed only some repair work, but it is almost impossible to assess the changes that this area of the town may have undergone. The documents are silent, and the medieval *qaṣba* was later completely overlaid by the massive angle-bastion fort that the English sappers blew up when evacuating Tangier in the seventeenth century. At Safi,

---

[36] Baião, *Corpo*, 57–9 (ANTT, CC I–13–62, Duke of Bragança to the King, 30 September 1513), 61–2 (ANTT, CC I–14–4, D. João de Menezes to the King, 1 December 1513), 75–8 (ANTT, CC I–15–14, Francisco and Diogo de Arruda and Vasco da Pina to the King, 30–1 March 1514); ANTT, CC I–14–30, Nuno Gato to the King, 18 December 1513; Leo Africanus, *Description*, 125–7.

[37] Rui de Pina, *D. Duarte*, Cap. 24, 139.

[38] Rui de Pina, *Chronica d'El-Rei D. Affonso V*, Vol. III (Lisbon, 1903), Cap. 165, 61–4.

[39] ANTT, Gavetas, 20–4–65.

[40] For the old Islamic fortifications of the Ḥafr al-Suhāj, see Vallvé Bermejo, "Ceuta musulmana," 429.

[41] The gate is shown in some detail by Hollar in "View from Peterburgh [*sic*] Tower" and in "The Lower Part of Tangier from the Hill West of Whitehall," in Routh, *Tangier*, ills. facing 146 and 299.

[42] Redman, *Qsar*, 144.

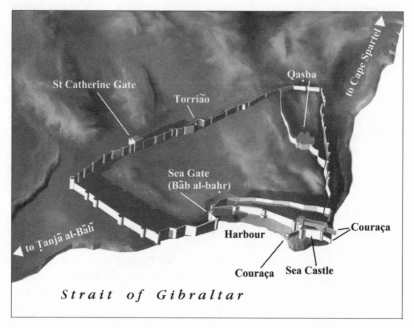

Figure 12.3. Perspective model of the fortifications of Tangier, fifteenth–early sixteenth centuries.

however, the dilapidated tapia-walled *qaṣba* was transformed into a strong Manueline bastioned fortress.[43]

Second, it was vital to keep open access to the sea, the lifeline of the Portuguese settlements. While at Ceuta the castle at the Ḥafr al-Suhāj doubled as both a landward bulwark and a stronghold dominating the anchorage, at Tangier and at Safi the latter role fell to a separate "sea castle" (*castelo do mar*). Although a Muslim fortification may have preceded the medieval Sea Castle (*Castelo do Mar*) of Tangier, located on a spur of high ground above the port from where projectiles could reach ships riding at anchor below, the castle documented in the English engravings of the seventeenth century dated to the reign of D. João II (Fig. 12.3).[44] The castle's inner ward was an irregular elongated pentagon enclosed by high curtain walls. Four of the corner towers were round, and the fifth was a high, square, battlemented and barti-

---

[43] See page 370, this chapter.

[44] The documentation is sparse, but a legend in Braun and Hogenberg's *Civitates orbis terrarum* identifies the castle and the adjoining works as *"arx ædificata a D. Johane Lusitanie regis, eius nominis II."*

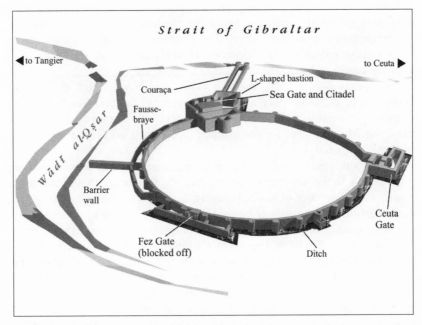

Figure 12.4. Perspective model of the fortifications of Alcácer Ceguer, fifteenth
–sixteenth centuries. Based on Charles L. Redman, *Qsar es-Seghir. An Archaeological View of Medieval Life* (Academic Press, 1986), 144, Fig. 5.2, and other
evidence.

zaned donjon. A *fausse-braye* ran along the outer foot of the curtain,
and beyond it, on the landward side, lay an L-shaped, sunken outer
ward defended by another curtain wall with corner towers. A gate
tower in this outer curtain guarded access to a wooden bridge, probably with a lifting section, which led to the inner bailey.[45] Smaller and
less complex, the Sea Castle of Safi (known, like that of Tangier, as
Castelo do Mar), built only in 1515–17, was conceived in the same style.
The rectangular bailey was surrounded by a curtain wall with one

---

[45] The castle is shown from all sides in the following engravings by Hollar: "The South-
East Corner of Tangier," "Tangier from the East," "The Town, with York Castle, from
the South-East," "York Castle from the North-West," and "The West Side of York
Castle," in Routh, *Tangier*, ills. facing 54, 114, 280, 294, 346. The somewhat less
accurate plan of Tangier by John Seller (1675), reproduced in *Early Maps*, ed. Tony
Campbell (New York, 1981), 114–15, presents a bird's-eye view of the structure. A
bartizan is a small projecting turretlike attachment, often affixed to the top four
corners of a tower. A *fausse-braye* is a low wall parallel to the main curtain and some
distance to the front; it constituted a first line of defense.

square and two round corner towers, a square donjon occupied the middle of one of the curtains, and a fourth detached tower was linked to the castle by a masonry arch. The positioning of the gateway, in a corner dominated by the donjon, is reminiscent of the fifteenth-century castle of Fuensaldaño in Spain.[46] At Alcácer the Muslim double bent-axis Bāb al-baḥr, the Sea Gate, was blocked up and transformed into a citadel playing the same role as the Sea Castle of Safi, namely commanding the town's vital beach.[47] At Arzilla and at Azemmur, the Muslim *qaṣba*s were already positioned so as to function as natural "sea castles."

The other typical and enduring element expressing preoccupation with access to the seashore was the *couraça*. Generally this was a long straight wall or pair of walls running from a tower or bastion in the main fortification to a river bank, the edge of the beach, or even well into the coastal shallows. Another tower or bastion stood at its further end, and at least part of the *couraça*'s length might be roofed over. It gave the defenders sheltered access to the waterfront, blocked the approach to the seaside or riverside walls, and integrated natural obstacles such as a beach or a river more closely into the defensive perimeter, creating a virtual outer bailey at low cost. Several *couraças* were sometimes combined to enhance the defensive potential by partitioning such a natural outer bailey into sectors.[48]

The *couraça* had a long line of venerable ancestors. These included the long screen wall between the lower bailey gate of the Byzantine castle of Anadoli Kavak (Heiron castle) and a customs post on the shore of the Bosphorus, dating to about the middle of the twelfth century; the screen walls jutting out across the outer bailey at Harlech Castle, Merioneth, built in 1285–90, or at the Castello della Rocca in Cesena (Italy; 1380); the two thirteenth-century screen walls at Conway, each with a tower at its further extremity; and the medieval Portuguese *couraças* at Montemôr-o-Velho, Coimbra, Caminha, Silves (where a Muslim *couraça* existed already in 1189), Melgaço, Monção,

---

[46] See plan and illustrations in Goulven, *Safi*. The beginning of the castle's construction is documented in ANTT, CC I–17–61, Alvaro de Athaíde to the King, 25 January 1515. Athaíde specifically assigns the castle the role of protecting the anchorage. On Fuensaldaño, see Sidney Toy, *A History of Fortification from 3000 B.C. to A.D. 1700* (London, 1955), 226.

[47] Redman, *Qsar*, 146.

[48] At Alcácer, the long double *couraça* linking the town to the sea, and a barrier wall jutting from the enceinte in the direction of the river, partitioned the space around the town into three defensive sectors. The importance of the barrier wall running towards the river is stressed in ANTT, Núcleo Antigo [henceforth NA] 769, "Livro da medição das obras de Alcácere, Ceuta, Tángere e Arzilla, 1514."

Mértola, and Spanish ones at Badajoz, Toledo, Burgos, Escalona, Simancas, and elsewhere. The *couraça* at Montemôr, consisting of two parallel walls terminating in twin towers or *albarrãs*, prefigured the double *couraça* of Alcácer. *Couraças* or *corachas* were also a feature of many Andalusian fortifications, as well as those of Muslim Granada and Málaga.[49] Some of these earlier screen walls served the same role as those built in Morocco, while others covered the access to a well or spring outside the main enceinte.

The Muslim defenses that the Portuguese took over already incorporated *couraças*.[50] At Ceuta, several *couraças* predating the Portuguese occupation are documented in 1415–19: the *couraça* "of Ruy Mendes," another *couraça* near the *Taraçenas* (the naval arsenal), and the *couraça* that ran in the direction of Barbaçote (on the Almadraba Bay [Baḥr Abū 'l-Sūl] side, towards Tetuan), which still existed in 1648. The latter had a mate jutting out as a mirror image towards Ceuta Bay and later called the *Couraça Alta* or the *espigão del Albacar*. It is clearly shown in the classic vista of Ceuta in the 1572 edition of Braun and Hogenberg's *Civitates Orbis Terrarum*. The *couraça* of the *Taraçenas* was most probably located on the Ceuta Bay side, at the northwestern corner of the town's Middle Quarter, somewhere in the area of the modern-day Muelle de los Pescadores.[51] At Tangier, there was in 1437 a Muslim *couraça* attached to the northwestern wall of the town, which doubled as a jetty and a tactical screen that sheltered the access to the open beach and prevented the enemy from effecting an easy lodgment under the sea wall.[52]

The new Portuguese *couraças* included the one at Alcácer, built in its initial form the year after the Portuguese conquest, between late March and late June 1459. It ran from the Islamic gate complex of the Bāb al-baḥr or Sea Gate (the *Porta da Ribeira*) across the strand to the sea, and when completely finished consisted of two parallel screen walls 110 meters long, and a ditch that brought water to the moat that surrounded three quarters of the town wall (Fig. 12.4).[53] At Tangier, a

---

[49] For plans and illustrations of Anadoli Kavak, Conway (indicating the emplacement of now destroyed or partially obliterated elements), and Harlech Castle, see Toy, *History of Fortification*, 90, 168, 179. The Iberian *couraças* are discussed in Ricard, "Couraça et coracha," *Etudes*, 465–92. A new *couraça* was also being built at Viana da Foz de Lima in 1410–40. Silva Marques, *Descobrimentos* I: 402–3, doc. 317.

[50] *Couraças* also existed in Muslim-held Larache in 1416 or 1417, at Tīt near Mazagan, and probably at Rabat-Salé. See Ricard, *Etudes*, 487–9.

[51] *Sources, Port.*, IV: 295; Mascarenhas, *Historia de Ceuta*, Cap. 4, 15; see also "Uma planta de Ceuta" (seventeenth century), published by A. Dornelas in *História e genealogia*, Vol. I (Lisbon, 1913), 11–21; Ricard, *Etudes*, 479–81.

[52] Rui de Pina, *D. Duarte*, Cap. 34.

[53] Rui de Pina, *D. Affonso V*, Caps. 141 and 142; Gomes Eanes de Zurara, *Crónica do*

stubby but imposing *couraça* extended down the steep slope between the waterfront and the keep (*Torre de Menajem*) of the Sea Castle, and its twin long walls ended in a great, stout round tower. It remained a prominent feature of Tangier's harbor vista until the seventeenth century.[54] Two other *couraças* of unknown date stretched down to the strand from the Sea Castle's two northern towers. One of them figures prominently in the *Civitates Orbis Terrarum* view of Tangier, and we still find it included in John Seller's plan of Tangier published in 1675, although by that time little remained of it. Wenceslaus Hollar's 1669 close-up view of the Sea Castle from the northwest clearly depicts the ruined stumps of both *couraças*.[55] At Arzilla, a new *couraça* was built between 1508 and 1512. It extended into the sea from the bastion called the *Baluarte da Couraça*, located at the western extremity of the town, and barred the approach to the seafront.[56]

By the late 1470s, the growing importance of offensive artillery fire directed against the enemy from a fortification, already clearly acknowledged, for instance, during the two sieges of Alcácer by Moroccan forces in 1458–9,[57] prompted further improvements in the Portuguese defenses. Most of these works are poorly documented and were carried out possibly under D. João II, or in the early years of D. Manuel. Although Joanine construction efforts tapered off in the last years of the reign, by the later 1490s the peace that had prevailed along the military frontier in northern Morocco since 1489–90 was failing. As early as 1495, the Moroccan outposts began to receive generous reinforcements in men, ammunition, and weapons, while captains and soldiers saw their pay and allowances increase. There followed a series of quick strikes at Portuguese targets by the Waṭṭāsid sultan Muḥammad al-Shaykh in 1501, 1502, and 1504.[58] Simultane-

---

Conde D. Duarte de Meneses (Lisbon, 1978), Caps. 70 and 82; ANTT, NA 769; Ricard, *Etudes*, 482; Redman, *Qsar*, 145.

[54] Probably built under D. João II (1481–95), it is shown in the following Hollar engravings: "The South-East Corner of Tangier," "Tangier from the East," and "The Town, with York Castle, from the South-East," in Routh, *Tangier*, ills. facing 280, 294, 544. There are some indications that the upward passage between the long walls was barred at regular intervals by transversal walls equipped with gates, according to the medieval principle of providing multiple lines of defense along a path of retreat to the main keep. The only plan that shows the transversal walls is a schematic English engraving of "The Little Mole, Wharf, and the Customs House (of Tangier)," dated December 1675, in Routh, *Tangier*, ill. facing 354.

[55] Seller, "Plan of Tangier," in *Early Maps*, 114–15; Wenceslaus Hollar, "York Castle from the North-West," in Routh, *Tangier*, ill. facing 346.

[56] Ricard, *Etudes*, 484.

[57] Zurara, *Duarte de Meneses*, Caps. 41 to 60, and 74 to 85; Rui de Pina, *D. Affonso V*, Vol. II, Caps. 139 through 140; Vol. III, Caps. 141 through 142.

[58] The Waṭṭāsids attacked Tangier and Arzila in 1501 and 1502, opposed the Portuguese

ously, in 1503, the Cortes of Lisbon approved a subsidy of 50,000 *cruzados* for war in Morocco. Liberal gifts of revenue and perquisites were granted to persons and institutions connected in various ways with the outposts, and the overhaul of fortifications seems to have begun in the same buoyant and expansive spirit, even though on a modest scale.[59] Given the tactical thinking embodied in these late Phase A additions, they cannot be indiscriminately lumped together with the subsequent Manueline constructions of Phase B. Embodying changes in design that had appeared in Italy forty years earlier, they look more back toward an earlier generation of military engineering than forward to the age of the mature bastion.

The round tower at the extremity of the most prominent Tangier *couraça* was reinforced with a lower, massive, round or polygonal tower bastion (*torrião*). Its gently sloping walls appear to have been more strongly scarped at the base, and a series of gunports opened halfway or two-thirds of the way to an apparently massive top parapet. If this tower bastion was indeed polygonal (the evidence is unfortunately inconclusive), it would match the scarped *torrioni* documented in Italy from as early as the 1440s. A rather late Italian example of reinforcing a tower with a bastion or *torrione* is found in Rome's Castel Sant Angelo, where Antonio da San Gallo modernized the round corner towers by surrounding them with seven-sided bastions in 1492.[60] There also seem to have been gunslits in the round tower at the extremity of one of the other two *couraças* attached to Tangier's Sea Castle, shown in the *Civitates Orbis Terrarum* view, as well as at the base of the southeast corner tower on the other side of the harbour.[61] Between them, the three emplacements would have effectively swept the harbor and its approaches with their gunfire. If these features do indeed date, like the reinforcing *torrião*, to the end of

---

at Mazagan in 1502, and once again besieged Arzilla in 1504. After the Portuguese attempt to establish a fortress at Graciosa in 1489, the sultan had also refortified Larache (al-ʿArāʾish). Cook, *Hundred Years' War*, 150; Lopes, *A expansão*, 27–8, 46–7.

[59] Lopes, *A expansão*, 28.

[60] J.R. Hale, "The Early Development of the Bastion: An Italian Chronology, c. 1450–c. 1534," in *Europe in the Late Middle Ages*, ed. J.R. Hale (London, 1965), 478–9 (fifteenth-century *torrioni* at Corinaldo, Morro d'Alba, Ostra, S. Arcangelo di Roma), 483. The pictorial evidence for the Tangier *torrião* includes Braun and Hogenberg's *Civitates*; the English engraving of "The Little Mole, Wharf, and Custom House" of Tangier (December 1675), in Routh, *Tangier*, ill. facing p. 354; and Wenceslaus Hollar's vistas of "The South-East Corner of Tangier," "Tangier from the East," and the "The Town, with York Castle, from the South-East." Thomas Phillips' vista of "Tangier and the Mole, Before it was Demolished, 1683" is much less accurate, but also supports, at least vaguely, the idea of a polygonal bastion.

[61] Braun and Hogenberg, *Civitates*; ANTT, NA 769.

the fifteenth century, they would confirm a mounting emphasis on intelligently disposed artillery positions.

Ceuta's defenses seem to have remained inadequate until the beginning of the reign of D. João II, if the lamentable state of the town's artillery park during the governorship of Rui Mendes de Vasconcellos Ribeiro, 1479–81, is any indication.[62] Soon, however, suitable gun platforms began to be documented here that parallel the improvements at Tangier. A *torrião* was constructed near the Almina Gate, and a bastion gun tower (already called *baluarte*) integrated with the gate was probably completed in the 1490s or in the early 1500s.[63] The third outpost, Arzilla, seems to have been left behind in this construction drive, and no substantial improvements were undertaken before the Muslim assault of 19 October 1508. Waṭṭāsid artillery having mauled the walls, the *madīna* was briefly overrun and the defenders had to take refuge in the *qaṣba* before the tide of battle turned back in their favor. Only following this near disaster was Arzilla's entire complex of *madīna* and *qaṣba* systematically fortified and reinforced with additional artillery, so that during the attack led the following year by *wazīr* Mawlāy Naṣr al-Waṭṭās, the Moroccan forces were forced to fight a losing gun battle under the walls of the town. Nonetheless, Arzilla marked a turning point. Never again would the Portuguese be able to dimiss Moroccan firepower with a cavalier shrug, at least not in the Waṭṭāsid north.[64]

The next phase in the development of Portuguese military architecture in Morocco, Phase B, coincided as already mentioned with a new concerted push to enlarge and consolidate the European sphere of control in Morocco. Its landmarks were the fresh acquisitions and newly founded forts on the central and southern coasts: Safi, Santa Cruz, Mazagan, and Azemmur. By 1514–15, the Portuguese were raiding to the very walls of Marrakech, and both the northern and southern sectors of the frontier were ablaze. In 1508, not only Arzilla, but also Tangier and newly occupied Safi had come under attack. From then on, Muslim forces would appear before Arzilla almost every year until 1513. In 1510, Safi was besieged by the Hintāta rulers of Marrakech and the Waṭṭāsids, and in 1511 it was Tangier's turn once again, while in the south Santa Cruz was being attacked by the Saʿdian Sharīf Muḥammad al-Qāʾim.[65] In 1514, Mawlāy Naṣr made an attempt to

[62] Mascarenhas, *Historia de Ceuta*, 249–50.
[63] ANTT, CDM, Livro 31, fo. 22 (expenditures for work done in 1494 and 1496); ANTT, CDM, Livro 38, fo. 62 (expenditure for work carried out from 27 June 1503 to 7 May 1506); ANTT, NA 769.
[64] Cook, *Hundred Years' War*, 145; Leo Africanus, *Description*, 262.
[65] The father of Amad al-ʾAʿraj and Muḥammad al-Shaykh.

retake Azemmur, and in 1516 Arzilla endured a stupendous siege in the course of which artillery pounding reduced large sections of the landward curtain walls to rubble. A year earlier, the ill-fated Portuguese bid to establish a new fortress at Mamora had ended in a disastrous defeat at the hands of the Waṭṭāsids, with the loss of many pieces of artillery, which were salvaged by the Moroccans and arrayed against Arzilla. With the exception of the Saʿdian assault on Santa Cruz in 1511, all the operations were marked by steadily increasing proficiency in the use of gunfire on the part of Moroccan forces.[66]

The Portuguese response was to repair, improve, and expand all the frontier defenses. The pace at which some of the outdated northern fortifications were being overhauled had quickened as early as 1503, and reached a peak between 1508 and 1518.[67] In the south, the newly secured localities often jumped straight from Phase A, the compromise-filled phase of initial occupation, to Phase B in the space of a few years. With the exception of Ceuta, Tangier, and Mazagan, where the works of Phase D and later rebuilding subsequently obliterated many of the early-sixteenth-century features, this Manueline construction stage gave the Portuguese fortifications the basic appearance they retained until they were lost or evacuated. It is to this particular stage that the bulk of the surviving Portuguese military architecture in Morocco belongs.[68]

The salient feature of Phase B was a more systematic introduction

---

[66] Cook, *Hundred Years' War*, 145–6, 150, 152–5; Lopes, *A expansão*, 38–40; Godinho, *Descobrimentos*, III:259; Bernardo Rodrigues, *Anais de Arzila*, ed. D. Lopes (Lisbon, 1915 and 1919–20), I:112–16, 158–202.

[67] For expenditures on work carried out at Ceuta, see, e.g., ANTT, CDM, Livro 38, fo. 62 (1503–06); CDM, Livro 5, fo. 3v (1508); for Arzilla see CDM, Livro 5, fo. 3v (1508); for Azemmur, see ANTT, *Chancelaria de D. João III*, Livro 1 de Doações, fo. 48 (1515–17); for Safi, see, e.g., ANTT, *Chancelaria de D. João III*, Livro 1 de Doações, fo. 49v (1517–21); for Tangier, ANTT, CC I–3–50, 9 June 1504; for the frauds and peculation connected with the reconstruction of Alcácer, see ANTT, CC I–19–31, 15 November 1515.

[68] Among the men responsible for shaping the plans of the Manueline fortifications and supervising their execution were the engineers and master builders Diogo and Francisco de Arruda, who worked at Azemmur, Mazagan, and Safi (Baião, *Corpo*, 75–9 [ANTT, CC I–14–14, 30 March 1514]); Correia, *Lugares*, 80–3. Diogo de Arruda is documented as *mestre das obras* in Safi in 1512; Francisco de Arruda worked there in 1514; Martim Lourenço, who was employed at Alcácer (Baião, *Corpo*, 36 [ANTT, CC I–8–22, Martim Lourenço to the King, 13 July 1509]). Francisco de la Encina, also briefly involved with the fortifications of Alcácer (Baião, *Corpo*, 49–50 [ANTT, CC I–11–89, D. Rodrigo de Sousa to the King, 26 May 1512]). Henrique de Porada, who directed the building of the bastions at Safi (ANTT, CC II–60–118, 15 September 1515); the stonemason João Luis, who was *mestre de obras* in Safi until 1526 (Correia, *Lugares*, 80–3); and Bastiam Fernandes, the *mestre* at Santa Cruz in 1514 (Baião, *Corpo*, 120 [ANTT, CC I–16–11, 11 September 1514]).

of the bastion as an artillery emplacement. At Ceuta, two bastions are documented by 1514 – the *Baluarte de Sta Anna* and the already mentioned *Baluarte da Porta d'Almina*.[69] At Alcácer Seguer, two bastions, the *Baluarte da Porta de Ceuta* and the *Baluarte da Praia*, were attached by 1514 to the two medieval Islamic gate complexes known to the Portuguese as the *Porta da Ribeira* and the *Porta de Ceuta*. A third L-shaped bastion, equipped with two tiers of staggered gun casemates, enclosed the space between the town end of the *couraça* and the *Porta da Ribeira*.[70] At Arzilla, at least two bastions, the *Baluarte da Praia* and the *Baluarte da Couraça*, were completed prior to 1514. The second of these occupied the southwestern corner of the walls and served as anchor for the already mentioned new *couraça*.[71] At Azemmur, the refurbished *qaṣba* was equipped with four bastions faced with dressed stone by the end of May 1514.[72] At Safi, work on the walls connecting the sea front to the *qaṣba*, and on the bastions spaced along them, was underway by 1511–12. In January 1515, Alvaro de Athaíde proposed that the *qaṣba*'s crumbling tapia walls be at long last pulled down, and argued in favor of building bastions backed by strong towers.[73] The modified version that was finally adopted comprised the two corner bastions that now flank the great drum *torrião* of the present-day Kechla (for the *torrião*, see Fig. 12.5). At Santa Cruz, the seven towers completed in 1513–16 included a bastion called the *Baluarte de S. Simão*, and a terrace serving as artillery platform was attached to the keep or *Torre de Menajem*. Such gun terraces compensated for the fact that the archaic round towers and *torres de menajem* of transitional forts like Santa Cruz were too high to permit accurate fire from their tops.[74]

Many of the new Manueline bastions were semicircular or

[69] ANTT, NA 769.
[70] The bastions were still under construction in May 1512, but seem to have been completed by 1514. ANTT, NA 769; Baião, *Corpo*, 50 (ANTT, CC I–11–8, 26 May 1512). The space enclosed by the L-shaped bastion is the one designated as the *patio d'armes* by the Redman excavation team; Redman, *Qsar*, 146–8. The *couraça* had been allowed to decay, however, while the adjoining keep (*torre de menajem*) remained unfinished in 1512. To the governor's great chagrin, the crown stubbornly dragged its feet about having these vital works repaired and completed. Baião, *Documentos*, 36 (ANTT, CC I–8–22, Martim Lourenço to the King, 13 July 1509), 45–6 (ANTT, CC I–11–45, D. Rodrigo de Sousa to the King, 24 May 1512), 49–50 (ANTT, CC I–11–89, D. Rodrigo de Sousa to the King, 26 May 1512).
[71] ANTT, NA 769; Ricard, *Etudes*, 484.
[72] Baião, *Corpo*, 75–9 (ANTT, CC I–14–14, 30 March 1514).
[73] Correia, *Lugares*, 80–3; ANTT, CC I–11–75, 12 May 1512; ANTT, CC I–17–61, 25 January 1515; ANTT, CC II–60–118, 15 September 1515.
[74] Figanier, *Santa Cruz*, 40–1, 73–5. Concerning gun terraces and the problem of height, see Hale, "Bastion," 480 n. 1.

Figure 12.5. The Manueline *torrião* of the Kechla, in the *qaṣba* of Safi.

U-shaped, although square and oblong bastions are also found. Indiscriminately called *baluartes* in the documents, they still were, however, mostly gun towers rather than true bastions (i.e., completely solid artillery platforms). The larger ones, for instance at Azemmur or Safi, were two-storied structures, with rows of gun embrasures at both levels and crenellated parapets. The lower gun ports were designed for heavier guns, while the upper row often consisted of letterbox slits for lighter pieces or small arms such as arquebuses. The gun chambers of the more solid bastions had vaulted ceilings, but giving a major bastion only a timber ceiling would not be considered unusual at Safi as late as 1540.[75] The vaulting was not always very solid, and in two of the Arzilla bastions it had collapsed by 1541, about twelve years from the date of construction, rendering them completely unserviceable.[76] Structural weaknesses apart, the gun towers imposed serious limitations on the use of artillery. Heavy guns simply could not be fired safely and to the best effect from inside enclosed casemates that

---

[75] *Sources, Port.*, III:250 (ANTT CC I–67–110, D. Rodrigo de Castro to the King, 24 June 1540).

[76] *Sources, Port.*, III:528 (ANTT, CC 1–70–103, Conde de Redondo to the King, 1 October 1541).

quickly filled up with smoke, and the guns' traverse was constricted by the thickness of the walls.[77] Finally, in front of each rounded tower bastion there lay a wedge of dead ground that could not be covered by flanking fire, a handicap that left the works vulnerable to sapping and mining. This became a serious concern as the Moroccans improved their siege techniques throughout the late fifteenth and early sixteenth centuries.[78]

The disadvantages of the gun tower, as opposed to a completely solid artillery platform, were obvious to the Portuguese by 1512–14. True bastion platforms began to appear here and there throughout Phase B. At Alcácer, for instance, the citadel built around the Islamic Bāb al-baḥr or Sea Gate featured a platform contrived by reinforcing one of the original bent-axis Islamic gate chambers with internal partitions and packing the remaining space with loose rubble.[79] Another solution was to use open-backed casemates, such as were built into the great L-shaped bastion in the citadel of Alcácer, and into the rectangular bastion in front of that town's Ceuta Gate.[80] This architectural expedient at least diminished a little the smoke congestion, deafening noise, and structural reverberations that went with firing heavy guns.

No matter how imperfectly however, the gun chambers within the Manueline tower bastions combined the all-important dual functions of fire toward the field and flanking fire along curtain walls and toward adjacent bastions. The fields of fire were often poorly systematized, partly because of the impossibility of achieving this without tearing down or extensively reshaping the old Muslim fortifications.[81] Yet in no instance, perhaps with the exception of the harbour front at Tangier, did the guns have to shoot further than 250 meters, the span later on advocated by fortification theorists as the ideal distance be-

---

[77] A letter from Nuno Gato, sent from Azemmur in 1514, makes it quite clear that the heaviest artillery was in fact placed on the very top of those gun towers that were solid enough, and that only lighter pieces were mounted in the lower chambers, something that we would not expect just from looking at the design and size of the gun ports. Baião, *Documentos*, 82 (ANTT, CC I–15–16, Nuno Gato to the King, 30 March 1514).

[78] As early as the 1510 siege of Safi, Muslim sappers nearly breached the walls. *Sources, Port.*, I:265–9, 284–96, 356–8.

[79] Redman, *Qsar*, 146–8. At Safi, the interior of the *Baluarte da Couraça* was filled up with sand in 1541, to make it more akin to a true bastion. ANTT, CC 1–70–1, 21 June 1541; *Sources, Port.*, III:447.

[80] Redman, *Qsar*, 146–8.

[81] The round shape of Alcácer made systematizing fields of fire from the bastions particularly challenging.

tween the points of two adjacent bastions.[82] It would be quite errone-
ous, however, to imagine that the Manueline Phase B additions were
entirely up to the twin task of breaking up enemy attacks at a distance
and resisting bombardment by Muslim artillery.

First, only true bastions could have achieved that, and they were
still rare. Second, this was a phase of experimentation *and* ceaseless
emergencies, when moderately workable solutions had to be devised
in wartime conditions by people on the spot, who were not experts
acquainted with the latest refinements of Italian military engineering.
Third, throughout the Manueline period the fact that the Portuguese
could not ignore Moroccan gunpowder siegecraft did not prevent
them from chronically underestimating it, and the hit-and-run raids
by small parties that characterized day-to-day frontier warfare did not
seem to call for sophisticated defenses.[83] Finally, the disparities between the best of contemporary Italian fortification techniques and the
ones used in Portuguese Morocco reflected both the lag between central Italy as the focal point of innovation in military architecture and
the rest of Europe, and the additional constraints imposed by the
environment of the North African military frontier.

In localities newly conquered during the Manueline expansion, the
first rounds of adapting and reinforcing old Muslim fortifications were
usually carried out by the soldiers and civilians of the various expeditionary forces under the orders of the field commanders, without
the expertise of skilled masons, carpenters, or engineers.[84] The vagaries of local topography, as well as enemy pressure, made it often
difficult to obtain a sufficient supply of good stone.[85] Heavy timber
normally had to be brought in by ship from Madeira, Portugal, or
Spain.[86] Mortar made with local lime was either considered too brittle
and not weather-resistant enough, or there was not enough firewood

---

[82] Quentin Hughes, *Military Architecture* (New York, 1974), 103.

[83] See, e.g., R. Ricard, "A propos de 'rebato.' Note sur la tactique militaire dans les
places portugaises du Maroc," in Ricard, *Etudes*, 345–57. Baião, *Corpo*, 95–8 (ANTT,
CC I–15–98, 27 July 1514), furnishes a good representative example.

[84] See, e.g., ANTT, CC I–6–69, Diogo de Azambuja to the King, 12 December 1507. It
was also notoriously difficult to attract skilled artisans to the Moroccan outposts.
During the period of neglect in 1536, the situation was so bad in Safi that it prompted
Manuel de Sande to quip bitterly that there was "no one who could as much as drive
in a nail, or knew into what kind of wood he might drive it." ANTT, CC I–57–107,
Manuel de Sande to the King, 21 September 1536.

[85] See, e.g., Baião, *Corpo*, 50 (ANTT, CC I–11–89, D. Rodrigo de Sousa to the King, 26
May 1512).

[86] See, e.g., ANTT, CC II–15–2, 1 June 1508; ANTT, CC II–15–37, 10 August 1508; ANTT,
CC II–15–87, 20 October 1508.

available to burn lime. All the outposts made frequent requests that it be shipped in from Portugal, but deliveries were always insufficient and in the end local lime was used everywhere except in critical dressed-stone facings of bastions and in the lower courses of walls. The works therefore tended to decay faster, shortening the maintenance cycle and only prompting more futile requests for quality materials. Repairs were more often than not again carried out by such workmen as happened to be at hand, who were typically used to older and less sophisticated techniques.[87] Moreover, although the military finances of the Manueline era still await their historian, it seems that despite the manifest commitment to press the Portuguese advantage in Morocco in 1508–18, fortification budgets were never more than barely sufficient.[88] Financial pressures left little room for innovation, and there was a tendency to follow well-tried and therefore bureaucratically justifiable practices.

The old thus rubbed shoulders with the new throughout Phase B. The medieval concept of vertical defense was not entirely defunct, as attested by the prominent use of machicolations at Azemmur. Other transitional or archaic elements, such as the *couraça*[89] and the *torrião*, also remained part of the Portuguese military builder's bag of tricks. The construction of a new Manueline *torrião* is documented at Ceuta, and another one dating to about 1515 survives at Azemmur.[90] The latter combines the provision of flanking fire with fire to the field and along the adjacent curtain by heavy artillery, through a very large square window port allowing for ample traverse (Fig. 12.6). The machicolations, which rise flush with the surface of the *torrião's* squat drum and are supported on long vertical buttresses, represent, however, a transitional combination of modern artillery-based and archaic vertical defense, reminiscent of Francesco di Giorgio's late fifteenth-century towers at Cagli (ca. 1484) and in the Rocca of Mondavio (1490–2).[91] At Tangier, a massive drum *torrião* similar to Safi's Kechla

---

[87] ANTT, CC I–15–14, Francisco and Diogo de Arruda and Vasco da Pina to the King, 30–1 March 1514.

[88] A staggering mass of documents in the ANTT illustrates this point. One representative example is provided by Baião, *Corpo*, 36 (ANTT, CC I–8–22).

[89] At Arzilla, as already mentioned, a new *couraça* was built between 1508 and 1512. Another *couraça* was constructed at Ceuta, at the head of the main ditch near the Bastion of Santa Anna, sometime prior to 1514 (ANTT, NA 769). At Safi, a *couraça* was installed sometime before 1540 by the master builder Lourenço Argueiro (ANTT, CC I–67–110; *Sources, Port.*, III:250).

[90] ANTT, NA 769; John Bury, "Francisco de Holanda: A Little Known Source for the History of Fortification in the Sixteenth Century," *Arquivo do Centro Cultural Português* 14 (Paris, 1979): 190.

[91] Hale, "Bastion," pls. 26 and 27.

Figure 12.6. The Manueline *torrião* at Azemmur (ca. 1515).

was built roughly in the middle of the long straight western (land-ward) wall of the town (Fig. 12.3).[92]

The traditional medieval round tower or *cubelo* continued in wide use. In 1509, a two-storied tower was under construction at Alcácer in

[92] Wenceslaus Hollar, "Tangier from the South-West," and "The Lower Part of Tangier from the Hill West of Whitehall," in Routh, *Tangier*, ills. facing 146 and 156.

a position where it could bolster the defense of the *couraça*.[93] The defences of Santa Cruz (1513–16) comprised seven *cubelos*, with artillery mounted in most of them. The fact that such *cubelos* were hollow, like all medieval towers, made it tempting to store gunpowder in the cellar or on the ground floor, close to the guns above, a dangerous practice responsible for such tragedies as the explosion in the *Torre do Facho* during the final siege of Santa Cruz by Muslim forces in 1541.[94] Serviceable existing *cubelos* of Muslim origin were widely retained until the end of the Portuguese occupation. At Alcácer, they survived even the demolition of the top part (approximately half) of the wall, although the Portuguese engineers razed them down to wall level and filled them with large stones and mortar. This made them less vulnerable and provided an acceptable support for light pieces, transforming them into bastions in all but shape and tactical spacing.[95] Similarly, at Tangier archaic *cubelos*, or half-*cubelos*, cut almost flush with the parapet everywhere except in the northwestern wall dominating the steep escarpment that faced the sea, constituted the main feature of the town walls as late as the seventeenth century.[96] As far as Ceuta is concerned, for whatever the evidence is worth, the sixteenth-century vista in Braun and Hogenberg's *Civitates* still clearly shows a typical medieval enceinte with tall towers.

Finally, the small new fortresses of Phase B were decidedly not laid out with a view to optimal use of or resistance to artillery. The first Manueline castle of Mazagan (Mazagan I), built in 1515–17, represented a quaint throwback. It consisted of a rectangular bailey surrounded by vertical curtain walls with four corner towers, three of which were round. The fourth, square and higher than its counterparts, served as the donjon (*torre de menajem*). The castle gate was defended by a barbican. This thoroughly traditional medieval design resembled that of the already discussed Sea Castle at Safi, its exact contemporary.[97] The small fort at São João da Mamora seems to have differed only in having corner tower bastions instead of towers.[98] Even

---

[93] Baião, *Corpo*, 36 (ANTT, CC I–8–22, 13 July 1509). It remains difficult, at present, to identify this particular tower with any known feature of the citadel.

[94] Figanier, *Santa Cruz*, 73–5; *Sources, Port.*, III:369 (ANTT, Gavetas, 2–6–16, 2 April 1541).

[95] Redman, *Qsar*, 145.

[96] Wenceslaus Hollar, "The North Side of Tangier," "The Bowling Green at Whitehall," "The Lower Part of Tangier," "Tangier from the South-West," in Routh, *Tangier*, ills. facing 146, 156, 244, 284, and other engravings.

[97] Bury, "Francisco de Holanda," 190–1; Correia, *Lugares*, 57; *Sources, Port.*, III:88–9 (doc. 33, ANTT, CC II–210–94, Manuel de Sande to the *provedor mor dos contos*, March 1537), 390–4 (doc. 108, Biblioteca Nacional de Lisboa, Manuscritos, MS 1758, fo. 62, The King to Luis de Loureiro, 13 April 1541).

[98] ANTT, CC I–18–39, Mestre Duarte to the King, 19 June 1515.

more primitive fortifications were used in small civilian settlements. The one adjacent to the castle of Mazagan was defended as late as 1541 only by walls of tapia and weak stonework, partially surrounded by a moat filled with seawater.[99]

It was during the following phase of neglect and vacillation, Phase C, that the Portuguese made the first tentative moves toward adopting the full-blown new Italian style that had been maturing quickly under the influence of such figures as Giuliano da Sangallo (1445?–1516), his brother Antonio da Sangallo the Elder (1455–1534), and the latter's nephew Antonio da Sangallo the Younger (1483–1546).[100] Initially, however, the tendency manifested itself more in token patronage appointments than in architectural reality: at Safi, for instance, one García "da Bologna" became the *mestre de obras* in 1526, replacing the stonemason João Luis.[101] Instead of something being done to ensure the defense of the Moroccan outposts, symbolic steps were taken to create an impression that something was about to be done. Little more could be expected in the absence of political will to invest in expensive fortifications in North Africa. Far from a mere hiatus between two periods of building activity, Phase C was a crucial watershed that saw the colonial defense infrastructure in Morocco sink, through lack of commitment, into a decay that could not be redressed without allocating to this particular military frontier a larger share of the Portuguese empire's resources. The balance of factional and economic interests, at court and within the empire's administrative machinery, made such a choice impracticable.

Between 1480 and 1520, the cost of keeping the Moroccan outposts had nearly doubled, and as early as 1516–17 austerity measures had begun to whittle down garrison sizes and force the outposts to become more self-reliant. The cost-cutting trend was reinforced by the fact that from 1514 until ca. 1522–3 the consolidation of Portuguese influence, no matter how fragile, over large portions of the province of Dukkāla,

---

[99] *Sources, Port.*, III:63 (doc. 25, ANTT CC I–57–107, Manuel de Sande to the King, 21 September 1536), 390–4 (doc. 108, Biblioteca Nacional, Manuscritos, MS 1758, fo. 62, The King to Luis de Loureiro, 13 April 1541), 502–6 (doc. 130, ANTT CC I–70–75, Luis de Loureiro to the King, 25 August 1541).

[100] Correia, *Lugares*, 43–4, dates the turning point to 1529, the year marked by the first prominent stirrings of organized factional opposition at the Portuguese court to continued full-scale involvement in Morocco. There is no contradiction involved, however. The realization of what modernizing all the installations in Morocco would entail must have made many people think twice. Incidentally, this was the year of the Ottoman siege of Vienna and of the fall of Algiers to the forces of Khayr-ed-Dīn Barbarossa. Regarding the ripple effects of these developments, see Cook, *Hundred Years' War*, 179–81.

[101] Correia, *Lugares*, 80–3.

in the hinterland of Safi and Azemmur, made it somewhat easier for the local outposts to feed themselves. The colonists were now able to sow grain, friendly areas paid tribute in kind, and local trade flowed more freely, filling the marketplaces. Nevertheless, the droughts and epidemics that struck Morocco in 1517–22 and culminated in the great famine of 1521, together with Moroccan raids and a volatile situation in the hinterland, gave rise to periodic emergencies requiring expensive aid.[102] This was enough to tarnish the entire North African venture as a pointless money pit, above all in the eyes of those dazzled with prospects of gain in the Indian Ocean.

As famine depleted the ranks of Moroccan armies and the pressure on the Portuguese frontier eased by 1521–2, it became more and more difficult to justify military expenditures. Outright neglect set in as first the Saʿdian Sharīfs and then the Waṭṭāsids concluded truces with Portugal in 1524–6 and braced for a mutual confrontation.[103] The breathing space that Portuguese Morocco enjoyed at this point postponed the necessity to make hard decisions, despite the alarming prospect that one of the contestants might achieve a quick victory and then strike at the Portuguese with the combined resources of a reunited Morocco.[104] By the late 1520s, however, at the same time as it half-heartedly contemplated modernizing some of the outposts, the Portuguese crown began to veer much more clearly in favor of retrenchment. Two main factors were responsible for this trend.

First, the shrinking of the zone of influence in the region of Dukkāla and a resumption of Moroccan military pressure in the south made the outposts ever more dependent on outside assistance, including deliveries of grain from Europe and the Azores. Second, an influential bloc of courtiers and prominent personalities either favored expansion

---

[102] For trends in the balance between local and external supply, see Godinho, *Descobrimentos*, III:250–1, 260–5, 280–5; for general background, Cook, *Hundred Years' War*, 155.

[103] De Sousa, *D. João III*, 12–25. For the circumstances of the truce between the outposts of Safi and Azemmur and the new Saʿdian ruler of Marrakech, see *Sources, Port.*, II: 317, 320, 351–3, 357–8, 365–6, 367–70, and a summary in Godinho, *Descobrimentos*, III:264–5. For the truce with the Waṭṭāsids following the death of Muḥammad al-Burtuqālī, see *Sources, Port.*, II:382–3, 385–6, and Cook, *Hundred Years' War*, 176–7. Both before and after the truce, however, intermittent warfare simmered on in the north. In 1524 the Waṭṭāsids raided the immediate hinterland of Arzilla and Tangier, and continued to do so whenever most of their forces were not committed against the Saʿdians. Godinho, *Descobrimentos*, 250; De Sousa, *João III*, 99; Rodrigues, *Anais de Arzila*, I:469.

[104] The situation at Azemmur in 1527 illustrates very well the state of affairs. The colony was disastrously neglected, undermanned, and military pay was massively in arrears. Walls and gates were in total disrepair. By 1530, the inhabitants were literally at the end of their rope, psychologically and physically. Lopes, *A expansão*, 67–8.

in India as opposed to continued involvement in Africa, or even advocated overall colonial divestment. The agonizing doubts about whether to keep Ceuta, which had surfaced in the 1420s and 1430s, now reasserted themselves, at a distance of one hundred years, in the guise of doubts about whether to keep more than two or three enclaves in Morocco. Similar arguments, similar counterarguments, echoed across the time gap.[105]

In the spring of 1530, Santa Cruz do Cabo de Gué came very close to being abandoned and dismantled.[106] In 1532, D. João III requested from the pope a bull justifying the evacuation of Safi and Azemmur, even though domestic opinion on the subject was divided, with many favoring continued commitment. By 1535, mounting Sa'dian military pressure and their impressive use of artillery at the 1534 siege of Safi made gradual evacuation of both Safi and Azemmur appear urgent. Garrisons in both places were reduced, and troops kept being switched back and forth to plug gaps.[107] In the fall of 1535, the garrison of Mazagan was a small, heterogeneous, hungry, and undersupplied band of men who wanted nothing more than to return to Portugal to take care of their wives and children. At Safi, conditions were not much better, and the siege of Azemmur in 1537 only further aggravated the already bad situation.[108]

At this point, peace agreements concluded with both Fez and the Sa'dian Sharīfian forces in the south only further sapped the will to

---

[105] Regarding problems of supply and the implosion of the southern hinterland zone of influence, see Godinho, *Descobrimentos*, III:265–7. After tentative probings in 1528–9, Santa Cruz do Cabo de Gué came under attack in 1530 and 1531, and in 1532 it was the turn of Azemmur. Cook, *Hundred Years' War*, 182; Pierre de Cénival, ed. and trans., *Chronique de Santa Cruz du Cap de Gué* (Paris, 1934), 44–79. For the balance of opinion in Portugal, see Ricard, "L'évacuation," 357–81. The opponents of involvement in Morocco included the duke of Bragança, paradoxically the conqueror of Azemmur, who by 1529 advised keeping only Azemmur and Safi. Among the advocates of retrenchment in the East was the count of Vidigueira. Lopes, *A expansão*, 70–1. For the famous debates concerning Ceuta, further expansion in Morocco, and especially the vocal opposition of Infante D. Pedro and the count of Barcelos to further conquests, see Lopes, *A expansão*, 12–16, 20–1, and Silva Marques, *Descobrimentos*, 352–60 (doc. 286), 360–3 (doc. 287), 363–5 (doc. 288), 373–4 (doc. 293).

[106] *Sources, Port.*, III:xvi.

[107] Lopes, *A expansão*, 71–2 (by 1532, the plan was to keep Mazagan and Santa Cruz, Tangier and Arzilla, and reduce Ceuta to a mere *presidio* with reduced fortifications and skeleton garrison); Cook, *Hundred Years' War*, 182–3; *Sources, Port.*, III:1–14 (doc. 1, ANTT, Gavetas, 2–7–9, Aires de Sousa to the King, 1 January 1535), 18–21 (doc. 4, ANTT, CC I–54–43, D. Fadrique Manuel to the King, 7 January 1535), 31–3 (doc. 10, D. João III to the Conde de Castanheira).

[108] Mazagan: *Sources, Port.*, III:60–4 (doc. 25, ANTT, CC I–57–107, Manuel de Sande to the King, 21 September 1536). Safi: *Sources, Port.*, III:60–4, and also 131–2 (doc. 46, ANTT, CC I–59–109, D. Rodrigo de Castro to the King, 14 October 1537). Azemmur: Lopes, *A expansão*, 73.

maintain, not to say improve, the Portuguese fortifications. The pressure exerted on the Waṭṭāsids by the Sharīfs had already channeled the energies of Mawlāy Ibrahīm, the friend and right-hand man of the Waṭṭāsid sultan, away from the traditional frontier warfare with the Portuguese in the north as early as 1533. After the Waṭṭāsid defeat by the Saʿdian army at the Battle of Wādī al-ʿAbīd (also known as Battle of Bū ʿAqba, 24 July 1536), Mawlāy Ibrahīm pressed hard for a peace with Portugal, and on 8 May 1538 an eleven-year peace treaty was concluded between D. João III of Portugal and Abū ʾl-ʿAbbās al-Waṭṭāsī of Fez. Localized truces for up to three years were also concluded between the southern outposts and the Sharīfs in 1536–7.[109]

In the meantime, after a decade and a half of little more than perfunctory maintenance, the state of the Portuguese fortifications had become truly parlous. When the military architects Benedetto de Ravenna and Miguel de Arruda inspected Ceuta in the spring of 1541, they were appalled by what they saw, and reported to the crown that the city was in no condition to withstand a well-conducted modern siege using artillery. The governor insisted that he alone accompany the architects, for fear that the dismal findings might spark uncontrollable panic in the colony.[110] The fortifications of Arzilla were in complete disrepair. Not only had the vaults of some of the bastions collapsed, but the scarping of the moat had given way in several places, the walls facing the sea were heavily eroded, and walls and houses inside the *qaṣba* were crumbling.[111] At Safi, work on the great *torrião* of the Kechla had stopped sometime before June 1540 for lack of support from the crown.[112] With the exception of repairs or very small additions due to local initiative and realized with local resources, none of the places slated for evacuation saw any real improvement until the last Portuguese settler and soldier had left. While Moroccan siegecraft

---

[109] For the peace treaty with Fez, see *Sources, Port.*, III:158–65; for the role of Mawlāy Ibrahīm, *Sources, Port.*, III:146–57. Regarding the Saʿdian truces, see *Sources, Port.*, III: 35 (doc. 12, ANTT, CC II–206–86, Luis de Loureiro to factor Vicencio Embrum, 28 March 1536), 38 (doc. 14, ANTT, CC II–207–62, Luis de Loureiro to Vicencio Embrum, 1 June 1536), 73 (doc. 29, ANTT, CC II–210–7, Luis de Loureiro to the King, 1537), 96–102 (doc. 35, ANTT, CC I–58–86, Proclamation of Peace, 25 April 1537), 104–8 (doc. 37, ANTT, CC I–58–101, Rodrigo de Castro to the King, 4 June 1537); also Lopes, *A expansão*, 48.

[110] *Sources, Port.*, III:434–46 (doc. 118, ANTT, CC I–69–125, D. Affonso de Noronha to the King, 7 June 1541); the walls were partly in ruins, see *Sources, Port.*, III:, 499–501 (doc. 129, ANTT, CC I–70–55, D. Affonso de Noronha to the King, 12 August 1541). The report containing the confidential recommendations of the two architects is filed in ANTT, *Gavetas*, 15–17–9.

[111] *Sources, Port.*, III:528 (doc. 136, ANTT, CC I–70–103, Conde de Redondo to the King, 1 October 1541).

[112] ANTT, CC I–67–110; *Sources, Port.*, III:250 (24 June 1540).

continued to improve, constantly honed through internal warfare if not through skirmishes with the Portuguese, on the Portuguese side the clock seemed to move backwards as walls and bastions crumbled.

The full-blown Italianate Phase D began, ironically, with the 1541 evacuation of the southern outposts. This move all of a sudden resolved past confusions and clarified the new and much more limited strategic objectives and requirements. The architectural transition that had been in abeyance over the past decade became reality in one year. The previously much neglected Mazagan became the new solitary showpiece, the one and only thoroughly modernized fortress town in sixteenth-century Morocco. The choice was not only strategic but also financial: There was nothing to tear down here and level except the settlers' jury-rigged mud walls. The original design of Mazagan II is undoubtedly to be attributed to Francisco de Holanda, who has explicitly claimed its authorship. De Holanda drew on the lessons learned during a tour of Italian fortresses, on which he had embarked in the fall of 1537. What caught his eye above all was the Florentine *Fortezza da Basso*, designed in 1533 by Antonio da Sangallo the Younger, "the finest fort in Europe" in De Holanda's words.[113] The execution of the project was entrusted, however, to two other engineers, working in cooperation with the royal master builders João de Castilho and João Ribeiro. The Italian on the team, Benedetto de Ravenna, made his main contribution to the design in 1542, while on a tour of the Moroccan fortresses in the company of Miguel de Arruda, the younger member of the Arruda family of engineers and military architects. The fort was more or less completely finished by the summer of 1542.[114]

The plans drawn up in 1541 preserved the old, small Manueline castle as a keep at the center of the new fortress, but little remains of it today except the former *sala de armas* transformed into a cistern. The curtain walls of Mazagan II were designed to enclose the better part of the previous settlement, transforming it into a fortress town. They receded slightly back at an angle roughly in the middle of each side, emulating the *cortine oblique* with which Antonio da Sangallo the Younger was experimenting in the 1530s and 1540s.[115] The three-meter-

---

[113] Bury, "Francisco de Holanda," 164, 191–2; Hale, "Bastion," 489.

[114] Bury, "Francisco de Holanda," 191; R. Ricard, "Les inscriptions portugaises de Mazagan," in Ricard, *Etudes*, 385–412; *Sources, Port.*, III:502–06 (doc. 130, ANTT CC I–70–75, Luis de Loureiro to the King, 25 August 1541).

[115] Bury, "Francisco de Holanda," 193. Inward-bent curtains are documented particularly well in Antoine de Ville Tholosain, *Les fortifications* (Lyon, 1641), bk. I, pt. I, ch. 28 and pl. XII.

high and eleven-meter-thick ramparts were well capable of withstanding artillery bombardment. At each corner of the fort stood an angle
bastion or half-bastion (*S. Antonio, S. Esprito, S. Anjo, S. Sebastião*)
surmounted by a block platform or cavalier, the whole six meters high,
and the batteries in the retired flanks were protected by orillions. The
fort was surrounded by a ditch thirty-five meters wide and three to
six metres deep, filled with seawater at high tide, and the water level
was controlled by a lock. A triangular ravelin defended the landward
gate in the middle of the east curtain, and the counterscarp on the
outer side of the ditch seems to have incorporated a covered walk
from which arquebus-firing infantry could engage the enemy.[116] The
general trace of Mazagan II prefigured, for instance, the sketch of a
sea fort found in the *Della fortificazione delle città* of Girolamo Maggi
and Iacomo Castriotto (Venice, 1564).

Ceuta, however, had to wait until the later 1540s for the modern
defenses that finally replaced the medieval castle at the root of the
peninsula. The Muslim Ḥafr al-Suhāj (Foso de San Felipe) became the
wet ditch for an Italian-style fortified frontage (the Muralla Real) (Fig.
12.7), with two massive angle bastions controlling the southeastern
and northwestern ends of the canal. The model chosen for the bastions
was the round-shouldered one adopted by Giuliano da Sangallo as
early as 1500–3 at Borgo San Sepolcro, Nettuno, and Arezzo.[117] The
shoulders or orillions protected retired flanks containing gun chambers that provided flanking fire along the curtain and the faces of the
adjacent bastion. The bastions were surmounted by high cavaliers. On
the landward side, the engineers subsequently razed the remnants of
old ruined structures in the Rabaḍ al-barrānī, as well as suburban
dwellings in the section of the Rabaḍ called the Albacar, as already
proposed by Benedetto de Ravenna and Miguel de Arruda in 1541,
and filled the no-man's-land along the canal with a maze of modern
forward works consisting of two half-bastions connected by a curtain
wall, ravelins, lunettes, and a zigzag glacis.[118] At Tangier, modernization seems to have proceeded even more haltingly, and was even less
extensive than at Ceuta. Only the Upper Castle (*qaṣba*) was enclosed,

---

[116] ANTT, CC I–70–76, Luis de Loureiro to the King, 28 August 1541; ANTT, CC I–72–
68, João de Castilho to the King, 1542; R. Ricard, *Un document portugais sur la place de
Mazagan* (Paris, 1932); Bury, "Francisco de Holanda," 192–3 and sources cited there.

[117] Hale, "Bastion," 488.

[118] An impression of the works in the configuration they had taken by the middle of the
eighteenth century can be obtained from such plans of Ceuta as the one compiled
for the marquis of Pombal and printed with a French legend in 1774, or the 1791
plan reproduced in José Carlos de Luna, *Historia de Gibraltar*, 338–9.

Figure 12.7. The Muralla Real and the Foso de San Felipe, Ceuta, with orillioned bastion.

sometime prior to 1660, within a bastioned fort of irregular shape partly abutting on the old Muslim/Portuguese town wall.[119]

Contemplated as a whole, the progression from the fifteenth-century Portuguese reuse of Muslim defensive works to the acceptance of perfected Italian fortification techniques in the 1540s shows a pattern of prolonged and ultimately destructive spells of neglect followed by feverish bouts of catching up. The pattern reflected the ebb and flow of frontier warfare, the political battles at the Portuguese court and in the kingdom's *Cortes* about the cost of maintaining the outposts, the fluctuating commitment of the Portuguese crown, and the progress in Moroccan mastery of gunpowder tactics and siege methods from the 1490s onward.

The reign of D. João II and the beginning of the reign of D. Manuel I constituted the first catch-up period. Despite the medieval flavor of the major works of that era, the best of the defenses then built attempted to take artillery more or less systematically into account as a formidable weapon against massed human wave attacks, and constituted standard examples of contemporary military engineering. Such works as the tower bastion in Tangier harbor were as good (or as bad) as whatever could be found in Italy (at Forlimpopoli, Imola, Pesaro, or Forlì and Nepi) and elsewhere in southern Europe in the late 1470s and early 1480s.[120] From this point on, however, the gap between the Portuguese defenses in Morocco and state-of-the-art fortifications in north-central Italy grew ever wider.

The second spell of building activity was concentrated in the later Manueline period (ca. 1508–18), when war flared up all along the seaboard frontier and when, despite increasing Moroccan firepower and incessant sieges of outposts, Portuguese control over large areas of Moroccan hinterland and the conquest of Marrakech, or perhaps even Fez, seemed more than an idle dream. The Manueline defenses, however, unquestionably lagged behind the best of contemporary Italian fortifications. The lag was most pronounced in the case of newly built detached forts, little more than old-fashioned medieval castles. Moreover, the Portuguese continued to use the older type of round or U-shaped bastion or gun tower even in such fort like contexts as the qaṣba of Azemmur (1514), whereas in new or renovated Italian fortresses such forms quickly yielded to the full-fledged angle bastion by about 1508.[121] In the case of urban fortifications, the disparity was less

---

[119] A good bird's-eye view of this fortification is provided by Seller, "Plan of Tangier," in *Early Maps*, 114–15.
[120] For comparison, see Hale, "Bastion," 479–80 and passim.
[121] Hale, "Bastion," 488–9.

noticeable, partly because the process of adapting long stretches of town walls to the requirements of the new era was more awkward and expensive whatever the location, and even in north-central Italy the same attention was not always lavished on towns as on showpiece fortresses. The round bastion, in particular, had by no means become an outdated feature of Italian city walls: Angle bastions made only a hesitant appearance here, and did not truly come into their own until the later 1520s and early 1530s.[122]

Even in the urban context, however, the gap widened as the infrastructure of Portuguese Morocco was allowed to decay in the 1520s and 1530s and as defensive technology along the military frontier ceased to keep pace with the offensive technology of the Muslim opponent. The situation was not remedied until the last spell of modernization, from the early 1540s onward, and then only under the pressure of an impending military catastrophe and through copying Italian models with the help of Italian engineers. By then, Moroccan firepower and siegecraft had more than caught up with the fortifications of the transitional Manueline stage, and could only be effectively countered using advanced contemporary designs. The cost of modernizing entire urban enceintes, however, besides rebuilding all the forts, would have been staggering and politically unacceptable. It is suggestive that of the three localities the crown finally decided to keep, Mazagan was only a small fort with a flimsy adjacent settlement, so that the new showpiece fortress was built virtually on virgin ground. At Ceuta, from the very first moment of its occupation, it was considered sufficient to refortify the isthmus, and the forward works shielding the Foso de San Felipe were largely constructed in the already virtually empty no-man's-land of the Rabaḍ al-barrānī. At Tangier, finally, where centuries of accreted defenses would have had to be razed and remodeled, the job was simply never completed, regardless of the threat of Moroccan artillery. The dictates of expediency and affordability prevailed in the final count over technologically optimal solutions.

[122] Hale, "Bastion," 489–90.

CHAPTER 13

The artillery fortress as an engine of European overseas expansion, 1480–1750

GEOFFREY PARKER

HISTORIANS used to explain the "rise of the West" in one of two ways: either in terms of some "moral superiority" or "manifest destiny" that justified the white man's efforts to seek and retain world domination, or in terms of a presumed advantage of European commercial techniques and organization over all competitors, of joint stock over atomized capital, of companies over "peddlers," of seamen over landsmen. But subsequent developments have largely discredited the first of these views: the humiliating defeat and temporary collapse of European power in Asia in the mid-twentieth century quickly eroded the idea of white "moral superiority," while the growth of secular‘ thought rendered Christian triumphalism unfashionable in most quarters. The second "explanation," however, does retain some value. Although modern research has revealed that "native" Asian and African economic practices in the sixteenth century were superior to those of contemporary Europe, permanent corporate structures, found only in the West, from the *Casa di San Giorgio* of twelfth-century Genoa to the various East India companies and public banks of the seventeenth-century Atlantic states, nevertheless did confer a continuity and longevity far greater than that of any non-European merchant consortium.[1]

I am grateful to Tonio Andraed, Thomas Arnold, Bernard Bachrach, Edward Farmer, Alan Gallay, Richard Kagan, George Milner, John Nolan, John Richards, Sanjay Subrahmanyam, James Tracy, and Nancy van Deusen for valuable suggestions concerning this essay.
[1] Niels Steensgaard discerned two stages in this process: first the arrival of the Portuguese, who enjoyed a crucial advantage over Asian traders because they did not have to sell their stock within a single monsoon season like their "native" rivals, and the arrival of the Dutch, who deployed a centralized trade system and a single stock of capital (whereas the Portuguese had maintained hundreds of entrepreneurs under

And yet that advantage reflects social organization as well as business practice. It constitutes but one manifestation of the remarkable ability of relatively small groups of Europeans to function effectively, even when somewhat divided, in the interests of the same general goals. In fact, this "economy of effort" – from the Crusaders through Cortés and Pizarro, Albuquerque and Coen, to Clive and Cornwallis – appeared most clearly and most decisively in the military and diplomatic spheres, for the West made all its major territorial gains with amazingly small resources.[2] Before 1800, scarcely any triumphs came through superior numbers; rather they arose through a combination, in the terse phrase of Anthony Reid, of "superior firepower, particularly on shipboard, and fortresses, which they could make virtually impregnable; and [local] allies."[3] These three related aspects of the efficient use of violence to acquire and maintain supremacy constitute, in effect, a new paradigm for the "rise of the West": the military explanation.[4]

THE GENESIS OF THE ARTILLERY FORTRESS

But what was the precise role of "fortresses" within this new paradigm? According to Lynn White, doyen of European historians of technology, writing in 1967:

The early sixteenth century in Europe witnessed two revolutions, both of which altered habits of the previous thousand years and each of which, by the later 1500s, had crystallized into patterns that remained nearly intact until the end of the nineteenth century. One was the Protestant Reformation and the defensive response to it in the regions still loyal to Rome. The other was a sudden and profound change in military technology, the chief element of which was the development of light, highly mobile cannon that shot iron balls in fairly flat trajectories. Since the older style of fortifications crumbled before

---

their protection). See "Tourists, tents and traders. An interview with Niels Steensgaard," *Itinerario* 18/1 (1994): 36–7.

[2] See R. Hassig, *Aztec Warfare: Imperial Expansion and Political Control* (Norman, 1988), 105–9, 208–20; Sanjay Subramanyam, *The Political Economy of Commerce: Southern India, 1500–1650* (Cambridge, 1990), ch. 5; and S. Chaudhury, "Trade, bullion and conquest. Bengal in the mid-eighteenth century," *Itinerario* 15/2 (1990): 21–32.

[3] Anthony R. Reid, *Southeast Asia in the Age of Commerce 1450–1680*; vol. 2, *Expansion and Crisis* (New Haven, 1993), 271.

[4] The concept first appeared in F.C. Lane, *Venice and History* (Baltimore, 1966), chs. 23 and 24, and was developed by Niels Steensgaard, "Violence and the Rise of Capitalism: F.C. Lane's Theory of Protection and Tribute," *Review* 5 (1983): 247–73. See also Geoffrey Parker, *The Military Revolution. Military Innovation and the Rise of the West, 1500–1800*, rev. ed. (Cambridge, 1996), chs. 3–4; and *The Cambridge Illustrated History of Warfare: The Triumph of the West*, ed. Geoffrey Parker (Cambridge, 1995).

such devices, an entirely new, and enormously costly, apparatus of defense was required. It would be hard to decide which of these simultaneous revolutions had the greater impact on European life, or the most lasting effects.[5]

Appreciation of the value of the new "apparatus of defense," commonly referred to as the artillery fortress, did not remain confined to Europe. In September 1584, for example, the devout but pragmatic Matteo Ricci in China wrote scathingly of the pusillanimity of his hosts:

Because when two or three Japanese warships come and land on the coast of China, they burn their boats and capture villages and even large cities, putting everything to the torch and sack, without anyone offering resistance. . . . It is true that the Chinese have many fortresses, and the towns all have their walls with which to resist the fury of the pirates; but the walls are not of geometric design [i.e., they lacked provision for flanking defensive crossfire] nor do they have traverses or moats.[6]

Ricci perceived the absence of artillery fortresses, at least in the coastal areas, as a critical weakness in China's military effectiveness which, he felt, might facilitate Western conquest and (his real objective) the Christianization of East Asia. Lacking bastions, the Ming empire, he believed for all its apparent strength, might crumble in the face of modest European pressure.[7]

The chronology of the evolution of the artillery fortress in Europe is now relatively clear. Although cannon first appeared in the West in

---

[5] Lynn White Jr., *Medieval Religion and Technology. Collected Essays* (Berkeley, 1986), 149 (from "Jacopo Aconcio as an engineer," first published in *American Historical Review* 62 [1967]).

[6] *Catálogo de los documentos relativos a las Islas Filipinas existentes en el Archivo General de Indias de Sevilla*, eds. P. Torres Lanzas and F. Navas del Valle (Barcelona, 1926), 2: clxxxiii–iv; and Matteo Ricci to Juan Bautista Román, 13 September 1584, in F. Colin and P. Pastells, *Labor evangélica de los obreros de la Compañía de Jesús en las islas Filipinas* (Barcelona, 1902), 3:448–52. On Ricci's acute military sense (and contempt for Chinese military skills), see J.D. Spence, *The Memory Palace of Matteo Ricci* (London, 1983); on the terror that paralyzed maritime China at the time, see K.W. So, *Japanese Piracy in Ming China during the Sixteenth Century* (East Lansing, MI, 1975). However Ricci was not quite correct: some geometrical defenses have been discovered in Chinese sources: see J. Needham and R.D.S. Yates, *Science and Civilisation in China*; Vol. 5, *Chemistry and Chemical Technology*; pt. vi, *Military Technology: Missiles and Sieges* (Cambridge, 1994), 260–5. Moreover, some Chinese vertical walls proved thick enough to resist even the most ferocious artillery bombardment: see pages 408–9 of this chapter; on the very different response of Japan, see pages 412–14.

[7] Ricci by no means stood alone in this: see the optimistic views of other Europeans in the Orient quoted in Geoffrey Parker, "David or Goliath? Philip II and his World in the 1580s," in *Spain, Europe and the Atlantic World. Essays in Honour of John H. Elliott*, eds. Richard L. Kagan and Geoffrey Parker (Cambridge, 1995), 254–6; and J.M. Headley, "Spain's Asian Presence, 1565–1590: Structures and Aspirations," *Hispanic American Historical Review* 75 (1995): 623–46.

the 1320s, they do not seem to have been used to batter down walls before the 1370s, and the practice remained fairly rare until the 1420s.[8] Nevertheless, from the late fourteenth century onwards, a number of important innovations increased the capacity of fortifications to withstand gunpowder bombardment: first the addition of guns and gun ports for offensive use as a counterbattery; then a variety of new structural designs, such as "countersinking" the fort, to minimize the damage done by incoming fire; and later the introduction of polygonal defensive designs to maximize the opportunities for outgoing fire. But such innovations proved the exception; in most areas the traditonal "vertical system" remained the principal means of defense even though, for a century after 1430, whenever good siege artillery bombarded vertical walls, the outcome was predictable.[9] The verdict of Andreas Barnaldez on the conquest of Granada in the 1480s – "Great towns, which once would have held out a year against all foes but hunger, now fell within a month" – was echoed by Niccolo Machiavelli concerning the French invasion of Italy of the 1490s: "No walls exist, however thick, that artillery cannot destroy in a few days."[10]

In the 1520s, however, this ceased to be true. Thanks to its low, thick walls, broad moats, and geometrical bastions, the "artillery fortress" defied bombardment (see Fig. 13.1). In a report commissioned by the government of Florence in 1526, Machiavelli himself perceived three distinct ways of turning a town into an artillery fortress. Two involved starting from scratch: tearing down the existing walls and either building a new defensive system beyond them, so as to include the suburbs and all points (such as neighboring high ground) from which an enemy might threaten; or else building a smaller circuit than before, abandoning (and leveling) all exterior areas deemed to be indefensible. However, both of these methods involved substantial expense: not

---

[8] See H. Koller, "Die mittelalterliche Stadtmauer als Grundlage staatliche Selbstbewusstseins," in *Stadt und Krieg*, eds. B. Kirchgässner and G. Scholz; Stadt in der Geschichte (Sigmaringer, 1989), 9–25. France soon became the European center of artillery warfare, but by the 1490s Spain had 180 large and medium pieces and five state-run gun and powder factories: see W.F. Cook, "The cannon conquest of Nasrid Spain and the end of the Reconquista," *Journal of Military History* 57 (1993): 52.

[9] See the important chronology of the increasing force of artillery in C.J. Rogers, "The military revolutions of the Hundred Years' War," in *The Military Revolution Debate*, ed. C.J. Rogers (Boulder, 1995), 68–73.

[10] Bernaldez, *Memorias*, quoted in Cook, "The cannon conquest," 43; Machiavelli, *Art of War*, quoted in Parker, *The Military Revolution*, 10. See also the similar views of the late fifteenth-century military engineer di Giorgio discussed in F.P. Fiore, "L'architettura militare de Francesco di Giorgio: realizzazioni e trattati," in *Architettura militare nell' Europa del XVI secolo*, ed. C. Cresti, A. Fara, and D. Lamberini (Siena, 1988), 40.

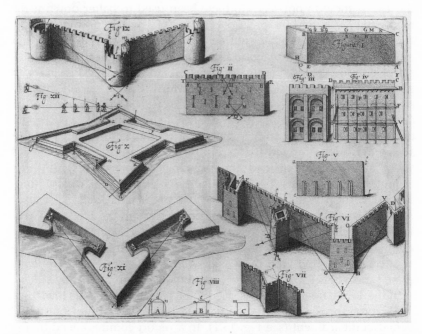

Figure 13.1. The development of modern fortifications in Europe was already portrayed by Matthias Dögen, a German military theorist, in 1647. In a single illustration he showed the evolution from the high walls of the classical period and the Middle Ages, through the round towers of the Renaissance, to the geometric designs pioneered in Italy in the sixteenth century, which the Europeans soon spread throughout the world. Matthias Dögen, *Architectura militaris moderna* (Amsterdam, 1647), 12–13. Courtesy of the Beinecke Library, Yale University.

only the money to build the fortress itself, but also high social costs, because the suburbs scheduled for demolition just beyond the medieval walls often contained important buildings such as hospitals, religious houses, and industrial plants (mills and furnaces). Machiavelli's report of 1526 therefore considered a third technique of installing modern defenses which, although less permanent than the others, proved both far quicker and far cheaper: a drastic modification of the existing fortifications, reducing the height and increasing the depth of the existing walls, redesigning the towers and gateways into bastions, and creating an escarpment to give a proper field of fire. Of course earthen ramparts, when unprotected by brick and stone, would not last long (contemporary estimates ranged from four years, with minimal maintenance, up to ten) before the weather eroded them. But they proved relatively fast and cheap to erect; they could absorb incoming fire effectively, and, with enough determined defenders (as at Metz in 1552 or at Haarlem in 1572–3), they could defy even the largest and best-led armies of the day.[11]

By then, however, the new bastioned fortifications – called *alla moderna* in Italy and "Italian style" or *trace italienne* everywhere else – had proliferated. Small European states such as Mantua, Monferrat, Lucca, and Geneva concentrated on building a single "impregnable" super-fortress, capable of holding out almost indefinitely, while larger polities invested not in one but in many artillery fortresses in order to create a layered defense-in-depth.[12] Thus, soon after they gained control of the duchy of Milan in the 1530s, the Habsburgs began a comprehensive program of fortifications: Cremona and Lodi against Venice in the east; Alessandria and Novara against Savoy in the west; Pavia and, above all, Milan itself as a strategic reserve.[13] Meanwhile, two similar systems evolved in the Low Countries. Already by 1572, when the Dutch Revolt began, twelve Netherlands towns had been turned into artillery fortresses and the walls of eighteen more had been partly rebuilt in the Italian style – a total of twenty-seven miles of new walls. By 1648, however, when the Revolt ended, the Spanish Netherlands alone boasted twenty-eight artillery fortresses and a further twenty-seven towns with partially modernized walls; and the provinces of Holland and Utrecht in the Dutch Republic, which, in 1572 had possessed only one artillery fortress and three more towns with one or two bastions, by 1648 had thirteen of the former and fourteen of the latter.[14]

---

[11] Machiavelli's "Relazione di una vista fatta per fortificare Firenze," in *Niccolo Machiavelli: Arte della guerra e scritti politici minori*, ed. S. Bertelli (Milan, 1961), 295. See also the perceptive discussion of D. Lamberini, "La politica del guasto. L'impatto del fronte bastionato sulle preesistenze urbane," in *Architettura militare*, 223–34. For Metz, see G. Zeller, *Le siège de Metz* (Nancy, 1943), 219; for Haarlem, see Geoffrey Parker, *The Dutch Revolt*, 2nd ed. (London, 1984), 159–60.

[12] See the interesting discussion in J.F. Pernot, "Guerre de siège et places-fortes," in *Guerre et pouvoir au XVIIᵉ siècle*, ed. V. Barrie-Curien (Paris, 1991), 129–50; and in T. Arnold, "Fortifications and the Military Revolution: The Gonzaga Experience, 1530–1630," in *The Military Revolution Debate*, 201–26.

[13] See A.S. Tosini, "Cittadelle lombarde di fine '500: il castello di Milano nella prima età spagnola," in *Architettura militare*, 207–17; and S. Leydi, *Le cavalcate dell' ingegnero. L'opera di Gianmaria Olgiati, ingegnere militare di Carlo V* (Modena, 1989). The Venetian Republic did the same: see M.E. Mallett and J.R. Hale, *The Military Organization of a Renaissance State. Venice c. 1400 to 1617* (Cambridge, 1984), 409–28.

[14] Data taken from W. Brulez, "Het gewicht van de oorlog in de nieuwe tijden. Enkele aspecten," *Tijdschrift voor Geschiedenis* 91 (1978): 386–406, based *inter alia* on a comparison of the town plans made by Jacob van Deventer in the 1560s and by Johan Blaeu

Wherever they appeared in Europe, fortifications *alla moderna* dominated the conduct of warfare. As John Cruso, an English military writer, observed in 1632, "The actions of the modern warres consist chiefly in sieges, assaults, sallies, skirmishes etc., and so affoard but few set battels." According to Roger Boyle, Lord Orrery, in 1677, "Battells do not now decide national quarrels, and expose countries to the pillage of conquerors, as formerly. For we make war more like foxes, than like lyons; and you will have twenty sieges for one batell;" while in exactly the same year Johann Behr stated that, in Germany, "Field battles are in comparison scarcely a topic of conversation . . . Indeed at the present time the whole art of war seems to come down to shrewd attacks and artful fortification."[15]

The point was expressed most cogently by the principal military engineer of Louis XIV of France, Sébastien le Prestre de Vauban, in a tract written ca. 1670:

The attack on fortresses has with justice always been considered one of the most essential elements of the art of war. But since the number of strongholds has increased to the point where one can no longer enter enemy territory without encountering many fortified towns, its importance has increased to the point where one can say that today it alone offers the means of conquest and conservation. To be sure, winning a battle leaves the victor in control of the countryside for the time being, but only taking the fortresses will give him the entire country.[16]

In the Netherlands, for example, where (as noted above) few towns in his day lacked modern fortifications, in spite of "over 60 battles and 200 sieges" the country had never been totally subdued. According to Vauban:

The reason is obvious. A battle lost in the Low Countries normally has few consequences, for the pursuit of a defeated army continues for only two, three or four leagues, because the neighboring fortresses of the enemy halt the

in the 1640s. M. van Hemelrijck, *De Vlaamse Krijgsbouwkunde* (Tielt, 1950), 131–307, still provides the best overall survey of fortifications constructed in Belgium and northern France by the Habsburgs.

[15] J. Cruso, *Militarie instructions for the cavallrie* (Cambridge, 1632), 105; Roger Boyle, earl of Orrery, *A Treatise of the Art of War* (1677), quoted in Parker, *Military Revolution*, 16; J. Behr, *Der aufs Neu-verschantzte Turenne* (1677), quoted in Christopher Duffy, *The Fortress in the Age of Vauban and Frederick the Great, 1660–1789* (London, 1985), 13–14. See also the useful discussion in F. Tallett, *War and Society in Early Modern Europe 1495–1715* (London, 1992), 50–4.

[16] Sébastien le Prestre de Vauban, *Mémoire pour servir d'instruction dans la conduite des sièges et dans la défense des places* (ca. 1670, but misdated 1704: Leiden, 1740), 3–5, checked against the manuscript copy in the Anne S.K. Brown Military Collection at the Hay Library, Providence, Rhode Island, fols. 1–1v.

victors and provide a refuge for the vanquished, saving them from being totally ruined.[17]

As the construction of preclusive frontiers of artillery fortresses continued, in one region of Europe after another sieges eclipsed battles in importance and wars eternalized themselves.[18]

THE EUROPEAN ARTILLERY FORTRESS OUTSIDE EUROPE

But what was the chronology and the role of the artillery fortress outside Europe? The first early modern castle built by the Europeans in the course of their overseas expansion – indeed, significantly, the first European building in the Tropics – went up at São Jorge da Mina in West Africa in 1482, following a naval encounter between Portuguese and Castilian vessels in the area two years previously. Given the perceived need for speed, the Portuguese crown sent out an expeditionary force carrying some pre-cut masonry (the foundations, gates, and window frames; the rest was to be supplied locally); and the completed edifice, although traditional in design (with one fortified enclosure for defense and another for trade), bore thirty cannon.[19] The construction of fortified beachheads had long formed part of the Western military tradition – William the Conqueror had built a castle at Pevensey as soon as he landed in England in 1066; the Crusaders, the Venetians, and the Genoese all fortified their settlements around the coasts of the Levant, the Aegean, and the Black Sea – and it offered a crucial strategic advantage for expansion. Writing between 1505 and 1508 of his experience in Africa and India, the Portuguese conquistador Duarte Pacheco Pereira could already boast that in "fortresses

---

[17] Vauban, *Traité de l'attaque des places* (manuscript in the Anne S.K. Brown Military Collection at the Hay Library, Providence, Rhode Island, in the same volume as the *Mémoire*, second pagination, 1–2). This passage does not appear in Sébastien le Prestre de Vauban, *De l'attaque et de la défense des places*, 2 vols. (The Hague, 1737–42, but written ca. 1704), although in other respects the two works are almost identical. The Brown manuscript appears to be an interim draft, written at some point between 1670 and 1704.

[18] This ceased to be true only when various governments in the later eighteenth century chose to invest in roads rather than in walls. The cost was much the same, but the speed of movement permitted by the new road network finally rendered a defensive system based on heavily fortified strongpoints both ineffective and uneconomical. See Parker, *Military Revolution*, ch. 5; reinforced by H. Eichberg, "Zirkel der Vernichtung oder Kreislauf des Kriegsgewinns? Zur Ökonomie der Festung im 17. Jahrhundert," in *Stadt und Krieg*, 105–24.

[19] See details in J. Vogt, *Portuguese Rule on the Gold Coast, 1469–1682* (Athens, GA, 1979), 19–31; and A.W. Lawrence, *Trade Castles and Forts of West Africa* (Stanford, 1964), 103–79, and pls. 2–36.

surrounded by walls ... Europe excels Asia and Africa." Islamic sources agreed. The *Tuhfat-al-Mujâhidîn*, a chronicle of the struggle of the Malabar Muslims against "the Franks" in southern India, devoted special attention to – and heaped special abuse upon – the large number of forts erected by the Portuguese (starting at Cochin in 1503), which made it almost impossible to drive the newcomers out, for "their forts could never be taken."[20] Nevertheless, the traditional vertical designs of the Portuguese described by these writers had become inadequate by the late sixteenth century, when traders from other European states made their presence felt: bastions, ravelins, and moats were now added to older constructions like São Jorge, and all new forts were constructed on geometric principles. In the seventeenth and eighteenth centuries, nine European states maintained forty-three fortified stations along the West African coast, from Arguim to Whydah (thirty-one of them crammed into the 300-mile stretch of the Gold Coast); by 1800, almost all were artillery fortresses.[21]

Portuguese expansion in East Africa, Asia, and South America followed much the same course. The coastal fortifications erected in the first phase, often by Portuguese engineers, followed the vertical pattern; from the 1540s, however, new-style complexes, often conceived and directed by Italians, sprang up – starting with the huge bastions of Mazagão (Morocco), Diu (India), and Salvador (Brazil). Everywhere, "Renaissance" defenses gradually gave way to modern ones; from 1558–60, for example, a huge Italian-style fortress encircled and replaced Albuquerque's smaller structure at Ormuz, erected in 1507–15.[22] The process proved slow, however. The splendid drawings by the military engineer Pedro Barreto de Resende, appended to António Bocarro's *Book of plans of the fortifications, cities and settlements of the*

---

[20] D. Pacheco Pereira, *Esmeraldo de situ orbis*, ed. J. Barradas de Carvalho (Lisbon, 1991), 190–1; Zain al-Din, *Tohfut-ul-Mujahideen*, in *Historia do Portugueses no Malabar por Zinadim*, ed. D. Lopes (Lisbon, 1898), 73 (see further data on the forts of the "Franks" on 36, 47, and 58–9). Pacheco, who played a prominent role in the exploration of the West African coast in the 1480s and served in Portuguese Asia in 1500–5, wrote his treatise between 1505 and 1508. Zain al-Din composed his account in the 1580s.

[21] Full details in Lawrence, *Trade Castles and Forts*. This concentration is easily explained. Elsewhere in West Africa, the inlets and lagoons allowed the Europeans to control trade with the artillery aboard their ships, but the "Gold Coast" offered no natural harbors, and the ships therefore had to anchor some distance from the coast; hence the need for fortresses ashore. (My thanks to Graham Connah for this point.)

[22] See the magnificent illustrations of these locations in *História das fortificaçoes portuguesas no mundo*, ed. R. Moreira (Lisbon, 1989), 114, 150–3, 170–1, 176–9, 256–7, 259. The same late transition from medieval to modern architecture occurred in Spanish North Africa: see J.B. Vilar, *Mapas, planos y fortificaciones hispánicos de Tunez (siglos XVI–XIX)* (Madrid, 1991), 354–474, and *Mapas, planos y fortificaciones hispánicos de Marruecos (s. XVI–XX)* (Madrid, 1992), 337–454.

State of India, completed in 1635, depicted fifty-three seaside strong-holds between Sofala and Macao, but scarcely ten of them could boast fortifications *alla moderna*: Mascate and Fort Jesus at Mombasa in Africa (the latter specially laid out to a geometrical plan by an Italian architect, Giovanni Battista Cairati, in the 1590s);[23] Baçaim, Chaul, Diu, Damão, and São Thomé in India; Jaffna (1618) and Batticaloa (1628) in Ceylon; Melaka (1564–8); and the Monte fortress (1620) at Macao.[24] Moreover, even in 1635 some of those still lacked adequate artillery for their defense. Diu, with its massive walls (rebuilt in 1624), possessed only forty-five large and twelve small guns (the rest, according to Bocarro, had been taken on an expedition to relieve Melaka in 1629 "where most of them were lost"); Damão had only twenty-seven guns for its eleven bastions, and Chaul only thirteen guns for its nine bastions. Worst of all, five of the forts defending Goa, the viceregal capital, boasted only six guns between them, and the wall alongside the river had none at all.[25]

Three considerations explain the slow spread of the new defensive technology. First, it cost a great deal of money: the pentagonal citadel at Antwerp, with walls stretching some 1,500 yards, cost 800,000 florins to build between 1567 and 1571; and although using forced labor could reduce the initial cost substantially, the *trace italienne* required a larger garrison. Building "modern" defenses thus represented a major and lasting investment of resources that most taxpayers would gladly avoid for as long as possible.[26] Second, even a state-of-the-art fortress

---

[23] Cairati also supervised the construction of artillery fortresses at Basseim and Damão in India. See details in C.R. Boxer and C. de Azevedo, *Fort Jesus and the Portuguese in Mombasa 1593–1729* (London, 1960); J. Kirkman, *Fort Jesus. A Portuguese Fortress on the East African Coast* (Oxford, 1974); and W.A. Nelson, *Fort Jesus of Mombasa* (Edinburgh, 1994).

[24] *O livro das plantas de todas as fortalezas, cidades e povoações do Estado da India oriental*, ed. I. Cid, 3 vols. (Lisbon, 1992), is a modern version of the manuscript in the Evora public library containing color depictions of forty-eight forts (a sketch-map of their location may be found in I:21). The manuscript was also published, with black and white plates and many additional subsequent printed sources, in A.B. de Bragança Pereira, *Arquivo Português Oriental*, tomo 4, Vol. 2 (3 parts, Bastorá, 1937–8). Another manuscript copy in the Biblioteca Nacional, Madrid (MS 1190 and MS Res 202) contains fifty-three plates. For details on these and three other extant manuscript copies of the work, see A. Cortesão and A. Teixeira da Mota, *Portugaliae Monumenta Cartographiae* (Lisbon, 1960), 5:59ff. On the new circuit of walls at Melaka, see P.Y. Manguin, "Of fortress and galleys. The 1568 Acehnese siege of Melaka, after a contemporary bird's-eye view," *Modern Asian Studies* 22 (1988): 607–28.

[25] *O livro*, 2:132–5.

[26] H. Soly, "De bouw van de Antwerpse citadel (1567–71). Sociaal-economische aspecten," *Tijdschrift voor Geschiedenis* 21 (1976): 549–78. Because every part of the construction process was paid for (by the citizens of Antwerp), the detailed surviving accounts of this enterprise offer an important index of overall cost. Labor represented almost

possessed only defensive capacity. It served to protect merchants and their property, and to supply and shelter ships, but that was all. A few outposts and the occasional raid could extend the Europeans' influence perhaps fifty or sixty miles into the hinterland, but no single stronghold could, by itself, control the interior. Construction of isolated fortifications overseas therefore tended to make sense where the Westerners sought to trade, rather than where they sought to settle. As in Europe, to render an entire frontier secure required a defense-in-depth. Third and finally, the military geography of many regions made the costly new foritifications seem irrelevant. In the early sixteenth century, only a few Muslim cities along the shores of the Indian Ocean possessed stone gates and towers, and only one, Aden, possessed a complete circuit of fortifications: "very well surrounded by walls, towers and turrets, with battlements after our own fashion [*há nossa maneira*]," according to a Portuguese observer in 1513.[27] Most of the other port cities of South Asia sheltered behind wooden stockades, sometimes reinforced with earth, and posed no serious challenge to the Westerners. A few, such as Diu, acquired a citadel, and a former Ottoman engineer fortified Surat in the 1540s, but for most of the sixteenth century the "fidalgos" lacked any indigenous pressure to introduce state-of-the-art fortifications.[28]

The conquest of Melaka by the Portuguese in 1511 epitomized the situation. The city, although a huge trading metropolis (its waterfront was said to measure nine miles and its population exceeded 100,000), lacked regular fortifications. Moreover, "most of its artillery – such as it has – resembles muskets," and "they are very short of gunners and powder."[29] When the Portuguese arrived, however, the sultan "greatly

three-quarters of the expenditure. Cf. Rijksarchief in Gelderland, Arnhem, *Archief van het huis Bergh* 539, unfol., Herman van den Berg to Archduke Albert, 24 January 1604, claiming that he had managed to fortify Venlo in the "new style" for 9,000 florins instead of 60,000, through the use of forced labor. For the higher cost of defending Italian-style defenses, see Mallett and Hale, *Military Organization*, 445.

[27] "O livro Duarte Barbosa" in *Coleccçõ de noticias para a historia e geografa das nações ultramarinas* 2, 2nd ed. (Lisbon, 1867), 262.

[28] The view of W.G.L. Randles, "The artilleries and land fortifications of the Portuguese and of their adversaries in the early period of the discoveries" (unpublished typescript).

[29] *Lettera di Giovanni da Empoli [1514]*, ed. A. Bausani (Rome, 1970), 132; letter from nineteen Portuguese captives in Melaka to Albuquerque, 6 February 1510, in *Cartas de affonso de Albuquerque*, ed. R.A. de Bulhão Pato (Lisbon, 1893), 3:5. The captives claimed that Melaka's 10,000 buildings included only 500 of adobe, the rest being of "straw like those of India." However, the mosques at least were made of stone because, as Empoli recorded, Albuquerque recycled them for "A famosa." For a brilliant survey of Melaka before the conquest, see L.F.F.R. Thomaz, "The Malay

fortified their seaboard with stockades of huge thick trees full of numerous cannon large and small and cases crammed with gunpowder." So the Portuguese commander, Afonso de Albuquerque, burnt a few Muslim ships in order to secure from the sultan a favorable agreement, which included not only restitution for damage done to Portuguese property and advantageous terms of trade but also the demand that the ruler "should send people to a place that he would tell him of to build a fortress at his own expense."[30] Since these terms were contemptuously dismissed, Albuquerque at first tried to capture Melaka by naval bombardment (bringing to bear, according to one source, 400 guns).[31] When this failed, the 1,500 Portuguese, plus 800 allies (Chinese and Indian), stormed the stockade and the inhabitants fled.

Now, having gained a lodgement, Albuquerque and his men:

> with great haste by day, and the use of torches by night, [were] intent on building a castle of timber, with many large trees for the interior and a goodly quantity of cannon, and in a month it had been made strong; and as soon as it had been made secure, we prepared one of stone which we built by dismantling the houses of the Moors, the mosques and other of their buildings. We erected it with great hardship bearing the stones on our backs; and each one of us was day-labourer, mason and stone-cutter.[32]

The work endured and this castle, known as "A famosa," still formed part of the defenses of the city 130 years later when, despite a complete circuit of walls constructed in the 1560s, which had resisted numerous sieges by its Asian neighbors, it fell to the Dutch.

Throughout the sixteenth century, fortifications built in the cheaper vertical style (like São Jorge da Mina or A Famosa) or with hollow round towers (like the walls of Melaka) proved perfectly adequate

---

Sultanate of Melaka," in *Southeast Asia in the Early Modern Era. Trade, Power and Belief*, ed. Anthony R. Reid (Ithaca, 1993), 69–90.

[30] *Lettera di Giovanni da Empoli*, 135–6. The explicit reference to gunpowder weapons among the defenders of Melaka contradicts the oft-quoted account in the "Sejarah Melayu," which stresses the fear and surprise caused by the Europeans' bombardment: "What may be this round weapon that yet is sharp enough to kill us?" "Serajah Melayu or 'Malay Annals'," ed. C.C. Brown, *Journal of the Malay Branch of the Royal Asiatic Society* 25/2–3 (1952): 158. However, the Serajah was compiled from oral traditions in 1612, whereas Empoli (an eyewitness) wrote in 1514; moreover, although the Melakans may have possessed gunpowder weapons, it seems unlikely that they were as effective, or were deployed as effectively, as those of the Europeans.

[31] A. De Gubernatis, *Storia dei viaggatori italiani nelle Indie orientali* (Livorno, 1875), 376 (from an anonymous Italian account of the fall of Melaka).

[32] *Lettera di Giovanni da Empoli*, 138. Empoli reported the same pattern at the capture of Goa in 1510: as soon as the city fell, Albuquerque began to construct a stone castle (121).

against local rulers. Admittedly, improvements became advisable from time to time – as early as 1513, Albuquerque complained that in western India "the people we are fighting are different now, and [their] artillery, arms and fortresses have now all been transformed to our way of using them"[33] – but the Europeans always seemed to retain a decisive advantage. Thus when the sultan of Ahmadnagar laid siege to Portuguese Chaul in 1571, his army of 140,000 men dwarfed the 1,100 European defenders, while at the same time other Indian rulers attacked several other Portuguese outposts, thus reducing the chances of relief. The garrison a perimeter of no more than 600 by 450 yards, but could shelter behind improvised walls and bastions bearing artillery; moreover, since Chaul was never cut off from the sea, Portuguese ships managed to land reinforcements and supplies, and also used their guns against the besiegers. Nevertheless, the forces of Ahmadnagar gradually took all the outworks until, after six months, they launched a full-scale assault. But it was repulsed and, in the furious counterattack that followed, the Portuguese captured or spiked all the enemy's artillery. The siege was over.[34]

European adversaries were not so easily driven off, however. With the arrival of the Dutch in the Indian Ocean in the 1590s, the Portuguese realized that they faced a new and far more dangerous threat and began to construct new geometrical fortifications there. As Philip III observed in 1607: "Ever since the beginning of the discovery of India, experience has demonstrated the importance of fortresses; and now this seems even greater with the appearance of the [Dutch] rebels in those parts." The viceroy of Portuguese India was therefore ordered to spend money, first and foremost, on completing "modern style" fortifications already begun, then on founding artillery to defend them, and finally on building more warships.[35] Many other royal letters reiterated the point in increasingly strident tones.[36] At the same

---

[33] Albuquerque to King Manuel, 30 November 1513, in *Cartas de . . . Albuquerque*, 1:127; "*artelheria e armas e fortalezas he ja tudo tornado a nosa husamça*"– alas, he did not provide the details.

[34] See R.O.W. Goertz, "Attack and defence techniques in the siege of Chaul, 1570–1," in *II Seminário internacional de história indo-portuguesa*, eds. L. de Albuquerque and I. Guerreiro (Lisbon, 1985), 265–92. See also the useful general overview of M.N. Pearson, *The Portuguese in India*, The New Cambridge History of India, Vol. I, bk. 1 (Cambridge, 1991), 56–9.

[35] Philip III to the viceroy of India, 18 January 1607, in *Documentos remetidos da India ou livros das Monções*, ed. R.A. de Bulhão Pato (Lisbon, 1893), 1:90–100. Characteristically, the king concluded his long hortatory letter by regretting that he could send no money to implement any of the new policies enjoined.

[36] See, for example, Philip III to the viceroy of India, 26 February 1605, in *Documentos remetidos*, 1:1–18, inquiring about the progress of fortification in all the major centers

time, the Portuguese tried to organize their troops in India to fight in the European manner, for whereas "street gang" tactics normally worked against native rulers, fire control and superior discipline proved imperative against the Dutch. "We have tried many times to reorganize our troops in India according to the European manner," Philip III reported wistfully in 1617, "since experience has shown that without it we have suffered several important losses. But now that we are at war with the Dutch, who are disciplined soldiers, it is more important than ever."[37] Yet the losses continued and even multiplied until all the Portuguese fortresses in Ceylon and south India, although they had resisted numerous attacks by Asian rulers, fell to the Dutch between 1638 and 1663. The victors, however, took no chances and fortified their gains on a far more impressive scale: thus the walls of Galle in Ceylon, with twelve bastions (some of them ninety feet thick), ran for over a mile, while those of Colombo (with eight bastions) and those of Negapatam (with twelve) stretched further still.[38]

The same defensive pattern prevailed elsewhere in Asia: Expensive geometrical fortifications normally only sprang up when and where other Europeans threatened. Thus, as they spread out across Siberia from the 1580s, the Russian explorers and fur traders built forts at river crossings to protect themselves from local attack and safeguard their links with Muscovy, but these wooden constructions remained modest.[39] In the Philippines, too, the sophisticiation of Spanish fortifications remained limited until other Europeans began to threaten. Even the castle of Santiago at Manila began inauspiciously. In 1588, one Spanish official there informed the king that the fortifications

of Portuguese India; and same to same, 13 and 17 February 1610, in *Documentos remetidos*, 1:322–36, ordering improvements to the fortification of numerous bases with artillery bastions (while again regretting that no money could be sent). After a hiatus following the conclusion of a truce with the Dutch, the pressure resumed: see same to same, 20 January 1618, in *Documentos remetidos*, 4:273ff, ordering the viceroy to repair and modernize all fortifications in the "Estado da India;" same to same, 22 and 24 March 1620, in *Documentos remetidos*, 6:297ff and 439f; and so on.

[37] Philip III: instructions to Viceroy Redondo, 21 March 1617, in *Documentos remetidos*, 4: 168–9. See also the reminder, Philip III to viceroy, 23 January 1618, and the viceroy's discouraging replies of 8 February 1619 and 8 February 1620, *Documentos remetidos*, 4: 287–8 and 5:326–8.

[38] Details from P.E. Peiris, *Some Documents Relating to the Rise of the Dutch Power in Ceylon, 1602–1670* (Colombo, 1929), 67–8; and P. Baldaeus, *Naauwkeurige beschrijvinge van Malabar en Choromandel* (Amsterdam, 1672), 1:155 (Negapatam) and 2:106 (Colombo). See also the excellent illustrated descriptions in W.A. Nelson, *The Dutch Forts of Sri Lanka: The Military Monuments of Ceylon* (Edinburgh, 1984).

[39] See *Russia's Conquest of Siberia*, eds. B. Dmytryshyn, E.A.P. Crownhart-Vaughan, and T. Vaughan (Portland, 1985), 22 and 41 (a woodcut illustration of an *ostrog*); and G.V. Lantzeff and R.A. Pierce, *Eastward to Empire: Exploration and Conquest on the Russian Open Frontier to 1750* (London, 1973), 110–14, 124.

under construction were "a waste of time and money, because . . . they are made with round towers in the old fashion . . . without a moat or parapet" and thus could not offer interlocking fields of fire. Moreover, "with what this costs, we could make a fortress in the modern style, with three bastions, instead of a structure so useless that any English or French troops who might besiege it would force it to surrender on the first day of the battery." The military commandant three years later could only agree, since the defenses were "somewhat out of proportion, being made without architect, advice or plan."[40] However, the repeated Dutch blockades and attacks after 1600 soon changed the situation, and by 1650 a full enceinte with eleven bastions had been built to surround the heart of the bustling town, while several outlying strategic points (most notably the Cavite peninsula) were also fortified in the "modern manner."[41]

In the Americas, fortress building by the Europeans began early. Between 1509 and 1569, the Spanish crown issued over 100 orders to erect fortifications in the New World.[42] However, little construction actually took place until the 1550s, when the presence of European enemies threatened the security of the region. The principal ports of the Caribbean began to receive modern fortifications in the reign of Philip II, starting with Havana (briefly captured by the French in 1555) between 1558 and 1577, and accelerating after the devastation caused by Francis Drake's West India raid of 1585–6.[43] By then, however, Drake's circumnavigation in 1577–81 had also provoked a program of fortification in South America. According to the king himself:

Many fortresses have been founded and many large garrisons have been established in the Americas in order to discipline and punish the daring of the pirates, who with such defiance and persistence come to those ports in order to rob and cause other damage.[44]

---

[40] Juan Bautista Román to Philip II, 6 July 1588, and Governor Desmariñas to Philip II, 20 June 1591, in M. L. Díaz-Trechuelo Spínola, *Arquitectura española en Filipinas (1565–1800)* (Seville, 1959), 43–4.

[41] Díaz-Trechuelo Spínola, *Arquitectura*, passim; and R. Reed, *Colonial Manila: The Context of Hispanic Urbanism and Process of Morphogenesis* (Berkeley, 1978), ch. 5.

[42] See the list of cédulas in A. de Altolaguirre y Duvale, *Gubernación espiritual y temporal de las Indias*, 6 vols., Colección de documentos inéditos de Ultramar, 2a series, 21–6 (Madrid, 1927–32), 2:36–52, under the rubric "De las fortificaciones y fuerzas."

[43] See P.E. Hoffman, *The Spanish Crown and the Defense of the Spanish Caribbean, 1535–85: Precedent, Patrimonialism and Royal Parsimony* (Baton Rouge, 1980), passim; and K.R. Andrews, *The Spanish Caribbean: Trade and Plunder, 1530–1630* (New Haven, 1978), 81–107. See also the instructions given to Juan de Texeda in 1588 and to Juan Bautista Antonelli in 1593 to fortify the main harbors of the Caribbean in D. de Encinas, *Cedulario indiano* (Madrid, 1596; 4 vols., facs. ed., Madrid, 1945–6), 4:46–52 and 68–70.

[44] Philip II to the viceroy of Peru, 9 April 1582, in G. Lohmann Villena, *Las defensas militares de Lima y Callao* (Seville, 1964), 1. See also the useful survey of J.A. Calderón

Philip II here referred primarily to the construction of forts in the straits of Magellan and at Callao, the principal port of Peru; but more soon followed as other English and later Dutch expeditions entered the Pacific, albeit amid controversy: "Your Majesty well knows," a minister wearily complained in 1576, "the disputes that divide engineers: they never agree."[45] The defenses therefore went up slowly; in Chile, the government only fortified Valparaíso in 1594, following a raid on the port by Richard Hawkins, and garrisoned the fort erected by the Dutch at Valdivia during a brief occupation in 1643. Further north, the same Dutch raid stimulated the construction of a complete enceinte around Callao (at a cost of 876,000 pesos), and other artillery-bearing fortifications went up around the Spanish Caribbean and along the Pacific coast of Latin America throughout the seventeenth century.[46] Across the Andes, the Portuguese colonists in Brazil also slowly fortified their principal coastal settlements; then, in the eighteenth century, they began to plan impressive polygonal fortifications in the interior to defend the gold mines from possible Spanish attack.[47]

In North America, the various groups of Europeans soon began to build geometrical defenses too, first against each other, and later against the indigenous population. At New Amsterdam, the Dutch began a quadrilateral artillery fort with four bastions "faced outside entirely with stone" in 1635, and along the north side of Wall Street, in 1653, constructed a palisade of sharpened stakes, each twelve feet long, "to make this city of New Amsterdam defensible," adding two stone bastions in 1660. They also maintained garrisons – at least intermittently – in eight other redoubts patterned on Fort Amsterdam in rural or outlying areas of New Netherland.[48] In the later seventeenth

---

Quijano, *Las defensas indianas en la Recopilación de 1680. Precedentes y regulación legal* (Seville, 1994).

[45] Archivo General de Simancas, *Guerra Antiqua* 81, fol. 346, consulta of 20 November 1576, concerning Giovanni Battista Antonelli's criticism of planned fortifications at Cartagena de Indias. See also D. Angulo Iñiguez, *Bautista Antonelli. Las fortificaciones americanas del siglo XVI* (Madrid, 1942).

[46] Lohmann Villena, *Las defensas*, 93, 116; J.A. Calderón Quijano, *Fortificaciones en Nueva España*, 2nd. ed. (Madrid, 1984), passim; and G. Guarda, *Flandes Indiano. Las fortificaciones del reino de Chile, 1541–1826* (Santiago de Chile, 1990), 13–14 and 60–74 (Valdivia), 49–55 (the Straits of Magellan), and 150–1 (Valparaíso). See also J. Gorbea Trueba, "La arquitectura militar en la Nueva España," *Estudios de historia Novohispana* 2 (1967): 213–32.

[47] See F.A. Dutra, "Matías de Albuquerque and the Defense of Northeastern Brazil, 1620–1626," *Studia* 36 (1973): 117–66; and R.M. Delson, "The beginnings of professionalization in the Brazilian military: The Eighteenth Century Corps of Engineers," *The Americas* 51 (1995): 562–4.

[48] See *Documents relative to the Colonial History of the State of New York*, eds. E.B. O'Callaghan and B. Fernow, 15 vols. (Albany, 1853–67), 1:365, 422, 440–1, 499; 5:280;

century, the English erected a complete set of bastions around the capital of their new conquest, renamed New York, while the Spaniards built a citadel at St. Augustine (Florida) and the French fortified Qué-bec with bastions.[49] Inland, however, where no other Europeans threatened, at first defenses generally remained more modest. At Flowerdew Hundred on the James River in Virginia, the colonists erected a small fort in the 1620s with an "earthen rampart, amounting to half of a bastioned fort, which protected the artillery positioned to guard the stretch of the James River around Windmill Point against cannon fire from sailing vessels; while to the west, a shallower ditch-set stockade, or 'quick-set' hedge, defended the settlement from land assault by Native Americans" – a perfect example of the two defen-sive styles. Not far away, at Harbor View (near the confluence of the Nansemond and the James), a simpler structure went up in the 1640s, with two bastions set into opposite ends of rectangular walls; it formed the precursor of the American frontier "Indian" forts whose typological descendants can be traced all the way to California.[50]

The Spaniards proved equally pragmatic. Although initially the crown ordered fortresses to be erected in numerous inland locations (even in Mexico City), the conquerors of New Spain – both spiritual and secular – preferred to build their churches to serve as forts in case of need and to construct portable blockhouses along the main roads leading north from the capital (for example, to Zacatecas and Guada-lajara) in the 1570s.[51] In the south, officials and settlers constructed numerous forts for defense against their indigenous foes – over 150 of them in Chile alone (96 in the present state of Arauco) – many of them sharing the same rectangular design as those of New England, with two bastions at opposite corners.[52]

The French, however, decided to build full artillery fortresses even

The records of New Amsterdam from 1653 to 1674, ed. B. Fernow, 7 vols. (Albany, 1897), 1:72–3; and Alan C. Aimone, "New Netherland's Military Experience," *De halve maen* 51 (October, 1976): 15–17, and 51 (January, 1977): 13–14.

[49] On these and other fortresses, see A. Gallay, *Colonial Wars of North America, 1512–1763. An Encyclopedia* (New York, 1966), 600–11 (Québec), 664–7 (St. Augustine), and so on; and I.K. Steele, *Warpaths. Invasions of North America* (Oxford, 1994), chs. 2–6.

[50] C.T. Hodges, "Private Fortifications in 17th-century Virginia: A Study of Six Repre-sentative Works," in *The Archaeology of Seventeenth-Century Virginia*, eds. T.R. Reinhard and D.J. Pogue (Richmond, 1993), 192–3, 199; and the numerous entries in Gallay, *Colonial Wars*.

[51] For details, see P.W. Powell, *Soldiers, Indians and Silver: The Northward Advance of New Spain, 1550–1600*, 2nd. ed. (Berkeley, 1969), 151. For the order to create a fortress in Mexico City, see Altolaguirre y Duvale, *Gobernación espiritual*, 2:45 (cédula of May 1536).

[52] Guarda, *Flandes Indiano*, 182–98 ("El frente interno"). A plan of Angol in 1637 shows the typical geometrical design used against the Araucanians (see 198).

in the interior of early modern North America. A popular work on world travel commented laconically on an early French expedition down the Mississippi in the 1680s: "The Chevalier de la Salle left with a detachment, entered the Illinois area, took possession of the country in the name of Louis XIV, called it Louisiana in honor of this prince, and constructed a fort there; the Spaniards would have built a church, the English a tavern."[53] In fact, La Salle built two quadrilateral structures in the Mississippi valley, with bastions at each corner (Fort Crèvecoeur in 1680 and Fort Louis in 1682), and others followed, but at first all were made of timber and thus possessed limited durability. Fort de Chartres in Illinois, for example, built in 1720 of "logs the size of a man's leg, square in shape, having two bastions which commanded all the curtains," was soon described as decayed. But in 1753, as part of a chain of forts designed to contain the expansion of the English colonies to the east, the foundations of a large stone fortress with four bastions were laid which, eleven years later, earned praise from a British officer as "the most commodious and best built fort in North America." Its precise geometrical shape still stands today – Vauban would have been proud – although the loss of Quebec in 1759 rendered the work useless, for the French were forced to cede all their American possessions, and so Fort de Chartres became Fort Cavendish.[54]

In America as in Asia, however, isolated fortresses proved of limited use. They served to create a safe environment for trade and a defense against low-intensity threats, but they could not resist a major assault. The forts erected along the northern frontier of New Spain did not always protect their defenders, let alone the surrounding towns and plantations. Likewise, during "Bacon's Rebellion" in Virginia, the strongholds built in 1676 to protect the settlements against Indian attack failed to achieve their goal. The French did indeed erect forts that ranged from South Dakota to the Ohio River and south to Louisiana, but only because the local Indian nations welcomed them for purposes of trade and mutual defense: they too repeatedly proved incapable of resisting a full-scale attack. Even the more sophisticated forts of New Netherland all fell to the English in 1664 without a shot

---

[53] Abbé Delaporte, *Le voyageur françois* (Paris, 1769), quoted by S. Wilson, "Colonial Fortifications and Military Architecture in the Mississippi Valley," in *The French in the Mississippi Valley*, ed. J.F. McDermott (Urbana, 1965), 103.

[54] Wilson, "Colonial Fortifications," 119; Gallay, *Colonial Wars*, 114–16; and D. Buisseret, *Historic Illinois from the Air* (Chicago, 1990), 28–9, 38–9, and 40 (an excellent map of the French fortresses in North America during the Seven Years War). Fort de Chartres has now been restored to its mid-eighteenth-century condition (information kindly supplied by Benjamin Rota).

being fired, and in 1673 the Dutch regained them almost as easily. Only the few fully-fledged "Italian style" defenses, such as Fort San Marcos in Florida (which successfully resisted sieges by the English in 1702 and 1750), proved their worth.[55] But San Marcos, too, could not serve as a base for large-scale offensive operations in the interior. The Westerners in North America – whether French, Dutch, English, or Spanish – could neither transport their artillery inland nor could they move their own troops fast enough to catch their adversaries in the field. Indeed, they could seldom find their enemies' settlements: "Every swamp is a castle to them," lamented Increase Mather during King Philip's War in New England (1675), "knowing where to find us, but we know not where to find them." Even in the mid-eighteenth century, the repeated attempts of the French to destroy the Chickasaw failed because they could not locate the Chickasaw towns and, when they did, they found their fortifications (constructed with English assistance) impregnable. Normally, therefore, the Westerners relied on Indian allies and auxiliaries to do their fighting for them.[56]

NON-EUROPEAN ARTILLERY FORTRESSES AND THE MILITARY BALANCE OF POWER

The native peoples of the Americas, Siberia, and the Philippines, although they succeeded in emulating many military techniques of the European invaders, normally failed to build artillery fortresses. Admittedly a number of locations in Mexico and Peru were fortified before the Spanish invasion, but only with vertical defenses; others, like Mexico City, possessed vast temples designed like (and, in the event, used like) citadels; while other Indian strongholds boasted such inaccessible locations that further fortifications seemed unnecessary.[57] The Inca fastness of Ollantaytambo, for example, stood on a rock outcrop so steep that artillery could be used for neither attack nor defense. Apparently, a full process of replication only took place in the north of the continent, where the constant rivalry of the various European invaders led them to teach their Indian allies to construct true Western-style defenses. Although in the "Pequot War" of 1637 the

---

[55] For useful sketches, see Gallay, *Colonial Wars*, 58 (Bacon's Rebellion), 489–91 (the loss of New Netherland) and 499–500 (its recovery), and 666 (San Marcos). On New Spain, see Powell, *Soldiers, Indians and Silver*, passim.

[56] Mather quoted by J.L. Axtell, *The European and the Indian. Essays in the Ethnohistory of Colonial North America* (Oxford, 1981), 145; Gallay, *Colonial Wars*, 124–9, on the Chickasaw. I thank Alan Gallay for enlightenment on this point.

[57] See Hassig, *Aztec Warfare*, and Hassig, *War and Society in Ancient Mesoamerica* (Berkeley, 1992), passim.

Native Americans still relied on their traditional circular palisade fortifications, forty years later, during "King Philip's War," their military
repertory had expanded dramatically. For the Narragansetts of Rhode
Island, besides owning molds and a forge able to make musket and
pistol balls and parts for firearms, constructed a fort on a natural
island in the "Great Swamp" which, although it only had palisades
for the curtains, "at one corner ... they had placed a kind of block-
house ... from whence they sorely galled our men that first entered"
and a "flanker" at the other. In December 1675, the fort's capture cost
the lives of over seventy colonists.[58] Meanwhile the Susquehannock
Fort in Maryland defied a siege by English colonists for six weeks in
the same year, thanks to its "high banks of earth, with flankers having
many loopholes and a ditch around all." Other examples of Indian
forts with bastions and "flankers" are reported in New York state,
eastern Canada, and, later, Illinois, where in 1730 the Italian-style
defenses constructed by the Indians around Fort Fox defied a full-
dress French siege for a month.[59] In the end, the Native Americans
lost ground, not so much through any technical inferiority but because
their numbers dwindled (largely thanks to the inroads of European
diseases), while those of the Westerners (largely thanks to immigra-
tion) relentlessly increased.[60]

Elsewhere, efforts to emulate European techniques of defense and
attack proved more successful. Most of the Muslim states of the Middle East possessed an extensive and sophisticated military tradition
(both written and practical) of their own and rapidly assimilated Western firearms into their military repertory, albeit often by a process of

---

[58] Details in W. Hubbard, *The History of the Indian Wars in New England* (Boston, 1677;
ed. S.G. Drake, Roxbury, 1865), 1:146–7; and P.M. Malone, *The Skulking Way of War:
Technology and Tactics among the New England Indians* (Lanham, 1991), 73–4. The fort
in the "Great Swamp" thus resembled an Irish "crannog": see the description of one
from the 1650s in J. Ohlmeyer, *Ireland from Independence to Occupation, 1641–1660*
(Cambridge, 1995), 83. The Narragansetts also constructed a stone fort with two
bastions that remained undiscovered by the colonists until after the war; Malone,
Skulking Way, 74–5.

[59] Thomas Mathew's contemporary account, quoted by A.L. Ferguson, "The Susquehannock fort on Pitscataway Creek," *Maryland Historical Magazine* 36 (1941): 1–9. For
other examples, see George Milner, "Palisaded Settlements in Prehistoric Eastern
North America," ch. 2 of this volume; Steel, *Warpaths*, 66–7 and 113; and Gallay,
Colonial Wars, 219–22 (on Fort Fox, with two contemporary maps) and 424–5 (Indian
forts in Maryland). See also the judicious remarks of L.H. Keeley, *War Before Civilization* (Oxford, 1996), 71–81.

[60] For another surprisingly successful indigenous replication of European techniques of
fortification, albeit from outside this period, see J. Belich, *The New Zealand Wars and
the Victorian Interpretation of Racial Conflict* (Harmondsworth, 1986), 49–50, 106–7, 251–
2, and 294–7.

routine mimesis, copying captured weapons and importing foreign specialists.[61] The Ottoman Turks, for example, at first seemed particularly adept against the West. In 1453 their artillery (mostly cast by Western renegades) demolished the walls of Constantinople; in 1520–1 they captured the strategic strongholds of Rhodes and Belgrade; and in the 1570s they captured both the "modern" Venetian fortifications of Cyprus (Nicosia, with its eleven bastions, was at the time the most sophisticated fortress-city yet built by Europeans), and the heavily fortified Spanish outposts of Tunis and La Goletta.[62] However, these Turkish successes resulted more from overwhelming force than from the surgical precision with relatively modest forces practiced in the West; moreover, after each success the Turks did relatively little to maintain or improve the fortifications they captured. According to Alain Manesson Mallet in the late seventeenth century:

Once they [the Turks] have them, they are content to repair the breaches and scarcely take the trouble to preserve the defenses, believing that it is useless to spend money to maintain strongholds which the Christians will never attack, thanks to the divisions amongst them. . . . As for bastions, these infidels never construct them – unless some renegade shows them how.

Mallet included plates of several fortresses previously taken by the Turks to demonstrate either the lack of subsequent improvements or the imperfect attempts at modernization and, by way of constrast, he also depicted two state-of-the-art artillery fortresses built in Habsburg Hungary.[63] Nevertheless, the Turks almost succeeded with their gam-

[61] See the perceptive remarks of J. Aubin in _Bulletin critique des annales islamologiques_ 6 (1990): 153–5. D. Ralston, _Importing the European Army: The Introduction of European Military Techniques and Institutions into the Extra-European World, 1600–1914_ (Chicago, 1990), 43–78, only begins his analysis of "the reform of the Ottoman army" in 1750 and therefore sheds little light on this; but see the interesting case studies of C.F. Finkel, "French mercenaries in the Habsburg-Ottoman war of 1593–1606: the desertion of the Papa garrison to the Ottomans in 1600," _Bulletin of the School of Oriental and African Studies_ 55 (1992): 451–71; R. Murphey, "The Ottoman attitude towards the Adoption of Western Technology: The Role of the _Efrenci_ Technicians in Civil and Military Applications," in _Contributions à l'histoire économique et sociale de l'empire ottoman_, eds. J.L. Bacqué-Grammont and P. Dumont (Louvain, 1983), 287–98; and S. Christensen, "European-Ottoman military acculturation in the late Middle Ages," in _War and Peace in the Middle Ages_, ed. B.P. McGuire (Copenhagen, 1987), 227–51.

[62] On the Venetian fortification program in Croatia/Dalmatia, see Mallett and Hale, _Military Organization_, 429–60; and Josip Vrandecic, "The military revolution comes to Croatia," (publication forthcoming). On Habsburg efforts in Hungary, see L. Zangheri, "Gli architetti italiani e la difesa dei territori dell'Impero minacciati dai turchi," in _Architettura militare_, 243–51; and R. Schäfer, "Festungsbau an der Türkengrenze. Die Pfandschaft Rann im 16. Jahrhundert," _Zeitschrift des historiches Vereins für Steiermark_ 75 (1984): 31–59.

[63] Alain Manesson Mallet, _Les travaux de Mars, ou l'art de la guerre_, 3rd ed. (The Hague, 1696), 3:317–33, from "Livre sixième: De la milice des Turcs," with a discussion of

ble (if such it was: we rely here only on Western sources). Although they failed to take Vienna in 1683, it should be remembered, first, that the relief army, drawn from several European states, arrived just as the Ottoman siege army neared victory, and second, that it was the Turks at the gates of Vienna and not the Europeans at the gates of Istanbul.[64]

Furthermore, the Turks gladly shared their expertise with others. An interesting early transmission of the "Military Revolution" of early modern Europe to a Muslim society occurred in Saʿdian Morocco in the sixteenth century. As early as 1541, following the fall of a Portuguese outpost, King John III observed:

We must recognize that warfare in Morocco has changed. The enemy is now very adept in the arts of war and siegecraft, due in part to the aid of many Turks and renegades, numerous artillery weapons, and the important materials of war.[65]

John III's grandson, Sebastian, experienced the truth of this in spectacular fashion in 1578, when he and his army met defeat and death at the hands of Turkish-trained Saʿdian forces in the battle of Alcazarquiver, while the subsequent conquest of the sub-Saharan Songhay empire in 1590–1 by Moroccan troops – led by a Spanish Muslim renegade and including a detachment of Ottoman musketeers – offered a "textbook gunpowder conquest," to rank with those of Cortés in Mexico, Pizarro in Peru, and Legazpi in the Philippines.[66]

In fact, "Turks and renegades" made their influence felt all over the Islamic world. The sultanate of Acheh in Sumatra, for example, established direct contact with the "Raja Rum" (the Ottoman sultan, "king of the West") in the sixteenth century; letters and gifts were exchanged, and a stream of Turkish military experts came to Indonesia to cast cannon and to fight (according to Malay sources, some 300

---

prints of Satu Mare, Budapest, Szolnok,and Neuhausel (Nové Zámsky). This section did not appear in Mallet's first edition of 1672, but was added in the second in 1684–5, following the relief of Vienna.

[64] A point made by W.J. Hamblin, "Gunpowder weapons and medieval Islamic military theory" (a paper graciously sent to me by Dr. Hamblin in October 1989). On the remarkable logistical achievements of the Ottoman empire, see C. Finkel, *The Administration of Warfare: The Ottoman Military Campaigns in Hungary, 1593–1606*; Beihefte zur Wiener Zeitschrift für die Kunde des Morgenlandes 14 (Vienna, 1988).

[65] See W.F. Cook, *The Hundred Years' War for Morocco. Gunpowder and the Military Revolution in the Early Modern Muslim World* (Boulder, 1994), 193. On the spread of Western military techniques to other Islamic states in North Africa, see A.C. Hess, *The Forgotten Frontier. A History of the Sixteenth-Century Ibero-African Frontier* (Chicago, 1978), and "Firearms and the decline of Ibn Khaldun's military elite," *Archivum ottomanicum* 4 (1972): 173–99.

[66] See Cook, *The Hundred Years' War*, 258.

Turks with firearms were fighting for Acheh by 1537). In 1567, the
Ottoman sultan even promised to send a fleet to Indonesia to drive
out the Portuguese, but in the event it sailed to suppress a revolt in
Yemen instead.[67] Sultan Iskandar Muda of Acheh (1607–36) maintained a corps of military slaves, captured when young and trained
specially (just like the janissaries), and his soldiers constructed siege-
works of such sophistication that (according to a Portuguese account)
"not even the Romans could have made such works stronger or more
quickly."[68] Elsewhere in south Asia, "Turks and renegades" frequently
rubbed shoulders. At the capture of Goa in 1510, for example, an
Italian participant reported that the victors "killed around two thousand persons of those who resisted us. And these were almost all
Turks, and renegade Christians of all sorts; among whom were Venetians and Genoese in largest numbers."[69] In spite of this salutary
example, the total "renegade Christians" who earned their living from
the local rulers in the region continued to rise – to perhaps 5,000 by
1600 – with an even larger number of Turks. Their presence dwindled
somewhat in the course of the seventeenth century, at least in Mughal
India, and their rewards diminished as native artificers became more
experienced; nevertheless, during the civil war between Aurangzeb
and his brothers for the Mughal throne in the 1650s, several hundred
Europeans and Turks served both as mercenaries and as technical
advisers, especially for artillery and siegecraft. Thus, according to
François Bernier, Aurangzeb captured the port city of Surat in 1658
only because some Dutch experts "showed his generals how to use
gunpowder mines."[70]

[67] Details from Anthony R. Reid, "Sixteenth-century Turkish Influence in Western Indonesia," *Journal of Southeast Asian History* 10/3 (1969): 395–414.

[68] See C.R. Boxer, "The Achinese attack on Malacca in 1629, as Described in Contemporary Portuguese sources," in *Malayan and Indonesian Studies: Essays Presented to Sir
Richard Winstedt on his 85th Birthday*, eds. J. Bastin and R. Roolvink (Oxford, 1964),
105–21, reprinted in Boxer, *Portuguese Conquest and Commerce in Southeast Asia, 1500–
1750* (London, 1985), ch. 5.

[69] Piero Strozzi – a Florentine, hence his rejoicing – writing on 10 December 1510, just
after the capture of Goa, quoted by Subrahmanyam, *Political Economy*, 255. See numerous other examples of "renegades" in A.D. da Costa, "Os Portugueses e os Reis
da India," *Boletim do Instituto Vasco da Gama* 13 (1932): 1–45; 15 (1932): 1–38; 18 (1933):
1–28; and 20 (1933): 1–40; and M.A. Lima Cruz, "Exiles and Renegades in Early
Sixteenth-century Portuguese Asia," *Indian Economic and Social History Review* 23
(1986): 249–62, esp. 259–62.

[70] Donald F. Lach and Edwin J. van Kley, *Asia in the Making of Europe*, 3 vols. (Chicago,
1993), 3:726, quoting Bernier and Fryer. See also Sanjay Subrahmanyam, "The *Kage-
musha* Effect: The Portuguese, Firearms and the State in Early Modern South Asia,"
Moyen Orient et Océan Indien 4 (1987): 97–123; J.F. Richards, *The Mughal Empire*, The
New Cambridge History of India, vol. 1, bk. 5 (Cambridge, 1993), 220–2; N. Manucci,
Storia do Mogor, or Mogul India 1653–1708, ed. W. Irvine, 4 Vols. (London, 1906–8),

However, Indian rulers seem to have taken few steps to imitate European fortification styles. According to Niccolo Manucci, an Italian in Mughal service, the Mughal capital at Delhi boasted walls in the 1650s "one half of brick and the rest of stone. At every hundred paces is a strengthening bastion, but on these there is no artillery." Slightly earlier, William Methwold of the English East India Company reported that the inland state of Golconda (later Hyderabad) possessed sixty-six fortresses, most of them perched on high rocks or hills and accessible by only one route. Most were of massive construction: the walls of the Purana Qila at Delhi, built between 1530 and 1545, stood some fifty feet thick and sixty feet high; those of Golconda, four miles in circumference and later adapted to include artillery platforms, were no less imposing. Against such targets, even the heaviest early modern artillery bombardment (supposing siege guns could be brought up) made little impression, and sieges tended to be decided by blockade rather than cannonade. Thus Aurangzeb brought about 100 siege guns and 100,000 troops against Golconda in 1687, and also set three mines (each containing sixteen tons of gunpowder) under the walls; but the guns never came close enough to be effective, and when the mines were sprung two had been countermined and blew back on the attackers while the third failed to ignite. In the end, after an eight-month siege, Golconda only fell by treachery when a disaffected nobleman opened one of the gates to the Mughals during a night attack.[71]

Early modern China conformed to much the same pattern. Admittedly China lacked castles, but instead most towns boasted impressive fortifications; indeed, the Chinese character most often translated as "wall" (*cheng*) is also the character most often translated as city. Thus "*cheng*, a wall, always implies a city; *cheng*, a city, always has walls."[72] According to a European general in 1860, the walls of Peking stood "upwards of fifty feet in breadth, very nearly the same in height, in excellent repair, and paved on the top where, I am sure, five coaches-and-four could, with little management, have been driven abreast

---

1:309, 313; and F. Bernier, *Travels in the Mogul Empire, AD 1656–68*, ed. A. Constable (London, 1891), 31–2. (Bernier served as Aurangzeb's personal physician.)

[71] Manucci, *Storia do Mogor*, 1:183–4; William Methwold (writing in the 1620s) quoted in Lach and Van Kley, *Asia in the Making of Europe*, 3:1023. See also Sidney Toy, *The Strongholds of India* (London, 1957), 53–60 (Golconda) and 123 (Delhi); and J.F. Richards, *Mughal Administration in Golconda* (Oxford, 1975), 48–51.

[72] See Nancy Schatzman Steinhardt, "Representations of Chinese Walled Cities in the Pictorial and Graphic Arts," ch. 14 of this volume. Even the earliest Chinese pictograms denoting "town," in the Shang oracle bones of the second millennium B.C. were written in the shape of a square or rectangular enclosure, above the drawing of a man: see Needham and Yates, *Science and Civilisation in China*, 5:pt. 4, 243.

[along them]." Those of Nanking, equally formidable, stretched for twenty-two miles. In the event, the strength of these defenses was never tested by Western guns, but in 1841, during the Opium War, a two-hour bombardment from warships of the Royal Navy on the batteries of Amoy, according to an eye-witness, "produced no effect whatever; not a gun being found disabled and but few of the enemy killed in them when our troops entered. The principle of their construction was such as to render them almost impervious to the efforts of horizontal fire, even from the 32-pounders."[73] Small wonder then that (as Matteo Ricci noted) China chose to ignore the "artillery fortress."[74]

At the time of the fall of Melaka to the Portuguese in 1511, no town in Southeast Asia seems to have possessed stone walls, and the situation changed only slowly.[75] In Siam, even in the late seventeenth century, only Bangkok had any walled defenses: a chain of small forts along the Chao Phrya river, manned by 100 Christian Luso-Asiatic soldiers under captains "who drill them every day." Elsewhere, according to European visitors, the Siamese disdained to fortify strong places "for fear of losing them, and not being able to retake them."[76] Likewise, the early modern Vietnamese burnt their wooden settlements when invasion threatened, fleeing to the mountains until security returned. Despite an almost constant state of civil war in the country, the only permanent fortifications remained the walls built across central Vietnam to divide Tongking from Cochin-China; towns and cities were surrounded at most by a bamboo fence (although Hue,

[73] Quotations from H. Knollys, *Incidents in the China War of 1860, Compiled from the Private Journals of General Sir Hope Grant* (Edinburgh, 1875), 198–9; and J. Ouchterlony, *The Chinese War* (London, 1844), 174–5. Note, however, that (according to Ouchterlony) rapid naval broadsides did destroy the granite-built gun batteries on the Pearl River defending Canton.

[74] Conversely, Western fortifications might succumb to Chinese attack: in 1661–2 the Ming loyalist leader Coxinga – albeit with the aid of a renegade – conducted a successful siege of Fort Zeelandia, the Dutch headquarters on Taiwan; see the account of C.R. Boxer, "The siege of Fort Zeelandia and the capture of Formosa from the Dutch, 1661–2," *Transactions and Proceedings of the Japan Society of London* 24 (1926–7): 16–47, reprinted in Boxer, *Dutch Merchants and Mariners in Asia, 1602–1795* (London, 1988), ch. 3. For the role of the renegade, see 41. See also H. Franke, "Siege and defense of towns in medieval China," in *Chinese Ways in Warfare*, eds. F.A. Kierman and J.K. Fairbank (Cambridge, MA, 1974), 151–201; and Needham and Yates, *Science and Civilisation in China*, 5:pt. 4, 260–5.

[75] See *Lettera di Giovanni da Empoli*, 132–3, written in 1514, and specifically contrasting the "walled cities, houses, buildings, castles of great strength, and artillery of every sort like our own" found in China with the lack of fortifications in Indonesia.

[76] Lach and Van Kley, *Asia in the Making of Europe*, 3:1202, 1216 (based on the accounts of Louis XIV's envoy to the court of Siam, Simon de la Loubère, published in 1691, and of the French missionary, Nicholas Gervaise, published in 1688).

at least, boasted a considerable stock of Western artillery by the 1680s).[77] Only Burma proved different; the unification of the country by the Mons of Pegu in the mid-sixteenth century clearly owed a lot to their ability to construct "impregnable" fortifications in the European manner, although this ability seems to have waned in the seventeenth century.[78]

These mainland states, however, rarely faced a major and sustained European challenge: Felipe de Brito Nicote and his motley crew of mercenaries in Burma (1599–1613) and Louis XIV's naval and military expedition to Siam (1687–8), although surprisingly successful, proved to be isolated episodes.[79] Matters in the Indonesian archipelago were very different, with first the Portuguese and then the Spanish, Dutch, English, and French all striving to create permanent fortified bases and to control both the production and trade of certain items. Although the inhabitants of most cities in the archipelago also responded to unstable political conditions by flight, some cities began to acquire walls. To begin with, many urban areas already boasted fortified residential compounds for the great men, and solid stone "godowns" in which merchants stored their goods against the threat of theft and fire. Furthermore, by 1600 the Javanese cities of Banten, Japara, Tuban, Pati, and Surabaya had all acquired perimeter walls – although the largest metropolis in the archipelago, Acheh, rejected them: "This city [according to a chronicler] is not fortified like other cities because of the very large number of war elephants" able to protect it.[80] The sultan of Makassar displayed rather more ambition. By the 1630s, his capital possessed a large fortress (Sombaopu) around the royal palace which, on the seaward side, boasted walls fourteen feet thick, and four bastions equipped with twenty heavy guns donated by Europeans (the Danes, English, and Portuguese all maintained factories in the city) and commanded by an Englishman who had converted to Islam.[81]

---

[77] L. Cadière, "Le quartier des Arènes. I. Jean de la Croix et les premiers Jésuites," *Bulletin des amis du Vieux Hué* 14/4 (1924): 312 (citing a report of 1683); Lach and Van Kley, *Asia in the Making of Europe*, 3:1264 (from the 1631 "Relation" to Christoforo Borri); 1281 (citing Alexandre de Rhodes in 1641); and 1298. For other examples of "flight" as a reaction, see also Parker, *Military Revolution*, 122 (Malaya).

[78] See V.B. Lieberman, "Europeans, Trade and the Unification of Burma c. 1540–1620," *Oriens extremus* 27/2 (1980): 203–26; Reid, *Southeast Asia*, 78–82; and Lach and Van Kley, *Asia in the Making of Europe*, 3:1122–46.

[79] See Lach and Van Kley, *Asia in the Making of Europe*, 3:1124–8 and 1193–4 for details.

[80] See Reid, *Southeast Asia*, 87–8.

[81] Details from Lach and Van Kley, *Asia in the Making of Europe*, 3:1444 (from the eyewitness description of Seyger van Rechteren, who visited Makassar in 1635); G. Vermeulen, *De gedenkwaerdige Voyagie* (Amsterdam, 1677), 67; and Reid, *Southeast Asia*, 88. A map of this date from the "Secret Atlas of the East India Company" showing

Other forts of brick also sprang up, until in the 1660s a solid defensive wall studded with forts stretched along the seafront of the city for over seven miles.[82] Both the design of the forts and contemporary documents indicate Portuguese influence, and this should come as no surprise: Makassar had been consistently friendly towards the Portuguese since the arrival of the Dutch in the area, and provided a crucial refuge for them as the Dutch noose tightened elsewhere. After the fall of Melaka in 1641, for example, between 2,000 and 3,000 Portuguese transferred their activities from Malaysia to Makassar.[83] The Dutch resented this challenge, and in 1667 a fleet of thirty-five ships (including eleven warships) sailed up from Batavia and bombarded the forts along the seafront. Despite a barrage of "12, 18 and 24 pound balls from the enemy," which damaged the masts, sails, and rigging of the Dutch ships, the fortresses fell one by one and eventually Makassar made peace (Fig. 13.2). Two years later, however, when it seemed that the sultan had disregarded the agreement, the Dutch returned with Bugis allies and began a formal siege. In June 1669, after six months of bitter fighting, the Dutch managed to explode a mine under the walls of Sombaopu and create a breach twenty yards wide. They then launched an assault that involved fighting so heavy "That old soldiers have perhaps never heard its like in Europe itself": the Dutch musketeers allegedly fired off 30,000 rounds, yet it still took ten days to complete the capture of the fort.[84]

However, the most remarkable early modern Asian response to Europe's gunpowder revolution occurred in Japan. Writing in the 1590s, the Jesuit missionary Luis Fróis dismissed Japanese fortifications almost as contemptuously as his colleague Matteo Ricci had previously deprecated those of China. Describing Toyotomi Hideyoshi's new fortress at Kyoto, Fróis wrote: "Although for Japan, where

Sombaopu, in color, is in Reid, "Southeast Asian Cities before Colonialism," *Hemisphere* 28/3 (1983): 144.

[82] A.R. Reid, "The rise of Makassar," *Review of Indonesian and Malaysian Affairs* 17 (1983: 141–2. However (Professor Reid informs me) one can see today from the substantial ruins that the bricks used were thinner than European ones.

[83] Personal communication from Anthony Reid, 24 March 1995; see also Lach and Van Kley, *Asia in the Making of Europe*, 3:1446 (citing Domingo Fernández de Navarrete, who visited Makassar in 1657).

[84] Details from the eyewitness accounts in Reid, "The Rise of Makassar," 150; Vermeulen, *Voyagie*, 53–71; and W. Schouten, *Reys-togten naar en door Oost Indien*, 2nd ed. (Amsterdam, 1708), 85–93. See also the pictures of the Dutch bombardment of Pannakkukang in Reid, *Southeast Asia in the Age of Commerce*, 2:279, and in Schouten, *Reys-togten* (Fig. 13.2). L. Andaya, *The Heritage of Arung Palakka: A History of South Sulawesi (Celebes) in the Seventeenth Century* (The Hague, 1981), 130–3, offers a good account of the fall of Makassar to the combined forces of the Dutch and of Arung Palakka's Bugis.

Figure 13.2. The Renaissance-style fortifications around Makassar proved unable to withstand bombardment by a Dutch fleet in June 1667. The Dutch first forced the outlying fort of Panakoke (in the foreground) to surrender and then attacked Fort Ioupandan (on the skyline) and Sombaopu (labeled "Hooft Casteel" or citadel). The sultan sued for peace after one day's bombardment. Wouter Schouten, *Reys-togten naar en door Oost Indien*, 2nd ed. (Amsterdam, 1708), plate facing p. 92. Courtesy of the Universiteitsbibliotheek, Leiden.

artillery is not used, it is very strong, nevertheless in comparison with Europe it is very weak, because with four pieces of artillery, everything would be destroyed in half a day." But, even as he wrote, Japan was adapting. In 1578, according to Fróis himself, for the first time the nobles of the island of Kyushu (many of them newly converted to Christianity) began to deploy "some artillery pieces" in their wars; and, at the same time, the dominant military leader on the main island, Oda Nobunaga, built a new type of defensive fortification at Azuchi, near lake Biwa, by surrounding a promontory with angled stone walls in such a way that they constituted a solid mass of rock and earth, in which each part offered flanking fire to the rest.[85] Al-

[85] Ricci, quoted on page 388 of this chapter; L. Fróis, *História do Japão*, ed. J. Wicki (Lisbon, 1984), 5:315 (sub anno 1591–2, part of an interesting chapter comparing various types of building in Europe and Japan); see also, 3:41–2 (for 1578), 4:54–5 (for 1584), and so on. See the interesting discussion in J.P. Oliveira e Costa, "A introdução

though Azuchi was destroyed in 1582, numerous other cannon-proof castles of similar design followed between 1580 and 1630, of which some sixty survive, and Japanese forces built more during the invasion of Korea during the 1590s (just after Fróis wrote). Several of the new fortresses were enormous: The star-shaped walls of Kumamoto castle, with forty-nine towers and two keeps, extended for almost eight miles; so did those of Osaka castle, composed in part of rocks weighing between 120 and 130 tons each, to a depth in places of almost sixty feet.[86] Although artillery (both Japanese and Western) was occasionally deployed against these targets – most notably at the siege of Osaka in 1614–15 and during the Shimabara rebellion of 1636–7 – it proved indecisive; the walls were too thick.

The striking resemblance between the geometrical form of these fortifications and the *trace italienne* might suggest that the Japanese imitated the Western design; and, indeed, military conversation with Westerners, among others, formed one of Nobunaga's principal passions. However, no surviving documents demonstrate a connection, and it is noteworthy that Nobunaga also devised the idea of the musketry volley some twenty years *before* it emerged in the West! It seems more likely that the same problem – the vulnerability of vertical defenses to artillery bombardment – gave rise to the same solution in both countries. In any case, the impressive network of artillery fortresses developed in early modern Japan helped to preserve its integrity against the West.[87]

But no immunity lasts forever. In most Islamic societies, the founding and management of artillery became the exclusive preserve of small cadres of foreign specialists, most of them renegades and adventurers with little training and less experience in their craft. In China and Japan, too, technological innovation ceased and by the nineteenth century the military elite had lost the capacity to use their "new" weapons. Instead of changing their armed forces in order to make the best use of Western military technology, they attempted to adapt Western technology to their existing ideas of warfare; and in this they failed.[88]

das armas de fogo no Japão pelos Portugueses a luz da história do Japão de Luís Fróis," *Estudos orientais* 3 (1992): 126–8. Other, more favorable, European descriptions of Japanese castles appear in *They Came to Japan. An Anthology of European Reports on Japan, 1543–1640*, ed. M. Cooper (Berkeley, 1965), 131–41.

[86] See Parker, *Military Revolution*, 142–3 and references on 232.

[87] For Nobunaga's love of military conversation, see A. Valignano, *Sumario de las cosas de Japón* (1583; ed. J.L. Alvarez-Taladriz, Tokyo, 1954), 152. For the spontaneous development of musketry volley, see Parker, *Military Revolution*, 140.

[88] Richards, *The Mughal Empire*, 288–9; and N. Perrin, *Giving up the Gun. Japan's Reversion*

CONCLUSION

The artillery fortress of early modern Europe played a key role in the rise of the West in two distinct respects, one defensive and the other offensive. The sixteenth century saw a strong phase of Islamic expansion, with the Mughals gaining control of some 1.25 million square miles of India, and the Ottomans creating an empire of roughly 1 million square miles, which stretched from Morocco, through Egypt and Iraq, to the Balkans and Hungary. So many states and societies succumbed that the resistance of the West to this Islamic tide stands out as unusual. And it was a close-run thing: At Mohacs (1526) and Mezokeresztes (1596) in Hungary, the Turks triumphed; and if they were routed at Lepanto in the Mediterranean in 1571, they nevertheless conquered Cyprus and Tunis in the 1570s and Crete in the 1650s. The artillery fortress proved crucial in limiting the damage. On the one hand, as Vauban rightly observed, "Winning a battle leaves the victor in control of the countryside for the time being, but only taking the fortresses will give him the entire country;" and where artillery fortresses had proliferated to create a defense-in-depth, as in the Maghreb, Hungary, and Dalmatia, a rapid Muslim advance proved impossible. On the other hand, the resistance of even a solitary artillery fortress could waste a powerful army, because it could only be starved out and few non-European states could maintain their forces in the field beyond a single campaigning season. The fortress also proved remarkably cost-effective: After the initial outlay (crippling though that could be), the expense of maintaining the masonry and an adequate garrison amounted to far less than the upkeep of an army capable of defeating adversaries in the field.

Finally, even though they alone did not suffice to create a continental empire, the Europeans' fortified cities overseas nevertheless served to extend their power inland. This occurred in two ways. First, the fortresses offered advantages to indigenous rulers, especially those who lived in fear of a more powerful neighbor: to the king of Malindi in East Africa, faced by the sultan of Mombasa; to the king of Cochin in South India, threatened by the Samorin of Calicut; to the Mohawks in northeastern America, beset by the Iroquois. Granting the Europeans permission to erect a fort, and concluding a treaty with them,

---

to the Sword (New York, 1979). In Ch'ing China too, despite the keen interest of many government officials in military technology, most innovations involving firearms remained the work of foreigners of limited practical experience: see J. Waley-Cohen, "China and Western Technology in the Later Eighteenth Century," *American Historical Review* 98 (1993): 1525–44. See also Ralston, *Importing the European Army*.

improved their local importance and their overall security. Without forts capable of offering sustained resistance, alliance with the Europeans, without which Western power would surely have remained confined to the coasts, might not have seemed so attractive to native rulers. Second, and scarcely less important, the capacity of European fortresses to withstand even a prolonged siege offered obvious advantages to local merchants fearful that the wars endemic in most regions might destroy their trading stock. The history of the Europeans in Asia, Africa, and North America provides numerous examples of local merchants keeping their goods inside fortified European bases, despite the high tolls and duties exacted, and even lending money to preserve the Western presence in the region. Thus João de Castro, viceroy of India, financed his relief of Diu in 1539 largely from loans provided by Indian merchants living in Goa; and from the 1680s onwards Indian merchants in southeast India began to make substantial deposits in cash with the agents of the English East India Company in Madras.[89]

The military effectiveness of Western fortifications of course predated the "Age of Expansion." Following a wave of invasions during the third century A.D., the Romans constructed a network of fortresses along the empire's Rhine frontier – the earliest known example of a defense-in-depth. Then, from the 900s, Fulk Nerra, count of the Angevins, began to construct stone castles to form a similar preclusive frontier around his territory, a technique that quickly spread along all the major land frontiers of medieval Europe: between Capetians and Plantagenets along the Norman border; in the Welsh Marches and around the Pale in Ireland; in Spain during the "Reconquest." Castles also served to guard overseas enclaves during the Middle Ages, as discussed earlier in this chapter; adding bastions merely allowed the strategy to survive into the gunpowder age. To return to the "military paradigm" summarized by Anthony Reid, the artillery fortress constituted the crucial link between the Europeans' naval mastery and their ability to attract and exploit local allies. The invention and diffusion of the "Italian style" of fortification thus represented an important step in the West's continuing – perhaps unique – ability to make the most of its smaller resources in order, first, to hold its own and, later, to expand to global dominance.[90]

---

[89] Information kindly provided by Sanjay Subrahmanyam and Blair B. Kling. See also Parker, *Military Revolution*, 134; and H. Furber, *John Company at Work. A Study of European Expansion in India in the Late Eighteenth Century* (Cambridge, MA, 1948), 204f.

[90] For a discussion of the continuing characteristics of western warfare, see Parker, *Cambridge Illustrated History of Warfare*.

PART III

Signifying walls

CHAPTER 14

Representations of Chinese walled cities in the pictorial and graphic arts

NANCY SHATZMAN STEINHARDT

THE Chinese have built walls for as long as they have built cities. The archaeological record confirms that a wall enclosed a Chinese city 4,500 years ago and there is no reason to believe the practice is this new.[1] What is remarkable, even for Chinese civilization, which is replete with examples of continuities over millennia, is that the excavators' description of a city wall in Shandong province from 2500 B.C. so closely describes walls from north or south China from any of the five thousand years between then and now:

First, on the surface there was scooped out a round-bottomed foundation trench about 13.8 meters wide and 1.5 meters deep. Then, using sterile loess, the workers packed the ditch full, layer by layer, forming a firm foundation for the wall.... In the sterile loess that was used were mixed "dry ginger stones" to increase its cohesive strength. The layers of earth that were formed were very regular in thickness, being between 0.12–0.14 meters, and they were very even and in good order. If one bored into the packed earth he could see traces of the tamping preserved between the layers of earth, small circular convexities and irregularities about 3.0–4.0 centimeters in diameter. The main body of the wall was then built on top of this foundation and it, too, was formed by repeated layers of earth about 0.12–0.14 meters thick. Each layer upward, measuring from the wall face inward, was narrowed 3.0 centimeters, and this formed the batter of the face of the wall (Fig. 14.1).[2]

Excavators estimated this wall to have been about nine meters wide at the top and to have risen six meters in height.

[1] The city was Chengziyai, in Shandong province. On it see Li Chi (Ji), *Chengziyai*, Archaeologia Sinica no. 1 (Nanjing, 1934) and *Ch'eng-tzu-yai*, trans. K.M. Starr (New Haven, 1956).

[2] *Ch'eng-tzu-yai*, 62–3. This passage is also quoted in Kwang-chih Chang, *The Archaeology of Ancient China*, 4th ed. (New Haven, 1986), 248.

419

Figure 14.1. Remains of wall of Liao Shangjing, Balinzuoqi, Inner Mongolia, built in the tenth century, 3,500 years after the wall described in this passage. Balinzuoqi is approximately 1,000 kilometers from Chengziyai. Photo: Steinhardt.

The Chinese have also drawn, painted, engraved, carved, and printed pictures of walls for almost as long as the respective techniques have existed. As we shall see below, line drawings, paintings, engravings, and relief sculptures of walled cities were made in the first millennium B.C. or within two centuries afterward; city walls frequently are portrayed in printed books. The earliest printed book illustration of a city wall has never been determined, but examples exist by the Song dynasty (960–1279).

The Chinese wall has a life independent of the Chinese city. It has provided China with her most powerful symbol, the Great Wall. Great Wall (the image-laden English translation of the Chinese *chang cheng*, literally "long wall"), as Arthur Waldron has explained, has a primary meaning as the symbol of the "fundamental incompatibility of the agrarian society of China with the nomadic world of the steppe."[3] Upon beginning the study of Chinese, one is taught that the first character of *Zhong guo* (the Chinese name for China) means center and

---

[3] Arthur Waldron, *The Great Wall of China* (Cambridge, 1990), 3.

that it is drawn as a central, vertical line in a four-sided enclosure.[4] In introductory courses in Chinese civilization, one learns that this character is a strikingly appropriate image of the sinocentric world view, in which China is the center and the boundaries (or limits) of the world around it are clearly, even rigidly, defined.[5] As a student of sinology one discovers that the character most often translated as wall, *cheng*, is also the character most often translated as city. It is through context that the non-native determines which to use in translation; but the native reader may not feel the need to differentiate. *Cheng*, a wall, always implies a city. *Cheng*, a city, always has a wall. The premodern Chinese city has no life independent of walls.

In the West, one's first encounter with China almost invariably includes an image of her walls. In *Mei Li*, the story of a Chinese girl at the time of the New Year's celebration for which author and illustrator Thomas Handforth won a Caldecott Medal in 1939, the opening lines are, "In North China, near the Great Wall, is a city shut in by a Wall. Not far from the city in the snow-covered country is a house with a wall around it, too."[6] In the next sentence we learn it is the day before the Chinese New Year, the subject of the story, and not until the fourth sentence do we meet Mei Li, the main character. The first information Handforth chose to convey to an English-speaking child about China was that it is a place of courtyard walls within city walls within the national wall. The picture on the front and back cover pages is dominated by those walls (Fig. 14.2).

The most popular image of China for adults in the 1930s, similarly, was that of a nation of walls. Ripley's (*Believe It or Not*) infamous claim that the Great Wall, "mightiest work of man," was "the only one that would be visible to the human eye from the moon," was probably made in the same decade.[7] The more specialized reader might have been aware of Wulf Diether Graf zu Castell's air views of China,

---

[4] Actually, the character represents an arrow in a target. See L. Wieger, S.J., *Chinese Characters* (New York, 1965), 31.

[5] A long bibliography is available on China's view of herself and in relation to the world. See, for example, Marcel Granet, *La pensée chinoise* (Paris, 1934); Frederick Mote, *Intellectual Foundations of China* (New York, 1971); Mark Elvin, *The Pattern of the Chinese Past* (Stanford, 1973); and Benjamin Schwartz, *The World of Thought in Ancient China* (Cambridge, MA, 1985).

[6] Thomas Handforth, *Mei Li* (Garden City and New York, 1938), pages not numbered. Handforth wrote the book based on experience; the artist lived in China in 1931. His etchings and lithographs are in United States museum collections. Thus his artistic ability suggests he would have been capable of a more sophisticated illustration, and further, that he intentionally chose the one shown here as Fig. 14.2.

[7] Waldron, *The Great Wall*, 213, says it was introduced in ca. 1932.

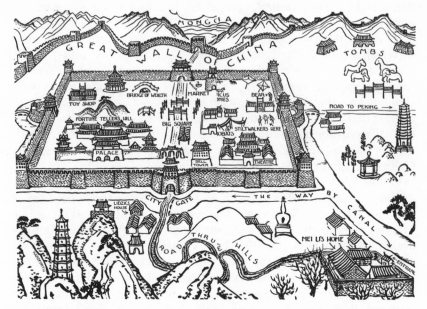

Figure 14.2. City in North China. Thomas Handforth, *Mei Li* (Garden City, NY, 1931), inside back cover.

among which no city he photographed was without at least one walled boundary.[8] Indeed, walls dominated the image of China and her cities two hundred years before the children's or popular books by Handforth and Ripley, or Graf zu Castell's photographs. From Beijing to a prefectural town to outposts in the environs of the Great Wall, the illustrations in J.B. Du Halde's four-volume *Déscription geographique, historique, chronologique, politique et physique de l'empire de la China et de la Tartarie chinoise,* published in 1736, presented, first and foremost, an image of walled cities.

The Western image of China and her cities has not been one of Western manufacture. It was simply a transfer westward of the message that China communicated in her own pictorial representations of herself. That message, that cities were and had always been walled, was true. (Thus Mao's destruction of Beijing's outer walls was the clearest possible signal that old China was to exist no longer.) That construction methods for city walls could be traced to Neolithic times also bore some truth. More nuanced are Chinese representations of

[8] Wulf Diether Graf zu Castell, *Chinaflug* (Berlin and Zurich, 1938).

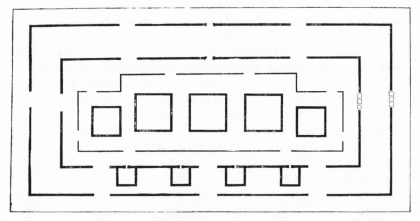

Figure 14.3. *Zhaoyu tu*. Tomb of King Cuo, Zhongshan kingdom, Pingshan, Hebei, late fourth century B.C. After *Wenwu* no. 1 (1979).

walled cities. This essay explores those representations with the hope of determining: Do representations of Chinese walled cities change in response to evolving pictorial traditions, or, if they seem not to change, why? Can techniques or details of representation exclusive to Chinese walled cities be identified or are pictures of Chinese city walls part of the mainstream of the Chinese arts? Are representations of Chinese walled cities specific enough to inform us about the actual cities or their construction techniques, or are they more often nonspecific renderings, perhaps purposeful ones? Are there instances in which cities spill beyond their walls and how does the Chinese art tradition deal with that phenomenon? Finally, are there contexts in which Chinese painters, designers, printers, or decorators choose walled cities rather than other possible subject matter?

EARLY REPRESENTATIONS OF CHINESE WALLS

The oldest known Chinese site plan is a walled enclosure inside a walled enclosure (Fig. 14.3). The illustration is engraved on a 94 × 48 cm bronze plate, less than one centimeter thick. Excavated in Pingshan county of Hebei province, the labeled diagram is a design of a late-fourth-century-B.C. burial site of a ruler of the Zhongshan kingdom, two of his wives, and two other royal members of his household.[9]

---

[9] On this plate see Fu Xinian, "Zhanguo Zhongshanwang Cuo mu chutu de zhaoyutu ji qi lingyuan guizhi de yanjiu" ["Research on the plan of the tomb of King Cuo of the

Funerary temples for each of them are shown as a row of four-sided buildings inside the two sets of walls. Engraved on the bronze plate is a detailed, scaled rendering with descriptions, dimensions, and symbols. This first incised example of Chinese walls is evidence that by the fourth century B.C. a fundamental and sophisticated principle of cartography – the transfer of three-dimensional space to a scaled, two-dimensional drawing – was in place in China; and it makes clear that walls were crucial to the scheme of royal funerary space. In Chinese, the plate is known as *zhaoyu tu* or *zhaobian tu*, the second a more explicit indication that the drawing is of a necropolis.[10] Thus the roots of illustrations of walled, Chinese royal funerary cities can be traced to the fourth century B.C.

In fact, China's earliest maps are also some of the earliest examples of illustrations of Chinese walled cities. Two maps, drawn in colors on silk, found in Tomb no. 3 at the site Mawangdui near Changsha, Hunan province, include illustrations of Chinese walls. Both predate the year 168 B.C., the year the son of the marquis of Dai was buried in that tomb.[11] In addition to keys and symbols, both standard in Chinese cartography by the second century B.C.,[12] military command posts are

Zhongshan kingdom of the Warring States period and the arrangement of the surrounding tombs"], *Kaogu xuebao* no. 1 (1980): 97–118; Yang Hongxun, "Zhanguo Zhongshanwang ling ji zhaoyu tu yanjiu" ["Research on the tomb and plan of the Zhongshan kings of the Warrings States period"], *Kaogu xuebao* no. 1 (1980): 119–38; and "Hebeisheng Pingshanxian Zhanguo shiqi Zhongshanguo muzan fajue jianbao" ["Excavation report on the tomb of the Zhongshan kings of the Warring States period in Pingshan county, Hebei"], *Wenwu* no. 1 (1979): 1–31.

10   The articles cited here, like most later literature, use the term "*zhaoyu tu*," literally, "picture of the omen area." *Zhaobian tu* is employed by Cao Wanru, ed., in her discussion of the plate in *Zhongguo gudai ditu ji* [*Atlas of Ancient Chinese Maps*], Vol. 1, Warring States period through the Yuan dynasty (Beijing, 1990), esp. 1–3. *Bian* means burial, and thus Cao's term can be translated "picture of a burial [area]." Here, I follow the Chinese name through which the piece is generally known, the one used in publications other than Cao Wanru's.

11   The bibliography on the Mawangdui tomb excavations is extensive. Standard references are Hunan Provincial Museum and Institute of Archaeology, Academica Sinica, *Changsha Mawangdui yihao Hanmu* [Han Tomb no. 1 at Mawangdui, Changsha] (Beijing, 1973); Annelise G. Bulling, "The 'Guide to the Souls' Picture in the Western Han Tomb at Ma-wang-tui Near Ch'ang-sha," *Oriental Art* 20/2 (1974): 158–73; Fang Chow, "Ma-wang-tui: A Treasure Trove from the Western Han Dynasty," *Artibus Asiae* 35/1–2 (1973): 5–23; Michael Loewe, *Ways to Paradise* (Boston and London, 1979); and Jeffrey Riegel, "A Summary of the Excavation of Han Tombs 2 and 3 at Ma-wang-tui, Ch'ang-sha," *Chinese Sociology and Anthropology* (Winter 1977–8): 51–103.

12   In addition to discussion in Cao, *Ditu ji*, 4–17, see several articles in each of *Wenwu* no. 2 (1975) and no. 1 (1976); Mei-Ling Hsu, "The Han Maps and Early Chinese Cartography," *Annals of the Association of American Geographers* 68 (1978): 45–60; R.R.C. de Crespigny, "Two maps from Mawangdui," *Cartography* 11/4 (1980): 211–22; and Annelise G. Bulling, "Ancient Chinese Maps," *Expeditions* 20/2 (1978):16–24. Most Chinese maps discussed in this chapter are also discussed in J.B. Harley and David

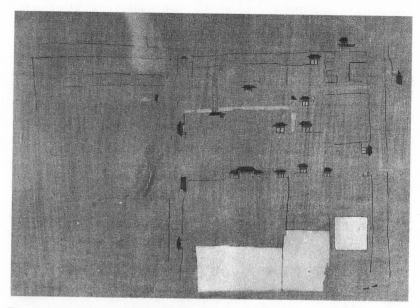

Figure 14.4. Redrawing of "Walled Enclosure." Mawangdui tomb no. 3, Hunan, second century B.C. After Cao, ed., *Zhongguo gudai ditu ji* (*Atlas of Ancient Chinese Maps*), fig. 26.

indicated by lines that probably signify walls. Black lines also define mountains, which, as we shall see later, can stand in the place of walls in the Chinese pictorial arts. It is likely but not certain that the outer boundary designated a walled area. It is known that the centrally located triangle designated a walled, military fortification with corner or side lookout towers. The second silk map found in Mawangdui Tomb no. 3 has been identified as part of a larger map of a county or the map of a tomb.[13] There is no question that it depicts a wall-enclosed region (Fig. 14.4).

Although both were uncovered in the same tomb, the two Mawangdui maps are different in purpose. Through them, it is clear that the divergent forms in which illustrations of city walls can be found were forged more than two thousand years ago. The military map is the most accurate drawing we shall encounter in this study. It is also the

Woodward, eds., *The History of Cartography*, Vol. 2, bk. 2, *Cartography in the Traditional East and Southeast Asian Societies* (Chicago and London, 1994).

[13] On these two maps see Cao, *Ditu ji*, captions for Figs. 26–9. Figure 26 is the military map.

only military map. Even in its sketchy state, accuracy could mean the critical difference between military success and failure. Walls need not be beautiful, but their relative positions on the map had to be correct. The county or tumulus map, by contrast, is a fine example of second-century-B.C. Chinese painting on silk. Its four straight boundaries and the lines between them anticipate many of the pictures of cities that will be discussed below. Yet unlike the military map, there is no reason to believe or even suppose accuracy in the layout of the streets stretching from city wall to city wall, perpendicular to one another, or elsewhere.

Probably the reasons so few military maps survive in comparison to the number of other Chinese maps are because they were not intended for general consumption, and because they never were carved or painted on walls. They were not, in other words, art. Thus it is very important to note that in this one military example, an outermost line is drawn, and the most likely purpose of that line is the same as the purposes, it is suggested, for similar lines in "pictures" of city walls: It may be an actual wall around the territory represented in the map, or it may be a compositional device easily perceived as a wall that increasingly had become part of the visual expectations of two-dimensional representations of places since earlier in the first millennium B.C.

Some of the images of Chinese walled cities most similar to those on the Mawangdui silk map (Fig. 14.4) survive in wall paintings from several centuries later, but still in the Han dynasty. In other words, to address a question raised above, a style of city wall can be observed through the four centuries of Han rule. Five scenes with city walls were painted in a second-century-A.D. tomb in Helinge'er, Inner Mongolia. As on the silk map from Mawangdui, walls are represented in the murals by thick lines (Fig.14. 5).[14] But close examination shows a difference from the silk map: The outer walls are fortified. Inside the walls stand multilevel buildings, and gate towers join the fortified wall faces. Moats surround the walls of some of the cities painted in the Helinge'er tomb. Inscriptions identify subjects as *cheng*, and provide names for specific buildings inside them. Walls and architecture are shown both from the top and the side, depending on which view is more instructive.

Other walled cities painted on the Inner Mongolian tomb walls are

---

[14] Again, we are dealing with a long bibliography for this tomb. The best single source is Gai Shanlin, *Helinge'er Hanmu bihua* [*The Han tomb with wall paintings at Helinge'er*] (Huhehaote, 1978). In English see Annelise G. Bulling, "The Eastern Han Tomb at Holin-ko-ehr (Holingol)," *Archives of Asian Art* 31 (1977–8): 79–103.

Figure 14.5. "Lishicheng" detail. Tomb at Helinge'er, Inner Mongolia, second century A.D. After Gai Shanlin, *Helinge'er Hanmu bihua* (Huhehaote, 1978), fig. 9.

more complex (Fig. 14.6). One, Fanyangcheng, offers both a bird's-eye view of city walls and a version of three-quarters perspective that remains a common format for the rest of the history of premodern East Asian painting of architecture. In "Fanyangcheng," an inner city is included within the outer wall. The smaller enclosure, sometimes inside a larger city, other times adjacent to it, had been a feature of Chinese cities since the Warring States period in the first millennium B.C.[15] It was the hub of a city's government, the local or regional

---

[15] On this feature and on Warring States cities, see Steinhardt, *Chinese Imperial City Planning* (Honolulu, 1990), esp. 43–50.

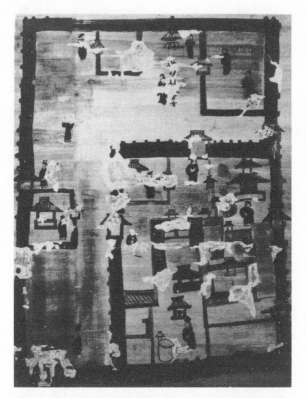

Figure 14.6. "Fanyangcheng" detail. Tomb at Helinge'er, Inner Mongolia, second century A.D. After Gai
Shanlin, *Helinge'er Hanmu bihua* (Huhehaote, 1978),
fig. 10.

equivalent of a ruler's palace-city inside a national capital or a prince's
quarters in a provincial capital.

One might be surprised at the complexity of city and city life
painted on the walls of a Han official's tomb in Inner Mongolia.
Fanyangcheng, for instance, is a city of walls, gates, towers, commerce,
official and other residences, food preparation, entertainment, and
movement (on horseback). Indeed, one observes more varied activity
on the painted wall than in the main intersection of Ningcheng today![16]

---

[16] This statement is based on my visit to Ningcheng in 1992. However, Gai Shanlin
takes a different view. He writes that features in the paintings can be seen in other

The city image from the Helinge'er tomb is not unique. The same sort of activity is painted on the walls of a contemporary tomb farther south, in Anping, Hebei province. In the Anping tomb painting, a greater number of city walls and four-sided walled enclosures is painted.[17]

One cannot but wonder how closely the tomb paintings represent the actual life inside the walls of a Han city. Perhaps we are dealing with visualizations of recounted images of second-century-A.D. cities more diverse and active than outposts like Ningcheng or Fanyangcheng; perhaps the murals are renderings by artists familiar with life in more major Chinese metropolitan centers, perhaps one that tomb occupants at command posts in Inner Mongolia called home; or perhaps the manor of a second-century A.D. official stationed in a provincial town was really this active and complex.[18] In any of these cases, the city walls play a prominent role in the composition. Walls not only enclosed (or were supposed to enclose if in actuality they were never completed) every Chinese city (*cheng*) since before the first millennium B.C., they defined a city's literary, visual, and actual image from these early times.

The most profound literary image of a Chinese city was cast in the first millennium B.C. It is recorded in the *Kaogong ji* (Record of Trades) section of the *Zhouli* (Rituals of Zhou).[19] The often-recorded passage reads:

The *jiangren* [man under official employ responsible for directing building projects] constructs the state capitals. He makes a square nine *li* on each side; each side has three gates. Within the capital are nine north–south and nine east–west streets. The north–south streets are nine carriage tracks in width.[20]

Although similarities between the written description and the Han paintings may not seem obvious, they are considerably clearer in

---

small cities of Inner Mongolia that have survived from the Han dynasty. See Gai, *Helinge'er Hanmu*, 29.

[17] On the Anping tomb, see Hebei Province Cultural Relics Research Institute, *Anping Dong Han bihua mu* [*A Wall-painted Eastern Han tomb in Anping*] (Beijing, 1990). Details of city walls are shown in pls. 51 and 52. The city scene in the Anping tomb is not so different from cities photographed from the air by Graf zu Castell (mentioned above) 1,800 years later.

[18] As Gai Shanlin suggests (see footnote 16).

[19] The importance of this passage in the literary history of Chinese urbanism cannot be overemphasized. He Yeju wrote a book on the subject; see his *'Kaogong ji' yingzuo zhidu yanjiu* [*Research on the building system via the* Kaogong ji] (Beijing, 1985). The majority of Chinese histories of the Chinese city begin with the passage.

[20] My translation is from *Kaogong ji* in *Guanzhong congshu* [*Collected writings of the Guanzhong region*], Vol. 6, *juan* 2/11a–12b. A French translation also exists. See Edouard Biot, trans., *Le Tcheou-li*, 2 vols. (Paris 1851), 2:553–9.

illustrations of the *Kaogong ji* that survive alongside the passage in books (Fig. 14.7). The outer walls are fortified, and fortifications are drawn inward from the wall, both in the second-century wall paintings and in the printed map from the early fifteenth century (Figs. 14.5, 14.6, and 14.7). Once inside the city walls, streets run due north–south or east–west, blocked only by residences of the city's chief occupant or government offices. In Wangcheng (Fig. 14.7), the ruler governed and resided in the center, and in Fanyangcheng (Fig. 14.6) he occupied the southeastern city sector. Such a walled city, with the ruler's enclosure in a southern corner, has been excavated at Linzi, capital of the state of Qi in Shandong province. Its date is Warring States period, 403–221 B.C.[21]

Most impressive are the number of shared details one finds in Handforth's image of Beijing (Fig. 14.2), the illlustration of Wangcheng (Fig. 14.7), and the second-century A.D. representations of cities on the Helinge'er tomb walls (Fig. 14.6). Comparing Mei Li's Beijing with Wangcheng or with a later image of a capital city, the capital of the Northern Song dynasty (960–1125) at today's Kaifeng in Henan province, printed in a fourteenth-century encyclopedia (Fig. 14.8), one observes the uniformity of corner and other gate towers and the evenly placed parapets. In both Mei Li's city and the Eastern Han painting in Inner Mongolia, one finds entertainment space as well as the ruler's residence inside city walls. No historian would have reason to suggest that everyone's day-to-day life in a Chinese city was one of excitement and entertainment. Yet the image of the city for a twentieth-century Chinese girl and the American child who reads about her, like the image of the city painted on walls of a Han official for posterity, is one of wealth, entertainment, enjoyment, and excitement – the high points of life.

It is unlikely that Thomas Handforth saw Han tomb wall paintings. He probably never read the fourteenth- and fifteenth-century compilations in which Figures 14.7 and 14.8 were printed. Rather, Handforth's ability to so closely capture profoundly Chinese images of ideal walled cities of China's classical age is due to the fact that the pictorial image of Chinese walls and what was found inside them, cast by the Han dynasty, was perpetuated for two millennia. (Ironically, the profoundly formulaic yet unambiguous lines of Han painters and later Chinese woodblock designers lend themselves to illustrations for Western children.) Those images included fortified walls with corner and other gate towers, moats around the walls, and orthogonal lines

---

[21] For an illustration see Steinhardt, *Chinese Imperial City Planning*, fig. 52.

inside them. The images and descriptions of Chinese cities in classical texts reinforced one another. Moreover, they were the same images preserved on the earliest extant maps of China and her cities, and on painted and brick-lined walls of underground tombs. Those familiar with Chinese civilization should not be surprised with the correspondences between images and the written word.

Not only do continuities over millennia characterize all aspects of Chinese culture, but both funerary art and territorial maps are serious enough in purpose that they are the most likely media for these continuities. Funerary art is generally considered to serve one primary purpose: the re-creation in microcosm of the world of life for continuation in the afterlife. Crucial to this re-creation are paintings with architecture and its walls or comparable symbols that identify an underground structural shell. Minor arts buried with the dead, and decoration on these small objects, can enhance the postmortem world; only structures can define it. Sometimes, architecture alone, a pillar and bracket set above it, for example, can suffice to identify the world underground. Other times, boundaries can be rendered by mountains alone.[22] Thus one would like to discover additional purposes or meanings when cities or city walls are present. Perhaps there are three of them, one visual and the others more symbolic. First, walls are straight and regular and thus help clarify images. They suggest where the viewer should look for an important subject such as the ruler's or official's residence. The use of boundaries is so ubiquitous that they seem almost as necessary as walls, one might argue, to the Chinese visualization of space. Second, since walls signify cities, the wall-painted scenes can be thought of as maps. Yet, since the painted images are not purely bird's-eye-view representations, they are easier to read than actual maps (and easy reading is fine because their purpose is not military). Third, perhaps paintings of walls serve the same purpose as walls themselves: They divide the public world outside from the private world inside. In a tomb, a picture of a wall can separate the occupant's private life from his public one. Symbolically, walls can distinguish the world of the tomb from the outside world.

---

[22] A Han-dynasty wall painting in tomb no. 61 from Luoyang shows the mountains (but not the wall) that define this border between China and the territory beyond. For an illustration see *Han-Tang bihua* [*Murals from Han through Tang*] (Beijing, 1974), pl. 2. Symbolically, the mountains may stand for walls. In the minor arts, man-made structures may replace walls for the same purpose. A Warring States–period lacquer box excavated at Changsha, Hunan, for example, has architectural detail but no walls. See Michael Sullivan, *The Birth of Landscape Painting in China* (Berkeley and Los Angeles, 1962), fig. 6; for examples in bronze, see Sullivan, *The Birth of Landscape*, fig. 15.

Walls might be interpreted as protection of the Chinese funerary world from outside incursions. Walls lend security and order to the world. They symbolize China's central role in this world order. With such profound ideology behind them, it is no wonder that the representation of city walls had such a long history with such little noticeable change.

CITY WALLS IN FOURTH- THROUGH SIXTH-CENTURY CHINA

In a civilization whose ideology was written and represented before the early centuries of the first millennium A.D. had ended, and with unequaled reverence for past ideals, only very powerful forces motivate change. One such force was a new and foreign religion, Buddhism. Another was a change in rulership. Buddhism entered China in the first century A.D. and made serious inroads toward the fall of the Han dynasty in 220. By the fourth century, small dynasties and kingdoms, some with non-Chinese rulers, coexisted in the north and south. Unification would not come again until the 580s.

From this less politically stable China, images of city walls are abundant. Tomb walls, especially in Gansu province, remain a main source of the representations. A painting of a "fortified house," according to the Chinese description, is found on the lower register of the north wall of Dingjiazha Tomb no. 5 in Jiuquan (Fig. 14.9), dated 386–441, during the reign of one of two rulers of the Later Liang or Northern Liang kingdom. The painter(s) of this scene and indeed the entire wall lacked the skill of Han mural painters at Helinge'er two centuries earlier.[23] The format of three scenes along horizontal registers clearly derives from Han precedents,[24] but elements of the composition of each register float in space with neither scaled nor spatial relation. Since Han painters had been capable of significantly better planned compositions over larger spaces, one readily concludes that either the provincial location along the road to Central Asia or the lack of funds of the very short-lived kingdoms were likely responsible for the limitations in compositional excitement and articulation of detail in the two fortresses shown in Figure 14.9.

[23] On the wall paintings from Dingjiazha tomb no. 5, see Gansu Province Cultural Relics and Archaeology Research Institute, *Jiuquan Shiliuguomu bihua* [*Walls paintings from the Sixteen Kingdoms tomb in Jiuquan*] (Beijing, 1989).

[24] For example, from wall-painted tombs in Helinge'er and Anping, discussed above, or from Wangdu. On the tomb at Wangdu see *Wangdu erhao Hanmu* [*Han tomb no. 2 from Wangdu*] (Beijing, 1959).

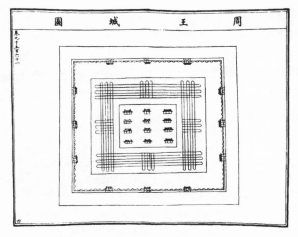

Figure 14.7. "Wangcheng" (ruler's city). *Henan zhi* (Record of Henan province), preserved in *Yongle dadian, juan* 9561, dated 1408.

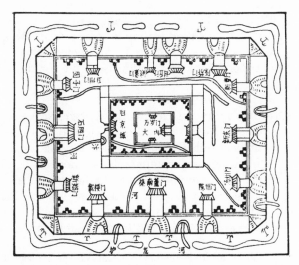

Figure 14.8. Idealized plan of Northern Song capital, Bianliang. *Shilin guangji*, 1330s. After Dong Jianhong et al., *Zhongguo chengshi jianshe shi* [History of Chinese city construction] (Beijing, 1982), 42.

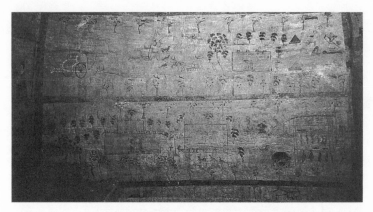

Figure 14.9. Painting showing "fortification." Detail of north wall, Dingjiazha tomb no. 5, Jiuquan, Gansu, 386–441. After *Jiuquan Shiliugumu bihua* (Beijing, 1989), west wall section, pl. 1 (plates not numbered).

Yet quality aside, the fortresses and what appears to be a wall with one gate next to the two-story fortress are prominent. The message the otherwise uninspired rendering offers: fortification. Through the picture of the occupant's residence in this dangerous, war-torn desert spot, apparently drawn by a true amateur, perhaps we have come to a "realistic" image of a fortified wall in no-man's land. It appears that like the Han Chinese several hundred years before, the occupant of Dingjiazha Tomb no. 5 took inspiration from life for the wall of his afterlife.

About twenty kilometers northwest in the same region of Gansu (the Hexi corridor), numerous tombs have been excavated near the town of Jiayuguan.[25] Dated to the third and fourth centuries, they are believed to be tombs of military officials, local officials, or local lords.[26] In quality, the paintings are comparable to those from Dingjiazha Tomb no. 5. Scenes from daily life dominate the paintings, whose line quality might be described as crude. Yet amateurish as the painters may have been, city walls and corner gate towers are clear and evident in some of the compositions (Fig. 14.10). Different from the Dingjiazha

---

[25] The town is best known for the portion of the Great Wall that remains there. On the tombs from Jiayuguan see Gansu Provincial Cultural Relics Team, Gansu Provincial Museum, and Jiayuguan City Cultural Relics Commission, *Jiayuguan bihuamu fajue baogao* [*Excavation report on wall-painted tombs in Jiayuguan*] (Beijing, 1985) and Wang Tianyi, *Underground Art Gallery* (Beijing, 1989).

[26] Wang Tianyi, *Underground Art Gallery*, 125.

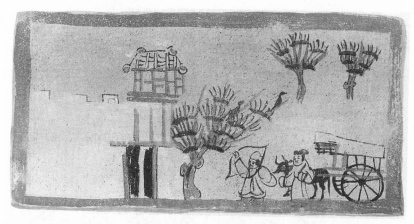

Figure 14.10. "Shooting Birds." Brick from tomb in Jiayuguan, Gansu province, showing city walls with battlements and gate towers on the left side, third–fourth century. After Wang Tianyi, *Underground Art Gallery* (Beijing, 1989), pl. 30.

tomb, in the Jiuquan tombs pictures were painted on individual bricks that were placed into the wall alongside undecorated bricks. No attempt at a unified composition with a large cult figure and scenes in registers beneath it, such as was found at the Jiuquan tomb, can be discerned. As in Han tomb wall painting, scenes are often labeled and outlined.

At both Gansu sites (Figs. 14.9 and 14.10), walls with parapets are represented. Either might be a picture of the residence of a desert lord. Necessary details, such as the parapets and a raised watch tower, are present. Again, the purposeful aspect of walls in a Chinese funerary context is apparent. And again, the technique by which painters portray them is a reflection of the place and times. Isolated from the cities and cultural entrepôts of China, these are the walls painted by local craftsmen in the third and fourth centuries.

City walls at the Magao caves

The most famous city in Gansu province is Dunhuang, take-off point for the Mogao and other Buddhist cave temples. It is also one of the westernmost towns in Gansu and thus China proper, traditionally recognized as the terminus of the Silk Road into and out of China. It is a site of nearly 500 caves painted over nine centuries. If laid out in

Figure 14.11. Line drawing of city wall. Mogao cave 257, Gansu, Northern Dynasties (386–581). Xiao Mo, "Dunhuang Mogaoku Beichao bihua de jian-zhu," *Kaogu* no. 2 (1976): 110.

a line, the paintings would stretch some twenty-five kilometers.[27] Paintings of architecture comprise a subset of these images.[28] Representations of city walls are a subset of the architectural paintings. The paintings of city walls are easily divided into a Northern and Southern Dynasties group (ca. 386–589) and a later one.

Representing the earlier period are paintings in caves 249, 257, and 296.[29] In cave 257, the city wall is shown from three views and the corner towers jut out in a back corner and in the foreground (Fig. 14.11). Compositionally, one observes little advancement beyond the

---

[27] The bibliography on the Mogao Cave paintings, one group of those referred to as the "Dunhuang cave paintings," is immense. On them see, for example, *Tonk bakuk kutsu* [*Dunhuang Mogao Caves*], 5 vols. (Tokyo 1980–2); Dunhuang Institute for Cultural Relics, *The Art Treasures of Dunhuang* (Hong Kong and New York, 1981); and Anil de Silva, *The Art of Chinese Landscape Painting in the Caves of Tun-huang* (New York, 1964).

[28] On architectural painting at the Mogao Caves see Xiao Mo, *Dunhuang jianzhu yanjiu* [*Research on architecture at Dunhuang*] (Beijing, 1989); "Tonko kutsu hekigani mieru jiin kenchiku" ["Monastery architecture seen in Mogao Cave wall paintings"], *Tonko bakuko kutsu*, 4:192–215; and Xiao Mo, "Dunhuang Mogaoku Beichao bihua de jian-zhu" ["Architecture in Northern Dynasties wall paintings at the Mogao Caves, Dun-huang"], *Kaogu* no. 2 (1976): 109–20.

[29] The numbering system used here for Mogao caves is the Chinese one. It is purely arbitrary. An earlier system employed by Paul Pelliot is no longer in use. For illustra-tions of other paintings with architecture and walls, see publications of Xiao Mo cited above. The painting in cave 249 is found in *Kaogu* no. 2 (1976): 110.

Figure 14.12. "City Scene." Relief sculpture from tomb in Chengdu, Sichuan province, Eastern Han dynasty (A.D. 23–220). After Gao Wen, ed., *Sichuan Handai huaxiang zhuan* [*Pictorial bricks of the Han dynasty in Sichuan*] (Shanghai, 1987), fig. 25.

depiction of walls and a gate tower in a Han-dynasty relief sculpture from Sichuan (Fig. 14.12). In cave 257, the purpose of the city is purely backdrop for Buddhist narrative. Still, as always thus far, city walls are heavily fortified and four-sided.

A comparison can also be made between architecture in a Jiayuguan tomb mural and that found in the Mogao caves. The quality of line in cave 257 is more controlled and definite than that which delineates walls and buildings in Figure 14.10, but examination of details of ceramic roof tiling, specifically the curvature of "owls' tails" at the top ends of the main roof ridge, and the layering of tiles on roof purlins, is strikingly similar. Stylistically, both are products of Gansu in the late fourth or fifth century.

The painting in cave 249 (Fig. 14.13) shows only the front of a city. The central entry gate is prominent, walls are high and heavily forti-fied, and conventions for crenelations are apparent: either they are

Figure 14.13. Line drawing of city wall. Mogao cave 249, Gansu, Northern Dynasties. Xiao Mo, "Dunhuang Mogaoku Beichao bihua de jianzhu," *Kaogu* no. 2 (1976): 110.

triangular like those in cave 257 or they are rectangular. Another feature is noticeably part of the representation: City walls are backed (or fronted) by mountains which, as noted above, can serve in the pictorial tradition in place of walls. More impressive is a painting such as the one in cave 296 in which one sees a squarish wall with prominent front and back towers and major buildings lined up along them.[30] A main hall inside these walls is two-storied. Not only are the walls fortified in the conventional manner, including corner towers (only two are shown), but one also sees a moat and mountains beyond it. It is unclear from these two paintings with mountains if the intent is for them to be on only one side of the city. If so, they would play a geomantically protective role.[31] Mountains also protect cities by making access to their boundaries difficult. Numerous capital cities, including Beijing and Luoyang, were constructed south of mountains. Mountains also, we have suggested above, may be symbols of the walls themselves.

Occasionally, city walls are irregular. In cave 296, source of the painting described above, one also finds ambiguously-connected walls of a city whose outer boundaries may not be straight. Nevertheless, the expected components are there – the focus on a central, high building, corner gate towers, and, for the first time among material presented here, alternating colored rectangles to represent bricks at the base of buildings or walls. In fact, this feature has become a convention in sixth-century Chinese wall painting. It also appears in a

---

[30] A line drawing of the painting in cave 296 can be seen in Xiao, *Kaogu* no. 2 (1976): 110.

[31] Jeffrey Meyer discusses the importance of mountains in Chinese geomancy in "Feng-shui of the Chinese City," *History of Religions* 18/2 (1978): 138–55.

walled enclosure dated to the first half of the sixth century from cave 127 at Maijishan, in far eastern Gansu province, and it will persist.[32]

Possible meanings or purposes for the representation of city walls in Buddhist cave painting can be determined only when they are viewed as part of larger compositions. Both illustrations from cave 296 are painted at the tops of walls that bend inward toward the ceiling. Upper walls of numerous Mogao caves show panoramic sweeps of figures, daily life scenes, architecture (including city walls), and land-scape. Keeping in mind that the purpose of all the Mogao cave illus-trations is Buddhist, city walls still come forth as a backdrop for narrative, offering borders and highlights for specific events, and as punctuation of space so that deities and mortals can move from scene to scene. Mountains are abundant on these Mogao cave walls and appear to serve the same purposes as they did in Gansu tomb paint-ing. Perhaps they, too, are symbols of walls, or perhaps here, walls symbolize mountains.

The most grandiose murals with city walls begin to appear in Mo-gao caves dated to the second half of the sixth century and "peak" in Tang-period (618–906) caves. Painting of panoramic scenes became more complex, and with time, representations of city walls and what they enclose were executed by artists who seem surer of delineation and were willing to experiment with the shapes of city walls, probably. A painting in Mogao cave 420, dated to the Sui dynasty (581/9–618), shows outer walls with twenty sides (Fig. 14.14). In a Tang-period cave, no. 323, an irregularly shaped outer wall has been identified as the Western Han (206 B.C.–A.D. 23) capital, Chang'an, whose fifteen-sided outer wall was uniquely irregular.[33]

The Tang dynasty is also the period from which clearer and more elaborate renditions of cities and their walls survive at the Mogao caves. Usually the boundary of an individual city is squarish (Fig. 14.15), with corner towers and prominent gates on most wall faces. When corner structures have rounded or otherwise unusual roofs, such as is the case in Figure 14.15, there is a reason. Recognizably non-Chinese to the Chinese eye, the image is a signal that Buddhism originated in India and its legends and imagery were accumulated en

---

[32] For an illustration of the cave from Maijishan, see Akiyama Terukazu and Matsubara Saburo, *The Arts of China*, vol. 2, *Buddhist Cave Temples, New Researches*, trans. Alexan-der C. Soper (Tokyo and Palo Alto, 1969), 116. The same feature of wall construction appears in gate-towers of the Tang capital, Chang'an, painted on the tomb walls of Crown Prince Yide in 706. This image is frequently published. See, for example, *Han-Tang bihua* [*Wall-painting Han to Tang*] (Beijing, 1974), pl. 86.

[33] On this point, see Xiao, *Dunhuang jianzhu yanjiu*, 123–5. For an illustration see *Tonk bakuk kutsu*, 3:pl. 63.

Figure 14.14. Architecture and walls in panorama. South side of ceiling, Mogao cave 420, Gansu province, Sui dynasty (581–618). After *Tonkō bakukō kutsu*, (Tokyo, 1980–2), 2:pl. 74.

route eastward to China. Even if the artisans had not seen Indian cities, they had heard of them; and they knew their appearances to be distinct from what could be seen in China. Still, except for the roofs of towers, walls and architecture otherwise conform to established Chinese pictorial patterns.

Some of the representations of non-Chinese cities or their walls are details of Buddhist pilgrimage sites. By the tenth century, at least one road map of a pilgrimage route was painted. The walls of cave 61 are covered with panoramas of the route to one of China's holiest Buddhist mountains, Wutai, in northern Shanxi province.[34] Although the images alone would not suffice to relate the way from neighboring provinces or across China to Wutai, the paintings do serve as a kind of checklist for the pilgrim. Illustrated are monasteries or other holy sites he should have passed, or should plan to visit on the way back. As for the role of walls, each monastery is a self-contained, walled

---

[34] On these wall paintings, see Hibino Jbu, "Tonk no Godaisanzu ni tsuite" ["On a map of Mt. Wutai at Dunhuang"], *Bukky bijitsu* 34 (1958): 75–86; Ernesta Marchand, "The Panorama of Wu-T'ai Shan as an Example of Tenth Century Cartography," *Oriental Art* 22/2 (1976): 158–73; and Dorothy Wong, "A Reassessment of the *Representation of Mt. Wutai* from Dunhuang Cave 61," *Archives of Asian Art* 46 (1993): 27–52.

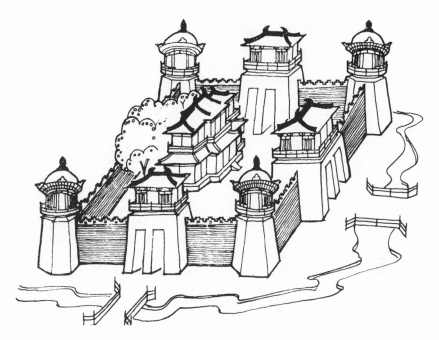

Figure 14.15. Line drawing of walled city. Mogao cave 85, Gansu, Tang period. After Xiao Mo, *Dunhuang jianzhu yanjiu* (Beijing, 1989), 123.

compound with the kind of gates and towers wall painters of city walls have been shown to have executed. Walled compounds have labels, features we have seen accompanying paintings of city walls since the Han dynasty.

Illustrations dated to the tenth century, such as those on the walls of cave 61, relate important information about the Chinese conception of a map. Although a second-century-B.C. military map could be detailed and accurate, a millennium later, under different circumstances, city walls in landscape were painted with somewhat more accomplishment but with less accurate detail and still lacking in scaled distance. The purpose of a wall map was not accuracy. It was merely a record of what might be found in the general vicinity of its subject. (The same role is played by maps on walls in Chinese hotels today.) Pilgrims and travelers throughout Chinese history have relied on word of mouth more than other means for getting from place to place. As landscape became an increasingly important component of Chinese painting on silk or on walls, beginning in the Tang dynasty and surging into prominence in the tenth century, so, too, it became a more and more complicated part of paintings of city walls. Sophisticated compositional devices and details that survive in their earliest versions on cave walls flourished and became independent subject matter in the late Tang and later centuries. Nevertheless, the purposes of walled enclosures in wall-painted panoramas or other landscapes remained to highlight significant areas and to lead the eye or would-be pilgrim through time and space. Even by the twelfth century, the subjects of paintings with wall-enclosed spaces remained religious or didactic. In contrast to paintings on silk with architectural details, murals were never purely decorative and wall painters did not write essays about the meanings of their paintings.[35]

Yet, walled enclosures have one unique role in Mogao cave painting. It is the representation of Buddhist paradise (Fig. 14.16). The purposes of the Buddhist paradise paintings have been studied, and three have been suggested.[36] First, and generally agreed upon, the paintings are visualizations of Buddhist paradise (especially Pure Land Buddhist paradise) for devotees, visions of the benign and wonderful world to come. Second, it has been suggested that the paradise imagery functions as a "mediation," or link between the world of man and the world of the deity.[37] Thus it is fitting that deities are placed inside man-made walls. Yet different from actual Chinese cities and representations of cities observed so far, the walls of paradise are not heavily fortified. Walls are straight, but joined to a host of towers, pavilions, and multistory structures. Often the connectors are bridges. As in other examples of Buddhist walled enclosures, architecture and walls are backdrop, not subject. Last, representations of paradise may be thought of as *mandala*, according to the very general definition: a diagram of a Buddhist universe.[38]

Another question that must be addressed regarding the wall paintings of paradise is whether they ever represented or were inspired by

---

[35] During the tenth to eleventh centuries, some of the most renowned Chinese painters of landscape, such as Fan Kuan (ca. 960–1030) and Guo Xi (ca. 1001–1090), also wrote treatises on the meaning of their art. For examples of their writings see Osvald Sirén, *The Chinese on the Art of Painting* (New York, 1963).

[36] In addition to writings of Xiao Mo cited in footnote 28, see Puay-peng Ho, "Paradise on Earth: Architectural Depiction in Pure Land Illustrations of High Tang Caves at Dunhuang," *Oriental Art* 41/3 (1995): 22–31.

[37] The three ideas are put forth in Ho, "Paradise on Earth."

[38] On the definition of *mandala* and related subjects see Okazaki Jji, *Pure Land Buddhist Painting*, trans. and adapt. Elizabeth ten Grotenhuis (Tokyo, New York, and San Francisco, 1977).

Figure 14.16. Line drawing of Buddhist paradise. Mogao cave 217, Tang dynasty. After Xiao Mo, *Dunhuang jianzhu yanjiu* (Beijing, 1989), 66.

anything other than, or more specific than, textual descriptions of the paradise of a Buddha (most often Amitabha's Pure Land in the western regions), for example, a specific monastery. Taking the viewpoint that paradise imagery is a generalized representation of existing structures, it is possible to place Buddhist paradise scenes from the Tang-period Mogao caves alongside plans of extant, partially extant, or described (but now lost) monasteries and palaces of the Tang period and slightly later and find similar features. The similarities begin with the transposition of the house of the ruler into the house of a deity, a phenomenon that occurred several centuries earlier when architectural space for the imported Buddhist faith was initially conceived in China. Similarities may also include a series of buildings (often three) along a main building line, principal structures marked either by multiple stories or hipped roofs (or both), curved ("rainbow-shaped" to use the Chinese term) bridges joining buildings to covered arcades, and covered arcades or walls surrounding the entire enclosure as well as front courtyards.[39]

Yet in spite of the details from a variety of Tang building complexes that align with those in murals, no single site perfectly matches any one wall painting. Probably, Buddhist cave paintings of wall-enclosed spaces are nonspecific because their purposes are religious. The interior cave space should be interpreted as four walls (the walls of the Buddhist world) around a center (usually a Buddha, sometimes a pagoda or pillar that represents him). The paintings should be interpreted as two-dimensional visualizations of the three-dimensional world that symbolizes the boundless world of faith.

CITY WALLS IN LINE DRAWING (PRINTED BOOKS AND RELIEF)

One exception might refute the argument that no one source for paintings of Buddhist paradises can be put forward. It is a monastery that has been considered ideal, and therefore has been suggested, since the sixth century, as a prototype for Chinese Buddhist monastic space. Known as Jetavana (*Jietaisi* in Chinese), in vast, central India, this site of the Buddha's "Great Miracle" was described and illustrated by the Chinese Buddhist monk Daoxuan (596–667) in 667 (Fig. 14.17).[40] Due to the buildings along the main axis in the center, the multistoried pavilions and gate towers, the covered corridors and courtyards surrounded by them, and individual building precincts on the sides and above, the illustration has been studied alongside Buddhist paradise imagery at Tang-period Mogao caves. This picture of the Jetavana monastery is an appropriate starting point for discussion of Chinese city walls in line-drawn form.

Chinese examples of walled cities in this medium, line drawing, are countless. They are found in the illustrated section of almost every Chinese local record, and local records, or gazetteers, were kept for every prefecture, prefectural town, and important city. Often records survive in several and revised editions for each place. Here just a few examples are discussed.

---

[39] Puay-peng Ho addresses this issue in "Paradise on Earth." For more on standard plans of Tang monastery architecture and their possible relation to Mogao cave painting, see Annelise G. Bulling, "Buddhist Temples in the T'ang Period," *Oriental Art*, n.s. 1/2 (1955): 3–10, and 1/3 (1955): 3–10.

[40] On this subject, see Puay-peng Ho, "The Ideal Monastery: Daoxuan's Description of the Central Indian Jetavana Vihra," *East Asian History* 10 (1995): 1–18; and Bulling, "Buddhist Temples in the T'ang Period," both parts.

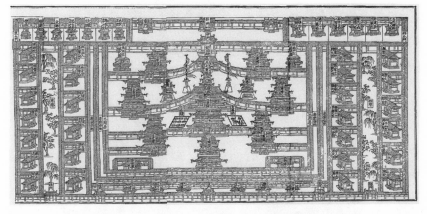

Figure 14.17. "Jetavana Monastery." Daoxuan, *Zhong Tianzhu Sheweiguo Zhi-huasi tujing* 45/812–13; A.D. 667. After Ho, "The Ideal Monastery: Daozuan's Description of the Central Indian Jetavana Vihra," *East Asian History* 10 (1995): 2–3. Courtesy of Puay-peng Ho.

Representation of city walls and wall-enclosed building complexes is more standardized in printed books and stelae on which line drawings are based than it is even in wall painting. One can begin with an illustration of the Temple of the Earthgod (Houtu huangdi Qinmiao xuantu), preserved on a stone stele dated to 1136 (Fig. 14.18). The line drawing taken from that stele has been compared with both the Jetavana monastery illustration (Fig. 14.17) and with the line drawing made after the twelfth- or thirteenth-century stele of the Temple to the Central Peak (Zhongyuemiao).[41] In all three, the building complex dominates a north-south line, its main hall is joined to side enclosures by arched ("rainbow-shaped") causeways, and walls are inside of walls. All are drawn in the standardized manner noted above. The walls are so pronounced that the primary visual impact is one of walled enclosure and nonspecificity, in spite of the fact that the building complex layouts are far from identical.

Turning to images of cities in printed books, the nineteenth-century plan of Datong in northern Shanxi province, just south of the border with Inner Mongolia, from *Datongxian zhi* (the record of Datong city and its immediate environs), shows a city enclosed by a layered wall,[42]

---

[41] Illustrations of the Temple to the Central Peak stele are found in Cao, *Ditu ji*, pls. 76–8. For more information on both stelae, see Cao, *Ditu ji*, discussion of pls. 67–9 and 76–8.

[42] For an example of a wall built of pounded earthen layers see Fig. 14.1.

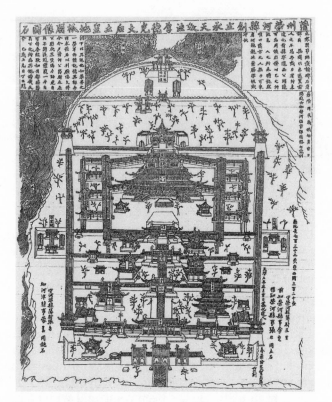

Figure 14.18. Line drawing of *Houtu huangdi qinmiao
xiangtu* (Earthgod temple) stele, 1136. After Cao, ed.,
Zhongguao gudai ditu ji (Beijing, 1990), pl. 69.

an entry gate at the center of each wall face, four corner towers, and
additional walled regions beyond the main city gates (Fig. 14.19).
Beyond each gate and tower were additional walled fortifications that
an attacker would have to penetrate before getting to the gate and
wall itself. Such defensive projections existed. They were known as
wengcheng and *mamian* (or *yangma*). A *wengcheng* survived from Khub-
lai Khan's capital Dadu (predecessor to Beijing) until the 1960s.[43]
Wengcheng still can be seen in the walled portion of Qufu, Shandong
province. *Mamian* are illustrated in a line drawing from the Song
treatise, *Wujing zongyao* (Collection of military techniques), edited by
Zeng Gongliang in ca. 1040 (Fig. 14.20) and survive in wall remains

[43] An illustration of the Dadu *wengcheng* is found in *Kaogu* no. 1 (1972), pl. 8.

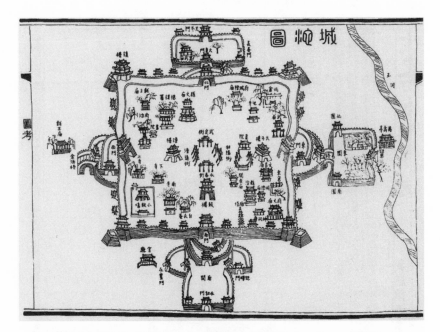

Figure 14.19. "Datong city," *Datongxian zhi, juan* 1; A.D. 1830.

from Ming-period Xi'an (Fig. 14.21). The drawing of Datong's wall (Fig. 14.19) is not to scale, so we cannot be certain that the number of parapets is accurate; but the important messages of the image are sparkling: First and foremost, this is a heavily fortified city; inside are numerous religious and governmental buildings. One can easily anticipate straight streets from gate to gate even though no road is indicated. Knowledge of the idealized Chinese city, Wangcheng, must have been part of the stored imagery of the line drawing's designer.

Larger cities are purposefully, if not accurately, rendered in line drawings as well. One example is the plan of the beautiful southern town Suzhou (Pingjiang in the Song dynasty), carved on a stele in 1229 (Fig. 14.22).[44] Prominent is the walled, governmental compound with central gate and corner towers and the fortified walls of that compound and the entire city. Unlike some of the stelae (or line drawings) we have seen, perpendicularly-crossing streets are indicated. Mountains along the western city side are highly noticeable, but ex-

---

[44] In addition to Cao, *Ditu ji*, discussion of pls. 79–81, see Frederick Mote, "A Millennium of Chinese Urban History: Form, Time, and Space Concepts in Soochow," *Rice University Studies* 59/4 (1974): 35–65.

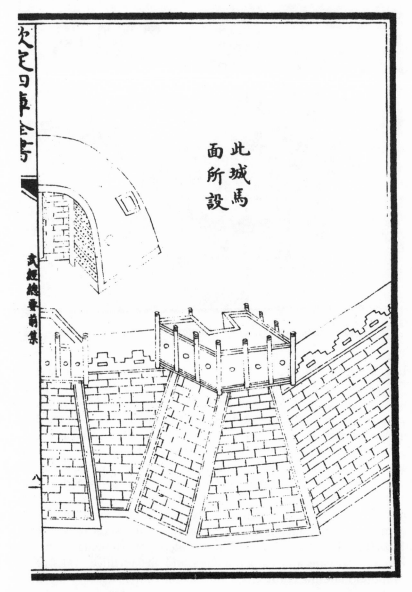

Figure 14.20. Illustration of city wall with towers and of *mamian*, ca. 1040. Zeng Gongliang, ed., *Wujing zongyao* [Collection of important military techniques], *juan* 1/8a–b.

Figure 14.21. Wall of Xi'an, Shaanxi province, Ming period. Photo: Steinhardt.

cept for the moat that surrounds the fortified wall, a common feature in actual walled cities and in pictures of them, one is not aware that Suzhou is a city of canals (Marco Polo compared Suzhou to Venice). Instead, the image of straight, walled regions is overpowering. Thus, the pictorial representation of Southern Song (1126–1279) Suzhou lends itself to comparisons with the central regions of line drawings of the Jetavana monastery, the Temple to the Central Peak, and the Earthgod Temple (see Figs. 14.17 and 14.18) and to the fortified outer boundary of Datong (Fig. 14.19). Covered corridors of temple complexes in Figures 14.17 and 14.18 have become fortified walls, and monastic courtyards have been turned into enclosed neighborhoods in the illustration of Datong.

City walls and walled cities appear rigidly uniform in Chinese printed books and stelae. Like the line drawing of Datong (Fig. 14.19), illustrations of earlier capital cities in the fifteenth-century encyclopedia *Yongle dadian* are clearly derived from the famous illustration of

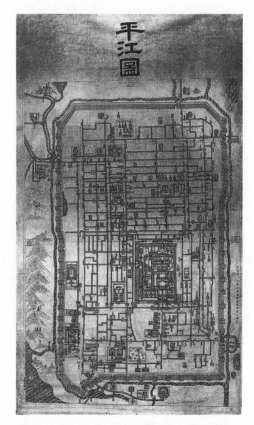

Figure 14.22. Line drawing of *Pingjiang tu*
[illustration of Pingjiang (Suzhou)] stele,
1229. After Cao, *Zhongguao gudai ditu ji* (Beijing, 1990), pl. 81.

Wangcheng (Fig. 14.7).[45] So is the plan of the Northern Song capital
Bianliang (Fig. 14.8) from the encyclopedia *Shilin guangji* of the 1330s.
In actuality, none of these cities, nor Suzhou, nor the Southern Song
capital Lin'an (today Hangzhou) were squarish in plan. It is only due
to their printed images, perpetuated for posterity long after the city
streets and walls had been torn down, destroyed, or decayed, that

---

[45] For a study of these illustrations see Xia Nai, *"Yongle dadian juan* 9561 *yin Yuan Henan
zhi* de gudai Luoyang tu shisi fu" ["Fourteen illustrations of Luoyang from *Yuan
Henan zhi* according to *juan* 9561 of the *Yongle dadian"*], *Kaogu xuebao* no. 2 (1959): 37–
55.

they have been considered reflections of an idealized walled city of China's classical age.[46] Only in the case of a city that obviously contradicted the conventions for a walled enclosure, such as the Western Han capital Chang'an (mentioned above and see Fig. 14.15), might an irregular wall shape be recognized. In the context of Chinese cartography, the exaggerated, even fictitious, representations of cities were purposeful. Maps legitimated China's urban history, including its textual history, so that it began with the description of Wangcheng in the *Kaogong ji* and continued with little alteration in later cities. In two dimensions, topographical factors like water could be discounted in the name of a uniform configuration whose history spanned millennia.

Representations of city walls are one component, but arguably the most significant illustrated one, in the legitimation of a city as "Chinese" according to traditions of China's hallowed past. The desire to draw and print standard images is all pervasive, from the oldest printed examples to current drawings of old or traditional walled cities. Even in twentieth-century urban histories of China, crooked walls and noncentrally placed or aligned palaces are represented as orthogonally and concentrically planned inheritors of a city-building tradition generated by Wangcheng.[47] Truly, it now seems that Handforth could have used almost any model and ended up with no illustration of Beijing other than the one he did (Fig. 14.2).

Thus the worlds of locally, regionally, and state-sponsored printed records and of Buddhism employed simply drawn, straight, fortified city walls to define China's image. Although specific details such as an additional palace area or a multistory structure were often shown, usually those details were hardly noticeable. Sometimes they were concealed, or even omitted, in the name of the ideal depiction. Military maps of the scope employed by Han generals were of a different purpose, and became a separate tradition from published plans of Chinese walled cities or guides through panoramic landscapes. Thus the final question a study of Chinese city walls must pose is if, in any instance, a creatively, exquisitely, profoundly rendered, and/or artis-

---

[46] I have discussed this aspect of the plans of both Song capitals, and of Chinese plans of capitals, more generally, in "Why Were Chang'an and Beijing So Different?" *Journal of the Society of Architectural Historians* 45/4 (1986): 339–57; *Chinese Imperial City Planning*, esp. 137–60; and "Mapping the Chinese City: The Image and the Reality," in *Envisioning the City: Six Studies in Urban Cartography*, ed. David Buisseret (Chicago, 1998).

[47] Almost every Chinese city has been subject to reconfiguration in published plans. Some of the most startling transformations are found in illustrations of the Western Han capital, Chang'an, and in capitals of the Northern and Southern Song dynasties.

tically rendered city wall can be found. The logical place to search is among the works of China's greatest artists.

GREAT PAINTERS DEPICT CHINESE CITY WALLS

This last section, of which the subject matter is defined as works by "great painters," focuses on key examples of Chinese painting on silk or paper. For most of these works, the painter or painters were trained, educated, and worked in ways that set them apart from the artisans or workshop members who decorated the walls of tombs of nonroyal Chinese occupants and from the officials who drew maps for printed books or supervised the drawing of maps in printed books or the carving of stelae. Often, but not always, China's greatest painters were educated at a level high enough to warrant an official title, a means by which many of China's recognized (if not great) painters earned a salary while executing court-sponsored projects. Recognition of skill was usually an important means by which a painter, his biography, and his oeuvre came to be included in the literary history of Chinese painting and sometimes in the official historical record.[48]

The paintings that might be discussed in this section probably number at least one hundred, but not nearly as many as the pictures of city walls found in gazetteers. Five paintings of cities and their walls from the twelfth through fifteenth centuries are selected for this discussion.

The first and earliest is perhaps the most famous painting of a Chinese city, "Spring Festival on the River" (*Qingming shanghe tu*), by Zhang Zeduan, who was active in the first decades of the twelfth century. The festival is "tomb-sweeping." It occurs in early spring as an occasion to clean up ancestral graves after winter damage. The greatest achievement in the painting is often considered its detailed and realistic depiction of life and activity in the Northern Song capital, Bianliang, during the painter's residence there.[49] The details are such

---

[48] This paragraph grossly overgeneralizes a complex situation. Some of China's most famous painters were not educated, some great painters were wall painters. For a recent, general introduction to the role of the Chinese painter in society, see Li Chu-tsing, ed., *Artists and Patrons: Some Social and Economic Aspects of Chinese Painting* (Seattle, 1989). For information on the kinds of writings I refer to as the "literary history" of Chinese painting, see Hin-cheung Lovell, *An Annotated Bibliography of Chinese Painting Catalogues and Related Texts*, Michigan Papers in Chinese Studies no. 16 (Ann Arbor, 1973).

[49] On this painting see Roderick Whitfield, "Chang Tse-tuan's *Ch'ing-ming shang-he t'u*," (Ph. D. diss., Princeton University, 1965); Whitfield, "Chang Tse-tuan's *Ching-ming*

Figure 14.23. Zhang Zeduan, *Qingming shanghe tu*, detail, 12th century. Palace Museum, Beijing.

that only someone familiar with the innermost workings of the city could have painted it. Max Loehr wrote of the painting, "There seems to be no other Song painting of such intense realism, so given to full and accurate description and so sovereignly indifferent to formalistic concerns."[50]

Yet this same attention to detail and concern for minutiae (Fig. 14.23) has caused painting and painter to be categorized in less than esteemed light in China's own history of the field. "Spring Festival on the River" is an example, albeit an extraordinary one, of a type of Chinese painting labeled *jiehua*, a term translated as "boundary painting" or "ruled-line painting" to denote the use of straight edges in its execution. Ruled-line painters were considered skilled executioners of art for commemorating or recording important, sometimes historic events, or for purchase: Chinese histories do not place them among China's greatest painters.[51] (When ruled-line elements occur in works by "great" painters such as tenth-century painter Li Cheng, they are details in compositions for other purposes, and classed according to a different and more highly regarded category, such as landscape.[52])

shang-ho t'u," *Proceedings of the International Symposium on Chinese Painting* (Taibei, 1972): 349–88, and Zhang Anzhi, *Qingming shanghe tu* [The painting "Spring Festival on the River"] (Beijing, 1979). For new interpretations of the painting, see Linda Cooke Johnson, "The Place of *Qingming shanghe tu* in the Historical Geography of Song Dynasty Dongjing," *Journal of Sung-Yuan Studies* 26 (1996): 145–82; and Valerie Hansen, "The Mystery of the Qingming Scroll and Its Subject: The Case against Kaifeng," *Journal of Sung-Yuan Studies* 26 (1996): 183–200.

[50] Max Loehr, *The Great Painters of China* (New York, 1980), 165.

[51] For introductions to *jiehua*, see William Trousdale, "Architectural Landscapes Attributed to Chao Po-chü," *Ars Orientalis* (1963): 285–313; Robert Maeda, "*Chieh-hua*: Ruled-Line Painting in China," *Ars Orientalis* 10 (1975): 123–41; and You Xinmin, ed., *Jiehua yifa* [*Techniques of* jiehua], (Beijing, 1989).

[52] The painting attributed to Li Cheng, "A Solitary Temple amid Clearing Peaks," in the

With time, "great painters" came to be separated from court work-shops. Those who worked for the government or otherwise as "pro-fessionals" included among their ranks *jiehua* painters.

In the context of this study, it is noteworthy that in "Spring Festival on the River," even though the subject is a city, the only sign of its wall is the gate shown in Figures 14.23. Ruled lines, however, are everywhere (and landscape detail is abundant and extremely fine), but those lines are used mostly for buildings and for one extraordinary bridge.

Three factors may have contributed to Zhang Zeduan's decision not to paint Bianliang's wall. First, in this truly urbane commercial center, the outer wall was not straight (in spite of the picture of it in printed books such as Fig. 14.8). The Song capital grew and grew as popula-tion flooded to it to make money. The mid-tenth-century outer wall was completed about the time the Northern Song came to power, and it skirted around to accommodate the urban sprawl, but the popula-tion quickly expanded beyond it.[53] Thus perhaps the wall did not have the somber aura or pervasive presence in Bianliang that it had in earlier cities or would have in later Beijing.

Second, perhaps it was such common knowledge that Chinese cities were walled that Zhang Zeduan, the artist, decided it was not neces-sary to paint this wall. Perhaps the prominent gate was considered sufficient indication of an entire wall.[54] Related to this, a third possi-bility is that it was an artistic or compositional decision that the pres-ence of city walls might detract from the rest of the detail. Perhaps the focus on a gate, which stands out so much because no wall joins it, offered the compositional hub sought by Zhang Zeduan to lead the viewer to land. If so, it can be said that among "great" painters, or at least from the brush of a silk painter who had studied in the painting academy in the Northern Song capital (and would flee south with the dynasty to educate others in the painting academy at the Southern Song capital Lin'an), finally, we find a city without its wall.

The second painting with a *jiehua* rendering of a gate tower and adjoining wall is by an unknown painter and of ambiguous subject matter. The painting has been labeled "Zhao Yu's Pacification of the Barbarians South of Lu." Based on stylistic details, it has been dated

Nelson Gallery-Atkins Museum, Kansas City, for example, is one of the tenth-century paintings in which a philosophical exploration of nature is an important theme.

[53] See Steinhardt, *Chinese Imperial City Planning*, 137–44 and n. 44, for a list of published plans.

[54] In the version of Zhang Zeduan's painting in the British Museum, one sees a fortified city wall and a much less prominent bridge.

Figure 14.24. Anonymous, *Zhao Yu's Pacification of the Barbarians South of Lu*, detail, Jin period(?). Courtesy of the Nelson Gallery-Atkins Museum, Kansas City.

to the period of Jin rule (1126–1234) (Fig. 14.24).[55] Like Zhang Zeduan's "Spring Festival," this is a hand scroll in which much of the painter's energy has focused on elements other than architecture. One of the most telling details, for instance, what appears to be the chopping down of trees, has led to the identification of the subject as a Liao (947–1125) countermeasure to the planting of trees by Song. Forestation under the Song dynasty was an effort to deter attacking Liao forces from the north. The painting offers one of the most detailed depictions of a city gate of early (pre-Yuan) date.

Besides the amount of landscape imagery compared to architecture, another similarity is found in the two *jiehua* silk paintings with city walls. The gateways are focal points of both. (This feature is especially noticeable when the paintings are extended to full length.) The very prominent and beautiful gates are more than adequate signs of the walls they were known to join. Furthermore, as we have observed above, when it comes to representations of city walls, general format

[55] For discussion of this controversial painting, see *Eight Dynasties of Chinese Painting: The Collections of the Nelson Gallery-Atkins Museum, Kansas City, and The Cleveland Museum of Art* (Cleveland 1980), 37–40.

Figure 14.25. Wang Zhenpeng, "The Dragon Boat Regatta on Qingming Lake," 1312–20. Courtesy of the Metropolitan Museum of Art, New York.

and specific details can be traced back hundreds of years. This fact is clear in a comparison of Figures 14.24 and 14.13, in which, through the bolder, more casual strokes in Mogao cave 249 on the one hand, and the detail of a *jiehua*-painter's brush on silk on the other, the eye confronts a central, dominant, hipped roof above an entryway. The set of front corner towers of the U-shaped structure in the silk painting can also be traced to wall painting and architectural remains of the Tang period. Four towers in a diagonal row are found on a wall of Crown Prince Yide's tomb and three are part of the reconstruction of Hanyuan Hall from the palace compound Daminggong.[56]

The third painting is a work by a painter at the Mongolian court. His name was Wang Zhenpeng. His known period of activity was 1312–20, during the reign of Emperor Renzong. Among Wang's subjects was "The Dragon Boat Regatta on Qingming Lake" (Fig. 14.25).[57]

[56] The wall painting is the one referred to in footnote 32. For illustrations of Hanyuan Hall, see Steinhardt, *Chinese Traditional Architecture* (New York, 1984), 92–9.

[57] On Wang Zhenpeng and his painting, see Marsha S. Weidner, "Painting and Patronage at the Mongol Court of China, 1260–1368" (Ph.D. diss., University of California–Berkeley, 1982). The authenticity of the "Dragon Boat Regatta" painting in the Metropolitan Museum of Art is disputed. It is not a concern here. Our interest in the painting is in the representation of walls.

The version of this painting in the Metropolitan Museum, New York, combines wall and bridge. The arched bridge is a detail observed in Zhang Zeduan's "Springtime Festival on the River." Here, however, wall, bridge, and the architecture they join appear more as subjects than in Zhang Zeduan's painting. We cannot go so far as to say that the subject is a wall: As in Zhang Zeduan's painting, it is a festival. In fact, my search for a painting whose subject is a wall (except for modern consumer-oriented paintings of the Great Wall) is ongoing.

"Dragon Boat Regatta" is chosen for discussion here to consider a possible motive or purpose for the painting of walls by great painters. In "Dragon Boat Regatta," although the wall represents a city, that is, a palace-city, the purpose of the painting is not associated with a city. By contrast, on tomb walls, even though a city could be implied by a small piece of a wall, a fortified gateway, or just a bridge, the city and its walls were fundamental to the definition of spatial boundaries in the afterlife. In the two silk paintings discussed previously, the city and its walls represented the locus of the subject for Zhang Zeduan, and the boundary between the Chinese world and the non-Chinese for the other painter. These were not Wang Zhenpeng's intentions. For Wang Zhenpeng, it may be suggested, the wall that joins palace to pavilion is part of the fanciful, decorative detail professionally rendered by a master of *jiehua* tradition at the court. This painting has been chosen for discussion here as an exceptional one in which a wall stands without its profound and age-old symbolism. At best, it can be likened to the representation of city walls or other architectural elements in the minor arts, shown above to function as backdrop; but here it is just as much fanciful detail.

Wang Zhenpeng's purpose (or lack of purpose) in painting a wall is unusual. Most often, including in later painting, Chinese artists whose subject is walls somehow make it clear that a city is represented. In every painting discussed so far, except Wang Zhenpeng's, walls have been purposeful. One later example of this feature of Chinese paintings with city walls is found in Wang Fu's (1362–1412) "The Eight Views of Beijing."[58] Wang Fu was born in Jiansu province of southeastern China. During the initial decade of transition from the Yuan to the Ming dynasty, the 1370s, he was banished to the north where he served as a frontier guard until about the year 1400.[59] By the beginning

---

[58] On this painting, see Kathlyn Liscomb, *"The Eight Views of Beijing*: Politics in Literati Art," *Artibus Asiae* 49 (1988–9), 127–52. Numerous illustrations of this painting can be found in Liscomb's article.

[59] On Wang Fu's biography, in addition to Liscomb, see James Cahill, *Hills beyond a River: Chinese Painting of the Yüan Dynasty, 1279–1368* (New York and Tokyo, 1976),

of the fifteenth century, Wang Fu received an appointment at the imperial palace in Nanjing where he worked as a calligrapher and eventually drafter. In 1414, two years before his death, he moved to the northern capital, Beijing. "The Eight Views of Beijing" is dated to December of this year by a colophon.

Wang Fu's painting has been interpreted as part of a political program of justification for moving the capital northward. The "eight views" are intended to show the beauties of the capital, the same purpose as some contemporary poetry, whereas memorials to the throne served to show the strategic advantages of Beijing.[60] It is noteworthy that only one of the eight views recognizes Beijing as a walled city and the other seven present it as a place of natural beauty or scenic spot. (The last scene, with a bridge, is not a symbol of a wall but the famous tourist spot Lugouqiao [Marco Polo Bridge].) The Jimen fortification shown in Wang Fu's painting stands for a wall, but out of context, no one would mistake it for a symbol of the famous walled city or one of its northern passes. Nor would one assume the scene represents a strategically fortified capital. In context, however, the piece of wall is purposeful subject matter by a painter who, as part of a political agenda, was commissioned to paint a city's details.

The last painting with city walls discussed here is by a "follower," in a sense, of Wang Fu. It is "Twelve Views of Tiger Hill" and the painter is Shen Zhou (1427–1509), probably Suzhou's most famous painter. Shen Zhou was a rare painter in the history of China, for he was born and died in prosperous times and circumstances. His life as a country gentleman is reflected in his paintings.[61] Yet even in Shen Zhou's paintings of Suzhou, a city best known for its estates and gardens, and where defense was rarely an issue, many walls are found. The view from a distance is of small open buildings, elevated on a high wall formed of horizontal layers. Another wall, also the bottom of a foundation platform, is stone. Yet another is made of plaster. And in this idyllic beauty spot one can even find a mud wall (Fig. 14.26).[62] Indeed, when a man of wealth, painting in the privacy

58–9, and Cahill, *Parting at the Shore: Chinese Painting of the Early and Middle Ming Dynasty, 1368–1580* (New York and Tokyo, 1978), 58–9. The exact chronology of events in Wang Fu's life is not definite.

[60] Liscomb makes this point. On memorials relevant to the movement of the capital, see Edward Farmer, *Early Ming Government: The Evolution of Dual Capitals* (Cambridge, MA, 1976).

[61] Of the long bibliography on Shen Zhou see, for example, Cahill, *Parting at the Shore*, 82–96; and Richard Edwards, *The Field of Stones: A Study of Shen Chou*, Oriental Studies no. 5 (Washington, DC, 1962).

[62] "Twelve Views of Tiger Hill" is published in its entirety in *Eight Dynasties of Chinese Painting*, 188–90.

Figure 14.26. Shen Zhou, Chinese, 1427–1509, Ming dynasty. *Tiger-Flight Spring at the Back Gate* from the album *Twelve Views of Tiger Hill*. Album leaf, ink and slight color on paper, 31.1 × 40.2 cm. © The Cleveland Museum of Art, 1998, Leonard C. Hanna, Jr., Fund, 1964.371.

of his prosperous Suzhou estate, painted a city or its architecture, or even hinted that a city was his subject, he painted walls.

CONCLUSIONS

Neither Shen Zhou nor other painters or designers or carvers of walls had reason to strive to represent realistic details. Instead, the representation of walls in the Chinese pictorial arts is part of a widespread and always purposeful ideology of walls and cities. The images are standard. The essential features – fortifications, gates, corner towers, earthen layers or bricks of which they are composed – are present, and the depictions can be traced back more than a millennium. Choosing or instructed to draw a city wall, a painter's image is one ingrained in his psyche since infancy.

Walls represented cities, cities had walls, and the city wall was among China's most powerful symbols. Symbols of security from the national to the personal level, a feature without which China could not defend herself, a private citizen dared not enter the next world, and a wealthy citizen of leisure chose not to represent a garden pavilion, walls were not symbols taken lightly or with which one pondered creativity. A "great painter" might take the liberty of not painting the entire wall around a city, but both he and a stele carver or cartographer were equally likely to show crooked walls as ideally rigid or to place them where they in actuality did not exist. Among the cultures and time periods considered here, for China, walls are uniquely pre-eminent.

CHAPTER 15

The hierarchy of Ming city walls

EDWARD L. FARMER

T HIS essay will explore the portrayal of city walls in Ming dynasty gazetteers.[1] Ming representations of city walls and frontier fortifications reveal important elements of the Ming project to revive and reconstruct the Chinese world in the wake of the era of Mongol conquest. Wall building was essential not just for defensive purposes but also to distinguish levels of the administrative hierarchy of the empire and symbolically to delineate the extent of the Han Chinese cultural realm.

After surveying depictions of Ming walls I have concluded that it is not useful to draw a sharp line between those that housed civil units of government and those that were purely military. Rather, they were all defensive structures ranged across a broad spectrum from great cities of the heartland, fortified to withstand siege, to tiny, isolated military outposts on remote frontiers. The uniformity with which these walls were described and portrayed in official and semi-official publications speaks both to the strength of Ming cartographic conventions and to the conviction of Ming authors and illustrators that theirs was a culturally unified world.

As the last ethnically-Chinese dynasty,[2] the Ming era (1368–1644) was the only time in the last millennium that the Han people, today

---

I should like to express my gratitude to the Graduate School of the University of Minnesota for supporting the research on which this essay is based.

[1] Chinese history is conventionally divided into dynastic eras. The last three dynasties were the Yuan, Mongol rule from 1279 to 1368; the Ming, indigenous rule from 1368 to 1644; and the Qing (or Ch'ing), Manchu rule from 1644 to 1911. *Note:* Unless otherwise specified, all gazetteers are reproductions from the Tianyige collection, a famous private library in Ningbo, reprinted in a standard format by the Shanghai guji chubanshe in the early 1960s.

[2] Chinese is here equated with Han. Largest of the current nationalities in China, the Han include speakers of the major Chinese dialects, approximately ninety-four percent of the population.

the dominant group in the multinational People's Republic of China, governed all of China proper. The Ming empire endured for nearly three centuries but its territory was far less extensive than that of the Mongol (Yuan) and Manchu (Qing) conquest states that preceded and followed it. The Ming controlled only the Chinese heartland, the central provinces where the agricultural Han population was most densely concentrated. Aside from brief forays in the early years, the Ming adopted a defensive posture toward the outside world.[3] Defensive works were erected across the northern frontier; to the west and southwest the edges of its territory were dotted with military outposts, and along its eastern and southern coasts a maritime prohibition was enforced.

In a fundamental sense the Ming era saw a conscious pulling back, an effort to wrest Chinese territory away from the control of Inner Asian conquerors, to isolate as much as possible the world of farming villages from contact with the peoples of the steppe, and to promote and disseminate traditional values and institutions throughout the realm. Wall building was a concrete manifestation of the extension of Ming governmental authority in both its military and civil aspects. In form, Ming city walls embodied the essential features of Chinese city walls as they appeared early in the historical record. Square bodies of rammed earth oriented on a north–south axis, studded by prominent gates, and surrounded by moats were established features well before the advent of the common era. In this context the cultural conservatism and traditional character of city walls in the post-Mongol period can be viewed in part as expressions of what Arthur Wright called "the fervent Chinese restorationism of the Ming."[4]

MING WALLS

To place Ming representations of walls in their historical context a number of observations are in order.

First of all, we ought not succumb to the temptation to seize upon the Great Wall, the complex of fortifications along the interface between the farmland and grassland, as a defining symbol of imperial China. Arthur Waldron has shown that the Great Wall indelibly etched on our minds had no iconographic value in Chinese thinking until the rise of nationalism in the nineteenth century, when modern patriots,

---

[3] I have in mind imperial expeditions into Mongolia, a short-lived effort to annex Annam, and the naval expeditions of the eunuch admiral Zheng He.

[4] Arthur F. Wright, "The Cosmology of the Chinese City," in *The City in Late Imperial China*, ed. G. William Skinner (Stanford, 1977), 73.

anxious to resist the inroads of imperialism, embraced a Western stereotype.[5] The concept of a Great Wall, in Chinese "long wall" (*changcheng*), does not dominate Ming writings – these tend to distinguish between the regions within and beyond the passes. What does occur over and over again are references to the "Nine Defense Areas" (*jiubian*),[6] a series of heavily armed sectors spanning the strategic northern border. Ming maps portray the northern defense areas as fortified garrisons with numerous subordinate strong points all surrounded by defensive walls. In both a physical and a functional way these military structures embody the essential character of Ming city walls.

A second point to bear in mind is that Chinese cities are closely identified with their walls. In Chinese usage the concepts of wall and city are intimately connected: The character *cheng* means both "wall" and "city." The term invites the assumption that a city is enclosed by a wall. The most common word for "city" in modern Chinese is *chengshi*, a term that links two characters: *cheng* (wall) and *shi* (market). Divided, the two halves of *chengshi* suggest two classes of cities: seats of government and commercial centers. Three decades ago G. William Skinner drew scholarly attention to the interpenetrating hierarchies of administrative centers and nodes in the pyramids of market systems.[7] Whereas markets were produced by economic forces of supply and demand, administrative centers were manifestations of a political system consciously designed to express relative standing within a carefully graded structure of government. In Ming times the administrative hierarchy still dominated society at the expense of the commercial system. Chinese cities were classified and portrayed primarily in terms of the governmental units they housed.

A third and related point has to do with the way in which walled cities reflected the political structure of the dynasty and its orthodox ideology. In an article contrasting the cultural style of Beijing and Shanghai, Yang Dongping has argued that the two cities represent substantially different phenomena.[8] Beijing is an example of a political,

---

[5] Arthur Waldron, *The Great Wall of China: From History to Myth* (Cambridge, 1990), 4–6, 194–226.

[6] Here I follow *The Cambridge History of China*, Vol. 7, *The Ming Dynasty, 1368–1644, Part I*, eds. Frederick W. Mote and Denis Twitchett (Cambridge, 1988), 937, in favor of Charles O. Hucker, *A Dictionary of Official Titles in Imperial China* (Stanford, 1985), 80, who calls them frontiers. The Chinese term specifically refers to the frontier (*bian*), which implies the northern border.

[7] G. William Skinner, "Cities and the Hierarchy of Local Systems," in *City in Late Imperial China*, 275–351.

[8] Yang Dongping, "Xiandai Zhongguo di 'Shuangcheng ji' – Beijing yu Shanghai di chengshi wenhua mingyun" ("Modern China's 'Tale of Two Cities' – the urban cultural destiny of Beijing and Shanghai") *Dongfang* (Orient) 1 (1993):45.

administrative, military center with a high wall (*cheng*), whereas Shanghai represents a center of commerce and trade, essentially a coastal market (*shi*). Yang's contrast brings to mind Robert Redfield and Milton Singer's distinction between "orthogenetic" cities – typically inland centers, the products and bearers of indigenous cultural traditions – and "heterogenetic" cities – typically located on the seacoast, brought about by maritime interaction between diverse cultures, home to degradation, alienation, and anomie.[9] If we are to search for the meaning of Ming city walls we must look first and foremost at the walled cities of the heartland, for they best expressed the aspirations of those who created and maintained the Ming order. Shanghai, the quintessential cultural crossbreed, did not emerge until the nineteenth century.[10] It represented an intrusion of Western power that would have been unthinkable in Ming times.[11]

A fourth observation bears on the character of Ming city walls as the products of an early modern, land-based empire. The threat of invasion from the north by Inner Asian peoples was not the only danger to Chinese social order. It can be argued that Chinese culture faced another challenge from the south – the encroachment of the world trade system, based on the order (or disorder) of the market, the corrosive disruption brought about by the unseen logic of commercial opportunity. It is true that by the sixteenth century Ming China was linked to the emerging global market by increased maritime trade along the southern coast, and a lively commercial culture flourished in the lower Yangzi region, but the stimulus of early Western contact was not yet strong enough to affect Chinese conceptions of city wall construction. Artillery pieces of various kinds were employed throughout the Ming period, but we find no reflection in

[9] Robert Redfield and Milton Singer, "The Cultural Role of Cities," *Economic Development and Social Change* 3/1 (1954): 58.

[10] One could argue that Beijing, erected on the site of Khitan, Jurchen, and Mongol capitals, and a terminus for camel caravans from the north and west, was not free of external influences from across the Inner Asian frontier. While there may be some truth to this, it can be countered that Beijing was reconstructed in the Ming era as a military and political center for the protection of Han China to the south. It took on yet another character in the Qing era when Manchu banner forces were garrisoned in the northern half, leading to the distinction between the two walled sections known as the Chinese City and the Tartar City.

[11] However, the commercial transformation of China was well underway by the middle of the Ming period. Gilbert Rozman, *Urban Networks in Ch'ing China and Tokugawa Japan* (Princeton, 1973), 44–5, characterizes the process in terms of maturation of the market system: increasing numbers of periodic markets and the formation of a national market by the seventeenth century.

Chinese wall construction of the European conventions and innovations of bastion design referred to elsewhere in this volume.

THE HIERARCHY OF CITY WALLS

An appreciation of Ming city walls can best be gained by viewing them in terms of their standing in a hierarchy of central places. That hierarchy can be seen as the expression of Ming conceptions of social order. Romeyn Taylor has characterized premodern China as a society which "in its entirety came to be hierarchically organized in an empire, and this empire-society was understood by its members to be universal."[12] While Taylor's observation was concerned largely with the official orthodoxy of the imperial era, I assume that the Ming effort to embody Chinese ideals of cultural order was not limited to religious activities and is also clearly expressed in the hierarchy of walled cities.

A tidy example of the Ming sense of hierarchy is provided by the essay on geography (*dili zhi*) in the official dynastic history (*Mingshi*). In that work the administrative units of the empire are described beginning with the capitals and then descending through the provinces, starting with those nearest to Beijing and ending with those farthest away. The sequence is: The Capital, Nanjing, Shandong, Shanxi, Henan, Shaanxi, Sichuan, Jiangxi, Huguang, Zhejiang, Fujian, Guangdong, Guangxi, Yunnan, and Guizhou. Under each province, prefectures are listed in descending order from the center, and under them subprefectures and counties are arranged in the same manner.[13] This simple listing of the names of places embodies a sequential, and spatial, manifestation of Ming assumptions about the hierarchical character of the empire.

Terminology also provides clues to the hierarchy of Chinese cities. At the apex of the hierarchy stand the capitals demarcated by the terms *jing* and *du*. The principal Ming capitals were The Capital (Jingshi, i.e., Beijing) and Nanjing (Southern Capital), suitably protected by the largest city walls in all of China.[14] Next in stature to the imperial

---

[12] Romeyn Taylor, "Chinese Hierarchy in Comparative Perspective," *Journal of Asian Studies* 48/3 (1989): 493.

[13] *Mingshi* (*Ming history*; Beijing, 1974), *juan* 40–6, 881–1221.

[14] Administratively, they were the centers of two province-sized metropolitan areas, Nanzhili and Beizhili, respectively. Both were seats of the imperial government but their status was not equal. "The Capital" (Jingshi) was the name applied first to Nanjing and then to Beijing after the court moved north in 1420. The terminology was not finally stabilized until 1441. See Edward L. Farmer, *Early Ming Government: The Evolution of Dual Capitals* (Cambridge, MA, 1976), 123.

capitals were two quasi-capitals erected to honor homes of imperial ancestors. The "Middle Capital," Zhongdu, at Fengyang was erected by the Ming founder at his native place. While it had many of the attributes of an imperial city its role was modest and the term *du* appears to signify a status lower than that of the Capital. The other example, Xingdu, honored the home of the emperor Shizong, the son of a prince enthroned in 1522 when the emperor died without an heir.[15]

Below the capital level, city walls were built to mark and protect the seats of government within the two metropolitan areas and thirteen provinces of the Chinese heartland. The set included 159 prefectures (*fu*), 234 subprefectures (*zhou*), and 1,144 districts or counties (*xian*).[16] These were the centers in which civil service officials were stationed and from which they exerted imperial authority. At lower levels walls might be found encompassing smaller cities, towns, and even villages, not to mention innumerable military commands, installations, and frontier posts.

In his article on "The Morphology of Walled Capitals," Sen-dou Chang surveys a number of ways in which Chinese walled cities as a group displayed principles of hierarchy.[17] First, the area of higher ranking cities was usually greater than that of lower ranking cities. Thus the capitals had the longest walls, enclosing a greater territory than the walls of provincial capitals, and the walled area of prefectural capitals was greater on average than that of county capitals.[18] Second, higher ranked cities had more gates in their walls than lower ranked cities.[19] Third, higher ranked cities had more regularly shaped walls than did lower ranked cities. This observation correlates with another, that city walls approximating a square or rectangular shape were more likely to be found in the north or northwest than in the south.[20] This phenomenon Chang attributes to the obvious fact that there is more flat terrain in the north than in the south.

Another contrast Chang makes between northern and southern cities is that, thanks to the greater abundance of water, moats are more prevalent and wider in the south. A related phenomenon is that northern cities tend to have lower ratios of population to land and to have

---

[15] Farmer, *Early Ming Government*, 176–7.
[16] Hucker, *Dictionary of Official Titles*, 76–8.
[17] Chang Sen-Dou, "Some Observations on the Morphology of Chinese Walled Cities," *Annals of the Association of American Geographers* 60/1 (1970): 63–91.
[18] Chang, "Chinese Walled Cities," 91.
[19] Chang, "Chinese Walled Cities," 96.
[20] Chang, "Chinese Walled Cities," 88.

more bodies of water and crop land within the walls, attributes which enhanced their capacity to withstand siege.[21] We can add to Chang's analysis by noting that the major military threat was from the north and that national political centers historically tended to be located north of the Yangzi.[22] Thus there was a rough congruence between standing in the hierarchy, size, regularity of shape, and military power. Water transport, both riverine and maritime, may have been more developed south of the Yangzi where commerce flourished, but military power and political authority tended to gravitate toward the defense perimeter in the north, and that is where the walls were most apt to assume square shapes.

The number of walled cities in Ming China is difficult to estimate, but it is clearly in the thousands. The basic levels of government, listed above, from capitals down to districts, would require about a thousand urban areas enclosed by walls. The numbers are not neatly cumulative because higher-level units usually had lower-level ones nested within them. The capitals, for example, had one prefectural office and two county offices situated inside their walls. Likewise, a prefectural city would also serve as home to one of its subordinate districts. How many towns and villages below the district or county level had walls built around them is difficult to say but an average of only two or three per district could send the total into the thousands.

In addition to urban concentrations of civilian population, Ming China was also dotted by thousands of military installations, many surrounded by walls. The territory of the empire was divided under the jurisdiction of five regional military commissions that supervised local garrisons (*wei*, nominally 5,600 men), typically attached to prefectures or subprefectures. The subdivisions of the garrison, the battalions (*qianhusuo*, nominally 1,120 men) and their subordinate companies (*baihusuo*), often were housed separately from the garrison headquarters and so accounted for another class of walled enclosure.[23] Across the northern frontier stretched a network of defense commands with numerous walled strong points and fortifications. Last, along the southern and western fringes of Han settlement, the Ming established pacification offices (*xuanweisi*) and pacification commissions (*xuanweifu*) intended to control non-Han peoples such as the Dai,

[21] Chang, "Chinese Walled Cities," 94–5.
[22] The exceptions are Hangzhou during the Southern Song, a capital which governed only the southern portion of China, and Nanjing in the early Ming. Nanjing was soon displaced by Beijing, presumably because the northern city had a more strategic location.
[23] See Hucker, *Dictionary of Official Titles*, 78–80.

Miao, Yao, Yi, and Zhuang, whose tribal chiefs typically held the offices. These accounted for many outposts and stockades in remote regions.[24]

STRUCTURES AND INSTITUTIONS

The wall and its surrounding moat gave a Chinese city its essential shape, but there were other elements critical to its orientation and definition. South of the city one would expect to find the altar to the gods of mountains and streams (shanquantan). To the south or west, only rarely to the north, one could find the altar to the gods of soil and grain (shejitan). North of the city wall, in a far less auspicious location, the abandoned ghost altar (liyitan)[25] was situated (Fig. 15.1). Altars such as these helped to integrate the city into a national system of cults. Throughout the empire the son of heaven, high metropolitan officials, and local magistrates were expected to carry out parallel rituals according to a fixed calendar and protocol. Within the walls were located the administrative compounds of the civil offices. These were generally designed to be the most imposing structures in the city. A higher-level administrative center might contain multiple offices. In addition to the administrative seats one could find branch offices of the provincial administration (buzhengsi) and provincial surveillance commission (anchasi), granaries (cang), and relay stations (yi). Other features prominently marked on a gazetteer map are the temple of the city god (literally, the temple of the gods of the wall and moat, chenghuangmiao), the Confucian school (ruxue), and perhaps one or more local schools (shexue). Daoist and Buddhist monasteries (guan and si respectively) were also often labeled. A drum tower (gulou), used to mark the passage of time by sounding the watches, provided a sense of rhythm to life within the walls while the bell tower (zhonglou) was used to issue alarms and rally the populace in an emergency.

The city god temple deserves some attention here because in it we see the city portrayed symbolically in terms of the spirits of walls

---

[24] Liew Foon Ming, "An Annotated Translation of the Military Treatises One and Two from the Ming Dynastic History: A Documentation of Ming-Qing Historiography (Mingshi, juan 89 and 90, Bing 1 and 2)," 3 vols., unpublished habilitationsschrift (Hamburg, 1992), 415–94. Liew lists these aboriginal units (tusi) by province: Sichuan, 68; Guangxi, 6; Yunnan, 58; Guizhou 97; Huguang, 43.

[25] Romeyn Taylor, "Official and Popular Religion and the Political Organization of Chinese Society in the Ming," in Orthodoxy in Late Imperial China, ed. Kwang-Ching Liu (Berkeley, 1990), 146, notes that the Ming founder was so concerned about the danger of unrequited ghosts that he ordered these altars erected clear down to the township level.

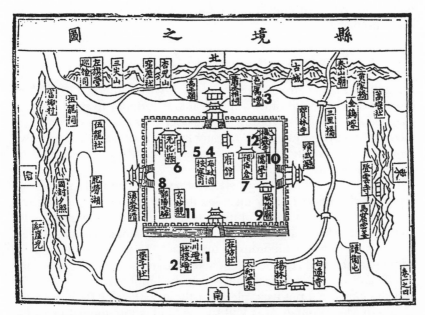

Figure 15.1 Guanghua *xian* (Huguang). Outside the wall note: (1) altar to gods of mountains and streams; (2) altar to gods of soil and grain; (3) abandoned ghost altar. Inside the wall: (4) branch office of provincial administration; (5) branch office of provincial surveillance commission; (6) district office; (7) a granary; (8) a relay station; (9) temple to gods of wall and moat; (10) Confucian school; (11) a Daoist monastery; (12) a Buddhist monastery. *Source: Guanghua xian zhi.*

(*cheng*) and moats (*huang*). The Ming founder, who had strong convictions about matters of religion, took steps to placate the gods and keep them working on behalf of his dynastic enterprise. In one of the more striking innovations of his reign, he tried to reorganize the hierarchy of city gods on his own behalf by granting them noble titles.[26] His motive, in part, was to enlist the gods of walls and moats as his spiritual representatives and to charge them with oversight of the local officials. This initiative, and the official status of the gods of walls and moats, is emblematic of the extent to which walled cities were seen by Chinese rulers, and the educated elite they co-opted, to be extensions

[26] His effort was not entirely successful. The gods of walls and moats stood at the interface between the national and the local, their loyalties claimed simultaneously by the resident community and the remote emperor. See Romeyn Taylor, "Ming T'ai-tsu and the Gods of Walls and Moats," *Ming Studies* 3 (1977): 31–49.

downward of a centralized order and not the homes of autonomous communities.

THE REPRESENTATION OF CITY WALLS

Ming literati had a strong sense of place. It was common for members of the local elite, with official approval and support, to produce local gazetteers (*difangzhi*) recording the history, virtues, and accomplishments of their communities. Wolfgang Franke estimates that some two thousand local gazetteers were published in the Ming period, of which more than 900 are extant.[27]

The opening section of a gazetteer typically is devoted to the geography of the district. This includes its location, its mountains and rivers, the history of its evolution as an administrative entity with emphasis on changes in level and terminology under various dynasties, its superior and subordinate units, and the physical layout of its administrative seat. This last item takes the form of an account of the "walls and moats" (*chengchi*) in which the emphasis is on the walls and the gates. A brief example from the gazetteer of Bazhou in the Northern Metropolitan Area will suffice to illustrate the nature of the information provided:

Wall and Moat. The wall's circumference is 6 *li*, 320 *bu* [3.8 kilometers]. Its height is 2 *zhang*, 7 *chi* [8.3 meters]. It is 2 *zhang* wide [6.2 meters] at the base and one *zhang* [3.1 meters] wide at the top. The moat is 8 *li*, 152 *bu* [4.7 kilometers] in circumference. It is 7 *zhang* [21.7 meters] wide. There are three gates in the wall: north, Zhanji Gate; south, Wenming Gate; east, Linjin Gate. Tradition has it that King Zhao of Yan built the wall. The Song general Yang Yanlang repaired it to defend against the Khitans. There was an earthen wall all the way around. It continued in the Jin and Yuan dynasties. Under the Present Dynasty, in the year Hongzhi *xinhai* [1491] the subprefect Xu Yizhen built eastern and northern wall towers. . . .[28]

Illustrations normally are placed at the front of gazetteers just behind the preface(s) and contents but before the beginning of the text proper. While there is some variation in the numbers of illustrations, a few standard patterns predominate. The most frequent sequence of illustrations would include maps of (1) the territory of the district indicating the location of the administrative seat in relation to the natural terrain features and subordinate units of government; (2) the

---

[27] Wolfgang Franke, *An Introduction to the Sources of Ming History* (Kuala Lumpur, 1968), 236.

[28] *Bazhouzhi*, 1/4ab. The illustration, not reproduced here, shows the wall with three gates and surrounding moat. The north gate is protected by an enceinte wall.

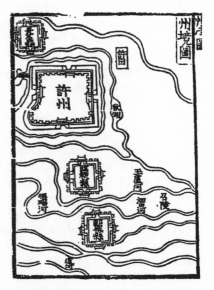

Figure 15.2 Xuzhou (Henan). Xuzhou had subordinate districts: Linyin (just below Xuzhou), Liangcheng (on far left), Yancheng (at bottom), and Yuzhou (at top). See *Mingshi* (Ming History, Beijing, 1974), *juan* 40–6, 980–1. *Source: Xuzhou zhi.*

walls and moats of the administrative seat showing locations of key offices, temples, and other installations inside and outside the wall; (3) the administrative compound with various buildings labeled; and (4) a similar portrayal of the Confucian temple (*ruxue*). The emphasis given administrative offices and the Confucian school reflect, no doubt, the conviction of the compilers that governmental authority and orthodox learning were the most important forces unifying their cultural universe. With less regularity gazetteers contain maps depicting changes in various dynasties, subordinate units, scenic prospects, mountains and waterways, altars and temples, and routes of travel.

A minimal depiction of the hierarchy of administrative units can be seen in the portrayal of Shouzhou, a subprefecture attached to Feng-yang *fu* in Nanzhili. In the bird's eye view provided in the gazetteer, Shouzhou is split across two pages while its two district seats are relegated to the upper and lower left-hand corners of the map.[29] A more symbolic treatment of subordination is shown in the map of Xuzhou, a subprefecture subordinate to Kaifeng in Henan (Fig. 15.2).

[29] *Shouzhouzhi.*

In this depiction of the territory of the unit, spread across two pages, the subprefectural seat is shown at a larger size than its four subordinate districts.[30] Each of the cities is represented by a crenelated, square wall with four gates.[31] Only Xuzhou itself is shown with a slight irregularity in the shape of its wall, a bulge in the southwest corner that also appears on a larger map of the city wall.[32]

A somewhat more elaborate set of administrative arrangements is portrayed in a map of the territory of Daming prefecture in the Northern Metropolitan area (Fig. 15.3). Daming *fu* had one subordinate subprefecture, Kaizhou, and ten districts.[33] The two districts under Kaizhou appear to border the Yellow River, which flows across the bottom of the map in wavy lines. On this map Daming *fu* is depicted as a large square with triple lines and four gates, the districts by smaller double-lined squares, and the subprefecture by a double-lined half circle. One of the districts is shown by name only inside the prefectural city. In the northeast quadrant of the map a jagged, double-lined circular form indicates the location of an earlier Daming *fu* city wall.

Kaifeng, a former imperial capital and capital of Henan during the Ming era, is shown on a regional map in relation to nearby districts along a stretch of the Yellow River (Fig. 15.4). In this map, which has north at the bottom, we see the Henan provincial capital (*buzhengshisi*) in the southwest (upper right) corner with six nearby district offices, two south of the river and four to the north. Not seen are the jurisdiction boundaries, which place three of the *xian* in Henan, three in the Capital, and one in Shandong. Defense points along the road paralleling the northern bank of the river are indicated by pointed flags.[34] The map comes from the gazetteer of Zhangyuan *xian* in the Capital area.[35] Its own city map (Fig. 15.5) shows a square city wall with four gates, each protected by a curved outer wall (*yuecheng*, literally, moon wall) surrounded by a moat. Beyond the moat is shown a circular outer wall with four additional gate complexes. Here, I believe the cartog-

---

[30] See *Mingshi*, 980–1.
[31] City walls and military walls are depicted with crenelations in most cases. I assume that they were in fact crenelated even when gazetteer illustrations, perhaps due to variations in the style of illustrations, do not show crenelations.
[32] *Xuzhou zhi.*
[33] *Mingshi*, 898–9.
[34] For similar symbols see Cordell D. K. Yee, "Reinterpreting Traditional Chinese Geographical Maps," in *The History of Cartography*, Vol. 2, bk. 2, *Cartography in the Traditional East and Southeast Asian Societies*, eds. J. B. Harley and David Woodward (Chicago, 1994), 64, legend of fig. 3.29. I am indebted to Peite Kang for bringing this to my attention.
[35] *Zhangyuan xian zhi.*

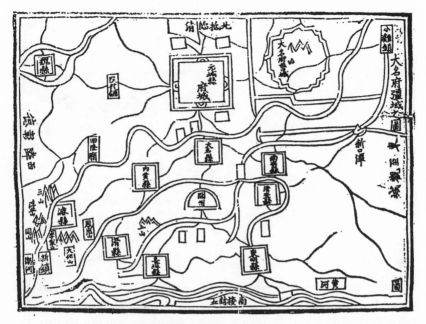

Figure 15.3 Daming *fu* (Beizhili). Daming *fu* is shown as a three-line square in the upper center of the map; the location of an old city wall is shown to its right. One of its ten subordinate districts, Yuancheng, is indicated by name inside the prefectural seat; the others are marked by double-line squares. The single subprefecture, Kaizhou, is symbolized by a half circle directly below the prefecture. Vertical rectangles in the upper right and lower left corners indicate two *zhen* in which police offices (*xunjiansi*) were located. *Mingshi* (Ming History, Beijing, 1974), *juan* 40–6, 898–9; Charles O. Hucker, *A Dictionary of Official Titles in Imperial China* [Stanford, 1989], 254. *Source: Daming fu zhi.*

rapher has exaggerated certain features to accentuate the ideal properties of the city's layout. The effect is a cosmogram depicting a square (earth) encompassed by a circle (heaven).

CITY WALLS IN THE HEARTLAND

If the capitals represented the apex of the city hierarchy in Ming China, they are each in their way imperfect examples of the ideals they were meant to embody. Historical circumstances and uneven terrain were the causes of the irregularities in their walls.

The soon-to-be Ming founder, Zhu Yuanzhang, crossed to the south

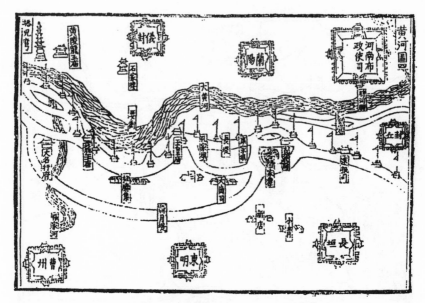

Figure 15.4 Kaifeng (Henan). Kaifeng, in the upper right-hand corner, is labeled "Henan Provincial Administration Commission" (buzhengshisi). The
two smaller cities in the upper half of the map (Yifeng and Lanyang) and the
one just across the river at the far right (Fengqiu) are districts subordinate to
Kaifeng prefecture. The city in the lower left corner (Caozhou) is in Shandong,
while the cities in the lower center (Dongming) and lower right (Zhangyuan)
are in Beizhili. See *Zhongguo lishi dituji* (Historical Atlas of China), Vol. 7, *Yuan,
Ming shiqi* (Yuan, Ming period), ed. Tan Qixiang (Shanghai, 1982), 57–8. In fig.
4, south is at the top and river flow is from right to left [eastward]. *Source*:
Zhangyuan xian zhi.

bank of the Yangzi and seized the city of Jiqing (Nanjing) in 1356. The
location was a strategic one; it gave access to the vast wealth of
the lower Yangzi while insulating him from Mongol power north of
the river. However, its location on rugged terrain adjacent to the river
precluded the construction of a neatly symmetrical city on the order
of the contemporary Dadu (Khanbalig, i.e., Beijing). Instead, when the
old walled city was to be expanded at the time of the dynastic founding, the result was an irregular shape, like the right and lower parts
of a "T" but with the left arm bent upward to the northwest (Fig.
15.6).[36] When completed, the outer wall was truly heroic. It ranged in

---

[36] F. W. Mote, "The Transformation of Nanking, 1350–1400," in *City in Late Imperial
China*, map 135.

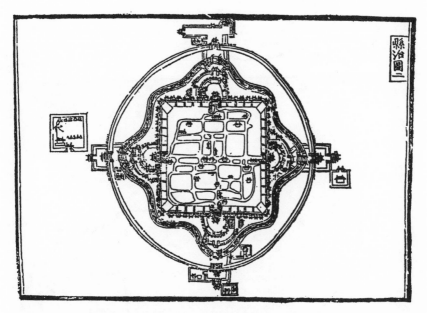

Figure 15.5. Zhangyuan *xian* (Beizhili). Note exaggerated enceinte walls around the four gates, rhythmic curve of the moat, and circular outer wall with four additional gate complexes. The text describes a long history of repairs and improvements to the walls throughout the fifteenth century, resulting in an inner wall of 8 *li* [4.5 km] and an outer wall of 12 *li* [6.7 km]. *Source: Zhangyuan xian zhi*, 1/4b–6a.

height from fifteen to eighteen meters and its length has been estimated at thirty-nine kilometers.[37]

The imperial city was roughly centered in the right arm of the T. The north–south axis that ran through the palace complex and out the Zhengyang Gate thus did not provide a defining center for the city as a whole. The drum and bell towers lay halfway across the city to the northwest of the palace.

A far more regular shape was achieved in the early fifteenth century when Zhu Di, the "second founder" of the Ming, usurped the throne and moved the capital to his old fief at Beiping (formerly Dadu) in the north. His reconstruction of the old Mongol capital preserved the rectangular walls on three sides but contracted the north wall south-

---

[37] Mote, "The Transformation of Nanking, 1350–1400," 134–6. I have converted his estimate to a metric equivalent. Chinese sources give widely varying figures for the length of the Nanjing wall. Mote made his estimate by measuring modern maps.

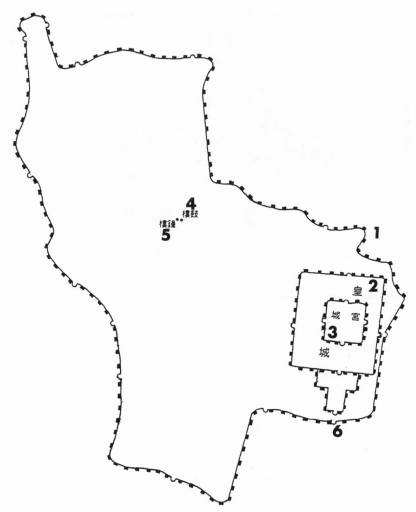

Figure 15.6. Nanjing. The southern capital, showing (1) outer city wall; (2) imperial city wall; (3) palace wall; (4) drum tower; (5) bell tower; (6) Zheng-yang Gate. This drawing is adapted from *Zhongguo lishi ditu* (*Historical Atlas of China*), ed. Zhang Qiyun (Taibei, 1980), 2:7.

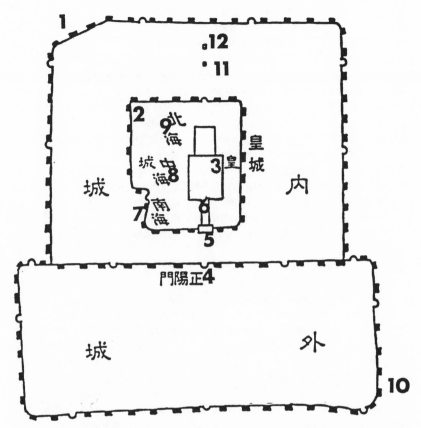

Figure 15.7. The Capital. Ming Beijing, showing (1) new northern wall; (2) imperial city wall; (3) palace or "Forbidden City" (Zijincheng); (4) Zhengyang Gate; (5) Chengtian Gate; (6) Meridian Gate (Wumen); (7) Nanhai; (8) Zhonghai; (9) Beihai; (10) outer wall of 1552; (11) drum tower; (12) bell tower. This sketch map is adapted from *Zhongguo lishi ditu* (*Historical Atlas of China*), ed. Zhang Qiyun (Taibei, 1980), 2:6.

ward (with a slight angle on the northwest corner), cutting off the two northernmost gates on the eastern and western walls (Fig. 15.7). The circumference of the outer wall was more than twenty-two kilometers, considerably smaller than Nanjing but far more impressive to behold because of its straight lines, square corners, and the fact that it rose from a level plain.

The interior of Beijing reproduced an imperial city and palace complex similar to that at Nanjing (even repeating many of the names of gates and buildings) on a grander scale and with a much more symmetrical layout. The north–south axis ran straight through the Zhengyang Gate, now truly the center of the southern wall, and on through the gate of the imperial city (Zhengtianmen) and into the Meridian Gate (Wumen) at the southern or main entrance to the palace or Forbidden City (Zijincheng). The drum tower and bell tower were located north of the imperial city on the same axis. Asymmetry was to be found chiefly in the placement of the imperial city wall (*huangcheng*), which was extended on the west side to enclose the three great lakes (Nanhai, Zhonghai, Beihai) left from Mongol times.[38] Another feature of the city surviving from Mongol times is the term *hutong*, which refers to the narrow lanes penetrating the great blocs between the broad boulevards. A major modification of the Beijing walls was undertaken in 1552, when the southern suburbs were enclosed by an outer wall.

The best opportunity the early Ming regime had to actualize ideal conceptions of how a capital should be laid out was the construction of the Middle Capital (Zhongdu). Zhongdu was what I have called a quasi-capital, erected by the dynastic founder at his ancestral home in Fengyang in present day Anhui.[39] Despite the fact that the capital city was created *de novo*, the builders were unable to give the outer walls a perfectly square or even rectangular shape. This was due to the limitations of the site, which lay on hilly ground just south of the Huai River. These constraints led the builders to move the imperial city southward so that an existing spine of hills would provide a protective backing to the palace complex. The original plan of the square, outer city wall was twice distorted to encompass high points. The western wall was extended southward creating a square projection on the southwest corner of the city. The entire eastern wall of the city was moved eastward with the result that the north–south axis running through the imperial city and the palace no longer intersected the northern and southern walls at their midpoints.[40] The result was a rectangular outer city wall of 27.9 kilometers, 9.3 meters in height. The

---

[38] For the layout of the capital see *Zhongguo lishi ditu* (*Historical Atlas of China*), eds. Zhang Qiyun et al. (Taibei, 1984), 2:5–6.

[39] Sen-dou Chang, "Chinese Walled Cities," 89, remarks that it is surprising that Fengyang *fu* has a round wall in light of the fact that it was built by the Ming founder at his native place. The story is a complicated one, but the relationship between the Middle Capital and the seat of Fengyang *fu* is clarified by a map of the Middle Capital in Wang Jianying, *Ming Zhongdu*; Gazetteer of the Ming Middle Capital (Beijing, 1992), last page of unnumbered illustrations preceding page 1.

[40] Wang Jianying, *Ming Zhongdu*, 69–71.

imperial city was 7.2 kilometers in circumference, 6.2 meters in height, surrounding a palace or "forbidden city" wall 3.4 kilometers long and 12 meters high.[41] Because of its cost and the impracticability of its location, the Middle Capital was downgraded in status and construction was ordered halted in 1375.[42]

A better example of early Ming ideals, and perhaps the site with the most regular of Ming walls, is Xi'an. Xi'an was built on a new site east and north of the remains of old capital cities. Work began in 1370 and was completed eight years later. The result was a wall 13.74 kilometers in length, 12 meters high. It had four major gates, one facing in each of the cardinal directions.[43]

Walls of irregular shape existed in great profusion. Sometimes it is apparent from the gazetteer maps that the rectangular ideals were still held strongly in mind even when they could not be perfectly realized. This appears to be the case in Xiangcheng *xian* in Henan, where the southern half of the wall is square but the northern half consists of indentations, odd angles, and curves. Within the walls, a regular grid of north–south and east–west streets is indicated. In addition to five city gates, corner towers are depicted at six points on the wall. No such effort at regularity is attempted in the portrayal of Lueyang *xian* in southern Shaanxi. In rugged terrain, surrounded by mountains with passes (*guan*) indicated in three directions, the wall traces a "U" shape capped by a slightly convex northern horizontal. Oval and round shapes, more efficient in terms of material and labor required for construction, are commonly occurring wall shapes. Examples of each type are found in the map of Ningguo *fu* and its subordinate Ningguo *xian* in Nanzhili.

CITY WALLS ON THE PERIPHERY

Ming China had three defensive frontiers: the northern border, subject to invasion by Inner Asian peoples on horseback; the seacoast, plagued by pirates; and the southwest, where an expanding Han agricultural population lived interspersed with indigenous groups resistant to assimilation. City walls assumed different forms in each region. Across the northern frontier the Ming built and maintained an

---

[41] Wang Jianying, *Ming Zhongdu*, 71. I have converted the Chinese units to metric equivalents.

[42] Wang Jianying, *Ming Zhongdu*, 7.

[43] Su Yongqi, "Woguo sizuo gu chengqiang" ("China's four ancient city walls"), *Renmin ribao* (*People's Daily*, overseas edition, 21 January, 1994):8. Jiang Yonglin brought this article to my attention.

awesome array of fortifications, including the long walls, passes (*guan*), watch towers and beacon mounds (*dun*), barracks (*ying*), fortresses (*bao*), and evacuated points (*kong*). Along the seacoast the installations were smaller and more widely spaced. In the southwest, Chinese and aboriginal commands blended into a patchwork of relatively modest installations stretching the definition of city wall to the extreme.

From east to west the nine defense areas were Liaodong (in Manchuria but administered from Shandong), Jizhen (Jizhou), Xuanfu, Datong, Shanxi, Yansui, Ningxia, Guyuan, and Gansu. At the eastern end Ming forces were extended far up into Manchuria. In the illustrated gazetteer of the Kaiyuan area we find minimal descriptions of lonely fortified outposts along the defense perimeter. One is Zhenyi *bao* (literally, "Repress the Barbarian's Fort;" see Fig. 15.8).[44] It is shown as a square fortification with a single gate facing a border with inner and outer rows of lookout towers (*tai*) behind what appear to be inner and outer frontier walls (*bian*, barriers?) on either side of a river. The fort had a complement of one officer and 112 men. Subordinate to it were three civilian settlements (*tun*, not shown), and seventeen towers.[45] In the foreground, beyond the frontier, are depicted felt tents with the comment that this is the pasturage of seven non-Han units.

Ningxia is toward the other end of the northern defense line, just west of the Yellow River (Fig. 15.9). There, on the western edge of the Ordos region, the Ming built an intense concentration of walls and fortifications. Ningxia has the status of a guard (*wei*) with four subordinate battalions (*qianhusuo*).[46] The city is shown with six gates while lower units, mostly fortresses (*bao*) and barracks (*ying*), are drawn smaller, with only one or two gates. The Yellow River and a range of mountains course gracefully across the page but there are only two discontinuous segments of long wall. Quite a different impression of the same region can be gained by looking at the *Jiubian tushuo* (*Illustrated Account of the Nine Defense Areas*). This work, compiled by the Ming ministry of war, depicts the entire span of the northern frontier in text and maps from Liaodong in the east to Gansu in the west. One panel shows Huamachi *ying*, which appeared as an isolated unit in

[44] *Kaiyuan tushuo* (*Cartographic Account of Kaiyuan*), comp. Feng Yuan (Wanli period, photographic reproduction by National Central Library, Taibei, 1981), 365. For rich details on the Liaodong defense sector, including maps, diagrams, and photographs of surviving structures, see Liu Qian, *Ming Liaodongzhen changcheng ji fanyu kao* (*Study of the Great Wall and defense in Liaodongzhen in the Ming*; Beijing, 1989). A map following page 6 shows Zhenyi *bao* to be close to the northern extremity of Ming defenses.
[45] *Kaiyuan tushuo*, 366–7.
[46] *Mingshi*, 1012–13.

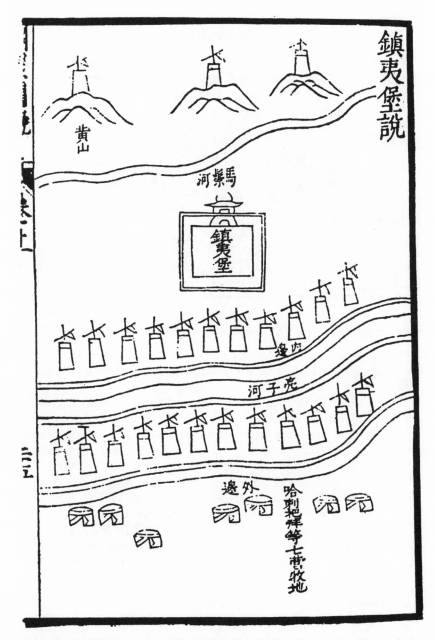

Figure 15.8. Zhenyi *bao* (Liaodong). An isolated fort facing a double defense line on either side of a river in Manchuria. Beyond the border, seven pasturages are indicated by felt tents in the lower foreground. *Source: Kaiyuan tushuo,* 365.

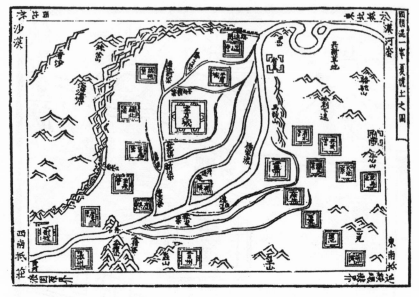

Figure 15.9. Ningxia (Shaanxi). A constellation of walled units along the Yellow River and the Great Wall (not shown). *Source: Ningzia xin zhi.*

the Ningxia gazetteer, close to a flag-bedecked section of the Great Wall.[47]

Threats to the eastern seacoast were of a different character than the danger of invasion faced in the north. On the coast the problem was piracy, short-term raiding rather than conquest or permanent annexation of territory. The Ming responded to coastal marauders, generically referred to as Japanese pirates although Chinese and others also participated, by discouraging subjects of the empire from going to sea and by stationing military units along the coast. Walled cities and fortifications were the foundations of this defensive effort.

A glimpse of Ming coastal defense is provided by the gazetteer of Qingzhou prefecture in Shandong. The administrative seat of Rizhao district is shown bordering the sea. Rizhao had a modest wall of 1.1

---

[47] *Jiubian tushuo* (*Cartographic Account of the Nine Defense Areas*; compiled by the Ming Ministry of War, 1569), Photographic reproduction by National Central Library (Taibei, 1981), 248. For details on the westernmost end of the Ming Great Wall, including diagrams and photographs of Jiayu guan, see *Jiayuguan ji Ming changcheng* (*Jiau Pass and the Ming Great Wall*), eds. Gao Fengshan and Zhang Junwu (Beijing, 1989).

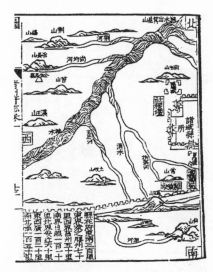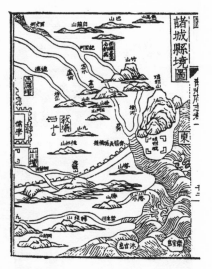

Figure 15.10. Zhucheng *xian* (Shandong). The text of the gazetteer (11/31b–32a) indicates the existence of five stone-walled defense structures within the district in addition to the long wall shown. Text in the lower left corner describes the location and borders of the district. *Source: Qingzhou fu zhi.*

kilometers with three gates.[48] Closer to the sea are a walled guard (*wei*) and two walled stockades (*zhai*). Farther up the coast Zhucheng district is shown as a bigger city with five gates in its wall (Fig. 15.10). Between the city and the sea stretches a long, crenelated wall.

Even more extensive fortifications can be seen south of the Shandong peninsula at Haizhou (Fig. 15.11). There, the city wall was separated from the surrounding mainland by a body of water. The prefecture's one district is depicted as an L-shaped wall with three gates in the upper left-hand corner of the map. A barbell-shaped island just off the coast is the site of a battalion (*qianhusuo*) in a double-walled enclosure on its southern part and a walled barracks (*ying*) on its northern part. Eight other walled entities are depicted in the map in addition to numerous lookout towers (*dun*) marked with military flags. Postal stations (*pu*) are indicated by a row of single-peaked houses on the left side of the map.

The scale of warfare, and the threat to the Chinese heartland, were much smaller along the inland frontier of the empire. Often it was

[48] *Qingzhoufu zhi*, 11/3b.

Figure 15.11. Haizhou (Nanzhili). City wall of Haizhou subprefecture is shown in the center of the left panel. Above it is the walled seat of its sole subordinate district. The island in the right panel has a walled battalion in the lower part and a walled barracks in the upper part. Lookout towers are marked with military flags and a line of postal stations appears as single-peak houses on the left side of the left panel. *Source: Haizhou zhi.*

proximity between settled communities of Han Chinese and other peoples that provoked local conflict and encouraged the Ming state to create institutions for joint governance. In many areas it was simply local banditry or other violence that impelled the construction of city walls. An example is provided by Yunyang, a district on the upper reaches of the Yangzi in northern Sichuan (Fig. 15.12). Initially, the district seat had no defensive wall, relying on the steep hills to its back and the wetlands in front for protection. When in the Chenghua reign (1465–87) bandits emerged from the wilds to harass the city, the magistrate built wooden palisades (*muzha*) across the approaches and stone defense works on the high ground. This discouraged the bandits and gave the townspeople a sense of security. A proper city wall was built in 1510. It was a free-standing wall on the south but on the north it took advantage of the existing mountains. A moat surrounding the southern wall was spanned by five bridges.[49]

[49] *Yunyang zian zhi,* 1/3a–4b.

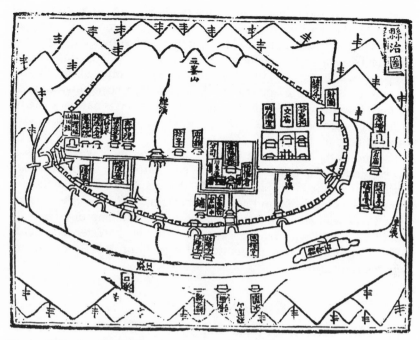

Figure 15.12. Yunyan *xian* (Sichuan). Note integration of wall into hills behind the city. Two types of gates appear: four large gates with full tower and five small gates, possibly water gates. *Source: Yunyang xian zhi.*

Guizhou is one of the poorest and most remote parts of China proper. It was the last province incorporated into the Ming empire and it was ranked last in the hierarchy of provinces in the dynastic history. The two-page map of Sinan prefecture gives us an idea of this remote region. When first established the prefecture had no wall and relied on the hills behind and the river in front for protection. Then, in 1501, a wooden palisade was built to the south and an earth wall was raised on the north. In the Zhengde period (1506–21), after Sichuan bandits attacked, a solid wall was built and a moat dug. Outside the gates, bridges were built in such a way that the planks could be laid on them in the day and taken up at night.[50] Despite its remote location Sinan had many of the features of a walled city in a more central location, such as an altar to the gods of mountains and streams, an altar to the gods of earth and grain, a temple to the gods of the wall and moat, a Confucian school, and a drum tower.

---

[50] *Sinan fu zhi,* 2/13a.

Sinan was home to many aboriginal people. Within the prefectural wall a "Barbarian Office" (*manyisi*) and two residences of barbarian officials (*tuguanzhai*) are to be seen. The map also shows the exhibition pavilion (*shenmingting*) where moral instruction was to be imparted to the populace. In this instance it might have been utilized in an effort to give the indigenous people guidance on Han social and cultural norms. How successfully ideas were communicated is hard to imagine in light of comment in the gazetteer that barbarian languages were impossible to understand.[51]

The end of the line administratively, and in terms of walled cities, is represented by the office of the Langyuan Barbarian Authority (*manyisishu*) subordinate to Sinan *fu*. On the map a central pavilion is shown, as is a compound for the aboriginal officials. There is no formal city wall as such. Round about, where the map of a Han city would be dotted with temples, we see only the character *tian* (field), perhaps indicating that promotion of agriculture was the primary administrative function.

CONCLUSION

Until it was succeeded by the Qing dynasty, Ming China undertook the construction and reconstruction of the largest constellation of walled cities on earth. It is my contention that the commonalties of these walled cities, their designations, and their positions in a hierarchy were all products of powerful conservative (or restorationist) impulses in Chinese society. Ming cultural conservatism was manifested both in a defensive stance toward the outside world and in a preoccupation – obsession would not be too strong a word – with ritual production of social order. This preoccupation was itself the product of a long history, but, most immediately, of recent centuries of subjugation by non-Han peoples.

Viewed from this perspective Chinese city walls had defensive, administrative, and ritual significance. Our brief tour of examples from the heartland to the periphery, from the top to the bottom, was designed to show a wide range of examples. But we can see running through the whole range the three forces of military imperative, administrative authority, and cultural hegemony shaping and defining city walls.

Much more could be done to fill out the picture. Careful classification and comparison of design and construction could provide us with

---

[51] *Sinan fu zhi*, 1/10a.

a history of Chinese military architecture. City gates alone deserve to be studied, not just for their design, but for the ideological content of their names. Quantitative study of the dates of construction and repair of walls and when they were faced with brick and stone would add substance to Ming military and political history. The few illustrations included here should suffice to show that a systematic survey of the hundreds of extant gazetteers would be a richly rewarding project.

CHAPTER 16

Decoration of city walls in the medieval Islamic world: The epigraphic message

SHEILA S. BLAIR

T HE walls around medieval Islamic cities, like most other buildings and art objects made in Islamic lands, were richly decorated with inscriptions. Carved in relief, these long bands on gates, towers, salients, and other parts of the walls conveyed significant messages to both residents and visitors by their location, content, and style. The inscriptions are important furthermore as some of the few contemporary texts dealing with the walls. The purpose of this essay is to investigate what medieval Muslim patrons had inscribed on their walls. What message did they want to convey? Where and when did they add inscriptions? What forms did they use? What styles of script? What decorative motifs accompanied these texts?

To answer these questions, I decided to focus on the most lavish program of city walls extant – those on the city in southeastern Anatolia, on the upper Tigris, known today as Diyarbekir.[1] The walls, established in the fourth century A.D., are decorated with forty-four inscriptions recording repairs from the tenth century to the sixteenth, as well as a few figural representations. The inscriptions are not only numerous but also well published. Half of them were analyzed by Max van Berchem, the Swiss scholar who founded the study of Islamic epigraphy, in his 1910 monograph on the city with Josef Strzygowski and Gertrude Bell.[2] These served as the basis for a paleographic study of the eleventh-century inscriptions by Samuel Flury.[3] Other inscrip-

---

[1] For a history of the city, see *Encyclopaedia of Islam*, 2nd ed. (Leiden and London, 1960–), s.v. "Diyār Bakr (iii)," and Albert Gabriel, *Voyages Archéologiques dans la Turquie Orientale* (Paris, 1940), 87–90.

[2] Max van Berchem, Josef Stryzgowski, and Gertrude Bell, *Amida* (Heidelberg, 1910).

[3] Samuel Flury, *Islamische Schriftbänder Amida-Diarbekr XI. Jahrhundert* (Basel and Paris, 1920), translated as "Bandeaux ornementés à inscriptions arabes: Amida-Diarbekr, XI siècle," *Syria* 1 (1920): 235–49 and 318–28; and 2 (1921): 54–62.

tions from the city were recorded by Jean Sauvaget in his appendix to Albert Gabriel's study of the monuments of eastern Anatolia.[4] The political implications of some of this work, particularly from the medieval period, were analyzed by Estelle Whelan in a long and still unpublished dissertation.[5]

The large corpus and broad chronological sweep of the inscriptions at Diyarbekir allow me to investigate changes over time. To simplify matters, I have maintained the dynastic rubrics and numbering used by earlier scholars, dividing the forty-four texts into eight groups that correspond to the changing political situation from the tenth century to the sixteenth (see Appendix 16.1).[6] A first group (38–43) dates to the period of ʿAbbasid rule in the early tenth century, when the strong centralized empire of the late eighth and early ninth centuries was beginning to disintegrate, and the six inscriptions represent the imposition of caliphal authority over the city. A second group (44–56), done under the Marwanids, a Kurdish dynasty who carved out a buffer state in the late tenth century, reflects the vigorous cultural life under these local patrons. At the end of the eleventh century, the Marwanids were replaced briefly by the Saljuqs, a Turkish dynasty whose domains stretched from the Mediterranean to Central Asia, and the five inscriptions in the third group (57–61) belong to a concerted plan of reconstruction and document the incorporation of Diyarbekir into a wider political net. The city soon reverted to local control, however, and during most of the twelfth century it was in the hands of two families, the Inalids and Nisanids, and the few inscriptions they added (62–5) reflect the city's return to relative isolation. A major change occurred in 579/1183[7] when Diyarbekir was taken by the great Ayyubid conqueror Saladin, who gave the city to his vassals, the Turcoman family of Artuqids, and the eleven inscriptions left on the walls by the

---

[4] Gabriel, *Voyages*, 310–38.

[5] Estelle Whelan, "The Public Figure: Political Iconography in Medieval Mesopotamia" (Ph.D. diss., New York University, 1979). Unfortunately this monumental three-volume work was unavailable to me, but the author kindly shared some of her work on the inscriptions with me and corrected several of my misapprehensions. In this scholarly world often marked by rivalries and petty jealousies, it is a pleasure to thank a colleague for such generosity and intellectual integrity.

[6] I have maintained Sauvaget's numbers, with references to those published by Van Berchem and those in the standard corpus of Islamic inscriptions, *Répertoire chronologique d'épigraphie arabe* (henceforth RCEA), ed. Étienne Combe, Jean Sauvaget, and Gaston Wiet (Cairo, 1930–). Numbers in the text in parentheses refer to these inscriptions.

[7] Yearly dates are given in two calendars, the hegira calendar, the one that was prevalent in the Muslim lands, followed by a slash and the corresponding year in the Common Era (e.g., 579/1183). For simplicity's sake, regnal dates (e.g., r. 1075–96) and centuries (e.g., thirteenth century) are given only in the Common Era.

Artuqids (66–76) belong to a program of fortification reflecting the unsettled conditions of the times. The refortifying of the walls continued (77–8) after Diyarbekir was retaken by the Ayyubids in 630/1232.

After the Mongol conquests in the mid-thirteenth century, Diyarbekir played a less important role. It changed hands frequently, and the unsettled political situation is clear from a two-century gap in the epigraphic evidence. In the fifteenth century the city became the capital of the Aq Qoyunlu, or White Sheep, a Turcoman confederation under whose patronage three inscriptions (79–81) were added to the walls. In the sixteenth century the city changed hands again, but eventually passed to the control of the Ottomans ruling from Istanbul, who incorporated it into their empire and refortified the citadel (81).

In addition to a chronological survey that illustrates diachronic changes in the conception of walls and the messages on them, the large number of inscriptions from Diyarbekir allows me to draw general conclusions about such subjects as the kinds of people involved and their sources of funding. Although the inscriptions on the walls of Diyarbekir are notable for their number and fine state of preservation, they are not unique, and many of the texts can be compared to similar ones found on walls in other Islamic cities from Central Asia to the Maghrib (or Islamic west). Diyarbekir thus presents a basis for comparison with other programs of city walls in the Islamic lands over a period of six centuries.

The modern name Diyarbekir derives from the name of the province, literally the abode of [the tribe of] Bakr, a tribe descended from Bakr b. Wa'il that inhabited the region in the seventh century. In medieval times the city was called Amid, from the Greek Amida. The city has a long history because of its advantageous siting on a wide plateau that dominates the right or western bank of the Tigris (Fig. 16.1). The river flows from north to south, passing in a gentle bend beneath the eastern side of the city. The site, an entrepôt for caravans, stands at the crossroads of major trade routes from Mesopotamia to the Black Sea and from Anatolia to Iran. The city also enjoyed a riparian advantage: The Tigris becomes navigable there, and even in the twentieth century long trains of rafts, known as *kelek*, descended from Diyarbekir to Mosul. These rafts, constructed on the banks of the Tigris from wood in nearby forests, were dismantled at Mosul and the wood sold. The site also offered an abundant supply of water, brought by aqueduct from the northwest.

The walls around Diyarbekir (Fig. 16.2) have a roughly elliptical trace, measuring some 1,700 by 1,300 meters or more than five kilo-

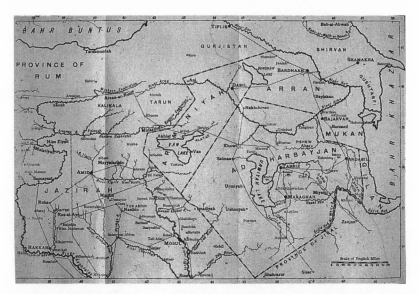

Figure 16.1. Map of the Jazira showing the location of Amid/Diyarbekir. After LeStrange, *Lands of the Eastern Caliphate* (Cambridge, 1905), map III.

meters in circumference, and are broken by two main protrusions – a salient on the southwest defended by two big round towers, and the citadel on the northeast. Ranging from eight to twelve meters high and three to five meters wide, the curtain wall is built of masonry rubble between ashlar facings of basalt. The dark color of the hard volcanic stone gave rise to the medieval name of the city, Qara Amid, or Black Amid. The sturdy material also means that the walls are some of the best preserved examples of medieval military architecture, although their fine preservation is also due to the relatively minor role the city played after the mid-thirteenth century. Some twelve meters in front of the curtain wall are traces of another wall, 1.80 meters thick. Beyond that lay a moat, now filled in.

The walls are pierced on the four cardinal axes by gates, known in modern times as the Kharput Gate on the north, the Urfa Gate on the west, the Mardin Gate on the south, and the New Gate on the east. The New Gate commands a ramp leading down to the Tigris, and the other three gates mark the departure point for the three great routes that lead respectively to Kharput (medieval Hisn Ziyad) and the Euphrates; Urfa (medieval al-Ruha', Edessa) and northern Syria; and Mardin and Mesopotamia. A north–south artery connects the Kharput

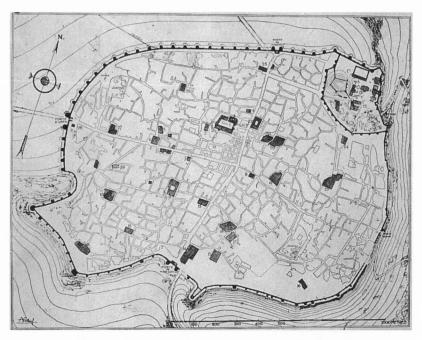

Figure 16.2. Plan of the walls of Diyarbekir. After Albert Gabriel, *Voyages Archéologiques dans la Turquie Orentale* (Paris, 1940), fig. 69.

and Mardin Gates, with a branch leading off to the Urfa Gate on the west. In addition to the gates, the walls are punctuated by seventy-eight square, round, and polygonal towers. The more complex towers are concentrated on the north and west sides of the enceinte, which are also defended by a large ditch preceded by an advance wall, for the land beyond is flat and open and therefore more vulnerable to attack.

Gabriel's study established the chronology of the walls. Until the fourth century A.D., Amida was a minor city defended by a fortress. The original walls were erected by the emperor Constantine ca. 330. After the peace of Jovian in 363, when the inhabitants of Nasibis (medieval Nasibin, modern Nusaybin) took refuge in Amida, its surface area was doubled and the ramparts took on their definitive aspect. This work can be dated ca. 375 on the basis of a Latin inscription on the Kharput Gate mentioning the emperors Valentinian, Valens, and Gratian and stating that the *civitas a fundamentis fabricata est*.[8] The

[8] Text given in Gabriel, *Voyages*, 136.

Figure 16.3. Diyarbekir, view of the Kharput Gate, showing inscription 42, dated 297/909–10. Photo: Sheila S. Blair and Jonathan M. Bloom.

enceinte is therefore the most important and complete example of Roman fortification to survive from the fourth century A.D., as well as a major source for tracing the evolving concept of city walls over the centuries.

The first campaign carried out on the walls of Diyarbekir in the Islamic period was undertaken under the ʿAbbasid caliph al-Muqtadir in 297/909–10. Since the ʿAbbasid inscriptions set the standard for the later ones in terms of placement, form, and the types of people mentioned, it is important to look at them in some detail. The ʿAbbasid work is recorded in six inscriptions (Fig. 16.3): three on or adjacent to the Mardin Gate (38–40) and three on the Kharput Gate (41–3). A three-line band of simple Kufic (or angular) script carved on the tower east of the Mardin Gate (38) gives the basic information about the work. Following the invocation of the name of God, the merciful and compassionate, and the profession of faith that there is no god but God, the inscription tells us that the work was ordered by the ʿAbbasid caliph al-Muqtadir (r. 908–32). At the end is a relief showing confronted quadrupeds. A second and longer three-line text (39) to the left of the first adds that the work was executed in 297/909–10 under the supervision of Yahya b. Ishaq al-Jarjara'i and Ahmad b. Jamil al-Muqtadiri.[9] A block several courses below the second inscription depicts an eight-rayed sun in a medallion flanked by animals. The third inscription on the curtain wall west of the Mardin Gate (40) is a long band (1200 × 20 cm) sculpted at mid-height in the facing. Its longer length permits a fuller text: It repeats the information given in the first two inscriptions but adds that the work was ordered by al-Muqtadir to glorify religion and protect Muslims, that the work was executed under the supervision of the vizier Abu'l-Hasan ʿAli b. Muhammad, and that the two people mentioned before, Yahya b. Ishaq al-Jarjara'i and Ahmad b. Jamil al-Muqtadiri, were in charge of expenditure.

We learn much the same information from the corresponding inscriptions on the Kharput Gate. A four-line text sculpted above the gate (41) gives the same text as the long band on the southern enceinte.[10] Another inscription (42) is set on the towers flanking the Kharput Gate, much like the one near the Mardin Gate, but the text continues from the right side to the left and gives the full information about patron and supervisors. It runs above two niches; the one on the right has a shell hood atop five blocks with animals, and the one on the left has a semicircular hood supported on columns. Finally, a sixth inscription to the left of the niche on the left at ground level (43) contains four blocks with different bits and pieces from different inscriptions and several reliefs.[11] The last one contains the invocation of God written backwards (from left to right), in what the Germans call *wappenstil*. The inscription cannot have been molded, for the letters are carved in relief. Rather, the carver must have been working from a paper copy, which he inadvertently reversed.

In his classic study of the inscriptions of Diyarbekir, published at the beginning of the century, Van Berchem set these inscriptions in their historical context and pointed out their political importance in showing how ʿAbbasid authority over the city was reestablished after

---

[9] The Arabic text given by Sauvaget in Gabriel, *Voyages*, no. 39, is different from the text as given in Van Berchem and the RCEA, the translation in all three sources, and the photograph. Van Berchem, Stryzgowski, and Bell, *Amida*, pl. II/2. I presume it is just a misprint.

[10] The only difference between this text and the long band next to the Mardin Gate (39) is that this text omits the epithet al-Amidi after the name of Ahmad b. Jamil.

[11] In addition to these historical inscriptions, on stylistic grounds a Koranic text seems to date from the same period. It contains Koran 2:255, the so-called Throne Verse, written in simple Kufic, and is known only from an old photograph showing four blocks piled on top of each other for the picture. Van Berchem, Stryzgowski, and Bell, *Amida*, fig. 7.

the local governors had asserted their independence. Diyarbekir had been governed since the mid-eighth century by a native family which, like many in the ʿAbbasid empire, played a role midway between the simple provincial governors of earlier times and the almost independent dynasties of the later period. Since 284/897, the family had been headed by Muhammad b. Ahmad b. ʿIsa b. al-Shaykh, whose father and grandfather had governed the city before him. Muhammad revolted against the ʿAbbasid caliph al-Muʿtadid (r. 892–902), who marched against Diyarbekir in late 285/898, besieged the city, and breached the walls in Rabiʿ II 286/April–May 899. The following month, the governor Muhammad sued for peace, which the caliph granted, adding presents as a sign of amnesty but also damaging the walls as a mark of prudence. The inscriptions tell us that eleven years later the caliph al-Muqtadir, son and second successor of al-Muʿtadid, had the walls repaired.

The inscriptions also tell us a lot more about the political agenda in (re)building city walls in the early tenth century. The texts were clearly drawn up in advance in the chancery, since they all conform to proper protocol. They use a very general formula to describe the work, "this is what was ordered by" (*mimmā amara bihi*). They all include the four elements of the caliph's name: his proper name Jaʿfar, his title imam (leader), his surname al-Muqtadir billah ("the powerful through God"), and his caliphal title *amīr al-muʾminīn* (commander of believers). Repeating the caliph's full name six times over the southern and northern gates was obviously a mark of sovereignty designed to show that the ʿAbbasids had reasserted control over the rebellious city.

The need for the ʿAbbasids to mark their sovereignty at this precise moment (297/909–10) was particularly pressing. Al-Muqtadir, the eighteenth ʿAbbasid caliph, had been raised to the throne two years earlier at age thirteen, at a time when the power of the central authority was on the decline and squabbling for the throne rampant. Many at court favored another claimant, al-Muqtadir's cousin Ibn al-Muʿtazz, a noted poet and son of the thirteenth caliph. Following the murder of the vizier al-ʿAbbas b. al-Hasan b. Ahmad al-Jarjaraʾi in the fourth month of his reign, al-Muqtadir was deposed in favor of his cousin. The revolt lasted only one day (20 Rabiʿ I 296/17 December 908), until the eunuch general Muʾnis al-Muzaffar came forward to save the young al-Muqtadir. Ibn al-Muʿtazz was executed, and the reinstated al-Muqtadir appointed a new vizier, Abuʾl-Hasan ʿAli b. Muhammad, better known as Ibn al-Furat. He is precisely the vizier mentioned in the two longest inscriptions at Diyarbekir, the band to the west of the Mardin Gate (40) and the text over the Kharput Gate

(41), only partially clear in Van Berchem's time. Ibn al-Furat became all powerful at the ʿAbbasid court for the next two years, until he was accused of lavish expenditures and embezzlement. He was dismissed, reappointed twice more, and finally executed in 312/924.[12] The young caliph's impotence at the hands of his viziers is clear from these inscriptions at Diyarbekir, which give the vizier Ibn al-Furat the same benediction as the caliph al-Muqtadir: "may God extend his life."

In addition to the caliph and his vizier, the ʿAbbasid inscriptions on the walls at Diyarbekir mention two other individuals involved in the construction project, and examining the words used tells us about the role these people played. Yahya b. Ishaq bears the patronymic al-Jarjaraʾi, showing that he or his family came from Jarjara, a village on the left bank of the Tigris between Baghdad and Wasit. This patronymic was borne by several viziers of this period, including Ibn al-Furat's precedessor. Yahya b. Ishaq supervised the expenditure (*al-nafaqa*) for the walls, and in the inscription flanking the Kharput Gate (42), he is described as an agent (*al-ʿāmil*). In Umayyad times this term had designated a provincial governor, but when financial matters were separated from other administration under the ʿAbbasids, the term usually designated the director of finances in a provincial capital.[13] Yahya b. Ishaq was in charge of accounts.

The other person, Ahmad b. Jamil, is called an engineer (*muhandis*) in the inscriptions near the Mardin Gate (39–40). In the one on the curtain wall (40), he bears the patronymic al-Amidi, showing that he was a local boy, and in the one on the tower (39), he bears the patronymic al-Muqtadiri, showing that he was a servant of the caliph. The inscription flanking the Kharput Gate (42) adds that he was the agent in charge of the work (*al-wakīl ʿalā thalik*). Ahmad b. Jamil was the master of works.

Van Berchem also noted that the inscriptions at Diyarbekir were remarkable for their style as well as their content. He commented on their paleographic significance as some of the rare inscriptions in simple Kufic from Mesopotamia. They are distinguished from contemporary inscriptions in Syria and Egypt by their thinner letters, awkward forms, and pronounced triangular endings. This last feature may well have given rise to the report by modern travelers that the inscriptions sculpted on the walls were in Syriac, Persian, or even cuneiform. Their style probably derived from the metropolitan style known from

---

[12] *Encyclopaedia of Islam*, 2nd ed., s.v. "Ibn al-Furāt (2) Abuʾl-Ḥasan ʿAli b. Muḥammad;" "Ibn al-Muʿtazz" and "al-Muktadir." Dominique Sourdel, *Le Vizirat ʿAbbāside de 749 à 936* (Damascus, 1959).

[13] *Encyclopaedia of Islam*, 2nd ed., s.v. " ʿĀmil."

now lost inscriptions in the capital Baghdad, but executed by local craftsmen.[14]

The inscriptions at Diyarbekir are also noteworthy because of the effort involved in carving them, their readability, and the planning in setting them out. They are all carved in relief, a technique much more laborious than incising, and the texts were manipulated to fit the space available, with a phrase added or dropped from a benediction to expand or shorten the text. Despite the same date on the two gates, the inscriptions suggest that the Kharput Gate was more important, for the inscriptions there are better planned and more finely executed. The main text there (42) reads continuously in a single line from one side of the gate to the other, and the letters are widely spaced to enhance legibility. The text was planned so that the caliph's name and titles, the imam al-Muqtadir billah, sit directly over the niche decorated with animals. The animals – a bird with raised wings, two zebus, and two lions – are finely sculpted and regularly placed along a line at the springing of the niche. In contrast, the confronted animals on the Mardin Gate are squeezed in at the end of the first inscription as space fillers and are so roughly carved and abraded that their identity is unclear.

The 'Abbasids' attempt at reasserting central control was unsuccessful, and over the course of the tenth century, more and more provinces slipped into the hands of local dynasts. The second set of restorations to the walls of Diyarbekir was carried out under one such family, the Marwanids, who ruled the city from 380/990–1 to 478/1085.[15] The founder, a Kurdish chief named Badh, had first seized various strongholds in Armenia and Kurdistan, then took Diyarbekir, and even threatened Baghdad. The dynasty's name, however, derived not from the founder, but from his brother-in-law Marwan, a miller who had married Badh's sister. Their son Abu 'Ali al-Hasan, who married his uncle's widow, routed the Hamdanids, an Arab dynasty that had exercised control in the area, and reoccupied Diyarbekir, establishing it as the Marwanid capital. Following Abu 'Ali's murder in 387/997, he was succeeded successively by his two brothers, Mumahhid (r. 997–1011) and Nasr al-Dawla Ahmad, whose fifty-year reign (1011–61) marks the apogee of Marwanid power, when Diyarbekir enjoyed a high level of stability and a prosperous and thriving cultural life.[16]

---

[14] This point is well argued by Whelan, "The Public Figure," 777–8.

[15] For an outline of the dynasty's dates, see C.E. Bosworth, *The Islamic Dynasties* (Edinburgh, 1967), 53–4; see also *Encyclopaedia of Islam*, 2nd ed., s.v. "Marwānids" with further references.

[16] For a brief biography, see *Encyclopaedia of Islam*, 2nd ed., s.v. "Naṣr al-Dawla."

Figure 16.4. Diyarbekir, detail of tower LVI, showing part of inscription 47, dated 437/1045–6. Photo: Estelle Whelan.

Following Nasr al-Dawla's death at an advanced age, the power and prestige of the Marwanids waned. His territories were divided between his sons, with Saʿd ruler in Diyarbekir and his younger brother Nizam al-Din Nasr ruler in Mayyafariqin, the second city of the province and two days march east of Diyarbekir.[17] Within two years Nizam al-Din Nasr ousted his older brother and took over Diyarbekir as well. At his death in 472/1079, he was succeeded by his eldest son Mansur, who ruled for six years before being deposed by the Saljuqs.

The thirteen inscriptions left by the Marwanids on the walls of Diyarbekir exemplify the rule of a local dynasty which managed to maintain its independence by a skillful policy of accommodation and self-preservation. The first Marwanid inscription at Diyarbekir (44), a 3.5-meter band set over the Kharput Gate, commemorates Abu ʿAli's occupation of the city. Six inscriptions on the walls (45–50) attest to work by the third and most important Marwanid, Nasr al-Dawla (Fig. 16.4). Although he had established himself in Mayyafariqin in 401/

---

[17] Textual sources give the name as Saʿid, but one inscription (47) on the walls of Diyarbekir was read by both Van Berchem and Sauvaget as Saʿd.

1010–11, he only obtained effective control of Diyarbekir in 415/1024–5, and the six inscriptions he left there span the latter part of his rule over the city. Six more inscriptions (51–6) mark work on the walls undertaken by the last two Marwanids, Nizam al-Dawla and his son Mansur.

In general, the Marwanid texts at Diyarbekir follow the form established in the ʿAbbasid inscriptions. They use a slightly more fulsome but still generalized formula that so-and-so ordered the work (*mimmā amara bi-ʿamalihi*), without identifying any specific construction. As is standard for the time, the ruler bears longer and more elaborate titles. Nasr al-Dawla, for example, is called our lord, the amir, the great lord, he who is assisted by God, the victorious, the glory of Islam, Saʿd al-Din (he who brings good fortune to religion), Nasr al-Dawla (the victor of the state), Rukn al-Milla (the pillar of the religion), Majd al-Umma (the glory of the religious community), the honor of amirs, Abu Nasr Ahmad b. Marwan, and the benediction asks God to extend his life and prolong his royalty.

The other people mentioned in the Marwanid inscriptions are the same types as those mentioned in the ʿAbbasid inscriptions. The inscription on the Kharput Gate (49), for example, includes the name of the vizier Abu Nasr Muhammad b. Muhammad b. Jahir, better known as Ibn Jahir.[18] His peripatetic career exemplifies the shifting political fortunes in the area in the eleventh century, when power was shared between a variety of local rulers like the Marwanids and the increasingly impotent ʿAbbasid caliphs in Baghdad, themselves under the protection of the Great Saljuqs, Turkish chieftains who had moved from the central Asian steppe to take Baghdad in 447/1055. Born at Mosul to a family of rich merchants, Ibn Jahir first served the Shiʿite Uqaylid princes there, then moved to Urfa, where he became vizier to the local Mirdasid ruler Muʿizz al-Dawla, and subsequently shifted to Diyarbekir, where he was vizier to Nasr al-Dawla from 430/1039 to 453/1061. After his patron's death, Ibn Jahir persuaded the ʿAbbasid caliph to offer him the vizierate, and his family maintained that position for half a century.

The supervisors, too, are similar. The Marwanid ones include one agent (*ʿāmil*) Abu Tahir b. Kaghid b. Sahl, mentioned in the inscription on tower XLIX (46), and several local qadis, or judges. Abu ʿAli al-Hasan b. ʿAli b. Ahmad al-Amidi is mentioned in the inscriptions (47–8) done under Nasr al-Dawla, and a family of qadis supervised work under his son and grandson. Abuʾl-Hasan ʿAbd al-Wahid b. Muham-

---

[18] Encyclopaedia of Islam, 2nd ed., s.v. "Djahīr [Banu]."

mad b. ʿAbd al-Wahid is mentioned in three inscriptions (51–3) on the walls restored by Nizam al-Dawla in the early 460s (1067–72), as well as on a bridge he had built three years earlier south of the city.[19] His son Abu Nasr Muhammad b. ʿAbd al-Wahid supervised the work (54) on tower V executed under Mansur. Three different builders (*al-bannāʾ*) are also mentioned: Nusayr b. Habib worked under Nasr al-Dawla (47–8), Musa b. Mazid under Nizam al-Dawla (51–2), and Abu Saʿd b. Humayd under Mansur (54).

The Marwanids also continued the ʿAbbasid tradition of using sculptural reliefs to accompany their texts. For example, when tower LII was rebuilt in 444/1052–3 (48), the decoration included two niches, the left one decorated with birds in the spandrels and a Kufic text, and the right one decorated with a scalloped shell. Other towers show the occasional bird or animal. Such relief decoration was typical of the time. For example, the gate erected in 451/1059 by the third ruler of the local Numayrid dynasty at Harran, a day's march southeast of Urfa, had reliefs of dogs and birds.[20]

The first Marwanid inscription at Diyarbekir (44), set at the top of the projecting wall through which the Kharput Gate is pierced, continues the tradition of marking sovereignty seen in the ʿAbbasid inscriptions at the Kharput and Mardin Gates. The Marwanid inscription uses the same kind of script, small simple Kufic letters, and contains the same kind of text.[21] After invoking God's blessing, it records that the work was ordered in 386 (996) by the victorious amir Abu ʿAli al-Hasan b. Marwan, may God glorify his victory. The text is composed to underscore the prince's triumphant role: He is called victorious (*al-manṣūr*) and the benediction asks God to glorify his victories (*aʿzza naṣrahu*). The Marwanid inscription confirms the point made by the ʿAbbasid inscriptions about the primary importance of the northern Kharput Gate: Putting one's name over that gate showed sovereignty over the city. The text on tower LVI (47), dated 437/1045–6, mentions that the work was executed during the governorship (*fī wilāya*) of Nasr al-Dawla's son, the amir Saʿd al-Dawla Abuʾl-Hasan Muhammad. The inscription thus gives us a date by which time Nasr al-Dawla had

---

[19] Van Berchem, Stryzgowski, and Bell, *Amida*, no. 13; RCEA 2657; Sauvaget in Gabriel, *Voyages*, no. 105. The text, dated 457/1065, also mentions the builder ʿUbayd.

[20] D.S. Rice, "Medieval Ḥarrān: Studies on its Topography and Monuments, I," *Anatolian Studies* 2 (1952): 36–84, esp. 49–51; Terry Allen, *A Classical Revival in Islamic Architecture* (Wiesbaden, 1986), 35–7.

[21] Unfortunately, no photograph was included in Gabriel's work and Van Berchem did not know of this text.

appointed his son ruler of the city and follows the traditional type of gate inscription in marking political changes.

Most of the other Marwanid inscriptions, however, mark different kinds of work from that recorded by the earlier ʿAbbasid inscriptions. The Marwanid inscriptions are set not on gates, but on towers and salients on the south, north, and east walls. These walls must have been damaged in the upheavals of the previous century, when the town was the target of several attacks by the Byzantines before passing to the Hamdanids and then briefly (ca. 368/978) to the Buyids, a Shiʿite dynasty from Iran who had seized control of Baghdad. The insecurities of the eleventh and twelfth centuries meant that the walls of many cities throughout the Islamic lands were built or extensively repaired at this time. The walls erected around the central Iranian city of Isfahan by the local Kakuyid ruler ʿAla al-Dawla Muhammad b. Dushmanziyar in 429/1037, for example, are said to have measured more than 15,000 paces in circumference, not including the extensions around several suburbs; the nearby city of Yazd was fortified three years later.[22] The same situation occurred in the Maghrib, and cities such as Fez, Rabat, and Marrakech received stunning walls under the Almoravids (r. 1056–1147) and Almohads (r. 1130–1269).[23]

While many Islamic cities were walled in the eleventh and twelfth centuries, the walls around Marwanid Diyarbekir were particularly famous in their own time. In 438/1046, during Nasr al-Dawla's reign, the Persian traveler Nasir-i Khusraw visited the city, and his admiring description shows how the walls of Diyarbekir were appraised in their own day:

On the 6th of Day, old reckoning, we arrived in Amid, the foundation of which is laid on a monolith rock. The length of the city is two thousand paces, and the breadth the same. There is a wall all around made of black rock, each slab weighing between a hundred and a thousand maunds. The facing of these stones is so expert that they fit together exactly, needing no mud or plaster in between. The height of the wall is twenty cubits, and the width ten. Every hundred ells there is a tower, the half circumference of which is eighty ells. The crenellations are also of this same black stone. Inside the city are many stone stairs by means of which one can go up onto the ramparts, and atop every tower is an embrasure. The city has four gates, all of iron with no wood, and each gate faces one of the four cardinal directions. The east gate is called the Tigris Gate, the west gate the Byzantine Gate, the north the Arme-

---

[22] Sheila S. Blair, *The Monumental Inscriptions from Early Islamic Iran and Transoxiana* (Leiden, 1992), no. 41, 111–14.

[23] H. Basset and H. Terrasse, *Sanctuaires et forteresses almohades* (Paris, 1932).

nian Gate, and the south the Tell Gate. Outside this wall just described is yet another wall, made of that same stone, the height of which is ten ells and the top of which is completely covered with crenellations. Inside the crenellation is a passageway wide enough for a totally armed man to pass and to stop and fight with ease. The outside wall has iron gates, placed directly opposite the gate in the inside wall so that when one passes from a gate in the first wall one must traverse a space of 15 ells before reaching the gate in the second wall. Inside the city is a spring that flows from a granite rock about the size of five millstones. The water is extremely pleasant, but no one knows where the source is. The city has many orchards and trees thanks to that water. The ruling prince of the city is a son of that Nasr al-Dawla who has been mentioned.

I have seen many a city and fortress around the world in the lands of the Arabs, Persians, Hindus, and Turks, but never have I seen the likes of Amid on the face of the earth or have I heard anyone else say that he had seen its equal.[24]

Nasir-i Khusraw's description of the walls around Diyarbekir, which he calls the strongest in the world, draws attention to the material, fine construction, towers, and gates. It does not mention the inscriptions. One reason may be that he considered them a standard and therefore unremarkable part of city walls, but a better explanation is that his description was part of his unwritten agenda for the journey. A civic administrator in Merv in northeast Persia before his travels, Nasir-i Khusraw belonged to the Isma'ili sect, a Shi'ite schismatic movement whose supporters believed that the legitimate successors to the prophet Muhammad were his lineal descendants through his daughter Fatima. The center of Isma'ili Shi'ism in Nasir-i Khusraw's time was Egypt, ruled since 358/969 by the Fatimids (r. 909–1171), a heterodox Shi'ite dynasty from North Africa. Nasir-i Khusraw's journey was a veritable grand tour of Isma'ili sites, culminating in a three-year sojourn in Cairo, where he was undoubtedly trained as a missionary and propagandist (dā'ī).[25] His descriptions of the cities he visited en route concentrate on defensive and topographic features, particularly the location of the water supply, features that would have attracted the attention of those interested in forcibly extending the Isma'ili state. Nasir-i Khusraw's lack of interest in the inscriptions extolling the sovereignty of other rulers is therefore understandable. His omission also shows that the message sent out by patrons of

---

[24] Nāṣir-i Khusraw, *Safarnāma*, trans. W.M. Thackston Jr. as *Nāṣer-e Khosrāw's Book of Travels* (Albany, 1986), 8.

[25] On his life and mission, see the introduction to Thackston's translation, ix–xii, and *Encyclopaedia of Islam*, 2nd ed., s.v. "Naṣir-i Khusraw." On the Isma'ili mission, see *Encyclopaedia of Islam*, 2nd ed., s.v. "Dā'ī."

inscriptions on city walls was not always the one received by passers-by.

Nasir-i Khusraw's failure to mention the inscriptions at Diyarbekir is all the more remarkable as the Marwanid ones stand out from the earlier ones in their technique and style. Most are superbly carved in an exuberant floriated script on limestone blocks inserted into the basalt walls (Fig.16. 4).[26] The color contrast thus heightens their visibility and allows particularly fine relief carving. Indeed, one modern scholar considered them the finest examples of floriated Kufic and some of the most beautiful inscriptions of their time, more sophisticated than those of contemporary Egypt.[27] They reflect a flourishing local tradition and confirm what texts tell us about the rich cultural life in Diyarbekir under the Marwanids. The local authority is clear from a new element introduced in the texts – the source of funding, as the inscriptions on towers LVI and LII (47–8) add that the costs were covered by Nasr al-Dawla's personal wealth.

The Marwanid inscriptions were directed to the city's inhabitants as well as to outsiders, for some are found on the interior face of the walls. Inscription 46, for example, is a two-line text set on the city side of the wall closing the gorge of the salient. Inscription 49 is a long band set around the three sides of the Kharput Gate facing the town. The text begins with a Koranic verse (9:18) that mosques should be visited and maintained by believers and that Nasr al-Dawla ordered the work out of love for God and his Prophet Muhammad. Unlike the other inscriptions, this one is dated to a specific month (Dhu'l-Hijja 447/March 1056). It clearly commemorates a specific work, probably the construction of the mosque in the second floor of the nearby salient. The work confirms the description of Nasr al-Dawla as a pious man who, despite his love of luxury and his 360 concubines, was meticulous in his observance of daily prayer. According to another inscription in Jerusalem, he endowed two houses for pilgrims there in 445/1053–4.[28]

---

[26] The first Marwanid inscription (44), set up over the Kharput Gate in 386/996, is a partial exception as it is not in floriated but in simple Kufic, but Whelan, "The Public Figure," 805–10, has shown that Marwanid inscriptions from the late tenth century at Mayyafariqin show the trend toward greater elaboration, foliation, and use of curved forms.

[27] Indeed, Flury (*Islamische Schriftbänder*) omitted the ʿAbbasid inscriptions from his study of the inscriptions at Diyarbekir because he considered them inferior to the eleventh-century work, but Whelan, "The Public Figure," showed that many of the features he considered characteristic of the local style are already present in the earlier work.

[28] Michael H. Burgoyne, "A Recently Discovered Marwānid Inscription in Jerusalem," *Levant* 14 (1982): 118–21.

Figure 16.5. Diyarbekir, detail of tower XXX, showing part of inscription 57, dated 481/1088. Photo: Estelle Whelan.

Nasr al-Dawla maintained his independence by judiciously balancing outside powers, taking care to pay homage to the increasingly strong Saljuqs of Iran. In 441/1049–50 he had inserted the name of the Saljuq chieftain Toghril in the *khutba*, or Friday bidding prayer, and several times when the Saljuq chief or his successor made a triumphal tour through the region, Nasr al-Dawla renewed his allegiance. Nasr al-Dawla's successors were not as successful in maintaining their independence, and they were eventually brought down by a Saljuq army under Ibn Jahir, the one-time vizier to Nasr al-Dawla. Turning against his erstwhile patrons, Ibn Jahir persuaded the Saljuq sultan Malik-Shah to send an army to invade Marwanid territory. After stiff opposition, the Saljuqs under Ibn Jahir defeated the Marwanids in 478/1085, and Diyarbekir and other cities were incorporated into the Saljuq domain.

The walls of Diyarbekir may have been damaged in the Saljuq siege, for five inscriptions (57–61) on the west, south, and north sides of the enceinte record restorations carried out under Saljuq auspices immediately after the city was taken (Fig. 16.5). The work was a concerted program of restoration, for the inscriptions are dated to five of six successive years between 480 and 486 (1088–93), and one inscription (59), a two-meter band on tower XIV, contains only the phrase "restored in 484" (1091). The texts show not only the damage incurred during the siege but also the broader scope of Saljuq power as Diyarbekir was incorporated into political conflicts of the whole Mediterranean-Mesopotamian-Iranian region.

The inscriptions carried out under the most powerful Saljuq ruler, Malik-Shah (57–60), contain texts modeled on earlier forms, naming the ruler, the governor, a local qadi, and a builder. The Saljuq receives splendid titles appropriate to his new position as sultan. He is the great sultan, the august king of kings (*shāhanshāh*), the sultan of God's land, the ruler of God's country, the auxiliary of God's caliph, Mu'izz al-Dunya wa'l-Din (glory of the world and religion), majesty of the state and beauty of the faith, Abu'l-Fath (the father of victory), Malik-Shah, son of Alp Arslan. Two different governors are named within the five-year span: Qawam al-Mulk Abu ʿAli al-Hasan, mentioned in inscriptions 57 and 58, was replaced by Ibn Jahir's son in inscription 59. The office of qadi was more stable, for the same qadi who had supervised the work done for the Marwanid Mansur on tower V in 476/1083 also supervised the work done for Malik-Shah. A new builder was involved, Muhammad b. Salama from al-Ruhaʾ (modern Urfa). That city must have had a strong tradition of builders, for the Cairene antiquarian al-Maqrizi reported that three brothers from there rebuilt the gates of Cairo at this time.[29]

The power of the Saljuq state is shown by the length and size of the texts naming Malik-Shah, which majestically unfurl in three or four lines of floriated script across the faces of three large towers at Diyarbekir. Malik-Shah's role as overlord of the city is underscored by a similar text, dated 484/1091–2, in a large band across the west side of the façade of the prayer hall of the congregational mosque in the city.[30] These large texts are accompanied by prominent figural reliefs. Centered above the inscription on tower XXX (57) is a frame band enclosing a composition carved in high relief with confronted bulls.[31] The text band itself is also decorated with other animals, including felines, birds, and horned sheep. The inscription on tower XL (58) has con-

---

[29] Abu'l-ʿAbbās Aḥmad al-Maqrīzī, *Al-mawāʿiz waʾl-iʿtibār bi-dhikr al-khiṭāṭ waʾl-āthār* (Cairo, 1294/1877), I: 381; K.A.C. Creswell, *The Muslim Architecture of Egypt*, 2 vols. (Oxford, 1952–9, rprt., New York, 1979), I:162; Allen, *Classical Revival*, 29–37 and note 22. For the Cairene walls see below.

[30] Van Berchem, Stryzgowski, and Bell, *Amida*, no. 18; RCEA 2792, with additions and corrections in VIII, 293; Sauvaget in Gabriel, *Voyages*, no. 82.

[31] Gabriel thought that there was a badly worn figure in the center, but Dr. Whelan informs me that he was wrong.

fronted horses, as well as felines and birds decorating the text. The pictures were presumably meant to reinforce the meaning of the text on the two towers just beyond the southwest salient.

The fifth inscription added to the walls under the Saljuqs (61) is a six-meter band on the curtain wall east of tower XI, near the aqueduct, in the name of Malik-Shah's brother, Tutush. After Malik-Shah's death in 485/1092, his son Berk-yaruq succeeded to the throne, but Malik-Shah's brother, who had been sent to hold Syria as an appanage, occupied Diyarbekir the following year. This inscription dated in that year marks Tutush's sovereignty over the city. The Saljuq ruler is lauded in the same way that the Marwanid Abu 'Ali had been in the inscription (44) he had installed over the Kharput Gate after taking the city: in both cases the benedictions ask God to glorify the rulers' victories.

Tutush's inscription is also designed to set him apart from previous rulers. The text uses a different grammatical construction from all earlier inscriptions at Diyarbekir: this construction was executed during the reign of . . . (*jarat hadha al-'imāra fī ayyām*), a construction closer to the kind used in Syria, for example, at the mosque of Aleppo restored under Malik-Shah in 483/1090.[32] The inscription also mentions a new qadi who supervised the work, Thiqat al-Mulk Abu'l-Makarim Mahdi b. 'Ali. Unlike the earlier qadis, he is called the chief qadi (*qāḍī al-quḍāt*), and he bears the epithet al-Shami ("from Syria"), suggesting that he was installed by Tutush.

The most startling variations in the text, however, are the honorifics (Arabic *laqab*) added to Tutush's name.[33] The Marwanid Nasr al-Dawla had already borne compound honorifics in the inscription he had erected on the Kharput Gate (49), where he was Nasr al-Dawla (the victor of the state), Rukn al-Milla (the pillar of the religion), and Majd al-Umma (glory of the religious community). In this inscription Tutush bears a similar triple crown: He is Taj al-Dawla (crown of the state), Siraj al-Umma (torch of the religious community), and Sharaf al-Milla (nobility of the religion). What is extraordinary is that each of Tutush's three honorifics is followed by a rhyming adjective: Tutush is Taj al-Dawla al-Qahira (crown of the victorious state), Siraj al-Umma al-Zahira (torch of the splendid religious community) and Sharaf al-Milla al-Bahira (nobility of the dazzling religion).

The adjectives used in Tutush's inscriptions were chosen not only

---

[32] Ernst Herzfeld, *Matériaux pour un corpus Inscriptionum arabicarum, Syrie du Nord, Inscriptions et Monuments d'Alep* (Cairo, 1955), no. 75.

[33] See *Encyclopaedia of Islam*, 2nd ed., s.v. "Laḳab."

for their rhyme but also in reference to contemporary events, notably the Saljuqs' rivalry with the Fatimids, who had conquered Egypt in 358/969 and established a new capital there.[34] The adjectives *al-qāhira* and *al-zāhira* are immediately associated with the Fatimids, who made frequent plays on words in their inscriptions. Their newly founded capital was Cairo (*al-qāhira*).[35] The first mosque established there by the Fatimids became known as the Azhar Mosque.[36] The name is generally thought to derive from the epithet *zahrā'* ("splendid") applied to Fatima, the daughter of the Prophet Muhammad and ancestress of the Fatimid imams, for the masculine form is *azhar*.[37] The same root furnishes the second adjective in Tutush's honorifics, *al-zāhira*. The third adjective used in Tutush's inscription, *al-bāhira*, may have been included for euphony and rhyme.

Tutush's choice of adjectives with loaded connotations invoking the Fatimids in an inscription recording the Saljuq restoration to the walls of Diyarbekir must have been a deliberate reposte to the Fatimid caliphs, who had just begun a major campaign rebuilding the walls of Cairo under the supervision of the Armenian general Badr al-Jamali, supposedly by builders from Urfa.[38] The Cairene walls are a masterpiece of Islamic military architecture and the finest masonry ever executed in Egypt (Fig. 16.6). The gates are particularly magnificent, and their inscriptions masterfully carved. Work was begun in Muharram 480/April-May 1087, and continued at least four years, according to the inscription on Bab Zuwayla dated 484/1091–92. The Fatimid work at Cairo is thus exactly contemporary with the Saljuq restoration at Diyarbekir.

The texts carved on the walls of Cairo on or near Bab al-Nasr,[39] Bab al-Futuh,[40] Bab Zuwayla,[41] and Bab Barqiya[42] are very similar. They

[34] For the latest on the Fatimids, see Yaacov Lev, *State & Society in Fatimid Egypt* (Leiden, 1991).
[35] *Encyclopaedia of Islam*, 2nd ed., s.v. "al-Kāhira."
[36] This form is already used in the endowment deed of the caliph al-Hakim dated 400/1009, preserved by the historian al-Maqrizi, *Khitat*, II: 273–5; translated in Gaston Wiet, *Matériaux pour un corpus inscriptionum arabicarum: Egypte II* (Cairo, 1929), 106–12.
[37] Creswell, *Muslim Architecture of Egypt*, I:36.
[38] Creswell, *Muslim Architecture of Egypt*, I:161–217; Allen, *Classical Revival*, 29–35.
[39] Van Berchem, *Matériaux pour un Corpus Inscriptionum Arabicarum, Egypte I* (Cairo, 1894), no. 33; RCEA 2762.
[40] Van Berchem, *Egypte I*, no. 36; corrected by Gaston Wiet, "Nouvelles inscriptions fatimides," *Bulletin de l'Institut de Egypte* 24 (1941–2), 149–55; RCEA 2762, corrected in RCEA XI:264–5.
[41] Van Berchem, *Egypte I*, no. 37, corrected under no. 520.
[42] Gaston Wiet, "Une nouvelle inscription fatimide au Caire," *Journal asiatique* 249 (1961): 13–20.

Figure 16.6. Cairo, Bab al-Nasr, begun in Muharram 480/April–May 1087.
Photo: Sheila S. Blair and Jonathan M. Bloom.

begin with the invocation of God (In the name of God the Merciful, the Compassionate), the Shi'ite profession of faith (There is no god but God alone, without partner; Muhammad is his prophet; and 'Ali, peace be upon him and upon all the imams who follow him, is God's friend), and the Throne Verse (Koran 2:255). They then report that the walls were restored by a servant of the caliph al-Mustansir billah, the commander Badr al-Jamali. The text on the Bab al-Nasr can be used as a sample:

It is by the glory of God, the strong and powerful, that Islam is protected and that fortresses and walls are raised. This gate of strength and the surrounding wall of al-Mu'izz's Cairo the well-guarded, may God protect it, were raised by the servant of our master and our lord, the imam al-Mustansir billah, commander of the faithful (God's blessings upon him, his pure ancestors, and his noble descendants), the most noble lord, the amir of the armies, the sword of Islam, the defender of the imam, the guarantor of the judges of the Muslims and the director of the missionaries of true believers, Abu'l-Najm Badr al-Mustansiri, may God affirm the religion through him, may God make the commander of the faithful profit from the extension of his life, and may God perpetuate his stature and raise his word; through the integrity of his government God has fortified the state and its people and caused his justice to extend to the small and the great. By this work he hopes to obtain God's reward and grace, he seeks God's grace and goodness and his protection of the throne of the caliphate, and asks God to surround him with favors. This work was begun in Muharram of the year 480 (April–May 1087).

The Fatimid text picks up certain themes by repeating words with the same root but different forms. One theme is glory ('izz): God possesses glory ('izz), he is the strong ('azīz), the gate (although popularly known as the Bab al-Nasr after the earlier gate on the same side of the city)[43] is actually the Gate of Glory (bāb al-'izz) in the city founded by the caliph al-Mu'izz (literally, he who glorifies). Similar plays are made with the roots ḥāṭa (to guard or protect) and nasha'a (to rise) and between similar roots such as ḥarasa (to guard) and ḥamiya (to become hot) and ḥaṣuna (to be well fortified) and ṣāna (to preserve). The historical section of the text was also adapted to echo the Koranic verse (Koran 2:255) at the beginning. The Koranic excerpt, known as the Throne Verse, states that God's throne (kursī) extends over the heavens and the earth, and the end of the historical text asks God to protect the throne (kursī) of the caliphate. The entire text, which must have been drawn up in the Fatimid chancery, was carefully composed, learned, and witty.

---

[43] See Creswell, *Muslim Architecture of Egypt*, I:162, for the names of the gates.

Like most Fatimid texts, the texts on the gates of Cairo proclaim the Fatimids' adherence to Shi'ism. The profession of faith refers to 'Ali and the imams descended from him, including the Fatimids, whose legitimacy was based on their descent from the Prophet's family. Blessing is invoked on al-Mustansir billah, commander of the faithful, his pure ancestors, and his noble descendants, further references to the Shi'ite line.

The Cairene inscriptions also allude to contemporary events. The reference to God's fortifying the state and people because of the integrity of Badr al-Jamali's government refers to the events that brought the general to power. A revolt by the Turkish guard who pillaged the city, civil war, and famine had brought Cairo to ruin and the Fatimid dynasty to the verge of collapse. As a last resort, the caliph recalled the governor of Syria, Badr al-Jamali, who arrived in Egypt in 466/1073. After quickly restoring order, Badr al-Jamali rose to become the most powerful man in the realm and the one who ordered the walls rebuilt as a sign of renewed Fatimid dominance over the city.

The Fatimid inscriptions are not only carefully composed but also meticulously laid out, with a few words added or omitted so that the texts fit the exact space available. On the Bab al-Nasr, for example, the text is laid out in a long band sculpted under the cornice at mid-height. It begins on the front of the west salient, runs along the side of the salient and over the entrance, and finishes on the side and front of the east salient. The text thus forms a long line broken into five parts, with the historical section beginning over the central gateway and the name and titles of the caliph over the top of the arch. Anyone entering through the gate would then ride beneath the name of the caliph. The carefully composed and laid out text is executed in a superb floriated Kufic, with large letters readable from afar.

The inscription on Bab al-Futuh is even more formidable. It is a fifty-nine-meter band of marble set at mid-height on the outer face of the curtain wall to the east of the gate. It begins at the angle between the gate and the curtain wall and continues along the big square salient that supports one of the minarets of the mosque of al-Hakim. The floriated Kufic letters are carved in relief, and the blocks are held in place by forty-two bronze nails, which may have been gilded and would have twinkled in the smooth marble ground surrounding the raised letters.

Tutush's inscription on the northern curtain wall of Diyarbekir is a pale imitation of the erudite and expensive text repeated on all the sides of Fatimid Cairo. Had Tutush's rule over Diyarbekir been extended, perhaps his text too would have been repeated, but during the struggles among the successors of Malik-Shah, Diyarbekir soon passed into the hands of a Turcoman chief, Inal. His successors, the Inalids, remained in control of the city for almost a century, but they were forced to yield real power in the city to a rich native family, the Nisanids, who served as viziers.[44] Under these two families, Diyarbekir continued to prosper, in part because it was somewhat removed from mainstream developments elsewhere in the Islamic lands. The congregational mosque in the city was restored several times in the twelfth century,[45] and a minaret added to the mosque on the citadel in 555/1160.[46] Work on the walls was restrained during this period, and the four inscriptions there (62–5) document not only the city's relative isolation, but also the changing balance of power between Inalids and Nisanids.

According to inscription 62, tower LXIII next to the New Gate was rebuilt by the Inalid Mahmud b. Ilaldi soon after his accession in 536/1141. In the following decade the vizier Abu ʿAli al-Hasan b. Ahmad b. Nisan had the west bay of the Mardin Gate walled up, according to inscription 63. The third and most informative inscription (64) records the rebuilding of tower XV in the northwest corner of the city in 558/1162. The Nisanid vizier's power over the nominal Inalid ruler is clear, as the inscription uses a variant form, naming the Nisanid at the beginning of the inscription as the person who directed and paid for the construction of the tower during the reign of the Inalid Mahmud b. Ilaldi. For the first time the work is specified as *al-burj* ("the tower"), and the text notes that it was totally rebuilt. The final inscription (65) of this period, done twenty years later, records the opening of a postern in the rampart near tower LVII by the Nisanid Bahaʾ al-Din in 578/1182. It does not even mention the Inalid ruler.

Inscription 65 also alludes to the growing political storm and the increasing threat of outside forces, for in the last month of that year the Ayyubid Saladin besieged the city, taking it in the first month of 579/May 1183. He then gave it to his allies, the Artuqids, who had ruled Hisn Kayfa, several days' journey downstream on the Tigris, since the opening years of the eleventh century. The brief and distinctive text on the postern at Diyarbekir begins, "I put my faith in God," and includes a phrase invoking God's mercy. The hidden postern is

---

[44] The obscurity of these two families is shown by the two brief entries in *Encyclopaedia of Islam*, 2nd ed., s.v. "Inālids" and "Nīsānids." Much of the information about them comes from the inscriptions on the city walls.

[45] Sauvaget in Gabriel, *Voyages*, nos. 83–9, dated 511/1117–18, 518/1124–5, 535/1141, 550/1155–6, and 559/1163–4.

[46] Sauvaget in Gabriel, *Voyages*, no. 96.

called the Gate of Happiness (Bab al-Saʿada), perhaps in reference to its use as an emergency exit by the last Nisanid.

This last Nisanid inscription is also important for its style, for it is written not in the bold floriated Kufic used in earlier inscriptions, but in a sober cursive script. This type of cursive became a hallmark of the Ayyubid dynasty, and some scholars view the change from angular to cursive as motivated by political concerns, particularly the revival of Sunni Islam from the mid-twelfth century.[47] The use of cursive script here, a year before the Ayyubids conquered the city, shows that epigraphic changes were not the result of dynastic change. Rather, politicians in the twelfth century were quick to seize upon stylistic changes and could turn epigraphic style to their advantage, transforming the newly evolved cursive script into a dynastic hallmark.

With the installation of the Artuqids at Diyarbekir, the walls again became the focus of major construction, as shown by the eleven inscriptions (66–76) done over a period of twenty-five years. The first ones set up by Nur al-Din Muhammad b. Qara Arslan (66–7) show that he redid the Urfa Gate. The two southern passageways of the antique triple gate were blocked, leaving only the northern doorway open, and the profile of the door frames was redone, with new iron doors that pivoted on basalt crapaudines added. As with his predecessors, Muhammad's role as sovereign is clear not only from the location of the inscriptions – over the gate that leads to northern Syria and Aleppo, homeland of the Ayyubids – but also from the text. Inscription 66 invokes victory from God and imminent conquest (*naṣr min allāh wa fatḥ qarīb*), a phrase from Koran 61:13 that had been used by the early Fatimids on textiles and other goods in reference to their forthcoming conquest of Cairo.[48] The text was appropriated by the Artuqids here to reflect their taking of Diyarbekir, similarly a long-sought goal.

Nur al-Din Muhammad's religious zeal is evident from the long titles he bears; he is lauded as:

our lord, the one knowledgeable in religious science, the just, the one assisted by God, the vanquisher, the victor, Nur al-Dunya waʾl-Din (light of the world and religion), the defender of Islam, the aid to the imam, the crown of the state, the support of the faith (Qawam al-Milla), the majesty of the religious community (Jalal al-Umma), the pride of kings and sultans, the suppressor of infidels and polytheists, the subjugator of schismatics and apostates, chief of

---

[47] For the latest statement of this view, see Yasser Tabbaa, "The Transformation of Arabic Writing, Part 2: The Public Text," *Ars Orientalis* 24 (1994): 119–47.

[48] Jonathan M. Bloom, "The Origins of Fatimid Art," *Muqarnas* 1 (1985): 30–8, esp. 31 and nn. 103–5.

Figure 16.7. Diyarbekir, tower XXXIX known as the Yedi Kardaş, with inscription 75 done in 605/1208–9. Photo: Estelle Whelan.

the Muslim armies, defender of the champions of the holy war, sphere of the high qualities, treasure of the caliphate, hero of the world, the Khusraw of Iran, king of amirs, the sure, the falcon, the illustrious, father of victory (Abu'l-Fath) Muhammad.

Not only are the titles ever increasing and often rhyming, but they derive from a range of Arabic, Persian, and Turkish sources. The titles are similar to those carried by other princes of the times, particularly the Zangids, a Turkish dynasty that controlled the southern Jazira and Syria in the twelfth and thirteenth centuries.[49] The titles show the increasing zeal of orthodox Sunnis of the time in face of both internal and external enemies, notably the Crusaders.

Artuqid titles reflect the unsettled times, and indeed the most important change to Diyarbekir under the Artuqids was the increased fortification. The big round towers on the west – XXXI, known as the Ulu Badan or Great Tower, and XXXIX, the Yedi Kardaş or Seven Brothers (supposedly for the seven rooms in it) – were built up (Fig.16.7). Some work was carried out under Muhammad (68) and his

---

[49] On Zangid titulature, see Niketa Elisséeff, "La titulature de Nur al-Din d'après ses inscriptions," *Bulletin des Études orientales* 14 (1952–4): 155–96.

successor Qutb al-Din Sökmen (70), but the major campaign dates to
the reign of Nasir al-Din Mahmud (74 and 75) in 605/1208–9.[50] Even
more important was the development of the citadel. According to
inscription 69, Sökmen had the Gate of Deliverance (Bab al-Faraj) on
the north wall of the citadel built in 595/1199. Nasir al-Din Mahmud
was responsible for more work. According to inscription 72, he had
the large rectangular building now serving as a prison built in 600/
1203–4. The old wall separating the citadel from the town is dated
603/1206–7 (73), and the gate was finished three years later (76). The
wall enclosed a pentagonal chateau, presumably the site of the Artuqid palace. Nothing remains of the palace, but Gabriel suggested that
the figural reliefs now in the Çinili Koşk in Istanbul were taken from
the site.[51]

Artuqid work on the city walls was part of an ambitious campaign
of urban reconstruction under Sökmen. At least two *madrasas* (legal
schools) were founded near the congregational mosque: the Mas'udiya
Madrasa founded between 590 and 596 (1193–1200) and the contemporary Zinjiriya.[52] Many of the same people were involved in the
construction. 'Isa Abu Dirham, the person who built the Gate of Deliverance (69), is called the builder of houses (*bannā' al-dūr*). He was a
master builder, and his signature is also found on a reused block (71)
installed on tower X just over the aqueduct and on the Zinjiriya
Madrasa.[53] The inscriptions suggest that building projects became
more complicated in these years. The builder Ibrahim b. Ja'far is mentioned in the inscription 74 on tower XXXI, and Yahya b. Ibrahim,
perhaps his son, is mentioned (75) on the corresponding tower, XXXIX.
According to the inscription, he executed the work on the plans (*tarsīm*) of the Artuqid ruler Mahmud, suggesting that this was part of a
sophisticated program with advance planning and that princes were
involved in military construction.

Building up citadels and strengthening fortifications was commonplace in the Islamic lands during the twelfth and thirteenth centuries
as a result of the interdynastic wars among Muslim princes and the
external threat of the Crusades, and many of the features seen at
Diyarbekir can be found elsewhere. Some of the most impressive

[50] Nos. 74 and 75 are reversed on Gabriel's plan according to the locations given by
    Sauvaget and Van Berchem.
[51] Gabriel, *Voyages*, 157; the reliefs are published in Van Berchem, Stryzgowski, and Bell,
    Amida, 354ff.
[52] Gabriel, *Voyages*, 195–9; inscriptions in Sauvaget in Gabriel, *Voyages*, nos. 97–101; Van
    Berchem, Stryzgowski, and Bell, *Amida*, no. 28.
[53] Sauvaget in Gabriel, *Voyages*, no. 101.

fortifications survive at Damascus, Aleppo, and Cairo, seats of the Artuqids' overlords, the Ayyubids, but the phenomenon was widespread. The walls of Baku in Azerbaijan, for example, were rebuilt in the twelfth century under the local Sharvanshah ruler Manuchihr II (r. 1120–49).[54] The work included a strong citadel and the Maiden's Tower, a circular tower 17 meters in diameter and 30 meters high with eight internal stories, comparable to the complicated towers with several stories of rooms built at Diyarbekir. The three-story Ulu Badan is 25.50 meters in diameter and some 25 meters high; the Yedi Kardaş measures 27.80 meters in diameter.

Artuqid work on the walls of Diyarbekir also fits the contemporary tradition of figural sculpture on city walls. The relieving arch in the doorway of the Urfa Gate is surmounted by a sculpture with a bird of prey atop a bull's head holding a ring or wreath. The text band with the date inscribed in the relieving arch itself has dragons at either end. The two big round towers, Ulu Badan and Yedi Kardaş, are more elaborately decorated with double-headed eagles, sphinxes, griffins, winged lions, and other motifs. A figural relief reused on tower XI may also date to this period. It depicts a seated figure with a nimbus holding a scorpion in his right hand and a hatchet or scepter in his left. He has been interpreted as representing the planet Mars.[55] Another relief on tower X depicts a sphinx or winged lion.[56] The iron doors of the Urfa Gate are decorated with lions' and rams' heads.[57]

The reliefs are too varied to be emblematic and their exact message is unclear, but they belong to a widespread use of figural imagery under the Artuqids.[58] They issued bronze coins with reliefs, and in the late twelfth century the Artuqid court sponsored a school of manuscript painting, where several illustrated copies of al-Jazari's treatise on automata and other works were produced.[59] The syncretist figural style associated with the Artuqids is clear from the Innsbruck Plate, an enameled bronze bowl with a central seated figure, usually called

[54] M.A. Useynov, *Pamyatniki azerbaydzhanskogo zodchestva* (Moscow, 1951), 37–8. See also Blair, *Monumental Inscriptions*, 155.
[55] Gabriel, *Voyages*, 168 and fig. 138.
[56] Gabriel, *Voyages*, fig. 139.
[57] Gabriel, *Voyages*, fig. 140.
[58] Dr. Whelan concluded that the reliefs were meant to underscore the sovereign message of the inscriptions, but could not find any one-to-one correspondence between figural reliefs and text.
[59] See the articles by Nicholas Lowick, "The Religious, the Royal and the Popular in the Figural Coinage of the Jazīra;" Rachel Ward, "Evidence for a School of Painting at the Artuqid Court;" and Nahla Nasar, "Saljuq or Byzantine: Related Styles of Jazīran Miniature Painting," in *The Art of Syria and the Jazira 1100–1250*, ed. Julian Raby, Oxford Studies in Islamic Art 1 (Oxford, 1985).

the apotheosis of Alexander, surrounded by six roundels containing birds and animals. The inscription around the interior gives the names and titles of the Artuqid ruler, Rukn al-Dawla Da'ud b. Sökmen.[60]

The taste for figural imagery was widespread throughout the region and often involved the reuse of classical elements. A good example is the temple of Baal at Palmyra, converted into a fortress in 527/1132 by Yusuf b. Firuz, chamberlain to the Burid ruler of Damascus. The upper machicoulis is flanked by projecting consoles, each supporting a relief showing a male figure seated on a rocky pedestal and holding some object. The figures have been identified as Hermes and Heracles and dated to the second century A.D.[61] Similarly, when the Saljuqs of Anatolia rebuilt the walls around Alanya, Sinop, Konya, and other cities in the first half of the thirteenth century, they incoporated figural reliefs. The walls of Konya, for example, were richly decorated with spolia as well as other figural reliefs carved for the occasion. A colossal headless statue of Heracles from classical times was placed at the side of one gate, which was surmounted by a newly carved double-headed eagle. Other Saljuq reliefs depicted angels, lions, a sphinx, a dragon, fish, and two foot soldiers wearing chain mail and grasping broad-swords.[62]

Following the fall of the Great Saljuqs, two major powers had emerged in the central Islamic lands: the Saljuqs of Anatolia, with their capital at Konya, and the Ayyubids of Cairo. Diyarbekir was delicately poised between them, and the Artuqid rulers submitted to one and the other in turn to maintain their independence. By the end of 629/1232, however, the Ayyubid sultan in Cairo, Saladin's nephew al-Malik al-Kamil (r. 1218–38), had had enough and he sent an army under his son, Najm al-Din Ayyub, to take Diyarbekir. Following Najm al-Din's conquest of the city, his father arrived on the first day of 630 (18 October 1232), expelled the last Artuqid ruler, and confirmed Najm al-Din as governor.

Two inscriptions (77–8), dated 634/1236–7 on towers XI and X on the north side of the enceinte, mark Najm al-Din Ayyub's rule over Diyarbekir. The texts soliciting glory for the sultan Najm al-din Ayyub are virtually identical, including the grammatical mistakes. As with Artuqid inscriptions, the texts show the increasing sophistication of city wall builders in this period. The work was done by the builder

---

[60] Scott Redford, "How Islamic Is it? The Innsbruck Plate and its Setting," *Muqarnas* 7 (1990): 119–35; *Die Artuqiden-Schale im Tiroler Landesmuseum Ferdinandeum Innsbruck* (Munich, 1995).

[61] Allen, *Classical Revival*, 57–8.

[62] Scott Redford, "The Seljuqs of Rum and the Antique," *Muqarnas* 10 (1993): 148–56.

Abu'l-Faraj on the plans (*tarsīm*) of Jaʿfar b. Mahmud al-Halabi. The designer's epithet, literally meaning from Aleppo, shows that Jaʿfar or his family hailed from Aleppo, a city with a long tradition of fine stone architecture where the citadel had just been refortified under Saladin's son al-Malik al-Zahir (r. 1186–1216).[63] Jaʿfar had previously worked for the Artuqids in 620/1223–34, for his name is found in two inscriptions in the congregational mosque (90 and 108) and in one on the adjacent Masʿudiya Madrasa (100). In the earlier inscriptions Jaʿfar was called master (*ustādh*). By the time of the Ayyubid work fourteen years later, he was more important, for he bears the honorific Shujaʿ al-Din (hero of religion) and the title *muqaddam* (major or commander). Jaʿfar's earlier work was executed by the builder Masʿud. He may well be the same person who had worked on towers XI and X, and just as Master Jaʿfar became Commander Shujaʿ al-Din Jaʿfar, so Masʿud became Abu'l-Faraj.

In the thirteenth and fourteenth centuries, Diyarbekir was attacked repeatedly and changed hands frequently, passing between the Saljuqs of Anatolia, the Ayyubids, the Mongols, and the Artuqids of Mardin. Political stability was only reestablished when the city became the seat of the Turcoman confederation of the Aq Qoyunlu in 805/1402.[64] The dynasty's founder, Qara ʿUthman, had fought on the side of Timur against the Ottoman Bayezid at the battle of Ankara, and in return for his support, Qara ʿUthman was rewarded with a grant of the lands of Diyarbekir. Diyarbekir served as the Aq Qoyunlu capital for the following seventy years. In 873/1469, with the death of the Timurid sultan Abu Saʿid, the Aq Qoyunlu became the uncontested power in Persia. To mark their new role, Uzun Hasan transferred the capital from Diyarbekir to Tabriz in northwestern Iran.

Three inscriptions mark the period of Aq Qoyunlu rule at Diyarbekir. The name of Qara ʿUthman's grandson, Jahangir (r. 1444–53), was inscribed (79) on the interior of the wall between towers LXXV and LXXVI in 853/1449–50. The same text was probably inscribed between the next two towers to the west, LXXIV and LXXV. In the summer of 857/1453, during Jahangir's absence, his brother Uzun Hasan seized Diyarbekir, and in spite of dogged attempts, Jahangir never managed to regain the city and was finally defeated in 861/1457. Uzun Hasan's control of the capital is commemorated by an inscription (80) dated 864/1459–60 on tower XX to the right of the

---

[63] Herzfeld, *Alep*; and Allen, *Classical Revival*.
[64] On them, see *Encyclopaedia of Islam*, 2nd ed., s.v. "Aḳ Ḳoyunlu;" *Encyclopaedia Iranica* s.v. "Āq Qoyunlū;" and John E. Woods, *The Aqquyunlu: Clan, Confederation, Empire* (Minneapolis, 1976).

Urfa Gate. Gabriel noted that the repairs to the gate were limited to repairing a gap in the surface.[65] A final inscription in Uzun Hasan's name (81) is a band supposedly dated Shawwal 883/December 1478–January 1479 on tower XIII.[66]

Following the decline of the Aq Qoyunlu, Diyarbekir passed briefly to the Safavids of Iran in the opening decades of the sixteenth century, until 923/1517, when the district was conquered by the Ottomans as part of their great campaign in the eastern Mediterranean following the disastrous defeat of the Safavids at Chaldiran in 920/1514. Diyarbekir became the center of an extensive province of newly conquered territories, and during the next four centuries of Ottoman government, the city, protected from wars and invasions, recovered some of its earlier prosperity. Many mosques and khans were built.[67] The congregational mosque was restored in 935/1528–9, and the revenues from a shop in the suq were used to build a fountain in it.[68] The major work on the fortifications was a new curtain wall separating the citadel from the city; a Persian inscription (81 bis) on the gate commemorates its construction by the Ottoman sultan Süleyman in 933/1526–7.[69] Without archaeological investigation, Gabriel was unable to determine whether the new wall rested on older foundations.

What, then, do we learn from the forty-four inscriptions set up on the walls and gates of Diyarbekir between the tenth century and the sixteenth? A first important point is that the inscriptions do not record forty-four discrete and complete campaigns of rebuilding the walls around the same city. In his pioneering study, Van Berchem already noted that classical Arabic texts describing the destruction or razing of city walls should not be taken literally, for it would have been foolish to dismantle such a vast and precious resource. Rather, the

---

[65] Gabriel, *Voyages*, 172.

[66] The date of no. 80, written out in words, is problematic, for it is one year later than the death of the sultan, usually reported as the eve of 'Id al-Fitr 882/5 January 1478. See, for example, Woods, *Aqquyunlu*, 274 and n. 142, with various dates in the same year. The inscription includes a benediction for a living person, "may God perpetuate his reign and sultanate," so it must have been drafted while the sultan was alive. The text is not illustrated, so one cannot check whether Sauvaget misread the large cursive letters.

[67] Gabriel, *Voyages*, 199–200 and 202–3; inscriptions by Sauvaget in Gabriel, *Voyages*, nos. 103–4.

[68] Sauvaget in Gabriel, *Voyages*, nos. 94–5; Van Berchem, Stryzkowski, and Bell, *Amida*, nos. 37–8.

[69] Only mentioned by Sauvaget in Gabriel, *Voyages*; the text is reportedly given in Basrı Konyar, *Diarbekir tarihi, kitābeleri, yıllığı* (Ankara, 1936), II:130–3, a work unavailable to me.

texts should be interpreted as meaning that the tops of the walls were damaged or specific areas dismantled. The inscriptions refer to some kind of restoration work, but in order to interpret what that work was, it is necessary to view the inscriptions along with archeological investigations of the walls. In short, epigraphy is helpful but insufficient for establishing a chronology of walls. Gabriel's work showed that the walls of Diyarbekir were almost constantly under repair or restoration, even more frequently than the forty-four times noted in the inscriptions.

Although the inscriptions at Diyarbekir do not record a complete history of the rebuilding of the city's walls, they do suggest hypotheses about other aspects of urban, political, social, and economic history. The inscriptions point, for example, to changes in urban patterns, as different areas of the walls were earmarked for work at different times. The Kharput Gate seems to have been the main entrance to the city in Byzantine times, as Greek and Latin inscriptions were found there too.[70] The Greek one was reused, but the Latin inscription on the fourteenth course of masonry, six meters above ground level, was embedded over the opening of the antique door. The Kharput Gate retained its importance in early Islamic times, as inscriptions and reliefs were added under the ʿAbbasids (41–3) and Marwanids (44), and the Marwanid ruler Nasr al-Dawla had a mosque added in the second floor of the nearby salient (49). The gate's importance under the Marwanids may have been due to its accessibility to Mayyafariqin, an important city in the Marwanid realm. Most Islamic cities, however, lay to the south of Diyarbekir, and the Kharput Gate opened onto a north–south artery that connected to the Mardin Gate, also inscribed in ʿAbbasid times (38–40).

In medieval times, the Urfa Gate on the west seems to have become more important. The last Marwanid Mansur already had some work done there at the end of the eleventh century (56), and the first Artuqid Nur al-Din Muhammad marked his takeover of the city in the late twelfth century there (66–7), as did the Aq Qoyunlu Uzun Hasan in the mid-fifteenth (80). The corresponding gate on the east, New Gate, was strengthened by building up the adjacent tower in the mid-eleventh century (51) and again in the mid-twelfth (62).

The change of axis coincided with the increased concern for urban security in medieval Islamic times, as towers and walls were built up on many sides and antique gates narrowed. The sense of security is underscored by the one inscription (64) that does not identify the work

---

[70] Gabriel, *Voyages*, 134–6.

on the walls as a generic "it" but uses the specific word "tower" (*al-burj*). The citadel became another focus of work. Built up under the Artuqids (69, 72, and 76), it maintained its importance under the Aq Qoyunlu, who repaired the towers just to its west (79). During the Ottoman period, when Diyarbekir was incorporated within a vast empire, security was not a matter of concern, but the citadel was the locus of administration and the heart of the city, as is shown by the new wall erected around it (81).[71]

The inscriptions at Diyarbekir also point to political changes. These political changes are clear from the wording used in the inscriptions. Texts were manipulated to play up the role of the ruler as victor. The Marwanid who took the city, Abu ʿAli, is lauded as the victorious amir (44), and the benedictions for both him and the Saljuq Tutush (61) ask God to glorify their victories. The Artuqid inscription over the Urfa Gate (66) invokes victory from God and imminent conquest (Koran 61:13). The Ayyubid inscriptions (77–8) on the towers near the aqueduct do not even mention construction but merely hail the glory of our lord, sultan Najm al-Din Ayyub, referring to the person who had just taken the city.

Placement and layout of the text were also important. Words were added or dropped so that the sovereign's name fell over a niche or gateway or in the middle of a long band. This attention to layout is already clear in the ʿAbbasid inscription over the Kharput Gate (42), which was planned so that the caliph's name and titles, the imam al-Muqtadir billah, sit directly over the niche decorated with animals. Over time, the sculptors became increasingly sophisticated in laying out the texts. The inscriptions done for the Artuqids (74–5) on the big round towers XXXI and XXXIX, for example, are set off by heavy moldings so that they resemble large *tabulae ansatae*. The round, almost three-dimensional relief of the accompanying figures calls further attention to the text.

The texts usually contain the full protocol of a sovereign, particularly his evolving titles, which reflect the concerns of the society. Notable are the increasingly zealous titles from the late eleventh century, when rulers are warriors of the faith, defenders of Islam, and pillars of religion. The Artuqid conqueror Nur al-Din Muhammad, for example, is lauded over the Urfa Gate (66) in 579/1183 as the suppressor of infidels and polytheists, subjugator of schismatists and apostates, chief of the Muslim armies, and defender of the champions of the holy

[71] This was also the reason that Gabriel was denied access to it.

war. These epithets could have been aimed at either internal or external foes. The city of Urfa, for example, had a large Christian population and changed hands many times until 1098, when Baldwin took it during the First Crusade and made the County of Edessa the first Latin state in the East. Some scholars have interpreted such texts as spreading the spirit of holy war (*jihād*) and representing the triumph of Islam over the Crusaders in Syria and the Jazira.[72]

When read closely, however, the inscriptions at Diyarbekir hint that internal foes were more important. Reading the inscriptions in chronological order suggests that the titles are part of a gradual expansion of titulature, not a sudden or immediate response to the Crusader presence. Moreover, the inscriptions lack any particular twist alluding to a specific event like Baldwin's conquest. On the contrary, one of the clear allusions to contemporary events, Tutush's bizarre titles with *al-qāhira* and *al-zāhira* in the inscription dated 486/1093 on the north curtain wall (61), is a pointed reference to the Fatimids, the heterodox Shi'ite dynasty that ruled Egypt and the great rival to Saljuq power in the Levant. While not denying the undoubted ambiguity of the message and duality of the audience, the Diyarbekir inscriptions suggest that the internal Muslim community, who knew and read Arabic, were the prime recipients.

The inscriptions on the walls of Diyarbekir also show the increasing complexity of the Islamic polity after the mid-tenth century. The 'Abbasid inscriptions (40–1) mention the well-known vizier Ibn al-Furat and present the model of the 'Abbasid caliph and his servant, the vizier who executes caliphal orders. By the eleventh century the appanage system had evolved, and the lines of organization were not as clear. The most famous vizier under the long-lived Marwanid ruler, Nasr al-Dawla, was Ibn Jahir, who served as vizier for twenty-three years. Like his 'Abbasid predecessor, Ibn Jahir is mentioned in the inscription commemorating Nasr al-Dawla's building of a mosque (49). In terms of political succession, however, Nasr al-Dawla had made his son, Sa'd, governor of Diyarbekir, as is mentioned on tower LVI (47). The vizierate changed frequently in these years, and four different viziers are mentioned: Kafi al-Dawla (50) and Za'im al-Dawla (52–3), who both served the Marwanids, and Qawam al-Mulk Abu 'Ali al-Hasan (57–8) and Ibn Jahir's son Jahir (60), who both served

---

[72] See, for example, Yasser Tabbaa, "Monuments with a Message: Propagation of Jihād under Nūr al-Dīn (1146–1174)," in *The Meeting of Two Worlds: Cultural Exchange between East and West during the Period of the Crusades*, ed. Vladimir P. Goss and C.V. Bornstein (Kalamazoo, 1986), 223–40.

the Saljuq Malik-Shah. The increasing power of the vizierate is seen in the local Nisanid family who eventually displaced their nominal overlords, the Inalids, in the twelfth century.

The evolution of fiscal administration in Islamic times and the changing sources of funding for city walls are also apparent from the inscriptions at Diyarbekir. The 'Abbasid work (40) was done to fortify religion and assure the protection of Muslims. Although no source of funding is stated, the inscription suggests that monies were taken from the state treasury since the work was overseen by an *'amil*, director of finances in a provincial capital. This situation may have continued into the early eleventh century as someone of the same rank supervised the work carried out by the Marwanid Nasr al-Dawla on tower XLIX (46).

This was not the case in later times. Not only are there no references to fortifying Islam or protecting Muslims, but the Marwanid Nasr al-Dawla states that the costs of rebuilding towers LVI and LII (47–8) were covered by his own money. Similarly, the Nisanid vizier directed and paid for the reconstruction of tower XV a century later (64). Personal funding was accompanied by local supervision, and during most of the eleventh century work on the walls at Diyarbekir under the Marwanids and Saljuqs was supervised by a qadi. Four such judges are named. Abu 'Ali al-Hasan b. 'Ali b. Ahmad al-Amidi supervised the work for Nasr al-Dawla (47–8) between 437/1045–6 and 444/1052–3; and a father-son pair, Abu'l-Hasan 'Abd al-Wahid b. Muhammad b. 'Abd al-Wahid and his son Abu Nasr, worked for the Marwanids and Saljuqs from 457/1065–6 to 485/1092 (51–4, 57–60, 105). These three people were clearly local judges, for Abu 'Ali bears the epithet al-Amidi ("from Amid") and the filial relationship between the other two suggests local affiliation. The fourth qadi (61) was different: Thiqat al-Mulk Abu'l-Makarim Mahdi b. 'Ali al-Shami ("from Syria") was probably brought in by the Saljuq ruler Tutush from Syria, his home base. From this point onward, no sources or supervisors of funds are mentioned in the inscriptions.

The inscriptions at Diyarbekir also show the increasing complexity of design and construction, as many of the texts include the name of a master builder. The 'Abbasid work (40–1) was carried out by Ahmad b. Jamil, a local engineer (*muhandis*). All subsequent builders are called *al-bannā*'. Three different ones worked for three successive Marwanid rulers over a forty-year period in the mid-eleventh century: Nusayr b. Habib worked for Nasr al-Dawla (47–8), Musa b. Mazid for Nizam al-Dawla (51–2), and Abu Sa'd b. Humayd for Mansur (54). Work carried out under the Saljuqs was spread out around the enceinte, and the scale of work is reflected in the foreign origins of the builder who worked for the Saljuq sultan Malik-shah (57–60) – Muhammad b. Salama from Edessa. No builder is mentioned in any Inalid or Nisanid inscription, implying perhaps that the work was of less consequence, particularly as we return to named builders with the major urban reconstruction carried out under the Artuqids. 'Isa Abu Dirham, who signed the citadel gate (69), the walls (71), and the Zinjiriya Madrasa (101), is also credited as a builder of houses (*bannā' al-dūr*). The builder Ibrahim b. Ja'far is mentioned in the inscription (74) on tower XXXI dated 605/1208–9, and Yahya b. Ibrahim, perhaps his son, is mentioned on the corresponding tower XXXIX (75).

The inscriptions show that construction of city walls had become increasingly complex by the early thirteenth century, when builders are distinguished from designers. The builder Yahya b. Ibrahim (75) executed work on the big round tower XXXIX according to plans (*tarsīm*) drawn up by his Artuqid overlord Mahmud. Another builder-designer pair worked in the succeeding generation for the Ayyubids (77–8): The builder Abu'l-Faraj executed the plans of the Shuja' al-Din Ja'far b. Mahmud from Aleppo. The increased status of designers is clear from their increasing titles: Mahmud was an Artuqid prince, and Ja'far is a commander (*muqaddam*) with a title Shuja' al-Din (hero of religion). None of the post-Mongol inscriptions carries the name of a builder, suggesting that their work had political implications rather than structural importance.

The figural reliefs that accompany these inscriptions have roused much interest, particularly from Western scholars, and many different interpretations have been put forward. Looking at them in a broad chronological sweep suggests that they reflect a continuous tradition which became more important in medieval times. Already in classical times the gates and walls at Diyarbekir were decorated with arched niches, inscriptions, and crosses in relief, and these reliefs were sometimes reused in Islamic times. The Kharput Gate, for example, includes several elements reused from the Byzantine gate, including niches and capitals on pilasters and one Latin and four Greek inscriptions. The 'Abbasid texts were also decorated with reliefs of animals and birds. They seem to follow a long Near Eastern tradition of decoration with trees, animals, birds, and stars, although their exact meaning is unclear.

The reliefs get bigger and finer in medieval times. The 'Abbasid reliefs are crude, but those added under the Artuqids show real artistry. They may well have had some astral associations, just as an inscription (92) in the congregational mosque implores God to raise the stature and situation of the patron, the Artuqid of Mardin Shams al-din Salih, to the level of Arcturus, a star of the first magnitude. An illustration to one of the copies of al-Jaziri's treatise made for the Artuqids in 602/1205–6 shows a palace façade on a zodiacal clock with two-headed eagles in the spandrels.[73] In all cases, however, the figural reliefs are smaller and presumably less significant than the texts they accompany, and it is the inscriptions that help us in charting the changing concept of city walls through the centuries.

It is thus clear that inscriptions were not always put up on the walls of Diyarbekir to record repairs. What other motives were there for writing on city walls? To answer this question, we can look at the places where the inscriptions were added. Some were inscribed on the curtain wall or towers and mark significant campaigns, reconstructing sections that must have been damaged in attacks or building up the fortifications in vulnerable areas. The southwest projection, for example, was fortified in medieval times. The salients flanking it carry inscriptions (57–8) in the name of the Saljuq Malik-Shah, and the big towers known as Ulu Badan (XXXI) and Yedi Kardaş (XXXIX) were rebuilt by Artuqids (70, 74, and 75), who also transformed the citadel (69, 72, and 76).

Another prime spot for reconstruction was the north side of the enceinte where an aqueduct brought water to the city. Five inscriptions (53, 61, 71, 77, and 78) commemorate work there under the Marwanids, Saljuqs, Artuqids, and Ayyubids from the late eleventh century to the early thirteenth. The proximity and number of these inscriptions point up the importance of securing the water supply to the city. This was particularly true in the troubled Middle Ages, and Terry Allen noted how the extension of the ancient water system of Aleppo by the Zangid ruler, Nur al-Din (r. 1146–74), affected urban development there.[74] The same situation pertains elsewhere. The earliest inscription from Fatehpur Sikri, the fiat city used as a capital by the emperor Akbar (1556–1605), was a text inscribed on the wall near the Ajmer Gate noting the completing of a well by the Mughal emperor Babur in 933/1526–7.[75]

[73] Istanbul, Topkapi Palace Library, MS Ahmet III, 3472, 10, reproduced in Ward, "Artuqid Painting," fig. 8. Color illustration in Filiz Çağman and Zeren Tanındı, *The Topkapi Saray Museum: The Albums and Illustrated Manuscripts*, trans., exp., and ed. J.M. Rogers (Boston, 1986), fig. 7.
[74] Allen, *Classical Revival*, 9–10.
[75] M. Ashraf Husain, "Inscriptions of Emperor Babur," *Epigraphia Indica – Arabic and Persian Supplement* (1965): 49–51; a translation is given in *Fatehpur-Sikri: A Sourcebook*, eds. Michael Brand and Glenn D. Lowry (Cambridge, MA, 1985), 225, no. 8; the earlier inscriptions come from cemeteries and mosques.

By far the most common place to add inscriptions, however, was on or near city gates, and more than one-third of the forty-four inscriptions at Diyarbekir are located there. All the ʿAbbasid inscriptions are on gates: three (38–40) on the Mardin Gate and three (41–3) on the Kharput Gate. The first Marwanid inscription to survive (44) is set over the Kharput Gate atop the ʿAbbasid inscription (41) and marks Abu ʿAli's occupation of the city a short time before. The first work by his nephew Nizam al-Dawla after he ousted his brother from the city was to set up an inscription (51) on tower LXIII beside New Gate. This was the same place chosen by the Inalid Mahmud to put up an inscription (62) just after he succeeded his father in 536/1141–2. In the same year that the Artuqids took control of the city, they set up inscriptions (66–7) over the Urfa Gate, a site that had already seen some work under a previous dynasty (56). The Aq Qoyunlu ruler Uzun Hasan chose a tower to the right of the same gate to commemorate his takeover of the Aq Qoyunlu capital (80).

Sometimes these inscriptions mark actual work to the gates, especially blocking bays in antique triple gates. For example, the west bay of the Mardin Gate was blocked (63) by the Nisanid vizier Abu ʿAli al-Hasan in the 540s/1145–56. The Artuqid Nur al-Din Muhammad (66–7) had the two southern passageways of the Urfa Gate blocked in 579/1183. At other times, however, work on the gates was mainly cosmetic, as for example with Uzun Hasan's work on the Urfa Gate (80). In such cases, the inscriptions were set up solely for rhetorical purposes, particularly to mark sovereignty.

The traditional signs of Muslim sovereignty are to mint coins and to insert one's name in the Friday bidding prayer at the congregational mosque. The inscriptions at Diyarbekir show that another sign of sovereignty was to put one's name on the walls of a major city. Indeed it is interesting that the Marwanid Nasr al-Dawla, who, texts say, acknowledged the authority of Tughril and the Saljuqs by inserting their names in the Friday bidding prayer, never acknowledged the Saljuqs in his inscriptions.

Putting one's name over the city gate was an important tradition throughout the Islamic lands, and a few examples must suffice to show how long-lasting and widespread the tradition was. According to the thirteenth-century historian Ibn Shaddad, the ʿAbbasid caliph Harun al-Rashid (r. 786–809) had his name added to the Bab al-Sibal, the eastern gate of al-Raqqa/al-Rafiqa, when he refortified the site as the new capital of the region of Diyar Mudar in the Jazira.[76] The

[76] Cited in *Encyclopedia of Siam*, 2nd ed., s.v. "al-Raḳḳa."

Ayyubid ruler al-Malik al-ʿAdil did the same thing in adding his name to the Aleppo Gate at Harran when he had the citadel rebuilt after his brother Saladin gave him the city in 587/1191.[77] The Qajar ruler of Iran, Nasir al-Din Shah (r. 1848–96), had gateways with his name set up outside Tehran, Qazvin, Isfahan, Shiraz, Simnan, and other large cities; these were eclectic confections with undulating façades topped by multistory minarets somewhat like candles. The one at Semnan, for example, has murals depicting scenes from Persian epic literature on the front and the name and titles of the Qajar monarch in bold gold letters on the back.[78]

Inscriptions, then, cannot replace archaeology in charting the construction of city walls. Rather, these written texts are more important as historical documents. They show the complex and changing settings of the city in Islamic times. The inscriptions were carefully manipulated and reflect contemporary concerns, particularly that of advertising one's sovereignty over the city.

APPENDIX 16.1

Chronological List of Inscriptions on the Walls of Diyarbekir

ʿABBASIDS

(38) [297/909–10], Mardin Gate
  Van Berchem, no. 1; RCEA 894
(39) 297/909–10, Mardin Gate
  Van Berchem, no. 2; RCEA 889
(40) 297/909–10, Mardin Gate
  Van Berchem, no. 3; RCEA 890; corrected in RCEA V, p. 190
(41) 297/909–10, Kharput Gate
  Van Berchem, no. 4; RCEA 891; corrected in RCEA V, p. 191

---

[77] D.S. Rice, "Unique Dog Sculptures of Mediaeval Islam: Recent Discoveries in the Ancient Mesopotamian City of Harran and Light on the Little-known Numairid Dynasty," *Illustrated London News* 221 (1952): 467.

[78] These gates are only occasionally mentioned: e.g., Robert Hillenbrand, "The Role of Tradition in Qajar Religious Architecture" in *Qajar Iran: Political, Social and Cultural Change 1800–1925*, ed. E. Bosworth and C. Hillenbrand (Edinburgh, 1983), 355, or illustrated: e.g., A.U. Pope and P. Ackerman, eds., *A Survey of Persian Art* (Oxford and London, 1939), pl. 472a. The inscriptions are even less well published. For example, all that Nosratollah Meshkati, *A List of the Historical Sites and Ancient Monuments of Iran* (Tehran, n.d.) says about the Arg Gateway at Simnan (National Iranian Monument no. 395) is that "This structure also belongs to the Qajar period."

(42) 297/909–10, Kharput Gate
  Van Berchem, nos. 5 and 6; RCEA 892 and 895
(43) 297/909–10, Kharput Gate
  Van Berchem, no. 7; RCEA 893

MARWANIDS

(44) 386/996, Kharput Gate
  RCEA no. 2049
(45) 426/1034–5, Tower LVIII
  Van Berchem, no. 8; RCEA no. 2411
(46) 42x/1030s, Tower XLIX
  Van Berchem, no. 9; RCEA 2469
(47) 437/1045–6, Tower LVI
  Van Berchem, no. 10; RCEA 2522
(48) 444/1052–3, Tower LII
  Van Berchem, no. 11; RCEA 2561
(49) Dhu'l Hijja 447/March 1056, interior of Kharput Gate
  Van Berchem, no. 12; RCEA 2576
(50) 450/1058, curtain wall north of Tower XIX
  RCEA 2621
(51) 460/1067–8, Tower LXIII near New Gate
  Van Berchem, no. 14; RCEA 2666
(52) 464/1071, rampart north of Tower LXX
  RCEA 2679
(53) 465/1072, curtain wall east of Tower X
  RCEA 2700
(54) 476/1083, Tower V
  Van Berchem, no. 15; RCEA 2743
(55) Tower V
  RCEA 2755
(56) Urfa Gate

SALJUQS

(57) 481/1088, Tower XXX
  RCEA 2773
(58) 482/1089, Tower XL
  Van Berchem, no. 16; RCEA 2780
(59) 484/1091, Tower XIV
  RCEA 2793
(60) 485/1092, Tower LIX
  Van Berchem, no. 17; RCEA 2798

(61) 486/1093, curtain wall east of Tower XI
RCEA 2804

INALIDS and NISANIDS

(62) [ca. 540/1145], Tower LXIII near New Gate
Van Berchem, no. 25; RCEA 3204
(63) 54x/1145–56, Mardin Gate
RCEA 3165
(64) 558/1162, Tower XV
RCEA 3251
(65) 578/1182, postern in rampart against Tower LVII
Van Berchem, no. 26; RCEA 3378

ARTUQIDS

(66) 579/1183, Urfa Gate
Van Berchem, no. 27; RCEA 3383
(67) Urfa Gate
RCEA 3404
(68) Tower XXXXI
RCEA 3405
(69) 595/1199 citadel, Gate of Deliverance
RCEA 3523
(70) Tower XXXI
RCEA 3534
(71) Tower X
RCEA 3524
(72) 600/1203–4, citadel
RCEA 3573
(73) 603/1206–7, citadel
RCEA 3625
(74) 605/1208–9, Tower XXXI
Van Berchem, no. 29; RCEA 3642
(75) Tower XXXXIX
Van Berchem, no. 30; RCEA 3643
(76) citadel
Van Berchem, no. 31; RCEA 3644 and 3645

AYYUBIDS

(77) 634/1236–7, Tower XI
Van Berchem, no. 34; RCEA 4136

(78) 634/1237, Tower X
    Van Berchem, no. 33; RCEA 4137

AQ QOYUNLU

(79) 853/1449–50, interior wall between Towers LXXV and LXXVI
(79bis) interior wall between Towers LXXIV and LXXV
(80) 864/1459–60, Urfa Gate
(81) Shawwal 883/December 1478–January 1479, Tower XIII

OTTOMANS

(81bis) 933/1526–7, citadel
(81ter) citadel, salient O

CHAPTER 17

Medieval French representations of city and other walls

WOLFGANG G. VAN EMDEN

In Henri Pirenne's classic work on the city, there is a trenchant statement about walls as a necessary condition of medieval urban status: "It is impossible to imagine a town existing at that era [the Middle Ages in general] without walls. It was an attribute by which towns were distinguished from villages. It was a right, or, to use the expression of that time, it was a *privilege* which none of them lacked."[1] This view is hardly controversial today; it has indeed been normal to consider a protective stone girdle to be part of the very definition of the city in many places and periods up to the eighteenth century.

In examining works of medieval French and Anglo-Norman literature, mainly from the twelfth and thirteenth centuries, in this context, I aim first to establish how far, in fact, they reflect this automatic link between cities and walls. After a search for expressions making such a connection (and on an obvious, almost formulaic level they are not hard to find), I discuss some methodological complications which apply in this field. This discussion in itself throws some light on the ways in which walls were used, both in the texts and in reality. I then apply the view of walls as part of the status of a town or city to a specific, little known example, that of the walling of New Ross in Ireland about 1265. It will be seen in this first part of the chapter that the generally held view described above is not fully borne out by the literary evidence examined here. In the second part, I examine in greater detail the vocabulary, motifs, and themes that appear when walls are narratively exploited in French-language works of imagina-

---

[1] Henri Pirenne, *Medieval Cities. Their Origin and the Revival of Trade*, trans. Frank D. Halsey (Princeton, 1952; rprt. 1970), 150.

Figure 17.1. Town wall at Autun, basically Gallo-Roman. Photo: van Emden.

tion in the Middle Ages, in order to lay some foundations for a para-digmatic approach to the thematics of the subject.

In the necessarily circumscribed corpus of Old French literary texts which underlies this essay, detailed descriptions and narrative exploi-tation of city walls, as distinct from those of castles or small fortified bourgs, have in fact proved hard to find. One reason for this dearth, *pace* Pirenne, is to be seen, at least as far as France is concerned, in some of the other contributions to the present volume: medieval cam-paigns of walling towns and cities tend, largely and with exceptions such as Philippe-Auguste's Paris, to date from the fourteenth and fifteenth centuries with the threat from the English.[2] The use and maintenance of Roman and Gallo-Roman enceintes, such as that at Autun, for example (Fig. 17.1), is of course an altogether different matter, as Bernard Bachrach shows in Chapter 7 of this volume.

Certainly, the phrase *clos de mur(s)* is a more or less formulaic ad-junct to the names of cities in significant numbers of medieval French

---

[2] Notably those of Kay Reyerson, Chapter 4, and Michael Wolfe, Chapter 11. Cf. Jim Bradbury, *The Medieval Siege* (Woodbridge, Suffolk, 1992), 1–2.

texts, not only epic ones.[3] Béroul's late-twelfth-century *Tristran*[4] has a typical example, in which the fact that Carlisle is walled contributes nothing to the story:

> Di ton nevo q'au roi Artur,   649
> A Carduel, qui est clos de mur,
> Covienge qu'il aut par matin; [. . .]

[Tell your nephew that he must go in the morning to King Arthur at Carlisle, which is walled . . .]

The same expression comes, equally automatically, in the entirely fantastic, nightmarish yet idealized context of the subterranean search for her wounded lover by the heroine of Marie de France's roughly contemporary *lai*, *Yonec*.[5] After following the trail of his blood, and passing through a hill corresponding no doubt to the magical *sidhe* of the Celtic Otherworld,[6] she emerges on to a meadow:

> Asez pres ot une cité;   360
> De mur fu close tut entur;
> N'i ot mesun, sale ne tur,
> Que ne parust tute d'argent;
> Mut sunt riche li mandement.

[Quite close, there was a city, walled all around; there was not a house, hall nor tower which did not seem to be all of silver; the buildings are very rich.]

The significant thing for our purposes is that, even in this surrealistic setting, the word *cité* is at once followed by the wall that encloses it.

It is curious that Ovid's famous reference to Babylon's walls of brick, said to have been built by Queen Semiramis, at the start of his tale of Pyramus and Thisbe in Book IV of the *Metamorphoses*, is not

---

[3] On the thematics of the city, with many thought-provoking analyses and interpretations from an historian's point of view, see "Warriors and Conquering Bourgeois: the Image of the City in Twelfth-century French Literature," in Jacques le Goff, *The Medieval Imagination*, trans. Arthur Goldhammer (Chicago and London, 1988), 151–76. Walls and their adjuncts are very much part of the discussion.

[4] Béroul, *The Romance of Tristran*, ed. A. Ewert, 2 Vols. (Oxford, 1939), vol. 1, ll. 649–51. For other references to walls and related motifs in Arthurian and Arthurian-related texts, see E.H. Ruck, *An Index of Themes and Motifs in 12th-century French Arthurian Poetry; Arthurian Studies* 25 (Woodbridge, Suffolk, 1991), 31.

[5] Marie de France, *Lais*, ed. A. Ewert (Oxford, 1944, and rprt.), 91. All references to Marie de France will be from this edition.

[6] See P. Ménard, *Les Lais de Marie de France* (Paris, 1979), 157–8. Some of the details of this passage, ll. 360–74, may imply the division of the town into *bourg* and *cité* which is discussed below, but the text is not wholly clear in its details.

taken up in the Old French Ovidian adaptation of the twelfth century. But *Floire et Blanchefleur*,[7] of the same period though not a work of particularly Ovidian inspiration, alludes to "li murs qui le [Babiloine] clot" [the wall which encloses it] at l. 1789, though of course that city *is* the site of the harem which the hero must infiltrate disguised as a basket of flowers.

The second part of Wace's *Roman de Rou*,[8] written in alexandrines, again at about the same date, describes Rouen as a city enclosed by a wall and a ditch, the context then showing us some of the elements of this city wall:

> la cité estoit close de mur et de fossé.   3319
> Francheiz et Alemanz, quant il furent armé,
> ont a ceuls de Roem un grant assaut donné;
> Normanz se deffendirent comme vassal prové,
> as berteiches monterent et au mur quernelé,
> n'i ont rienz par assaut cil dehors conquesté.

[The city was enclosed by a wall and a ditch. The French and the Germans, when they had armed, made a great assault on those of Rouen; the Normans defended themselves like hardened vassals, climbing up to the brattices and the crenellated walls; those outside have gained nothing from their attack.]

The ideal of protection afforded by such walls is made clear – if clarification on so obvious a point is needed – by the following simile in Chrétien de Troyes's *Yvain*[9] (ca. 1177 in my view), the context of which is a victorious pursuit:

> mes il les chace molt de pres   3255
> et tuit si conpaignon aprés
> que lez lui sont ausi seür
> con s'il fussent tuit clos a mur
> haut et espés de pierre dure.

---

[7] *Floire et Blanchefleur*, ed. Jean-Luc Leclanche (Paris, 1980); it has to be said that this poem identifies, as is common in the Middle Ages, ancient Babylon with Cairo, and there is no reference to Semiramis. The wall of Semiramis is not forgotten by Christine de Pizan, *Le Livre de la Cité des Dames*, see the translation by Earl Jeffrey Richards (London, 1982), pt. 1, ch. 15, 39.

[8] Wace, *Roman de Rou*, ed. A.J. Holden, 3 vols. (Paris, 1970), 1:123–4.

[9] Chrétien de Troyes, *Yvain*, ed. Mario Roques (Paris, 1963); the equivalent passage in the manuscript edited by Foerster and Reid [see ed. T.B.W. Reid (Manchester, 1942, and rprt.], ll.3259–63, has no significant variants. In general, I will be less interested than usual in variants in this essay, since the essential point for present purposes is normally that the description or statement has been made by a medieval man, whether author, *remanieur*, or scribe (unless of course the details are important for the course of the narrative).

[But he pursues them very closely, and all his comrades after him, for alongside him they feel as much in safety as if they had all been enclosed by a high, thick wall of hard stone.]

Epic references are naturally at least equally common, and are to be found, for example, in *Girart de Roussillon*,[10] again from the same period:

> A mige nuit, abanz que can li cos, 6278
> Fun Roissillons traïs, qu'est de mur clos.

[At midnight, before cockcrow, was Roussillon which is walled betrayed.]

In *Aymeri de Narbonne*,[11] late twelfth or early thirteenth century:

> Desus un pui vit une vile ester 160
> Que Sarrazin i orent fet fermer.
> Molt bien fu close de mur et de piler;
> Onques plus fort ne vit hom conpasser.

[On a hill he (Charlemagne) saw a city (Narbonne) standing, fortified by the Saracens. It was well circled by wall and buttress; never did a man see a stronger constructed.]

In the roughly contemporary *Anseïs de Cartage*[12]:

> Voient la vile, qui tant fu bien muree. 276

[They see the city, which was so excellently walled.]

The oldest and most famous *chanson de geste*, the *Chanson de Roland*,[13] dating from the very start of the twelfth century in the view of most specialists, similarly associates *murs* and *citét* in its very first *laisse* (epic stanza):

> N'i ad castel ki devant lui remaigne, 4
> Mur ne citét n'i est remés a fraindre,
> Fors Sarracuce, [. . .]

---

[10] *Girart de Roussillon*, ed. W. Mary Hackett, 3 vols. (Paris, 1953–5); all references to *Girart de Roussillon* in the original language will be from this edition.

[11] *Aymeri de Narbonne*, ed. Louis Demaison, 2 vols. (Paris, 1887), ll. 160–4.

[12] *Anseïs de Cartage*, ed. A.F. Kerr (unpublished Ph.D. diss., University of Reading, 1994), l. 276. Cf. ll. 196, 1465, 2460, 2563, 3485, 3876, 4472–3, 5311, 8701, 10176–8, 10420, for the automatic association of walls with a common noun for city or with the name of a city. (I have not had access to the old edition of J. Alton [Tübingen, 1892]).

[13] *La Chanson de Roland*, Frederick Whitehead's text with notes and introduction by T.D. Hemming (London, 1993), ll. 4–6.

Figure 17.2. Semur-en-Auxois. Photo: van Emden.

[There is no castle which remains in his (Charlemagne's) way, no wall or city has remained to be broken down, except Saragossa . . .]

Similarly, a little further on, we are told:

> Cordres ad prise et les murs peceiez, 97
> Od ses cadables les turs en abatiéd.

[He (Charlemagne) has taken Cordoba and reduced its walls to rubble, he brought down its towers with his catapults.]

It would be easy to go on with such brief references to city walls, but it is important to note that, in general, these are not exploited narratively. In my experience, walls are much more commonly encountered in the context of individual castles or at most bourgs, small fortified towns, also commonly called *chastels*, in relation to which, as Reyerson stresses, the twelfth century was historically the beginning of a great period for wall building. Such fortresses still exist in numbers today, though of course the preserved walls are often later. One may cite, at random, examples at Semur-en-Auxois (Fig. 17.2) or the nearby Chateauneuf, and Flavigny, all in Burgundy, at Bar-sur-Aube in Champagne,[14] Cordes-sur-Ciel (Tarn), Penne d'Agenais (Lot-et-Garonne), and other *bastides*,[15] or the Templar fortress village of La Couvertoirade (Aveyron), which goes back to the twelfth century. It is mainly in such places that the fiction of the twelfth and thirteenth centuries describes walls and puts them to narrative use.

Castelfort, in *La Chevalerie Ogier*, seems to provide a fictional example of this type of fortification, since, after describing its position on a rock in a valley, and saying it was founded by Cain and the sons of Israel (a type of claim to which we shall return), the poet specifically refers to it as a *borc* on the Rhône.[16] Roussillon, in *Girart de Roussillon*,[17] is clearly another, as Girart loses it on the first of two occasions by asking the *bordeis* (bourgeois) to guard the walls:

> But the count [Girart] acts like a man with a foolish disposition, having his wall occupied by his bourgeois whom he asks to watch as if their lives depended on it: "If Charles comes and attacks you here, hurl stones and rocks with such violence that you force them to retreat far back!" Who cares what he asks of them? God curse them! He who has a nice little wife goes and dallies with her, and he who has no mistress goes and grabs one. They go off to sleep everywhere throughout the fortified town [*castel*].

That it is a matter of a small fortified town rather than a castle is shown by references not just to the bourgeois, inhabitants of a *bourg*, but also to the royal troops searching the roads within the enceinte (ll. 1002–3). Later, during the second treacherous capture of Roussillon (ll. 6278 ff; see above for the first two lines), the squires are described

---

[14] To which Bertrand de Bar-sur-Aube, in *Girart de Vienne*, ed. Wolfgang van Emden (Paris, 1977), l. 99, refers as a *chastel*, as he does later to Dijon (l. 415). For the terminology of such places in France, cf. also Susan Reynolds, *Kingdoms and Communities in Western Europe, 900–1300* (Oxford, 1984), 107.

[15] *Bastides* and *villeneuves*, interesting in that they are artificial small towns built for specific purposes, seem generally to have had walls built as part of their design. The same may be said, no doubt, for Aigues-Mortes, whose celebrated fortifications were certainly necessary for the protection of Louis IX's strategic harbor, in the wake of the Albigensian Crusade.

[16] I quote perforce for the present (cf. footnote 55) from the widely available but unreliable edition of Mario Eusebi (Milano, Varese, 1963), ll. 6632–46.

[17] Ed. cit., ll. 906–16; in view of the linguistic difficulty of this Franco-Provençal text, I acknowledge here, in providing an English version, the recent translation into modern French in *La Chanson de Girart de Roussillon*, trans. with intro. and notes Micheline de Combarieu du Grès and Gérard Gouiran (Paris, 1993), 105, as well as the much older translation by Paul Meyer (Paris, 1884). There may be here a reflection of the traditional defensive practice by which inhabitants, including Jews, were commonly required to defend that part of the wall nearest to which they lived (see the contribution of Bernard Bachrach to this volume); on the other hand, this poet is generally hard on non-nobles, though it would be hazardous to infer from this that the poem was necessarily composed for the aristocracy.

searching crypts and cellars, setting fire to the thatched *borc* (l. 6283), in which bell towers and stores of food go up in vivid flames.

One of the most precise descriptions of a small town fortified for defensive purposes comes from another of Chrétien's late-twelfth-century romances, *Cligés*,[18] in which the traitor Angrés prepares to be besieged in Windsor (Guinesores) by King Arthur and an army including Alixandre, father of the eponymous hero:

A ce jor, comant qu'il soit ores,	1228
Qui le chastel volsist desfandre,	
Ne fust mie legiers a prandre,	
Car li traïtres le ferma,	
Des que la traïson soucha,	1232
De dobles murs et de fossez,	
Et s'avoit les murs adossez	
De pex aguz et de darciere,	
Qu'il ne cheïssent par derriere.	1236
Au fermer avoit mis grant coust.	
Tot juing, et juingnet, et aoust	
Mist au feire le roilleïz,	
Et fossez, et pont torneïz,	1240
Tranchiees, et barres, et lices,	
Et portes de fer coleïces,	
Et grant tor de pierre quarree.	
Onques n'i ot porte fermee	1244
Ne por peor, ne por assaut.	
Li chastiax sist en un pui haut,	
Et par desoz li cort Tamise.	

[At that time, however things may be today, if one wanted to defend the fortified town, it would not have been easy to take; for the traitor fortified it, as soon as he hatched his treason, with double walls and with ditches, and he had supported the walls behind with sharp stakes and props[19] to stop them from falling inwards. He had used much wealth in fortifying the place. He spent all June, July and August making the palisade and ditches, and a drawbridge, trenches, draw-bars and barriers, iron portcullises and a great tower of ashlar. There was never a door closed there out of fear or because of assault. The fortified town stood on a high hill and below it ran the Thames.]

The interest of this description lies in the apparently ad hoc combination, for immediate military needs, of archaic, perhaps temporary, features like the palisade supported by stakes with others – a tower

[18] Chrétien de Troyes, *Cligés*, ed. Alexandre Micha (Paris, 1965).
[19] Conjectural translation: the word used, *darciere*, is a hapax.

Figure 17.3. Château Gaillard. Photo: van Emden.

made of ashlar[20] (Fig. 17.3), portcullises and drawbridges – which
suggest permanence. We see here the siege preparations of the lord
of a small town over a period of three months, which is the time it
takes for Arthur, having heard of the treason in Brittany, to raise
and bring forces to Windsor. How far are they true to reality? The
outcome of the siege is fortuitous, in that the traitor is captured by
means of a stratagem involving the use of a postern:[21] the defenses
are not really put to the test. In this sense, the walling and fortification described here in no way defines the status of the town, but
it is fairly typical of the way in which the authors I have to deal
with use walls narratively: preparations for, and descriptions of,

---

[20] Chrétien, who may well have worked for Henry II and seems to know the geography
of England (see Glyn S. Burgess, *Chrétien de Troyes. Erec et Enide* [London, 1984], 97–8;
Beate Schmolke-Hasselmann, "Henry II Plantagenêt, roi d'Angleterre, et la genèse
d'Erec et Enide," *Cahiers de Civilisation médiévale* 24 [1981]: 241–6), would in that case
certainly have known at least the stone shell-keep or curtain wall which predates that
king's round keep, (still extant under the top half added by Wyatville in the early
nineteenth century), if not Henry's keep itself.

[21] For the postern as part of the narrative thematics of the castle wall, see Wolfgang van
Emden, "The Castle in Some Works of Medieval French Literature," in *The Medieval
Castle. Romance and Reality*, eds. Kathryn Reyerson and Faye Powe (Dubuque, 1984),
17–22.

sieges, even if in this case the siege is brought to a swift close by rather unusual means.

Vienne, in *Girart de Vienne*,[22] must be seen as a larger town, indeed a city (it has a bishop, ll.1526, 6675 – even an archbishop, ll. 6827, 6873, as in contemporary reality – and so Saint Maurice is undoubtedly a cathedral) that is fortified, and needs no ad hoc preparation:

> Grant fu le siege entor Vïenne mis,   2593
> onques gregnor ne vit hom qui soit vis;
> Ch[arles] en jure, le roi de Seint Denis,
> n'en partira tant qu'i[l] les avra pris.
> Li dus Girart voit son chastel assis,
> n'est pas merveille s'il fu espooris.

[Great was the siege laid around Vienne, never did living man see a greater; Charles, the king of Saint Denis, swears that he will never leave until he has captured them. Duke Girart sees his fortified town besieged, and it is no surprise if he was terrified.]

In the case of this epic, the high marble walls are, for once, part of the idealization of the city, of its definition, almost, when its future lord first sees it (ll.343–9):

> voient Vïenne la fort cité vaillant,
> les murs de marbre qui molt sont haut et grant.
> Girart parla, qui le cuer ot vaillant,   345
> dit a Renier: "Vez cité bien seant!
> Ne vi si noble en trestot mon vivant.
> Cil qui la tient doit estre molt poissant;
> si n'avoit plus, s'est il riche menant."

[They see Vienne, that strong, powerful city, with its marble walls so high and great. Girart of the valiant heart said to Renier: "Look at that beautifully sited city! I never saw a nobler one in all my life. He who holds it must be a very powerful man; if he had nothing else, he is rich and mighty."]

Later the walls are occasionally mentioned in the course of the siege combats that ensue (e.g., ll. 3665–75, 4579–634, though, uncharacteristically, both these examples end with a conversation between Aude, high up on the wall, and Roland, who will of course be betrothed to her at the end of the story). So Vienne is one example of a major city whose walls *are* exploited narratively, as well as being part of its status.

There are certainly also references to the walls of great and famous

---

[22] Ed. cit.; at pages xxx–xxxiv, I explain my reasons for dating this poem from ca. 1180.

cities such as Jerusalem, Rome, and Troy in both epic and romance; but this is usually in the rather stereotypical context of siege warfare, in which the narrative material might just as well be in respect to an individual castle. It is not primarily a matter of definition or city status. This is a provisional impression, based on years of varied research in which my attention has been on aspects other than the one which is the subject in hand, so that I may well have missed relevant passages; on the other hand, appeals to respected British colleagues for *compléments d'information* have not produced major examples of which I had been ignorant or forgetful.[23] It may be that other medieval literatures might produce more directly relevant material, but, as is stated above, I confine myself here to French literature of the Middle Ages, mainly, though not exclusively, of the twelfth and thirteenth centuries. In this area, the gleanings are not lacking, but they do not commonly present great walls as part of the *definition* of a city. I hope, however, that even an untypical balance sheet may be of interest and significance.

One methodological problem, though it is progressively being reduced, is the absence of easily accessible and comprehensive computer-based concordances of many Old French texts for the identification of interesting passages for analysis. Few glossaries list all words used in the work in question, and common ones like *mur, muraille* are invariably the most obvious candidates for omission. Those seeking to create a data base allowing an exhaustive study of the thematics of the subject are thus frustrated, and many illuminating examples are bound to be missed.

Another preliminary methodological consideration is the use of the word *cité* in Old French. There are two reflexes in Old French of Latin *civitas, civitatem* : first *cit*, based on a form of the subject case, *civite*, which lost its unstressed penultimate vowel in the Gallo-Roman period,[24] and second *cité*, from the accusative case. Either may, quite commonly, mean simply "city," "town," as in the following typical examples:

> Atant s'en tornent a grant esperonnee
> Vers la cit de Vïenne.[25]

---

[23] I am grateful in particular to Dr. Sarah Kay, Professor Angus Kennedy, Dr. Tony Hunt; my Reading colleagues Dr. Peter Noble and Dr. Sara Poole; and to Dr. Marianne Ailes, Mrs. Mary Alexander, Dr. Judith Belam, Dr. Alex Kerr, Dr. Claude Sinzelle, and Dr. Karen Pratt for references and suggestions.

[24] Pierre Fouché, *Phonétique historique du français*, 2nd ed., 2 vols. (Paris, 1969), 2:464.

[25] Ed. cit., ll. 2411–12.

Figure 17.4. Carcassone (citadel). Photo: van Emden.

[Then they return, spurring hard, towards the city of Vienne.]

> Ore ot Vïenne, la fort cité loee,
> Li dus Girart [. . .][26]

[Now duke Girart had Vienne, the strong, renowned city . . .]

There is however also another use of *cité*, differentiating it from *ville*, which reflects the position in a good many medieval towns: a fortified quarter, a citadel, often including a castle, within the bounds of the town itself. This is a configuration preserved in many places today, such as Caernarvon and Conway in Wales, or Saint Malo and Carcassonne (Fig. 17.4) in France. As Samuel Kinser says of Arras in the time of Philippe Commynes:

Most medieval cities had a fortified castle, or citadel, at the center of the town where representatives of the feudal territory surrounding the city lodged. Very

---

[26] Ed. cit., ll. 1477–8.

often, as at Arras here, town government and citadel government were at swords' points.[27]

It happens that two texts, very different in nature and nearly three hundred years apart in time, both refer to this arrangement in Arras. We shall return to Commynes's description shortly; in Jean Bodel's play, *Le Jeu de Saint Nicolas*, which dates from around 1200, a distinction is made between two parts of the town, administered by different bodies of men:

> CONNARS: Amis, on m'apele Connart;
>   Crïeres sui par naïté
>   As eskievins de la chité [. . .]
>
> RAOULÉS: J'ai non Raouls qui le vin cri
>   Si sui as homes de le vile.[28]

[CONNART: My friend, they call me Connart; I am by right of birth the crier of the magistrates of the city (. . .) RAOULET: My name is Raoul, and I cry the wine; I serve the men of the town.]

As Warne observes in his note to ll. 604, 609, which relies on a review by A. Guesnon, Arras was, from the time of the royal charter of 1194, divided into two separate quarters, the episcopal *cité*, based on the cathedral and administered by twelve *eschevins*, and the fortified *ville*, built round the Abbey of Saint Vaast and administered by twelve *prud'hommes*.[29] In Bodel's text, the emphasis is on the administrative competition between the two, but Kinser's "swords' points" are clearly hinted at in the behavior of the two rival criers, who reach the point of pushing and shoving each other and of threatening to come to blows (ll. 614–25) before the innkeeper succeeds in restoring peace and a compromise.

A later, more military view of this arrangement comes, as has al-

---

[27] *The Memoirs of Philippe Commynes*, ed. Samuel Kinser, trans. Isabelle Cazeaux, 2 vols. (Columbia, SC, 1969), 1:341 n. 127. Cf. a very similar point in Le Goff, *The Medieval Imagination*, 163. Many such *cités*, often referred to by the Latin name of *arx*, were based on the walls of a Roman *civitas*, and consequently were often, as at Arras, episcopal administrative centers; cf. Pirenne, *Medieval Cities*, 59–62; by contrast, the fifteenth-century castle built within Dijon by Louis XI after the defeat of Charles the Bold was designed to intimidate the inhabitants, and was much hated. It was systematically and totally destroyed in the nineteenth century, an indication of the hatred which it aroused. See Henri Chabeuf, *Dijon à travers les âges. Histoire et description* (Dijon, 1897; rprt., 1982), 45–51, 56–8.

[28] Jean Bodel, *Le Jeu de Saint Nicolas*, ed. F.J. Warne (Oxford, 1951; rprt. 1968), ll. 602–4, 608–9. For the dating, see Warne's discussion, xv–xvii.

[29] A. Guesnon, *Le moyen age* 21 (1908): 67–86, esp. 74.

ready been indicated, in the fifteenth chapter of the fifth book of Commynes's *Mémoires*,[30] which I quote both in French and in the English translation of Michael Jones.[31]

[1477] Ja avoit ledit seigneur bonne intelligence avec mons^r des Cordes, et, conseillé et advisé de luy, qui estoit chief et maistre dedans Arras, requist ausdits ambassadeurs qu'ilz luy feissent faire ouverture par ledit seigneur des Cordes de la cité d'Arras; car lors y avoit muraille et foussé entre la ville d'Arras et la cité, et portes fermans contre ladite cité; et maintenant est à l'opposite, car la cité ferme contre la ville.

[Already the King[32] had reached a good understanding with my lord of Cordes, who was commander and master of Arras. Counseled and advised by him, the King requested the ambassadors to order the lord of Cordes to open the citadel of Arras to him, because at that time there were walls and a moat between the town of Arras and the citadel and gates closed against the citadel, while at present it is the other way round with the citadel closed against the town.]

There is something intriguing about this passage, for the implication is that the *cité*, or citadel, was less effectively fortified than the town in 1477, which is the reverse of the usual pattern where there is a *cité* within a *ville*. This is corroborated by the fact that the *cité* was entered on 4 March 1477 by the royal troops, while the *ville* was not occupied until 4 May. Pirenne makes the general point that, once the commercial towns built around the older citadel had been defensively walled, the now redundant fortifications of the *arx* were often allowed to fall into decay.[33] This may explain the point at issue; in any event, at the time when Commynes was writing (between 1489 and 1498) the position had been reversed, it seems; the start of the process may perhaps be seen in the sequel to the surrender of the *cité* in 1477 for, as Jones's translation puts it, "As soon as the King was inside the citadel he had earthworks thrown up against the gate and at other places near the town. . . ."

---

[30] Philippe de Commynes, *Mémoires*, intro. Philippe Contamine (Paris, 1994), 339.

[31] Philippe de Commynes, *Memoirs*, trans. with intro. Michael Jones (Harmondsworth, 1972). Jones's translation is based on the Calmette/Durville edition, (1924–5; rprt. 1964), in the series *Les Classiques de l'histoire de France au moyen âge*, which was not accessible to me. This no doubt accounts for his translation of "the King" where Contamine's edition has "ledit seigneur"; it makes no practical difference, for, if the manuscript used by Contamine is referring to the lord of Humbercourt rather than the king, it merely has the latter's representative speaking for him. The context is the surrender to Louis XI of Arras, and other towns held by des Cordes for Mary of Burgundy, in the aftermath of the death at Nancy in January 1477 of her father, Charles the Rash.

[32] See the preceding note.

[33] Pirenne, *Medieval Cities*, 149–50.

The case of Arras may serve to illustrate the potential lack of correspondence between the medieval word *cité* and its apparent modern equivalent; nevertheless discussion will henceforth examine the walls of towns and the use made of them in medieval French literature on the assumption that *cité* and *ville* are in practice largely synonymous, unless the context in a particular case makes it very clear that the Arras pattern, common as it was and is, applies. I shall also have to enlist walls from castles and bourgs for the reasons stated; there is in any case no clear dividing line in the spectrum ranging from *chastiaus* (a term often, though not always, used for a bourg with defenses) through fortified towns to walled cities.

Given the implication in the quotation with which I started, and indeed in the close connection between *mur* and *cité* in many of the examples I have examined so far, that the possession of a wall is somehow a test of status,[34] then the only Old French account known to me of the actual acquisition of a wall by a town is anomalous. The *Walling of New Ross*, an account in Anglo-Norman of the first stages of this process in the town of New Ross in southeast Ireland seems contemporary with the events: the last line states that "Ce fu fet l'an de l'incarnation Nostre Seignur .M.CC.LXV." [This was made in the year of our Lord 1265],[35] and the poem deals only with the digging out of the ditch; it would seem that the poet moved on after the first campaign, or at any rate wrote at or before its completion.

Whatever the motive for this abrupt end, the reasons for building a wall at New Ross seem to have had little to do with civic pride or city status. Aside from a rather engaging legend reported three centuries later by Richard Stanihurst and involving a thieving Irish "pezzant" and a generous widow called Rose[36] – and the rarity of walled cities

---

[34] Cf., in addition to the introduction to this chapter, R. Muir, *History from the Air* (London, 1983), 215: ". . . in the medieval period and probably in the Roman period too, walls also proclaimed the urban status and prestige of the defended settlement. . . ."

[35] I shall use the edition and translation by Hugh Shields, "*The Walling of New Ross*: A Thirteenth-century Poem in French," *Long Room* 12–13 (1975–6): 24–33. (*Long Room* is the journal for publications by the Friends of the Library, Trinity College, Dublin.) I am grateful to Dr. Shields for drawing my attention, in a private communication, to the description of the walls and environs of another Irish town, Limerick, in *Durmart le Gallois*, which I was not able to take into consideration for this essay. Dr. Shields considers it wholly imaginary, without relation to present-day topography.

[36] See Shields, "*The Walling of New Ross*," 24; and *Holinshed's Chronicles of England, Scotland and Ireland in Six Volumes*, vol. 6, *Ireland* (London, 1808), 30–3. The legend had to do with the theft of a "peece of cloth" by a "pezzant" who made off on horseback after pretending to be about to pay, and the reaction to this crime of a wealthy and "chast" widow named Rose, who put up the money for the wall. The lady is compared with Dido, and the labors of the citizens of Ross to those of the

in Anglo-Norman Ireland no doubt explains the arising of legends about so parochial an event – the reality was more prosaic and perhaps revealing. The poet announces that he will tell of an Irish town:

La plus bele de sa grand	the finest of its size	8
Qe je sache en nule tere.	I know in any country.	
Mes poure avoint de un gerre	But they were fearful of a war	
Qe fu par entre deus barouns;	that was [going on] between two barons;	
Vei ci escrit amdeus lur nuns:	here are their two names in writing:	12
Sire Morice e sire Wauter.	lord Maurice and lord Walter.	
Le noun de la vile voil nomer:	I shall tell you the name of the town:	
'Ros' le devez apeler,	'Ros' you are to call it,	
C'est le novel pont de Ros.	it is the new bridge of Ross.	16
Ce fu lur poure ke ne furent clos.	What they feared was that they had no town walls.	
A lur conseil un joure alerent	To their council one day they went	
E tot la commune ensemblerent;	and the whole commons assembled [?].	
Lur conseil pristerent en tele maner:	They made a resolution thus:	20
Qe un mure de morter e de pere	that a wall of stone and mortar	
Voilent enture la vile feire,	they would build round the town,	
Qe pour avoint de cel geere.	for that war was causing them concern.[37]	

Here, as in the first examples I quoted, the word *clos* is used (l. 17); but it is the fear of not being protected in an unstable situation, and indeed one might call it a panic reaction, which is stressed (cf. also l.23).[38] When the hired laborers proved slow workers (ll. 29–33), the

Carthaginians in Book I of the *Aeneid*, ll. 423–36! At least Holinshed describes the completed walls and turrets, saying that the walls are equal "in circuit" to those of London.

[37] I quote from Shields's edition and translation of these basically octosyllabic (but often highly faulty) lines, keeping the double columns which the short lines permit.

[38] See Shields, *"The Walling of New Ross,"* 24: Maurice Fitzgerald and Walter de Burgh, magnates from the south and the north respectively, had been at odds for some years when Maurice provoked a new outbreak of fighting by his arrest of Henry III's *justiciar*, Richard de la Rochelle, on 6 December 1264; his against the background of general strife between Henry and this English barons, which seems to have spilt over into Norman Ireland. The start of work at Candlemas 1265 (l. 24: 2 February) may legitimately be explained as a panic reaction to the arrest of Richard and the resumption of hostilities, for the date is surely a surprisingly early one for outdoor construction work.

council sat again and decided on a plan unprecedented in England or France (ll. 36–7): All the people of the town would go on a rota basis by trade or profession to work on the fosse, vintners, mercers, merchants, and drapers on Monday, from dawn till *nune* (probably the ninth hour, 3 P.M., rather than "noon"), with their banners and music, singing and dancing (ll. 44–61). The priests, after singing Mass, are part of the Monday shift and work particularly well because young and eager ((ll.62–7); they are joined on the site by the seamen (with their banner), six hundred of them (ll. 68–77). On Tuesday, tailors, robe-trimmers, dyers, fullers, and saddlers make up a rather smaller shift (ll. 78–85). And so on, with different trades specified for each day, with banners, music, and dancing. It was no doubt this collaborative effort – whatever the fear that had motivated the decision in the first place, it shows high morale and a strong sense of civic solidarity – that made the episode legendary. Shields rightly, I am sure, considers that there is nothing to show that the poem was known to Stanihurst, but the latter does report the communal effort with some verve, adding an exemption for the physically infirm which the poem does not mention, and ascribing the whole idea, the finance and the detailed rostering (though not by trades) to Dame Rose, in simple reaction to the escapade of the Irish "pezzant":

Hir deuise was, that the towne should incontinentlie be inclosed with wals, & therewithall promised to discharge the charges, so that they would not sticke to find out labourers. The deuise of this worthie matrone being wise, and the offer liberall, the townesmen agreed to follow the one, and to put their helping hands to the atchiuing of the other. The worke was begun, which thorough the multitude of hands seemed light. For the whole towne was assembled, tag and rag, cut and long taile: none exempted, but such as were bedred and impotent. Some were tasked to delue, others appointed with mattocks to dig, diuerse allotted to the unheaping of rubbish, manie bestowed to the cariage of stones, sundrie occupied in tempering of morter, the better sort busied in ouerseeing the workmen, ech one according to his vocation imploied, as though the ciuitie of Carthage were afresh in building. . . .[39]

(There follows the quotation from the *Aeneid* I referred to earlier, in translation.)

---

[39] Holinshed, *Ireland*, 30–1. Cf. Muir, *History from the Air*: "Walls could also play a useful role in towns where trading was a vital function and market tolls an important source of revenue, because the provision of a limited number of gates helped to control the comings and goings of traders." The same purpose was served by a wall erected within Dijon as late as 1852 to prevent merchants from avoiding the tax known as the *Octroi*, a tax not revoked until 1948; see Chabeuf, *Dijon à travers les âges*, 45. The legend repeated by Holinshed clearly has a similar function in mind, as distinct from the poem, which concentrates on defense in the troubled circumstances described above.

The differences in the two accounts are considerable, aside from the motivation of the exercise and the exemption of the bedridden: In Stanihurst's account, there is a certain contradiction between the generous money offer, which causes all to volunteer, and the element of drafting implied by the exemption. Further, allocation of work seems to be by skills, whereas in the poem, all trades seem to do all types of work. The poem reserves one surprise on this front, of which there is no mention in the later account: On Sundays, the ladies take their turn, and with no punches pulled:

Le demainge les dames i vont;	On Sunday the ladies go;	122
Sachez de veires, bon óvere i font.	and in truth they do good work.	
Le nombre ne sai de cert nomer:	I cannot say for sure how many there were:	124
Nule hom vivant ne les puit conter.	no one could possibly count them.	
Totz la pere i vont jeter	They all go to heave the stone	
E hors de fosse a porter.	and carry it out of the fosse.	
Ki qe la fut pur esgarder	Had you been there to witness it	128
Meint bele dame y put il veer	you would have seen many a lovely lady,	
Meint mantel de escarlet	many a mantle of scarlet,	
E de verd e de burnet,	green and fine dark brown,	
E meint bone roket bien ridee,	many a good well-smocked gown,	132
Meint blank fem[?] ben colouree;	many a fair-skinned, rosy wife[?].	
Ke unkes en tere ou je ai esté	Never in any land where I have been	
Tantz bele dames ne vi en fossee.	did I see so many fine ladies in a fosse.	

There may be an element of poetic posturing here; not only does our halting poet try to use anaphora (ll. 129–33) and makes a little joke about so many ladies in one ditch in the last two lines; he also goes on, after praising their beauty and describing their banner and musical contribution, to tell us that they propose to build one of the gates, to call it "La port de Dames," and to build their prison there, in which any man would willingly lose his liberty (ll. 136–57)! There are clear, literary, courtly overtones here,[40] which have little to do with the

---

[40] For a close parallel, see Chrétien de Troyes, *Yvain*, ed. M. Roques (Paris, 1963), ll. 1921–44, where there is a highly sophisticated and detailed exploration of the idea of the prison of love.

matter in hand, to which the poet returns at l. 158, describing the
benefits of the fosse when it is completed (he does not seem to envis-
age the wall in this assessment):

De dames ore me voil lesser	Of ladies now I shall leave 158
	off talking
E du fossé plus en parler.	and say more about the fosse.
Le fossé est vint pees parfunt	The fosse is twenty feet deep 160
E une lue de vei teint ben de	and extends for a full league.
lung.	
A l'oure qe serra tot parfeit	When it is complete
Ja n'avera mester de aver gayte,	there will be no need to have a
	watch;
Mes dormir púunt surement.	they can sleep soundly. 164
Ja n'averunt gard de male gent;	They will have no cause to fear
	evildoers;
Me ke venissent quarant mile	should they come forty thou-
	sand strong
Ja nen entrunt dedens la vile.	They will not get into the town.

There is here a reference to one of the motifs that we shall identify in
the second part of this essay as being typical of the literary description
of walls – the width of the ditches protecting them – and what I shall
call the impregnability topos (ll. 166–7); the latter is then amplified by
a disquisition on the amount of armor and weapons and the number
of crossbowmen and men at arms in the town (ll.168–91). But the poet
returns at once to the essentially *defensive* nature of the fortification:

Me je vous die tot sanz faille:	Yet I can truly say 192
Eus ne desirent nule bataile,	that they do not wish for battle:
Mes lur vile voleint garder	they only want to protect their
	town
De maveis gent a lur pouer.	from marauders by whatever
	means they can.
Nule home de ce ne lez dut	No one should blame them 196
blamer	
Qe lur vile voleint fermer;	for wanting to enclose their
	town;
Qe qant la vile serra fermé	when the town is securely
	closed
E le mure tot vironé	and the wall encircles it com-
	pletely,
N'ad Irés en Irland si hardi	not an Irishman in Ireland 200
	will be so bold
Qi l'oserént asailler, je vus plevi;	as to dare attack it, I guarantee.

In this stress on defense, the poet is entirely consistent, given the real
reasons (as distinct from the surely apocryphal version about the

peasant's escapade motivating the widow Rose) for the enterprise. It contrasts interestingly with R. Allen Brown's emphasis on the offensive role of the castle: here is a town fortifying itself against a perceived threat at a precise moment in time.[41] The insistance on the impregnable nature of the defences, as well as the remarkable story of united effort the poet tells ties in well with a comment of Lewis Mumford's in his seminal *The City in History*: "The psychological importance of the wall must not be forgotten. When the portcullis was drawn and the town gates were locked at sundown, the city was sealed off from the outside world. Such enclosure helps create a feeling of unity as well as security."[42]

It is worthy of note that these feelings appear to have been generated with only the fosse under construction, though it is clear that Ross did finish the program with a set of walls subsequently. In literature, too, the defensive aspect of the fortifications of a town or a castle tends to receive greater attention in practice.[43] This is connected with the interminable sieges that characterize the Old French epics, particularly those dealing with the subject of revolt.[44] The siege is the necessary expression of a personal vendetta against a baron who has to remain a basically sympathetic victim, but it is also easy to control narratively because of the variety of incidents that can be imagined to enliven a static situation, and, because of its length, it can easily lead to a resolution with honor for both sides.

Having established this narrative perspective, we may now turn to an examination of the vocabulary used in Old and Middle French in the semantic field under discussion, and the often formulaic, if not cliché'd, contexts in which words designating walls find themselves. The purpose of this second part of my essay is tentatively to lay some foundations for a paradigm or taxonomy of literary descriptions of walls, be they those of castle or city.

Mur is of course the commonest word employed, but it is accompanied by an astonishing number of cognates: *murail, muraille, mural, murage,* and *muret* (the latter apparently a diminutive) are all to be found. The word *mandement*, basically an abstract noun ("command," "precept"), can be used for a building, as in the quotation from *Yonec*

---

[41] See R. Allen Brown, *English Castles*, 3rd ed. (London, 1976), 186, 198–9.

[42] Lewis Mumford, *The City in History* (Harmondsworth, 1961), 350.

[43] A point I developed in "The Castle in Some Works of Medieval French Literature," 1–26.

[44] Van Emden, "The Castle in Some Works of Medieval French Literature," 2–3; cf. Howard Bloch, *Medieval French Literature and Law* (Berkeley, Los Angeles, and London, 1977), 96–7.

above, but also for a fortification, as in this quotation from *Girart de Vienne* (a reference to the destruction of Troy, a motif to which we shall return):

> [...] par devant Troie, en la bataille grant,   4949
> la ou Paris, le fiz au roi Priant,
> n'Estor, ses freres, n'orent de mort garant.
> Tuit furent mort, veincu et recreant,
> et trebuchié tuit li haut mendement;
> n'i remest tor ne haut mur en estant [...]

[... before Troy, in the great battle in which neither Paris, son of King Priam, nor his brother Hector had any protection from death. They were all killed or defeated, and all the high fortifications were brought down; no tower or high wall remained standing ...]

The late twelfth-century *Prise d'Orange*, in its *AB* redaction, confirms this interpretation, which does not figure in the Tobler-Lommatzsch:[45]

> "Gillebert, frere," ce dit li cuens Bertran,   1767
> "Assaudrons nos Orenge la vaillant?
> Fraindrons cez murs et cez hauz mandemenz?"
> Dist Gilebert: "Vos parlez de neant;
> Ne la prendrez a jor de vo vivant."

["Gilbert, my brother in arms," said count Bertrand, "shall we attack Orange the rich? Shall we smash those walls and those high fortifications?" Gilbert said: "You are talking nonsense; you will never take it as long as you live."]

Or again, from a rather earlier poem in the Cycle de Guillaume d'Orange, the *Charroi de Nîme*[46]:

> "Done moi, roi, Nauseüre la grant   494
> Et avec Nymes et le fort mandement, [...]"

["Give me, King, great Nauseüre, and with it Nîmes and its strong fortification ... "]

says Guillaume to King Louis, who is unable to give him a fief at home. Significantly, at the beginning of the next *laisse*, a *laisse parallèle* in which similar material is used to echo the lines just quoted, Nîmes

---

[45] *Prise d'Orange*, ed. C. Régnier, *editio major* (Paris, 1965); our reading is closely supported by redaction *D*, ll. 1435–41. The *editio minor*, in all its editions, has the *AB* text. Régnier's glossary supports my interpretation of the meaning of the word. However, also see Adolf Tobler and Erhard Lommatzsch, *Tobler-Lommatzsch altfranzosisches Worterbuch* (Wiesbaden and Berlin, 1915–1952).

[46] *Le Charroi de Nîmes*, ed. Duncan McMillan, 2nd rev. ed. (Paris, 1978), ll. 494–5. This poem dates from ca. 1150.

is qualified (ll. 501–2) "o les granz tors aguës" ["with its great pointed-roofed towers"]; *mandement* is thus defined in terms of strong towers, confirming the interpretation given above, and it is in general the case, as one might expect, that towers are very much part of the semantic field in which walls figure.

Both walls and towers are ritually high, thick, strong, even impregnable, crenellated, protected by earthworks, the sea, rivers and/or ditches, by-passed by tunnels (in some cases), ancient, made by Old Testament figures, pagans or Saracens, *listé* (banded), of many colors and materials[47]

One of the most striking features of the description of city and castle walls, not only in epic, is the emphasis on the rich materials of which they are made and the sometimes rather improbable colour schemes adopted. There may well be influence in some, especially non-epic, cases from learned sources, particularly the description of the walls of the New Jerusalem in Revelation XXI, 10–21, which, in another art form, inspired the famous chandelier in the cathedral at Aachen. Such imitation is obvious in the description of the walls of Paradise in the *Voyage of Saint Brendan*, which dates from the first quarter of the twelfth century. This is, of course, no city wall as such, but several of the motifs common in description of such earthly defenses are almost paradigmatically seen here, some *a contrario*, so that the passage is worth quoting; the motifs which seem paradigmatic are highlighted in boldface type in the translation[48]:

Tut en primers uns murs lur pert	1669
Desque as nües qui halcez ert:	
N'i out chernel ne aleür	
Ne bretache ne nule tur.	1672
Nuls d'els ne set en feid veire	
Quel il seit faiz de materie,	
Mais blancs esteit sur tutes neifs:	
Faitres fud li suverains reis.	1676
Tuz ert entrins, sanz antaile,	
Unc al faire n'out travaile,	
Mais les gemmes funt granz lüurs	
Dum purplantez esteit li murs.	1680
As gutes d'or grisolites	

---

[47] They obviously have main gates, portcullises, and posterns too, but these have not been at the forefront of my attention on this occasion; I dealt with them at some length in my article "The Castle in Some Works of Medieval French Literature," 15–22.

[48] Benedeit, *The Anglo-Norman Voyage of Saint Brendan*, eds. Ian Short and Brian Merrilees (Manchester, 1979), ll. 1669–1700.

Mult i aveit d'isselites;
Li murs flammet, tut abrase,
De topaze, grisopase,   1684
De jargunce, calcedoine,
D'esmaragde et sardoine;
Jaspes od les amestistes
Forment luisent par les listes;   1688
Li jacinctes clers i est il
Od le cristal e od le beril;
L'un a l'altre dunet clartét:
Chis asist fud mult enartét.   1692
Lüur grande s'entreportent
Des colurs chi si resortent.
Li munt sunt halt, de marbre dur,
U la mer bat mult luign del mur;   1696
E desur le munt marbrin
La muntaine est tute d'or fin;
E puis desus esteit li murs
De paraïs qui clot les flurs.   1700

[First they see a wall, rising up to the clouds, without **crenellations** or **wall-walk, brattices** or any sort of **tower**. None of them (the monks accompanying Brendan) knows, in faith, **of what material it is constructed**, but it was **whiter** than any snow: **its maker was** the Sovereign King. He made it without any labor, in one piece and **without any gap**. But the gems with which the wall was garnished shed a bright light: there were many choice chrysolites [ornamented] with drops of gold; the wall burns and blazes all over with topaz, with chrysoprase, with jacinth, with chalcedony, with emerald and sardonyx; jaspers and amethysts shine brilliantly at the edges; the bright jacinth is there, along with the crystal and the beryl, each reflecting back the light of the other: he who set them was a skilled artist. They send from one to the other the great light of their reflecting colors. Far from the wall, **the sea** laps against the high mountains of hard marble, and on this marble range of hills rises another mountain, all of pure gold; and **on top of this was the wall** of Paradise whose flowers it encloses.]

The great height of this wall is no doubt from Revelation (XXI, 12), but it also corresponds to one of the most obvious qualities required for the earthly walls we have to deal with, even if the adjective *haut* is not always as automatic in the vicinity of *mur* as one might expect (see below). The details of the fortifications it does *not* have tell us, by contraries, how city defenses are seen (as has already been evident in some of the quotations used above, and will be obvious from others to follow). Towers are very commonly associated, obviously, with walls and with the concept of height; crenellations too are frequently mentioned, brattices sometimes; wall-walks are perhaps more often assumed to exist than routinely evoked. The end of the quoted passage also shows a hint of another feature of man-made fortifications: Ideally, they are built on the living rock, and therefore immune from mining. The reference to the sea, which here lies some way from the wall, nevertheless resembles fairly common descriptions of fortifications that are lapped by the sea or wide rivers, and/or are surrounded by deep ditches, whether wet or dry. We shall need to return to these aspects, which are part of a general topos of impregnability, perhaps hinted at also in the *Brendan* poet's description of his wall as made "in one piece without any gap," but first we will consider the aspect that led me to evoke this idealized wall: the remarkable claims about its construction.

The material of which the wall is made and its color are common features of such descriptions. The jewels in the *Brendan* passage, which are clearly based on the account in Revelation, are not a feature of even idealized city walls in general, though there is a reference to beating down "the stone and the enamel" from the walls of the Holy City in the *Chanson de Jérusalem*.[49] Muriel A. Whitaker, discussing otherworld castles in her contribution to *The Medieval Castle*, draws attention to the crystal castle in the much later Middle English *Sir Orfeo* (ca. 1300): "Its hundred towers are wonderfully high, its buttresses pure gold, its vaulting elaborately enameled, its spacious apartments radiant with precious stones, its poorest pillar of burnished gold." Here, the idealization is both exterior and interior; Whitaker also refers to "the Gawain-poet's splendid Hautdesert, which is as real as the castles at Windsor and Carlisle and as ideal as those in Gothic illuminations, with their pink stone walls, azure pinnacles, and gilded gables."[50]

The snowy whiteness of the walls of Paradise as described in *Brendan* has decidedly more analogues among humanly built walls, as they are depicted in works of the imagination, whether visual or narrative. One thinks of the idealised castles in the *Très Riches Heures* and elsewhere, and castles were of course sometimes whitewashed, as was the case, for example, with Guildford Castle in Surrey in 1251,[51] Conway

---

[49] *Chanson de Jérusalem*, ed. N.R. Thorp, in *The Old French Crusade Cycle*, Vol. 6 (Tuscaloosa and London, 1992), l. 3244: "Por abatre des murs et le piere et l'esmal;" it may be significant that the *laisse*, in *-al*, earlier describes the Temple as being made with enamel, l. 3231 (cf. l. 3274, etc.).

[50] Muriel A. Whitaker, "Otherworld Castles in Middle English Arthurian Romance," in *The Medieval Castle*, 27–45, esp. 27.

[51] See *The History of the King's Works*, gen. ed. H.M. Colvin, Vol. 2, *The Middle Ages* (London, 1963), 658.

Castle in Wales, and London's White Tower.[52] This evidence, though, is mid-thirteenth century at the earliest.[53]

Literary parallels to our supernatural paradigm may be found, for example, in *Aymeri de Narbonne*[54]:

> Voient la terre de la crestienté;   3619
> De Terrasconne, le bon pais loé,
> Li mur blanchoient comme flor en esté.
> De sa cité [Narbonne] voit les murs blanchoier [. . .]   3821

[3619 They come in sight of Christian land; the walls of Tarragona, that good renowned land, shine white like flowers in summer. 3821 He sees the walls of his city shining white.]

Color cannot, of course, be altogether dissociated from construction materials. Marble walls, which must represent an idealization of the normal ashlar, and which imply whiteness, are common, indeed become a cliché. In *La Chevalerie d'Ogier de Danemarche*,[55] Charlemagne bargains with an "engineer," Malrin, for the construction of siege engines to destroy Castelfort, in which Ogier has taken refuge; he promises Malrin enormous wealth:

> Se il li rent cel fort castel marbrin.   6674
> Li engignieres maintenant respondi:
> "Ja n'en arai [qi] valle un angevin
> Dusqu'a la tor qi est de marbre bis
> Qui plus est blance que ne soit un hermin,
> Verrés cha jus de la roche caÿr, [. . .]"

[if he delivers to him that strong marble castle. The engineer replies immediately: "I will not take an Anjou penny's worth until you see that tower of

---

[52] A point already made in my article "The Castle in Some Works of Medieval French Literature," esp. 6. There will inevitably be overlap between that essay and the present one. See *The History of the King's Works*, 2:714, for an order of 1240 to whitewash the White Tower inside and out.

[53] On the *Très Riches Heures* and similar illustrations as evidence, see A. Dean McKenzie, "French Medieval Castles in Gothic Manuscript Painting," in *The Medieval Castle*, 199–214. The author stresses the accuracy, as measured by surviving evidence, of most of these miniatures from the fourteenth century onwards; earlier illustrations tend, however, to be more schematic. R. Allen Brown, in *Castles. A History and Guide*, ed. Brown (Poole and Dorset, 1980), 16, refers also to whitewashed castles at Whitecastle, Monmouthshire, and La Tour Blanche, Philippe-Auguste's fortress at Issoudun (Indre).

[54] Ed. cit., ll. 3619–21, 3821. See also l. 3099, where the same verb describes the tower of Narbonne. For another, non-epic example, see Chrétien's *Yvain*, ed. cit., ll. 4870–1.

[55] Ed. cit., ll. 6661–79; I have added in square brackets an essential correction (though other readings might also be corrected) from the critical edition prepared, under my direction, by Dr. Judith Belam (as yet unpublished Ph.D. diss. of the University of Reading, 1994).

dark marble, which is whiter than an ermine, tumble down here from that rock . . ."]

The clichéd nature of the motif is accentuated here by the adjective *bis*, which means "grey-brown" or simply "dark." It is used merely for the rhyme, and the poet has not noticed that it contradicts the rest of the passage which, like those quoted earlier, stresses the whiteness of the walls and tower to the extent of using a fairly hackneyed simile comparing them with the winter coat of the stoat, ermine. Many other perhaps less striking examples could be found.[56] A variant on it appears to be *la chaux*, lime, or in the context of castle and wall construction, presumably limestone.[57] Some authors have their own favorite material; thus limestone is repeatedly found, usually at the rhyme, in the description of walls (and other constructions) in *Girart de Roussillon*:

> Asejaz Vaucolor sendemanes;   3749
> Mar i remanra tor ne mur cauces.

[Besiege Vaucouleurs without delay; see that no tower or wall made of limestone remains.]

> Dedinz iste clausure de mur chaucin, [. . .][58]   8841

[(prisoners are asked to give parole, promising if no agreement is reached, to return to custody) within this curtain of limestone walls.]

The same material is mentioned also, if *a contrario*, in *Anseïs de Cartage*:

> Esturges voient, qui siet en un vaucel;   4472
> li murs n'est pas de cauch ne de quarel,
> ains est de terre, dont haut sont li crestel
> et les tours hautes du plus maistre castel.

[They see Astorga, which lies in a valley; the wall is not of limestone or ashlar, but of earth [i.e., earthworks],[59] the crenellations of which are high, and high the towers of the main castle.]

---

[56] E.g., *Girart de Vienne*, ed. cit., l. 344; *Renaut de Montauban*, ed. Jacques Thomas (Genève, 1989), ll. 4306–36, esp. ll. 4313–25 (the whole of this passage compares interestingly in several respects with that from the *Voyage of Saint Brendan*); see also ll. 364 (though here the marble is "green"and "banded"), 12001; *La Prise d'Orange*, ed. C. Régnier (Paris, 1970), ll. 288, 357, 1738; *Anseïs de Cartage*, ed. cit., ll. 450; *La Chanson de Jérusalem*, ed. cit., ll. 1007 (*marbre bis*), 1496 (*marbre . . . piere polie*), 2106 (*marbre cler*).

[57] On its treatment and use, see J.-F. Finó, *Forteresses de la France médiévale* (Paris, 1967), 128.

[58] Cf. also ll. 1015, 7199; also *La Chevalerie Ogier*, ed. cit., l. 6740.

[59] For a combination of walls and earthworks, see also *La Chevalerie Ogier*, ed. cit., l. 8127.

The same poem has another term for the construction material of walls: *arainne*. This, derived from Latin *arena*, represents sandstone, and it is not uncommon in *chansons de geste* in this context, e.g., from *Anseïs de Cartage*:

> cil a l'assaut cel jor bien maintenu   2805
> As murs d'arainne ont paien assalu;
>
> Or sont paien devant Katesoris,   7140
> le castel ont de l'une part assis,
> souvent assalent as murs d'arainne bis;

[2805 He has kept the assault going hard all that day. They have attacked the pagans on the sandstone walls; 7140 Now the pagans are before Katesoris and have besieged the castle from one direction, often attacking the walls of dark sandstone.]

The use of the adjective *bis* in the second quotation suggests that this material is, rightly, seen as not giving the brilliance provided by the marble and limestone materials mentioned earlier; the use of the word does not go against the grain of the rest of the text, as it does in the *Ogier* passage above. The same combination is to be found at least once in *Renaut de Montauban*, in reference to the palace of Dordone at ll. 2534-5: "Les murs d'araine bis."[60]

These examples by no means exhaust the variations on the color of walls in texts examined for this essay. In Marie de France's *Guigemar*, ll. 221-2, a secondary castle wall below the keep, enclosing a pleasure garden in which the heroine is imprisoned, has a thick, high wall in "green marble," like that of the fortifications of Aigremont at l. 364 of *Renaut de Montauban* (referred to in a note above and quoted below). In *Anseïs de Cartage*, in which we have already seen walls of marble and of dark sandstone, the more improbable color of bright red (*vermeil*) is alleged for the walls of two different Saracen towns, the second of which is the mythical Luiserne,[61] to whose Jericho-like end we shall return.

> Karles li rois a Connimbres assise,   10177
> qui fu fremee desor cele falise;
> li mur en sont vermeil comme cerise,

---

[60] For further examples of this material, see, e.g., *Renaut de Montauban*, ed. cit., l. 3535; *Li Romans de Claris et Laris*, ed. J. Alton (Tübingen, 1884), ll. 2987-9; *Blancandin et Orgueilleuse d'Amour*, ed. H. Michelant (Paris, 1867), l. 930; Lambert li Tors and Alexandre de Bernay, *Li Romans d'Alixandre*, ed. H. Michelant (Stüttgart, 1846), 9, 35.

[61] The same color is applied to Luiserne by the poet of *Gui de Bourgogne*, eds. F. Guessard and H. Michelant (Paris, 1859), 130.

> n'i a quarrel qui a ciment ne gise.
> Ne crient assaut une pelice grise, [. . .]
>
> voient Luisernes, dont li mur sont plenier 10420
> et plus vermeil que carbon de brasier.

[10177 Charles the King has besieged Coimbra, which was constructed on that cliff; its walls are bright red like a cherry and there is no block of ashlar which is not laid on cement. It does not fear assault the value of a grey tunic . . . 10420 they see Luisernes, whose walls are vast and brighter red than coal on a brazier.]

This flight of fancy recalls another description of a town with elements of fantasy in the way in which the author presents it: I refer to Tintagel in the *Folie Tristan d'Oxford*[62] (late twelfth century), one of the two short verse stories attached to the Tristan legend in which the eponymous hero succeeds in seeing his beloved Iseut by disguising himself as a madman. It is the author, not the madman, who speaks, a few lines (132–9) after the passage concerned, of the enchanted nature of the castle, which disappears twice a year, and who here describes the colors of the stone in terms which are as fancifully idealized as those evoked immediately above and in the lines which follow:

> Tintagel esteit un chastel 99
> Ki mult par ert fort e bel.
> Ne cremeit asalt ne engin
> . . . .
> . . . . .ki vaile
> Sur la mer en Cornuaile
> La tur querree fort e grant.
> Jadis la fermerent jëant.
> De marbre sunt tut li quarel,
> Asis e junt mult ben e bel.
> Eschekerez esteit le mur
> Si cum de sinopre e d'azur.[63]

[Tintagel was a castle [or: fortified town] which was very strong and fine indeed. It feared neither assault nor siege engine [one line and a half are missing] on the sea in Cornwall. The tower was square, strong and large; long ago, the giants fortified it. The facing stones are all of marble, placed and

---

[62] *La Folie Tristan d'Oxford*, ed. Ernest Hoepffner (Paris, 1938).
[63] I examined this description in "The Castle in Some Works of Medieval French Literature," 5–6, but for the sake of completeness quote it here once more. In passing, the use of the "impregnability topos" at ll. 100–1 may be noted. We shall return to this later.

jointed well and beautifully. The wall was squared like a chessboard as though in red and blue.]

A fine and probably influential example of this kind of decoration is in the *Roman d'Eneas* [64] (ca. 1160) in a passage which has little contact with the corresponding moment in the *Aeneid*, and which describes a city whose walls, highly colored, are only one aspect of the total defenses. It is worth quoting in full, but, given its length, I will give here only a translation, with key Old French expressions in brackets:

Dido's city was called Carthage, built upon the shore in Libya. The sea beats against it on one side – it will not be attacked from there – while on the other are the fishponds and the marshes wide and even and great ditches with barbicans made in the Libyan manner, and trenches, palisades, walls, barriers, a drawbridge. Before one gets into Carthage, there is many a twist and turn. In a bend upstream, towards the shore, stands a great mound of living rock [420 *roche naïve*]; on it the walls are founded. The stone blocks are of dark marble, white and blue and vermilion [422 *Li carrel sont de marbre bis,*[65]*/de blanc et d'inde et de vermoil*]; with great skill and cunning they are placed very regularly; all are of marble and adamant. The walls are built with columns, with pillars and with geometrical designs, with hinds, birds, and flowers; along with the marble in a hundred colors, the walls are painted outside without vermilion or azure [430 *o le marbre de cent colors/sont painturé defors li mur,/sanz vermeillon et sanz azur*]. All around three rows of magnets had been made from an extremely hard stone; the magnet is of such a nature that no armed man might approach without the stone attracting him to itself: men in hauberks might approach in any number; they would at once be stuck to the wall. The walls were thick and high [441 *espés et halt*] and they fear no attack; there were five hundred towers all around, apart from the principal keep; on the side facing towards the town, the walls were decorated with arcades, arches and canopies, and all were made with great blocks of marble.

This passage includes many fanciful features ensuring impregnability, but the (slightly self-contradictory) details about color are the main reason for quoting it here. Such highly colorful decoration as is

---

[64] *Roman d'Eneas*, ed. J.-J. Salverda de Grave, 2 vols. (Paris, 1925; rprt. 1964), Vol. 1, ll. 407–47. The passage, with its *accumulatio* of words representing defensive elements, has more than one point of resemblance with that from *Cligés* quoted above; as *Eneas* undoubtedly influenced Chrétien in his Ovidian love-analysis in *Cligés*, there is every reason to suspect other areas of imitation also. Similarly, E. Hoepffner argued, in his edition of the *Folie Tristan d'Oxford* (Paris, 1938), 17–18, that the *Eneas* passage, or one of those inspired by it (e.g., *Roman de Troie*, ed. Constans, Vol. 1, ll. 3009 ff and 3063 ff, which constitute truly brilliant and original developments), may well have served as the model for the details of Tintagel in the *Folie* just quoted.

[65] Cf. the same clichéd expression in *La Chevalerie Ogier*, quoted above. I have coined the name "epic automatism" for this kind of unthinking use of words, where rhyme and meter take precedence over sense.

claimed in several of these quotations is not, to my knowledge, paralleled in reality, though the artistic inspiration may not be dissimilar from that which gives Guillaume's palace in Caen, as represented in the Bayeux Tapestry, alternate patches of black and buff on squares of white "stone."[66] I assume that such examples are at the extreme end of a scale of idealization which begins in dazzling white marble; few actual castles or town walls will have corresponded even to the brilliant whiteness claimed for this material, though obviously some sorts of stone are lighter in color than others. The walls of, for example, Chinon or Stupor Mundi's Castel del Monte are perhaps sufficiently smooth and light in tone to come near the description at certain times of the day. It is true also that patterned walls as such are not uncommon: One thinks (apart from very early buildings like the Torhalle in Lorsch) of the fortifications of Edwardian castles in Wales such as Caernarvon or Beaumaris, of those of Fougères (Fig. 17.5) and Angers, or the section of barred ashlar remaining on the Grosse Tour at Château Gaillard (Fig. 17.3), and Angers, or again of the striking banding of the tower wall of Trévoux (Ain), near Lyon (Fig. 17.6). The banded walls at Caernarvon, together with their polygonal towers, are considered by Michael Prestwich to represent "a conscious echo of the defences of the imperial city of Constantinople," as an affirmation of an old Welsh legend placing Constantine's birth in the town.[67]

All these real patterns, of course, are not in primary colors, but in differing tones of gray or brown. This would appear to be the meaning, in the context of castle walls, of the common adjective *listé*, which can mean "bordered" or "banded" in relation to masonry, but also to rooms, marble objects, shields, etc. The big dictionaries give numerous examples; *Anseïs de Cartage* supplies a typical one:

> Dïent François: "Or i soient maufé!   10172
> Ja tant com vive ne serons reposé;
> li jouene enfant seront ançois barbé
> que pris aions les murs qui sont listé!"

[The French say: "Now may the devils be in it! We will never be at rest while he [Charlemagne] is alive; the young children will be bearded before we have captured these walls which are banded."]

The same word is applied to the walls of the palace within the town of Vienne in *Girart de Vienne*, ll. 2441, 6247, and I was probably wrong,

---

[66] Cf. A. Dean McKenzie, "French Medieval Castles in Gothic Manuscript Painting," in *The Medieval Castle*, 199–214, esp. 199.

[67] In Brown, ed., *Castles. A History and Guide*, 53–4.

Figure 17.5. Fougères. Photo: van Emden.

Figure 17.6. Trévoux. Photo: van Emden.

in my glossary of that text,[68] to suggest that the adjective implies a mottling of the marble: It is more likely to be, as in the other real and fictional examples referred to, an effect of banding obtained by using contrasting shades of stone. The word is used of the marble walls of the Tower of David, the citadel lying halfway along the western wall of Jerusalem, in the *Chanson de Jérusalem*, l. 3842. The same poem describes the Holy City walls as constructed of porphyry on at least two occasions (ll. 2285, 3108), a reddish-purple rock that is not one of the precious stones associated with the New Jerusalem in Revelation XXI, but an unusual, colorful choice, perhaps motivated by the rhyme.

It may well be, on the other hand, that the more multicolored examples may partake of the eleventh- and twelfth-century love of improbable color sometimes expressed in representations of other objects, such as horses, which are seen in many different shades in the Bayeux Tapestry (I have already alluded to Guillaume's castle at Caen), and in the thirteenth-century Norwegian Baldishol Tapestry. Turpin's famous horse in *La Chanson de Roland* (ll. 1490–6) is moderate in comparison, having only a white tail, a yellow mane, and a tawny head, but there are other, more gaudy examples.[69]

If we continue to take the *Brendan* passage as a partial paradigm, we note the ascription of the making of the wall to God. The usual analogue to this in more secular literature is the claim that the castle or city wall is very ancient, and ascribed to antique or pagan makers. We may return here, in passing, to the claim that the walls of Tintagel in the *Folie Tristan d'Oxford* had been fortified "long ago" by "giants," another variant on the same motif. This element of description is no doubt another manifestation of epic idealization, at least where the earlier texts are concerned, for in fact stone fortifications for castles, as distinct from Gallo-Roman enceintes round some towns, were a relatively recent phenomenon in the early twelfth century. It is well known that the castles thrown up by the Normans during and after the Conquest were at first made of wood, and that Lambert d'Ardres describes a very complex wooden structure, including three stories and a chapel, made for Arnould, lord of Ardres, by one Lodewick as

---

[68] Ed. cit., 389.

[69] See, e.g., Enide's parti-colored palfrey, and the vivid *berbioletes*, in Chrétien de Troyes's *Erec et Enide*, ed. M. Roques (Paris, 1978), ll. 5268–81 and 6732–41, respectively. Cf. Glyn S. Burgess and John L. Curry, " 'Si ont berbïoletes non' (*Erec et Enide*, l. 6739)," *French Studies* 43 (1989): 129–39: the *berbioletes* have somewhat different colors in the manuscript used by Foerster and referred to in this article, but are certainly more gaudy even than the douc langour, with which a tentative identification is suggested. Burgess remarks appositely that "Chrétien shares his contemporaries' love of colour."

late as 1120,[70] even if Fulk Nerra's Langeais and William's Caen pre-date it in stone by 130 and 70 years respectively.[71]

Authors must surely have been aware of the relative youth of the stone castle fortification when they idealized their fortified towns and castles by ascribing their building, typically, to "the Saracens," or even to Cain and Abel or other Old Testament figures, though no doubt such claims were inspired to some extent by the existence of Gallo-Roman town walls. I have already referred to such a claim in the *Chevalerie Ogier*, ll. 6632–46. Here the rock on which Castel Fort is built is said to be "du tans Abel" (from the time of Abel – a strange conception of geological time, but one consonant with the belief that the world was created about 4000 B.C.), and the actual builders are Cain and the sons of Israel. At l. 6612, the constructors are the sadly celebrated sons of Eve themselves, the younger of whom is also cred-ited by the *Chanson de Jérusalem* with being around, at least, at the building of a tower that is part of the walls of Jerusalem itself:

> Lors vint ens en le tor qui fu del tans Abel, [...]   2068

[Then he came into the tower which dated from the time of Abel ...]

However, the same poem usually ascribes the building of these fortifications to the Saracens:

> [...]Vés ci Jerusalem: molt i a grans defois   1240
> Des hautes tors de piere, des murs sarasinois.
> Nus assaus sans engien n'i valt pas une nois! [...]
> Par engien vaurais prendre ces murs sarrasinois. [...]"   1247

[1240 "See Jerusalem here before you: there is very great defense of the high stone towers and Saracen walls. Any attack without siege engines is not worth a walnut ... 1247 I intend to take these Saracen walls with engines ..."]

Given the crusading context, there is of course no necessary sugges-tion that the fortifications are old because of their Saracen origin: One

---

[70] See Finó, *Forteresses*, 110–11, and, for more detail, Robert Higham and Philip Barker, *Timber Castles* (London, 1992), esp. 115–17; for Langeais, see Bernard S. Bachrach in *The Medieval Castle*, 46–62.

[71] The recently excavated Doué-la-Fontaine is of course older still, having become what may properly be called a castle in its second, mid-tenth-century phase. But at the time our authors were writing, it had already disappeared under a motte crowned by another short-lived castle, and would hardly, therefore have entered into the thinking of the poets. On this castle, see R. Allen Brown, *Castles from the Air* (Cambridge, 1989), 32–3, and Michel de Boüard, "De l'aula au donjon: les fouilles de la motte de la Chapelle à Doué-la-Fontaine (Xe-XIe siècle)," *Archéologie Médiévale* 3–4 (1973–4): 5–110.

might expect the defenses to be of recent construction. Nevertheless, and with due allowance for the formulaic style of our poems, the allusion to Saracen walls seems often to imply antiquity also, and later in the *Jérusalem*, as well as in the lines referring to Old Testament figures quoted above, the fortifications of the Holy City are stated to be of venerable age, e.g., the following, which refer to the Tower of David, the citadel halfway along the western wall:

> Isnelement devale de la grant tor antie.   2598

> Li rois de Jursalam fu en la tor antie, [. . .]   3123

[2598 He comes quickly down from the great ancient tower. 3123 The King of Jerusalem was in the ancient tower.]

Certainly, Bertrand de Bar-sur-Aube closely connects the Saracen origin of the walls of Vienne with their great age. Naimon advises Charlemagne:

> "[. . .] cuidiez vos prendre par force la cité   4597
> et les forz murs, qui haut sont crenelez,
> et les fors tors, qui sont d'antequité,
> que paien firent par lor grant poosté? [. . .]"

> "[. . .] Hauz est li murs, que fist gent paiennie.   4614
> Par cele foi que doi seinte Marie,
> devant .VII. anz ne la prendrïez mie.
> Mendez en France et secors et aïe,
> engingneors qui sachent de mestrie;
> si abatront les murs d'ancesorie."

[4597 ". . . do you expect to capture the city by force and its strong walls with their high crenellations, and its strong towers, which have stood from ancient times, which the pagans built with their great power? . . . 4614 " . . . High is the wall made by the pagan people. By the faith I owe holy Mary, you would not be able to take it before seven years were out. Send for help from France, engineers skilled in their art, and they will bring down the ancient walls."]

The great age of the fortifications of Vienne is also brought out at ll. 3667, 4629, 4701, and the Saracen connection again at l. 6094.

Interestingly, in view of the contention of some scholars, myself included, that *Aymeri de Narbonne* is also by Bertrand de Bar-sur-Aube,[72] the connection between the age of fortifications and Saracen

---

[72] See *Girart de Vienne*, ed. cit., xxxv–xxxvii; for a contrary view, see W.W. Kibler, "Bertrand de Bar-sur-Aube, Author of *Aymeri de Narbonne*?" *Speculum* 47 (1973): 277–92.

builders is not explicitly made in that poem: the defenses of Narbonne are credited to *Sarrazin* and *paien* respectively at ll. 160–3, 171–4, and *paien* are also said to have repaired the walls and ditches at ll. 295–8; the city is described as *entie* (ancient) at ll. 1090, 1109 (at the rhyme), so that there is a logical link, but given the formulaic style and the distance between the references, one cannot say that the link is necessarily deliberate.

Girart de Vienne and *Aymeri de Narbonne* do, however, share a feature found also in other *chansons de geste* such as *La Prise d'Orange, Renaut de Montauban, La Chevalerie Ogier*, and the satirical non-epic *Roman de Renart*: a subterranean passage or *croute*,[73] described as *antie* in *Aymeri*, l. 3469, and often used, as it is there, by Saracens. Such features, which certainly had equivalents in real fortifications, such as those of Dover Castle, are generally exploited for escapes, infiltration, replenishment of food supplies, and surprise attacks during the sieges that are such a large part of the literary function of city and castle walls. They are often held back narratively by the author, who informs the hearer or reader of their existence only at the point at which they are required.

To return to our paradigm of fortification description from the *Brendan*, we have not yet specifically considered height as a feature, though a number of quotations made in other contexts include the concept. The absence of an exhaustive corpus of Old French literature in a machine-readable form prevents one from making a calculation of the percentage of references to *mur*, etc., accompanied by the adjective *haut*, as in the examples from *Girart de Vienne* quoted earlier (ll. 4598, 4614). One might expect it to be appreciable, especially in the formulaic style of the epic. Yet in *Girart*, the adjective accompanies the noun in seven out of twenty-five occurrences of the latter; in *Aymeri*, in only three out of twenty-five; in *Anseïs*, only one out of forty. What is striking is that *haut* is closely associated with *mandement* in most of the examples I have quoted here or seen in the Old French dictionaries. This is a very small sample. More work on the formulaic contexts of our key words would no doubt be rewarding. For the moment, the concordances required for such work are not available. It remains true, and natural, that height is mentioned in many of our contexts, if not

---

[73] For the references, and the literary uses made of this type of tunnel, also called *sosterrain* or *bove*, see my article "The Castle in Some Works of Medieval French Literature," 18–22. It is interesting to note that the long tunnels which lie under modern Arras, and from which the stone of the city was extracted in the Middle Ages, are still called *boves* today; military use was made of them during the First World War, both for sheltering and moving troops.

always in the immediate vicinity of the word *mur*.[74] The thickness of fortifications is also a motif that has occurred several times in the quotations used so far.

A final paradigmatic feature hinted at in the *Brendan* passage, with its wall of Paradise supported by a mountain of pure gold, itself arising from a marble range[75] of hills, is the idealized setting of a wall on living rock, which prevents mining. This feature has been picked out so far only at l. 420 of the *Eneas* quotation, with its reference to the building of Carthage on the *roche naïve*, preceded by the references to the water surrounding the city[76] (note again the presence of the sea, though it is not directly in contact with the wall of Paradise, in the *Brendan* quotation, l. 1696). Such features are again common parts, along with wet and dry ditches, of the description of idealized fortifications that are deemed impregnable except to treachery or starvation. This, which may be described as the "impregnability topos," is part of the wider paradigm we are exploring; Paradise has no direct use for it, yet seems, as I have suggested, to hint at one element of it.[77]

A significant passage from *La Chevalerie Ogier* (ll. 6618–26),[78] stressing the simultaneous presence of living rock as a foundation and of river and marsh water on all sides, is introduced by the impregnability topos:

> Mais je croi ben q'il a folle pensee: 6614
> Lonc tans i puet faire la demoree,

[74] The great height of fortifications is a recurrent theme in Le Goff, *The Medieval Imagination*. For a non-epic example, see also Chrétien's *Yvain*, ed. cit., ll. 3766–72.

[75] This is the interpretation by Ian Short of the singular of l. 1697 in the context of ll. 1695–6 of the *Brendan* passage in the French version, with translation, of his and B. Merrilees's edition already quoted. See Benedeit, *Le Voyage de Saint Brandan*, text and trans. Ian Short; intro. and notes Brian Merrilees (Paris, 1984), 123. I am naturally indebted to Short's translation in making my English version above.

[76] On this combination and the military benefits for cities that deliberately made use of the military potential of their sites, see Philippe Contamine, *War in the Middle Ages*, trans. Michael Jones (Oxford, 1984), 106–7; also Brown, *English Castles*, 182.

[77] Cf. another example in *Anseïs*, ll. 10176–80. Claims of impregnability are sometimes made without explicit reference to foundations on rock or the presence of water, and are indeed explained at times by the hardness of the stone of which the wall is made, e.g., *Jérusalem*, ll. 2063–5, 3624–5. For some related examples from non-epic texts, see Chrétien's *Erec et Enide*, ed. cit., ll. 3657–78, and *Perceval ou le Conte du Graal*, ed. William Roach, 2nd ed. (Genève and Paris, 1971), ll. 1326–50, 5754–7, 6659–71.

[78] This passage is quoted and discussed in van Emden, "The Castle in Some Works of Medieval French Literature," 14–15. It is perhaps worth quoting the translation given there for convenience: "Castel Fort is built on a gorge, on a rock from ancient times. The marshland is very large all around it which quakes [?] there for the distance a laburnum bow can shoot. Neither sergeant nor vavasor, mule nor packhorse, steed nor war horse could enter it and ever get out of the mire. On the other side flows a rapid stream, black and hideous, which washes there against the tower."

Ne le prendroit ne rois ne emperere
Se la gent n'est per dedens afamee.

[But I believe that he (Charlemagne) is thinking foolishly: he may stay there a long time, for neither king nor emperor would be able to take it unless the people inside it are starved out.]

The impregnability topos is repeated at the end of the next stanza, which contains the passage alluded to, and the themes of water and living rock, together with that of the great age of the site referred to earlier, are interwoven between lines 6608 and 6646. An earlier, unnamed castle, which briefly offers shelter to the Dane, has similar features (ll. 5986ff). At l. 5988, it is specified that it stands alone, not as part of a town (which, by implying the opposite possibility, is relevant to our earlier discussion of definitions; Castel Fort, to which Ogier flees next, is both town and castle, as has been shown above); ll. 6041–6 have the details of water and rock, repeated at ll. 6089–92, with a modified impregnability topos from Naimon: "[. . .] Ja per assalt le Danois ne prendrés: [. . .]." The advice is given to fill the ditches and to attack the walls with ladders; in the event, the combination of siege engines and men at arms with picks leads to the collapse of part of the wall, so that it is seen that even water and rock are not a defense against attack on the walls unless the water is such as to prevent close approach (cf. the castles at Fougères in France [Fig. 17.6], or Caerphilly, Beaumaris, or Bodiam in Great Britain).[79]

Lines 6094–100 of *Girart de Vienne* similarly mix several of the by now familiar motifs: the height of walls made by the pagans, the presence of the Rhône to prevent attack (though the "living rock" motif is missing) with a description of the precision with which the ashlar is laid to arrive at the conclusion that Charles could be there for twenty-seven years before taking the town. One may, I think, accept this last as an understated version of the impregnability topos.

Similar stress on the value of rock as a foundation is to be found at several points in *Renaut de Montauban*, in the episode of the building of Montauban, ll. 4255–336, as well as in the earlier siege in Montessor, ll. 2407–10. Another excerpt from the same epic (ll. 357–65), referring to the castle of Beuve d'Aigremont (to which allusion has already been

---

[79] In the case of Bodiam, the appearance is more important than the substance, in the view of Charles Coulson, see his contribution: "Some Analysis of the Castle of Bodiam, East Sussex" in *Proceedings of the Medieval Knights Conference, Strawberry Hill, April, 1990* (1992). Cf. R. Allen Brown's comments on the primary purpose of preventing the enemy from coming to close quarters with the fortification in *English Castles*, 182.

made in passing), and one from the First Branch of the *Roman de Renart*[80] (both not far distant in time from 1200) have so many of our paradigmatic features that it is worth quoting them to sum up this part of my essay; as before, the parts of the paradigm are printed in boldface type in the translation:

> [. . .] il virent Aigremont sor le tertre monté,   357
> Qui estoit forz et dur, de vielle antequité:
> La tors en est molt haute et li fossé chevé,
> .ii.c. piez orrent bien par ou il sont mains lé;
> Il n'a arbalestier deci a Duresté
> Qui tresist pas si haut por Paris la cité
> Com la tors estoit haute, de vielle antequité,
> Et par desus estoit de vert marbre listé;
> Elle ne crient assaut .i. denier moneé [. . .]

[. . . they saw Aspremont, **raised upon the hillock**, strong and hard, **of great antiquity** its **tower** is **very high** and the **ditches** are deep, a good 200 feet **wide** at their narrowest point; there is no crossbowman from here to Duresté who could shoot **so high** if he were offered the city of Paris, as the **ancient tower** was **high** and in its upper parts it was of **green, banded marble**; it **fears attack not one penny's worth**.]

> Messires Nobles l'enperiere   1679
> vint au chastel ou Renart ere
> et vit mout fort le plaissaïz,
> les torz, les murs, les roilleïz,
> les forteresces, les donjons,
> ausi haut ne traisist nus hons;   1684
> tout en viron son li fossé,
> parfont et haut et reparé;
> vit les torneles et les murs,
> forz et espés et hauz et durs;   1688
> vit les creniaz desus la mote
> par ou l'en entre en la croute;
> gardé sont et levé li pont
> et la chaaine contremont.   1692
> Li chastiaus sist en une roche. [. . .]
> Li assauz fu molt merveillos, [. . .]   1813
> Onques ne laissierent nul jor   1825
> que n'asaillisent a la tor,

---

[80] *Le Roman de Renart*, Première Branche, ed. M. Roques (Paris, 1967); I quoted this in "The Castle in Some Works of Medieval French Literature," 20–1, but its parodic, and *therefore* paradigmatic, nature makes it particularly illuminating.

> mes ne la porent enpirier
> dont el vausist mains un denier.

[1679 My lord the Emperor Noble came to the castle where Renart was and saw the exceedingly strong enclosure, the **towers**, the **walls**, the palisades, the fortresses and the keeps so **high** that no man might reach the top with an arrow; all around are the **ditches**, deep and with high sides and in good repair; he saw the turrets and the walls, **strong** and **thick** and **high** and **hard**; he saw the **crenellations** above the motte by which one enters the **tunnel** [or subterranean vault]; the bridges are under guard and raised and the chain is up. The castle was **built on a rock**. . . . 1813 The assault was terrible . . . 1825 They never failed any day to assail the tower, but **they were unable to damage it by a penny's worth**.]

All these elaborate systems of interlocking motifs are a function of the stress on defense against sieges, which are the stuff of so many literary texts, rather than any part of the social definition of what constitutes "the city." In reality they may have been less important than the offensive aspect of fortifications, at any rate where castles as distinct from cities are concerned.[81] In real life it was an incompetent baron, like Hugues du Puiset in 1111, who allowed himself to be caught in his castle by a besieging army.[82] The defensive literary emphasis could now, but for restrictions on space, be examined under a number of headings (e.g., hoardings and projectiles from defenders).[83] It must suffice here to suggest a few headings for possible future investigation.

The analysis of various works in the preparation of this essay suggests that the description of assaults on town and castle fortifications could usefully be studied to establish a system of siege motifs and topoi comparable to those examined here in relation to defenses, and which could be more systematically compared with the manuals on siege warfare in reality.[84] A particularly rich source might be the *Chanson de la Croisade Albigeoise*, an occitan chronicle in *chanson de geste* form by two contemporaries of the Crusade, both very committed

---

[81] I make the same point in more detail in "The Castle in Some Works of Medieval French Literature," 3; cf. Brown, ed., *Castles. A History and Guide*, 14, 62, 75–9.

[82] On Hugues and his depredations, the offensive threat of his castle, and Louis VI's attacks on Le Puiset, see Suger's *The Deeds of Louis the Fat*, trans. with intro. and notes Richard C. Cusimano and John Moorhead (Washington, DC, 1992), esp. ch. 19, 84–91.

[83] Much as I did in "The Castle in Some Works of Medieval French Literature," 8–17; such fictional accounts may profitably be compared with monographs such as R. Allen Brown's *English Castles*, ch. 7.

[84] Jim Bradbury, *The Medieval Siege*, provides much corroboration of details found in fictional texts. In the present context, the section on siege tactics, 78–88, is particularly informative.

observers hostile to the Cathars, the anonymous second writer being, however, equally opposed to the northern invaders.[85] The earlier, Guillaume de Tudèle, who wrote the first 130 *laisses* (epic stanzas), seems to me (to give one example) to describe assaults on city walls characteristically by beginning with the motif of filling up the ditches with cartloads of wood, earth, rocks (e.g., *laisses* 68, 74, 80) before the attack on the walls with picks, ladders, and siege engines. This technique, which is mentioned sporadically in certain, but definitely not most, *chansons de geste*,[86] is less evident in the work of the anonymous second poet, perhaps partly because he describes sieges that are less rapidly won (though indeed there are long sieges in the first part also, and defenders are starved into surrender in certain cases). Both authors go into enormous detail about the technology of sieges, introducing *chattes*, rams, and engines of different types, which do much damage to walls (e.g., *laisses* 92, 123, 162). There are also many of the motifs, such as the impregnability topos, which we have identified in works of pure fiction; certainly, this fiery poetic chronicle[87] would repay more detailed study than I have been able to give it in the context of the motifs used in the fiction of siege warfare. The same is particularly true, too, of the *Chanson de Jérusalem*, which also purports to be history rather than fiction (though it contains a great deal of the latter), and which deserves closer study for its military aspects.[88] I have also, with regret, had to leave aside the prose historians, particularly Villehardouin, as he is clearly influenced by epic.

Much could be said about mining, which was often employed in reality, though perhaps not quite as frequently in the poems. There is a detailed episode of successful mining of the walls of the Holy City in the *Jérusalem* (contrary, I think, to historical reality), ll. 4704–19, and there are other references in *Anseïs*, ll. 8800–1, 8976–7, 9269–75 (the last

---

[85] *Chanson de la Croisade albigeoise*, adapt. Henri Gougaud, intro. Michel Zink (Paris, 1989).

[86] Among those analyzed for this essay, I note it in *Anseïs de Cartage*, l. 3050, *Aymeri de Narbonne*, l. 1099, *La Chevalerie Ogier*, l. 6093–100; I would not claim to have made exhaustive searches, however.

[87] Strangely, this occitan chronicle contains a parallel to that on the *Walling of New Ross*: There is a passage in *laisse* 158 in which a wall is built between the town and the besieged citadel of Beaucaire (another example of the Arras pattern) and where there is a communal effort involving ladies and singing, as at Ross. Perhaps that strange poem owes more to the world of topoi than its naive and crude poetic technique would lead us to expect.

[88] One very curious feature, to which attention has been drawn by its recent editor, Dr. Nigel Thorp, is that the position of each Christian leader in relation to the different gates of Jerusalem during the siege is given in the same order as in historical reality, but each is moved anti-clockwise by one gate.

quite elaborate); the major Old French dictionaries give examples from five other epics.[89]

Sieges and their effect on walls may be looked at also from the point of view of the besiegers (where these are in the right, as opposed to the model of the epic of revolt, discussed earlier). The walls of Troy are something of a topos in their own right, and not just in the *Roman de Troie* and the *Roman d'Eneas*. There are references to Ilion in *Anseïs*, ll. 803, 1465–7, 3875–6, 6100 and *Girart de Vienne*, ll. 4949–55; the Moisan *Répertoire des noms propres* quotes some twenty *chansons de geste* that refer to Troy. Related to it is what one might perhaps call the "Jericho topos": towns whose impregnable walls fall at the prayer of a Christian leader, specifically Charlemagne. *Anseïs de Cartage* has a long reference to the celebrated fall of the walls of Luiserne, ll. 10420–82, but this is certainly not its first appearance. The story is found in the mid-twelfth-century Latin *Pseudo-Turpin Chronicle* as well as *Gui de Bourgogne* (early thirteenth century) which, unlike *Anseïs*, agrees with *Pseudo-Turpin* in saying that the fallen walls disappear under water.[90]

Space prevents me from looking at allegorical writing, which would also have been profitable: The *Roman de la Rose* is an obvious absentee, as is Christine de Pizan's *Livre de la Cité des Dames*, in which the City is arguably a metaphor for the whole work, and in which Part I, Chapters 8 and following, deal with the construction of the Wall. Here (unlike the New Ross example), it is the first thing to be undertaken (though, as at New Ross, work starts with the – highly allegorized – digging of the ditch).

These are just some of the avenues which might be explored much further than I have been able to do here, particularly in the direction of identifying literary topoi and comparing them with reality. This essay has in part sought to draw attention to the methodological and practical issues involved in researching the treatment of city and other defensive walls in medieval literature and in comparing it with historical reality, in as much as that can be established. Other contributions to this volume have been cited on specific points, and this essay will no doubt take on an extra dimension from the whole context in which it appears, for the military realities of the need for protection, and the methods used to achieve it, changed only gradually over space and time. It is really only the development of the cannon, as Professor Parker's essay shows, which renders walls obsolete.[91]

---

[89] *Beuve de Hantone, Aiol, La Chanson des Saisnes, Beuvon de Conmarchis, Gaydon.*

[90] On this legend, see J. Bédier, *Les Légendes épiques*, 4 vols., 3rd ed. (Paris, 1929), 3:152–66.

[91] See Chapter 13 of this volume. And it is worth noting that, even in the late twentieth

In its second major aim, that of identifying motifs and themes which contribute towards what one might call a taxonomy of the literary exploitation of walls in the French Middle Ages, the essay invites comparisons with other periods and civilisations, comparisons that the present volume encourages, especially in the area of decoration, which is a major part of the paradigm sketched out here. Many of the physical, concrete elements of the paradigm are, as we have seen, a reflection of reality, though the idea of the wall as constitutive of city status, with which we started, has not appeared on the evidence assembled here to be a dominant one. But we have seen also that literature usually idealizes in other directions: those of impregnability and decorative splendor, directions which certainly find counterparts in other contributions to this volume. To this extent, the findings of this essay draw strength from corroboration from other times and places; but it remains to consolidate these tentative results for Old French literature by more exhaustive searches, and this brings me back in conclusion to stressing, because it is methodologically important, the practical limitations of much existing published material. In the absence of truly comprehensive lexical databases of Old French texts, I expect to be sitting for many years, as Charlemagne so often does before the cities he besieges, waiting for that technological wall to come down.

century, Crusader castles such as Beaufort have been used as protection from aerial bombardment by combatants in the continuing hostilities in the Middle East.

CHAPTER 18

Siege law, siege ritual, and the symbolism of city walls in Renaissance Europe

SIMON PEPPER

THIS essay sets out to explore the law and ritual associated with Renaissance siege warfare, and to relate these manifestations of military culture to the symbolism that attached to city walls, gates, and urban fortresses.[1] Events are used here to provide a key to meaning. Underlying a wide-ranging account of actual and ritual combat is the proposition that, despite new artillery, a revolution in military architecture, and increasing tactical sophistication, the Renaissance art of "modern" war embodied survivals from the medieval chivalric tradition and civic heritage that continued to inform the conduct of sieges, as well as the ways in which society regarded fortifications. City walls and other types of fortification are conventionally treated as a highly functional building type, perhaps the most purely functional architecture of all. Certainly this has been true of the military architecture of the gunpowder era and its response to the challenge of artillery. In this essay the functionalist view is compensated by an examination of some of the deeper values associated with fortifications in the Renaissance, values which sometimes seemed opposed to those of the modernizers, but perhaps even more commonly coexisted with them in a complex web of ideas that is best approached by considering the actions and statements of those who risked their lives in the attack and defense of city walls.

---

[1] Much of the material from this essay is taken from an unpublished chapter of Simon Pepper, *Problems in Sixteenth Century Military Architecture: A Study of Fortifications and Siege Warfare with Special Reference to the Siege of Siena, 1552–1556* (Ph.D. diss., University of Essex, 1972), part of which has been published before under the title "The Meaning of the Renaissance Fortress," *Architectural Association Quarterly* 5 (1973): 22–7. I am most grateful to Professor Geoffrey Parker and Professor Sydney Anglo for suggested readings when this volume gave the opportunity to publish a more complete essay.

573

The tension that existed between military science and the protocols of Renaissance siege warfare is well illustrated by the plan to bombard the city of Siena in January 1555, in the final phases of the Italian Wars. After nine months of fruitless blockade, the imperial Spanish and Florentine forces besieging the French-held city determined to shoot their way into Siena. The plan involved the collection of a large number of big guns, which were to be assembled from all over an extensive theatre of operations and hauled into position under cover of darkness so that, at dawn, their concentrated fire could be brought to bear on a neglected stretch of Siena's walls that the Imperialists hoped to breach before secondary lines of retrenchments could be constructed by the defenders. Security was strict. Orders for the positioning of assault troops and guns were confined to a small circle of senior officers until less than forty-eight hours before the attack. Yet only a few hours before the movements were completed, the defenders were alerted to the imminence of the threat when an imperial herald delivered a formal summons to surrender.[2] The garrison was of course aware of the build-up of artillery. Even so, the last-minute summons confirmed the immediacy of the attack and threw away the element of surprise, a lapse which cannot be explained by any hopes that Siena would meekly surrender. A call for surrender, after all, would have been more compelling when delivered across an open breach. The presentation of the summons remains a perplexing episode, which smacks more of protocol than of military expediency.

Another problem from the same war concerns the treatment of Franco-Sienese prisoners taken while defending fortified places. In marked contrast to the generally proper treatment of captives, the defenders of fortified places taken by storm were normally hanged by the Imperialists, who reported their actions as "well deserved punishment," words that seem to imply that some offense had been committed.[3] The notion of offense implies the existence of rules, the force of which can be indicated by a well-documented case where they were said to have been violated.

At the end of August 1554, the Sienese fortress of Monterriggioni

---

[2] The text of the summons is published in Antonio di Montalvo, *Relazione della guerra di Siena, scritta l'anno 1557 in lingua spagnola da don Antonio di Montalvo, e tradotta in lingua italiana da don Garcia di Montalvo suo figlio,* eds. C. Riccomani and F. Grottanelli, documents edited by L. Banchi (Turin, 1863), Doc. XI, 236–38.

[3] For instance, Marignano's report of the capture of Torre di Vignano *"dove fu necessario piantare l'artigliaria e non v'era dentro piu che dieci persone fra villani et soldati, alli quali e necessario dar' il debito castigo che si arresero a mia discretione . . ."* Archivio di Stato, Firenze (hereafter A.S.F.), *Mediceo del Principalo,* Filza 1853, Bartolommeo Concino to Cosimo I; 3 May 1554.

was captured by the Imperialists. After a day of bombardment the fortress was surrendered, to the bitter disappointment of the Sienese, who immediately accused the castellan of treachery. There were grounds for suspicion. The officer commanding the fortress, Captain Giovannino Zeti, was a Florentine exile (a rebel against the emperor as well as the duke of Florence), and one of the key clauses in the surrender document restored him and his nephew to their Florentine properties and to the favor of the duke. Monterriggioni would not have been the first fortress to be "sold" for an indemnity against treason. However, the officer who represented the Imperialists at the negotiations reported a very proper resistance to dishonorable surrender, with Zeti holding out for terms that would have allowed the fortress to remain in Sienese hands for another two weeks and surrendered only if it remained unrelieved by a supporting force.[4] The Imperialists hoped to take the place without force, and after a day of bombardment, which had opened a small breach in the walls, still hoped to avoid the bloodshed of an assault.[5] While the besiegers penned their reports, Zeti inspected the damage and found that the cistern containing the drinking water had been ruined.[6] A council of Zeti's officers (including the Sienese civil commissioner) recommended negotiation for terms. Next day the fortress was handed over under conditions that included the restoration of goods and favours to Zeti and his nephew, safe conduct for others, and "honors of war" for the garrison. By the evening of the same day the affair had been condemned by the Sienese, and Zeti had been invited to appear for trial – an invitation that was not accepted.[7]

However, the Sienese denunciation had some effect, for in October 1554 a wall poster was published in Florence setting out Zeti's side of the story. The *Manifesto et dichiaratione fatta per il Capitano Giovannino Zeti sopra la causa di Monterrigioni* replies to rumor mongers who "*male informati o per altri passioni*" had prevented his employment by the Republic of Venice.[8] Men of honor, declared Zeti, cannot remain con-

---

[4] The text of the surrender, 29 August 1554, is in A.S.F. *Mediceo del Principato*, 1854, in the hand of Concino, secretary to the Imperial Council of War (effectively chief of staff to Marignano). The negotiations, 28 August 1554, are recorded in 1854.

[5] 28 August 1554. A.S.F. *Mediceo del Principato*, 1853.

[6] "*. . . che non solo non si poteva bere di detta acqua, ma odorarla.*" The words are from Zeti's *Manifesto*, the original of which is bound into A.S.F. *Carte Strozziane*, I, XCV, carta 307.

[7] Alessandro Sozzini, "Diario delle cose avvenute in Siena dal 20 luglio 1550 al 28 giugno 1555," in *Archivio storico italiano*, 2 (1842), 228.

[8] It is not possible to determine the distribution of this poster. Was it to be displayed all over Italy, or Tuscany, or merely throughout the camps? The Marignano-Cosimo filza (see footnote 3) contains another printed poster, originating in Milan, which was

tent with a good conscience but must demonstrate the truth to the whole world. This he did at considerable length and in great detail, the only obvious omission being any mention of his personal restoration. The keystone of Zeti's defense was the destruction of the well, and in this he was supported by the testimony of ten local citizens, the Sienese ex-commissioner, and the imperial commander, the marquis of Marignano. All confirmed on their "honor and faith" that at the time of the surrender there had been no sweet drinking water in the place.

Our interest in the Monteriggioni affair lies in the climate of opinion governing the defence of fortified places, rather than in the innocence or guilt of Captain Zeti. The existence as much as the content of the *Manifesto* is important. It speaks to the chivalric standards of conduct in war familiar to any reader of Cervantes, Monluc, or the Chevalier Bayard's Loyal Servant and is tangible evidence that this was no mere literary tradition. Rumors of misconduct were, it seems, sufficient to prevent the employment of an obscure officer by a distant state; and the imperial commander was prepared to throw the weight of his own sworn statement into the melting pot of public opinion on behalf of a recent imperial rebel. The general's intervention may of course have been designed to counter the value of the affair to Franco-Sienese propaganda, but this qualification serves to emphasize international acceptance of the rules of conduct. Certainly the author of the *Manifesto* took for granted such acceptance. Not once in a lengthy public statement does he find it necessary to define the rules.

In the post-Vietnam era the laws of war have excited interest amongst a wide scholarly community. Late-twentieth-century conflicts such as the Gulf War, Bosnia-Herzegovina, and Somalia – to say nothing of the ubiquitous *petit guerre* of internal security and antiterrorist operations – have focused international concern on the way wars have been and are actually fought, and how their inevitable violence affects combatants and (particularly) noncombatants. For our purposes, it is

clearly distributed over a wide area for it calls upon soldiers who served at a particular siege to collect money due to them from the Milan paymaster within twelve months. Evidently the soldiers had been deprived of a sack and were now to be paid a share of the reparations raised by the town. In a covering letter Marignano explains to Cosimo that this matter is a debt of honor, owed by him to his troops, and he asks that the poster be displayed publicly throughout Florentine territory. The only other document I have encountered which resembles the Zeti *Manifesto* is a lengthy letter of supplication addressed to Carlo Emanuele I of Savoy on behalf of the ex-governor of Vercelli who had been imprisoned for misconduct in the siege of 1617: see the "Relazione dell'assedio della Citta di Vercelli, fatto nell'annon 1617 dall'esercito di Spagna, scritta dal Cap. Antonio Berardo," ed. Carlo Promis, *Archivio storico italiano*, XIII (1847), 453–528.

jus in bello (the laws or customs for the conduct of war) rather than *jus ad bellum* (the right to wage "just war" with a Christian conscience) that matters.[9] The period covered by this essay spans the fifteenth and the first half of the sixteenth centuries and – crucially – demands another important distinction, which has been elegantly made by Maurice Keen, between a siege and a field engagement. A medieval field engagement was regarded as a trial by battle arbitrated by God. "To accept a challenge to battle," argues Keen, "was to accept the judgement of God; it was also to accept one's adversary as of approximately equal standing to oneself."[10] Robert Stacey explains the reluctance of soldiers to risk all in a pitched battle: "God was a just judge, and where battle could not be avoided He would render a just verdict. But it was best not to tempt Him to a hasty decision."[11] The siege, however, was the closest that medieval and Renaissance conflict came to total war. God played no official part in it.[12] The siege, in Keen's analysis, was a test of the sovereignty of the princes involved; an issue that was reflected very clearly in the protocol of summons and defiance that initiated formal siege operations, as well as the harsh penalties applied to a place taken by storm.

In a city taken by storm almost any licence was condoned by the law. Only churches and churchmen were technically secure, but even they were not often spared. Women could be raped, and men killed out of hand. All the goods of the inhabitants were regarded as forfeit. If lives were spared, it was only through the clemency of the victorious captain; and spoliation was systematic.[13]

History gives us many examples of sacks carried out by mutinous or ill-disciplined troops, and in the heat of action there was often little that officers could do to restrain soldiers who had fought their way through the carnage of the breach to rape and pillage in the captured town, killing anyone who got in the way. Keen points out, however,

---

[9] An excellent recent summary of the debate is contained in Michael Howard, George J. Andreopoulos, and Mark R. Shulman, eds., *The Laws of War: Constraints on Warfare in the Western World* (New Haven and London, 1994), which contains good selective bibliographies for different periods. For our purposes, Robert C. Stacey's chapter on "The Age of Chivalry," 27–39, and Geoffrey Parker's chapter on "Early Modern Europe," 40–58, are particularly valuable. Theodore Meron, *Henry's Wars and Shakespeare's Laws: Perspectives on the Laws of War in the Later Middle Ages* (Oxford, 1993): 101–4, is also useful.

[10] M.J. Keen, *The Laws of War in the Late Middle Ages* (London, 1965), 123.

[11] Stacey, "The Age of Chivalry," 35.

[12] Michael Waltzer, *Just and Unjust Wars. A Moral Argument with Historical Illustrations* (New York, 1977), 160: "Siege is the oldest form of total war."

[13] Keen, *Laws of War*, 121–2.

that the sack was by no means always committed in hot blood. He cites the capture of Luxembourg by the Burgundians in 1463, when the troops remained at their standards while Philip the Good entered the city to give thanks at the Church of Notre Dame. After Philip had prayed, the word was given and the town plundered. The cold-blooded callousness of this event indicates its theoretical justification.

The goods and indeed the lives of the inhabitants of a conquered town, were not regarded as mere lawful spoil; they were forfeit to the contumacious disregard of a prince's summons to surrender. . . . Hence the scientific pillaging of towns, and the careful division of their spoil "by the sentence" of the king or his lieutenant, for this sentence was not an act of war, but the sentence of justice.[14]

Geoffrey Parker, commenting on the late-sixteenth-century Spanish campaigns to suppress the Dutch rebellion, points out that public policy sometimes placed limits on the degree of violence tolerated when towns were taken in controlled conditions. The classic legal view still maintained that an exemplary sack could terrify other rebellious towns into surrender (thus saving further bloodshed), as well as lining the pockets of unpaid troops, and removing a source of future resistance. However, no less a figure than the duke of Alba, commanding the Spanish forces in the Netherlands, argued that leniency in victory would be justified when the captured town had been occupied by the enemy after a siege, or had held out until artillery had been emplaced against it, or had yielded to the Dutch rebels in the absence of Spanish support.[15] But these were official policy positions, which depended for their enforcement on tight discipline that modified the traditional customs of war. Siege law itself was unrelenting. Moreover, it placed the castellan or governor, as well as his garrison and any civil population, in a seemingly impossible position. Resistance was contumacious, surrender a particularly reprehensible form of treason deserving of death and, for the nobility, degradation.[16] In practice the dilemma was resolved by the general concept of a reasonable defense and, in particular cases, by a precise definition of the conditions under

[14] Keen, *Laws of War*, 122–3.
[15] Parker, "Early Modern Europe," 49.
[16] Michel de Montaigne, *The Complete Essays of Montaigne*, trans. Donald M. Frame (Stanford, California, 1968), bk. 1, ch. 16, 49.

In our fathers' time the seigneur de Franget, formerly lieutenant of Marshal de Chastillon's company, having been made governor of Fonterrabia by the Marshal de Chabannes in place of Monsieur de Lude, and having surrendered the place to the Spaniards, was condemned to be deprived of his nobility, and both he and his posterity were declared commoners, taxable, and unfit to bear arms; this rough sentence was executed at Lyons. Later all the noblemen who were in Guise when the Count of Nassau entered it suffered the same punishment, and still others since.

which a position was to be defended. Lack of food could justify surrender, but this was difficult to prove.[17] Lack of drinking water was
more critical, but when Captain Zeti pinned his defense on this point
he was careful to obtain a good number of independent witnesses. To
the attackers it was reasonable to defend a position until a "practicable
breach" had been created in the wall, but not beyond that point:
Northern European practice in the seventeenth and eighteenth centuries demanded that the garrison should sustain at least one general
assault.[18] Both put the defenders beyond the pale on a strict interpretation of the law, but to avoid casualties and expense besiegers would
often offer terms at these stages. It was not considered reasonable to
expect a mercenary castellan to defend a hopeless position to the
death, and contracts of appointment often specified the duration of a
defense, thus opening the door to negotiations. When the summons
was presented the castellan would reply in conciliatory terms, stressing the strength of his position and proposing that if, after so many
days, it had not been relieved, the place would surrender and the
garrison be permitted to depart.[19] The place would be taken "by appointment" and there would be no sack. At Monterriggioni Captain
Zeti proposed just such an arrangement.

Finally, it was considered neither reasonable nor desirable that a

---

[17] Monluc, the French commander in Siena during a savage blockade which caused
severe starvation in some quarters, was never completely convinced that the city was
empty of food, and the apparent availability of hoarded supplies during the final
days of the siege seems to have confirmed these suspicions. Sozzini, "Diario," passim.

[18] These rules are discussed in M. Carnot, *De la Défense des Places Fortes* (Paris, 1812), 7.
He quotes a letter of Louis XIV to his Governors, dated 6 April 1705, noting that

> *il a été enjoint à tous les gouverneurs de places de guerre, par une clause expresse qui s'est toujours
> depuis inserée dans leurs provisions, de ne point se rendre, à moins qu'il n'y ait brèche considerable
> au corps de la place, et qu'après y avoir soutenu plusieurs assauts; j'ai jugé à propos de renouveler les
> mêmes ordres à tous les commandants des mes places.*

This directive of Louis XIV was enshrined in a law of 26 July 1792, art. 1:

> *Tout commandant de place forte ou bastionée, qui la rendre à l'ennemi, avant qu'il y ait brèche
> accessible et praticable au corps de place, et avant que le corps de ait soutenu au moins un assaut, si
> toutefois il y a un retranchement intérieur la brèche, sera puni de mort, à moins qu'il ne manque de
> munitions et de vivres.*

[19] Note Zeti's words, reported by Concino (secretary to the imperial Council of War):
"*no' desiderava altra cosa che d'esser servitore dell'ecca v.*" Such forms of words, however,
should not be taken as evidence of double-dealing. A defiance was a legal term, and
certainly did not imply abuse. Chevalier Bayard's defiance of the Herald at Mezières
was a model of courtesy:

> *Herault mon amy, vous vous en retournerez, et leur direz que le Roy mon maistre avoit beaucoup
> plus de suffisans personnaiges en Son Royaume que moy, pour envoyer garder ceste Ville, qui nous
> faict frontiere. Mais puis qu'il m'a faict cest honneur de s'en fier à moy, j'espere avec l'ayde de nostre
> Seigneur, la luy conserver si longuement, qu'il ennuyera beaucoup plus à vos maistres d'estre au
> siege, que à moy d'estre assiegé.*

Histoire du Chevalier Bayard, ed. Thedore Godefroy (Paris, 1616), ch. 63, 372–3.

weak position should obstinately defy a greatly superior force – the idea of superiority, as Montaigne cynically explains, being a special blend of physical and social force.

Valour has its limits like the other virtues, and these limits once transgressed, we find ourselves on the path of vice; so that we may pass through valour to temerity, obstinacy and madness, unless we know its limits well – and they are truly hard to discern near the borderlines. From this consideration is derived the custom, which we have in wars, of punishing even with death those who obstinately defend a place which by the rules of war cannot be held. Otherwise, in the hope of impunity, there would not be a chicken coop that would not hold up an army.... But the judgement of the strength or weakness of a place is formed by estimating the comparative strength of the forces attacking it; a man might properly hold out against two culverins who would be crazy to resist thirty cannon. Moreover there comes into account also the greatness of the conquering prince, his reputation, the respect that is owed to him, whence there is danger that the balance will be weighted a bit heavily on the side of the attackers. And it happens because of the same conditions that some have so great an opinion of themselves and their power that, since it seems unreasonable to them that there should be anything worthy to stand up against them, they put everyone to the sword wherever they find resistance....[20]

Some Italian writers convey the impression that a strict interpretation of the Laws of War was essentially a northern European preoccupation. Francesco Guicciardini's account of the disasters accompanying the French invasion of Italy in 1494–5 lays stress on the unprecedented ruthlessness of the massacres that followed the successful French assaults upon Fivissano, Mordano, and Monte di San Giovanni, and the shock effect that such events caused throughout Italy.[21] The Italian public, according to the same author, was both shocked and surprised by the hanging of the Venetian castellan of Peschiera in 1509 by the French, and the sack of Prato in 1512 at the hands of the Imperialists.[22] In 1522, however, Guicciardini himself

---

[20] Montaigne, *Essays*, I, 15, 47–8. The moral: "Thus above all we must be aware, if we can, of falling into the hands of an enemy judge who is victorious and armed."

[21] Francesco Guicciardini, *Storia d'Italia*, bk. 1. See also Simon Pepper, "Castles and Cannon in the Naples Campaign of 1494–95," in *The French Descent on Italy in 1494 and 1495*, ed. David Abulafia (London, 1995), 263–93, for further consideration of the French massacres.

[22] For Peschiera, *Storia d'Italia*, bk. 8, and for Prato, *Storia d'Italia*, bk. 11. The sack of Prato was one of the best documented tragedies of the Italian Wars: *Il sacco di Prato e il ritorno de' Medici in Firenze in 1512: Documenti*, ed. C. Guasti, 2 vols. (Bologna, 1880); V. Gori, *Storia documentata del sacco di Prato, sue cause e conseguenze* (Florence, 1895); J. Modesti, "Il miserando sacco dato alla terra di Prato dagli Spagnoli l'anno 1512," ed. A. Vanucci, *Archivio storico italiano*, series 1, I (1842), 233–51; and Simone di Goro Brami, "Narrazione del sacco di Prato," 253–60.

urged the citizens of Parma to assist him in the defense of the city "for the honour of their wives and daughters."[23] Although everyone was shocked by the sack of Rome, not even Guicciardini pretended to be surprised.

There is, in fact, every reason to believe that the finer points of siege law were well understood and practiced by fifteenth- and sixteenth-century Italians, as well as by more distant powers, such as the Ottoman Turks. Commines mentions the rule that anyone attempting to enter or leave a town during a siege "is worthy of death according to the laws of war" and asserts that this rule was observed in Italy, but not normally in France.[24] The herald who summoned Monte di San Giovanni in 1495 for Charles VIII of France was returned to the king minus his ears, an outrageous breach of heraldic immunity that may have been designed by the fortress commander to dispel all thought of surrender from the minds of the Neapolitan garrison.[25] Here the gravity of the insult was increased by the physical presence of the French king. The massacres by the Turks of the Venetian garrisons who lost Negropont in 1470 and Modon in 1500 – two of the Republic's most important possessions in Greece – were carried out in the

---

[23] *Storia d'Italia*, bk. 16.
[24] Philip de Commines, *The Memoirs of Philip de Commines, Lord of Argenton*, ed. Scoble, 2 vols. (London, 1855–6), I:bk. 5, ch. 6.
[25] Accounts of the war crime at Monte San Giovanni vary somewhat, but all are agreed that something unforgivable occurred. Sanuto says the heralds were hanged as well as mutilated, and (reporting the Venetian ambassador's letters) also that the French lost only ten dead and twenty-five wounded in the assault but killed 700 men, women, and children in the town and castle in reprisal. M. Sanuto, *La Spedizione di Carlo VIII in Italia raccontata da Marino Sanuto il Giovane* . . . , ed. Rinaldo Fulin (Venice, 1883), 209. Giovio says only that *"fecero quasi ingiuria a una trombetta Francese"* which had greatly inflamed *"gli animi di quella nation superba, perche in Francia stimano cosa mal fatta il fare ingiuria a una trombetta, ch'essi chiamano Araldo. . . ."* Many of the garrison managed to escape, he adds, leaving unarmed civilians to bear the brunt of the reprisals. Paolo Giovio, *Dell'Istoria del suo tempo di Mons. Paolo Giovio da Como, Vescovo de Nocera*, tradotta per M. Lodovico Domenichi (Firenze, 1555), 65. De la Vigne glosses over the insult to the heralds but stresses the bad character of the garrison, *"composé de plusiers gens ramassaez des diverses nations, scavoir des voleurs & bannis pour la pluspart, determinez & resolus à toutes sortes d'extremitez . . . ."* De la Vigne (also known as Le Vergier d'Honneur), "Extrait de l'Histoire du Voyage de Naples du Roy Charles VIII, mis par escrit, en forme de iournal de son exprés vouloir & commandement par ADLV, Secretaire d'Anne de Bretagne, Reyne de France," in Guillaume de Jaligny, *Histoire de Charles VIII*, ed. Tedore Godefroy (Paris, 1684), 129. Charles VIII himself, in a letter to his brother, glosses over the treatment of the herald(s) with the comment that the defenders had replied to his summons *"autrement qu'elle ne devoit."* The subsequent massacre was explained simply as a *"punition et grant example pour ceux qui vouldroient faire semblablement à l'encontre de moy."* The letter dated 9 February 1495 is published in Jules de la Pilorgerie, *Campagne et Bulletins de la Grand Armée d'Italie commandée par Charles VIII, 1494–1495* (Nantes & Paris, 1866), 176–7.

presence of the sultan, who had been personally as well as legally insulted at the first of those celebrated eastern sieges.[26] The "Islamic" customs of war, which at once authorized and limited the sack of Constantinople to the three days of terror following the fall of the city in 1453, were essentially no different from those governing western conduct in similar circumstances although here, as with the cases previously cited, the presence of Mehmed II added considerable force in military law to the momentous events.[27] But the physical presence of the sovereign was by no means an essential element. Guicciardini records an incident in 1504 when Cesare Borgia, whilst in papal custody, was persuaded to surrender the fortress of Cesena. Pietro D'Oviedo, a Spaniard, went to receive the place in the name of His Holiness and was hanged by Cesare Borgia's governor, who said that "it would be a disgrace to him to obey his master while he was a prisoner, and therefore he who presumed to request it of him deserved to be punished."[28] This seems to be putting a very fine point on the meaning of contumacy.

It is tempting to rationalize the peculiar severity of siege law in

[26] L. Fincati, "La perdita di Negroponte (luglio 1470)," *Archivio veneto*, n.s. 32 (1886), 263–307, gives the most detailed account; Polidori, ed., "Due ritmi e una narrazione in prosa di autori contemporanei intorno all presa di Negroponte fatta dai Turchi a danno dei Veneziani nel MCCCCLXX," *Archivio storico italiano*, Appendice, 9 (1853), 403–40, includes the eyewitness account of Fra Jacopo della Castellano, one of the very few survivors spared after the surrender of the Castle of Euripos at Negropont; William Miller, *The Latins in the Levant: A History of Frankish Greece, 1204–1566* (London, 1908), 471–7, gives a vivid account of the fall of Negropont, including the insults offered to the sultan by the defenders at an early stage of the siege. For the massacre following the fall of Modon, see Archivio di Stato Venezia, *Senato del Mar*, reg. 15, fol. 34v (19 September 1500); Andrea Balastro, "Progressi seguiti di tempo in tempo delle cose aricordate et fatte per cagione dell'infelice obsidione della città di Modon et miserandi pupilli," in Donado da Lezze (or Leze), *Historia Turchesca, 1300–1514*, ed. I. Ursu (Bucharest, 1909), 258; Simon Pepper, "The Defence of Venice's Mainland Greek Colonies in the Late Fifteenth Century," in *War, Culture and Society in Renaissance Venice: Essays in Honour of John Hale*, eds. David S. Chambers, Cecil H. Clough, and Michael E. Mallet (London, 1993), 53.

[27] The only substantive difference between Turkish and Christian siege law concerned the treatment of churches, which could be transformed into mosques only when the city had been taken by storm. "They were regarded as part of the lawful booty and possessions of the Moslem conquerors. In cities that surrendered by treaty or that had capitulated voluntarily, they remained in Christian hands as is shown by many examples in Mistra, Athens, or Janina, or Berat in Albania and Prilep in Yugoslav Macadonia. Sometimes, in conquered cities, the churches were left to the Christians but could be taken at any time. In Thessaloniki and also in Istanbul this took place in several phases, one at the end of the fifteenth century and one at the end of the sixteenth century." Machiel Kiel, "Notes on some Turkish Monuments in Thessaloniki," *Balkan Studies* 11 (1970): 141.

[28] *Storia d'Italia*, bk. 6.

terms of the strategic importance of fortified positions. To some extent, no doubt, military discipline reflected the vital importance of a loyal defense. Again, no doubt, it was easier to regulate the duties of a fortress commander than to identify misconduct in the confusion of a field engagement. These are the utilitarian factors that appeal to the twentieth-century mind. The legal justification for what appears to us as a peculiarly harsh siege law rested upon the need to hold a fortified position as an issue of sovereignty and, this being so, it is hardly surprising that fortifications of all kinds and, to some extent, the component parts of fortifications – walls, towers, merli, and gates – themselves came to be associated with the sovereignty of a prince or the liberties of a free city.

To the inhabitants of a free city, the wall was an essential attribute of civic status and independence. The foundation of Renaissance cities, such as Filarete's Sforzinda, was described in terms which related directly to accounts of ancient foundation ceremonies, with their emphasis on the ritual ploughing of the first furrow for the wall, and the lifting of the plough for the gates.[29] Vasari's fresco, *The Foundation of Florence* (Florence, Palazzo Vecchio, Salone dei Cinquecento), shows the ploughing of the furrow, "the act of possession."[30] Pius II, a great admirer of walls, noted that Scottish towns lacked an enceinte, with the clear inference that towns without walls could scarcely be regarded as towns at all.[31] Many writers discussed the "Spartan Walls," and all of them agreed with Alberti that "it is certain that walls are a very powerful defence both of our persons and liberties. I cannot join in with those who are for having their city quite naked without any wall."[32] Francesco de Marchi explained their necessity in quasi-anthropological terms. Animals protect themselves, he said, by

going into desert places or, in good country, by retreating to high places, dense forests, dark valleys, caves and the like for their security, as did men before they discovered means of fortification . . . and with art assisted nature to defend themselves. It was then recognised that with artifice they could live in such a way that a small number could defend themselves from a greater.[33]

---

[29] Filarete, *Trattato*, ed. John R. Spencer (New Haven, 1965), bk. 4, ff. 24v, 25r; L.B. Alberti, *Ten Books on Architecture*, trans. James Leoni and ed. Joseph Rykwert (London, 1965), bk. 4, ch. 3; Francesco de Marchi, *Della architettura militare, Libri tre* (Brescia, 1599), bk. 1, ch. 27.

[30] John Hale, *Renaissance Fortification: Art or Engineering?* (London, 1977), 44–5.

[31] *Commentaries*, ed. Gabel, bk. 1, 33.

[32] Alberti, *Ten Books*, bk. 4, ch. 3.

[33] De' Marchi, *Della architettura militare*, bk. 1, ch. 11.

Man's ability to defend himself behind walls (and presumably with weapons) is seen here as a step in the march of progress towards civilization.

The purely defensive function of the wall was coupled to a constitutional role as the line dividing civic privilege from the economic and political subservience of the suburb, or *faubourg*. Siege law underlined this distinction by treating *faubourg*, city, and fortress as discrete units. Keen describes a case where separate treaties of surrender for the fortress and the city permitted the evacuation of troops and the payment of lump-sum indemnities in lieu of free pillage. These units had surrendered "by appointment" in legally separate sieges. The *faubourgs* that had surrendered "at discretion" were put to the sack.[34]

There is also some evidence that people became attached, not so much to the mere possession of a wall, but rather to a particular architectural image. The *merlatura* or crenellation – the tooth-and-gap pattern of merlons (the upstanding masonry that protected defenders on the battlements) and embrasures (through which they fired) – were highly regarded. In England and France, a royal license had to be obtained before a castle or town could be crenellated; crenellation thus becoming a mark of favor and prestige as well as of increased strength.[35] The *merlatura* is a prominent and somewhat anachronistic feature of many late-transitional fortresses in Italy, and it is by no means uncommon to find a vestigial *merlatura* in the form of a zig zag brickwork course near the frieze of a cheaply constructed tower. Similar attributes attached to the machicolations, the corbelling-out of the upper battlements, which permitted defenders to shoot or to drop heavy objects directly down the face of walls onto attackers who would otherwise be very difficult to hit at the foot of the fortifications. Here too vestigial machicolation survived long after that kind of defense had had its day in the form of blind brackets (and later still as corbelled moldings) under very different kinds of parapets. If something was important, it was worth wrecking. Marino Sanuto reported that the *merli* of Brescia were stripped off by the French when they captured the city in 1509.[36] Sanuto recorded the incident in connection with a number of French outrages. It may be that this kind of *merli-*

---

[34] Keen, *Laws of War*, 141.

[35] The *merlatura* appears widely in heraldry and, according to Edith Porada, as a representative symbol of a fortress, town, or fortress-temple in the ancient Near East. See "Battlements in the Military Architecture and Symbolism of the Ancient Near East," in *Essays in the History of Architecture Presented to Rudolf Wittkower*, eds. Douglas Frazer and others (London, 1967), I:1–12.

[36] Marino Sanuto, *I Diarii*, eds. N. Barozzi, G. Berchet, R. Fulin, and F. Stefani, 58 vols. (Venice, 1879–1903), 9:ch. 72.

stripping was regarded by the French and the Venetians as a form of civic degradation, for by this date it would probably not have fundamentally influenced the defensibility of the walls.

A somewhat similar problem was posed whenever medieval walls with their high towers and curtains were modified or replaced by low-profile earthworks. The walls of Florence were "modernized" in this way in 1526,[37] and it was the architectural loss of "almost all the towers which like a garland crowned the walls of Florence round and round" that distressed the patriotic contemporary historian, Benedetto Varchi, perhaps even more than the poor administration of the chief *procuratore* in charge of the works.[38] The replacement of old and outdated city walls was frequently a slow process, bedeviled by shortages of money and materials and often by lack of political will. However, to my knowledge, Varchi's remarks are the only expression of regret on purely aesthetic grounds to the removal of picturesque features by their owners.[39] Enemy demolition was quite different.[40] Yet the change in appearance of early modern fortifications was profound, and led inevitably to new aesthetic priorities.

As the military architectural revolution of the sixteenth century ran its course and new works increasingly took the form of low, thick ramparts sunk in deep ditches and, ideally, presenting a much simplified profile to the outside world, more architectural attention was paid to the gates. These had always been important, of course, and had often been highly developed in the Middle Ages as defensive works, security points, revenue collecting barriers, and residences for guards

---

[37] See Machiavelli's description in the "Relazione di una visita fatta per fortificare Firenze," in *L'Arte della guerra e scritti militari minori* (Firenze, 1929), 207ff.

[38] Benedetto Varchi, *Storia fiorentina*, ed. Gaetano Milanese, 3 vols. (Florence, 1888), bk. 2, ch. 21, 95–6. Mural towers were special, of course. Towers, or tower like features, gave what von Moos called "the military look" to many Renaissance palaces and civic buildings – often at the expense of their formal composition – despite the fact that many medieval Italian communes had struggled to rid themselves of the magnates' family towers which dominated their skylines. Stanislaus von Moos, "The Palace as a Fortress: Rome and Bologna under Pope Julius II," in *Art and Architecture in the Service of Politics*, eds. Henry A. Millon and Linda Nochlin (Cambridge, MA, and London, 1978), 46–78.

[39] Sir John Hale shares this view, see his *Renaissance Fortification. Art or Engineering?*, 44.

[40] Agnolo Bardi, commenting on the demolition in 1552 of seventeen magnates' family towers in Siena at the hands of the Spanish governor, declared that they too contributed to the "*bellezza della città.*" The demolitions formed part of the Spanish program of Sienese disarmament that accompanied the construction of the citadel and which eventually drove the city into open rebellion. Here there was evidently no love lost for "*questo insolente barbaro, che bene si può dire cosi per essere nato in Granata della stiatta de' mori, e barbari con tanta rabbia si mettesse à fare isbassare si belli, e superbi edifitij . . . che sonno el'ornamento della città.*" Agnolo Bardi, *Storia Senese 1512–1556*, MS Biblioteca Communale di Siena, A.VI.51, folio 538v.

and other civic officials. From a strictly military standpoint, the best-placed gates in the era of gunpowder artillery were probably those tucked close into the flanks of protective bastions, sometimes even placed in the flanks at right angles to the main rampart curtains to make them practically invisible and invulnerable to cannon shot fired from the front. The complicated dog-legs, ramps, bridges and pinch-points of the more elaborate late Renaissance gate systems must have provided a dramatic experience for the stranger entering the city; but externally these security systems lacked the architectural impact of the medieval mural gates. Yet in a surprising number of cases, security was compromised by the design of magnificent formal gateways, prominently placed in ways that owed much more to urban design than to the practical exigencies of fortification.

Michele Sanmichele's gates at Verona and Michelangelo's Roman Porta Pia are merely the best known of these enterprises, but the sheer number of drawings from Antonio da Sangallo and his circle dedicated to the design of the Porta Santo Spirito at the Vatican, or the gateway-keep of Florence's Fortezza da Basso, gives some idea of the effort to marry appropriate civic standing with function in this key component.[41] Sangallo's decision to incorporate the Etruscan Porta Marzio into the side entrance of the Rocca Paolina in Perugia suggests a concern for what today might be called conservation as well as urban design, but which also imparted some "instant tradition" to what was in reality a violent architectural intervention.[42] Gates could also dignify works which – whatever their military importance – were on the margins of anything that could be called architecture. The earthwork defense line, thrown up on the northern approaches to Siena during the period of tension before the fighting broke out in 1553, was supplied with a proper gateway and drawbridge, decorated with the arms of the Republic and the French crown, built at the personal expense of the cardinal of Ferrara, the French king's lieutenant in Italy. The gate was to be known as the Porta di Francia.[43] In Vasari's views of the siege of 1554–5 this gate can be seen rising somewhat above the level of the frontal curtain, mostly constructed in

---

[41] *The Architectural Drawings of Antonio da Sangallo the Younger and His Circle*, Vol. 1, *Fortifications, Machines, and Festival Architecture*, eds. Christoph L. Frommel and Nicholas Adams (Cambridge, MA, and London, 1994).

[42] For the Porta Marzia see Nicholas Adams and Simon Pepper, "The Fortification Drawings," in *Architectural Drawings of Antonio da Sangallo*, I:71.

[43] Simon Pepper and Nicholas Adams, *Firearms and Fortifications: Military Architecture and Siege Warfare in Sixteenth-Century Siena* (Chicago, 1986), 171–2.

brick but with prominent dressed-stone quoins and voussoirs at the arched opening. Beside Siena's spectacular medieval gate towers it no doubt seemed a modest structure, but the formal intention of the cardinal can hardly be in doubt. These earthworks were now part of the city walls, and were to be treated as civic architecture.

The building of great architecture was of course one of the chief means by which Renaissance princes could embellish both their cities and their personal reputations. In these terms new castles or city walls that added to the security of the realm were no less worthy of record than churches or palaces. Indeed, they had a unique political signifi-cance which emerges in numerous ways. The low-relief medals, which in the mid-fifteenth century became such an important medium of princely propaganda in Italy, featured castles prominently, leading Joanna Woods-Marsden to argue that Sigismondo Malatesta used his depiction of the new *rocca* at Rimini, which was identified on his medals by his own name in the inscription CASTELLUM SISMVNDVM ARIMINENSE, "as a personal symbol of princely au-thority and territorial dominion, and by extension, a badge of his rule over a state."[44] Exaggerated tall towers and a fictional hilltop site (Rimini is actually quite flat) confirmed "the symbolic association of a towering castle with the exercise of authority."[45] Such medals could be distributed as gifts to other rulers, carrying the message widely abroad, and buried in the walls as part of a foundation ceremony with profound local significance. Pier Maria Rossi of Parma also employed castles on his medal reverses and, in his castle at Torchiara, commis-sioned a fresco cycle that *inter alia* incorporated "portraits of some of the twenty castles, each carefully identified, that comprised his small state south of Parma."[46] The link between sovereignty and the posses-sion of fortresses, whether by defense or conquest, is one of the least elusive concepts of Renaissance iconography.

In the age of the modern "invisible military architecture" of low-profile bastions and ramparts, however, new artistic conventions were needed. Cosimo, first Duke and Grand Duke of Tuscany, celebrated his own fortification construction activities prominently in the cycle of

---

[44] Joanna Woods-Marsden, "How Quattrocento Princes Used Art: Sigismondo Pandolfo Malatesta of Rimini and *cose militari*," *Renaissance Studies* 3–4 (1989): 396.

[45] Woods-Marsden, "How Quattrocento Princes Used Art," 397.

[46] Woods-Marsden, "How Quattrocento Princes Used Art," 398. See also the same author's "Pictorial Legitimation of Territorial Gains in Emilia; the Iconography of the *camera peregrina aurea* in the Castle of Torchiara," *Renaissance Studies in Honor of Craig Hugh Smyth* (Florence, 1985), II:553–68.

frescoes by Vasari that decorated the Palazzo Vecchio in Florence.[47] Surrounded by his engineers and architects, with drawings rolled out to reveal bird's-eye views of the circuits of bastioned walls, Cosimo is shown discussing proposals for the new fortress city of Portoferraio on Elba, and dozens of less ambitious projects, which, taken together, made him one of the most active Italian fortress builders of the sixteenth century. What the new military architecture lost in picturesque profile it gained in the dramatic star-shaped plan forms. Pictures of models are sometimes employed too, in Vasari's fresco cycle, using the time-honored convention of the city in the hand of its patron saint. In some of the smaller panels Vasari has Cosimo bestowing the *corona muralis* on anthropomorphized representations of Tuscan towns, using a castellated crown of square *merli* to represent the walls that "honor" the place with the Roman military decoration given to the first man over the walls of a captured city.

It is not difficult to imagine the significance attached to the compulsory demolition of walls or gates. Jean de Troyes records that when the Liègeois were forced to surrender to the Burgundians in 1467, the duke demanded the handover of subject towns to the count of Charolois "besides giving him a vast sum of money and consenting to have their gates pulled down, and part of their walls demolished."[48] The emperor Henry VII imposed similar terms upon Cremona in 1311.[49] In both cases demolition of part of the walls would have rendered the town defenseless. That the gates were also pulled down suggests that these acts were intended more as gestures of civic humiliation. When God took a hand in the proceedings they became even more significant. Commines tells a story in this vein which supports his description of Charles VIII's entry into Rome in 1494 "as a prince who had authority to do what he pleased wherever he came." As Charles approached Rome on his triumphant march to Naples, Commines asks why King Alfonzo of Naples, who enjoyed a strong following in Rome, did not attempt to oppose Charles at this time:

God was willing to demonstrate to the world that all these things were beyond the contrivance and comprehension of human wisdom; and, as we said before, that above twenty fathoms of the city wall fell down, so now there fell down above fifteen fathoms of the outer wall of the Castle of St Angelo, as I have

---

[47] Kurt W. Forster, "Metaphors of Rule: Political Ideology and History in the Portraits of Cosimo I de' Medici," *Mitteilungen des Kunsthistorischen Institutes in Florenz* 15 (1971), 65–104.

[48] Jean de Troyes, *Chronique Scandaleuse*, ed. Scoble (London, 1855), 348.

[49] W.M. Bowsky, *Henry VII in Italy: The Conflict of Empire and City State, 1310–1313* (Lincoln, 1960), 112.

been told by several persons, and particularly by two Cardinals who were there.[50]

Probably Commines's stories were apocryphal. They may well, however, have been based upon a traditional conjunction between the arrival of great sovereigns and some ritual gesture concerning the walls; a tradition that perhaps motivated Julius II to have himself hoisted over the ramparts of Mirandola after that city had surrendered to him in 1511.[51] Sometimes the gesture was voluntary. When the emperor Charles V visited Siena in 1536, the imperial procession entered the Borgo di Camollia through a breach that had been made in the wall.[52] The gates of the Porta Camollia were taken off their hinges and laid on the ground as the supreme civic compliment.[53]

If walls and gates were associated with the identity and sovereignty of the city, the fortress was associated with the authority of a prince or an imperial power. The imposition of a new urban fortress carried particularly potent meaning, and Renaissance opinion generally cautioned against the political wisdom of such enterprises. Machiavelli advised against the use of fortresses as both provocative and useless,[54] but Bernardo Segni, himself a staunch Republican, implicitly accepted their effectiveness when he complained of the project for the Fortezza da Basso that the Medici were determined "to place on the necks of the Florentines a yoke of a kind never experienced before: a citadel, whereby the citizens lost all hope of ever living in freedom again."[55]

---

[50] Commines, *Memoirs*, 149.

[51] Guicciardini, *Storia d'Italia*, bk. 9, attempts to explain this action. "He caused himself to be mounted upon the walls, because the gates were beaten down, and from thence descended into the town." It is not clear, however, whether the pope wanted to find the best route into the town, or the most impressive. Bayard's Loyal Servant, in a slightly different version of the same story, suggests the latter: *"Le Pape ne daigna entrer dedans la ville de la Mirandole par la porte. Il fait faire un pont par dessus le fossé sur le quel il passa, & entra dedans par une des breches."* *Histoire du Chevalier Bayard*, 241.

[52] Sozzini, *Diario*, 21, cites the description in Marco Guazzo, *Historie . . . di tutte le cose degne di memoria . . . quel hanno principio l'anno MDIX* (Venetia, 1548).

[53] Sozzini, *Diario*, 21. A similar gesture was sometimes employed as a sign of peaceful intentions. To reassure the suspicious Scots escorting Mary Queen of Scots to the French court, the gates of the town of Morlaix were unhinged and the chains of the bridges broken after an accident to the drawbridge had alarmed the party. Antonia Frazer, *Mary Queen of Scots* (London, 1970), 60. Usually, the gesture was a compliment. Luca Landucci heard (incorrectly, as it turned out) that on 21 September 1494 "the King of France had entered Genoa, and that the Genoese were preparing to receive him with great honour, having decorated the whole city, and even taken down the gates and laid them on the ground to show more splendour and to ensure the King's safety." *Diario Fiorentino dal 1450 al 1516*, ed. Iadoco del Badia (Firenze, 1883), 70. Although the king did not finally enter Genoa, these preparations had been made.

[54] Machiavelli, *Discorsi*, II:24.

[55] Quoted in J.R. Hale, "The End of Florentine Liberty: The Fortezza da Basso," *Floren-*

Francesco de Marchi spoke for most sixteenth-century military treatise authors when he described fortresses as "like the bit in the mouths of wild horses, and like the rudder that guides the ships in the sea" and warned that "fortresses are dangerous to build in cities or places accustomed to live free."[56]

According to Alberti, this had not always been so. The ancients, he said, built fortresses within the city as places of refuge

> where the virtue of their virgins and matrons might be protected by the holiness of a sanctuary. But Tyrants afterwards usurped the Fortress to themselves, and overthrew the piety and religion of the place, converting it to their cruel and wicked purposes, and so made what was designed as a refuge to the miserable, a source of miseries.[57]

Many of Alberti's ideas on city planning derived from his belief in the need to control the commotions of the "scoundrel rabble," a necessity which overrode his earlier reservations on the misuse of the fortress. He conceded a difference between a palace for a king and castle for a tyrant.[58] In either event, however, "there should be a high watch-tower, from whence you may at any time see any commotion in the city."[59] It was this controlling role that was stressed by Francesco di Giorgio in his well-known anthropomorphic metaphor of the fortress-city relationship:

> Nature having shown them [the ancients] the head and face of the human body to be its most noble members, and that with the eyes one may see and judge all of the rest of the body, so the fortress should be placed in an eminent place that can see and judge all of the body of the city. Thus the castle must be the principal member of the body of the city just as the head is the principal member of the whole body. And if [the head] is lost the body is lost, [similarly] if the fortress is lost so too is the city ruled by it.[60]

The analogy is then expanded. Man has eyes with which to see and understand visible things and, similarly, he must have mental equipment (*occhi mentali*) to judge and understand future events. If he sees

---

tine Studies: Politics and Society in Renaissance Florence, ed. Nicolai Rubinstein (London, 1968), 504.

[56] de Marchi, *Della architettura militare*, bk. 1, chs. 13 and 18.
[57] Alberti, *Ten Books*, bk. 5, ch. 3, 86.
[58] Alberti, *Ten Books*, bk. 5, ch. 3, 86: "The Palace of a King should stand in the heart of a city, it should be easy of access, beautifully adorned, and rather delicate and polite than proud or stately: but a Tyrant should have rather a castle than a palace, and it should stand in a manner out of the city and in it at the same time."
[59] Alberti, *Ten Books*, bk. 5, ch. 3, 86
[60] Francesco di Giorgio Martini, *Trattati di architettura, ingegneria e arte militare*, eds. Bonelli and Portoghesi, 2 vols. (Milan, 1967), I:3. The citation is from the Codex *Torinese Saluzziano*, 148.

the body moving into small or major difficulties (*infermità*) he must move quickly to put things right, if necessary "with the help and advice of the physician." For often we see a small but badly tended injury become mortal and, contrariwise, a great and serious wound can often be cured with diligent care. So the governor of the city continues to observe vigilantly to see if the city is running into trouble, great or small, and takes appropriate measures.[61] This is perhaps the most positive gloss on the urban fortress to emerge from the literature of the quattrocento.

The distinction drawn by the treatise authors and others between the walls of free cities and the fortresses of their oppressors was well supported by political events in the sixteenth century as new regimes consolidated their often despotic rule. The precedents were already well established by the Angevin and Aragonese fortresses dominating Naples, by the Castello Sforzesca at Milan, by the Castello Estense at Ferrara, the Visconti Cittadella of Verona, the Malatesta castle at Rimini and numerous others.[62] The Florentines had themselves not been backward in reinforcing the Republic's control of Volterra by a fortress in 1472. Others were started by the Florentines at Borgo San Sepolcro in 1500, at Arezzo in 1502, at Pisa in 1509, and at Livorno in 1518.[63] They understood very clearly the politics of fortress construction but, as Nicolai Rubinstein has recently pointed out, "the Florentines, like the citizens of other republics, applied different criteria to liberty at home and in their dominions."[64] The Florentine Fortezza da Basso was started in 1534 by Alessandro de' Medici, shortly after the defeat of the last Republic, and completed in record time at enormous cost and with scant regard to the protests of libertarians and rebels alike, ironically after the assassination of its founder. Later Florence acquired yet another Medici fortress, the Belvedere, overlooking the other half of the city from the southern heights.

Pope Paul III's domination of Perugia was consolidated by the construction of the Rocca Paolina from 1540.[65] This represented a far more

---

[61] Di Giorgio Martini, *Trattati*, I:4.
[62] Recent studies include John E. Law, "The Cittadella of Verona," in *War, Culture and Society*, 9–27; Nicolai Rubinstein, "Fortified Enclosures in Italian Cities," in *War, Culture and Society*, 1–8; L. Green, "Il problema dell'*Augusta* e della villa di Castruccio Castracane," *Actum Luce* 13–14 (1984–5): 353–77; Joanna Woods-Marsden, "How Quattrocento Princes Used Art," 387–414, and "Images of Castles in the Renaissance: Symbols of *Signoria*: Symbols of Tyranny," *Art Journal* 48 (1989): 130–7.
[63] Hale, "End of Florentine Liberty," 504.
[64] Rubinstein, "Fortified enclosures in Italian Cities," 8.
[65] For the project's history, see Nicholas Adams and Simon Pepper, "Entry for Drawing U271A," in *Architectural Drawings of Antonio da Sangallo*, I:102–3.

overtly aggressive political act even than the construction of the Fortezza da Basso, for the works in the upper town of Perugia were built
over the ruins of the properties of the Baglioni family, who had taken
a leading role in the unsuccessful rebellion against a papacy that was
energetically reestablishing its control of the Church States following
the disasters of the Sack of Rome (1527). Where at Florence efforts had
been made to beautify both the interior and exterior of the Fortezza
da Basso, at Perugia the architecture of the Rocca Paolina was explicitly military in character. Visiting Perugia in September 1540, Paul III
is said to have expressed displeasure at the civic nature of the project
in its early form: "Seeing the palace already begun with its high walls
and iron-grated windows he said that it was not enough, I want you
to make a fortress here."[66]

The Spanish project to control Siena from a fortress took shape in
1549–50 and, although not the only cause, was certainly a major factor
in provoking the rebellion that expelled the Spanish troops of Charles
V, brought in the French, and set the scene for the war of reconquest,
which eventually cost the turbulent Sienese Republic its independence.[67] At Siena, the citadel was cleverly sited on a practically deserted hill just outside the medieval walls, from where it could both
contribute to the defense of the city against external enemies and
dominate the center with its guns. When rebellion broke out in 1552,
the incomplete citadel was captured after a short siege and its Spanish
garrison expelled.[68] The ceremonial involved the formal surrender of
the citadel by Spain to France, immediately followed by its formal
handing over by France to their new Sienese allies. The later stages of
this protocol were described carefully by the Sienese diarist, Alessandro Sozzini:

After the departure [of the Spaniards] the Most Illustrious Monsieur de Lan-
sach [French ambassador] went into the fortress, and at the Sixteenth Hour
the clergy entered in procession with the Lords and the Captain of the People;
and there the Most Illustrious Ambassador of the Most Christian King of
France consigned the fortress to the city with these words: "Most Illustrious
Lords, my Sire, having heard that the tyranny of Charles V had subjected you,
has sent me to liberate you, and because this place was the cause of holding
you in servitude, he returns to you Liberty, and hands over the said place: in
return for which my King wants nothing from you besides that you acknowl-

---

[66] Adams and Pepper, *Architectural Drawings of Antonio da Sangallo*, I:103 and 253–4.
[67] Pepper and Adams, *Firearms and Fortifications*, 58–78, for this episode and numerous
additional references.
[68] "La cacciata della guardia Spagnuola da Siena d'incerto autore," *Archivio storico
italiano*, I, II (1842), 481–524.

edge the gift from the hand of Blessed God, and be mindful of him who has struggled for your Liberty." And, the notary being summoned, he declared: "Notary, record that my King makes a gift to the City of Siena of all that she has to spend in his service." And, these words being spoken, he departed and left in the fortress the said most Illustrious Lords, who gave one turn inside, and with their own hands began to demolish and level it. . . .[69]

The formal act of demolition described at the end of Sozzini's account was quickly overtaken by a program of construction to complete the external facing ramparts and bastions using material taken from the inner works. This adjustment provided the most modern section of bastioned fortification in Siena's defensive system in the prelude to the siege of 1554–5 and retrospectively justified Emperor Charles V's claim that the hated citadel would serve to protect the city (for which reason the emperor expected the Sienese to contribute to its costs). What concerns us here is the close association in the public rhetoric of liberty and possession of the fortress and, an interesting touch, the willingness of the emperor's officers to surrender their incomplete works to the representative of the French king, rather than to the Sienese rebels who up to this point had done most of the fighting. Three years later, when the defenders of Siena were finally compelled to surrender to the emperor and his Florentine allies, the French took a very similar line, handing over their positions to the Sienese before evacuating the city under agreed terms. Blaise de Monluc, who had commanded Siena throughout many months of bitter resistance, was thus spared the need himself to make an act of surrender on behalf of his king.[70]

The protocols of siege warfare and the formalities associated with the defense or surrender of fortifications seem to find an echo in the use of castle and siege themes for medieval and Renaissance pageantry. Sieges and siege themes, of course, featured prominently in many of the courtly entertainments discussed by Sydney Anglo.[71] The fragmentary evidence of the following events suggests that the ritual siege combined features of conventional tournaments and the traditional battles of cities such as Pisa, Florence, Siena, and Perugia.[72] But

---

[69] Sozzini, *Diario*, 88.

[70] Pepper and Adams, *Firearms and Fortifications*, 138–9, for the surrender. For the text of the capitulation, see Giovanni Antonio Pecci, *Memorie storico-critiche della città di Siena dal 1480 al 1552*, 4 vols. (Siena, 1755–60), 4:219–24, and Blaise de Monluc, *Commentaires*, bk. 2, 94.

[71] Sydney Anglo, "The Evolution of the Early Tudor Disguising, Pageant, and Mask," in *Renaissance Drama*, n.s. 1 (1968): 3–44.

[72] William Heywood, *Palio e Ponte* (London, 1904), for Italian civic battles. More generally useful in this context are Sydney Anglo, *Spectacle, Pageant and Early Tudor Policy*

the phenomenon extended far beyond the Italian peninsula and found literary expression in the Siege of the Castle of Love, a common Renaissance and medieval theme which typically combined both an arduous assault and an honorable defense, more often than not terminating in storm and sack.[73] Accounts of some of these events, however, suggest that the brutal military penalties for unsuccessful defense were sometimes deliberately implemented in siege tournaments. In others the casualties were real enough, if not always intentional.

Jean de Troyes's description of the state entry into Paris of the newly crowned Louis XI in 1461 mentions that "in the Rue de la Boucherie there were large scaffolds erected in the form of the Bastille at Dieppe. And when the King passed by them the English who were within the Bastille were furiously attacked by the King's soldiers, taken prisoner, and had all their throats cut."[74] As Pius II moved through Viterbo during the feast of Corpus Christi in June 1462, he passed "a triumphal arch built like a citadel held by armed soldiers who imitated thunder with bronze engines and struck terror into the passers-by."[75] The Roman carnival of 1492 celebrated news of the capture of Granada "the last bastion of the Moors in the West," with a "triumph" featuring a six-wheeled cart decorated with likenesses of Ferdinand and Isabella, defeated Saracens at their feet, followed in the procession by "saracenorum captivorum infinitus numerus" and later by a battle in the Piazza Navona in which Spanish soldiers stormed and captured a timber castle gallantly held by Moors.[76] Indoor events had a much longer pedigree. In 1389, at the coronation of the French queen, the procession passed a tableau depicting Saracens attacking a Christian-held castle. After the ceremony there was a great banquet with a spectacle of "most ingenious devices which could have given great pleasure if they had been properly executed." Froissart goes on to tell of a large wooden castle, forty feet high by twenty square, with a tower at each corner and one in the center that was wheeled into the

(Oxford, 1969); K.G.T. Webster, "The Twelfth-Century Tourney," in *Anniversary Papers by Colleagues of G.L. Kittredge* (Boston, 1913), 227–34, and N. Denham Young, "The Tournament in the Thirteenth Century," in *Studies in Medieval History presented to F.M. Powicke* (Oxford, 1948), 240–68.

[73] This field was originally brought to my attention by Sir John Hale. See also Anglo, "Evolution," 10; R.S. Loomis, "The Allegorical Siege in the Art of the Middle Ages," *American Journal of Archaeology*, 2nd ser., 23 (1919): 255–69; G.R. Kernodle, *From Art to Theatre* (Chicago and London, 1944), 76–84.

[74] Jean de Troyes, *The Scandalous Chronicle or Secret History of Louis XI*, ed. Scoble (London, 1855), 308.

[75] *Memoirs of a Renaissance Pope: The Commentaries of Pius II*, ed. F.A. Gragg (New York, 1959), bk. 8.

[76] Filippo Clementi, *Il carnevale romano nelle cronache contemporanee* (Roma, 1899), 91–2.

hall. It depicted the city of Troy, the central tower being the Palace of Ilion, while near it was a partition and a wooden ship draped with the flags of Greece.

The men from the ship and partition fiercely attacked the castle which was stoutly defended. But the battle could not last long owing to the density of the crowd, and the people being stifled by the heat and the crush. One table at which a number of ladies were sitting near the door of the Parliamentary chamber was even knocked over, and the guests had to extricate themselves as best they could. The Queen was almost fainting, and a window had to be broken open to let in air. Lady de Coucy was also overcome, and the King had the banquet stopped.[77]

These affairs were prone to disaster. Luca Landucci, the Florentine diarist, described a mock-siege in 1513 around a wooden castle in the Piazza de' Signori, which was defended by one hundred men armed with lances, unbaked bricks, and "divers other weapons" against more than three hundred attackers. The fight got out of hand. A number of combatants were killed, together with some spectators whose platforms collapsed.[78] Cambi called it a "festa diabolica e tutta bestiale," explaining that the castle contained "certain ruffians, men of bad character, [while] outside were 400 soldiers of our own territory, in fact a number of those outside were injured and hardly any of those inside."[79]

According to the cavalier Giovanni Miniati, ritual battles and sieges occurred regularly in the city of Prato – similar to those in Florence – with skirmishes, assaults, retreats, ambushes, and tricks that pleased and amused many,

and they made strong castles, surrounded by ditches, and towers, with a keep inside, most ingenious and impressive, and they were attacked by an army that camped around it, with all the equipment of infantry, cavalry, artillery, sutlers, carters of a true, perfect and well regulated army, and people of quality took part, and a large part of the citizens, and ladies of Florence came to see it, enjoying and praising it highly.[80]

One of the largest Florentine displays formed part of a series of pageants devised by Don Vincenzo Borghini to celebrate the marriage of

---

[77] Jon Froissart, *Froissart's Chroniques*, ed. and trans. John Jolliffe (London, 1967), bk. 4, ch. 2, 324 and 327–8.

[78] Luca Landucci, *Diario Fiorentino dal 1450 al 1516 . . . continuato da un anonimo fino al 1542*, ed. Iadoco del Badia (Florence, 1883), 340.

[79] Giovanni Cambi, *Istorie di Giovanni Cambi . . .* , ed. Fr. Idelfonso di San Luigi, 4 vols. (Firenze, 1785–6), III:23–4.

[80] Giovanni Miniati, *Narrazione e disegno della terra di Prato in Toscana* (Firenze, 1596), 45–7.

Francesco de' Medici to Giovanna d'Austria, daughter of the emperor Ferdinand, a major triumph for the diplomacy of Cosimo I.[81] Lapini provides some details: "On 17 February 1565 [Florentine style] the castle which had been made at Santa Maria Novella, where today is the company of San Benedetto, was attacked with great salvoes of artillery and ten assaults. There were 300 inside and 800 outside; and after a stout defence the castle was taken in a splendid battle."[82]

One of the earliest of what might be called the "serious" outdoor siege tournaments took place in Venice in 1458, involving an attack on a timber "rivellino" and "rocheta intermedia" that had been built in the Piazza di San Marco.[83] The combat, described as a "pugna atrocissima," formed the third phase of a traditional tourney, the first two phases of which had been conventional jousting and fighting at the barriers (one competition restricted to the senior nobility and more important condottieri, the second open to all comers). Angelucci believed that the rivellino described in his text formed the outer wall surrounding an inner tower like structure: thus the fortification would have been a formidable double-walled obstacle demanding a hard struggle for its capture, in contrast to what in some of the other cases read more like parades or courtly entertainments – even if they were accident prone. Many events, like that in Venice, were indeed true battles.

The most detailed description of a ritual siege I have found is from the chronicle of Jean d'Auton, who tells of a spectacle staged after the entry into Milan in 1509 by the army of Louis XII, following the defeat of the Venetians at Agnadello.[84] A formal triumph "selon l'ancienne coustume des Romains"[85] was followed by many days of court entertainments, the most spectacular event being the attack on a *bastyon* that had been constructed by Charles d'Amboise.

He had had the bastion built in a garden close to his quarters in Milan, ditched all around and enclosed with great baulks [of timber] stuck into the ground and all around strengthened with heavy planks firmly fixed with nails and bolts: to the two front corners he had had made two defensible towers, each of which could hold twenty-five or thirty armed men to defend them, the

---

[81] *Feste e apparati medicei da Cosimo I a Cosimo II: mostra di disegni e incisioni*, Catalogo a cura di Giovanna Gaeta Berteli e Annamaria Petrioli-Tofani (Firenze, 1969), 19.

[82] Agostino Lapini, *Diario Fiorentino*, ed. Odoardo Carrazzini (Firenze, 1900), 151.

[83] A. Angelucci, *Armilustre e torneo con armi di battaglia tenuti a Venezia addi XXVIII e XXX Maggio MCCCCLVIII* (Torino, 1866), 22.

[84] *Chronique de Louis XII*, ed. Naulde, (Paris, 1891–5), ch. 34, 313.

[85] This phrase was used by Robert de la Marck, Seigneur de Fleuranges, *Histoire des choses memorables advenues du reigne de Louis XII et François I en Frnace, Italie, Allemagne et ès Pays-Bas, depuis l'an 1499 jusques en l'an 1521*, ed. Petitot (Paris, 1819), 181.

front and side walls, with the towers of the bastion, were six feet in height, and against the rear it had a high platform on which to seat the judges of the combat.[86]

The bastion was to be defended by one hundred men-at-arms drawn mainly from the company of the seigneur de Ravel, brother of Charles d'Amboise, and headed by a number of the most distinguished nobles; Francesco Gonzaga, marquis of Mantua; Jacques de Bourbon, count of Roussillon; and Jacques de Chabanes, seigneur de la Palisse. The defenders were armed with heavy blunted staves, swords without points, barrels of water, and long, forked poles with which to fend off scaling ladders. Against them were ranged four hundred men-at-arms led by Louis de Breze, grand senechal of Normandy; Robert Stuart with one hundred of his Scots; and Mercurio, the captain of the Albanian *stradiotti*. The attackers were supported by numerous pioneers who prepared to fill the ditch and to bring up ladders and bridges.

The first mishap concerned the timing of the banquet and the spectacle. At three o'clock in the afternoon the king had just ordered the first course served when the trumpets of the defenders sounded the alert, and those of the assailants the assault. Immediately the King left the table and ran to the source of the commotion followed by the court.

The tables remained covered with meats and garnished buffets on silver vessels and good wine in plenty. There were many rabble who had been waiting all morning up to that hour to see the combat. Some of them had a very good appetite and they, seeing that everyone had left the meal, took their places and set themselves to despatch the food, so that in a moment only bare cloths and empty vessels remained. Then, wiping their mouths, they too ran to the bastion which was assailed vigorously and stoutly defended.[87]

For two hours the combat was energetic but inconclusive. Soon the staves were all broken and the battle was fought with crowbars and the long forked poles. Great hoops were thrown down from the bastion to entangle the attackers. Barrels of water drenched them and filled the ditch with mud, which was thrown up at the defenders whenever they raised their visors. "They began to become embittered," reported d'Auton, "and one felt that if they got any closer mortal blows would be struck." So it proved. After a break for wine, Louis de Breze ordered bridges to be brought up and two Scots from

[86] Jean d'Auton, *Chroniques de Louis XII*, ed. R. de Maulde de la Clavière, 4 vols. (Paris, 1889–95), 4:313.
[87] Jean d'Auton, *Chroniques*, IV:315.

Robert Stuart's company fought their way into the bastion where they became separated from their comrades and were beaten insensible. One of them was "carried to his quarters, where the same night his brains fell down his nose, and he died, *dont fut domage.*" After the Scots went down, the attacks became even more furious and the man who struck them down was himself laid low. As casualties mounted, the King sent in his archers to separate the combatants and left the scene of the combat in great sorrow.[88]

For the marriage of the Duke of Urbino at Amboise in 1517, Francis I sponsored eight days of jousting, the finale of which included attacks on a fake town made of wood, of considerable size, surrounded by ditches and garrisoned by a hundred men-at-arms commanded by M. d'Alençon. Four large pieces of artillery were brought up and fired in volleys over the town, as if in a bombardment. Other bodies of men acted as a relief and a screening force, while an attempt was made to storm the town by a fourth column, and a sortie was made by d'Alençon; all leading to a general melée described by Fleuranges as "le plus beau combat qu'on ait oncques veu, et le plus approchant du naturel de la guerre."[89] Not surprisingly, there were many killed and wounded. At Amboise there were also attempts to introduce artillery – the new element on the battlefield – without causing a bloodbath. Besides the "live firing exercise" from the two cannon and two double-cannon over the besieged town, the town itself was equipped with large cannon made from wood bound in iron (like wine casks, it seems), which used gunpowder to fire large hollow balls as big as the bottom of a barrel.[90] These balls were fired through the besiegers, rolling along the ground without doing any damage, and amusing spectators with their bouncing. There were evidently limits to the kind of damage that could be inflicted, even in the savage sport of the tournament.

The great tournament at Nozeroy over Christmas and New Year of 1519–20 was sponsored by the Prince of Orange and featured six days of fighting culminating in the attack and defense of a "bastillion,"

---

[88] Fleuranges, *Histoire*, 181–2, provides (slightly different) details, and has the King amongst the 2,000 men at arms assaulting the *bastillon* which was defended by 300 men-at-arms and 200 archers. It was, he says, "*un merveilleusement grand desordre*" and it is surprising that the cost ran to no more than "*plus de quarante gentilshommes que tués qu'assolés.*" If the term *gentilshommes* is being used properly, it may be that the true casualties were much greater.

[89] Fleuranges, *Histoire*, 328.

[90] Fleuranges, *Histoire*, 328: "... *gros canons faicts de bois et cerclés de fer, qui tiroient avecques de la poudre, et les boulets, qui estoient grosses balles pleines de vent, et aussi grosses que le cul d'ung tonneau* ..."

which seems to have been an actual medieval fortification, remains of which were still to be seen in the eighteenth century.[91] This is the only case known to me in which a siege tourney used an existing fortification rather than a timber replica. The small castle used for the event was some distance from the Chateau de Nozeroy (which was destroyed in the Revolution). It had four towers, a drawbridge in front, a postern behind, and a deep ditch: one description gives sides of 100 feet, the original account mentions that it was well furnished with artillery, both big and small. It was defended by the prince and his retainers, plus fifty other noblemen, against the attacks of the seigneur de Montferrand and a thousand men with "grosse artillerie." After some preliminary skirmishing with about twenty-five Albanians (*stradiotti*), who had sallied out on their horses in an unsuccessful attempt to bring some sheep into the walls, bridging equipment and artillery was brought forward and a summons delivered by a herald. The siege proper then began and lasted two days with an overnight truce, but with many wounds on both sides in the frequent assaults, sallies, and other incidents of war before the defenders were judged to have won. The artillery on both sides, we are told, exchanged fire continuously, although in the absence of reported fatalities the guns must have been firing high, or using blanks, or employing something relatively harmless like the hollow balls used at Amboise. The use of *stradiotti* by both sides is an interesting recent borrowing from the Italian Wars, and there was obviously an effort to involve artillery – perhaps for dramatic effect, perhaps for the more serious purpose of accustoming men and horses to the noise, smoke, and smells of a modern battlefield. It was also clearly a very serious attempt to replicate the protocols and maneuvers of a regular siege.

At first sight these ritual sieges may appear as little more than exciting spectacles. Fleuranges describes how "the sieur d'Angoulesme, and the Young Adventurer, and other young gentlemen built bastions and attacked them all armed for both capture and defence *à coups d'espée*,"[92] and it is tempting to conclude that the full-scale

---

[91] Bernard Prost, *Traités du Duel Judiciaire: Relations de Pas d'Armes et Tournois par Olivier de la Marche . . .* (Paris, 1872), 235–59, for the entire story; see 254 for Father Joseph-Romain Joly's description of the site:

> Quelques pas au-delà de cette petite rivière (la Serpentine), au pied d'un coteau parallèle à celui de Nozeroi, du côté du levant, on rencontre une place quarrée, de cent pieds sur chaque face, entourée d'un fossé rempli des eaux d'une fontaine, qui descend d'une colline, avec un parapet. Elle avoit d'autres fortifications que l'on détruites en cultivant les terres, et dont il reste encore quelques vestiges. C'est là que Philibert de Châlons donna une fête d'armes l'an 1519, la denière qui se soit faite en France.

[92] Fleuranges, *Histoire*, 11.

combats were, so to speak, adults' games. Here it is important to distinguish between, on the one hand, fundamentally trivial sports or routine military training exercises and, on the other, events which together with their entertainment value embodied ritual and symbolic meaning. The participation of high nobility can by no means be construed as evidence for significance. Guilliame de Jaligny, for instance, described how Charles VIII and his courtiers amused themselves on the beach of Moncailler after lunch on 7 September 1495 with some target practice using small artillery pieces, which was almost pure fun and games (with perhaps a little training in the limitations of artillery) in the aftermath of Charles VIII's escape from Italy (where some of his loyal soldiers were still fighting for their lives in Naples and the south).[93] Even on the limited evidence available to us, it would be difficult to put the siege combats into quite the same sporting category. First, the context of the combat was often highly appropriate to a siege theme. The Bastille of Dieppe in the Rue de la Boucherie recorded a recent event at the end of the Hundred Years' War, a war which was seen by the French as a struggle for the territorial integrity of their nation. Moreover, the storming of the Bastille was staged after a coronation, an event closely identified with both sovereignty and nationalism. The Siege of Troy was a strikingly appropriate theme for the coronation banquet of a foreign-born queen.[94] Again, the siege theme of the combat organized by Charles d'Amboise formed part of a series of entertainments celebrating the French capture of Milan, while the Roman mock siege in 1492, in which "Spanish" troops assaulted a great wooden castle defended by "Moors," marked the final Christian victory in the reconquest of Spain at Granada.

This kind of contextual rationale is not suitable for all of the examples. Don Vincenzo Borghini who devised the Florentine combat for the state wedding of 1566, commented that "to keep the people peace-

---

[93] Guilliame de Jaligny, *Histoire de Charles VIII, Roy de France . . . depuis l'an 1483 jusques à 1498 par Guilliame de Jaligne, A. de la Vigne . . . et autres* (Paris, 1697), 224.

[94] A very similar context surrounded the first English indoor siege pageant described by Anglo, "Evolution," 8–10, one of a series of tilts, tourneys, and barriers within the lists, and by "disguisings" which celebrated the marriage in November 1501 of Catherine of Aragon to Prince Arthur, Henry VII's elder son. Castles on wheels were drawn into the banquet hall on chains of gold by various "great bestis" (lions, harts, ibex, etc.). Within were eight disguised ladies looking out of the windows, while at the top of each of four towers was a young girl "syngyng full swettly and ermenuously." A wheel-mounted ship then approached and, after anchoring next to the castle, disembarked Hope and Desire, representing themselves as ambassadors from the Knights of the Mount of Love. After the rejection of their overtures siege operations commenced, ending in the descent of the ladies who joined their conquerors in "many goodly daunces."

ful and harmonious, it is not enough to maintain them occupied and prosperous in their professions, it is necessary to keep them happy and satisfied,"and it may be that the combat was something of a "bread and circuses" affair.[95] But it was certainly no disorganized brawl. The grand duke's artillery and over one thousand men were involved. Agostino Lapini mentions ten assaults, which suggests a degree of control. Certainly this seems true of the Prato combats which, according to Nicastro, were regularly performed from the fourteenth to the seventeenth centuries.[96] Cavalier Miniati's description makes it clear that the Prato combats were organized to include all the components of a "true, perfect and well-regulated army" camped around castles "surrounded with ditches, towers and a keep inside, *molto artifiziozi, e belli.*" People of quality took part, including ladies from Florence, "*e molto li lodavano, e celebravano.*" Although good taste was not always associated with upper class participation, there is no hint of the "*festa diabolica e tutta bestiale*" that had so disgusted Cambi in 1513. Prato's function and the different Florentine events, however, all seem to be civic pageants that quite explicitly represented siege warfare.

Jean d'Auton's account of the 1509 Milan combat indicates that this affair was organized on principles similar to those of the tournament. There was a high platform "*pour assoir les juges du combat.*"[97] A challenge was issued in public and the leading participants named, just as happened before a conventional tournament.[98] Moreover, the combat at the Milan bastion was preceded and followed by jousting. At Amboise in 1517, and again at Nozeroy in 1519–20, the siege combat formed part of a more conventional tournament. Here too there was an explicit analogy to war, because of the danger, of course, and because the particular quality of the tournament was participation by the noble military caste and the manner in which men conducted themselves. In war, as in the tourney, one acquired honor by one's conduct as much as by one's success.

Today it is often said that the principal motive in sixteenth-century warfare was profit. To be sure, profit was a major factor, and one that recurs in accounts of siege warfare where an important issue at stake

[95] A. Lorenzoni, *Carteggio artistico inedito di Don Vincenso Borghini* (Firenze, 1912), Letter no. XXI, 42.
[96] Sebastione Nicastro, *Sulla storia di Prato dalle origini alla metà del secolo XIX, sei lezioni* (Prato, 1916), 217.
[97] Jean d'Auton, *Chroniques*, IV:313.
[98] *Lordonnance et ordre de tournoy ioustes et combat a pied et a cheval* (Paris, 1520); Rene d'Anjou, *Traittié de la Forme et Devis d'ung Tournoy* (Paris, n.d.).

was likely to be the rich plunder from a sacked town. It would, however, be misleading to overlook chivalric motives. One of the classic figures in sixteenth-century literature, after all, is the poor *hidalgo*, and real life gives us no better example than the figure of Blaise de Monluc, the minor noble from Gascony who climbed the ladder of military success in the Wars of Italy and of Religion and who dictated his *Commentaries* as he recovered from a disfiguring wound in the hope, as he repeatedly states, that they would be an inspiration to the young men of France.[99] For his defense of Siena in 1554–5, Monluc received gifts of money and the rare honor of *chevalier de l'ordre du roi*. A marshal's baton followed some years later after a period of eclipse. In a lengthy passage of self-justification, Monluc stresses the need to rid one's mind of such unreliable favors and to concentrate instead upon the acquisition of honor and the good opinion of one's fellow soldiers. The defense of a place, argues Monluc, offers quite singular possibilities for the acquisition of honor, and singular risks for eternal shame:

When your Prince shall give you a place to keep, you are to consider three things; first the honour he does you in reposing so much confidence in your valour and wisdom. . . . the honour he does you is no little one, forasmuch as he does not only honour you in your own person, but moreover sets a mark of reputation on your whole race, by entrusting in your hands a Key of his Kingdom or some City of very great importance to him. . . . The second thing that you ought to set before your eyes is to consider if you lose the place committed to you . . . you dishonour your own master, who shall read in the histories dedicated to eternity that in his reign such a town was lost. . . . Before you were honoured and esteemed . . . but should you once fall into a misfortune like this, instead of prayers and acclamation you shall meet with affronts and injuries, for prayers maledictions, and they will curse you . . . so that a hundred times a day you will curse the hour that you were not killed upon a platform or in a breach in the defence of your garrison rather than so shamefully to have given it up to the enemy.[100]

People will reproach your children as the sons of a cowardly father. Women will despise you, even your own wife "for the nature of all

---

[99] A useful biographical essay is to be found in Ian Roy, ed., *Blaise de Monluc: The Valois-Habsburg Wars and the French Wars of Religion* (London, 1971), 1–29. See also Paul Courteault, *Un Cadet de Gascogne au XVIe siécle: Blaise de Monluc* (Paris, 1909) and *Blaise de Monluc Historien, étude critique sur le texte et la valeur historique des Commentaires* (Paris, 1907).

[100] *The Commentaries of Messire Blaize de Montluc*, trans. Charles Cotton (London, 1674), 110–18. For this essay, I have used Cotton's translation, which catches the flavor of Monluc's robust language, as well as misspelling his name. Scholarly editions have been edited by Alphonse de Ruble, 5 vols. (Paris, 1864–72), Paul Courteault, 3 vols. (Paris, 1911–25), and Jean Giono (Paris, 1964).

women is such that they hate all poltrons, let them never be so proper men, or never so handsomely dressed and thus Monsieur le Gouverneur, you who have lost your place, you will be in a marvelous happy condition when you shall be cursed in your own bed."[101] Monluc's advice for the avoidance of such ill fortune is always to "imagine your Prince and master before you and to remember that your master has not entrusted this place in your hands in order to live there only, but to die there also bravely fighting if need be." Read too, or have read to you, books that speak of the honor of great captains. Martin de Bellay and Guicciardini are both recommended, although the old soldier regrets that more of his comrades in arms do not take up the pen.

Read then these books and meditate with yourselves, if I do like Antonio de Leva at Pavia, the Sieur de Lude at Fonterabia, the Seigneur de Bouillon at Peronne, the Seigneur de Sansac at Miranda, and Monluc at Siena, what will they say of me? What honour shall I carry back to my own house? And on the contrary, if I surrender, what shame and infamy for me and mine?[102]

This rhetoric recurs so frequently in Renaissance and early modern military literature that it cannot simply be overlooked. In 1495, Guillaume de Villeneuve, who was one of those left in Aragonese southern Italy to defend Charles VIII's conquests, defended Trani to his last gasp and, on his return to France from months of suffering in the Venetian and Neapolitan galleys, wrote a treatise justifying himself "for he would better die than to surrender without orders from his King and sovereign lord."[103] The chevalier de Ville concluded his seventeenth-century treatise with the proposition "that there is no post of responsibility in war with which one can acquire more honour and reputation than that of governor."[104] When Napoleonic France came under pressure on its frontiers, Carnot was brought out of retirement to write a treatise for the cadets at the School of Engineering "to make men feel the importance of the defence of fortresses, and to excite the enthusiasm of young soldiers by a great number of examples."[105] Among the documents that Carnot reproduced for the edification of

---

[101] Monluc, *Commentaries*, 115.
[102] Monluc, *Commentaries*, 118.
[103] *Mémoires de G. de Villeneuve commençant en 1494 et finissant en 1497, contenant la conquêt du Royaume de Naples pour Charles VIII et la manière dont les Français en furent chassés*, ed. Petitot (Paris, 1819), 14:302. Villeneuve works this bold statement into the text in reply to one of his captors who had asked him why he refused to surrender Trani, despite generous terms and his abandonment by a number of his cowardly and treacherous comrades.
[104] Antoine de la Ville, *De la Charge des Gouverneurs des Places* (Paris, 1639).
[105] Quoted by E.M. Lloyd, *Vauban, Montalembert, Carnot: Engineering Studies* (London, 1887), 184.

the cadets were the Napoleonic letters patent consigning the town of Sas-de-Grand to a certain Colonel Lafosse in terms that relate directly to medieval siege law:

We order you to hold that place for us, and never to surrender on any pretext. Always before your eyes will be the inevitable consequences of a contravention of our orders. We expect and wish that you will stand the hazards of an assault, to prolong the defence and increase the losses of the enemy. Before the surrender of the place you must be at the last extremity of all your efforts, and at the final and absolute impossibility of further resistance. We forbid you to bring forward that cursed event willingly, even if only by an hour, and under the pretext of obtaining by that more honourable terms. We wish that each time the Council of Defence meets to discuss operations these letters patent be read aloud in a loud and clear voice.[106]

The very longevity of these traditional attitudes to the honorable defence of fortified positions may well support the speculative conjunction drawn here between the tournament, the siege tourney, and the real military events that gave them significance. Such a line of conjecture seems to fall flat on its face when one recalls the spectacles described by Landucci, Cambi, Lapini, and the Cavalier Miniati. What could such civic affairs possibly have in common with the noble tourney? But then the defense of a city was an element of common ground shared by a republic and a king. For both of them the city and its walls were very real symbols of political integrity.

---

[106] M. Carnot, *De la Défense des Places Fortes* (Paris, 1812), 83. Many French places indeed, held out with great obstinacy in the face of superior allied forces. In the aftermath of yet another bitter defeat in 1870–1, that great restorer of fortresses and popularizer of French historic architecture, Viollet-le-Duc, included just such another incident in his patriotic fictional "history" of an imaginary Burgundian town. Summoned by a Prussian officer, accompanied by an emigre Bourbon royalist who urged him to surrender, the Bonapartist colonel commanding La Roche-Pont replied to the royalist Baron in words that could have come from Bayard and evidently satisfied the enemy soldier's sense of honour. " 'I am here on the authority of superior orders to defend the place against the enemies of the country. The political inducements which you urge have not the slightest weight with me. I utterly ignore them. I shall not surrender the place unless compelled by force or ordered to do so by the Emperor's government. Permit me to add, sir, that the part you are performing today is not an honourable one. What do you think of it, *Monsieur le capitaine?*' added he, turning to the German officer. The latter merely bowed slightly." E.E. Viollet-le-Duc, *Annals of a Fortress*, trans. B. Bucknall (London, 1874), 350.

CHAPTER 19

Representations of the city in siege views of the seventeenth century: The war of military images and their production

MARTHA POLLAK

In the early modern period war affected every aspect of human life, becoming, with plague and famine, one of the great trials of mankind.[1] By the seventeenth century a dominant military caste no longer existed, however, because all society was impregnated with military values. European governments were first and foremost machines for waging war, and the scale on which they fought increased dramatically throughout the century.[2] The widespread use of firearms, introduced in the sixteenth century, was compounded in the seventeenth century by the increased size of standing and temporary armies.[3]

The vocation for military service was no longer found exclusively among the nobility, as the army purged cities of the most dangerous and lowest classes of unemployed men through recruitment. Consequently, the "military participation ratio" rose as war became the livelihood of wide segments of the population rather than the privileged domain of the aristocracy. The scientific innovations in firearms revolutionized military practices and helped to economize on the training of recruits. Powerful weapons were put in the hands of the urban poor and the disinherited peasantry. Thus the practice of war was changed not only by the new firearms, but by the shift from the

---

[1] André Corvisier, "Guerre et mentalités au XVIIe siècle," *XVII Siècle* 148/37 (1985): 217–32.

[2] M.S. Anderson, *War and Society in Europe of the Old Regime, 1618–1789* (Leicester, 1986), 16.

[3] Geoffrey Parker, *The Military Revolution: Military Innovation and the Rise of the West, 1500–1800* (Cambridge, 1989 [1988]), 40–5.

605

individual to the mass unit.[4] The centrally-controlled professional armies led to the "industrialization" of military behavior and organization.[5] This societal condition is reflected in the appearance of more cities, which became heavily militarized throughout the century.

Since war in the early modern period was primarily carried out through siege, the city became the privileged site of war.[6] The objectives in most cases were strategically situated towns and cities, whose inhabitants dominated their surrounding territory financially and politically, or controlled strategically the entry and passage through an important region. The territorial expansions of the seventeenth century could not ignore the threat posed by these "fortified islands."[7] The siege was the most dramatic and direct civilian confrontation with the military, since often the suburbs of the city were destroyed and segments of the population expelled.

As cities became better fortified siege warfare continued, even though this was a costly method to resolve a conflict, since a "long siege ate up money, materials and often men in a manner that even the greatest battle hardly ever did."[8] In a manner not unlike the military competition of the Cold War, siege warfare in the seventeenth century became a mark of advanced civilization. It was a systematic and demanding way of fighting that required careful planning and detailed organization; concomitantly, a paucity of elaborately fortified cities and disregard of artillery and engineers came to be seen as a badge of backwardness. Louis XIV is said to have hated the surprise and chance of the battle in the open field where he risked failure; preferring a complete and planned organization, he favored sieges because everything could be organized in advance.[9] A great siege became one of the biggest engineering operations known to the age and, consequently, provinces covered with fortified cities became prohibitively expensive to conquer. It is my purpose in this essay to examine the extensive production of military images that represent the city preyed upon, menaced, and captured by a besieging army.

[4] Michael Roberts, *The Military Revolution, 1560–1660* (Belfast, 1956), 10–26.

[5] Anderson, *War and Society*, 40.

[6] Simon Pepper, "The Meaning of the Renaissance Fortress," *Architectural Association Quarterly* 2 (1973): 21–8. For the history of these sieges, Christopher Duffy, *Siege Warfare: The Fortress in the Early Modern World 1494–1660* (London, 1979).

[7] Galeazzo Gualdo Priorato, *Il Guerriero prudente e politico* (Venice, 1640), 140: "*sono le fortezze come i scogli nel mare, rendono malagevole la navigatione degli acquisti alle navi de'pensieri de'Principi.*" For Gualdo Priorato (1606–78) see Giuseppe Sticca, *Gli scrittori militari italiani* (Turin, 1912), ch. 5.

[8] Frank Tallett, *War and Society in Early Modern Europe, 1495–1715* (London and New York, 1992), 3.

[9] Joan DeJean, *Literary Fortifications* (Princeton, 1984), 31.

The striking views of Vienna which represent it while besieged in 1529 and 1683 provide persuasive images of the fundamental conservatism of siege warfare in the early modern period, as well as illustrate developments in the defense and attack of fortified cities. These two views (Figs. 19.1* and 19.2) reflect the technical development in siege warfare between the Renaissance and Baroque periods. More important, they illustrate the radical change in the means of representation available in the seventeenth century.

The earlier view by Hans Sebald Beham (1529) is a dizzying image, with concentric ("laid-down") layers, that has the cathedral of St. Stephen at its center, the walls forming the perimeter of the city, and the surrounding suburban landscape spread into a 360-degree panorama. The city and the area around it are populated by thousands of figures. The siege was conducted by the Turkish army which eventually raised it (recognizing that the distance from their home base was too great for the supply line to function), but not before giving Christian Europe the greatest scare of the century.[10] This massive view (812 × 856 mm), intended to dramatize the plight of Vienna as a bastion of the Christian faith, was sponsored by the city council of Nuremberg as a reflection of its pro-imperial policy, and was its only graphic commission during the first half of the sixteenth century.[11]

It is an extraordinary image in its conception, and it clarifies the hierarchy of elements that are involved in the conflict. What seems to matter is the following: the cathedral, illustrated in perspective view even though the image was drawn from its tower; the city walls; the imposing gates, all clearly shut; the immediate surroundings of the city; the vast numbers of soldiers, camels, tents, and officers shown individually and in geometrical groupings. A closer look reveals that the situation described is extremely grim for the besieged: There is a large breach in the wall where an explosion is just taking place (top center); the Turks are firing from very close up – having taken over the *Vorstadt* and using its buildings to stage their cannon fire (top left) – and an entire segment of the city wall seems ready to cave in. Made up of six blocks, the image must be "read" separately in four parts: the two central parts individually, the two pairs of side panels together. In order to examine details the viewer would have to rotate the woodcut continuously to see any part of the radial landscape. But the mural scale of the view suggests that it was probably mounted on

---

* All figures appear at the end of this chapter.

[10] J.R. Hale, *War and Society in Renaissance Europe, 1450–1620* (Glasgow, 1985), 16, 191.

[11] Keith Moxey, *Peasants, Warriors and Wives: Popular Imagery in the Reformation* (Chicago, 1989), 78.

canvas, and as a gift to Charles V this view was meant as less of a topographical document than a news account and instrument of praise and wonder.[12] As a graphic composition the imposition of a horizontal perspective scheme onto a ground-plan format is not appropriate for an accurate mapping of the city, but as an exercise in image-making this view of what at the time was considered the "siege of sieges" is unprecedented for a city view.[13] Furthermore, its circular outline echoes distantly a model adopted earlier in medieval *mappae mundi* and manuscript representations of heavenly Jerusalem, and thus claims a planetary centrality for Vienna's troubles.

The siege view of Vienna in 1683 is clearly derived from the representation of the earlier siege. The two military conflicts were both inflicted upon the city by Turkish besiegers, which turned its defense effectively into a crusade. The plight of the city in both instances brought about large popular response, and involved most western European governments.[14] Commensurate in size (879 × 883 mm), the composition of Henri Schmits' view (Fig. 19.2) echoes closely Beham's concentric view, but also differs from it greatly, representing the changed conditions of the city's walls and developments in cartographic representation. While the interior of the city is overlooked, the bastioned fortification enclosure is emphatically drawn, and is dramatized by a painstaking delineation in an ichnographic plan of the system of approaches and parallels made by the Turkish sappers, which appears bewilderingly elaborate but was admirably suited to the ground. The modernized city wall, with eleven polygonal bastions, had been built in response to the earlier siege and was already in place by 1547.[15] In this version of the siege the Turkish presence and menace is illustrated, not by its camp or large numbers of soldiers, but by the labyrinthine trenches made outside the Burgthur, between the Burg and the Löwel bastions. Thus Schmits combines the dramatic layout of Beham with topographic accuracy. Beyond that he adds the scientific military annotation of the trenches, which illustrates the exact site

[12] Richard Kagan, "The Art of Cityscapes," in *Art and History: Images and Their Meaning*, eds. Robert I. Rotberg and Theodore K. Rabb (Cambridge, 1988 [1986]), 133, discusses topographic accuracy vs. encomiastic purpose in city views.

[13] David Landau and Peter Parshall, *The Renaissance Print, 1470–1550* (New Haven, 1994), 226–8, 235, 240–4; J.R. Hale, *Artists and Warfare in the Renaissance* (New Haven and London, 1990), 17.

[14] For the siege of 1683, see Christopher Duffy, *The Fortress in the Age of Vauban and Frederick the Great, 1660–1789* (London, 1985), 230–3, and John Stoye, *The Siege of Vienna* (London, 1964), 157–90.

[15] As can be seen from the surveyed drawing of Augustin Hirschvogel, engraved in 1552, reproduced in Landau and Parshall, *The Renaissance Print*, 239–42.

of the last conflict and, in contrast to the tumult of Beham's view, provides a silent "anatomical" dissection of the event.

THE SIGNIFICANCE OF SIEGE VIEWS

Siege views were part of the wider interest in the representation of the city in the Renaissance.[16] The monumental city view and siege had been suggested as appropriate for the decoration of princely residences by Alberti and other early Renaissance humanists;[17] the works of art produced to commemorate, for instance, the Battle of Pavia fulfill this recommendation, linking military representation to Renaissance practices of artistic representation and thus also to antiquity. This established fully the military panorama as a bona fide work of art. Like the almost contemporary siege of Vienna, the Battle of Pavia (1525) caught the imagination of artists throughout Europe. In Jorg Breu's woodcut (Fig. 19.3) the city is allowed to loom large, occupying almost one quarter of the image, endowed with much greater detail than the countryside (though not necessarily accurate detail). In what is the most famed representation of this engagement – the fifth tapestry in the Battle of Pavia series designed by Bernard van Orley – the city reigns over the view of the bloody conflict from its central position in the composition (Fig. 19.4). This is the position that the city will occupy in most subsequent siege views. The view of the city is in profile, anchored to the landscape through the punctuation of medieval towers, while the attention lavished on topography and landscape goes well beyond the desire to describe accurately, enhancing the visual and sensual appeal of this image in flagrant contradiction to the subject depicted. The Pavia tapestries were offered as a symbolic war trophy to Charles V, whose imperial army emerged victorious from this engagement having captured a royal prisoner, in a manner similar (though on a much more lavish scale) to the offering of the siege view of Vienna that he received about the same time from the council of Nuremberg.[18]

The earliest siege views directly commissioned by a victorious commander, and intended as a political and dynastic instrument of propaganda, are the series on Charles V's conquest of Tunis.[19] The cam-

---

[16] Hendrik J. Horn, *Jan Cornelisz Vermeyen: Painter of Charles V and His Conquest of Tunis* (Doornspijk, 1989), 1:270.

[17] Landau and Parshall, *The Renaissance Print*, 234.

[18] Hale, *Artists and Warfare*, 189–90, 250; L. Casali et al., *Gli Arazzi della Battaglia di Pavia nel museo di Capodimonte a Napoli* (Pavia, 1993).

[19] Hale, *Artists and Warfare*, 137.

paign in Tunis provided ample material for the beginnings of a new pictorial tradition, one that claimed to revive ancient imperial practices. The drawings were prepared by the Flemish artist Jan Vermeyen, who accompanied Charles V on the African campaign in 1535. The artist, part of a whole cultural-commemorative entourage that attended the emperor, had been asked to record the expedition in prints, and the idea of a tapestry series only took shape consequently and required a long time to accomplish. The views of Pavia and the African campaign provided rich precedent for the large corpus of Renaissance and Baroque military tapestries that followed.

The representation of the imperial campaign is significant because, like the two defenses of Vienna discussed above, they took on the aura of a Christian crusade. Vermeyen, who was well versed in the geometry of surveying, provided the drawings for the engravings made by Franz Hogenberg (Fig. 19.5), as well as for the tapestries woven in Brussels. The picture of the imperial navy approaching the African coast combines the compositional strategy and information of portolan charts, land cartography, landscape painting, and portraiture. Charles V is seen from a high viewpoint in the lead ship of the imperial navy rounding the cape of Carthage; in the deep space of the view Goleta, Tunis, and the ruins of ancient Roman aqueducts are visible in this bird's-eye view of the north African coast. The broad panorama, the deep perspective view, the high horizon line that turns this view almost into a map, and the large numbers of boats and figures dramatize both versions of the image and draw the viewer into the picture.[20] The spatial disunity in the pictures of the conquest are the result of the combination of two features: the heroic figures, which act as wings to the telescoped, elevated view, and the detailed, clearly spaced action. Vermeyen successfully combined the monumental style of the Pavia tapestries with the minute genre of such works as Beham's siege of Vienna.

Numerous objects were spun off Vermeyen's images, partly because of their visual appeal – greater even than the Battle of Pavia series – partly because of their association with an imperial enterprise. The appeal of the siege and of the sack that followed as a decorative motif can be seen in a silver tray decorated with the assault of Tunis, where the city occupies the center of the composition and mimics the exciting density of the battlefield through its equivalent massing of buildings. This image constitutes, as well, a rather close reference to the 1529 siege view of Vienna in its concentric layering of city view, fortifica-

---

[20] Hale, *Artists and Warfare*, 250–2; Horn, *Jan Cornelisz Vermeyen*, 1:15–17, 256–80.

tions, besieging army, and surrounding seascape with ships. The fall of Tunis provided further subject matter for graphic artists who, far from the siege, could embroider upon the connections between war, city, and imperial action.

The European military moves of Charles V continued to provoke outstanding and influential examples of siege views. The siege and battle at Ingolstadt in 1546 was illustrated by Hans Mielich, and it is the only other sixteenth-century view of a siege taken from inside the city. Similar to Beham's view of Vienna, with the artist placed on top of a tall building, it provides a broad panorama of the landscape with huge armies amassed around the walls of the city. This encampment was of two opposing armies, that of Charles V and that of the Schmalkaldic League of his Protestant opponents, though Charles used this site because Ingolstadt was friendly to him.[21] The city is represented occupying the immediate foreground realistically foreshortened, unlike the cartographic and episodic treatment of Vienna, and the walls provide the picture line separating the few visible and peaceful buildings inside the city from the animatedly inhabited landscape beyond. The landscape view is in two parts: on the left, a large military settlement separated by a river from the plain beyond, on the right, a denser military camp beside which regiments in battle formation are preparing to enter a fray. Both panels constitute a balanced composition and thus can stand alone, but the main action is clearly on the right side, privileged also by the placement of the artist's viewpoint. The view suggests powerfully the din and dust of the clash, but also the pageantry of this meeting of armies.

The view of the imperial camp outside Wittenberg (Fig. 19.6) further celebrates the army, which occupies in a rational and clear way an area much larger than the existing town, and invites comparison between the two kinds of settlements, military and civilian. Charles's campaign against the Schmalkaldic League – his victory at Mühlberg, followed by his approach to Wittenberg – was justified, at least officially, by the League's war against Duke Heinrich of Brunswick-Wolfenbüttel and their siege of Wolfenbüttel (1542). In his siege view of Wolfenbüttel, the distinguished artist Lucas Cranach illustrated its bombing by the armies of Saxony and Hesse from a high viewpoint.[22] In its swampy site dominated by the camp of the besieging army, the city occupies three-fifths of the picture space while the camp takes up

---

[21] Karl Brandi, *The Emperor Charles V: The Growth and Destiny of a Man and of a World-Empire*, trans. C.V. Wedgewood (London, 1970 [1937]), 552–4; J.R. Hale, "Soldiers in German Art," in *Art and History*, 92, 97–8.

[22] Hale, *Artists and Warfare*, 19–23.

two-fifths. The trajectories described by the bombs testify to Cranach's acquaintance with ballistic theory, if not the actual works of Nicolò Tartaglia, a contemporary author of the most influential treatise on the subject.

Sieges as a decorative motif initially became popular in German art;[23] despite Alberti's and Castiglione's urgings to represent them, Italian artists preferred the complex melèe, like Paolo Ucello's knightly and medievalizing battle scenes or the detailed illustration of up-to-date military instruments such as Francesco di Giorgio Martini's decorative reliefs at the ducal palace of Urbino. Legitimized in the second quarter of the sixteenth century by imperial association and the desire for conquest, the celebration of military victories was carried out through every technique of art and form of representation, including intarsia, tapestry, wall painting, easel painting, low relief sculpture and, most important, through widely available engravings. War, siege, and assault became iconographic themes with great currency and popularity. The visual repertory through which these themes were expressed offers a great deal of information about strategy and military engineering, about the form of the city, and its defense.[24]

The inclination in the seventeenth century to exploit a successful siege politically and to popularize it, especially through the privileged medium of engraving, came with the requirement for authenticity of description. The "mapping impulse" as defined by Svetlana Alpers, which is a combination of pictorial format and descriptive interest, could be said to have characterized the desire to describe or record in pictures.[25] But this impulse, shared by surveyors, artists, and printers, was not limited to the Dutch context, even though an abundance of visual evidence from the Low Countries was influential in endowing images with content.[26] Purportedly accurate descriptions of military events became part of a war of images that came to parallel the war of pamphlets, and eventually helped define a significant seventeenth-century form of government, the warring monarchy.[27]

[23] Raimond Van Marle, *Iconographie de l'art profane au Moyen-Age et a la Renaissance* (The Hague, 1931), 1:326–39.

[24] Cesare de Seta, "Le mura simbolo della città," in *La città e le mura*, eds. Cesare de Seta and Jacques Le Goff (Bari, 1989), 11–57.

[25] Svetlana Alpers, *The Art of Describing: Dutch Art in the Seventeenth Century* (Chicago, 1983), 119–68.

[26] Kagan, "Cityscapes," 123.

[27] Roger Chartier, *The Cultural Uses of Print in Early Modern France*, trans. Lydia G. Cochrane (Princeton, 1987), 161; Jean Claude Boyer, "Les representations guerrieres et l'evolution des arts plastiques en France au XVII siècle," *XVIIᵉ Siècle* 148/37 (1985): 291–305.

These siege plans and views display the city as an object of political and military desire, and are of fundamental significance both for the formulation of the city's identity and for the documentation of military conflict focused on cities. The detailed rendering of military action must be seen in the context of the important place of military reportage in contemporary art, especially German art of the 1520s and 1530s. Thus the genre received more attention from the middle of the sixteenth century, and by the seventeenth century it became thoroughly widespread in France and the Netherlands as well as Germany, where a dominance of the aesthetic representation of fortification can be detected.[28]

These military representations of cities became mirrors for the relationship between political power and urban planning, in an age when military architecture was an openly accepted model for the appearance of the city, and cartography played a crucial role in defining the visual image and representation of the city. During the seventeenth century, bastioned city walls were sponsored and financed by ruling sovereigns. Their initiative asserted their military authority over municipal governments, which were, often obliged to contribute to the cost of the fortification construction.[29] The walls of the city constituted not only its military strength, but also the representation of that strength. Earlier, humanists like Alberti had underlined the expressive quality of the walls, not only defensive, but eloquent with the protective quality that is meant to frighten enemies.[30]

Representation of power and military culture are linked to theatrical imagery in the seventeenth century by the need to control – from a central, absolutist stance – the appearance of the city. This theatrical imagery is tied to public pageantry, which has a strong affinity with war in its wasteful character, suspension of moral standards, collective exultation, and diminution of the instinct of preservation. War, too, has a "ludic" character, like the public "festa" or party, most evident in the ceremonials associated with the beginning and the conclusion of the siege.[31] The idea of the siege as a social event gained great currency in seventeenth-century courtly practice.

In producing powerful images of famous sieges, artists and military

[28] Henning Eichberg, *Festung, Zentralmacht und Geometrie: Kriegsingenieurwesen des 17. Jahrhunderts in den Herzogtümern Bremen und Verden* (Cologne and Vienna, 1989).

[29] See my study of the expansions and fortification of an Italian city, *Turin 1564–1680: Urban Design, Military Culture, and the Creation of the Absolutist Capital* (Chicago, 1991).

[30] Hubertus Günther, "Die Kriegskunst in der Renaissance," in *Deutsche Architekturtheorie zwischen Gotik und Renaissance*, ed. Hubertus Günther (Darmstadt, 1988), 164–79.

[31] Franco Cardini, *Quell'antica festa crudele: Guerra e cultura della guerra dall'età feudale alla grande rivoluzione* (Florence, 1982).

architects were aided by the quickly developing techniques of Renaissance cartography which they wholeheartedly adopted and advanced. The plan became the fundamental tool in the siege of towns; the earliest accurately surveyed manuscript plans of cities known to us were made for military purposes.[32] The construction of new fortifications and the restoration of old ones, as well as the siege of a town, required elaborate and accurate topographical site plans. This vast western European cartographic development was fueled further by the great public appetite for visual descriptions of sieges. Thus military needs and public interest concurred in the production of profuse numbers of engraved siege views, some collected in albums or "battle books" (*Schlachtbücher*) that documented the early modern wars.[33]

The siege view of the most celebrated tactical victory of the century, that of the small town of St. Quentin, northwest of Paris, in 1556 (Fig. 19.7), is significantly like a much earlier manuscript image from the hand of Dürer (Fig. 19.8) of the siege of Hohenaspern in 1519.[34] Both illustrate a fortress that draws its strength from its location on a hill, with rows of cannon lined up against it, while soldiers attempt to assault it from below. As for his other bellic images, for the siege view of Hohenaspern Dürer drew upon his various artistic interests – perspective, landscape, cartography – but also on narrative history and scientific research. In St. Quentin, moreover, the view is synchronous, that is, a sequence of events is illustrated rather than one isolated moment. While Dürer's view is a "portrait" of the fortress desired by its besiegers, St. Quentin is part of a larger, cartographic landscape made visible by the high horizon line.

Towards the end of the sixteenth century some very significant changes occurred in both the form and the content of siege views. The engraving of the siege of Amiens by the army of Henri IV in 1597 shows that the attackers had built some important field fortifications (Fig. 19.9). These are double fortifications, of circumvallation and countervallation, with which the besiegers protected their encampment both against Amiens and a possible attack from a relieving army that might come to the aid of the city. These fortifications are illustrated clearly, though not to scale, in the siege view where Amiens is fully displayed with its streets, squares, buildings, and rather meager fortifications. The attempt to illustrate the surroundings of the city is

---

[32] Martha Pollak, "La storia delle città: testi, piante, palinsesto," *Quaderni Storici*, n.s. 67 (1988): 223–56.

[33] There are two extant volumes of these *Schlachtbücher* in the collection of Prince August in Herzog August Bibliothek in Wolfenbüttel, Germany.

[34] Hale, *Artists and Warfare*, 16.

not very successful, though the sections of the royal army are labeled separately, as are some neighboring towns.

The siege of the fortress of Montmellian in Piedmont by Henri IV is synthetically illustrated by the best royal topographer, Claude Chastillon, though the clarity of his picture is achieved at the expense of visual praise for the royal army, virtually nonexistent in this view where the immense polygonal bastions of the fortress hold pride of place. The siege itself is signaled only by groups of smoking cannon deployed on the surrounding hills. His high viewpoint facilitates the display of the site, but the army has no critical mass, and the view lacks dramatic punch.[35] Much more successful as a rhetorical image is Sebastien Leclerc's illustration of the "taking" of the same fortress of Montmellian by Catinat in 1691, where a three-dimensional model of the site is wheeled before the thrilled French audience at Versailles (Fig. 19.10), like a trophy in the triumph of a victorious military commander.[36]

SEVENTEENTH-CENTURY SIEGE VIEWS

The view of the blockade of Montauban, in 1621, shows the bastioned fortifications of the city in a radical departure from the state of St. Quentin and Amiens just a few years earlier. These lavish new fortifications enclose a relatively small town, still straitjacketed inside its medieval walls, and expand across the river with a verve that is matched by the extensive field fortifications of the besieging army. There are palpable problems of scale in this composition, which lead one to assume that the author of this siege view meant to illustrate

[35] For Henri IV's engineers, see David Buisseret, "Les ingénieurs du roi au temps de Henri IV," *Bulletin de la Section de Géographie* 77 (1976): 80.

[36] The performance of fictitious sieges for the entertainment of a court audience became widespread in the seventeenth century. An early example is the assault of the "Castle of Love," which took place in the Place Royale in Paris in 1612 as part of the wedding festivities of Louis XIII and Anne of Austria; see Jean Vanuxem, "Le carrousel de 1612 sur la Place Royale et ses devises," in *Les fêtes de la Renaissance*, ed. Jean Jacquot (Paris, 1956), 1:191–203, and Laugier de Porcherer, *Le camp de la place Royale* (1613). But in this case of ludic appropriation of a military enterprise, the imperial events under Charles V provided precedent once again, albeit in a military rather then civilian context. In the view by H.S. Beham of the military reception for the entry of Charles V into Munich in 1530, the party consists of the siege of a small castle at the right side of the picture, assaulted by foot soldiers and knights on horseback and bombed by mortars from the left. The arc of the bombs connects the central sheet and the right panel, while the central panel and the left one are linked by the arc of displayed cannon. The impact of military culture (linguistic, ceremonial, and aesthetic) and the reenaction of victorious sieges for public and court entertainment are considered in my larger study on Baroque cities, in preparation.

mainly the war machines put in place by the two warring factions; the city is only a pawn in this strategic conflict. The ambivalence of the illustration could also be explained by the inconclusiveness of the siege, which was raised by Louis XIII after three months.[37]

In strong contrast, the view of the siege of Royan by the king of France in 1622 shifts the interest back to the focus of the siege. Like Chastillon, the author of this view places the fortress at the center of the picture, focusing on the perimeter fortification with only a few hints of the interior layout of Royan. Naturally and artificially fortified, the city aggressively dominates the approaches by sea and land, making it an even more valuable prize. Numerous activities are simultaneously illustrated, including a scene of the king, in the right middle ground, accepting the surrender of the city. The legend and descriptive text that accompany the image give it the quality of journalistic reportage, as well as royal propaganda.

The Dutch victories against the Spanish during their long war were freely and loudly celebrated. In a publication of 1612 dedicated to the government of the United Provinces, *Warhafftige Beschreibung und Eigentliche Abbildung aller Zuge und Victorien*, symbolic and allegorical images are employed to convey the victories that Maurits of Nassau accomplished in the two decades preceding the truce of 1609.[38] The title page, brimming with Dutch riches, has at its base a pedestal ornamented with the view of a marching army, a battle, and a siege of a pentagonal citadel. Lavishly illustrated with copper plate engravings, the book is a compendium of Maurits's sieges, which are presented with remarkable stylistic consistency, and are intended to glorify Maurits at a time when he was being urged to assert himself against the leaders of the States of Holland.

The siege of Ostend (Fig. 19.11) provides a good illustration of the modernized fortification of the city – overhauled in 1572, in 1578 and again in 1596 – and its site by the sea. The excitement of the siege, which lasted from June 1601 to September 1604, is conveyed through grouped battalions and regiments with pikes and standards indicating the direction of movement. Given the length of the engagement these details represent not accuracy in reporting (though the archduke's army conducted a very active siege), but rather an attempt to show

---

[37] Yves-Marie Bercé, *La Naissance dramatique de l'absolutisme, 1598–1661* (Paris, 1992), chapter on "Louis XIII's Wars."

[38] *Warhafftige Beschreibung und Eigentliche Abbildung aller Zuge und Victorien* (Leyden, 1612); see also Herbert H. Rowen, *The Princes of Orange: The Stadholders in the Dutch Republic* (Cambridge, 1990 [1988]), 39–53.

how valiant the defense was.[39] Precise scale drawing has been put aside in favor of the immediacy and playfulness of a cartoon like illustration.

Some Dutch towns were taken and retaken several times, causing the successive sieges to be described and illustrated. Thus Groll was taken by Maurits of Nassau in 1597, and retaken by the Spanish in 1606; the condition of the city ca. 1610 is shown in the *Victorien* siege volume (Fig. 19.12). Fortified with five bastions, the city is being attacked from field works that form a crown around it; the orderly camp at top left is echoed in the disciplined regiments heading for Groll, while the cannon are battering it from close up. As in the other siege views in this book, the sketchy generic interior of the city and the out-of-scale representation of the army endow the picture with a game-like intimacy. In the single-sheet view by the influential cartographer and publisher Hendrick Hondius of the later siege of 1627, conducted by Frederick Henry of Nassau, this ludic and spectatorial quality has been suppressed in favor of a rationalistic plan (probably intended as the illustration to the text by Grotius describing the siege).[40] The city is shown to have six bastions, presumably built by the Spanish; there is no depiction of the interior of the city (Fig. 19.13). The polygonal fortifications are illustrated in true horizontal section, or ichnographic plan, and equally important, the relationship of the city and the circumvallation seems to be guided by a scale that allows actual distances to be measured off accurately. This "scientific view" is a thorough breakthrough; it brings together the orderly siege inherited from Maurits with the advanced technical abilities in surveying and cartography of Hondius.[41]

A fundamental contribution to the seventeenth-century siege view was made by the French graphic artist Jacques Callot.[42] His first work in this genre was the view of the siege of Gradisca, commanded by Giovanni de' Medici, which he made in 1618 in Florence, but his most

---

[39] Henri Haestens, *La nouvelle Troye ou Memorable histoire du Siege d'Ostende* (Leyden, 1615). The mechanics of the siege are closely examined in Christopher Duffy's chapter on the "80 Years' War in the Netherlands," in *Siege Warfare*; see also Geoffrey Parker, *Spain and the Netherlands, 1559–1659* (Glasgow, 1990 [1979]), 45–63.

[40] Hugo Grotius, *Grollae Obsidio* (Amsterdam, 1629).

[41] For the extensive oeuvre of Hondius, see Nadine Orenstein, *Hendrick Hondius and the Business of Prints in Seventeenth-Century Holland* (Roosendaal, 1994).

[42] For the most recent studies of Callot's work, see H. Diane Russell, *Jacques Callot: Prints and Related Drawings*, exh. cat. (Washington, 1975), esp. 179–87; and *Le incisioni di Jacques Callot nelle collezioni italiane*, exh. cat., Instituto Nazionale per la Grafica (Rome, 1992).

distinguished siege view is that of Breda, which he finished in 1628 (Fig. 19.14). It is a bird's-eye view combined with an ichnographic plan of the city and the field fortifications, landscape, and genre scenes in the foreground. Made of six sheets, the huge work (1200 × 1405 mm) was endowed with an engraved frame signaling that the intended purpose of this siege view was to be displayed like a wall painting or tapestry. Unlike the large view of Vienna by Beham, however, the entire image, made up of different representation systems ingeniously combined, can be taken in at one view. The horizon line is very close to the top of the picture allowing for most of it to be occupied by the military event. This is presented in a "curving perspective" with a panoramic view in the foreground, a perspective gradually tilted up in an artificial curve until the receding ground plane is almost parallel to the picture plane, as in a map.[43] The animated human activity in the foreground, and the canal that flows up from the left, lead the eye into the picture, which seems to be taken from a great height (though none exists in reality).[44] Like Jan Vermeyen and Hans Mielich, Callot incorporates his working persona into the picture, here at the bottom left; as in the military tapestries of the Battle of Pavia and the *Conquest of Tunis* there are chronologically disparate events occurring within the same picture plane.

Callot returns to the vivid depiction of the camp activities that the sixteenth-century German artists had so lovingly described. His figures, though small, are distinctly delineated; thousands of individuals populate this picture, including the festive entourage of Archduchess Isabella, which accompanied her to visit the siege. Callot made a similarly splendid view of the siege of La Rochelle, soon after he completed the siege view of Breda (Fig. 19.15). Both siege views were commissioned by the victorious party, and while Callot's pictures were not woven into costly tapestry, they constitute the most monumental siege images made in the seventeenth century. His work stands out not only because of size, but through the layout and detail of the illustration.

The siege of La Rochelle is even more sumptuously framed, with subsidiary military images woven into it as well as trophies and portraits of the king and the commanding general. The horizon line

---

[43] *Jacques Callot 1592–1635*, exh. cat., Brown University (Providence, 1970), cat. no. 35.

[44] Hermannus Hugo, *Obsidio Bredana* (Antwerp, 1626). For the most recent studies of this siege view and extensive documentation for the production of this engraving, see Simone Zurawski, "New Sources for Jacques Callot's Map of the Siege of Breda," *The Art Bulletin* 70 (1988): 621–39; and Jean-Marc Depluvrez, "Breda ou l'art du siege," in *Jacques Callot 1592–1635*, ed. Paulette Choné, exh. cat. (Nancy, 1992) 348–78.

having disappeared, the plan of La Rochelle occupies the center of the composition, faced across the bay by the dike with which the royal French army blockaded the city. The siege was begun by Louis XIII in September 1627 and employed 30,000 men, but their efforts were useless since the English navy commanded the approach by sea. The architect Clement Metezeau then conducted the construction of a dike to close the entry into the harbor of La Rochelle. The pharaonic size of this enterprise, employing thousands of masons and farmers, was widely and panegyrically praised as unprecedented.[45] Nonetheless, the population resisted for another year without outside help.

The engraving is a valuable document because, as at Breda, the most drastic punishment was meted out after the siege and the city's fortifications were demolished.[46] The surrounding landscape is littered with the French army, while the foreground is filled with great English galleons afloat outside the port. It is a dizzying perspective, characterized by the spatial disunity earlier employed by Vermeyen, in which the eye jumps from the large objects in the foreground to the abstracted buildings of the distantly observed city. Other views of this famous blockade were proposed, and Callot's student Stefano della Bella produced a much more peaceful image of the siege as seen from a ship's mast, and closer details of the dike and the city's silhouette, without the spatial jumps of Callot's composition.

In the siege views that della Bella produced between 1638 and 1650, he developed further Callot's compositional techniques, bringing in one major innovation.[47] This can be seen in the view of the siege of St. Omer of 1638 (Fig. 19.16), where della Bella thinks of his picture as a stage set upon which he lifts the curtain that also serves as the site for the legend. This pulling of the curtain on an endless view (without horizon) endows the picture, through a clever conceptual twist, with a theatrical quality that characterizes other Baroque art. Beyond the stagey composition, where a few large-scale figures emerge in the foreground and watch the siege with us, della Bella's contribution rests on the high quality of his vision and execution.

The siege of Casale in 1628 brought together the French and Spanish armies, freshly victorious at La Rochelle and Breda, respectively; the representation of this siege likewise draws on the devices employed

---

[45] Callot, text along the engraving: "... the great marvels of the world, the representation of the pyramids of Egypt, Colossus of Rhodes ... are less than the dike of La Rochelle...."

[46] Bercé, *La Naissance*, "Louis XIII's Wars."

[47] See Alexandre de Vesme, *Stefano Della Bella: catalogue raisonné*, with intro. and additions by Phyllis Dearborn Massar (New York, 1968).

to illustrate these previous conflicts. The siege, illustrated in a newsletter published by Melchior Tavernier in Paris, pitted the Spanish
army against the hexagonal citadel of the city, the largest in Italy. The
fortified walls and the citadel are shown in plan; the besiegers are
schematically illustrated, as is the surrounding area of the city. But
this is a dry cartographic representation in contrast with the livelier
view of Casale published in Paris in 1630 (Fig. 19.17). Here there is an
attempt to enliven the image of the city through three-dimensional
projection, which brings out the buildings of the city and the tents of
the camp that occupy the foreground and serves to draw one's eye
into the picture.

The cartographic plan, based on earlier representations of the city,
continued strongly in Dutch circles. The siege of 's Hertogenbosch in
1629 was illustrated by Jan Visscher, who was the prolific counterpart
of Hendrick Hondius in Amsterdam.[48] Part of a larger collection illustrating the continuing Dutch wars, Visscher's siege view offers a
graphic panegyric to this enormous effort by Frederick Henry of Nassau. The town, ranked with Brussels, Antwerp, and Louvain as one of
the chief places of Brabant, was well defended by its site between two
rivers, and by its large garrison. Like Hondius' siege view of Groll,
this is a cartographic plan. It is enlivened by the genre figures –
soldiers and officers shown at various military occupations – but the
map fills the entire sheet. This map illustrates the extensive circumvallation which took eleven hours to walk around and connected six
different camps, three major forts, and twelve hornworks, while dam-
ming two rivers,[49] displaying on a most impressive scale the laborious
and scientific siege methods of the Orange brothers. Thousands of
sightseers from the United Provinces assembled at 's Hertogenbosch
for the surrender of the city since, like the opening of trenches and the
laying of foundation stones, the ceremony of the surrender of a fortress was a spectacle of high dramatic interest.[50] The exit of the defeated was made through a breach in the fortified walls, then along a
path flanked by the besiegers, and to the sound of the exiting garrison's musicians, who played the music of the victorious army.[51]

The most important contemporary German artist involved in the

---

[48] For Visscher see Leo Bagrow, *History of Cartography*, 2nd ed., revised and enlarged by
R.A. Skelton (Chicago, 1985), 181–3, 277; and Tony Campbell, *Claes Jansz. Visscher: a
Hundred Maps Described* (London, 1968).
[49] Anderson, *War and Society*, 41.
[50] Pieter Geyl, *The Netherlands in the Seventeenth Century* (London, 1961), 1:84–95.
[51] John W. Wright, "Sieges and Customs of War at the Opening of the Eighteenth
Century," *American Historical Review* 39 (1934): 629–44.

making of siege views during the Thirty Years' War was Matthaeus Merian. His prodigious cartographic production included many war-related images, which are interspersed with peaceful city views and maps in his *Theatrum Europeum*, published from 1635.[52] His view of Frankfurt in 1631 shows the entry of the victorious king of Sweden, Gustavus Adolphus, who arrived through the fortified suburb of Sachsenhausen (Fig. 19.18). The horizon line is placed similarly to the earlier view of Casale, and the city occupies the center ground across the sheet. The lively profile of church bell towers forms an appropriate background to the marching regiments where the pikes are carried in formation. Merian's plan of Frankfurt emphasized the old city in his initial cartographic representation, and was used as the basis for later siege views.[53] In an earlier siege view of Frankfurt, made in 1552 by Conrad Faber, a higher bird's-eye view allowed the artist to represent the siege of the city more emphatically. The earlier view is splendid in its scope, creating a wide panorama of the broad plain around the city, but Merian's contributions emphasize the formidable modernized walls of Frankfurt, the polygonal bastions, and glacis that replace the medieval walls and moat still visible in 1552. Merian's views and plans, sold in collections or as single sheets, were well known throughout Europe, and with Callot and the Dutch cartographers Hondius and Visscher, he makes the most important contribution to the siege view in the first half of the seventeenth century.[54]

While the numerous victorious sieges of Maurits of Nassau were celebrated in the weighty publication of 1612, as we have seen above, the rapid victories of Marchese Spinola were reported in a comic strip (Fig. 19.19) whose spiral shape allowed for more towns to be added. Here the representation of each town is in fact only an ideogram, a generic sketch, though often with one recognizable element from the actual town. The emphasis here is on the collective effect of vanquishing numerous towns, and on the rhetorical aspect of this political arithmetic. This popular illustration is a powerful visual document for the argument that towns were indeed thought of as pawns in the protracted seventeenth-century wars. The type received reinforcement in 1631, when Gustavus Adolphus' successes in Germany were repre-

---

[52] Johann Philipp Abele, *Theatrum Europeum, oder Warhaffte Beschreibung ... vom Jahr Christi 1617 bis das Jahr 1629* (Frankfurt, 1635 [vol. II, 1637; vol. III, 1639]).

[53] Wilhelm Bingsohn, "Matthaeus Merian, ein soziales Umfeld und die Geschichte der Stadt Frankfurt am Mein 1590–1650," in *Matthaeus Merian*, exh. cat. (Frankfurt, 1993), 19–27.

[54] For Merian's prodigious production of city views, see Lucas H. Wüthrich, *Das druchgraphische Werk von Matthaeus Merian der Ältere* (Basel, 1966 and 1972), 1:ch. 14.

sented in a similar manner. His inventory of towns is much larger, and thus the strip coils five times around his portrait at the center, while the way in which he obtained these towns is forcefully illustrated in another broadsheet, also of 1631, where he is shown stabbing the papal representative in the belly and forcing him thus to "expel" the swallowed German cities. The Swedish winnings are at the center of a game of trick-track being played by the generals involved in the Thirty Years' War, vividly illustrating the significance of these towns as counters in what is seen as the cynical game of war.[55] The taking and retaking of towns in Germany was partly due to the poor level of fortifications, to which Merian's plans of German towns in his *Theatrum Europeum* testify.[56]

A significant contribution to the definition of the city at war in the seventeenth century was developed by military architects. Often these were artillery officers who endeavored to document their activities through treatises on the attack and defense of cities. Antoine de Ville provides a good example of this practice in the 1630s, since he wrote descriptions of specific sieges, as well as publishing his theoretical works on military architecture and the education of the military commander. His report on the sieges of Hesdin and Corbie, where he participated as a commanding officer, are illustrated with the plans of the respective towns and their siege layout (Fig. 19.20). The siege view is probably thoroughly accurate, and is a horizontal section of the city's fortifications and the temporary field fortifications. The representation of these field fortifications in engraved form is precious since they were destroyed immediately after the siege; the engraved illustration is the only trace left.[57] As with the hypothetical siege views incorporated into the treatises on military architecture, the siege view by de Ville is bereft of direct representation of human presence. This graphic convention renders the image "scientific" by eliminating the genre scenes and landscape effects that had made other military pieces aesthetically appealing.

Two views of Turin during the siege of 1640 (Figs. 19.21 and 19.22) clarify the distinctions brought about by mere graphic conventions. They are both ichnographic plans, though the one by Boetto (Fig. 19.21) is more finished and developed. But the main difference in his

[55] David Kunzle, *The Early Comic Strip, 1450–1825*, 70, 73–5. I owe this reference to Geoffrey Parker. See also John Roger Paas, *The German Political Broadsheet, 1620–1700* (Wiesbaden, 1991), 11:236–60.
[56] Parker, *The Military Revolution*, 26.
[57] As Simone Zurawski reminds us in her "New Sources," *The Art Bulletin* 70 (1988): 621–39.

illustration is the fact that it is populated by several armies, whose activities bring the picture to life but do not convey the nature of the circumvallation and countervallation in a single-minded way. His addition of the hills across the river and the dramatic scroll-like cartouches enhance the pleasure of the picture, making the place more desirable.[58]

Gustavus Adolphus' heirs continued his policy of wars fought in Denmark, Germany, Poland, and Russia, bringing the Swedish nobility closer to Europe and dramatically increasing its wealth. The scroll-like view (c. 250 × 1000 mm) of the siege of Copenhagen in 1658 provides a superlative example of how the conjunction of war and cartography can render a site thoroughly desirable (Fig. 19.23). Conducted by Charles Gustav of Sweden, this siege was part of the short war of 1657–60, and inconclusive despite a great display of Swedish force.[59] The illustration was designed by the military architect Erik Dahlbergh, and engraved later by the French artist Jean Lepautre.[60] Dahlbergh, whose stay in Frankfurt between 1650 and 1653 had brought him in close touch with the publishing house of Merian, succeeds through his high interpretive and technical skills in conveying graphically the beauty of Copenhagen's site and the desirability of this richly endowed and well fortified capital.[61] In his work, the ideal of cultivating draughtsmanship for cartography – urged by Alberti – is triumphantly achieved and realized through the availability and skills of seventeenth-century printers. The foreground is occupied by a procession of visitors who, similarly to the audience in Callot's view of Breda, came out to view the siege from a raised position. The scene is enlivened by the puffs of smoke from the cannon, and the curved trajectory of cannon balls exploding in mid-air orients one's eye towards the military prize. The background is a great naval scene, with a view of the distant hills of Malmö beyond. While this siege view is the panegyrical representation of a military event, its success is largely due to the skill and historical training of its designer, who displays a thorough acquaintance with treatises on cities.[62]

---

[58] I have discussed the siege of Turin in *Turin 1564–1680: Military Culture, Urban Design and the Creation of the Absolutist Capital* (Chicago, 1991), 119–21.

[59] On the siege of Copenhagen, see Stoye, *Europe Unfolding*, 153–4; and Duffy, *Siege Warfare*, 187–8.

[60] For the oeuvre of Jean Lepautre, see Maxime Préaud, *Graveurs du XVIIe Siècle: Les Lepautre*, Inventaire du fonds français, Bibliothéque Nationale (Paris, 1994).

[61] On Dahlbergh's draughtsmanship and career, see Börje Magnusson, *Att illustrera fäderneslandet: en studie i Erik Dahlberghs verksamhet som tecknare* (Uppsala, 1986), with English summary.

[62] The desirable aspects of the siting and appearance of cities formed an important part

The siege view of Copenhagen is replete with a lavish oak-wreath frame, enriched with military trophies, legend, and label. This siege view seems to bring out the best on both sides of the conflict, celebrated here by two canny artists. Dahlbergh was one of Sweden's great military talents, and like some military men of his time he was a polymath. Author of an entire collection of views celebrating Sweden's urban riches, he was also responsible for the staging of royal events.[63] His representation of the assault of Fredrichsodde (Fig. 19.24) is the most dramatic image of its kind, juxtaposing the scientific representation of the fortification as an orthogonal vertical section with the thousands of soldiers who constitute the assault column. The hero of this picture is clearly the military architect and his repertory of elements: glacis, covered street, parapet, scarp, and counterscarp. The carpet like humanity poured over the molded edge of the fortification section, their spiky lances, and the billowing smoke clouds dramatize the picture.

THE WARS OF LOUIS XIV

From the middle of the seventeenth century, in a positive retreat from the excesses of the "half-suicide" of the Thirty Years' War, military actions became more regulated and siege views were part of the attempt to create this regulating order. The military history of the last third of the seventeenth century is dominated by what can be called the "managed wars" of Louis XIV. He was personally involved in many sieges, which he preferred to battles in the open field.[64] For instance, he personally directed, with the help of Vauban, the siege of Lille in 1667. As at Spinola's siege of Breda, attended by the governing archdukes, Louis' court provided the audience at this well-staged military enterprise. Furthermore, at the siege of Lille, like Charles V in his African campaign, Louis was accompanied by a cultural entourage whose members, the writers Racine and Boileau, and the artist Adam van der Meulen, were brought along in order to celebrate the king's enterprise. These artists were responsible for the illustrations of Louis' achievements in war, which were spun out in numerous series

of most treatises on architecture in the fifteenth and sixteenth centuries, following the example of Vitruvius, and were further considered in publications by utopian moralists and political philosophers such as Botero and Campanella.

[63] Published under the title of *Suecia antiqua et moderna* (Stockholm, 1667–93).

[64] J. Meyer, "De la guerre," *XVIIe Siécle* 148/37 (1985): 269, 286.

of art works, as tapestries, painting cycles, suites of engravings, and decorative motifs for interior design.[65]

Van der Meulen's drawings of Lille, probably made during the campaign, were used for the composition of his painting of the siege, commissioned for the decoration of the royal château at Marly. His drawing was engraved in 1685, and it also served as the foundation for the tapestry in the series known as the *Histoire du Roy* woven at the Gobelins under the directorship of Jabach, which depicts events from Louis XIV's reign between 1654 and 1678.[66] Jabach, who became director of the Gobelins in 1671, provides an additional link between Louis XIV and the imperial program of Charles V since the collection of drawings that he donated to the king included the cartoons for the tapestry cycle of the siege of Pavia.[67] Van der Meulen's detailed and colored topographic sketches were probably also an inspiration for the collection of city models, the *plans-reliefs*, which the king commissioned soon after. These drawings brought siege views to a new level of verisimilitude while maintaining their high level of incidental appeal.[68] It was not easy to bring together the desire to heroicize the king and the accuracy that was indispensable for political propaganda. The decision was made to illustrate the king's victories without the heroic trappings of antique mythology, and from 1664 Van der Meulen relied on documentary evidence. Costumes and arms are contemporary, and the glorification is based on precise illustrations of actions and places, thus celebrating the triumphs of a policy rather than the personal virtues of the king.[69]

After Louis' successful siege, Lille was fortified by Vauban with a pentagonal citadel built at great cost (Fig. 19.25), as can be seen in a later view illustrating the siege of 1708.[70] Vauban realized here one of the favorite theoretical set pieces of early modern military architecture, the pentagonal fortress. The image of the city after the addition of this powerful geometrical and monumental building was strongly enhanced: It nearly bristles with military installations, while the besiegers attack across town in an attempt to avoid the formidable citadel.

---

[65] For the rhetoric of the royal image and its military content, see Peter Burke, *The Fabrication of Louis XIV* (New Haven, 1992), 71–93; and Antoine Schnapper, "French Kings as Collectors," in *Art and History*, eds. Rotberg and Rabb, 195–200.

[66] Daniel Meyer, *L'Histoire du Roy* (Paris, 1980).

[67] Casali, *Gli arazzi*, 1993.

[68] Laure C. Starcky, *Paris, Mobilier National: Dessins de Van der Meulen et son atelier*, exh. cat. (Paris, 1988), 10, 14, 51, 61, 94–6, 101–2, 176–7.

[69] Boyer, "Les representations guerrieres," 291–305.

[70] Anderson, *War and Society*, 88, 140.

Vauban proceeded similarly with the fortification of Luxembourg. He led the siege of the city (with Maréchal Créqui) in 1684, in an operation that lasted less than one month despite the powerful naturally fortified site of the city. Vauban led an army of 27,000 and directed the intensive artillery fire that protected the work of the sappers.[71] The excitement of this siege is well illustrated in a splendid image by Romeyn de Hooghe (Fig. 19.26),[72] which must be compared with Schmits' view of the contemporaneous siege of Vienna in 1683 (Fig. 19.2). They both illustrate accurately the points of attack, but use distinct representation methods. Where Schmits' view is entirely cartographic, de Hooghe includes buildings in isometric construction, fragments of landscape, and military genre. De Hooghe carried on, with considerable talent, the tradition established by Callot and della Bella; Schmits' work is modeled on that of cartographers and military architects like Henrik Hondius and Antoine de Ville.

Vauban had insisted on the strategic significance of Luxembourg, which, once it was taken, allowed for the demolition of neighboring French forts, simplifying the border reinforcements of Vauban's strategy for French national defense encoded by him as the *pré-carré*. The strategic desirability and visual appeal of Luxembourg, whose conquest was ratified through the treaty of Regensburg with Emperor Leopold – who was shaken by the recent siege of Vienna – is also illustrated in a portrait of Louis XIV made by Pierre Lepautre in 1684.[73] Though he is presented in the garb of an ancient Roman commander, Louis is holding the plan of a modern bastioned fortress whose outlines coincide precisely with those of Luxembourg (Fig. 19.27).

Louis XIV's victories were closely documented for the rest of the century, and became the primary inspiration for several large series of ornamental works and decorative motifs. The artist Sebastien Leclerc engraved twenty-nine plates for the series *Conquestes du Roi*, many after his own drawings.[74] Each siege is part of a monumental composition for which Leclerc designed two different frames. Each sheet contained the framed view of the siege, with besiegers on a hill in the foreground and the city occupying the center of the composition; above the large framed view is a smaller picture of the plan of the

---

[71] Duffy, *The Fortress in the Age of Vauban*, 27.
[72] John Landwehr, *Romeyn de Hooghe the Etcher: Contemporary Portrayal of Europe, 1662–1707* (Leiden and Dobbs Ferry, 1973); and Emile van der Vekena, "Eigentliche Relation der Belagerung von Luxemburg: Flugblätter, Flugschriften, und Pläne aus der Jahren 1683–85," *Luxembourg et Vauban*, exh. cat. (Luxembourg, 1984), 20–44.
[73] For the oeuvre of Pierre Lepautre, see Preaud, *Les Lepautre*, t. 9 (Paris, 1995).
[74] For the extensive production of Leclerc, see Maxime Préaud, *Graveurs du XVIIe Siècle: Sébastien Leclerc*, Inventaire du fonds français, Bibliothèque Nationale (Paris, 1980).

town framed in an oval, flanked by allegorical figures of fame and glory. The larger frame was woven of military trophies, fleurs de lis, and prisoners who flanked the pedestal where the explanatory text was engraved. Leclerc's accomplished siege views, in which several kinds of representation types are allowed to collude on a single sheet, show that he was steeped in the imagery of ferocious fortresses disseminated in countless seventeenth-century treatises on military architecture, such as those of Cellarius and Tensini.[75]

Later, in 1683, Leclerc engraved the tapestry series *Grandes Conquestes du Roi* after cartoons by Charles LeBrun, the king's first painter, and in 1702 he also engraved a reduced version of the sieges in a suite of eight plates known as the *Petits Conquests du Roi*.[76] But he did not limit himself to this self-imposed format. His bird's-eye view of the siege on Mons in 1691 shows the city with a crown of airborne cannon balls, and the king is part of the group illustrated in the foreground and recognizable by his great hat. Vauban had conscripted 21,000 peasants to work on this siege, but the year's almanac celebrated the courage of the king who, when he visited the trenches, bravely allowed his hat to be seen above the parapet in a gesture that cost the life of the officer next to him, promptly knocked down by a bullet intended for the king (Fig. 19.28). This siege view is taken from the trenches; the royal entourage forms the composition's stage wings through which our gaze is directed to the king and to Mons beyond. Well sited, strongly fortified, and richly filled with buildings, this town constitutes another object of political desire. Further military actions of the year were illustrated in almanac sheets through the standards that form part of the trophy, and others are offered as windows through the text of the almanac. The siege view reached apotheosis through its association with the royal person.

I have endeavoured through this essay to illustrate the dominant typologies of siege representation, and to document the critical mass of siege views that had been produced by the end of the seventeenth century. This production established the siege panorama as a significant variant among city views. Ranging from austere and abstract

---

[75] Andreas Cellarius, *Architectura militaris* (Amsterdam, 1656); Francesco Tensini, *La fortificatione, guardia, difesa et espugnatione delle fortezze esperimentata in diverse guerre* (Venice, 1624). For a critical evaluation of military treatises as a literary and graphic genre, see my *Military Architecture, Cartography and the Representation of the Early Modern European City* (Chicago, 1991).

[76] Daniel Meyer, "Les Conquêtes de Louis XIV," *La Revue du Louvre et des Musées de France* 20/3 (1970): 155–64.

plans of a scientific war to elaborately detailed and splashily seductive views of a "ludic" war, these images served as reportage, archival document, and scandal sheet. The representations of siege were as varied as the wars they commemorated, which ranged from violent interventions to "military promenades." The large quantity and variety of images, produced by a broad spectrum of artists, architects, and cartographers and carried through in fortification projects, books on fortification, single-sheet plans and views of cities, became in the seventeenth century a veritable cult of representation of military engagement.

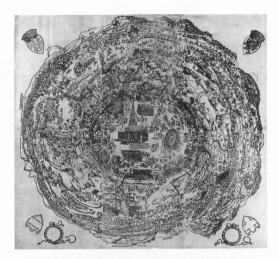

Figure 19.1. Siege of Vienna, 1529. Woodcut by Hans Sebald Beham, and Niclas Meldemann. Estampes Reserve, Bibliothéque Nationale, Paris.

Figure 19.2. Siege of Vienna, 1683. Engraving by Henry Schmits, dedicated to General Stahremberg, the commander in charge of Vienna's defense. Estampes, Bibliothéque Nationale, Paris.

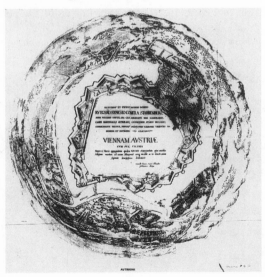

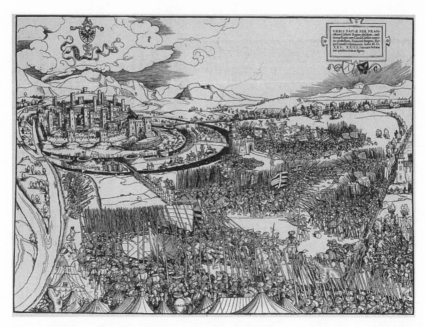

Figure 19.3. Battle of Pavia, 1525. Woodcut by Jorg Breu the Elder, from Max Geisberg, *The German Single-Leaf Woodcut, 1500–1550*, rev. and ed. Walter L. Strauss (New York, 1974), III:892.

Figure 19.4. Battle of Pavia, 1525. Fifth tapestry from the series woven in Brussels ca. 1529–30 after the design by Bernard van Orley, from L. Casali et al., *Gli arazzi della battaglia di Pavia nel Museo di Capodimonte a Napoli* (Pavia, 1993).

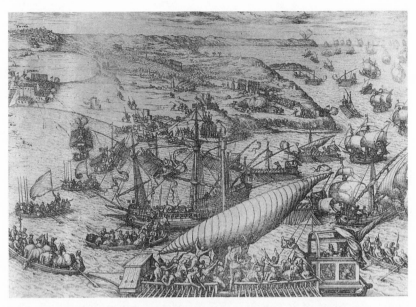

Figure 19.5. Conquest of Tunis by Emperor Charles V, 1535. Engraving by Franz Hogenberg after the design by Jan Cornelisz Vermeyen, ca. 1555, from *Kurze Verzeichniss wie Keyser Carolus der V in Africa. . . .* Herzog August Bibliothek, Wolfenbüttel.

Figure 19.6. The Imperial camp outside Wittenberg, 1547. Woodcut by Master MS, from Geisberg, *The German Woodcut*, II:1284.

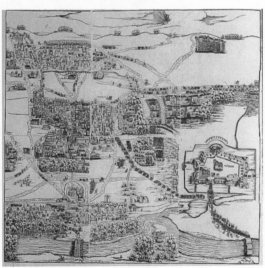

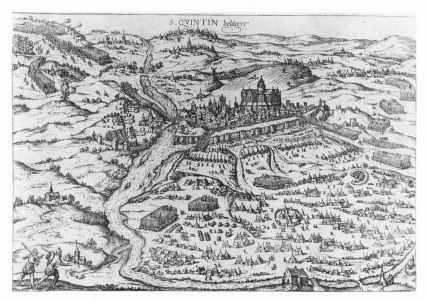

Figure 19.7. Siege of St. Quentin, 1557. Woodcut, German, *Schlachtbuch*, Herzog August Bibliothek, Wolfenbüttel.

Figure 19.8. Siege of Hohenaspern, 1519. Drawing by Albrecht Dürer, from J.R. Hale, *History and Warfare in the Renaisance* (New Haven and London, 1990), 16.

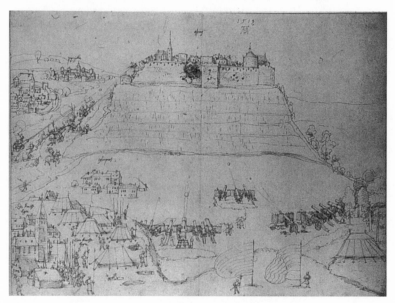

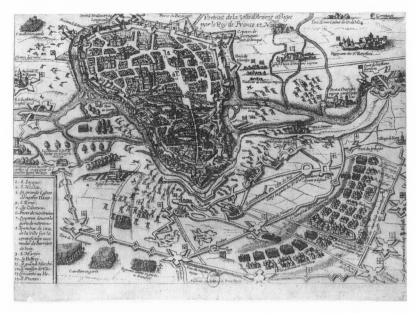

Figure 19.9. Siege of Amiens, 1597. Engraving, Estampes, Bibliothéque Nationale, Paris.

Figure 19.10. The conquest of Montmellian, 1691. Engraving by Sebastien Leclerc. Estampes, Bibliothéque Nationale, Paris.

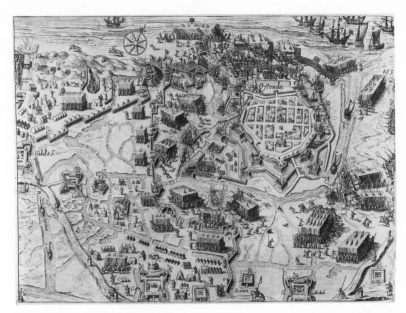

Figure 19.11. Siege of Ostend, 1601–4. Engraving from J. Orlers and H. van Hasten, *Warhafftige Beschreibung und Eigentliche Abbildung aller Zuge und Victorien* (Leyden, 1612). Herzog August Bibliothek, Wolfenbüttel.

Figure 19.12. Siege of Groll, 1597. Engraving from *Victorien*. Herzog August Bibliothek, Wolfenbüttel.

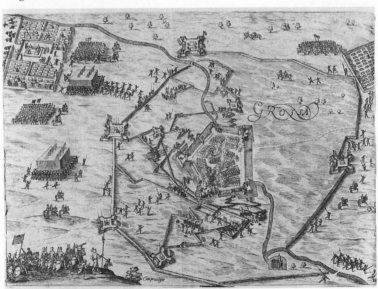

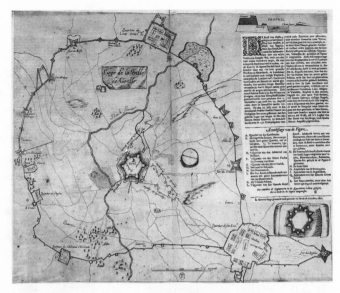

Figure 19.13. Siege of Groll, 1627. Engraving by Hendrick Hondius, 1627. Estampes, Bibliothéque Nationale, Paris.

Figure 19.14. Siege of Breda, 1625. Engraving by Jacques Callot, ca. 1628. National Gallery of Art, Washington, D.C. Rosenwald Collection.

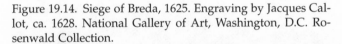

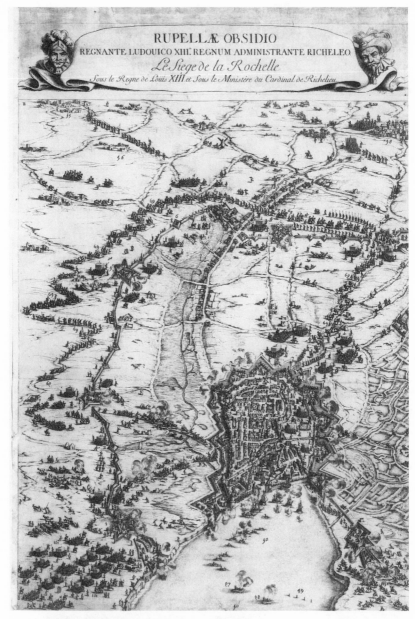

Figure 19.15a. Siege of La Rochelle, 1627. Engraving by Jacques Callot, ca. 1630, The Newberry Library, Chicago.

Figure 19.15b. (*continued*) Siege of La Rochelle, 1627.

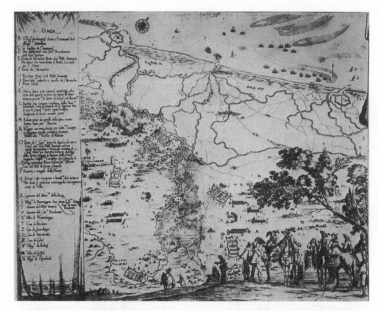

Figure 19.16. Siege of St. Omer, 1638. Etching by Stefano della Bella, 1638, from Alexandre de Vesme, *Stefano della Bella: catalogue raisonné*, with intro. and additions by Phyllis Dearborn Massar (New York, 1968).

Figure 19.17. Siege of Casale Monferrato, 1630. Engraving, Estampes, Bibliothéque Nationale, Paris.

Figure 19.18. The entry of the King of Sweden into Frankfurt, 1631. Engraving by Mathew Merian, ca. 1637, Estampes, Bibliothéque Nationale, Paris.

Figure 19.19. Victories of Marchese Spinola in Germany, 1620–1. Etching, Herzog Anton Ulrich-Museum, Braunschweig.

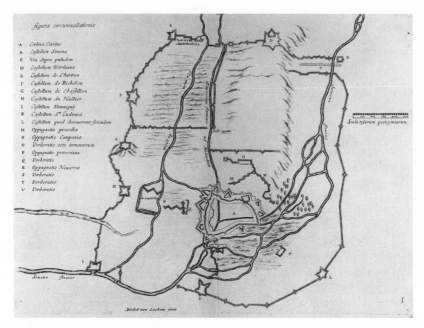

Figure 19.20. Siege of Corbie, 1636. Engraving by Michel van Lochom, 1637, from Antoine de Ville, *Obsidio Corbeiensis* (Paris, 1641). Herzog August Bibliothek, Wolfenbüttel.

Figure 19.21. (*facing page top*) Siege of Turin, 1640. Engraving by Giovenale Boetto, ca. 1645, Estampes, Bibliothéque Nationale, Paris.

Figure 19.22. (*facing page bottom*) Siege of Turin, 1640. Engraving, Herzog August Bibliothek, Wolfenbüttel.

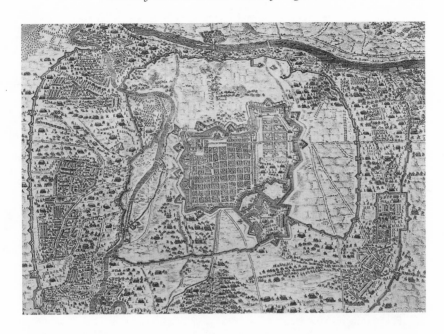

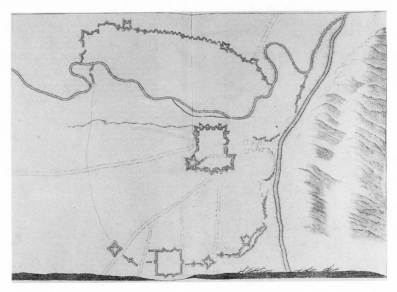

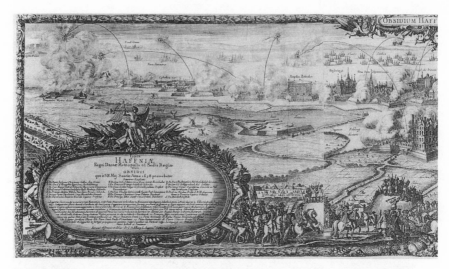

Figure 19.23a. Siege of Copenhagen, 1658. Engraving by Jean Lepautre after Erik Dahlbergh, Nicolai Collection, Württembergisches Landesbibliothek, Stuttgart.

Figure 19.24. Assault of Fredrichsodde, 1657. Engraving by Erik Dahlbergh, Nicolai Collection, Württembergisches Landesbibliothek, Stuttgart.

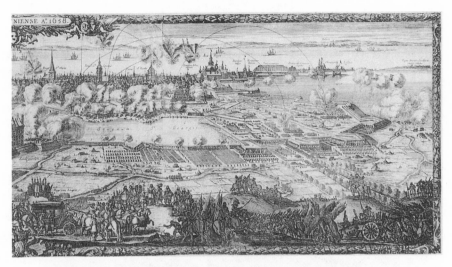

Figure 19.23b. Siege of Copenhagen, 1658 (continued).

Figure 19.25. Siege of Lille, 1708. Engraving by Peter van Call, Herzog August Bibliothek, Wolfenbüttel.

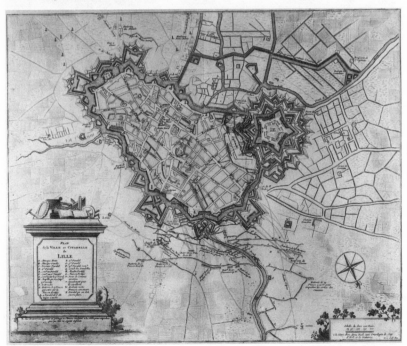

Figure 19.26. Siege of Luxembourg, 1684. Engraving by Romeyn de Hooghe, Herzog August Bibliothek, Wolfenbüttel.

Quis tot sustineat, Quis tanta negotia solus. Horat.

Figure 19.27. Portrait of Louis XIV, 1684. Engraving by Pierre Lepautre, National Gallery of Art, Washington.

Figure 19.28. Siege of Mons, 1691. Engraving by Langlois de Ciartes, Estampes, Bibliothèque Nationale, Paris.

Selected annotated bibliography of secondary works

The following bibliography is intended only as an introduction to the vast literature related to the study of city walls. Brief annotations have been added to most items by the editor or the authors to guide the reader who wishes to pursue particular topics or areas of study. In some instances, only one or two works by an author have been cited as examples of a more extensive *opera*. Readers should also refer to the footnotes in each chapter for additional works and suggestions for further reading.

INTRODUCTION

Chambers, David, et al., eds. *War, Culture and Society in Renaissance Venice: Essays in Honour of John Hale*. London, 1993.
    A collection of twelve articles, including discussion of Venetian architecture and fortifications. Contains several maps, photographs and illustrations (some in color). Also offers a truncated bibliography for John Hale, a leading scholar of early modern warfare.

De la Croix, Horst. *Military Considerations in Town Planning: Fortifications*. New York, 1972.
    A short survey covering themes in urban defense from prehistory to the modern era, complemented by numerous photographs and drawings.

Duffy, Christopher. *Siege Warfare: The Fortress in the Early Modern World, 1494–1660*. London, 1979.
    The author views Charles VIII's invasion into Italy in 1494 as marking a pivotal year for military architecture, which had to transform in order to withstand gunpowder artillery. The resulting struggle between attack and defense is then analyzed through the mid-seventeenth century.

The Fortress in the Age of Vauban and Frederick the Great, 1660–1789. London, 1985.
    The companion volume to Duffy's *Siege Warfare* (see above), it carries treatment into the late eighteenth century.

Hooper, Nicholas, and Matthew Bennett. *Cambridge Illustrated Atlas of Warfare: The Middle Ages, 768–1487*. Cambridge, 1996.

A lavishly illustrated and highly accessible work that incorporates much of the latest information. Unfortunately, the book begins with the wars of Charlemagne and thus omits late imperial and early medieval warfare.

Hughes, Quentin. *Military Architecture*. London, 1974.

From the ancient world to the Maginot Line, Hughes traces the constant struggle between weapons of attack and the fortifications designed to thwart them. Incorporates hundreds of illustrations, both contemporary and modern, and photographs.

Keegan, John. *A History of Warfare*. New York, 1993.

Departing from the purely political approach taken by Karl von Clausewitz in the nineteenth century, Keegan focuses instead on cultural determinants as the key to understanding warfare. Global in scope, the book ranges from ancient to modern.

McNeill, William H. *The Age of Gunpowder Empires, 1450–1800*. Washington, DC, 1989.

A brief, concise account of how gunpowder affected the dominant world powers through the eighteenth century. Includes treatment not only of Europe, but also of Muscovy, the Americas, the Muslim world, and East Asia.

Parker, Geoffrey, ed. *The Cambridge Illustrated History of Warfare: The Triumph of the West*. Cambridge, 1995.

A broad overview of the Western military tradition, ancient to present day, with chapters written by noted experts. Abounds with maps and contemporary illustrations, as well as many fascinating sidebars.

Parker, Geoffrey. *The Military Revolution: Military Innovation and the Rise of the West, 1500–1800*. 2nd ed. Cambridge, 1996.

A reworking of Michael Roberts's thesis, this work, first published in 1988, now denotes *the* military revolution in early modern Europe. As opposed to Roberts's revolution in field tactics, Parker places emphasis on the role of new-style fortifications and the importance of siege warfare. Though often attacked, this book remains the driving force behind early modern military studies. The second edition incorporates a more up-to-date bibliography, as well as an "afterward" chapter (also found in C. Rogers; see below).

Rogers, Clifford, ed. *The Military Revolution Debate: Readings on the Military Transformation of Early Modern Europe*. Boulder, 1995.

A collection of thirteen articles debating the accuracy of the military revolution thesis, its applicability in other areas of the world, and refinements in specific cases. Includes a reprint of Michael Roberts's seminal article of 1956, and a rejoinder by Geoffrey Parker to criticism of his own thesis.

Toy, Sidney. *A History of Fortification from 3000 B.C. to 1700 A.D.*, 2nd ed. London, 1966.

First published in 1955, this is a survey by one of this century's early masters on the topic of fortification. Offering many photographs, plans, and drawings, treatment remains limited mostly to Europe and the Near East.

Van Creveld, Martin. *Technology and War: From 2000 B.C. to the Present*. New York, 1989.

A sweeping survey of the role of technology in warfare, including chapters devoted to siege warfare. Though at times too simplistic or inaccurate, particularly for premodern warfare, it nevertheless reminds the reader of both the capabilities and the limitations of technology in martial enterprises.

Watson, Bruce. *Sieges: A Comparative Study*. Westport, CT, 1993.

The author analyzes five sieges, beginning with the siege of Jerusalem in 1099 and ending with the fall of Singapore in 1942. He then endeavors to illustrate the constants and variables encountered in this type of warfare. Aimed at a general audience and lacking reference notes.

PART I: TO WALL OR NOT TO WALL

Anderson, David. "Factional Competition and the Political Evolution of Mississippian Chiefdoms in the Southeastern United States." In *Factional Competition and Political Development in the New World*, eds. Elizabeth Brumfiel and John Fox, 61–76. Cambridge, 1994.

A quality overview of the unstable relations within and among Mississippian chiefdoms, including outright warfare. The author does not, however, describe the configuration of palisades.

Connah, Graham. *African Civilizations. Precolonial Cities and States in Tropical Africa: An Archaeological Perspective*. Cambridge, 1987.

A synthesis of disparate archaeological studies and suitable for a general audience, this work divides Africa geographically and then makes comparisons between the archaeological evidence for each region. Supplemented by maps, plans, photographs, and illustrations.

The Archaeology of Benin: Excavations and other Researches in and around Benin City, Nigeria. Oxford, 1975.

Containing many photographs, charts and tables, this study covers approximately 1,000 years of Benin's history by synthesizing archeological research on the city through the mid-1960s. Includes sections devoted to discussion of Benin's walls.

Contamine, Philippe. "Les fortifications urbaines en France à la fin du Moyen Age: aspects financiers et économiques." *Revue historique* 260 (1978): 23–47.

Argues that, instead of being viewed solely as a financial burden, the building of town walls was seen much like other public construction projects: a type of long-term investment.

Coquery-Vidrovitch, Catherine. *Histoire des villes d'Afrique Noire: des origines à la colonisation*. Paris, 1993.

A sweeping treatment of African cities from their earliest origins. Devotes sections to general questions on African urbanization, ancient cities, Bantu cities before the Muslims, Islamic cities, the Atlantic Age (sixteenth to eighteenth century), and the urban revolution of the nineteenth century. Offers several maps.

Corfis, Ivy, and Michael Wolfe, eds. *The Medieval City under Siege*. Rochester, 1995.

Thirteen articles, mostly devoted to the High and late Middle Ages, covering siege technology, the siege in literature, sieges as a particular form of warfare, and the changing nature of sieges in late medieval Europe.

Crouch, Dora P., et al., eds. *Spanish City Planning in North America*. Cambridge, MA, 1982.

In three parts, this volume includes translations of documents relating to early Spanish cities in the New World, discussion of the histories of three American cities (Santa Fe, St. Louis, and Los Angeles), and extended treatment of California for the period 1769–1850.

Curry, Anne, and Michael Hughes. *Arms, Armies and Fortifications in the Hundred Years' War*. Woodbridge, Suffolk, 1994.

Twelve articles by noted specialists. Among others, topics include the interplay between early gunpowder artillery and late medieval fortifications.

Engel, Evamaria. *Die deutsche Stadt des Mittelalters*. Munich, 1993.

A very approachable survey for anyone wishing to pursue further work on medieval German cities, though there is little by way of historiography. A mix of chronological and topical treatment.

Gutiérrez, Ramón. *Arquitectura y urbanismo en Iberoamérica*. Madrid, 1983.

Focusing on architecture, this study by a leading Argentine scholar offers a general introduction to urbanism in colonial America.

Hassig, Ross. *War and Society in Ancient Mesoamerica*. Berkeley, 1992.

Unlike most other works which treat warfare only post contact, Hassig gives an account of military conflict in Mesoamerica for 3,000 years prior to the arrival of Europeans.

Hull, Richard. *African Cities and Towns before the European Conquest*. New York, 1976.

A short study targeted at a lay audience, this synthesis covers cities and towns in Africa for the millennium prior to European colonization. Includes photographs, maps, and plans.

Kagan, Richard. *Urban Images of the Hispanic World, 1493–1750*. London and New Haven, 2000.

A profusely illustrated volume devoted to views and representations of Spain's American cities. Also examines some of the basic ideas underlying Spanish urbanism in the Americas.

Keeley, Lawrence. *War before Civilization: The Myth of the Peaceful Savage*. Cambridge, MA, 1996.

An anthropological study which seeks to refute the "peaceful savage" image by showing that premodern societies were, in reality, exceedingly violent. Estimates that the mortality rate in primitive warfare is significantly higher than in civilized warfare.

Keyser, Erich, et al., eds. *Deutsches Städtebuch*. 11 vols. Stuttgart, 1939- .
A massive ongoing study devoted to the study of German cities. The volumes, divided by province and encyclopedic in structure, offer detailed information on each city within a given province. Also includes data on urban fortifications for each entry.

Kubler, George. *Mexican Architecture in the Sixteenth Century*. New Haven, 1948.
A synthetic work that still serves as the classic study for all subsequent treatment of the topic.

Milner, George. "An Osteological Perspective on Prehistoric Warfare." In *Regional Approaches to Mortuary Analysis*, ed. Lane Beck. New York, 1995.
The skeletons of prehistoric war victims from the North American midcontinent are studied to provide insight on the nature of warfare prior to the arrival of Europeans. The author argues that warfare varied in intensity in the precontact Americas.

Moody, Harold. *The Walls and Gates of Kano City*. Nigeria, n.d. [1970].
This book is one of the very few specific studies of an African city wall system. Although he was neither a professional archaeologist nor historian, the author achieved a successful integration of the documentary, oral, and physical evidence and was able to demonstrate how the walls had expanded over time. His field observations are particularly valuable, made as they were in the 1960s before some of the evidence was lost to modern development.

Morse, Richard. "The Urban Development of Colonial Spanish America." In *The Cambridge History of Latin America*. Vol. 2: *Colonial Latin America*, ed. Leslie Bethell, 67–104. Cambridge, 1984.
A clear and concise introduction to Spanish urbanization policy and procedures in the New World.

Otterbein, Keith. *Feuding and Warfare: Selected Works of Keith F. Otterbein*. Langhorne, PA, 1974.
A collection of thirteen essays, many of which are cross-cultural comparisons, by one of the pioneers in the field of the anthropology of warfare. The articles are divided into three sections: "The Evolution of Warfare," "Fraternal Interest Group Theory," and "Overviews."

Payne, Claudine. "Mississippian Capitals: An Archaeological Investigation of Precolumbian Political Structure." Ph.D. diss., University of Florida, 1994.
A wide-ranging summary of major Mississippian period (A.D. 1000–1600) settlements in the southeastern United States. Gives attention to palisades and other aspects of community layouts, supplemented by archaeological data and sixteenth-century Spanish descriptions. Argues that large, politically important settlements were more likely to have palisades than outlying villages.

Reyerson, Kathryn, and John Drendel, eds. *Medieval Urban and Rural Communities in France: Provence and Languedoc, 1000–1500*. Leiden, 1998.

A collection of thirteen essays arranged in two parts. Part one, "Creating Communities," is further subdivided into sections on the town and village, and treats such topics as economics, law, and the family. Part two, "Communities at the Intersection of Village and Town," gives attention to the cities of Toulon, Montpellier, and Marseilles.

Rigaudière, Albert. "Le financement des fortifications urbaines en France du milieu du XIVe siècle à la fin du XVe siècle." *Revue historique* 273 (1985): 19–95.

Illustrates how the fortifications of many French cities were inadequate at the onset of the Hundred Years' War, as were the methods to procure construction funds. Discusses the ways France went about rewalling urban centers in the face of conflict.

Shaw, Thurstan, et al., eds. *The Archaeology of Africa: Food, Metals and Towns.* London, 1993.

At nearly 900 pages in length, this collection of forty-four essays by a multitude of scholars reaches back 20,000 years into African history. Essays thirty-three to forty-four are devoted to the archaeology of African cities and towns. Replete with tables, maps, and illustrations.

Smith, Robert. *Warfare and Diplomacy in Pre-Colonial West Africa.* 2nd ed. London, 1989.

First published in 1976, this analysis of warfare in West Africa prior to the arrival of Europeans also gives treatment to West African fortifications and sieges. The second edition has been revised and augmented by illustrations.

Solano, Francisco de. *Historia urbana de Iberoamérica.* 3 vols. Madrid, 1987.

A multi-volume, multi-authored introduction to Spanish and Portuguese cities in the Americas. Well illustrated with excellent maps and figures.

Stoob, Heinz. "Die Stadtbefestigung. Vergleichende Überlegungen zur bürgerlichen Siedlungs- und Baugeschichte, besonders der frühen Neuzeit." In *Europäische Städte im Zeitalter des Barock: Gestalt–Kultur–Sozialgefüge*, ed. Kersten Krüger, 25–54. Vienna and Cologne, 1988.

One of fourteen papers resulting from a 1984 conference held in Münster on the Baroque city. Stoob's study and the fold-out map which accompanies it (located inside the book's back cover) give a graphical representation of the concentration of fortifications in *Mitteleuropa* from the Middle Ages until 1945.

Sumption, Jonathan. *The Hundred Years' War.* Vol. 1: *Trial by Battle.* London and Boston, 1990.

Part of a massive multi-volume narrative covering the entire Hundred Years' War. Volume one concludes with the siege of Calais (1347).

Timbal, Pierre-Clément. *La guerre de cent ans vue à travers les registres du Parlement (1337–1369).* Paris, 1961.

A fascinating study that exploits the registers of *parlement*, a little-used but huge resource. Half of the volume consists of selected transcripts of these sources; the other half is divided into five main sections: recruitment, supply and transport, defense, military operations, and the treaty of Brétigny.

Toch, Michael. "The Medieval German City under Siege." In *The Medieval City under Siege*, eds. Ivy Corfis and Michael Wolfe, 35–48. Rochester, 1995.

Starting with the observation that sieges dominated medieval warfare in Germany, Toch then embarks on a further examination of thirteenth-century German sieges. Discusses defense technology, and shows that most sieges during this period failed in Germany.

Vayda, Andrew. "Warfare in Ecological Perspective." *Annual Review of Ecology and Systematics* 5 (1974): 183–93.

An excellent general reference work on conflicts in small-scale societies.

Warrick, Gary. *Reconstructing Ontario Iroquoian Village Organization*. Ottawa, 1984.

In what is possibly the best description of northeastern palisades, Warrick describes the organization of late prehistoric Iroquoian villages as part of a detailed study of the Fonger site. The settlements tended to be palisaded, and the longhouses that the walls encircled were closely spaced.

Willey, Patrick. *Prehistoric Warfare on the Great Plains*. New York, 1990.

An updated version of the author's 1982 Ph.D. dissertation, this is a report from the excavation and analysis of the Crow Creek massacre in South Dakota in A.D. 1325. Largely descriptive in nature, the report includes fifty tables, various photographs, and illustrations.

PART II: WALLS OF WAR

Adam, Jean-Pierre. *L'architecture militaire grecque*. Paris, 1982.

Covers a wide range of topics, from building materials to fortification design and artillery placement. Includes detailed treatment of the fortifications of the Peloponnesos, Greece north of the Isthmus, Asia Minor, and Greater Greece and Sicily. Contains many photographs and line drawings, plans, and four maps.

Asher, Catherine. *The Architecture of Mughal India*. Cambridge and New York, 1992.

A survey of the development of architecture under the Mughals. Calls attention to heavenly imagery in architecture that reached its apogee with the Taj Mahal.

Bachrach, Bernard S. "Medieval Siege Warfare: A Reconnaissance." *Journal of Military History* 58 (1993): 119–33.

Argues that sieges, not open-field battles, dominated the conduct of medieval warfare. Offers a corrective to Bradbury (see below) by contending that major urban centers, not castles, were the primary targets of sieges.

"Logistics in Pre-Crusade Europe." In *Feeding Mars: Logistics in Western Warfare from the Middle Ages to the Present*, ed. John Lynn, 65–72. Boulder, 1993.

Contends that, far from "living off the land" as is often supposed, medieval armies were the heirs to a sophisticated logistical network developed during the late Roman Empire, wherein the maintenance of older imperial fortifications played a key role.

"The Cost of Castle Building: The Case of the Tower at Langeais, 992–994." In *The Medieval Castle: Romance and Reality*, eds. Kathryn L. Reyerson and Faye Powe, 46–62. Dubuque, IA, 1984.

A quantitative study that demonstrates the massive amounts of manpower and materials required for the construction of even modest medieval fortifications, and shows why economic constraints thrust the maintenance and capture of such strongholds into the limelight of medieval warfare.

Bradbury, Jim. *The Medieval Siege*. Woodbridge, Suffolk, 1992.

A work of primary importance on medieval warfare. Breaking with most historians' emphasis on field warfare, Bradbury postulates that sieges were by far the most frequent and most important component of medieval warfare.

Calderon Quijano, Jose. *Historia de las fortificaciones en Nueva España*. 2nd ed. Madrid, 1984.

First published in 1953, this expanded edition on fortifications in New Spain from the sixteenth to late eighteenth centuries includes an updated bibliography, maps, and plans. Appendices contain nearly 200 photographs and illustrations, a glossary of terms, and editions of primary sources.

Chevalier, Bernard. *Les bonnes villes de France du XIVᵉ au XVIᵉ siècles*. Paris, 1982.

Investigates the emergence of *bonnes villes* (medium-sized cities) as autonomous political entities, and discusses the significance of town walls in the transformation from the medieval to the early modern world.

Contamine, Philippe. *War in the Middle Ages*. Trans. Michael Jones. New York, 1984.

Still the standard work on medieval warfare, though portions of it, especially those treating the early Middle Ages, are now out of date. Copious footnotes and a massive bibliography.

Contamine, Philippe, ed. *Histoire militaire de la France*. Vol. 1: *Des origines 1715*. Paris, 1992.

A collaborative grand synthesis that aims to cover the entirety of French military history. Ranging from Clovis (early sixth century) to Louis XIV, the authors pull in economic, religious, political, social, cultural and demographic history to place military affairs in their proper context. The volume lacks footnotes, but offers a substantial bibliography.

Cook, Jr., Weston. *The Hundred Years' War for Morocco: Gunpowder and the Military Revolution in the Early Modern Muslim World*. Boulder, 1994.

Traces Morocco's successful adoption of gunpowder weaponry, which allowed the Saʿdian state to thwart European and Ottoman domination.

Cresti, Carlo, et al., eds. *Architettura militare nell'Europa del XVI secolo*. Siena, 1988.

A collection of twenty-seven articles covering a wide array of topics regarding the methods of European fortification from ca. 1440 to ca. 1620.

Creswell, K.A.C. "Fortification in Islam before A.D. 1250." *Proceedings of the British Academy* 38 (1952): 89–125.

Argues that early Muslims patterned their fortifications and palaces on the older Roman *limes* which Muslims came to inhabit.

The Muslim Architecture of Egypt. 2 vols. Oxford, 1952–9; rprt, New York, 1979.

Including numerous illustrations and photographs, this study discusses every known monument for the period A.D. 939–1171 (vol. 1) and 1171–1326 (vol. 2). Meticulously referenced, this work is standard reading for any further research into the field.

Early Muslim Architecture. 2 vols. Oxford, 1932–40; 2nd ed., Oxford, 1969– .

An authoritative study by one of the masters of the field. The second edition has been thoroughly expanded, and includes many photographs and illustrations. Vol. one covers A.D. 622–750; vol. two treats 751–905.

Devries, Kelly. *Medieval Military Technology*. Peterborough, Ontario, 1992.

An excellent introduction to both the military equipment of the Middle Ages and its use and effect in medieval warfare. Devotes extended treatment to medieval fortifications.

Frykenberg, Robert, ed. *Delhi Through the Ages*. Delhi, 1986.

An extensive study of the city, consisting of twenty-eight articles, arranged chronologically from proto-history to modern.

Gallay, Allan, ed. *Colonial Wars of North America, 1512–1763: An Encyclopedia*. New York, 1996.

A collection of approximately 700 biographical, geographical, and subject entries written by more than 130 contributors. Articles vary in length and are followed by bibliographical references. The work covers the period from the conquistadors' first contact with North Americans to Pontiac's War of 1763.

Godinho, Vitorino de Magalhães. *Os descobrimentos e a economia mundial*. 4 vols. Lisbon, 1987.

Although Cook (see above) provides a much richer perspective on Moroccan and Portuguese-Moroccan history, Godinho remains useful for placing Portuguese expansion in Morocco into its proper context and has not yet been superseded in this respect.

Guarda, G. *Flandes indiano. Las fortificaciones del reino de Chile, 1541–1826*. Santiago de Chile, 1990.

Provides a lavishly illustrated account of the fortifications built by the various Spanish colonial administrations in Chile. The title, "Flandes indiano," comes from a seventeenth-century history which compared the struggle by the Spaniards in South America against the Araucanians with the war against the Dutch in the Netherlands.

Hess, Andrew. *The Forgotten Frontier: A History of the Sixteenth-Century Ibero-African Frontier*. Chicago, 1978.

Rejecting the Braudelian view of Mediterranean unity, Hess argues for separation of the region into distinct cultural spheres which witnessed continuous conflict between the Habsburgs and Ottomans. Focuses on two case studies, southeastern Spain and northern Africa, to show how each area developed its own distinct culture in the midst of this struggle.

Inalcik, Halil. *The Ottoman Empire: The Classical Age, 1300–1600*. Trans. Norman Itzkowitz and Colin Imber. London, 1973.

An abundantly documented study by an eminent Turkish historian. The author first shows how Mongol invasions weakened the Seljuk Turks, thereby facilitating subsequent Ottoman domination and resulting in a "classical age" in Ottoman history. Includes chapters on Ottoman economy, society, religion, and culture.

Johnson, Stephen. *Late Roman Fortifications*. Totowa, NJ, 1983.

Johnson traces the crisis of the late third century through the proliferating construction of fortifications in this period, from minor frontier posts to major urban centers. Includes many useful maps and plans, as well as archaeological data.

Kenyon, John. *Medieval Fortifications*. Leicester, 1990.

A synthesis of the archaeological scholarship since 1945 on English castles and towns. Parts one and two discuss the defensive and domestic components of castles; part three treats town defenses. The author covers the period from the Norman Conquest (1066) to the end of the fifteenth century, and offers many photographs and plans of excavated sites.

Kierman, F.A., and J.K. Fairbank, eds., *Chinese Ways in Warfare*. Cambridge, MA, 1974.

Comprised of an introductory chapter and seven essays, this volume covers Chinese warfare from its origins through the mid-sixteenth century. Of particular interest is Herbert Franke's paper, "Siege and Defense of Towns in Medieval China."

Lapidus, Ira. *Muslim Cities in the Later Middle Ages*. Student edition. Cambridge, 1984.

Treats Muslim cities during the Mamluk era (1250–1517) in Egypt and Syria, with special attention paid to Damascus and Aleppo. Very approachable to the general reader, with footnotes having been removed. For the complete scholarly apparatus, consult the first edition of 1967.

Lawrence, A.W. *Greek Aims in Fortifications*. Oxford, 1979.

Lawrence argues that the Greek science of fortification advanced significantly in the first part of the fourth century B.C. in reaction to advances in siegecraft. To this end, the author discusses every siege appearing in the literature for the period 432–189 B.C. With many photographs and plans, the work also incorporates a valuable list of over 500 fortified Greek sites.

Leriche, P., and H. Tréziny, eds. *La fortification dans l'histoire du monde grec.* Paris, 1986.

This volume is the culmination of a 1982 CNRS international colloquium. It contains forty-five articles in French, English, Italian, and German, which treat a broad spectrum of topics both geographically and thematically. Hundreds of photographs, line drawings, and maps.

Lopes, David. *A expansão em Marrocos.* Lisbon, 1989.

An adjusted reprint of the chapter written by David Lopes for the first volume of the monumental *História da expansão portuguesa no mundo*, edited by António Baião and others in 1937. Despite its age, the text offers a uniquely clear and concise survey of the Portuguese colonial expansion in Morocco from 1415 to 1589. It remains unsurpassed as a pocket reference work on the subject.

Marshall, Christopher. *Warfare in the Latin East, 1192–1291.* Cambridge, 1992.

Marshall gives an authoritative account of Crusader warfare from the Third Crusade to the fall of Acre. Chapter three, "Castles and Strongpoints," illustrates how Christian successes in the Holy Land depended heavily on systems of fortifications.

Moreira, R., ed. *Historia das fortificaes portuguesas no mundo.* Lisbon, 1989.

An account of the fortifications built by the Portuguese around the world. Well illustrated with photographs, prints, and plans.

Nelson, William. *The Dutch Forts of Sri Lanka: The Military Monuments of Ceylon.* Edinburgh, 1984.

Offers plans of thirty-one Dutch forts in Sri Lanka, arranged by location, complemented by photographs, illustrations, and explanatory text.

Ober, Josiah. *Fortress Attica: Defense of the Athenian Land Frontier, 404–322 B.C.* Mnemosyne Supplement 84. Leiden, 1985.

The author offers the view that, upon its defeat at the hands of the Spartans, Athens embarked on a new defensive policy based on an elaborate border fortification system. Includes a catalogue of the various strongholds that made up this network.

Pant, G.N. *Studies in Indian Weapons and Warfare.* New Delhi, 1970.

Arranged by weapons systems, this work covers Indian warfare from the stone age to the nineteenth century. Includes many line drawings, reproductions, and photographs.

Parry, V.J., and M.E. Yapp. *War, Technology and Society in the Middle East.* London, 1975.

A collection of twenty articles, most of which are in English but some French. Covers topics ranging from early Arab conquests to the twentieth century, including specific battles and campaigns, cases of technological transfer with the West, technological change, and military organization.

Perrin, Noel. *Giving up the Gun: Japan's Reversion to the Sword, 1543–1879.* Boston, 1979.

In searching for answers to the threat of nuclear arms and the Cold War then raging, Perrin looks to the stunning situation in Tokugawa Japan, where a conscious decision was made to abandon firearms in favor of more traditional weaponry. Written by a nonspecialist and suitable for a lay audience.

Ralston, David. *Importing the European Army: The Introduction of European Military Techniques and Institutions into the Extra-European World, 1600–1914.* Chicago, 1990.
Ralston examines the changes wrought on Russian, Ottoman, Egyptian, Chinese, and Japanese societies when they attempted to develop armies capable of withstanding Western incursions.

Redman, Charles. *Qsar es-Seghir: An Archaeological View of Medieval Life.* New York, 1986.
A synthesis of data and other studies concerning Qsar es-Seghir, a city on the northern shore of Morocco and the site of a huge international archaeological study. Captured by the Portuguese in 1458, the city was transformed to meet the needs of its new inhabitants. Offers numerous photographs of the finds from the excavation.

Reid, Anthony. *Southeast Asia in the Age of Commerce, 1450–1680.* Vol. 2: *Expansion and Crisis.* New Haven, 1993.
A broad survey giving the Southeast Asian perspective on political, religious, and economic changes caused by the arrival of Europeans.

Ricard, Robert. *Etudes sur l'histoire des Portugais au Maroc.* Coimbra, 1955.
Despite being somewhat dated, this work remains one of the essential introductory texts for anyone wanting to explore the history of the Portuguese outposts in Morocco.

Rogers, Randall. *Latin Siege Warfare in the Twelfth Century.* Oxford, 1992.
Investigates sieges at a time when fortifications were changing from wood to stone. Like Bachrach and Bradbury (see above), Rogers argues for the primacy of the siege in medieval warfare by investigating the Crusades and also conflicts in Italy, Sicily, Lombardy, and Iberia. Appendices give attention to various siege engines.

Sarkar, Jagadish. *The Art of War in Medieval India.* New Delhi, 1984.
A thematic approach including sections on artillery, fortifications, and sieges, and the laws of war. Covers the eighth to the tenth centuries.

Scranton, Robert. *Greek Walls.* Cambridge, MA, 1941.
Documents the chronology of four styles of Greek masonry. Appendix III is a list of all the walls studied by the author, arranged by type of wall. Includes several photographs.

Sharma, Y.D. *Delhi and Its Neighborhood.* New Delhi, 1964.
Divides the city of Delhi into its constituent areas for examination, and studies buildings and monuments of note in each. Includes twenty photographs and a fold-out map of Delhi and its environs.

Subrahmanyam, Sanjay. "The *Kagemusha* Effect: The Portuguese, Firearms and the State in Early Modern South India." *Moyen Orient et Océan Indien* 4 (1987): 97–123.
A look at the spread of firearms in South India in the sixteenth and seventeenth centuries, and how these weapons were perceived by indig-

enous populations. Concludes that the actual use of such weapons among South Indians was only limited.

Toy, Sidney. *The Strongholds of India*. London, 1957.

A richly illustrated, accessible description and examination of twenty-three medieval Indian fortresses. Also discusses weapons of attack and defense.

The Fortified Cities of India. London, 1965.

Examines eighteen cities, including some that were previously discussed in Toy's *The Strongholds of India* (see above).

Winter, Frederick. *Greek Fortifications*. Toronto, 1971.

A comprehensive study of extant Greek fortifications from antiquity, all of which were personally examined by the author. Incorporates a variety of photographs and plans.

Wolfe, Michael. "Siege Warfare and the *Bonnes Villes* of France during the Hundred Years War." In *The Medieval City Under Siege*, eds. Ivy Corfis and Michael Wolfe, 49–66. Rochester, NY, 1995.

Demonstrates how *bonnes villes* (medium-sized cities) came of age politically and militarily over the course of the Hundred Years' War, and how the king had to take them into account when trying to amass power.

PART III: SIGNIFYING WALLS

Allen, Terry. *A Classical Revival in Islamic Architecture*. Wiesbaden, 1986.

The study focuses on one edifice, the twelfth-century Madrasah al-Shu'aybiyah of Aleppo, and its place in Islamic architecture. Uses this as an example of an eleventh- and twelfth-century classical revival in Islamic architecture in Syria and surrounding areas.

Blair, Sheila. *The Monumental Inscriptions from Early Islamic Iran and Transoxiana*. Leiden, 1992.

Inscriptions from Iran and Transoxiana covering the period A.D. 622–1106. For each of the seventy-nine inscriptions, the author includes such information as location, type of inscription, references to other publications, text and translation, and discussion. Illustrated with photographs and drawings.

Boyd, Andrew. *Chinese Architecture and Town Planning, 1500 B.C.–A.D. 1911*. London, 1962.

A short and general introduction to the topic of Chinese architecture and urban planning covering almost 3,500 years. Though older, this remains a useful study.

Chang, Sen-Dou. "Some Observations on the Morphology of Chinese Walled Cities." *Annals of the Association of American Geographers* 60/1 (1970): 63–91.

Among other contentions, the author argues that topography could distort the typical square shape of town walls, that the size of walls was proportional to the administrative significance of the town, and that the internal structure of towns was nonetheless flexible. Incorporates several town plans.

Gabriel, Albert. *Voyages archéologiques dans la Turquie orientale.* 2 vols. Paris, 1940.

The standard work on the inscriptions of the city of Diyarbekir. Volume one consists of text, plans, line drawings, and editions of the inscriptions. The second volume contains hundreds of drawings and photographs, including those of the original inscriptions.

Hale, J.R. *Artists and Warfare in the Renaissance.* New Haven and London, 1990.

An examination of the depiction of Renaissance warfare and its participants in the works of Swiss, German, and Italian artists. Shows how the common soldier, though viewed as a necessary evil in Renaissance society, was typically portrayed as an outcast.

Harley, J.B., and David Woodward, eds. *The History of Cartography.* Vol. 2, Book 2: *Cartography in the Traditional East and Southeast Asian Societies.* Chicago and London, 1994.

A collection of twenty-one chapters written by a wide array of authors and taking a multi-disciplinary approach, this volume is replete with photographs, maps, drawings, and tables. Chapters three to nine cover cartography in China.

Howard, Michael, et al., eds. *The Laws of War: Constraints on Warfare in the Western World.* New Haven and London, 1994.

Twelve articles giving treatment to topics ranging from the classical Greek world to the twentieth century. Includes studies devoted to the laws of warfare in medieval and early modern Europe, and colonial America.

Keen, Maurice. *The Laws of War in the Late Middle Ages.* Toronto, 1965.

Contends that war proper could only be waged by sovereigns, and that late medieval soldiers were supposed to act within known limits of conduct. Focusing on England and France, the book also discusses particular problems encountered in siege warfare.

Landau, David, and Peter Parshall. *The Renaissance Print, 1470–1550.* New Haven, 1994.

Encyclopedic in structure and content, this reference work provides the reader with reproductions of hundreds of Renaissance prints, many in color. Covers virtually everything regarding prints for this period, including demand, production, and distribution.

Le Goff, Jacques. "Warriors and Conquering Bourgeois: The Image of the City in Twelfth-Century French Literature." In *The Medieval Imagination.* Trans. Arthur Goldhammer, 151–76. Chicago and London, 1988.

This essay, originally published in French in 1979, investigates the primarily rural-based warrior's attitudes towards the city and its inhabitants in twelfth-century France. The author detects two primary reactions of the warrior class to the city: that of heaven (Jerusalem) and of hell (Babylon).

Meron, Theodor. *Henry's Wars and Shakespeare's Laws: Perspectives on the Laws of Wars in the Later Middle Ages*. Oxford, 1994.

An insightful and thoroughly referenced examination of martial laws at the time of Henry V's Agincourt campaign (1415), and how these laws were later presented by William Shakespeare.

Pepper, Simon, and Nicholas Adams. *Firearms and Fortifications: Military Architecture and Siege Warfare in Sixteenth Century Siena*. Chicago, 1986.

Focuses on the ultimately fruitless attempt by the Republic of Siena to maintain its independence, resulting in a siege that lasted from 1554 to 1555. The authors chart the evolution of military architecture from medieval to early modern, capable of withstanding gunpowder artillery attack.

Pollak, Martha. *Turin 1564–1680: Urban Design, Military Culture, and the Creation of the Absolutist Capital*. Chicago, 1991.

An interdisciplinary examination of the architectural transformation of Turin at the hands of the dukes of Savoy, whereby the town became a landmark to its ruling dynasty. Investigates the marriage of political ideology with defensive necessity in fortifications.

Military Architecture, Cartography and the Representation of the Early Modern European City: A Checklist of Treatises on Fortification in The Newberry Library. Chicago, 1991.

A description of seventy-three treatises in The Newberry Library which treat the topic of urban fortifications. Each entry, arranged alphabetically by author, discusses the edition, references to modern works, and copies at other libraries.

Rotberg, Robert, and Theodore Rabb, eds. *Art and History: Images and Their Meanings*. Cambridge, 1988.

An interdisciplinary approach to the topic, the scope of the dozen articles contained in this volume ranges from Renaissance family portraits to the architecture of the Nazis. Also offers studies on Rome during the Renaissance (Christoph Frommel) and cityscapes commissioned by Philip II of Spain (Richard Kagan).

Skinner, G. William. "Cities and the Hierarchy of Local Systems." In *The City in Late Imperial China*, ed. Skinner, 275–351. Stanford, 1977.

Investigates the dual position of Chinese cities: one mandated by imperial, bureaucratic and administrative needs, the other determined by economic necessity. Offers several maps, tables, trade models, and an appendix discussing economic data.

Steinhardt, Nancy Shatzman. *Chinese Imperial City Planning*. Honolulu, 1990.

Covers Chinese imperial cities from the earliest evidence to twentieth-century Beijing. Includes dozens of city plans and illustrations.

Van Emden, Wolfgang. "The Castle in Some Works of Medieval French Literature." In *The Medieval Castle: Romance and Reality*, eds. Kathryn Reyerson and Faye Powe, 1–26. Dubuque, Iowa, 1984.

Discusses the differences found in the castle of literature as opposed to the historical castle, wherein the former appears as a highly idealized form of the latter. *Inter alia*, castles of literature were constructed of exotic materials, were often impregnable to storm attack techniques, and were built to incredibly large dimensions.

Von Berchem, Max, et al. *Amida*. Heidelburg, 1910.
The basic publication on the city of Diyarbekir. Part one is by von Berchem, the founder of the study of Islamic epigraphy. Includes photographs, line drawings, plans, and editions and translations of inscriptions from the town.

Waldron, Arthur. *The Great Wall of China: From History to Myth*. Cambridge, 1990.
Painstakingly referenced, this study shows how the Great Wall both bankrupted the Ming Dynasty and failed as a military strategy. Nevertheless, as the subtitle suggests, even in failure the Wall has taken on epic proportions in Chinese myth-building and national pride.

Waltzer, Michael. *Just and Unjust Wars: A Moral Argument with Historical Illustrations*. New York, 1977.
An attempt to formulate a modern concept of the "just war," based mostly on twentieth-century conflicts. Includes sections on "moral reality," "theory of aggression," "the war convention," "dilemmas of war," and "responsibility." Chapter 10 gives special treatment to problems encountered in sieges.

Wright, Arthur. "The Cosmology of the Chinese City." In *The City in Late Imperial China*, ed. G. William Skinner, 33–73. Stanford, 1977.
Shows how, even as Chinese society became more secular, the location and design of its cities were still heavily influenced by cosmology. The author offers several explanations for why this may have been the case.

Index